ORGANIZATIONS
AND
THEIR
MANAGING

ORGANIZATIONS
and
Their
MANAGING

A CONDENSED, ONE-VOLUME EDITION OF
The Managing of Organizations

BERTRAM M. GROSS

The Free Press, New York
Collier-Macmillan Limited, London

*T*O NORA, DAVID, LARRY, SAMMY, TEDDY, SHULA, AND ARIELA

PREFACE: *Systems Guidance in the 1970s*

A MAJOR PARADOX of the twentieth century is this: while organizations are becoming ever more important as a way of meeting human needs, they are also becoming less manageable.

The increasing importance of organizations is illustrated in every field of human activity. Wherever we look, we see them growing in significance, size, or both. We see this in private firms, government agencies (Federal, State and local), hospitals, schools, universities, research institutions, non-profit institutions (in health, education, welfare, and philanthropy), professional associations, trade associations, some labor unions and many community organizations.

In the past, all such organizations have faced new managerial (or administrative) difficulties whenever these conditions developed:

- more uncertainties in their environment
- more structural intricacy, or
- more performance complexity.

In the future, these conditions will become increasingly prevalent. During the 1970s, new environmental uncertainties will be brought into being by rapid, uneven, and often unpredictable changes in technology, social structure, human aspirations, government policies, coalitions of political power, and international relations in a world society experiencing unpredictable conflicts. New structural intricacies will be created by growth or reorganization, increased specialization and professionalism, new functions and interrelations. With more sophisticated demands on organizations, more varied activities, and more operations requiring co-ordination over larger expanses of space, time, and psychic or cultural distance, new complexities in performance will multiply. Under these conditions, managers and administrators at all levels will face greater difficulties in decision-making, communicating, planning, and control. Indeed, some organizations—business firms as well as government agencies, hospitals as well as universities, community as well as international bodies —will approach *unmanageability*. Some will reach it. . . .

"But what about modern management techniques? Won't they provide a solution?"

Unfortunately, when put into practice, all solutions—technical ones included—create problems. Good solutions create big problems. Excellent ones create fantastic problems. "Technological change of any significance whatsoever," as I point out later, "is a threat, real or imagined, to the power or security of someone, often of many people, in the organization. In its more obvious aspects, any technological change which enables the production of similar outputs with less labor threatens to reduce employment. But even where such an effect can be counterbalanced by expanded production or by transfers to other work, the change itself threatens established positions and expertise. It renders obsolete some of the accrued capital of knowledge in the hands and minds of those who operated in accordance with the previous processes. It may even suggest that the people responsible for the previous processes are inferior individuals, as compared with the wiser souls who promote the new processes. Furthermore, it may turn upside down the whole world of established relationships and lead to a complete reorganization of work groups, tasks, responsibilities, and individual status. . . ."[1] These observations are not limited to such areas as computerization, nuclear energy, supersonic flight, medical services, and the mass media. They are just as applicable to changes in managerial technology.

Besides, *during the 1970s we shall undoubtedly see a new wave of innovation in managerial and administrative techniques.* These new developments may well render obsolete many of the "modern" techniques developed in the 1950s and 1960s. In other words, they will usher in new opportunities for serving a greater variety of human interests more creatively and cheaply. But these opportunities can be recognized and ex-

1. "Production Technology" in "People-in-Organizations: Formal Aspects," Chapter 9, p. 205.

ploited only by managers able to perceive and understand them, to coddle, nurture, and coordinate the inventors and purveyors of new techniques—in short, to manage the technicians.

This will be rendered increasingly difficult by the burgeoning variety of specialization and subspecialization among the management technicians. There are already major varieties or subdivisions within such traditional technique areas as accounting, budgeting and finance, production and personnel management, public relations, marketing, procurement, and business and administrative law. The varieties are still greater in such newer areas as statistical decision-making, operations research, evaluation and control, human relations, benefit-cost analysis (or cost-effectiveness analysis) and systems analysis, design, and management. The major innovational tendencies point to still more specialization—with no clear indication as to whether many of the new "management specialists" will try to learn much about the broader dimensions of organizations and their managing.[2] For many organizations the result will be greater structural intricacy, structural complexity, and—because of differential effects on external agencies—environmental uncertainty.

To make matters worse, many of the new or improved techniques will probably continue in the future, as in the past, to be "initiated in a burst of grandiose claims of 'breakthroughs' and exaggerated application to irrelevant situations."[3] No matter how restricted a given set of techniques may be, their enthusiastic inventors or popularizers will probably continue the fancy labelling tradition initiated by Frederick Taylor at the turn of the century. New labels—even more flamboyant than such older phrases as "scientific management," "administrative science," and "management science"—will be used in high pressure sales talks to obtain funds from gullible managers.[4] Thus, in the 1970s even more than in the

2. A few years ago a middle-aged man from a nearby General Electric plant appeared as a student in my management seminar at Syracuse University. At the first session he revealed that his G.E. job was "management scientist." His purpose in joining the seminar was to learn something in "another" field, organization theory, and—more specifically—to find out why G.E.'s "management science" tended to become disconnected from general maangement. One of the many reasons, he reported later, was that too few people operating as "management scientists" had tried to think realistically about organizations and their managing from the viewpoint of general managers.

3. Bertram M. Gross, "The Newer Fields," in "Contributors from Other Fields," Chapter 8, *The Managing of Organizations*, Vol. I, p. 210.

4. "In his earlier days Taylor usually referred to his bundle of administrative techniques as the task system or task management. In 1910, however, a new and more popular label was provided by Louis Brandeis (later Supreme Court Justice), who represented Eastern shipping concerns in a struggle against a projected increase in railroad rates. The railroads had applied to the Interstate Commerce Commission for a rate increase, basing their plea on a recent increase in wages. Brandeis appeared before the Commission and contended that without any in-

past *the effect of the new management techniques on many organizations —particularly those lacking the capacity to test new claims, take new risks, and coordinate new specialists—could easily be greater unmanageability.*[5]

If this is the prospect in the "post-industrial" United States, the situation is much more foreboding in those nations (sometimes called developing" or "underdeveloped") beginning the industrializing process. In those countries, national leaders are usually firmly committed to the guidance of rapid economic, social, and political development. This requires more and more organizations with a genuine capacity to get things done. Yet in these countries, as I have pointed out in a survey prepared for the United Nations, we see the wide-spread "fallacy of administration as technical gadgetry."[6] This has led to superficial efforts at administrative improvement by importing techniques from industrialized countries and trying to apply them to situations they do not fit. To make matters worse, many high posts in these countries are manned by "Gentlemen Generalists" incapable of nurturing locally based technicians, let alone exploiting the fruit of their labors.[7]

DYNAMIC PEOPLE-RESOURCE SYSTEMS

A major purpose of this volume is to provide a "general systems language" to help anyone interested in learning more about the guidance of real-life organizations.[8]

---

crease in rates the railroads could maintain their profits by introducing more efficient methods of operation. He supported the position by using Taylor's ideas. But Brandeis felt that he needed a term which would be more popular than the severe-sounding 'task system.' He chose 'scientific management' (a term previously used only occasionally by Taylor) as *the* label."—"The 'Scientific Management' Movement" in "The Pioneers: The Gospel of Efficiency," Chapter 6, *The Managing of Organizations,* Vol. I, p. 126-127.

5. Does it seem impossible that new management techniques may lead to declining managerial capability? If so, reflect on the possibility that in the modern society faster transportation may have led to more congestion, more communication to less listening, and more knowledge to less wisdom.

6. U.N. Public Administration Division, *The Administration of Economic Development Planning.* United Nations, 15 August 1966, ST/TAO/M/32, p. 12.

7. The "Gentleman Generalist" and his origins in various colonial administrations are briefly touched on in "People-in-Organizations: Informal Aspects," Chapter 10, p. 249. Many former colonies, let it be added here, still suffer from a plethora of "Gentlemen Generalists" not able or willing to learn enough about the specialties that must be integrated (and promoted) if organizations are to be more effective.

8. To facilitate such application, other materials in the original *The Managing of Organizations* have been omitted. Those interested in the historical background of the "administrative revolution" and modern administrative

The approach set forth will provide useful starting points for both the managers (or administrators) and the managed (or administrated), the teachers and the taught, the academic observers and the observed. The aim is not to give prefabricated answers but to help managers and students of organizations ask better questions. Specifically, this volume can help in handling the increasingly complex problem of decision-making and planning discussed above: namely, how to make fruitful use of new managerial techniques of decision-making and planning, rather than be overwhelmed by fads and fashions.

The terms *system* and *systems analysis*, of course, have already become *fad terms*. "Sometimes—as in 'Randese' and 'McNamaranese'—they are used to refer to more logical efforts at rational calculation, with major attention to quantitative measures of benefits, outputs and inputs. Sometimes they refer to procedures, routines, rules or 'systematized' workflows, sometimes to machine systems, sometimes to man–machine systems."[9] One of the reasons for their growing popularity is that they mean different things to different people. These differences may be expected to grow.

In this volume any organization is viewed as a *dynamic people-resource system operating at specific locations in space and time*. Relevant information on any such system may relate to its environment, its internal structure, and its performance (or functioning).

Such information must be *general* in two senses:

1. It must relate to sequences of real problems—without being limited to what any one specialist in economics, statistics, sociology, psychology, politics, or other areas may want to provide.
2. It must bear upon any points touched by these problems—from the organization as a whole down to any unit thereof and outside to other organizations, no matter how different they may be.

---

thought are referred to Chapters 2-9 in Vol. I of same. A philosophical view of the future of the "administered society" and of administrative research and theory may be found in Chapters 30 and 31, respectively, in Vol. II of same. Anyone seeking a more technical presentation of the same general systems concepts is referred to my following publications: (1) "What Are Your Organization's Objectives? A General Systems Approach to Planning," *Human Relations*, August 1965, pp. 195-216; (2) "The Coming General Systems Models of Social Systems," *Human Relations*, November 1967, pp. 357-374; (3) *The State of the Nation: Social Systems Accounting*, London: Tavistock Publications, 1966; also published in Raymond A. Bauer, ed., *Social Indicators*, Cambridge: M.I.T. Press, 1966; (4) "The City of Man: A Social Systems Reckoning," in William Ewald, ed., *Man's Environment: Next 50 Years*, Bloomington, Ind.: Indiana University Press, 1967; and (5) "Political Process," *International Encyclopedia of the Social Sciences*, New York: Macmillan Co., 1968.

9. Bertram M. Gross, "The Coming General Systems Models of Social Systems," op. cit., pp. 129-140.

Above all, it must be based upon a frank recognition that organizations are people-resource systems of "organized complexity." This is "far more difficult to understand than the disorganized complexity of most nonliving systems, which is susceptible to statistical analysis based on probability theory."[10]

In this volume I present a bedrock minimum of the essential (although not sufficient) concepts needed to get such relevant information. Drawn from a variety of disciplines and professions, these concepts are formulated in supradisciplinary terms. They are presented not in "systems jargon" but rather at a moderate level of technical difficulty. Anyone with a good general education plus a moderate capacity for observing his (or her) own experiences in formal organizations—even including universities —will be able to adapt them to his (or her) own problems. They can be used as instruments in designing research plans, frustrating the designs of "the administration," or educating "higher management." Administrators and managers at all levels and in any country can—if they have enough skill—use them in defining the unique needs of specific organizations and responding to the unique challenges of the 1970s.

The forces making for the unmanageability of organizations, however, must not be underestimated. They include much more than the confusions of new technology, larger bureaucracies, and the insularity of an overspecialized world. They also include, as touched upon more generally in Chapter 1, many myths concerning organizations and many taboos as to how we should think and talk about their managing. Among these are the myths and taboos, often unwritten and unspoken, that may prevent an organization's members and managers from understanding

- certain unpleasant facts of life
- environmental turbulence
- the dynamics of structure
- the multi-dimensionality of performance
- the delicacy of guidance processes, and
- the improbability of managerial learning.

In the chapters that follow (except for the attention to "popular fallacies" in Chapters 5 and 8), a direct confrontation with other viewpoints is avoided—simply for lack of space. In the interest of presenting an integrated set of basic concepts, I have provided insufficient contrast with the accumulated burden of myth and taboo which I find in a large part of the conventional—even some of the latest—writings on organizations and management. In part, at least, I shall compensate for this defect by point-

10. Bertram M. Gross, *The State of the Nation: Social Systems Accounting,* op. cit., p. 171 (M.I.T. edition).

ing up some major contrasts as I briefly summarize in the remainder of this preface the substantive content of Parts I through VI.

UNPLEASANT FACTS OF LIFE

In Part I, "The Emerging Integration," I try to tear aside the verbal veils that conceal a growing consensus on matters that are often difficult to talk about frankly. Some of these veils are the inevitable result of normal defense mechanisms and standardized tactics of coping with conflict through bluff and deception. Others are used (or woven afresh) by those—both in the academic and practical world—who believe that the best way to deal with organized complexity is to assume it out of existence.

In "The Management of Organizations" (Chapter 2) I present some elementary axioms whose implications are developed later. Sharp warning signals are given against oversimplifying matters by maintaining either that all organizations are similar rather than different or different rather than similar. The emphasis is placed upon the coexistence of *both* similarities and differences—among all levels of management as well as among any group of organizations. The discussion of "generalists vs. specialists" may be construed as an equally sharp warning against over-general images of generalists, images that can easily erode rather than build upon the underlying consensus on the need for integrating activities to counter-balance the onward thrust of specialization. Management is presented as an integrating process that involves making decisions under conditions of uncertainty, communicating imperfect information through multiple channels and engaging in endless rounds of planning, activating and evaluating.

In Chapters 3, 4, and 5 I then proceed to deal with matters that managers and academics seem increasingly agreed upon but that are always difficult to bring into the open honestly or to study scientifically.

1. *The inevitability of conflict.* In terms I have used in a somewhat broader context, conflict management is viewed as "a stream of successive compromises punctuated by frequent occasions of deadlock and avoidance and occasional victories, defeats and integrations."[11]

2. *The imperatives of power.* I explain the difficulties in dealing more openly with the need for organizations and their managers to develop, use and maintain the power, or influence, required to overcome inevitable blockage. The viewpoint presented will itself be difficult for those incapable of appreciating the significance of the fundamental distinction—

11. "The Political Process," op. cit. A manager who dodges the internal politics in his organization is as inadequate as any humanities professor who cannot cope with campus politics or any pure scientist who cannot perceive the facts of science politics.

developed with care by many investigators over many decades—between power and authority.[12]

3. *The persistence of fallacies.* Although modern administrative thought has logically destroyed many time-honored administrative fallacies, they still haunt managerial offices and the groves of Academe. I shall never forget the dedicated manager (probably fresh from a quick reading course) who seized on the nine propositions at the beginning of Chapter 5 and praised me for having expressed his own wise views so succinctly. From him and others (plus some self-observation) I have come to learn the tremendous staying power of two oversimplifications in particular:

- the "prestige transference" fallacy that technical skill equals good administration, and
- the utopian fallacy that in good administration things run smoothly and easily.

ENVIRONMENTAL TURBULENCE

Although environmental concepts are at the forefront of modern thought, there is a serious tendency to think of environment exclusively in terms of land, water, air, and other nonhuman variables. This approach underestimates the importance of nonhuman resources by putting them "out there" rather than illuminating their role as significant components *within* people-resource systems.

It also leads to an under-appreciation of the significance of the social environment composed of other intertwined people-resource systems. In business administration, with major attention given to client-supplier relations, the political and cultural environment is often avoided. In public administration, with more attention usually given to inter-agency relations and politics, more immediate linkages tend to be neglected.

In "The Immediate Environment" (Chapter 6) I present a general systems model of any organization's linkages with clients: suppliers, associates and supporters; advisers; controllers and controllees; and adversaries of various types. Multidimensional role analysis is presented as a technique of analyzing the nature of linkages with external groups with multiple and shifting roles. To counter the myth of "public opinion" as an organic entity, I identify the problems involved in getting useful information on "publics with opinions" and particularly on elite opinions.

"The General Environment" (Chapter 7) presents an overview of all

12. A classic case of "scientistic" confusion on power-authority relations is provided by Robert L. Peabody, *Organizational Authority*, New York: Atherton Press, 1964.

the additional external systems that may suddenly thrust themselves into an organization's immediate environment in the future—or that may even in the present be the source of unseen constraints or opportunities. This takes us from external natural resources to a broad spectrum of social institutions (families, formal organizations, associations and political parties) and the power and value structure of the society.

Both the immediate and the general environments may include elements that are relatively placid or disturbed. With uneven change characterizing a growing number of nations and the world society as a whole, turbulence is becoming a major part of the environment of most organizations. The extent to which environmental turbulence is a constraint or an opportunity unquestionably depends, among other factors, on managerial ability to get, process and respond to relevant environmental information.

STRUCTURAL COMPLEXITIES

Some people think of organizations in terms of performance only. Taking structure for granted, they look only at activities. Others are concerned entirely with structure, looking only at functional roles and their interrelations. In both cases, the architectural or engineering metaphor underlying the word "structure" suggests something static, rigid, unyielding. Misled (or perhaps bored) by this false analogy, some sociologists have concentrated entirely on *informal* structure.

Part III presents a dynamic view of system structure—with internal conflict, tension and change viewed as inescapable parts of both a system's components and their interrelations.

"The Human Beings" (Chapter 8) deals with the basic "building blocks" of organizations: people. Here, without going too far into the analysis of personality structures, I present certain propositions useful as starting points in understanding organizational and managerial behavior. These deal with the multiplicity of human interests, the social roles of individuals, the individual's conflicts, the uniqueness of human personality, and the ir- and non-rationality that inevitably accompany human rationality.

Chapters 9 and 10, respectively, deal with the formal and informal *aspects* of organizational structure. The difference between the two (which are always closely intertwined) is that the former are prescribed by the holder of formal authority. The latter develop without—perhaps even against—such prescription.

The formal aspects are defined in terms of roles, interrelations and rules (or behavioral codes). I discuss the roles of individuals and units, the various bases of role combinations, the role conflicts arising from specialist-administrator combinations and the necessity of interlocking functions. In analyzing hierarchic relations, I present the idea of the "inverted pyramid" of formal authority "over" the top executives and indicate the many unavoidable forms of "multiple hierarchy." Hierarchy cannot operate successfully, it is argued, without many kinds of "poly-archic" (or lateral) relations. Centralization and decentralization are defined as mutually supporting factors that combine in shifting patterns. The discussion of behavioral codes is deferred until Chapter 19.

The ubiquity of informal roles, relations and codes is then discussed. A large number of informal role facets is identified. Some of these are played by any members of an organization. Some are peculiarly managerial. I then analyze the informal coalitions that complicate the internal distribution of power and introduce the concept of "organizational democracy."

MULTI-DIMENSIONAL PERFORMANCE

"Many managers are still too much the prisoners of outworn, single-purpose models erected by defunct economists, engineers, and public administration experts. Although they know better, they are apt to pay verbal obeisance to some single purpose: profitability in the case of the business executive, efficiency in the case of the public executive."[13]

In "The Matrix of Purposes" (Chapter 11) I portray the difficulties faced by any manager confronted by the embarrassing question "What are your organization's purposes?" One of these is the lack of an adequate language to deal with the multiplicity of performance dimensions. When such dimensions are conceptually spelled out, they may be used in plotting any sequences (or "scenarios") of desired future performance. They are also applicable to the description or evaluation of past performance. Seven dimensions are identified for discussion in the subsequent chapters.

1. *Satisfying interests* (Chapter 12). Although satisfying human interests is the *raison d'être* of any organization, interest satisfaction objectives —often referred to as *benefits, welfare, utility* value or payoff—are the hardest to formulate. There are many different "interesteds" both inside and outside an organization. Their interests are usually multiple, often hard to identify, always divergent, and sometimes sharply conflicting. Creative managers may promote new interests and aggregate or "integrate" existing ones into broader common interests. Yet common and public interests are also multiple, divergent, and changing. Satisfactions, moreover, cannot be directly observed. They must be inferred through

13. "What Are Your Organization's Objectives?" op. cit., pp. 195-196.

the use of various surrogates: information on (a) choices made, (b) payments given, (c) opinions expressed, and (d) presumed results. Moreover, satisfactions and dissatisfactions are often closely associated.

2. *Producing Outputs* (Chapters 13, 14 and 15). Output dimensions, it is shown, can best be expressed in terms of an "output mix" listing the various types of services or goods, with appropriate information on the quality and quantity of each. A theory of "output specification" is presented as a basis for distinguishing between different aspects of quality. Attention is given to the problems involved in using monetary measures of quantity and of "imputing" monetary value to nonmarketed products.

Special emphasis is placed upon intangible services that cannot be readily quantified. These may be counted, it is held, only by using such "service surrogates" as (a) the number of clients, (b) the duration of services, (c) more tangible intermediate products, or (d) the volume or value of input factors.

The definition of service output is shown to be critical in mission statements, performance rating, and performance budgeting. All output concepts are discussed in terms that are relevant not only to the end products of organizations but also to the output mix of internal units. These supply services to an internal "clientele network" within an organization.

3. *Using Resources Efficiently or Profitably* (Chapter 16). Both *efficiency* and *profitability* are terms referring to a variety of input-output relations. In addition to the many measures of output, there are many alternatives to be faced in identifying inputs and "creating" cost estimates. Thus there are always many ways of calculating profitability—as well as inescapable limitations on the meaning or (even the possibility) of such calculations. Attention is therefore given to other "broad" input-output relations, as well as to "partial" input-output ratios.

The major concepts needed in benefit-output-income analysis (sometimes referred to as cost-benefit analysis, cost-effectiveness analysis, or "systems budgeting") are set forth in the Chapters 12 through 16.

4. *Investing in the System* (Chapter 17). In addition to producing current output, organizations invest in their capacity for future performance. In a minimal sense viability means simple survival, which usually requires adaptation to new conditions if not recurring reorganization. Growth is usually characterized by disproportional change, changing rates of change, and delayed adaptation. Either survival or growth requires the expansion, replacement, conservation, or development of an organization's physical, human, and institutional assets.

5. *Mobilizing Resources* (Chapter 18). All other aspects of performance are dependent upon an organization's success in acquiring resources

from its environment. The inner logic of resource mobilization is different from that of resource use and often receives greater attention in planning. The key considerations in each are identified.

6. *Observing Codes* (Chapter 19). Organizational observance of various codes of behavior, I point out, is complicated by conflicting prescriptions, preferences, proscriptions, and permissions. Order, honesty, loyalty, distributive justice, secrecy, and opportunism, it is claimed, enter into a "universal inner core of organizational morality." This inner core is surrounded by outer layers of still greater variety. Under these circumstances enforcement entails strategies of "contained deviation" through external control, internal control, and code adjustment.

7. *Behaving rationally* (Chapter 20). This chapter rejects as insufficient the conventional "machine model" concepts of rationality as calculational (or cognitive) processes alone. Instead, rationality is defined in terms of satisfactory action patterns. Action may be judged more or less rational in accordance with three dimensions that are often conflicting: desirability, feasibility and consistency. The capacity for rational action is seen as rooted in the learning process and limited by external blockage as well as imperfections in information and adaptive ability. It is irrational to use "narrow" or "technical" rationality under circumstances requiring "broad" or "administrative" rationality. This is like a scientist trying to use controlled experiments in relations with his wife or a judge using courtroom rules of evidence in dealing with his children.

THE DELICACY OF GUIDANCE PROCESSES

Conventional models of administrative processes usually suffer from two defects. On the one hand, they often relate to crude and simplistic decision-making and communication processes—abstracted from the environmental, structural, and performance context of organizational and managerial action. On the other hand, they tend to ignore the "unpleasant" realities of conflict and power in complex intertwined systems. In contrast, Part V on "Administrative Processes" is based on the premise that people-resource systems are always partly unknowable and partly uncontrollable. In this sense, the managing of organizations is an exercise in the guidance of "unsystematic systems."[14] Five guidance processes are analyzed.

1. *Decision-making* (Chapter 21). This chapter is based on a blunt recognition of decision-making as a sequential process of struggle among

14. The concept of "unsystematic system" is brought forward more explicitly in *The State of the Nation: Social Systems Accounting*, op. cit., p. 178-179 (M.I.T. edition).

divergent considerations—as well as conflicting calculators. Defining the problem is a more critical aspect than searching for answers. But there are no problems apart from people or groups who *have* problems—that is, perceive some blockage in the path of their attaining various goals. Choosing among alternatives (along with imagining new ones) is closely associated with the justification (or rationalization) of any choice to one's self and other judges.

2. *Communicating* (Chapter 22). The many barriers between the senders and receivers of messages are rooted not only in the complications of coding and channels—but also within the messages, senders and receivers themselves. Aids in communication can help only as they alleviate specific blockages at these points. Perfect communication, however, might "blow the lid" off an organization.

3. *Planning* (Chapter 23). Meaningful rather than utopian planning is much more than making proposals or studies. It consists of making commitments to future action sequences. From this point of view the "real" planners are usually those involved in action. The real commitments may be overcentralized or over rigid. The real action sequences can never be fully embodied in documents and blueprints.

4. *Activating* (Chapter 24). One of the most difficult decision-making problems is the formulation of the question "How to get action under this or that plan?" Command alone is only one form of pressure—along with bargaining, manipulation, and physical force. Propaganda is only one form of persuasion—along with explanation, advice, example, and expectation. The promotion of self-activation goes beyond direct pressure and persuasion. The use of these various forms of influence depends not only on strategic timing but also on the mobilization of support and the management of crisis.

5. *Evaluating* (Chapter 25). The criteria of evaluation may be based on any permutation of performance, structural, or environmental dimensions. The use of any criteria—even those formulated with the aid of hindsight—requires the collection and interpretation of relevant information. These tasks are often made more difficult by the style and attitudes of evaluators. Any serious evaluation of managers requires special attention to the links between their performance and that of the organization.

LEARNING IMPROBABILITIES

The manageability of organizations in the 1970s will depend largely on the learning capability of their managers.

The one thing we can be sure of is that there will be a vast expansion in the quantity and variety of managerial education and training programs.

What and how much managers may really learn (from them, without them, or in spite of them) is the theme of the four brief chapters in Part VI, "The Future."

First of all, learning is a difficult and painful (although also exciting) personal experience in a social setting (Chapter 26). One of the reasons it is painful is the necessity of *un*learning.

Second, the acquisition of knowledge—no matter how intimately related to a people-resource system and its environment—is only one dimension of learning (Chapter 27). To use knowledge, managers must also develop broader interests and improve their skills. When this happens, skill may rise to the level of art, and art—hopefully—to the level of wisdom.

Third, a major role of managerial education in schools is to help people learn more from experience outside the schools (Chapter 28). This requires new links between advancement and learning (not just certificate acquisition) and better instructional methods both in schools and on the job.

Fourth, the greatest difficulty with the "school of experience" is that it has so many bad teachers. One of the aims of managerial education in universities and similar institutions should be to develop the image of the manager as teacher, as one who tries to promote personal learning capacities throughout the system he is trying to guide. This requires more acceptance—in universities as well as noneducational organizations—of the principle that "teachers too must learn."

This principle—particularly when applied to those whose major concern is management—goes right to the heart of the danger of unmanageability. Russell Ackoff, the world's leading technician in operations research, has illuminated this issue in his brilliant article "Management Misinformation Systems." He reports on the waste resulting from three new information systems prepared by enthusiastic "management specialists" and accepted by gullible managers (one in gasoline retailing, one in a department store, and one a computerized production-inventory control system in a factory). He concludes that managers who are not willing to invest some of their time in designing "a system that is to serve them, are not likely to use a management control system well, and their system, in turn, is likely to abuse them."[15]

The pressures on managerial time, of course, are rising rapidly. They can be handled responsibly only if there is enough general investment in broader learning activities that will allow managers to respond selectively and creatively—rather than routinely—to claims on their time. This in-

15. Russell L. Ackoff, "Management Misinformation Systems," *Management Science*, Dec. 1967, p. B-147–156.

volves a great leap from the over-simplified models they carry around in their heads (or are given by narrow technicians) to more sophisticated multi-dimensional models that, while dangerously complex at first blush, may help them acquire the arts of coping with organized complexity.

If this leap is not made, technical gadgetry is likely to abuse not only the managers—but also society as a whole. If more genuine learning can be accomplished, organizations may contribute more to the meeting of human needs.

B. M. G.

February, 1968

OUTLINE CONTENTS

PART V. *Administrative Processes*

PART VI. *The Future*

A Bibliographical Report

Indexes

DETAILED CONTENTS

ORGANIZATIONS
AND
THEIR
MANAGING

Chapter 1

AN ACTION-THEORY MARRIAGE

*T*HE STAGE is the entire planet. The plot and the settings are as diverse as life itself.

In New York, Moscow, Bombay, and Buenos Aires hundreds of men are engaged in getting thousands of others to run the machines that wrest materials from the earth, transport them near and far, and produce food, clothing, medicines, building materials, books, and other machines. In Berlin, Budapest, Shanghai, Cairo, and Jerusalem thousands more are employed in collecting taxes, and many more in spending money. In Accra, Manila, and La Paz critical minds find an Achilles' heel in ambitious plans for economic development: the shortage of managerial personnel. Steps are discussed to import or train the men who are needed.

In Paris, an automobile company pays out unexpected dividends to its stockholders. "The new management really knows its business," runs the comment on the Bourse. In London, the chief of a government corporation with a growing deficit announces his resignation. "He was a brilliant engineer," members of the Board of Directors tell each other, "but a wretched administrator." In Little Rock, Novosobirsk, and Barcelona the field representatives of national organizations exchange the standard jokes on "central office idiots." In even more standardized fashion they quietly interpret or sabotage the latest directives from headquarters. In thousands of places throughout the world foremen argue with workers' committees. Unit chiefs debate with workers on procedures and work methods. Advisers complain that their proposals for reorganization are ignored.

In scores of secret offices anonymous administrators work busily in organizing the super-secret work of the scientists and technicians who conduct the calculations and experiments which will enable a still larger group of people to prepare and perhaps deliver the latest missiles, gases, rays and whatnots that may yet destroy the stage itself.

All these activities differ from each other in innumerable ways. Many of them compete or even directly conflict with each other. Many are so far apart in objectives, methods and language that they might as well take place in different worlds. Yet they have two things in common: all involve people in organized groups or institutions and all involve the administration or management of organizations.[1]

The participants in these activities include presidents of corporations, governments, universities, and trade unions; generals, bishops, and kings; chairmen of government boards, councils, and executive committees; and the heads of ministries, agencies, banks, cooperatives, and cartels. Less conspicuous but of no less significance are the thousands upon thousands of officials who grease the wheels and control many parts of the administrative mechanism. Whether they will it or not, doctors, engineers lawyers, economists, statisticians, and physicists are drawn into the whirl of administrative activity. This even happens to many of the growing number of experts in administration itself. Most people, in fact, spend a large part of their waking hours as participants in the activities of administered organizations. For this aspect of human life has become increasingly important with the onward sweep throughout the world of an administrative (also referred to as "organizational," "managerial" or "bureaucratic") revolution which is enlarging the role of large and complex organizations in all societies.

The governance of organizations is an ancient human skill. No matter what our criteria, we find that many practitioners have raised it from a skill to an art. We find that others have gone still further and attained the level of administrative wisdom. Some have even provided examples that administration "is not only the faculty upon which social stability rests but it is possibly the highest faculty of the human mind" (Adams, 1913, p. 206.*

---

1. The terms *administration* and *management* are here used as synonyms. The reasons for this usage—together with a full consideration of the terms *organization* and *institution*—are given in "The Management of Organizations" (Chapt. 10).

* The "General Bibliography" contains the full citation for all documents referred to in the text. As explained on page 25, italicized references refer to books or articles covered by the bibliographical report in Volume II, "Research Studies in Organizational Behavior."

At the same time we see—perhaps more than in any other field—a persistent unevenness. In one and the same person we find skill associated with clumsiness, wisdom with shallowness. We see vast numbers of administrators who never rise above—or even up to—a level of deadly mediocrity. Above all, we find no simple relation between administrative skill and the purposes for which it is used. We see well-meaning organizations abominably administered and well-administered organizations spewing forth abominations. Within the same organization we see men and women rising higher than the angels and falling lower than the beasts.

If we look a little more closely, we can also see a new and immature area of human knowledge. We see a widening trend in many societies toward the ever more serious study of organizations and their administration. This trend brings together—with a certain degree of friction—experts from many disciplines. With still more friction it brings together the Men of Action and the Men of Academia. This book is part of that trend.

One of the purposes in writing this book has been to summarize and consolidate the progress that has been made in trying to understand the administration of organizations. From the viewpoint of man's previous history, this progress is tremendous. But from the viewpoint of what remains to be learned, we have barely started. Another purpose of the book, therefore, is to present a set of ideas that may stimulate others to move forward on the long road of creative action, theory, and research.

The major purpose of this introductory chapter is to provide a general perspective on the book and its subject matter. This can best be done by

- indicating the vital nature of the questions asked by those seeking to understand more about the administration of organizations;
- pointing out the seriousness of the obstacles to such understanding;
- identifying the limited aids to understanding that can be provided by theory and research;
- explaining the strategy I have used in presenting such aids to understanding; and
- discussing the methods I have used in finding and organizing my materials.

A. *The Vital Questions*

THERE ARE few questions more perplexing probably than those concerning the administration of organizations.

These questions arise not only in the minds of private and public administrators. They are asked even more frequently by the larger number of people subordinate to administrators or even inconvenienced by them. They are asked by aspirants to administrative posts. They are asked by all those who attempt to study and understand the behavior of people in organizations.

This does not mean that such questions are clearly identified. They may be asked by people with no concept of either an organization or its administration. They are asked in a variety of colloquial, technical, and academic terms that mask their relevance to the administration of organizations. Even when clearly stated, they are usually intertwined with nonadministrative questions.

This gives rise to a strange "nothing-everything" phenomenon. At times there seem to be no truly important questions concerning administration; the subject dwindles to nothing. At other times all-important questions relate to administration; the subject expands to include everything.

There is good reason for both viewpoints. Administration is merely an aspect of organizational activity. It is nothing by itself; it must always be seen with specific reference to just what it is that an organization is doing. Yet it is an essential—or at least unavoidable—aspect of all organizational activity and therefore of human society. Without it man's organizations would fall apart, his larger purposes would be will-of-the-wisps, his greatest hopes would be empty dreams.

1. WHAT WAS, IS, AND MIGHT BE?

The newcomer in any organization is apt to find himself faced with a big, booming, buzzing confusion. Even after he learns his own role, he may well ask, "What's going on here? How do things really work? How does anything ever get done?"

As he acquires experience, he learns partial answers to these questions in the form of what Michael Polanyi calls "tacit knowledge" (1958, p. 49 —65).[2] He knows how things get done in his immediate environment and uses this knowledge in doing things himself and getting other people to do things with him or for him. But an interest in better performance, intellectual curiosity, or both may impel him to ask more difficult questions. He seeks an understanding of the past to throw light upon the present. By looking at past and present, he tries to answer such questions as "What might happen in the future if I should do such-and-such?"

2. Polanyi's path-breaking *Personal Knowledge* on the philosophy of science is one of the few such books written as a long-term serious venture by a scientist of vast experience. To a considerable extent it represents the transformation of tacit knowledge gained by the author into systematically recorded knowledge.

If he rises to positions of higher responsibility in an organization, these questions concerning what has been, is, and might be are applied to a wider range of experience. They are asked concerning many different kinds of units at different hierarchic levels within an organization. They relate to a variety of external organizations: government agencies, business enterprises, associations, federations, and many others. They may even deal with organizations in other countries and very different cultures.

Experienced administrators develop amazing skills in answering these questions quickly. They learn how to ask questions, appraise the relevance of information, make judgments, and adjust judgments to changing circumstances. For this purpose they use rough-and-ready concepts, unstated premises, rules of thumb, and liberal doses of intuition.

But the more questions they may handle in this fashion, the more remain to be answered. Knowledge in the sense of personal acquaintance with (as expressed in the French *connâitre*) is quite different from knowledge in the sense of recorded and communicable facts and generalizations (as expressed more closely in the French *savoir*).[3] Although the tacit component of knowledge can never be fully expressed in words and other symbols, it can never become highly developed unless a significant part of it is so expressed. Unless this is done with some degree of precision and consistency, communication with others is haphazard and fragmentary. And organizational life constantly demands communication on such matters, particularly among and from administrators.

Thus even the most rough-and-ready administrators often become theorists despite themselves. They grab some simple set of principles, fully or partially expressed, and hang on for dear life. These crude theories help them grope their way through the vast jungle of information and misinformation about the past and the present. They help them make useful predictions about the future. And somehow or other things do get done.

But the *was*, *is*, and *might be* questions are so persistent and so challenging that many administrators feel the need for something more substantial. The more simple-minded try to use social science the way a drunk uses a lamp post—for support, not illumination (*Leighton*, p. 128). Or else they seek formulae that will produce prefabricated answers. Those with a little background in some substantive field of science or technology often seek the same degree of certainty in administrative thought. When they cannot find it, they complain that "the professors don't know what's

3. This discussion is based not only upon Polanyi's *Personal Knowledge*, but also upon the ideas developed in James, *The Principles of Psychology*, Vol. I, p. 221; Mayo, *The Social Problems of an Industrial Civilization*, p. 15-19; and Miller, Galenter, and Pribram, *Plans and the Structure of Behavior*, p. 81-93.

going on," "the textbooks are impractical," or "that may be all right in theory, but not in practice." Through this lament the men of action do more than proclaim their own superiority. They also suggest that they would be happier if professors "knew the score," textbooks provided more useful knowledge, and theory came into closer contact with reality.

The search for better answers is dramatically underscored by the rising popularity of "management training" and "executive development." These activities are based on the idea that responsible managers, although possibly "born administrators" and already clothed in the trappings of authority, may still have something to learn about management. Although this idea is always more readily accepted *vis-à-vis* one's subordinates, the important development of the last decade is that more and more frequently it is the King himself who declares "The King has no clothes."

The same uneasiness haunts the halls of academia. In universities and colleges throughout the world, teachers and students have the feeling that the ideas taught have too little relation to the questions of *was, is,* and *might be* in the wide world of organizational action. The same body of administrative thought damned by practical men as too theoretical and academic is looked down on by academic leaders as too practical. Many great institutions of splendid achievement disdain to enter a field which they regard as vocational instead of theoretical or scientific.

In greater part, perhaps, this feeling of uneasiness stems from self-criticism. The latecomers are dissatisfied with the patterns that they may have slavishly copied from others. The pioneers and the patternmakers are themselves seriously pondering new approaches—more practical and more theoretical—to *was, is,* and *might be* questions.

This sense of dissatisfaction reaches its peak when the teachers decide that they have little to teach and that their only contribution is to help students talk to each other about problems or case studies. The use of case studies and nondirected discussion springs to some extent from well-founded theory on the nature of the learning process. It also represents a jaundiced estimate of the present level of organized knowledge concerning administration. It expresses righteous refusal to bluff students by presenting them with empty principles or by drilling them in techniques of limited managerial use.

Despite these dissatisfactions, a growing number of serious thinkers from better-established disciplines have entered the management field. At first it was mainly political scientists, lawyers, and sociologists. Then came the psychologists, psychiatrists, anthropologists, and historians. More recently, the mathematicians and the economists have joined the undertaking. The result has been an unbelievable outpouring of books and articles, backed up by a growing body of research relating to organizations and their administration. The volume of relevant documents is already so great that anyone who tried to keep up with current writing on the subject would be drowned in a flood of paper.

2. WHAT SHOULD HAVE BEEN AND SHOULD BE?

Far more pressing than the *was, is,* and *might be* questions are those phrased in terms of *should have been* and *should be.*

All men and women sit in judgment of the activities of organizations and their administrators. Finding fault is a popular sport—particularly when directed at superiors or rivals. It is a form of self-expression, of personal relief from tension, and also a form of influence. Giving credit, albeit somewhat less popular, serves the same functions. In either case the evaluators may be more interested in what *should have been* than in what *was.*

Many men and women—administrators above all—are exceedingly active in trying to shape the future. They ask not only *what might be* but *what should be?*

In their simplest form these questions relate to the operations of a single unit of a single organization. What should its goals be? What should be done to help it achieve these goals more effectively?

In more complex form these questions relate to aggregations of organizations. How should scientific research, industry, transportation, trade, or banking be organized and administered? What is the best structure for agriculture—particularly in a country where there is a vigorous demand for land redistribution? How should trade unions be organized and collective bargaining handled? How should trade associations and national federations be organized? How should cooperatives be managed? How should the various agencies of government be related to one another and administered? What should be done, if anything, to strengthen various international organizations?

The *should* questions become still more perplexing when we turn from these huge aggregations and focus upon the individual in the era of the administrative revolution. What should a person—be he among the administrators or the administered—expect from organizational activity? What should be done, if anything, to help people escape the tyranny of organizations without becoming anonymous specks in a purposeless cloud of dust?

These *should be* questions are so overwhelmingly important that people are often impelled to seek answers in bland abstraction from the more mundane consideration of what *has been, is,* and *might be.* Thus much of administrative thought has been prescriptive and normative before attempting to be descriptive and analytical. This has been most obvious in the sphere of government organizations, where discussions of public administration often center around alternative approaches to philosophy and ethics. It is less obvious in the sphere of business administration. But even here we find a central role (although less frequently expressed) for various conceptions of the good life and the good society. The most practical-minded businessman may be a moralist or philosopher despite himself. He may be so passionately dedicated to a few *should be* conceptions that he has lost all sense of orientation to what really *has been, is,* or *might be.*

On the other hand, there are those who seek wherever possible to transform questions of desirability into questions of fact and probability. Consider the statement that "the administrator of this organization should take Action A instead of Action B." An analysis of facts relating to similar circumstances can lead to a restatement as follows: "If under such-and-such circumstances the administrator takes Action A instead of B, there is a much greater likelihood that his organization will achieve goal C." But what about C? Why should C be a goal? The reply: "If C, then a greater likelihood of achieving goal D."

So far so good. But the transformation cannot be extended *ad infinitum.* Somewhere between D and Z will come a point where an "ultimate value" may be found.

At this point some administrative theorists try to simplify their intellectual problems by drawing a sharp dividing line. "Here," they proclaim, "is where administrative thought stops and ethics begins. Administrative thought must limit itself solely to means. It cannot deal with ends."

This self-denying ordinance has some practical value for theorists. It allows them to sweep under the carpet some of the most puzzling of all organizational and administrative questions. It allows them to concentrate upon the more definitive handling of limited questions. It affords them the luxury of leaving unclear and unstated the specific aims toward which they themselves are motivated.

It also restricts the value of administrative theory to practical men. It introduces the fatally unrealistic conception of a clear and unmistakable separation between means and ends. It is usually based upon the still more unreal myth of some single ultimate end, as contrasted with the real world in which administrators are constantly making adjustments between a variety of highly desired ends.

Hence those who feel the need for a more realistic and more scientific orientation toward the vital questions of *was, is,* and *might be* find themselves increasingly obligated to face up to the still deeper questions of *should have been* and *should be.*

B. *The Obstacles to Understanding*

THERE IS NOTHING EASY about any effort to understand the world or any part of it. It is difficult even to ask the right questions. Final answers are impossible.

In the natural sciences the obstacles to understanding are difficult enough. As scientists and philosophers have repeatedly pointed out, the very act of observing has itself an effect on what is being observed. Although the observer may seek certainty, he must often be satisfied with probability. He is sure to find certainty and precision only when he puts them there in the first place through the assumptions he uses. These assumptions, in turn, are continually being replaced by new ones more useful in explaining larger arrays of phenomena. The new explanations invariably give rise to previously undreamed-of questions. The paradox of scientific progress is that it always opens up new areas of ignorance and greater challenges to future discovery.

The social scientist faces all these difficulties and many more. First of all, the people he observes observe him and react to him. The social scientist must always assume that the people he observes are in some way trying to influence the observational process. This may even take the form of deliberate efforts to deceive or exploit the observer. Second, the observer's values and biases can rarely, if ever, be disentangled from the recorded observations. At the very least the objects of observation are sensitive to—and influenced by—the observer's values and acts. Third, careful measurement is far more difficult in the social than in the physical sciences—and even where feasible, it may often be far less relevant. Nor are controlled experiments possible on any significant scale. The laboratory of the social scientist is society itself. What happens there is usually far beyond his puny power to control. Finally, the social scientist deals with more complex systems. The number of variables and of interrelationships between them is far greater than the relatively simple aspects of the world which physical scientists try to understand.

Yet when we try to understand the administration of organizations, we face still greater obstacles. Here we are confronted with higher degrees of complexity, deeply-rooted myths and taboos that thwart understanding, and an inevitable insularity on the part of all observers.

1. COMPLEXITY

In most of the social sciences theorists and researchers usually cope with complexity by acts of self-limitation. Political scientists tend to look at governments, economists at economies, psychologists at individuals, sociologists and anthropologists groups and societies. When their paths cross, the division of intellectual labor is preserved by using different concepts. In either case the object of study is simplified by excluding from the universe of discourse or attention all except certain aspects of human behavior and certain conceptual tools for its analysis.

The urge for deeper understanding, however, often leads social scientists to abjure these oversimplifications and more boldly to face human behavior in all its baffling complexity. In certain fields this seems to be required by the very nature of the subject matter. Historians are expected somehow or other to deal with the seamless web of the past, and the past includes every conceivable type of phenomena. The "policy scientists" —a term which refers to a small minority of pathfinders—orient themselves toward significant problems of the future. For this purpose they too must try to exploit all conceivable conceptual tools.

Administration is another of these fields. But here we cannot simplify matters by concentrating on the past or on the future. We must concern ourselves with both. We must behave like historian-policy scientists. In so doing we must look at the behavior of organizations and their administrators from many viewpoints, since we are dealing with life as a whole rather than an artificial or imaginary slice of life. Almost everything we look at is something that can be called a government or an economy (if only in a microscopic sense) and is composed of individuals and groups within a certain culture. We must therefore go very far in exploiting the aids to understanding that have been developed by political scientists, economists, psychologists, sociologists, anthropologists, and others.

In the effort to understand administration anyone can make his task simpler by concentrating on certain types of organizations or on certain aspects of administration. In fact, such concentration of effort is essential to the subdivision of intellectual labor. In the study of administration, as in anything else, if everyone tried to do everything, nothing would ever get done. But the deeper one goes at any one point, the more he will find an extremely large number of complex and interrelating variables. Not for him the luxury of *ceteris paribus* assumptions that allow him to "freeze" all variables except the one he is watching. Every situation is unique and to grapple with it he must help identify the *ceteris* rather than blithely ignore them. Administrative analysis, above all, is action-oriented. If his theoretical model is not close to reality he cannot, in good conscience, ignore the problem of building the bridges that connect it with reality.

The closer he gets to reality, however, the more it changes. Organizations change, people change, and circumstances change. Purposes change and methods change. There are even unanticipated changes in the rate of change. Under these circumstances one of the few things that is always certain is an important element of uncertainty. The better the resolution of any problem the more certain that it will give rise to new problems.

2. MYTHS AND TABOOS

It has become common practice to explode the fallacies, the folklore, or the proverbs which many people accept as a substitute for knowledge about administration. But as any logician can demonstrate, fallacies are ordinary obstacles to understanding. And as any expert can testify, they are found in every field of human thought.

Man's efforts to think rationally about administration, however, are impeded not only by fallacies but also by deeply-rooted myths and taboos. These cannot be readily dispelled by logic or demonstration.

One of the reasons for this is that myths and taboos are often born in the womb of organizational necessity. They are sired by administrators who see in them a way of enhancing their power, resolving or living with internal conflicts, or adjusting to a difficult environment

Some of these myths serve as filters through which many of us look at either single organizations or social organization in its broader aspects. Among these are the myths of ultimate authority and central omnipotence; these are referred to in Chapter 3.[4] Others are more narrow in focus— such as the myths of number magic and of impersonality and rationality in large-scale organizations.

The taboos serve as barriers to keep people from looking at certain things at all. Taboos on certain words and their referents often make it difficult to deal openly with such subjects as the use of power, pressure, propaganda, manipulation, or double bookkeeping—particularly by organizations and administrators enjoying high status in society. Other taboos surround any effort to deal scientifically with the referents of such "hurrah" words as democracy, freedom, justice, enterprise, and responsibility and such "boo" words as dictatorship, control, bureaucracy, frustration, and deviation. Above all, we all tend to surround with a fence of taboos anything we really hold dear—whether it be a form of social organization to which we feel ideologically committed, a way of organization life to which we are accustomed, or our own self-image of how we would act, or have acted, as administrators.

A person's status as a scientist does not automatically free him from the grip of myth and taboo. What he can readily see if he looks at another

4. They are discussed at greater length in "The Dispersion of Power in Organizations" (Gross, *The Managing of Organizations*, Chapt. 3).

society (particularly a primitive one) he may never be able to detect in his own environment. Nor does organizational and administrative experience do the trick. It may merely exchange one set of intellectual obstacles for another. Many experienced administrators will themselves become the most blinded by the myths and taboos that they have helped to propagate. The wiser administrators usually know better. But here, unfortunately, there is too much truth in the old adage that "those who know don't tell."

3. INSULARITY

Additional obstacles are provided by insularity in many forms.

One form of insularity is the culture-bound nature of most serious studies in the field. It is only natural for social scientists to focus their attention upon the phenomena near at hand in their own society. It is still more natural for the values and customs of their own society to affect their perception of other societies. Thus theorists and experts from the U.S.A. and Western Europe—where systematic administrative thought has thus far developed most intensively—have often blithely assumed the immediate relevance of their knowledge to countries of Asia, Africa, and Latin America. With the emergence of large-scale technical assistance programs in public and business administration, however, the naïveté of expecting saltwater fish to understand all the problems of freshwater fish has been revealed. The experts of the U.S.A. and Western Europe have begun to see that just as fish who have spent all their life in a big ocean cannot be good judges of the salinity of water, they themselves still have a long way to go in understanding their own environment.

A second form of insularity is the narrow and constricting environment in which most administrators learn about administration. The average administrator spends most of his life on a handful of islands on a vast, mysterious ocean. Even those who are most capable of learning from experience (and experience itself does not automatically produce this capability) are usually limited by a relatively small variety of experiences. This is particularly true of administrators who stay in one organization for most of their adult lives, for businessmen in general and for small businessmen in particular. It may be less true of the managers of large business enterprises and public administrators who deal with varied segments of their society. Even in these cases intensive experience with one sector may be counter-balanced by comparative ignorance of another sector. Both tacit and organized knowledge of administration tends to be parochial.

A third form is the intellectual insularity of social scientists. Many of those who presume to study administration cut themselves off from the knowledge that can be obtained only through some sort of personal experience. They study the deep waters of organizational and administrative life by looking at them from afar. They then "go into the field," fill out questionnaires, run cards through calculating machines and come out with the tentative and cautiously phrased hypothesis that water may be wet. . . .

Moreover, the growing specialization of scientific activity produces a special kind of insularity. C. P. Snow barely touched on this in his superficially stated lament that "the intellectual life of the whole of western society is increasingly being split into two polar groups . . . literary intellectuals at one pole—at the other scientists . . ." (1959, p. 4). He completely ignored the growing gap which separates each field and subfield of science from all the others.

To understand the predicament of social scientists we may regard the universe of human behavior as a vast jigsaw puzzle composed of thousands of multicolored pieces.[5] Because the puzzle is so large, some subdivision of labor is needed among those who try to piece it together. So the labor is divided—with some concentrating on pieces of a certain size, some on pieces of certain colors. The system works when the pieces are put together in sight of all the others and people can exchange information on the pieces they hold and others hold. Only in this way can one person capitalize on the progress of others or know what next steps are required.

But this does not happen so frequently or so easily. The task of examining single pieces is so difficult that not many have time to look at what is being done by those working on different sizes, shapes, or colors. Nor is this easy to do. The specialized tasks call for specialized terminologies. Thus each group invents new terms of its own or uses old words in new ways. They find themselves using different words to talk about the same things and the same words to talk about different things. The edifice in which they work, therefore, becomes more and more like the tower of Babel. The flood of published documents in all fields leads many people to give up the effort to keep up with anything outside of their own subspecialities.

5. I am indebted for this metaphor to Michael Polanyi's *Logic of Liberty*, p. 35. However, Polanyi assumes—as I cannot assume—a full flow of information. On the basis of this assumption he concludes that "a series of independent initiatives are organized to a joint achievement by mutually adjusting themselves at every successive stage to the situation created by all the others who are acting likewise."

c. *Aids to Understanding*

DESPITE THE OBSTACLES described above, administrative thought can already aid in the handling of the vital questions of *was, is,* and *might be,* and of *should have been* and *should be.*

This aid can appear in the form of:

> ✓ a language of administration,
> ✓ generalizations at various levels, and
> ✓ an identification of major values.

In this book I have tried to provide each of these aids to understanding. I have done this by synthesizing major ideas developed by others and adding certain ideas of my own. The aim is not to present final answers but to stimulate closer cooperation on these matters between men of action and social scientists and among social scientists themselves. Only thus can a more mature body of administrative knowledge come into being.

But even the maturation of administrative knowledge would not yield automatic answers to the extremely complex questions that will always plague private and public organizations. Theory and research can supply nothing more than intellectual tools. These tools can never take the place of the abilities and values of those who may want to use them or of the power that such users can organize to transform human purposes into living reality.

1. A LANGUAGE OF ADMINISTRATION

The need for a rich and vigorously growing language of administration is by no means limited to theorists and researchers. It is a practical problem facing all administrators.

Every organization has its own language of administrative action. In larger and older organizations these languages become part of the spirit of the place and perform a morale-sustaining function. They are picked up slowly by newly initiated insiders and are never fully understood by outsiders. In smaller and younger organizations they tend to reflect the idiosyncrasies and folklore of an economic sector, a geographic area, or an entire culture.

When people from different organizations get together to discuss common problems, communication between them is impossible unless they have a common language adequate to deal with the complexities of the problems they face. A similar impasse often occurs among the administrators of federations and international "peak associations." It also occurs within single organizations wherever the common language of administration is not sufficiently sophisticated or widely enough shared to span the widely divergent approaches of people from highly specialized units within the organization.

But it would be a mistake to think of language as only a means of communication, as a means of expressing ideas already well formulated. Language is much closer to the very substance of idea. Its more mature development always means that we have more to communicate. Thus the maturation of the language of administration will mean not only that administrators will be better able to share their experiences, but that they will be able to experience administrative action more richly, and organize their experience more consciously, and benefit more deeply from the lessons that can be provided in the school of experience. For theorists and researchers, on the other hand, the maturing language of administration will provide the basic concepts without which facts cannot be classified and generalizations cannot be shaped.

In moving toward a general language of organization and administration I have tried to use a vocabulary that is "both small enough and simple enough to be learned, precise enough to communicate, and large enough so that all of the important ideas that are contending can be comfortably and easily described" (Kahn, p. 5). In so doing I present many terms and concepts that until now have been regarded as the special property of business, military, or public administration or of one or another discipline or profession. The reader will thus find liberal use of such terms as aspiration level, bureaucracy, clientele, goods and services, input, output, polyarchy, power, pressure, products (both end and intermediate), product mix, propaganda, and rule. This will be disconcerting to those who regard some of these terms—such as bureaucracy, double bookkeeping, power, and pressure as "nasty words" with derogatory connotations. I have therefore used specific definitions in the effort to convert their nastiness to neutrality.

My usage may also prove initially confusing to some specialists who will find that my use of "their" term differs from their own use. Thus "end product" as herein used is not the same as "end product" in national economic accounting. Here, as in other cases, I have had to adapt technical terms to the special requirements of organization theory. My approach is to specify the usage I am employing, often after a full identification of alternative usages.

This approach is carried furthest in my presentation of a language of organizational purpose, which in my judgment must become the most important element in a general language of organization and administration. Here I provide an arbitrary division of labor between the words purpose, objective, goal, target, and norm, and have related these terms to needs, interests, drives, and motives. I give concentrated attention to the formulation of concepts relevant to the key categories of organizational purpose: the satisfaction of human interests, the production of goods and services, efficiency in the use of scarce resources, investment in organizational viability, resource mobilization, observance of codes, and technical and administrative rationality. Through the incorporation of accepted technical terms and the largest possible reliance on ordinary language I have been able to get along with no neologisms other than "commergence" for belonging or togetherness without pejorative connotations (Chapt. 8), "purpose surrogate" for an indirect measure of purposes, and "teletics" for the study of human purposes (both in Chapt. 11).

In presenting a presumably consistent set of terms, I am not suggesting that they are the "right" ones. To do so would be to indulge in word magic. Anyone has the right to use words, and other symbols, as he chooses. For purposes of sustained communication his symbols, apart from consistency in use, need only be useful and clear.

Utility, however, is a relative matter. "All definitions are essentially *ad hoc*. They are relevant to some purpose or situation, and consequently are applicable only over a restricted field or universe of discourse" (Ogden and Richards, 1946, p. 111). Here the universe of discourse is organization and administration. I am not suggesting that the terms I use here can be automatically transferred, without adaptation, to other spheres. Moreover, even with *ad hoc* definitions, there can be no "one best way." A frozen language is a dead language. The best test of the language herein offered will not be found in the degree of adoption but in its contribution to the continuing process of linguistic adaptation and growth in this field.

Clarity also is relative. Words merely "symbolize people's thoughts (or references) about things rather than things (or referents) directly" (*op. cit.*, p. 11).[6] The thoughts themselves, with their overtones of feeling and attitude, can probably never be fully expressed in any single set of terms. We grope for words to tell what we know, as Polanyi has pointed out, and our words hang together by these roots. "The true artists of speech remain always conscious of the metaphorical character of language. They go on correcting and supplementing one metaphor by

6. Here Ogden and Richards add: "But just as we say that the gardener mows the lawn when we know that is the lawn-mower which actually does the cutting, so, though we know that the direct relation of symbols is with thought, we also say that symbols record events and communicate facts. . . ."

another, allowing their words to contradict each other and attending only to the unity and certainty of their thought" (Polanyi, 1958, p. 102). Even if we eliminate metaphors, we can often express ourselves properly only by "successive definition"—by restating the same thought a number of times in different terms. Whenever someone goes too far in using identical and presumably consistent terms, there is reason to suspect that behind the words may lie deeply hidden ambiguities or, as in the case of the student who has learned his lesson by rote, an utter absence of thought.

2. GENERALIZATIONS AT VARIOUS LEVELS

Generalizations serve two purposes. In the jargon of medical doctors these may be termed "diagnosis" and "therapy." In military circles the same ideas are expressed by "evaluation of the situation" and "formulation of strategy and tactics."

In medical practice a good diagnosis is much more than merely providing a name for something that ails a patient. It applies to the patient's ailment some generalizations concerning how he got that way and what is likely to happen. Similarly administrative theory can do more than merely provide names. Its generalizations can help administrators and researchers in identifying the many aspects of problems and situations. It can help in the interpretation of situations by suggesting possible relations between various events. It can help in preparing an evaluation of what might happen in the future, if no special steps are taken.

Generalizations are equally valuable in developing the strategy and tactics of therapeutic action. They can contribute to an administrator's awareness of various ways of doing things, thereby broadening his perspective and freeing him from the chains of habit and routine. They can help in predicting the possible consequences of such alternatives, thereby aiding in the difficult process of choosing between them. They can be particularly helpful in the imaginative creation of new and previously unsuspected alternatives.

Whether generalizations are used for diagnosis or therapy, they also serve some extremely useful psychological functions. They provide the administrator and/or researcher with the indispensable "selector mechanisms" without which they are apt to be drowned in a flood of irrelevant or misleading information. By making him more aware of the universal aspects of even his most unique problems, they can free him from the overpowering onus of guilt which is apt to develop from the very natural feeling that he alone is in such a terrible predicament. They can provide a rational justification for action that he intuitively knows is correct but could not otherwise defend in communicable terms.

Generalizations, of course, can be made at many levels. At the lowest, we find singular generalizations. In the terms used by David Easton, these are "statements of observed uniformities between two isolated and easily identified variables." In the language of Robert Merton, these are "minor working hypotheses evolved . . . during the day-by-day routines of research."

At a somewhat higher level stands synthetic or narrow-gauge theory. For Easton, this is "a set of interrelated propositions that are designed to synthesize the data in an organized body of singular generalizations." This is similar to Merton's "theories of the middle range . . . special theories applicable to limited ranges of data."

A still higher level of generalization is provided by broad-gauge or systematic theory. For Easton this is "the conceptual framework within which a whole discipline is cast . . . those theories and assumptions which an investigator uses in undertaking an analysis within a given field." This is very close to what Merton refers to as a "master conceptual scheme" for deriving or consolidating all subsidiary theories.

These distinctions are often made in order to indicate that level of abstraction which, in the judgment of the author, needs major emphasis. Thus Easton attacks "hyperfactualism" and calls for more broad-gauge, systematic theory. Merton favors middle-range theory. By his sharp attacks on abstracted empiricism and grand theory, C. Wright Mills stakes out his own position along with Merton as a "middle of the roader."[7] A good case can indeed be made for the middle of the road. Theorists can easily go to the one extreme of getting lost in an unconnected mass of minor generalizations or the other extreme of vanishing in the cosmic distances of intellectual space.

In this book I have run up and down the ladder of abstraction. Some of the material in the following chapters consists of singular generalizations, some of synthetic theory, and some of broad-gauge theory. The greatest emphasis, perhaps, is upon broad-gauge theory. I would not want, however, to use Easton's term of systematic theory. While I have concentrated upon developing a broad conceptual framework I have deliberately tried not to oversystematize it. At this stage in the development of a subject there is greater merit in "dynamic openness" than in "premature closure" (Kaplan, p. 68-71).

The generalizations I have used may also be ranked in terms of the level of confidence expressed in them. This is the "fiduciary element of

7. The references referred to in the above paragraphs can be found in Easton, *The Political System*, p. 51-63; Merton, *Social Theory and Social Structure*, Chapt. 2, "The Bearing of Sociological Theory in Empirical Research"; and Mills, *The Sociological Imagination*, Chapts. 2 and 3.

an affirmation," which, according to Polanyi (1958, p. 29), enters openly or covertly into all assertions. At the lower levels of confidence such a generalization is merely an hypothesis. At the other extreme there are those generalizations which are regarded as necessary starting points and can therefore be called "axioms." In between there is a host of "principles," some analytic and descriptive, some prescriptive. In either case their truth can be verified by checking observable phenomena. Or else their validity can be demonstrated by deductions from axioms and empirically-supported principles.

3. A SUBSTANTIVE HANDLING OF VALUES

If social scientists were able to limit themselves to statements of fact, there might be little need for them to deal with values. Similarly, there would be little chance of dealing with values separately if it were completely impossible to formulate value-free statements or conclusions. The worlds of fact and value would be so indissolubly fused that any attempt to separate them would be wasted effort.

As Ernest Nagel (1961, p. 485-502) has cogently argued, neither of these extreme positions is a useful guide in the social sciences. On the one hand, social scientists must inevitably deal with many value judgments that cannot be reduced to purely factual or probabilistic terms. On the other hand, there are many statements about means-ends relations that (despite the values that might be placed on some means) may be value-free.

A major role of theory in the social sciences, therefore, is to help in the difficult process of distinguishing between the two kinds of statements. The effort to do this is difficult and drawn-out. "For the most part," as Nagel says, "we are unaware of many assumptions that enter into our analyses and actions, so that despite resolute efforts to make our preconceptions explicit some decisive ones may not even occur to us. But in any event, the difficulties generated for scientific inquiry by unconscious bias and tacit value orientations are rarely overcome by devout resolutions to eliminate bias. They are usually overcome, often only gradually, through the self-corrective mechanisms of science as a social enterprise. For modern science . . . progressively diminishes the effects of bias by retaining only those proposed conclusions of its inquiries that survive critical examination by an indefinitely large community of students, whatever be their value preferences or doctrinal commitments" (p. 489).

Administrative theory can assist in this process only if it specifically identifies various kinds of means and various kinds of ends and various types of means-end relations. It is not enough to speak of values in hushed terms as though they were gods or the spirits of the departed.

In this book, therefore, I have given considerable attention to the process of evaluation. I have tried to set forth in factual terms the various categories of criteria that are used in evaluating organizational and administrative performance. To do this I have had to identify the basic interests of human beings and the varying ways in which these interests are revealed in their nonpurposeful, purposeful, and evaluating behavior. In making this effort I have openly set forth a set of personal moral commitments. By so doing I think I can be most helpful to administrators and theorists in their constant checking back and forth between *was*, *is*, and *might be*, on the one hand, and *should have been* and *should be*, on the other.

D. *An Action-Theory Strategy*

THIS BOOK strives to achieve an action-theory marriage. It tries to deal with the major questions asked by both administrators and scholars concerning the governance of organizations. It tries to give some feeling for the art and wisdom of seasoned administrators. It tries to record the major aspects of such art and wisdom. It stresses the primacy of administrative action as both a source of theory and a test of theory's utility.

In my two-volume work, *The Managing of Organizations*, I have felt it essential to look at a much broader sphere of action than that of individual organizations at any one place in time. I have felt it essential to look also at the broad historical processes of social action and their interrelation with administrative theory in its various forms. This has meant probing back into the distant past. It has meant peering forward into the misty future.

Thus, in *The Managing of Organizations*, the chapters in "The Administrative Revolution" describe the historical sweep of the administration revolution through major parts of the world. Refuting the energetically propagated myths of "ultimate authority" and "central omnipotence," they present a flexible model for the distribution of authority within organizations. They identify the major threats that the administrative revolution has created with respect to the place of the individual in society, the nature of social organization, and man's survival on the planet.

The part on "The Development of Administrative Thought" approaches administrative thought as both an outgrowth of the administrative revolution and a factor in accelerating its onward sweep. It identifies many of the early, scattered and undifferentiated ideas on administration embedded in the political philosophy of previous centuries. It summaries the basic views of the outstanding "pioneers" in administrative thought: Henri Fayol, Frederick Taylor, Max Weber, Luther Gulick, Lyndall Urwick, Mary Follett, Elton Mayo, Fritz Roethlisberger, Chester Barnard, and Herbert Simon. It discusses the contributions to administrative thought from the various disciplines and surveys the rising flood of publications dealing directly with the major aspects of administration. Here, however, I concentrate on matters of more immediate relevance to managers and students of management.

1. THE UNDERLYING CONSENSUS

Despite the growing variety of administrative thought and research, a surprising degree of underlying consensus can be found on basic aspects of administration. Much of this consensus, however, is hidden by ter-minological ambiguity and substantive disagreements on other matters.

Part One, "The Emerging Integration," maps out this consensus in general terms. In Chapter 2 the question "What is administration?" is answered by indicating what the term usually refers to in modern ad-ministrative thought and by setting forth certain broad areas of agree-ment on the common characteristics of all administration and on its varying characteristics in different organizations, at different levels and in different environments. Special chapters then deal with the "conflict-cooperation nexus" and the relationships between power, authority and responsibility. Part One ends by discussing a number of traditional over-simplifications which, although still looming large in the belief-disbelief systems of many people, are being torpedoed by modern administrative thought.

2. THE DEEPER PENETRATION

The next four parts represent a penetration of the subject which, while built upon the emerging consensus, goes far beyond it.

Part Two, "The Environment," provides the essential background for looking at any organization. It starts with an organization's linkages to its immediate environment. The perspective is then broadened to include its general environment.

Part Three, "Structure," deals with the actors in the administrative drama: people-in-organizations. It starts by looking at the interests and motivations of human beings, apart from any particular roles they may play in organizations. It deals separately with the formal and informal aspects of organizational structure.

Part Four, "Performance," deals in detail with the major dimensions of organizational performance:

- the satisfaction of interests
- the output of services or goods
- efficiency or profitability
- investment in organizational viability
- mobilizations of resources
- observance of codes, and
- rationality.

Chapter 11, "The Matrix of Purposes," outlines these dimensions in summary form and discusses them in the context of purposefulness in organizations. The following nine chapters discuss each of these in detail, with output the subject of three separate chapters.

Parts Two, Three and Four deal with the substantive *content* of administrative decision-making and communication. In this context, Part Five analyzes major administrative processes. After the two "linch-pin" chapters of the "decision-making" struggle and the "recurring miracle" of communication, attention is then focused on the interrelated processes of planning, activating and evaluating.

3. THE FUTURE

Part Six, "The Future," concentrates on the expansion of administrative education. Emphasis is placed on the primacy of learning (and unlearning) and on the knowledge-ability-interest approach to what should be learned. The concluding note is one of work-learning and teacher-administrator combinations.

E. *The Methods*

THE MOST POPULAR METHOD of writing a book about administration is to rewrite the books written by others on the same subject during the previous decade. This method yields scores of new books every year, with little that is original beyond the re-editing and rearrangement of the same old stuff.

It would be presumptuous to say that I too have not used this method —at least in part. In fact, I have carried it to its logical extreme by exploiting all past writings that I could find on related subjects over many decades. Among other things, this has led me to a large body of empirical data which no one had previously tried to exploit. The process of exploitation, in turn, has required efforts at synthesis which have drawn heavily upon personal experience.

1. THE EVIDENCE SUPPLIED BY OTHERS

The essence of any attempt to study phenomena seriously is direct observation. Not just any observation. Rather, observation which is carefully directed, refined by the use of precise concepts, systematically recorded, systematically repeated, replicable by other observers, and enlivened by the imaginative formulation of hypotheses that try to explain the phenomena. From such observation comes the evidence that bears on the utility of a concept and the validity of a generalization.

In the late 1930's, when Chester Barnard wrote *The Functions of the Executive,* he had little more material and information to turn to (apart from personal experience) than the Hawthorne experiments and various then-new theorists in psychology and sociology (those theories themselves based upon but a sparse amount of carefully observed data).

Today, however, the situation is quite different. The observational basis for administrative and organizational theory is much stronger. What was then but a minor trickle of empirical research has swollen into a significant stream. Between 1940 and 1960, for example, at least four hundred articles and 200 books have been based largely, if not entirely, upon the empirical study of specific organizations. Although there is considerable discontinuity in the facets observed, this represents a rich fund of data and hypotheses. Nor does this include the less rigorous— but not to be neglected—observational data in case studies prepared for instructional purposes, in historical studies and in biographies and memoirs. All in all, the empirical study of organizational and administrative behavior has reached a stage where the records have already outrun the ability of most students of the subject to keep up with them. My own contribution here, rather than adding another empirical study to the growing accumulation, is more in the nature of review and consolidation of the specific studies done by others. The authors of such studies usually indicate that their purpose is to provide bricks for anyone interested in building the structure of more general theory. One of my purposes has been to use all such bricks that seem capable of helping support the weight of generalizations.

I have also had the benefit, as Barnard did not have, of the impressive forward thrust that has occurred during the last twenty-five years in the social sciences. Economics, political science, sociology, anthropology, and psychology have all moved forward at a rapid pace. Together with such newer points of focus as operations research, cybernetics, information theory, and general systems theory, they have provided theoretical, methodological, and factual aids to the study of administration.

Yet I have carefully refrained from attempting a thorough verification of the total body of these generalizations. Verification is a painstaking task that can better be handled one item at a time by those who concentrate on small sections of a subject. It is not appropriate to the task of presenting a general theory and a comprehensive survey.

Nor do I present all my generalizations in "operational terms"—that is, in terms immediately and automatically susceptible to measurement. In this sense many of the generalizations may therefore be regarded as more suggestive than definitive. This qualification is particularly important in any study that presumes to range over a wide array of subjects customarily dealt with by specialists. From the viewpoint of almost every specialist group there will be serious flaws in all of my generalizations touching upon their restricted areas. In some cases, I am sure, they will find outright errors and inconsistencies. But these are minor flaws that can readily be corrected. The more serious flaw is the built-in superficiality which is unavoidable when one refuses to dig down all the way in a small area. To some extent this is the unavoidable price that one must pay for a comprehensive viewpoint that attempts to avoid the Scylla of ignoring the wisdom in relevant disciplines and the Charybdis of getting mired down and lost forever in the endless depths of any one of them.

2. DOCUMENTATION AND INFORMATION RETRIEVAL

Because of the comprehensive scope of the book and the large amount of data drawn upon, I have adopted the strategy of building up a general body of documentation rather than attempting an intensive documentation of separate points.

The general documentation is found in three places.

The first is the survey of administrative thought presented in Part Two of *The Managing of Organizations*. Having thus summarized the views of other writers within one setting, I have not provided bibliographical surveys for each chapter or for each important subject. Nor have I attempted to survey all the most relevant views of others even on such crucial subjects as power, authority, responsibility, interests, purposes, structure, and process. Although documentation services of this type are sorely needed, it could not be a function of this book to provide them. As suggested in the discussion of information retrieval in the last chapter, it is to be hoped that they will someday be provided on a continuing and professional basis for both practitioners and academics.

The second is the bibliographical report, "Research Studies in Organizational Behavior." Although this selective bibliography includes only about a fourth of the available empirical studies, it highlights one of the great achievements of modern behavioral studies: the building up of a growing body of empirical data. The abstracts serve to indicate the various aspects of organization and administration dealt with, thereby tying the documents cited a little more closely to the structure of the book. They will also partly compensate for the skimpy nature of the references I have made to the tremendous amount of illustrative material now available.

The third is the "General Bibliography." This lists in traditional fashion all the other books, articles, and reports cited in the text.

Since there are two bibliographies, there are two forms of reference to them. References to the "Research Studies in Organizational Behavior" appear in italics, references to the "General Bibliography" in ordinary print. Thus *Argyris* (1953) refers to his *Executive Leadership,* which appears among the research studies, while Argyris (1957) refers to *Personality and Organization,* which appears in the "General Bibliography." At times, of course, the distinction between empirical studies and other documents is not very clear.

Having provided this rather high degree of general documentation, I have assiduously avoided the temptation of using footnotes for the purpose of marshalling "authorities" to support my views. The footnotes have been reserved for (a) expressing occasional "asides" (including comments on quoted sources) that depart somewhat from the continuity of the text, (b) providing more specific references than can be provided by text and bibliography alone to the sources of quotations, illustrations, and ideas borrowed from others, and (c) referring to related materials in other chapters.

3. THE ANALYSIS OF PERSONAL EXPERIENCE

In addition to the evidence obtained from others, personal observation in a variety of organizations and a number of countries have gone into the making of this book.

Most of these observations have been recorded in memory only. The flow of action has usually been too quick to allow for anything else. In piecing together my evidence I shall therefore rely upon a large amount of nondocumented personal observations and introspective analyses of my own failures and successes "recollected in tranquillity." This firsthand experience is supplemented by secondhand experiences gleaned from a multitude of discussions with other participants in organizational and administrative life. The last kind of evidence may not mean much to those with little experience of their own. For those with significant experience in organizational and administrative activity, it will often "ring a bell." It may just as often inspire counterobservations and alternative generalizations based on a different background of personal experience.

If the reader has reservations concerning evidence obtained from personal experience, so have I. Among the things I have learned from experience are the reasons why "those who know don't tell." One motive for not telling, of course, is a gentlemanly concern for those who might be injured by the telling (and I shall studiously refrain from disclosing information that could damage any specific individuals or organization). Another is to magnify one's reputation for wisdom by maintaining an impressive silence.

A more important reason is that telling is so terribly hard. It is much easier to speak of things that one does not know than to put "tacit knowledge" into intelligible words. Nor is it easy to acquire enough knowledge, tacit or otherwise, about any one organization in which one has been active. I could never "tell all" about my own organizational and administrative experience because I never succeeded in knowing all. Personal knowledge of administration is always partial.

Yet knowledge based upon personal experience has much to commend it. It provides clues that could never be obtained by looking on from the outside. The physicist, poor fellow, will never learn what it is like to be one of the electrons or mesons in the atoms he studies. This is the price he pays for the advantage of nature's not being against him. But the administrative practioner or theorist—so long as he follows the example of Antaeus and keeps his feet on the ground of personal experience—can always know what it is like to be among the administrators or the administered.

When administrative thought (and the various disciplines that nurture it) becomes more mature, there will of course be a much greater role for systematic, recorded and replicable observation. But this will not eliminate the analysis of personal experience. I suspect that it will merely provide a foundation for raising such analysis to still higher and more fruitful levels.

4. BALANCING THE QUALITATIVE AND THE QUANTITATIVE

One of the most striking things about modern social science is the great factional conflict between the "quantifiers" and the "imponderabilists."

The quantifiers know that any highly developed science requires precise observations. They maintain that until we can measure, we cannot really understand. They point out that many abstract concepts can never be elegantly formulated until put to use in the measurement process. Moreover, ordinary language may be too crude to handle the complex interrelations of many variables. They have therefore concentrated on rigorous efforts to measure various aspects of human behavior. They have applied the notational forms of modern mathematics to social phenomena. This often leads them into dealing with relatively unimportant aspects of administration. At times it leads to the most misleading forms of number magic, as pointed out in the final section of "The Matrix of Purposes" (Chapt. 19).

Their opponents know that many of the most important things in human life cannot be measured. They protest against misplaced or premature quantification. They would rather be vaguely right than precisely wrong. They honor the role of insight and intuition. This often leads them into dealing with the most important aspects of administration in a fashion more literary than scientific.

As for myself, I have one foot planted firmly in each camp. This is more than a matter of mere compromise; it is rather an effort at integration. Neither approach is by itself sufficient. Each has a lot to contribute, partly in its own terms and partly by way of correcting the excesses of the other.

I put more weight, however, on the foot in the qualitative camp. In every discipline there is probably a period of painful evolution from the predominantly-qualitative to the use of greater quantification. In administrative theory I believe we are still at a very early stage. Above all, genuine progress in quantification—as distinct from razzle-dazzle to impress *hoi polloi*—must rest on units within categories (which can also be referred to as sets, classes, or groups) having certain identifiable boundaries. Ordinal measurement rests on establishing relationships between such categories. The identification and definition of these boundaries and relation-ships are largely tasks in the formation of qualitative concepts.

By placing major emphasis upon these qualitative foundations, there-fore, it has been my aim to promote a stronger foundation for quantifica-tion and a framework more suitable for bringing the qualitative and quantitative approaches together in a fruitful balance.

Part I

THE EMERGING
INTEGRATION

Chapter 2

THE MANAGEMENT OF ORGANIZATIONS

*T*HE EMERGING CONSENSUS in modern administrative (or managerial)[1] thought seems to include three major elements:

- the identification of administrative (or managerial) activity as having something to do with the guidance or governance of the activities of organizations,
- attention to certain characteristics which all organizations and their administration—when viewed at a high enough level of abstraction—have in common, and
- awareness of the special or unique characteristics which differentiate every single organization—when viewed closely enough—from others.

To set forth this growing consensus involves more than summarization. At many points it requires a synthesis of diverse ideas and their expression in a consistent terminology.

Much of the emerging consensus, however, is concealed by different ways of saying similar things. Accordingly, this chapter is concluded

1. The terms "administration," "administrative" and "administrator" are here used as synonymous with "management," "managerial," and "manager." The reasons for this usage are discussed at the end of this chapter.

with an identification of some key terminological problems and a presentation of one way of meeting them.

A. *The Governance of Organizations*

IN MODERN THOUGHT the term "administration" (or management) usually refers to a great variety of activities engaged in by people who occupy positions of formal responsibility and authority in organizations—that is, by administrators (or managers). Without such words as "public" or "business" in front of it, the term refers to the activity of administrators in all types of organizations, armies, political parties, churches, trade unions and trade associations, as well as government and business organizations. Unless preceded by words like "top" or "lower level," it refers to the administrative activity of supervisors, sergeants, and others at lower hierarchic levels, as well as of presidents, department heads, generals, and boards of directors.

1. ADMINISTRATION AS GOVERNANCE

More specifically, how can we distinguish administrative from other activities?

In colloquial usage there are many ways of answering this question without detailing what administrators do. One of the best answers is that the administrator's activity is "getting things done through (or by) others." Similarly, people will often refer to an administrator as someone who is "in charge of others," has people working "for him," "under him," or "with him," is "responsible for the work of others," or as simply the chief, head, boss or "top dog." This usage has the advantage of clearly excluding various clerical activities and housekeeping services in such fields as supplies, maintenance accounts, files and correspondence.[2] On the other hand, by overemphasizing the administrator's concern with hierarchical subordinates, it diverts attention from his activities relating to the environment of his organization.

If we turn to more formal definitions of administration, we usually

2. The ambiguity created when "administration" is used in one phrase to refer *both* to running an organization and to handling housekeeping services or certain administrative tools is beautifully illustrated in positions with titles such as "Deputy-Administrator for Administration."

find an emphasis upon the two elements of (1) guiding or governing, (2) an organization, a unit of an organization or an aggregation of organizations. These two ideas are expressed in a remarkable variety of terms. Thus by combining any word from the first column with any word or phrase in the second column, we can get a hundred different ways of expressing a similar idea:

Managing	. . . an organization
Administering	. . . the activities of an organization
Governing	. . . organized human behavior
Guiding	. . . an enterprise
Coordinating	. . . an undertaking
Integrating	. . . a group of people
Running	. . . people
Directing	. . . the activities of people
Supervising	. . . subordinates
Controlling	. . . the use of resources

With a little ingenuity the number of combinations may be increased still further. Any combination may then be embroidered, as usually done in formal definitions, by reference to (a) purposes, (b) the physical resources used by people in organizations, (c) some criterion of successful administration, such as effectiveness or efficiency, and (d) processes or activities. Yet a careful examination of formal definitions—even though they may originate in the specialized fields of public or business administration—will usually show an explicit or implicit use of the ideas referred to in the two columns.[3]

3. A sampling of definitions from various sources yields the following:
Public Administration. White, 4th edit. (1955): "The direction, coordination and control of many persons to achieve some purpose or objective." Pfiffner and Presthus (1953): "The organization and direction of human and material resources to achieve desired ends." Millett (1954): "The process of directing and facilitating the work of people organized in formal groups to achieve a desired goal."
Business Administration. Newman (1951): "The guidance, leadership and control of the efforts of a group of individuals towards some common goal." Peterson and Plowman (1953): "A technique by which the purposes and objectives of a particular group of people are determined, clarified and effectuated." Koontz and O'Donnell (1955): "The function of getting things done through others." Terry (1956): "The accomplishment of a predetermined objective through the efforts of other people."
General. Adams (1913): "The capacity of coordinating many, and often conflicting, social energies in a single organism so adroitly that they shall operate as a unity." Tead (1951): "The conscious effort to direct, guide and integrate associated human strivings which are focussed towards some specified end or aims."

They thus provide a basis for distinguishing administrative activities from such nonadministrative activities as (a) spontaneous cooperation among people, (b) influencing others outside of an organizational context, (c) guiding the operations of machines, and (d) providing services which, while they may be used by others in an organization, are not designed to guide or coordinate the activity of others.

There are certain disadvantages to any key term in a shorthand definition. "Governance" may seem to imply that administration is an activity only at the highest levels of organization or that there are no important differences between public and private administration. "Guiding" may imply that the "pilot" is interested only in the external reefs and straits. "Coordinating" and "integrating" may suggest interest only in the internal problems. "Running" and "directing" may overemphasize the power and authority of the administrators. This is why formal definitions must always be handled with care and never taken too seriously. Far more significant is the broad context or network of symbols and meanings.

Although "governance" (or governing) is not commonly used in this context, there are various precedents. Fayol, it will be recalled, refers to "government" as the all-inclusive process of "directing an undertaking." Merriam finds that "obviously there is governance everywhere— government in heaven; government in hell; government and law among the outlaws; government in prison" (1944, p. 1). Ruml maintains that "it is in no sense a figure of speech to refer to a business company as a private government" (1950, p. 220). Eells uses the term in analyzing the "constitutional crisis" within the private corporation (1962).

This usage has many advantages. In the public sphere it helps focus attention on the political aspects of administration, thereby escaping the overconstrict dichotomy between public administration and politics. In the private sphere it facilitates attention to organizations as miniature polities with internal politics of their own. It helps bring out the element common in both political thought concerning sovereignty and administrative thought concerning authority. It suggests that the rule-making, rule-executing and rule-interpreting activities of public agencies may have parallels in private organizations. It suggests going beyond internal *minutiae* and dealing also with the guidance of an organization through the difficulties of its environment.[4]

4. This connotation ties in with the word's origin in the Greek *kubernan*, "to steer or control," which is also the source of the modern "cybernetics." The Sanskrit version is probably *kubhan*, which means "to dance or pirouette." This is not too remote from images of the intricate footwork of administrators in their efforts to maintain a balance among conflicting forces.

2. THE ADMINISTRATORS AND THE ADMINISTERED

Another widely accepted premise of administrative thought is a distinction between those who have and those who do not have administrative responsibility and authority—that is, between the administrators and the administered, the managers and the managed. This distinction is similar to that often made in political science between the rulers and the ruled, the governors and the governed. The governance of an organization cannot be "self-government" in the sense that all members have equal responsibility and authority. A "self-governing" organization, rather, is one whose members may participate to a certain extent in formulating purposes and selecting governing boards and top executives. Although the people so selected may be responsible to all the members (as in many associations and legislative bodies), they nevertheless stand apart from them. In any organization, moreover, there may be significant tension, if not conflict, between the two groups.

Yet this distinction cannot be seen as separating all members of organizations into two classes of people. There are at least four widely accepted limitations that tend to blur the dividing lines between the administrators and the administered.

First of all, most managers are themselves among the managed. All administrators except those at the highest levels of responsibility and authority are subject to the general guidance of other administrators.

Second, most administrators are also involved in a certain amount of nonadministrative activities. At the middle and lower levels of an hierarchy, as Fayol pointed out long ago, the proportion of nonadministrative to administrative activity tends to rise.

Third, formal designations may be rather misleading. On the one hand, people may be given administrative titles merely to justify a salary increase or raise their social status. Some people with titles of "administrative assistant" or "assistant to the administrator" may be engaged in little more than minor clerical work. On the other hand, professionals with administrative responsibilities often prefer to highlight their professional tasks and conceal or even evade their administrative responsibilities.[5]

Finally, administrative activities may be dispersed among various assistants and advisers. There is no clear line of demarcation that can always be drawn among those responsible for guiding an organization or unit and those responsible for helping them do this. As organizations become larger and more complex and as more specialized forms of

5. Note discussion of "The specialist-administrator" in "People-in-Organizations: Formal Aspects" (Chapt. 9).

administrative techniques are used, the circle of those with some form of administrative responsibility may widen. In highly decentralized and more democratic organizations it becomes still larger.

3. GENERALISTS vs. SPECIALISTS

There is also a wide consensus on the concept of administrators as generalists rather than specialists. This concept is particularly applicable to the higher level administrators, whose responsibilities usually include the coordination of the work of many specialists or experts. It may also be applied to other administrators as well—albeit in a more limited sense. Even though they operate at a lower level of generality, they are usually involved in the coordination of the work of different people with special problems and viewpoints. Also, in handling relations with the external environment of their units, they usually deal with a more varied array of problems than faced by their subordinates.

At the higher levels of organizations, where both external and internal relations are highly varied, administrators can never hope to master the details of all the problems with which they deal. The responsibility of keeping track of what is going on in many fields makes it impossible for the administrator to become, or remain, an up-to-date specialist in any field. In this sense, the top administrator's ignorance of many details is usually one of his outstanding characteristics. The top administrator who proudly proclaims that he knows everything that is going on in his organization (even without reference to its immediate environment) is invariably deceiving himself. The depth of his belief is probably exceeded only by the depth of his ignorance concerning those aspects of his organization's activities which he has neglected.

Yet the generalist-specialist distinction is also subject to various widely accepted limitations.

First of all, identifying someone as a generalist does not tell us what kind of generalist he is. Certainly, there are many varieties. At one extreme, there is the jack-of-all-trades who knows almost nothing about anything or flits aimlessly from one problem to another. At the other, there is the one who is able to fit diverse activities into a general framework.[6]

Second, administrators usually specialize in the problems of the organizations or units they are expected to guide. Administration has no significance unless specifically oriented toward a specific organization. "You

---

6. Note discussion of different generalist roles in "People-in-Organizations: Informal Aspects" (Chapt. 10).

can't administer administration."[7] Accordingly, administrators usually try to develop expertise in the specific purposes, problems and procedures of their organizations or units.

Finally, the generalist administrator may be something of a specialist in administration. He may be a specialist in handling one or more of the specialized tools of administration. This is not quite the same, it should be added, as being a professional production engineer, accountant or job analyst; in the former instance the expertise relates rather to the use of experts in these technical fields. The administrator may also be something of a specialist in the more general arts of governance. Expertise of this sort may come from broad experience in a variety of administrative posts, from study and learning and even from research and theory. In this sense, becoming a generalist may itself be a form of intense specialization.

B. *The Common Characteristics*

WHAT DO ADMINISTRATORS do when involved in the governance of organizations?

This question is a tricky one. When we look at administrative activities closely, we may see a variety of activities by the same administrator, a greater variety by different administrators in the same organization and still greater variety in different organizations in different countries and at different periods in history.

Despite this variety, there is growing consensus concerning certain characteristics that are common to all administrative activity. These will now be presented in a series of basic propositions, with a subsequent discussion of some of the more fundamental ideas in these propositions. In the following chapters these fundamental ideas, in turn, will be elaborated upon—but with less effort to remain within the area of the emerging consensus.

1. SOME BASIC PROPOSITIONS

The following propositions do not include all the valid or useful statements that have been or can be usefully made concerning administration. They are mainly of a rather obvious and axiomatic character. Instead of being looked upon as a revelation, they can be taken for granted

7. This is adapted from the title of Wendell Johnson's article "You Can't Write Writing" (1954).

by those who are seriously engaged in the solution of administrative problems, the conduct of administrative research or the improvement of administrative education. They are precisely the kinds of propositions that serve as the articulate or inarticulate major premises of experienced administrators. In one form or another, they are implicitly or explicitly stated in the best of modern administrative research and theory.

1. Administration, or governance, is the complex process through which administrators try to guide the activities of people in an organization toward formulating or achieving some accepted pattern of purposes.
2. The purposes of an organization are multiple, are given different degrees of emphasis by different members of the organization and are constantly changing in response to new situations.
3. The formulation and achievement of such purposes are blocked by conflicts, obstacles or changing circumstances within the organization or in the relations between the organization and its environment.
4. To achieve results, both organizations and their administrators try to cope with this blockage through the development, maintenance and use of power, or influence, with varying degrees of authority and responsibility.
5. In dealing with the members of an organization and with the external environment, administrators engage in or make use of the following:
    —the broad processes of making decisions and communicating information,
    —the fundamental administrative processes of planning, activating and evaluating, and
    —various technical administrative processes relating to production, budgeting and accounting, personnel, distribution of output, general internal services or research.

An aspect of all these propositions is that each can be reduced to the form of "A *is* B." In conformance with customary usage, the "is" may be interpreted as including "has been" and "will be," plus "any place." The word "always" is thus implied. If "always" seems overstrong, let us realize that it means "always to some degree." The propositions themselves are not confined to any particular degree. Nor are they limited to those variables which we are not as yet very adept at measuring, whether by cardinal numbers, scale analysis or other methods.

It will be noted that none of the propositions in the definition appears in the form "A *should be* B." They are not statements of value in the sense that the stater expresses his delight or regret that A is B. Centering on the *is*, they are conceptual and factual statements, not ethical statements.

Nevertheless, these propositions have many "should be" implications. The selection of these propositions from among a host of other possibilities is a way of saying that a serious analysis of administration *should* include these matters as starting points. This act of selection (as well as the selection of administration as a field of analysis) is itself an expression of certain ethical values and goals of the author. If A *is* B, one *should not* operate on the assumption that it is not. If B is composed of varying amounts of X, Y, and Z, one *should* under certain circumstances distinguish between different kinds of B. Moreover, many of these propositions deal even more directly with values. The purposes referred to in the first three propositions provide a basis for describing all organizational goals, "ultimate" as well as "instrumental." Thus they, in essence, assert as a *fact* that people in organizations are deeply concerned with *values*. It implies, as will be made clear later, that administrators are deeply concerned with adjustments among competing values.

These propositions do not constitute a model in the sense of Weber's "ideal type." There is no question of determining how administration at any particular time or place may conform to or depart from the model. There is thus no problem of building a bridge between model and reality to handle the distance that may be observed between the two. If the propositions are valid, *there can be no such distance.*

But are these propositions useful starting points for understanding the practice of administration?

To help answer this question, it is first essential to explain some of the underlying concepts embodied in them.

2. PEOPLE, ORGANIZATIONS, ENVIRONMENTS

Underlying all the propositions is the theme that administration involves people. In administration things are not merely *done.* "Administrators try to guide the activities of people." No matter what specific language be used, this modern approach to administration rips aside the veil of anonymity and abstraction. It breaks away from older ideas of the administrative world as one inhabited solely by structures, diagrams, rules and regulations. It parts company with those who have seen no difference between the management of men and the management of machines and materials. The material resources of an organization are important only because they are used by people (or "human resources"). This approach ties in with the Parsons-Shils view of social action as "the action of an individual actor or of a collectivity of actors" (1951, p. 4). It obliges us to relate the study of administration to the findings, controversies, and problems of all the disciplines and quasi-disciplines which throw any light on the behavior and misbehavior, the greatness and brutishness, the rationality and irrationality, the predictability and unpredictability of human beings. Nothing human is alien to administration. In this sense "human relations" is not a specialized technique; it is the very kernel of administration!

Moreover, administration involves organizations. The administrators are themselves members of organizations. They try to guide the activities of "people in organizations." They are interested in formulating and achieving the purposes of organizations. It is within organizations and the various formal and informal units or subdivisions of organizations that administrators occupy various "roles" or—what is almost the same—"organizational positions." For purposes of analysis it is often desirable to shift attention from individuals and focus it instead upon these roles (or positions) and other aspects of an organization's structure.

The administrator himself, it should be added, is often an integral part of a group, not an isolated individual. "The President Roosevelt of history, for example," as Bentley wrote with reference to the first of the American Presidents by that name, "is a very large amount of official activity involving many people" (1949, p. 176).

An organization, in turn, is not a closed system. It exists within a certain environment. According to the basic propositions, the environment may give rise to "conflicts, obstacles or changing circumstances." Administrators try to influence both the organization and its environment. In the form of climate, flora, fauna, and all sorts of physical resources, nature is a part of every organization's environment. Man is usually a more active part. The human environment is as broad as the community, state, society, and culture in which an organization operates. More narrowly, an organization's environment also takes the form of the "superior" organs of any larger organization to which it belongs. It consists of "outside" individuals, groups, and organizations acting to influence it in one way or another. These outsiders—which may include controllers and opponents as well as clients, suppliers, and advisers—enter into direct relationships with the organization. Often, their interaction goes so far as to be called "intervention." Hence we cannot reserve exclusively to the members of an organization the privilege of participation in its activities. Outsiders, as well as administrators and other members, may also be involved in shaping the pattern of an organization's structure or performance and the choice of measures designed to achieve goals for improvement in either.

These interrelated concepts of *people* in *organizations* that are *structured* in a certain way and *perform* within given *environments* are an integral part of the emerging consensus in modern administrative thought.

We have probably passed the stage when a serious thinker in this field could ignore the human basis of administration, the organizational framework, or the ecology of organizations.

Nevertheless, much still remains to be done in analyzing these three basic elements. In the various chapters of Parts II, III and IV, I shall go somewhat beyond the present consensus and develop these concepts on the basis of the progress already made in various fields of intellectual effort.

3. PURPOSES

The importance of purposefulness in the administration of organizations is universally recognized. In administrative life it is reflected in repeated exhortations to "clarify our objectives," "figure out just where we're going," or "get those fellows down there (or up there) to understand what our purposes really are." It is indicated by the large number of terms that are used to convey more or less similar ideas concerning purpose: objective, goal, target, norm, aim, end, intention, and function. One or another of these terms is used in most formal definitions or administration. The theme of purposes runs throughout the basic propositions.

The first proposition, it should be noted, refers to "formulating or achieving . . . purposes." This recognizes that higher level administrators may be more involved in broader or longer range purpose formulation, with lower level administrators often paying major attention to intermediate purposes or means. The proposition expresses the modern rejection of the idea that administration must necessarily be limited to narrowly conceived means of attaining fixed and predetermined purposes. It expresses the widespread acceptance of the inevitable interrelating of means and ends. It recognizes that administrators are often concerned with both and that the process of achieving purposes may itself lead to some kind of reformulation.

Throughout the propositions runs a strong emphasis upon the multiplicity of organizational purposes. This multiplicity reflects the diversity of interests by both members and outsiders and the many links in any purpose chain designed to satisfy any given interest. Any one purpose, moreover, may be "given different degrees of emphasis by different members of the organization." Purposes are "constantly changing in response to new situations."

Although the individual members of an organization usually have many differing individual purposes, these different purposes are brought together into an "accepted pattern of purposes." At one extreme, this pattern may consist of widespread dedication to common goals. At the other extreme, it may reflect *quid pro quo* bargains which give different returns to different members as rewards for their cooperation. Similarly, some purposes may be accepted with enthusiasm, some only through pressure. Some may be but grudgingly acceptable.

One of the great forward strides in modern administrative thought has been the increasing attention to the various categories of organizational purpose. Even those who see efficiency or profitability as the major purpose base their claim on the thesis that it serves to unify other purposes. Many kinds of purposes are thereby recognized. More explicit recognition has been provided by various classifications of objectives (Mooney and Reiley, 1931, p. 3-4; Davis, 1951, p. 90-126). There is now widespread acceptance of the idea of "a hierarchy of purposes" or "pyramid of values," as first presented by Waldo (1948, p. 204-205).

The kinds of performance purposes most frequently referred to may be listed as follows.

1. The satisfaction of various interests
2. Output of services or goods
3. Efficiency or profitability
4. Investment in organizational viability
5. Mobilization of resources
6. Observance of codes
7. Technical or administrative rationality

In Part IV, "Performance," this set of performance categories is presented as the "global matrix" of organizational purposes. Each of the seven elements is broken down into many component elements, together with a presentation of the many different terms used to express the same ideas. The fourth element—investment in the organization itself—provides a direct link with desired changes in the organization and its relation to the environment. Accordingly, the desired performance pattern of any organization may be expressed in some combination of these elements and subelements. Similarly, it is shown, the same concepts are used in formulating criteria for evaluating the performance of organizations and administrators. This effort at synthesis is feasible only because of the groundwork already laid by many writers in various disciplines.

4. PROCESSES

The "process approach" to administration is one of the great unifying trends in modern administrative thought, if not in all scientific inquiry. Yet to understand what is meant by this term, and by the reference to "complex process" in the first proposition, we must distinguish among three complementary concepts of process.

A. *Change and becoming.* The first concept is that of the administrative process as a continuing, ever changing activity. By this approach the realm of administration is one of flux and becoming, like the universe as Heraclitus saw it many centuries ago: "Into this same river you could not step twice, for other waters are flowing." It consists not of separate actions as disparate entities, but of interlocking activities. One activity blends into another. It is hard to find the beginning and still harder to find the end. Every achievement creates certain difficulties. Every solution creates new problems. Neither people nor purposes ever remain immobile. Organizations are born and they die. Their members enter and leave; of those who remain, some grow wiser and all get older. If the process of change is not evident from outside or is not formally legitimized, it takes place beneath the surface. This does not imply losing sight of the more static aspects of administration. They must be included as an essential part of the picture—just as the shifting sandbars and leafy banks are part of a rushing river. As Commons wrote about economics, "The organization of activity is merely the more stabilized aspect of activity. The form is part of the process" (1951, p. 21). Or, as put more positively by L. L. Whyte, "there is no sharp division between structure and process, because structure is a limiting case of process" (1950, p. 19-20).

To analyze and describe a process is far from easy. It is like trying to capture the flow of action on a football field with a still camera. We can make meaningful efforts to record what is going on only if we have instruments comparable to a battery of movie cameras equipped with color film and telescopic and panoramic lenses. But even thus the dynamics of motion, causation, and uncertainty are apt to elude us as spectators. The players and the captains "feel" what is happening. But even they probably never learn what is happening all over the field or why certain things have happened.

B. *The processes of various disciplines.* In his puny efforts to understand the ongoing flow of events, man tries to slice up his universe into various specific processes: physical, chemical, physiological, psychological, sociological, political, economic, administrative, and many others. Each of these represents a different aspect of, or a different way of thinking about, the same ongoing stream of action and becoming. Hence a strong emphasis upon the boundaries of academic disciplines—while helpful in the proper division of labor, funds and prestige within institutions of higher learning—can easily lead to aridity, sterility, and a breakdown of intellectual vigor within any discipline. This is particularly true in the field of administration. If one feels constrained from bringing to the study of administration concepts that have been developed by economists, political scientists, sociologists, psychologists, anthropologists and even biologists, mathematicians, and logicians, one cannot undertake a creative and meaningful study of administration.

This interweaving of "disciplinary processes" may be illustrated by a few comments concerning the interrelationship between administration and economic and political processes. The economic process is generally regarded as relating to the production, exchange, utilization, or accumulation of wealth or of goods and services. Yet the overwhelming bulk of goods and services are produced by organizations. These organizations could not operate unless they were administered. Thus, administration is an inevitable part of the economic process. From a broader point of view, the economic process can be seen as one of decision-making in the face of scarce resources. This conception is well presented in Lionel Robbins' famous definition of economics: "the science which studies human behavior as a relationship between ends and scarce means which have alternative uses" (1948, p. 16). Since the scarcity of means available for achieving organizational purposes is an inevitable part of administrative life, the economic process in turn becomes an integral part of the administrative process.

A similar interweaving is found with respect to political and administrative processes. In the more narrow sense, the political process is one of getting control of the machinery of the state through elections or any other means. Most of these means require some form of organization. Since any such organization must be administered, administration necessarily enters the political process. From a broader point of view, politics can be regarded as the general process of mobilizing, maintaining and using influence or power. In this sense politics enters into the life of all organizations, and thereby into the very essence of the administrative process.

Accordingly, the serious student of administration faces a formidable task. He must penetrate the terminological jungle developed in these many other fields. He must keep abreast not only of the growing flood of administrative literature, but also of a still greater flow of thought and research in many other fields. Moreover, to adapt conceptions from other disciplines to the needs of administration, he must sometimes enter boldly into these other domains and himself formulate hypotheses, conceptions, and theories which he cannot always obtain ready-made from those who are less aware of the needs in administrative thought.

c. *The administrative processes.* While administration as a whole may be seen as a "disciplinary process" in its own right, it too is sliced up into processes such as Fayol's "elements" or Gulick's POSDCORB. The maturation of administrative thought brings with it an increasing, rather than a decreasing, number of administrative processes. Thus, as indicated in the fifth basic proposition, modern administrative thought seems to distinguish among at least three levels of administrative processes. None of these replaces the others. Each represents different cross-sections of, or supplementary ways of looking at, the same multidimensional reality. The fact that some analyses conceive of administration in terms of one of these processes alone merely attests to the importance of specialized intellectual labor. It need not constitute an explicit—and cannot constitute an acceptable—rejection of the relevance of other processes.[8]

At a high level of generality we find the processes of decision-making and communication. The analysis of these processes may be relevant to administration even when there is no explicit recognition of any differences between administrative and nonadministrative decision-making and communication.

At a more specific level we find such processes as planning, activating, and evaluating.[9] Each of these, it may be noted, involves decision-making and communication. More important, each is part of a "seamless web" with three aspects: planning, activating, and evaluating. Frequently, these aspects of behavior take place simultaneously. When there is a time difference, there is no fixed sequence; any one may be followed by either or both of the others. Moreover, most larger (or molar) behavior units tend to be composed of smaller (or molecular) behavior units of the same type.[10] The planning aspect itself involves (a) making a plan for plan-

8. Thus, although Simon has preferred to concentrate upon the analysis of the process of decision-making and choice, he has never claimed that all aspects of administration must be subsumed under decision-making. In *Models of Man* (p. viii) for example, he refers to the dual mechanisms of influence and choice.

9. "Planning" is here used in the sense of "developing organizational purposefulness." Hence, it relates to all the categories of organizational purpose. "Activating" refers to all forms of initiating action. It therefore includes in a broader context "control" (in the sense of directing action), Fayol's "command," Gulick's "direction," and Simon's "mechanism of influence." The concepts of "activating" and "evaluating" represent a separate handling of two ideas often lumped together in the idea of "control" (in the sense of checking up on action and where needed, initiating corrective action). When these fundamental processes of planning, activating and evaluating are applied to the purpose of organizational survival or growth, we have the process traditionally described as "organizing." Their application to an organization's operations yields "coordinating."

10. In somewhat different terms (and at the level of individual instead of

ning, (b) activating the people and mental processes needed to develop the plan and (c) evaluating the plan that has been developed.

Finally, at a much more specialized level, we find a growing number of technical processes. These include production management, accounting, budgeting and finance, operations research, personnel management, and marketing. Some of these fields, particularly accounting, have developed into mature professions. Others are moving toward some degree of professional status. With the passage of time, old techniques in these fields are constantly being refurbished. The fields themselves are constantly being subdivided; it is already impossible for any one accountant to achieve significant expertise in all of accounting's many subdivisions. In addition, new techniques are constantly being devised. All of these constitute additional administrative processes which both contribute to and are based upon the processes of decision-making and communication and of planning, activating and evaluating.

These administrative processes are the central concern of administrative rationality. Accordingly, decision-making, communicating, planning, activating, and evaluating are discussed in Part V, "Administrative Processes." Although adequate attention to the administrative tools goes beyond the scope of this book, the managerial aspects of using some of these tools are discussed in earlier chapters. Thus the discussion of service specifications in Chapter 15 is related to job classification, merit rating and program budgeting. The discussion of costs in Chapter 16 and "mobilization logic" and "use logic" in Chapter 18 is related to budgeting and accounting.

5. COOPERATION, CONFLICT, POWER

The idea of cooperation is implicit in the entire set of propositions. An organization, as Barnard has pointed out, is a form of cooperative system. An accepted pattern of purposes is both an antecedent and a consequence of cooperation among the members of an organization. The maintenance of cooperation, it is generally agreed, is a major task of the administrator.

The modern recognition of the importance of cooperation developed largely as part of the "human relations" revolt against mechanistic models of administration. With certain conspicuous exceptions, such as Follett,

---

organizational behavior) this method of analyzing behavior is presented in G. A. Miller, Eugene Galanter, and K. H. Pribram (1960), particularly in Chapt. 2, "The Unit of Analysis," p. 21-39. The "molar-molecular" terminology was developed by Tolman (1951).

this often led to a neglect of conflict and power (or influence). Indeed, both of these ideas have long been sources of discomfort to many people. Like sex under the Victorians, they have often been regarded as subjects that, while obviously important, are not to be openly discussed in polite society.

The modern tendency in administrative thought is to accept conflict as an inevitable concomitant of cooperative action in organizations. Hence the third proposition states that the formulation and achievement of an organization's purpose pattern are "blocked by conflicts, obstacles ✓ or changing circumstances within the organization or in the relations between the organization and its environment." Indeed, any "accepted pattern of purposes" is itself embedded in a broader setting of divergent purposes. The accepted pattern itself always contains an element of open or latent conflict among its various elements. While conflict may weaken or destroy the cooperation required for organizational action, some forms and degrees of conflict may unify an organization and strengthen cooperation among its members.

Another aspect of the emerging consensus in administrative thought is a more frank and open approach to power (or influence). A distinctive characteristic of any organization is that it enables people to develop the power to do things together that they could not do so well, or at all, separately. This power is needed to cope with blockage and conflicts and achieve results despite them. Thus a distinctive characteristic of administrative action is the effort to influence—or activate—people and groups in the organization and the organization's environment. In whichever direction it may be exercised, it is now recognized that power should be distinguished from authority and that varying relationships may exist between authority and responsibility. Hence the proposition referring to "the development, maintenance and use of power, or influence, with varying degrees of authority and responsibility" by both organizations and their administrators.

To understand the dynamics of any organization, it is not enough to know its accepted purpose pattern. It is also essential to know something about its internal and external conflicts and the distribution of power within it. These are referred to when people talk about the "private politics" of a corporation, association, university, or trade union. They become public politics only when they are brought more fully into the clear, as often happens in the case of government agencies and political parties.

These two themes of power and conflict are fundamental to all aspects of organizations and their administration. Accordingly, before entering into the detailed materials of Parts II, III, IV and V, I shall develop each of them at greater length in "The Conflict-Cooperation Nexus" (Chapt. 3) and "The Power-Responsibility-Authority Triangle" (Chapt. 4).

c. *The Special and Unique Characteristics*

ANY DISCUSSION of the common characteristics of administration is apt to lead to the fallacious idea that administration is always the same and that differences are unimportant. On the other hand, single-minded attention to differences may lead to the equally fallacious denial of similarities. In modern administrative thought the tendency is to escape this dilemma by rejecting an either-or position. This means recognizing that two administrative situations may at one and the same time be *both* similar in some respects and different in others.

1. DANGER OF IGNORING DIFFERENCES

The danger of ignoring differences in administrative situations is dramatized by the mishaps of mobility. A successful Army officer becomes a business executive—and a flop. A successful business executive enters government service—and becomes a lost soul. A government official who has been successful in Washington or London is sent to Africa—and falls on his face. Or else, the individual stays in the same position, and the difference arises in his immediate environment. The able administrator of a small unit becomes unable to operate when he gets a new superior or when he himself is promoted to a higher administrative post. The founder of a small firm may be out of his depth when, as a result of his own achievements, it becomes a giant corporation. The brilliant organizer of revolution and war may, like Leon Trotsky, prove (and be pushed) out of place amid the more sober and less exciting tasks of consolidation and construction. Nor is administrative technology itself, for all its apparent impersonality, immune to the challenge of administrative differences. Methods of budgeting, recruitment and work simplification that are successful in one organization or country will often prove unworkable in another organization or country without adaptation or reconstruction.

Differences are also dramatized by the many misunderstandings that develop in interorganizational relationships. The chief of one section often deals with the chief of another section on the assumption that both sections operate in the same way. In dealing with other organizations administrators often assume a common language, or a common set of premises and values. This is an organizational variety of egocentrism; it is the fallacy of thinking that others are built in one's own image. It can lead to remarkable misunderstandings.

The importance of differences is accentuated by the fact that in a certain sense every organization—including those which are quite colorless as well as those with a highly developed sense of mission—has a unique personality of its own. To the outsider looking in, this quality may be lost. To him, everything may appear very similar to the administration of other organizations—just as most Chinese may look alike to a German or most Pakistanis may look alike to a Chinese. But when the outsider becomes an insider, when he passes through his period of groping and fumbling as a new initiate, when he "learns the ropes" and finds out "what makes things tick," when he in fact becomes a part of the spirit of the place, he will smile indulgently—and with some degree of justification—at the poor fool on the outside (be he professor, student or "practical man") who thinks he knows what administration in this place is all about.

On the other hand, the desire to feel that "we are different" is so great that actual differences are often vastly exaggerated. The need to regard one's self as different from others is one of the basic human needs, as discussed in more detail in "The Human Beings" (Chapt. 8). In organizations the satisfaction of this need is necessary in order to establish the identity of the group and provide the emotional basis for cooperation. Such satisfactions may be found either by being different or by seeing differences where they do not exist. I remember the government official of another country who tried to convince me that *his* government was different because, unlike the government of the United States of America, it was subject to influence by pressure groups. It took some time before his passion for difference was satisfied by finding more important—and more accurate—factors.

Similarly, the feeling that "they are different" may also be concretized in fallacious forms. This often happens when an American, for example, goes abroad as a technical adviser in a country just starting the industrialization process. The "culture shock" of finding certain differences in organizational activity in such a country may lead him to think that everything is different. He may see many differences that exist only in his imagination. He can compare what he sees only with his own image of his own country, which may be clouded by sheer ignorance and lack of self-knowledge. It is often easy for him to see the mote in a foreigner's eye without suspecting that the same kind of mote exists in his own eye. In any case, his standard of comparison will be his own limited field of experience.

2. BASES OF DIFFERENCES

A traditional approach to the differences in administration is based upon a simplistic differentiation which parallels the growth of special educational programs. This yields a taxonomy providing major distinctions among business, public, and military administration and minor distinctions among the administration of churches, schools, hospitals, libraries, welfare agencies, cooperatives, political parties, and others. As the basis for the division of labor in educational institutions, this has a lot to commend it, for it helps to focus attention on some of the special problems of administering these organizations.

But this "pigeonhole" form of classification does not go very far as an analytical tool for the study of differences. By itself, it provides no guidelines to the vast amount of differences among organizations in each category and at different places in any such organization. To be useful, it must be supplemented by additional methods of classifying various aspects of organizations and their administration. In other words it must be converted into a "depth" or "multifacet" classification. A multidimensional topology of this type would have to provide for the identification of differences in

- the characteristics not only of organizational membership and structure but also of environments and environmental relations;
- the purposes of organizations;
- the use of administrative processes; and
- the patterns of cooperation, conflict and power.

It should be immediately noted that these four categories are identical with those used in the previous section as the basis for identifying the most common characteristics of administration. The analysis of variety has not taken us away from, but has rather brought us back to, the unity of our subject matter. To put it another way, the basic propositions set forth in the first part of section B not only set forth the invariants of administration in all organizations. They also provide bases for discovering the variants. The variant factors are the constants themselves as they appear in different forms and patterns.

The special characteristics of any given group of organizations can usually be established without using facets at all of these four levels of analysis. It would never be necessary to use all facets at each of these levels even to identify the unique characteristics of administration in a given organization (or unit thereof) at a certain period of time in a given environment. How far one may want to go in using this instrument at any one time will depend upon the specific situation, the purpose of the analysis, and the availability of information. How far one may be able to go will depend also upon his skill in using the kind of concepts presented in the subsequent chapters.

D. *Key Terminological Problems*

To ROUND OUT our preliminary answer to "What is administration?" and prepare the ground for more detailed analysis of common, special and unique characteristics, it is essential to try to recognize the terminological ambiguities surrounding the terms "organization" and "administration." In so doing, I shall also present a consistent set of terminological preferences. Many of these may run counter to established usage in specific areas of administration in various countries. The reason is that much of present usage has developed within the confines of one or another specific area. My purpose is to produce a synthesis which, without ignoring the special characteristics of each field, can be fruitfully used in all of them.

1. "ORGANIZATION" AND RELATED TERMS

The term "organization" has thus far been used without any explicit definition. This gap must now be remedied. In addition, it is desirable to distinguish between "organization" and such closely related terms as "system," "bureaucracy," "institution," and "government."

A. *Organization.* In general usage the word "organization" has three different meanings:

i. The act of organizing—that is, of establishing an organization or changing its structure;
ii. Administration or management; or
iii. A certain kind of group—particularly a "formal organization."

For the first meaning, I think it more logical to use the participle "organizing." The second usage was developed by those who made the mistake of regarding organizing as the single or the major administrative process. It is already fading out; its demise should be accelerated. The third meaning—particularly in the sense of a "formal organization"—is the one used here.

But what kind of group is a formal organization? For our purposes, it is *not* a group in the sense of:

i. an abstract category of thought, such as "blue-eyed people" or even all people who are presumed to have a common interest, let us say, in studying administration or lowering taxes;

ii. a collection of individuals held together only by their common support for, and common attachment to, a religious, political, or intellectual leader;

iii. a "reference group"—that is, those people whose values an individual may refer to as he determines his own course of action;

iv. any type of system; or

v. any type of cooperation among people.

In positive terms, a formal organization may be regarded as a group or cooperative system, with the following characteristics:

i. An accepted pattern of purposes (as already discussed)

ii. A sense of identification or belonging

Both the directors and the workers of a telephone company regard themselves as part of an organization. This sense of identification is heightened by the felt distinction between "in-group" and "out-group." Despite their crucial importance to the organization, the people who merely talk on the telephone are "outsiders."

iii. Continuity of interaction

The members of an organization interact with each other with some minimum degree of regularity and continuity. Members leave an organization by falling below the required minimum—as when a factory worker does not appear on the job any more or when a union member stops paying dues.

iv. Differentiation of function

The activities of members of organizations are based upon some minimum amount of formal differentiation of roles. In small organizations this differentiation may be rudimentary. In larger organizations it becomes elaborate.

v. Conscious integration

The divided parts of an organization are held together not only by spontaneous cooperation but also by the conscious efforts of certain members responsible for bringing or holding them together. These, of course, are the administrators themselves, who bring people together for the formulation and achievement of an organization's purposes.

This definition necessarily involves the boundary-line problem of distinguishing between members and nonmembers or, in other terms, between "insiders" and "outsiders." The problem is peripheral in the case of organizations in which people work on a full-time basis. The employment relationship itself is a certificate of membership. It is acute, however, in the case of political and religious organizations, which invariably aim at the conscious integration of large numbers of people whose interaction may be irregular and discontinuous. Thus the person whose interaction with a political party may be expressed only on Election Day will usually be regarded as a "follower" of that party, a special form of "outsider," rather than as a member of the organization. A similar problem may also exist within an organization whenever a specific individual is assigned to part-time work in each of two subdivisions of the organization. Here, he is likely to be regarded as an outsider by both.

This discussion has already gone beyond mere terminology and has entered the sphere of organizational analysis. This analysis will be continued in the subsequent discussions of the formal and informal aspects of organizations (Chapts. 9, 10).

B. *System.* The term "system" is usually used to refer to "any set of interrelating elements." In this sense "system" may refer to

i. Any one of the concrete systems dealt with by general systems theorists from a solar system to the molecule and electron and from a cell to an organ, personality, small group, formal organization, political system, economic system, and social system;
ii. A system of rules or procedures influencing behavior; or
iii. A theoretical system bringing together various concepts and generalizations for the purpose of description, explanation, or prediction.

Any of these systems may be regarded as having boundaries (although these may be regions rather than lines) and as being either "open" or "closed."

Thus a formal organization is one type of system. Together with supplier, clients, and others beyond its boundaries, it may constitute a "cooperative system" in Barnard's sense. It may use various systems of rules and procedures. Its activities may presumably be explained by a theoretical system dealing with organizations and their administration.

C. *Bureaucracy.* In social science parlance, as distinguished from colloquial usage, the term "bureaucracy" is widely used to refer to certain aspects of complex formal organization. The most important of these aspects are the detailed subdivision of labor, hierarchical relationships, and general rules.

Some writers on the subject of bureaucracy, however, make the mistake of confusing bureaucracy with the entirety of certain formal organizations. This leads to an ignoring of certain important aspects of large-scale organizations—particularly the roles of nonbureaucrats. For larger organizations I find it desirable to make a threefold distinction between members of directorates, top executives, and bureaucrats.

D. *Institution*. The term "institution" is used in at least two ways that are directly relevant to our discussion. It may refer to:

i. A certain type of organization—namely, one which is important in society, has lasted a long time or has a strong sense of identity and tradition—or a cluster of such organizations (such as governmental, educational, and religious institutions); or

ii. Certain practices or traditions, which may be observed within organizations or without respect to organizational boundaries (such as the institutions of dating, marriage, and divorce).

The idea of "institutionalizing" something may comprehend either of these meanings. To institutionalize a group of informal advisors means to bring them within the confines of a formal organization. To institutionalize certain practices means to regularize them or to embody them in formal procedures.

The "administration of institutions" clearly relates only to the first of these meanings; it is a category of general administration. The idea of "institution building"—for example, in the sense that the building of new institutions is important for underdeveloped countries—is also usually used to relate to institutions in the organizational sense. The use of more honorific terms in the name of an organization—such as institute, center, foundation or authority—is often resorted to as a way of helping create a public image of a strong, durable institution. The term "establishment" is often used to refer pejoratively to a cluster of such institutions or their bureaucracies.

E. *Government*. What is the difference between "administration" in the sense here conceived and "government"?

To answer this question we must recognize that the word "government" may be used for at least five different referents:

i. Certain high officials of a state or the state itself;

ii. Exercising authority over the people of a state—in the sense of "running the country" or "ruling";

iii. The cluster of public agencies which comprise a state apparatus, or a central group thereof;

iv. Directing the state apparatus; or

v. Directing any organization, an activity for which the Board of Governors of a university or a hospital may be responsible.

The last two of these meanings relate to the administrative activity undertaken at the highest levels of authority by the members of directorates. They can thus be regarded as an important part of administration. To escape these restrictions, I have used "governance" to refer to the administrative process at any level in any organization.

2. "ADMINISTRATION" AND RELATED TERMS

At an early point I stated my intention of using "administration" and "management" as synonyms. In addition to management, however, there are many other words that have often been used in a similar fashion. I shall therefore try to explain the problems in this area and my preferences with respect to each of them.

A. *Managers and executives.* Our first terminological problem is what to do with three pairs of words: administrator and administration, manager and management, and executive and execution.

With respect to the first two pairs, no consistent usage can be found. For some, "administration" refers to the activities of those at the higher level of responsibility and authority in an organization. In the British civil service, for example, the "administrative class" is composed of officials at the top of the bureaucratic hierarchy, while the "executive class" takes care of the lower "management" functions. In the field of business, this usage is often reversed. Thus Brech, a British writer in the business field, maintains that "administration" should be seen as merely a part of "management." He regards it as a "useful label" for certain "tools of management" (1953, p. 15-16).

Under these circumstances, I have found it desirable to drop the differentiation between the first two pairs of terms and use "administrator" and "manager" more or less interchangeably. By this usage either word may be used—with appropriate modification—to refer to any hierarchic level or any type of administrative or managerial activity.

Unlike "administration" and "management," the term "execution" is rarely used as a direct analogue of its paired member, "executive." It usually appears as a member of the pair "planning (or policy-making) and execution." Although I see no inherent objection to this use of the term, it should not be used too hastily to gloss over a large number of separable administrative processes.

As for "executive," I have arbitrarily used it as part of the term "top executive" for those officials who are immediately below the level of the board of directors of a corporation or the cabinet of a government and above the level of the bureaucrats. This is more in keeping with American business terminology than with British public administration terminology.

The term "executive" also has a special meaning in the field of government, as explained in the following paragraphs.

B. *Executive, legislative, and judicial.* One of the most time-honored distinctions in political science is the distinction between the executive, the legislature and the judiciary. This distinction was first made by Aristotle, was developed by Locke and many others, and was dramatized by Montesquieu in his theory of "the separation of powers." It has led to considerable debate concerning the desirability of alternative types of relationships between the various branches of government. It has also led to an increasing tendency to distinguish between certain processes or functions rather than between branches of government. This makes it easier to recognize that legislatures may legitimately engage in certain executive or judicial functions, courts in legislative and executive functions, and executive agencies in legislative and judicial functions.

However, the emphasis on executive processes, coupled with the interchangeability of "executive" and "administrative" has given rise to a number of ambiguities in the use of the term "administrative process" as applied to government.

The first ambiguity is that "administrative process" is sometimes used very broadly to refer to the totality of all activities in the executive branch of government. In this sense "administration" becomes equivalent to the work done by the executive branch of the government. Thus all employees in the executive branch become executive officials or administrators. The idea of administration as an activity of people in organizations responsible for getting work done by the organization vanishes in a fog of ambiguity.

The second difficulty derives from the use of "administrative process" in a much more narrow sense. It may refer to the operations of certain administrative tribunals as distinguished from other executive agencies (Landis, 1938); or the operations of any executive agencies which promulgate "administrative law," that is, general rules and regulations which have the full force of statutory law (Schwartz, 1958).

These two ambiguities contribute, in part, to an explanation of the phenomenon that many experts in public administration have found ample room for important and creative work without coming very near to many of the administrative or managerial problems of government agencies in the same sense that they are dealt with by writers on business administration. Be that as it may, it would seem more desirable to use words other than "administration" to refer to these other areas. There is nothing lost in referring to the executive branch, executive functions, executive tribunals, the laws establishing executive agencies, executive rule-making, the laws establishing procedures for executive rule-making, and the rules and regulations produced by executive agencies. With laws establishing "administration" and "administrative law" relieved of all these unnecessary burdens, it now becomes possible—without adding additional ambiguity—to recognize the existence of administrative activity in executive, legislative, and judicial agencies.

Terminological clarification along those lines will also make easier constructive use of the legislative-executive-judicial distinction outside the sphere of government. In the sense that it deals with the process of formal rule-making, the legislative process is one that takes place within all organizations, not merely in those organizations or units representing holders of formal authority. Executive action takes place in all organizations. Nor is the judicial process—in the sense of the adjudication of individual claims, complaints and appeals—limited to differentiated or publicly labeled judicial bodies. In industry, judicial functions are often carried on not only by individual administrators but also by management-labor committees and mediation or arbitration boards (*Brown*).

c. *Direction, supervision, and control.* The word "direction" has been widely used to refer to two different activities:

i. Administration at the higher levels, a meaning associated with the use of such terms as director, director-general, and board of directors; or

ii. The issuing of "directions," that is, orders and instructions, or even the orders and instructions themselves.

The word "supervision" has also been given two meanings:

i. Administration at the lower levels, a meaning closely associated with the fact that intermediate and lower officials are sometimes "supervisors"; and

ii. Certain limited types of administrative activity, particularly the process of "looking over" what has been done or controlling.

In my judgment both these terms are useful to help distinguish between various levels of administration. Thus I have used the term "directorates" to refer generically to government cabinets, executive committees of boards of directors and any other body which stands above the top executives and below the general assemblies and larger boards from which they derive their formal authority. I see no need for using "direction" as a synonym for orders.

Similarly, there is no need for "supervision" to refer to certain aspects of administrative activity. It is more convenient to use the term "supervisor" to refer to administrators (irrespective of the administrative activities they perform) at the intermediate and lower levels of organization.

The word "control" also has two meanings:

i. Administration in the restricted sense of domination, or power and authority, as when reference is made to those "in control"; and
ii. Supervision in the sense of checking up on what has been done and taking corrective action where necessary.

In the first of these two meanings the term is occasionally useful. The second of these meanings contains ideas which may also be expressed, as indicated earlier, by the two concepts of "activation" and "evaluation."

D. *Development administration.* The term "development administration" has recently been used to refer to various forms of public and private administration in countries engaged in ambitious programs of economic, social and political development. The need for this term has arisen through the inordinate attention in schools of public and business administration to staff services and specialized techniques, at the expense of administration that is "action-oriented" and "pointing to programmatic values." Apart from this, the term has the merit of suggesting the special problems of administration in organizations with dynamic programs of innovation that may upset traditional social processes (Weidner, 1962). Swerdlow illustrates this usage by using the term to refer to the administration of an urban renewal program in an American city or of economic development activities in an underdeveloped country (1963, p. ix, xiv).

Chapter 3

THE CONFLICT-COOPERATION NEXUS

*I*N EARLIER DECADES many writers on administration neglected the processes of human cooperation or conflict. Some, while ignoring cooperation, stressed certain aspects of conflict. Others, in the joy of discovering the glories of cooperation, ignored conflict.

One of the major advances of modern administrative thought has been an ever-widening recognition that conflict and cooperation are inextricably intertwined in the life of any organization. Administrative thought is thus beginning to catch up with the tacit knowledge of administrators, for whom the problems of obtaining cooperation and handling conflict have always been objects of daily attention and nocturnal soul-searching.

At any specific moment an administrator also may neglect one or the other. He may romanticize cooperation in an effort to escape the stress of conflict. In the heat of battle he may neglect opportunities for cooperation. On the wings of mechanistic models of behavior he may even try to flee the exigencies of both. All such efforts are futile. If they lead to anything at all, it is merely a new situation of combined conflict and cooperation.

The complexity of this conflict-cooperation nexus can be revealed only through a deeper exploration of the environment, structure, performance and administrative processes of organizations. These are the subjects of Parts II, III, IV and V.

As a prelude to this exploration, let us now look briefly at the phenomena of cooperation, conflict, and conflict resolution. By considering cooperation and conflict as two aspects of social action, or two sides of the same coin, we may achieve an analytical separation of processes that are inseparably connected in action. Conflict "resolution" may thus be seen as a shift in a conflict-cooperation pattern rather than an "end to conflict" or a "final solution."

A. *The Necessity of Cooperation*

To STATE that cooperation is a necessary aspect of any organization is almost tautological. As already pointed out in Chapter 2, an organization is one form of cooperative system. The difference between it and looser cooperative systems is that within an organization cooperation is based upon a sense of "belonging," continuity of interaction, differentiation of function, efforts at conscious coordination or integration, and an accepted pattern of purposes. As a result of these factors, cooperation within an organization is much deeper than in a cooperative system which is not highly structured enough to be regarded as an organization. It is this depth of cooperation which makes organization a vital source of social power.

The idea of cooperation is so much a part of our everyday life that we tend to view cooperative phenomena as self-evident. If two men work together to roll a boulder off a road, we quickly identify the observed behavior as cooperative. But the reason we are sure we are seeing cooperation is that we impute a common interest or purpose: the removal of the boulder. If we have reason to think that the only purpose of one of them is trying to humiliate the other by demonstrating that he is too weak to move the boulder by himself, we will withdraw our identification. If we note that they are trying to move the boulder in different directions, we will call it conflict instead. Hence the central element in cooperative action is some communality of interest or purpose.

With this definition in mind, let us now look at the various sources of cooperation and note that it may have negative as well as positive aspects.

1. SOURCES OF COOPERATION

At the outset it is worthwhile to distinguish between the various loci of cooperation. Within an organization there is cooperation between formally and informally established subdivisions and between individuals. In the latter category we include cooperation between superiors and subordinates and leaders and followers, as well as between peers, colleagues, and others. Moreover, there is always some degree or type of cooperation between an organization and its environment. A human organization cannot be a completely closed system. Various relationships must exist with clients, advisers, controllers, and opponents. Unless these relationships embody some minimum degree of cooperation, the organization will wither.

In a deeper sense, however, the forms of cooperation at any one of these loci vary in terms of the degree of *actual or perceived communality of interests.*

On the one hand, cooperation may be based on a sharing of interests. These interests may be immediate, as when the members of a work group try to complete an unpleasant task rapidly or when an external threat to an organization's existence creates a deep interest in survival. They may be longer-range, with considerable divergence of views as to the immediate steps leading toward their satisfaction. In either case, whenever these common interests are intensely felt and are "salient" in the lives of a sufficient number of people, they may lead to a widespread sense of organizational mission and dedication.

On the other hand, cooperation may stem from a mere avoidance of dissatisfaction. This is the lowest level of communality. It occurs in all those cases when the interest of some of the cooperating parties is merely to avoid the penalties of noncooperation. Here we find the "enforced cooperation" that takes place through the overt or implied use of punishments or threats. Often, this is the cooperation of routinized acceptance, consent, acquiescence or compliance. Yet, if the sanctions are a "clear and present danger" rather than an empty bluff, they may yield considerable vigor of cooperative action.

Between these two points on the spectrum, there lies the cooperation which is based upon different but converging interests. Here differing interests are brought together—usually through negotiation or bargaining—into a *quid pro quo* agreement. This is, the kind of cooperation provided for by employment contracts, purchase contracts, lending and investing agreements, and "deals" or pacts between members of a coalition. On a temporary basis bargains of this type are apt to be unstable, to be overturned as soon as a new deal is negotiated. With the passage of time, however, they may congeal into shared interests whatever action is required to meet the terms of the bargain.

It would be a mistake to regard any one of these sources of cooperation as generally characteristic of one or another kind of organization. While shared interests may be spoken of more frequently in religious or political organizations, many members of such organizations cooperate largely because of the dissatisfactions that would result if they did not.

In armies, where the possibility of strong sanctions is obvious, there is considerable importance to be found in shared interests and *quid pro quo* bargains. For many people in employment organizations, the *quids* assured through the employment contract are rarely more than a partial basis of cooperation. The strongest foundation for cooperative activity in an organization is usually one which combines all three in generous proportions.

2. THE NEGATIVE SIDE OF COOPERATION

Since cooperation is a prerequisite of organization and the enlargement of cooperation an indispensable aspect of augmenting an organization's power, one is apt to regard it as an unmitigated good.

We are brought back to a more realistic viewpoint, however, by recalling such pejorative terms as "conspiracy," "collusion," "cabal," "plot," and "unholy alliance." All of these refer to cooperative efforts— often *sub rosa*—based upon interests or purposes which we do not favor. Thus, by virtue of its being oriented toward satisfying some interests, cooperation is often directed against other interests. Apart from the objects of cooperation and the parties to it, it is not an abstract value in itself. Thus, many ardent calls for increased cooperation often represent an effort to have people sacrifice legitimate interests. The cooperation of the Oysters with the Walrus, in Lewis Carroll's *Through the Looking-Glass*, soon led to their sliding down the Walrus' gullet. Nor did the Walrus' loudly expressed sympathy interfere with his eating more oysters than the Carpenter.

Another difficulty with cooperation lies in its possible association with stability and routinization. When cooperation is viewed in the negative sense of a mere absence of conflict, its extension is usually associated with an avoidance of change and the continuation of outmoded forms of action. In this sense a high level of cooperation may be a symptom of a low level of aspiration or effort. The extension of cooperation may mean adding to the organization's incapacity to act.

B. *The Inevitability of Conflict*

MANY OF THE earlier treatises on administration give the impression that administration is something smooth and easy. They suggest that tensions or disturbances develop because of administrative error or accident. Just follow sound principles and all will be well!

This approach to administration is associated with certain "smooth and easy" conceptions of social action in general. "There has always been a tendency in economics to gloss over interest conflicts" (Myrdal, 1954). Neoclassical economists in particular often jump from one extreme of seeing the market as an automatic adjustor of competing interests to the other extreme of failing to recognize the existence of competing interests. In sociology, as Coser has pointed out, some modern sociologists see conflict as a disease. With "the rise of bureaucratic structures requiring the services of social scientists in the task of administration," a sociologist often orients himself toward the provision of services to the higher administrators seeking formulas for harmony and prescriptions for avoiding conflicts (Coser, 1956, p. 29). Turning his back on sociological thought and research which identifies conflict as an integral part of social processes, he will often diagnose any kind of organizational conflict as pathological. He will prescribe therapy in the form of encouragement to this or that academic research or the hiring of this or that academic consultant.

Here also, as with power, there may be administrative reasons for the masking of conflict. In many situations of organizational conflict the bitterest enemies may follow the *Mahabhrata's* counsel to address an adversary "even more gently while delivering the deadly blow." Many administrators act on the principle that attention to basic conflicts exacerbates them and that the best remedy is to do nothing but pretend they do not exist. Social scientists at times have demonstrated the practicality of their wisdom by providing valuable aid in keeping up the pretense.

The practical administrator, however, usually takes conflict for granted. For him, conflict is neither incidental nor accidental. I have never yet found an experienced administrator who has been unwilling to accept the core of the following thought:

> Everything is very simple in administration, but the simplest thing is difficult. These difficulties accumulate and produce a friction of which no one can form a correct idea who has not seen administration.
>
> Friction is the only conception which in a fairly general way corresponds to what distinguishes real administration from administration on paper.
>
> This enormous friction which is not concentrated, as in mechanics, at a few points is, therefore, everywhere brought into contact with chance, and thus produces incidents quite impossible to foresee. . . .
>
> The knowledge of this friction is a chief part of that often boasted experience of administration which is required of a good administrator. . . . It is true that he is not the best administrator in whose mind this knowledge fills the largest space and who is most overawed by it . . . ; but an administrator must be aware of it that he may overcome it, where this is possible, and that he may not expect a degree of precision in his operations which just because of this friction is impossible.

This quotation is taken from Von Clausewitz's classic *On War* (Jolles trans., 1950, p. 53-55). For the purpose of highlighting the general relevance of Clausewitz's observations, I have taken the liberty of making two changes in his text: inserting "administration" in place of "war" and "administrator" in place of "general." One could just as well substitute "running a hospital" or "factory manager" or "division director."

"This enormous friction" is inherent in the use of power. If power takes the form of pressure, the result is resistance—or at least a struggle against inertia. If power takes the form of persuasion, it usually includes a good deal of bargaining.

1. LOCI OF CONFLICT

As with cooperation, here also we may start by distinguishing between the various loci of conflict.

One aspect of conflict is internal. In his classic study of social conflict, Simmel points out that conflict is the other side of the coin of cooperation. "A certain amount of discord, inner divergence and outer controversy is organically tied up with the very elements that ultimately hold the group together" (1955, p. 17-18). Individuals and groups within an organization never have identical interests. The differences in interests always produce some sort of conflict, overt, covert, or latent. The administrator, of course, must get people to cooperate in some fashion— in a wholehearted manner at best, and at the very least in such a way as not to interfere with others too much. But in either case the superior-subordinate relationship itself may be a source of conflict. Superordination is often resented by subordinates. The resentment may be all the greater when hidden under the mask of service acquiescence or tied up with an urge to be dominated.

The other part is external conflict. This fact is no less significant than the internal ones. Wherever there are objectives to be achieved, there are obstacles in the path. In part this may be merely the age-old story of Man against Nature. It is also the story of Man against Man, or group against group. In one case it may be a matter of merely passive resistance or friction. At times, however, it is a matter of head-on collision between two or more organizations. More frequently, it is competition, direct or indirect, for a larger share of scarce values, whether power, resources or social position (*Banfield*, 1951).

The line between external and internal conflicts, it should be noted, is not always clear. The internal struggles and tensions have an inevitable effect upon the kinds of conflict situations into which an organization moves, whether by steering or drift. The external conflicts in which it is engaged are inevitably reflected in the inner stresses of the organization. Both may be reflected in, and affect, the internal conflicts within any member of the organization. For an outsider, it is difficult to discuss this combination of internal and external conflicts, much of which is in the sphere of "organizational secrets." For an insider, privy though he may be to secrets, it is difficult to see these conflicts in perspective (just as it is probably impossible for one to serve as self-psychiatrist and objectively analyze his own internal conflicts). Yet no one can understand any organization very well until he achieves an awareness of its complex conflict pattern. Since the loci of cooperation are often the same points, this leads to the conflict-cooperation nexus as a whole.

2. SOURCES OF CONFLICT

Just as the sources of cooperation are found in actual or perceived communality of interests, the sources of conflict are found in some degree of actual or perceived divergence of interests.

At one extreme, conflict is rooted in a sharp incompatability—or head-on collision—of interests. Any satisfaction, or victory, for one side means dissatisfaction, or defeat, for the other. In game theory this limiting case is described as a "zero sum" game, that is, one in which the gains of one party in a two-party conflict plus the losses of the other party (a negative quantity) always add up to zero. In actual wars the conflict of interest need not be so extreme in order to evoke a considerable amount of antagonistic emotion and destructive action. Warfare itself can be "cold" as well as hot, repressed as well as open, psychological as well as military. Many conflicts within and among organizations often seem based upon a perceived incompatibility of interests and, even though physical destruction may not be resorted to, take on the characteristics of warfare.

At the other extreme, conflict may be rooted in interests that are different but not necessarily incompatible. Here, when conflict occurs, a large gain to one party may occur with little or no loss to others. Or else both may lose a little or gain a little at the same time. This is the conflict which may be found in rivalry and competition. It is found in the bargaining and negotiation situations which precede an agreed-upon exchange of services or goods. It is the irreducible minimum of conflict which is usually found among partners, colleagues, and members of any committee or unit within an organization.

Decision-making itself is a fundamental source of conflict, since it invariably involves conflicting considerations or pressures.[1] These conflicts are not particularly intense for the fortunate individual, unit, or organization which is faced with a choice between two goods, that is, two desirable forms of satisfaction. The choosing process becomes more painful, however, when—as is more often the case—the choice is between courses of action each one of which has many good aspects and many bad aspects. When the latter dominate attention, decision-making then becomes a search for the "lesser evil." Within organizations, decision-making conflicts are invariably enlivened by pressure for different solutions on the part of different individuals and groups in the organization or intervening in its activities from outside. These pressures, in turn, are internalized within the minds of various individual decision-makers and become the basis for the deep internal conflicts that characterize the life of many administrators.

Most conflicts are embedded in a multidimensional matrix of interests. They thus cannot be readily placed on a simple continuum from incompatible interests to different interests. Each conflict usually involves a complex set of interests, each one of which may be located at a different point on such a continuum. It can be properly identified only by a profile, or vector, of different points.

Such a conflict vector, moreover, is necessarily connected with a companion vector of points on various continua of shared interests. It is for this reason that Schelling has proposed that game theory should be extended to include common interest as well as total conflict games. He uses "bargaining game" and "mixed motive game" to refer to the "mixture of mutual dependence and conflict, of partnership and competition" (1960, p. 83-118). In using these terms he refers to the large proportion of conflict situations in which common and divergent interests are closely associated. Within organizations this relationship is fostered by procedures and rituals for the conduct of conflict on the part of cooperating individuals and groups. Similarly, the broader arena of conflicts between organizations and nations, opponents and bitter enemies often cooperate in the support of codes of competition and "civilized warfare."

3. NEGATIVE AND POSITIVE ASPECTS

The negative potentials of conflict are fairly obvious. Just as a deep enough internal conflict within the personality of an individual can destroy his ability to function, a deep enough internal conflict within

---

1. See Chapter 21, "The Decision-Making Struggle."

any organization will result in some form of dissolution. In sharply split dyads, such as certain man-wife relationships, it may lead to separation, divorce, or murder. In more complex organizations, the results may range from insurrection and schism to the creeping paralysis of deadlock and disinterest. For those who want to destroy an organization or its effectiveness, there is probably no more efficient method than the promotion of internal conflict.

The destructive possibilities of external conflict are even more apparent. Overwhelming outside power can be used to effect domination or annihilation. For the weak, even weak competition may be disastrous. When combined with internal dissension, external assault may be irresistible—as attested by the wreckage of ancient empires and the liquidation of business corporations. The possibilities of mutual annihilation by the two largest power-blocs in the world stare us all in the face.

Modern administrative thought, however, recognizes the constructive potentialities inherent in conflict. This theme was presaged in Simmel's analysis of how group unity is enhanced by internal conflicts among those who share basic values and by external conflicts with out groups (1955, p. 17-20). It was first stated in an administrative framework by Follett's observations that "we can set conflict to work and make it *do* something for us." It is restated by Simon, Smithburg, and Thompson's discussion of organizational conflict "as an important means of securing domestic control" (1950, p. 311). It is vigorously illustrated by Schlesinger's fascinating account of the "controlled competition" deliberately promoted by President Franklin Roosevelt:

> One of his favorite techniques was to keep grants of authority incomplete, jurisdictions uncertain and charters overlapping. . . . Roosevelt liked the competitive approach to administration not just because it reserved the big decisions for the President but perhaps even more because it enabled him to test and develop the ability of his subordinates (p. 535-539).

Looking back on a longer period of Presidential technique, Neustadt restates the theme in his observation that "Government is energized by a productive tension among its working parts" (*Presidential Power*, p. 183). In studying certain organizations operating across national and cultural boundaries, Cleveland, Mangone and Adams describe a field office as "a consciously-created system of tensions" (1960, p. 153). In terms of more general relevance to any unit, Cleveland summarizes many years of public and private organizational experience by stating that a major task of every administrator is to create a "web of tensions." Only thus will creative energies be released and cooperation made something more than dull routine (1960, p. 8, 16).

c. *The Outcomes of Conflict Resolution*

THE TERM "conflict resolution"—like "problem-solving"—is subject to various interpretations. On the one hand, it tends to suggest a certain finality that is inconsistent with a process concept of organizational and administrative behavior. It also suggests a purely intellectual operation which, like the solution of a mathematical equation, can be confined to what one does in one's head, on a piece of paper, or through operation of a computer.

In the sense herein used, however, "conflict resolution" is used to refer to the ongoing process of making certain changes in the multifaceted conflict-cooperation nexus. In this sense, no resolution or solution need be final. It may, indeed, be merely a prelude to new and sharper conflicts. Moreover, it refers to all the myriad forms of action, not rational thought alone, by which conflicts are resolved.

The term "outcomes" is here used to divert attention from the myriad processes of conflict resolution and focus it instead upon certain crucial types of change that are the immediate results of such processes. Analytically, these may take the form of avoidance, deadlock, domination-defeat, compromise, and integration. Any actual outcome of conflict resolution is usually a combination of two or more of these outcome forms. It is made all the more complex by virtue of the fact that each of these forms raises confusing problems with respect to the difference between what has really happened and the symbols or perception of that reality. In any case, there is considerable support for Dubin's proposition that "resolutions of conflict in continuing group relations determine the direction of social change" (1957, p. 193). Such resolutions, as Coser points out, highlight factors that are not deducible from the conduct of conflict and must hence be studied separately (1961).

1. AVOIDANCE

Interest divergence among human beings and groups is so great that it is highly doubtful whether social intercourse would be even tolerable without many forms of avoidance. In fact, withdrawal from conflict seems to be one of man's most natural and traditional ways of coping with conflicting interests. Internal conflicts may be unconsciously repressed. Family conflicts may be avoided by having children sleep in separate rooms, by taboos on the discussion of delicate subjects or—as in some societies—by rules against husbands talking with mothers-in-law (Murdock, 1949). Within organizations interpersonal conflicts are avoided by people "keeping out of each other's hair," by developing codes of noninterference in another's "territory," by suppressing deeply-felt differences of opinion, and by postponing or evading decisions. In conflicts among nations avoidance is achieved through disengagement, a *cordon sanitaire*, isolationism or the division of disputed territory into spheres of exclusive influence.

If avoidance is carried to an ultimate extreme, it may indeed mean the end of conflict—as when family troubles lead to divorce, members leave an organization or the organization is dissolved. Under such circumstances the price of peace is disorganization.

Normally, there are limits on the extent and duration of avoidance. The repression of conflict at one point can easily lead to its violent bursting forth at another. Or else one or more parties to the conflict may see in disengagement an opportunity to strengthen his forces for a more violent return to the fray at a more opportune moment. Today's truce may be but a transient calm before tomorrow's *Sturm und Drang*.

2. DEADLOCK

Like avoidance, deadlock is such a negative state that it may be difficult to regard it as an outcome. As with the stalemate conclusion of a chess game, no side can win. But unlike chess the broader game of social conflict can often continue in a state of deadlock for long periods of time.

> The possibility of deadlock—or to use a closely related term, stasis—is inherent in the democratic process of peaceful group conflict. When few victories are ever complete, when power is widely dispersed among many veto groups, when every solution is a compromise that is objectionable to many, and when every settlement itself creates new problems, you have the makings of a stalemate (*Gross*, 1953, p. 26).

The negative aspect of deadlock is probably one of the reasons why peace is not always as attractive as the hatred of war might suggest it should be. A "no win" peace is never as appealing as a victory. It becomes more desirable only when the dangers of defeat make "no loss" seem more comfortable. "Peace through stalemate, based on a coincident recognition by each side of the opponent's strength, is at least preferable to peace through common exhaustion" (Hart, 1954, p. 370).

From the long-time perspective of protracted conflict, however, deadlock may have more positive aspects. It may keep an opponent's energies concentrated upon a certain front while one tries to advance on other fronts. It may provide a breathing space, with or without withdrawal, during which one mobilizes forces for renewed and more conclusive efforts.

3. VICTORY-DEFEAT

Victory by one party to a conflict (or defeat to others) is the neatest of all outcomes. The victor receives a clear-cut gain. The defeated suffers an unambiguous loss.

It is also a highly circumscribed form of outcome. Even in games and debates, where there are agreed-upon rules for keeping the score, a victory in one round may be quickly followed by defeat in the next, and vice versa. In more complex forms of conflict, the possibility of such change is still greater. Clear defeat may be transformed into a psychological victory by propagandistic success in calling it something else—as when President Nasser of Egypt embellished his political victory over the forces that had seized the Suez Canal by convincing Egyptian supporters that it was military superiority which forced the withdrawal of the invaders from the canal region. The very act of surrender, as Coser pointed out, may involve an "assertion of power" (1961). It may be used to establish conditions for subsequent gains. The anguish of defeat may, in fact, be a contribution to future victories by providing the unseasoned with an invaluable baptism of fire and by teaching lessons that could otherwise never be learned.

Above all, victory or defeat on one issue may be inextricably associated with defeat or victory on other issues. Under such circumstances, either one is merely one aspect of a compromise outcome.

4. COMPROMISE

A compromise occurs when each party to a conflict wins something and loses something. It may take place with respect to a single issue, or it may emerge as the aggregate of a set of specific victories and defeats on various issues. It is thus the most widespread outcome of conflict resolution.

It is also the form most beclouded by the symbolic and deceptive tactics of bargaining and negotiation. A skillful leader who wants one loaf of bread will usually ask for two and be willing to "compromise" by accepting half of his stated demand. If he accepts the one loaf, he may then be violently accused of betrayal or opportunism by supporters whose energies he mobilized by dramatic visions of greater gains. To offset such criticism, he may take the offensive with his supporters by understating the negative aspects of a compromise and hailing the positive aspects as a great and historic (albeit limited) victory. Similarly, during the process of negotiation he may have to provide opportunities for his opponents to justify their participation in the compromise by parallel (albeit logically irreconcilable) claims of a great and historic victory. Like the confidence man in a con game, he may have to "cool the mark" (*Goffman, 1952*) by saving the face and assuaging the feelings of any who regard themselves as injured by the compromise. No wonder that the conflicting interpretations of many compromises are themselves the seeds of renewed conflict!

The necessity of compromise is something that can never be learned painlessly. Nor is the learning process easy for those who have learned too well the ease with which a purely logical problem can be solved through the processes of deduction but have not learned the difference between such a problem and a genuine social conflict. For these, as with nonrealistic idealists, compromise is often seen as an unmitigated evil. If it is to be tolerated, the condition is often laid down that at least there be no compromise on matters of principle. But principles are usually the first things to be yielded, for the simple reason that they are so rarely a clean-cut expression of fundamental high-priority interests. Because they are sometimes willing to sacrifice principles which are not directly related to basic interests but are rather propagandistic devices for the extension of support, the most effective leaders in the social struggle often appear to be totally unprincipled men. In a world of sharp divisions and dispersed power, they may even have to yield on basic interests. It may be added that since interests and principles are always multiple and diverse, the safeguarding or serving of some invariably requires a yielding or even sacrifice of others.

At the same time, to laud compromise as a value in itself may lead to an eating away of moral values and the growth of a cynical "anything goes" attitude toward life. It also leads to a major role in organizations for those who are skillful in serving as brokers and "go-betweens."[2] These are people who usually care more about making a deal or keeping peace for its own sake than about making progress toward achieving substantive goals.

2. See discussion of "middlemen" in "People-in-Organizations: Informal Aspects" (Chapt. 10).

5. INTEGRATION

As Follett pointed out long ago, integration is a conflict outcome in accordance with which the interests of all sides have found a place without any side sacrificing anything. The process of working toward an integration involves getting behind the symbols that may hide the state of true affairs and bringing conflicts out into the open so that the underlying interests can be analyzed and re-examined. This is very close to the "working through" process developed by psychoanalysts. Its application to organizational conflict is well illustrated in the way in which the Tavistock consultants helped bring about an integration as an outcome to certain managerial conflicts in the Glacier plant *(Jaques)*.

Enthusiasm for integration should not lead one to believe that it is possible to resolve all or most conflicts in this manner. Although such a resolution is generally more desirable and although integration probably plays a much greater role than many cynics would think, there are undoubtedly many occasions when nothing is possible except some sequence or combination of avoidance, deadlock, victory-defeat, or compromise. An integration of any complex conflict, moreover, is a multisided operation that must usually include within it some elements of mere compromise.

One of the reasons for the difficulty of attaining integration as an outcome of conflict is that it always involves a broadening of the framework. It requires the conflicting parties to become involved in issues beyond the current agenda of attention. It takes into account the many and diverse interests of the combatants, apart from those which are the basis of contention. It is based upon an examination of new and hitherto unexamined courses of action. This requires on the part of at least some of the participants a broad perspective toward life and a varied acquaintance with the total environment. To get beyond the narrow confines of mere compromise, one must be able to analyze the wide range of people's interests and have a sense of what is and is not feasible in a complex environment. These are not common capacities.

The role of imagination and creativity must also be mentioned. Here we find an essential link between Follett's analysis of integration and Barnard's concept of "moral creativity." As Barnard points out, an executive should be able to invent a new moral basis for the solution of moral conflicts, instead of relying on compromise alone. Similar inventiveness is needed in resolving any other type of conflict.

In conclusion, let it be noted that the process of integrating divergent or conflicting interests is part and parcel of the process of developing an organization's power. The ultimate source of any organization's power lies in the power of human beings. It is integration that brings together the interests of members and nonmembers and makes it possible for an organization to achieve influence that individuals could not possibly attain separately. By this same token, it should be remembered that integration, like power, is also a sword that can cut in any direction. It can unite the forces of the devil as well as of the angels. Whether any specific integration is to be regarded as good or evil must, like any other outcome of conflict, be determined entirely by one's ethical premises.

Chapter 4

THE POWER-AUTHORITY-
RESPONSIBILITY TRIANGLE

ONE COULD EASILY JUSTIFY an entire book on power, authority, and responsibility, or even a separate book on each. These subjects are of considerable importance beyond the realm of organizations and their administration. Within this realm, their significance has been repeatedly recognized throughout the history of administrative thought.

The myths and taboos associated with the public discussion of power, however, have often led to an excessive emphasis upon authority and responsibility. This imbalance is being redressed by the modern tendency to deal with power, or influence, more frankly. It thus becomes easier to consider the interrelations among all three.

The consideration of these interrelations can be facilitated, in my judgment, by thinking of the three as separate sides of a triangle. Thus, changes on one side must always affect one or both of the other sides. In this context the terms are used as follows:

Power (or influence) = the affecting of situations by human action
Authority   = the accepted right to engage in certain actions
Responsibility   = the obligation to act in a certain way

The major task of this chapter is to go beyond these oversimplified, nominal definitions and to present a synthesis of more substantive ideas that, apart from many terminological differences, are part of the emerging consensus in modern thought. These ideas will prove indispensable as provisionally fixed starting points for the detailed analysis of people and purposes in the administrative process. They will therefore be interwoven into the texture of the following chapters and *pari passu* elaborated upon and refined.

A. *Power: Cause-Effect Relations*

To GET RESULTS, as stated in one of the basic propositions (Chapt. 2), both organizations and their administrators develop, maintain and use power or influence. Any organization, from a ladies' club to an army, is a system through which people develop the power to do things that they could not do as well, or at all, by individual action. Any administrator is a person who is expected to exercise some kind of power in or on an organization.

Whether we refer to the power of organizations or their administrators, the concept may be used in the sense of either the *actual* or the *potential*. Actual (or kinetic) power is the production of certain results. Potential power is the capacity to bring about certain results. In either sense, the same idea—sometimes in more limited form—is referred to by "influence" (sometimes used only for weaker forms of power), "control" (sometimes reserved for stronger forms), "rule" or even "leadership." With all of these terms, reference is made to some cause-effect relation.[1]

---

1. The identification of power as a cause-effect relation is implicit in the common-sense view of a powerful organization or individual as one that "gets results" or "brings about action." It is explicitly stated by Simon and many other analysts of social power or influence, although some people try to deal with power without getting tangled in the dangerous web of philosophical controversy regarding causality. The difficulty of avoiding this web completely is suggested by the cause-effect relation inherent in all such definitions as the following:

⌁ the production of intended effects (Russell, 1938, p. 35)
⌁ making things happen, initiating change (Follett, "Power")
⌁ affecting policies of other than the self (Lasswell and Kaplan, 1950, p. 71)
⌁ the causation of behavior (Simon, 1957, p. 8)
⌁ any process in which a person or group of persons or organizations of persons determines, i.e. intentionally affects what another person or organization will do (Tannenbaum, "Control in Organizations")
⌁ the inducement of change (March, 1955)
⌁ every action which compels certain action on others (Mannheim, 1948, p. 167)
⌁ A's getting B to do what B would not otherwise do (paraphrased from Dahl, 1957)

In the broad sense herein used, the concept of power is by no means limited to the harshness of force and compulsion. As will be shown in the discussion of activation (Chapt. 24), the use of power takes the form of persuasion as well as pressure, of promoting self-activation as well as exercising external influence. It is always seen in the exercise of leadership.

1. THE MASKING AND UNMASKING OF POWER

The tremendous difficulties of measuring power often inhibit the use of the concept. Yet this inhibition is mild in comparison with the taboos of polite discourse. In public administration the idea of power-seeking and power-wielding by the public administrator interferes with the myth of the civil servant as a noble, neutral agent of the common will. Such words, it has often been felt, are used only by the violent critics of "power-mad government bureaucrats." They should not be used by the friends of public administration.

In business administration circles also, the public discussion of power has often been taboo. As Galbraith has pointed out, there is an unwritten "convention which outlaws ostensible pursuit of power and which leads to a constant search for euphemisms to disguise its possession" (1952, p. 28).[2] Recognition of the substantial power accumulated by business organizations clashes with the traditional model of a competitive economic system. It undermines the fiction that no entrepreneur has the power to fix the level of prices or the volume of production and that these decisions are made instead by the "impersonal forces" of the market. It also suggests the need for countervailing power in the form of labor organization or government regulation.

The taboo on the open recognition of power is all the more effective because, rather than being merely a restraint on intellectual speculation, it is itself a popular aid in the use of power. In many situations desired action can be better caused by concealment of power, by adroit manipulation and by what Liddell Hart calls "the strategy of the indirect approach" (1954).[3] The iron fist, after being encased in the velvet glove, is then

2. Despite Galbraith's limiting himself to the United States of America in the mid-twentieth century, the disguise of "ostensible pursuit" is hardly limited to one country or one period of history. It may be presumed, for example, that with women cosmetic disguise is minor in comparison with the disguise of their power over men.

3. Although Hart concentrates on the strategy of using military power, he maintains that his "idea of the indirect approach is closely related to all problems of the influence of mind upon mind—the most influential power in history.

hidden behind the back. The myths of ultimate authority and central omnipotence,[4] while magnifying the power at certain spots, by the same token minimize the power at other spots. To the extent that administrators or bureaucrats are regarded as the obedient and powerless slaves of top executives, directorates, legislatures, or "the people," their power may be greatly enhanced. Any unmasking of the actual distribution of power may serve to reduce the power of those operating behind the mask.

On top of all this, any open discussion of power or influence may conflict with deeply treasured ideals and powerful inarticulate premises. The idea of elites with power is offensive to many people who believe in utopian patterns of quasi-anarchic democracy. The idea of control is resented by people who have been subjected to onerous controls and believe in more autonomy for everyone. The idea of influence is soiled in the eyes of those who have witnessed the outrageous misuse of influence. For all these reasons power, like sex under the Victorians, has often been regarded as a subject not to be openly discussed but rather to be sought, thought about and used under the cover of darkness.

Nevertheless, the central role of power in administration has been brought to the fore by the seminal work of Follett, Key, Lasswell, and Long, and by the conceptual clarifications attempted by such recent analysts as Cartwright, Dahl, Dubin, March, Simon, and Tannenbaum. All of these commentators would probably accept Cartwright's comments on social psychology as applicable to other disciplines as well:

> Both early social psychology and modern society recognize the importance of power. If, however, we examine social psychology since the beginning of its scientific epoch, we search in vain for any concentrated attack on the problem. Surely this constitutes a weakness of modern social psychology. We can only conclude that twentieth century social psychologists have been "soft" on power. Direct investigation has been evaded in many ways. . . .
> But surely inability to deal with power within traditional theories does not mean that the problem should be ignored in the future. . . . The point may be stated differently: it is simply not possible to deal adequately with data which are clearly social psychological without getting involved with matters of power (1959, p. 2).

Similarly, it is now fairly widely agreed that it is simply not possible for administrator to administer without "getting involved with matters of power." Although a "concentrated attack on the problem" by empirical methods has not yet been launched, an indication of what might be

---

. . . The indirect approach is as fundamental to the realm of politics as to the realm of sex." p. 18-19.

4. See discussion of these myths in "The Dispersion of Power in Organizations" (Gross, *The Managing of Organizations*, Chapter 3).

expected is provided by Neustadt's pioneering analysis (1960) of administrative power-seeking by various Presidents of the United States—Harry S Truman, Dwight D. Eisenhower and, in the background, Franklin D. Roosevelt. Neustadt shows how they achieved varying degrees of personal power through ability in persuasion and in developing reputation and prestige among the "professionals" in their more immediate environment and among "publics" at large. By so doing, Neustadt has helped legitimate the analysis of the actions of administrators in "the development, maintenance and use of power." Case studies of top corporate executives have gone in the same direction—although writers on business administration have been less outspoken than those in public administration.

2. THE DIFFICULTIES IN ESTIMATING POWER

Although the growing literature on methods of measuring power[5] reveals many conceptual differences, these differences themselves stem from an ever broadening consensus on the importance of power in administration and other fields. They are also based upon widespread recognition that power is hard to measure (entirely apart from the complications introduced by taboos and masking) because of multiple causation, multiple effects, and the difficulty of tracing presumed results to specific causes.

A. *Multiple causes and effects.* The first difficulty is the large number of causal factors that always influence any action. Let us suppose that a unit chief tries to influence his superior to recommend a large budget increase for his unit. The unit chief uses various forms of direct or indirect influence. Some of these may be based upon the feedback information obtained from earlier attempts at influencing the same budgetary decision. At the same time his superior is also subjected to influences by other units, by advisers and by his superiors. He is also influenced by internal factors: his habits, interests, allegiances, and attitudes. Prominent among these internal influences may be his anticipations of what the unit chief may do in the future if the increase is or is not granted. Many of these influences, both external and internal, may stem from events that took place a long time ago: the past behavior of unit chiefs, his own experiences over the past ten years, or even occurrences during early childhood. If we go back far enough, we might even attribute the final

5. Among the most important recent papers on the subject are the following: Shapley and Shubik (1954); March (1955); Dahl (1957); Simon (1957, Part I); Tannenbaum (1962); Harsanyi (1962).

budget decision, at least in part, to the length of Cleopatra's nose.[6] Many influences, even the most recent, may be unnoticed and uncontrolled, to be taken for granted as parts of the situation, as contributing or conditioning factors or as "intervening variables." Those that are explicitly noticed—such as the superior's dislike for people in the unit or the adverse influence of his own superior—may prove both undesirable and uncontrollable. If we now turn from the unit chief to the organization as a whole and consider its power to get additional funds from a bank or legislature, we see the same situation. The causative power of the organization is also imbedded in a complex causation matrix that includes (a) various actions by the organization, (b) actions by others who may influence the financing agency, (c) internal influences, including habits, interests and anticipations within the bank or legislature, (d) the delayed or indirect influence of many actions in prior periods, and (e) unnoticed, uncontrolled, undesirable, or uncontrollable elements. The power wielder can probably never see all of these factors or appreciate the significance of all that he does see. This difficulty is enhanced by his need to concentrate upon those (the presumably "strategic" ones) that he can most readily manipulate.[7]

Resulting action is also multidimensional. Entirely apart from the budget decision itself, the effects of the budget dispute may include such things as (a) better morale in the unit because of the fight their chief put up, (b) deep animosities on the part of other units, (c) resentment on the part of the unit chief's superior which may contribute to retaliatory action at a later date. Similarly, the organization's effort to influence the financing agency may result in (a) better understanding of financial matters within the organization and (b) more external support in some quarters and more external opposition in others. In both cases, the effort

6. "All statesmanship, and all rational conduct of life, is based upon the method of the frivolous historical game, in which we discuss what the world would be if Cleopatra's nose had been half an inch longer" (Russell, 1950).

7. A noted physicist has described the problem of multiple causation as follows: "We do not have a simple event A causally connected with a simple event B, but the whole background of the system in which the events occur is included in the concept, and is a vital part of it" (Bridgman, 1946, p. 83). An anthropologist puts the problem this way: "It is the system as a whole which is involved in cause. To define the cause, one would have to define the whole system; one may not select out only certain factors" (Radcliffe-Brown, 1957, p. 42). One way of meeting the problem is to think not of causative factors but of "correlations" and "associations." While this approach may be helpful to researchers studying large arrays of events, the administrator must go further. He cannot dodge estimating the causative influence of specific acts, including acts of reciprocal influence.

to exercise power may result in delayed, unnoticed, unanticipated or undesired consequences. If the power wielder focuses entirely on a single intended result, he may lose sight of the whole matrix of significant consequences.

B. *Judging cause-effect relations.* As already indicated, the toughest problem in the estimation of power is establishing a relation between a particular causative factor and a presumed result. Let us suppose that the unit chief's superior does recommend the desired budget increase. Does this mean that causative influence must be attributed to any one or even the totality of the unit chief's efforts? Not at all! It is entirely possible that the same increase would have been recommended anyway. It is even possible that the unit chief's effort to influence the outcome may have in fact perilously endangered it, or may have even served to prevent a larger or a more enthusiastic recommendation.

These possibilities could be definitively determined if it were possible to know what would have happened if the unit chief had not tried to influence his superior's decision or had used different methods of attempted influence. To know this would require some way of isolating the unit chief's efforts at influence from the many other factors in the total causation matrix. In the laboratory of the scientist such knowledge may be obtained by a controlled experiment in which the results of introducing a specific variable are compared with the results obtained when everything is held constant except the same variable. When it is impossible to control all other variables (as in a biological laboratory), the experiment is repeated a large number of times, thus enabling a comparison of the "experimental group" results with "control group" results. In observing events outside of the scientist's laboratory, it is much more difficult to isolate variables, study large groups of comparable phenomena and establish control groups. Nevertheless, as Stouffer has pointed out, we can still keep in mind the model of a controlled experiment, even if in practice we may have to deviate from it ("Some Observations on Study Design"). Stouffer illustrates the controlled experiment model as follows:

	Before	*After*	*After — Before*
Experimental Group	x_1	x_2	$d = x_2 - x_1$
Control Group	x_1'	x_2'	$d' = x_2' - x_1'$

Here d symbolizes the results obtained with the factor which is being studied, d' the results without it. The difference between d and d' may be regarded as the measure of the power of the same factor.[8] Stouffer points out that in social science research, we often "have only one cell" instead of four and that "when this happens, we do not know much of anything. But we can still fill pages of social science journals with 'brilliant analysis' if we use plausible conjecture in supplying missing cells from our imagination." He advocates more careful research designs aimed at providing data on at least two or three, if not all of the four cells.[9]

Anyone trying to estimate the amount of social power also follows a similar procedure, implicitly or explicitly. Suppose we want to measure the power of an organization to make a certain kind of change in its environment—whether it be defeating an enemy, outdistancing a rival or influencing the behavior of clients. The essence of our analysis is a comparison between a presumed result (d) of a certain action and the presumed result if such an action had not been taken (d'). If we are starting from the present and estimating potential influence, we may have some data concerning x_1, but we shall have to use conjecture with respect

8. If one is interested in estimating future rather than past power, then both d and d' can be regarded as estimates of the probability that a given event will occur with and without the influence of a specific causative factor. In this case, as Dahl pointed out with a somewhat different set of symbols, no power relation exists if $d = d'$ and power is at a maximum if $d = 1$ and $d' = 0$ (1957, p. 205).

9. One of the limitations of Stouffer's model is that it does not directly suggest the multidimensional aspects of the phenomena to be described. Both the "before" and the "after" states of a system may be described more fully in terms of a vector. The transformation from an earlier to a later state (and to any subsequent state) may be expressed in terms of the operation upon an $n \times 1$ vector by an $n \times n$ "causation matrix." Similarly, the difference between the subsequent states may be expressed by the comparison between the appropriate system state vectors. Thus, let

  $C =$ causation matrix without action (or changed action) by given actor
  $A =$ causation matrix of action (or changed action) by given actor
  $P(A) =$ power of A
  $C' = C + A$
  $O =$ vector describing state of system; 0_1 (0_t) before (after) serving as object of influence by C or C';
  　$0'$ after serving as object of influence by C'
Then,

$$C \cdot 0^1 = 0_t$$
$$C' \cdot 0_1 = 0'_t$$
$$P(A) = 0'_t - 0_t$$

This formulation directs attention to the interrelation between many causal elements and many aspects of the system influenced. It also allows for inclusion within the causal matrix of internal as well as external influences. As with Stouffer's model, however, it is based upon the oversimplifying assumption that the transformations are linear and that the elements in the system states are additive.

to x_2. If we are looking back at actual influence already exerted, we may have more data concerning x_2 and shall have to use more conjecture with respect to the past. To estimate x'_1 and x'_2, we shall have to draw upon experience or working generalizations concerning similar circumstances. The whole situation is more complicated whenever d is a series of events extending over a long period of time or whenever it is necessary to compare d not only with d' but with a series of alternative situations.

The difficulties in estimating power become still greater when one turns to the power of an administrator. Here the relevant measure is not—despite popular ideas to the contrary—the administrator's power to get individuals to do what they would not otherwise have done. The d, rather, is the power of the organization or unit (as measured by one or more aspects of its performance), while d' is what we presume its power would be without him. Thus an administrator who throws his weight around to force people to do many things they would not otherwise do may exercise much less administrative power than one who gets people to do what they wanted to do anyway. The touchstone is found in our estimate of how the organization would have performed without him— or, better yet, with another administrator.

3. SOURCES OF POWER

Increasing attention has also been given to the sources of power—or what Simon refers to as the "influence base." As he points out, "if we can measure the magnitude of the influence base, we can infer from this the magnitude of the influence. (E.g., if wealth is the principal influence base in a particular situation—the principal means for exercising influence—then in that situation we may measure influence indirectly by wealth.)" (1957, p. 69.)

One way to analyze the influence base is provided by the proposition power is the product of the administration of resources.[10] An organization poor in resources may compensate for this weakness by better administration. An organization with weak administration may be powerful by reason of vast resources. The most powerful organizations are those which are strong in both. The most powerful administrators are

10. In an earlier formulation (*Gross*, 1953, p. 142-150) I identified the sources of power as (1) wealth, (2) numbers of people, (3) organization and leadership, (4) strategic position, and (5) combinations. The first two may be included under the concept of resources; the next three relate to administration.

those who contribute to the building up of a group of administrators capable of mobilizing and administering a significant quantity and quality of resources.

The term "resources" here refers to both material and human wealth. Material resources include the capital provided by nature, man-developed facilities, machinery and goods, and financial claims against physical resources. Human resources are people and organizations. These human resources are indeed the most elementary sources of power. Material resources are sources of power only to the extent that people value them and have the desire and ability—by individual or group action—to exploit them. Even the world-shaking power of nuclear fission and fusion exists only because of the knowledge and abilities of people and organizations.

The term "administration," as already explained, is here used to refer to the process of governing or guiding an organization. Administrators play a major role in bringing material and human resources together into an organization. The use, maintenance, conservation, and development of these resources is guided in turn by administrators with varying degrees of authority and responsibility. Thus any source of administrative capacity may be appropriately regarded as a source of power. Authority, particularly the formal authority associated with official position, has long been regarded, and properly so, as a source of power. To this must be added responsibility. Above all, emphasis must be placed on the knowledge, abilities, and interests of administrators.

When we contemplate the various sources of power, it is clear that under certain circumstances their use in the present may quickly produce depletion in the future. A military commander with a small supply of ammunition must hold his fire until the most appropriate moment. If he scatters his shots quickly, the fighting power of his organization may be destroyed. In many circumstances, however, the use of power may build up the power base, just as an automobile battery is charged through use or a muscle is strengthened through exercise. Also it is a dangerous oversimplification to think that the power base of one organization or person necessarily depends upon a complementary weakness on the part of another organization or person. Such an approach derives from analogies with areas of all-out conflict; it ignores the significance of cooperative efforts. The best analogy for the power of an organization is provided by the grid of electric power stations. The more electrical energy that can be originated in each station, the greater the power potential of the grid as a whole. Similarly, the more power that can be exercised by every member of an organization, the greater the power potential of the organization as a whole. If some become stronger, this does not mean that others automatically become weaker. In a well-administered organization it means that the organization as a whole is stronger (Tannenbaum, 1962; *Tannenbaum and Kahn*, 1958).

Above all, it is important to keep in mind Follett's observations on power as reciprocal influence. The power of an administrator is very much like love. The person who wants to be loved but is unwilling or unable to love is bound to fail. One must "give" love in order to "get" love. Similarly, one cannot develop his own power if he thinks only in unilateral terms and is unwilling to give others an opportunity to influence him.[11] "The man who exercises control gives more of himself to the organization. . . . While he controls more, he is not controlled less. . . . Members in the effective union pay for the increased control which they exercise (and for the effectiveness of their organization) not only in terms of the greater effort that they put into union activities, but also by their greater sensitivity and accession to controls within the union" (Tannenbaum, 1962, p. 244, 256-257). In this same sense, Likert (1961) describes an organization as an "interaction influence system" and regards the most effective organizations as those in which reciprocal influence by many members leads to greater influence as a whole.

4. ENERGY AND INFORMATION

The growing recognition of the importance of power in administration has been accompanied by increasing attention to the relation of social power to physical energy and information. From this point of view an organization is often viewed as a system for energy conversion and information processing.

Some disbursement of physical energy underlies all phenomena of organizational and administrative power. People and groups are not one side of a mind-matter dichotomy. Human life is a physical phenomenon. Action taken by an individual or organization to influence people by persuasion, even without any open or covert hint of physical force, involves significant energy disbursements. These may be measured in microunits by the electrical impulses in the nervous system or caloric consump-

---

11. This, of course, is much more than an analogy. Love itself is a form of power, "an active power in man, a power which breaks through the walls which separate man from his fellowmen, which unites him with others . . ." (Fromm, 1956, p. 20). One of the indices of maturity in administrative thought may be regarded as the ability not only to recognize the role of power in organizations (which may seem "tough") but to recognize love (which may appear "soft") as a form of power.

tion or in macrounits by various measures of individual or organizational performance. Although the stage of careful measurement has not yet been reached, important steps have been taken toward studying people and groups as energy-converting systems.[12]

In studying the power used by people and organizations, inertia and resistance are often the first phenomena to be noticed. In discussing the "poverty of power," Merriam makes the following observation:

> There is nothing more surprising to the holders of power, or perhaps to their subjects, than the frailty of their commands in certain types of crisis. . . . When the order is given, obedience is reluctant, partial; resistance widens; and as penalties are made heavier, opposition becomes stronger. . . . These forms of resistance are understood almost as well by the ignorant as by the learned—indeed, sometimes more perfectly . . ." (1950, p. 150, 183).

Such observations suggest interesting analogies with Newton's three laws of motion. These might be restated to deal with (1) the importance of social inertia, (2) the magnitude of power in relation to inertia and mass, and (3) the inevitability of counteracting power or resistance. Ohm's principle, according to which the electrical current in a circuit is inversely proportional to the resistance in the wire suggests another generalization on social power. In cybernetics the concept of entropy stated in the second law of thermodynamics is often applied to organizations and social systems.[13] This is often expressed as the tendency for an organization to run down for lack of energy available for specific purposes. In none of these cases, however, can one automatically transfer principles from one field to another. Although people and organizations are indeed physical systems, and as such subject to the laws of physics, they are special forms of physical systems (and from the cosmic viewpoint perhaps very exceptional cases). The general laws of physics, therefore, can provide only "starting point" ideas that must be considerably ad-

---

12. Neurology and psychology have long dealt with energy disbursements on the individual nervous system. Such concepts as Lewin's "psychical field" (1935) and Cattell's "synergy" (1948) broaden this approach. An anthropologist formulates an energy "law" of cultural evolution: "Other factors remaining constant, culture evolves as the amount of energy harnessed per capita per year is increased, or as the efficiency of the instrumental means of putting the energy to work is increased" (Leslie White, 1949, p. 368-369). A political scientist traces connections between growth of high-energy technology and increased government power (Cottrell, 1955).

13. See section on "Cyberneticists" in "Contributors from Other Fields" (Gross, *The Managing of Organizations*, Chapter 8).

justed and combined with other concepts in order to be applicable to human organizations.[14]

One of the bridges between physical systems and human organizations is provided by emerging theories on information transfer and processing. Even when power takes the form of violence (as with warfare or the harsher forms of disciplinary action), its effective application depends upon a considerable amount of information processing to develop the required physical energy and direct its use. A little violence becomes much more influential when information on its actual use and possible future use is widely transmitted. If we remove from consideration the direct contact of mass upon mass which is provided by violence, we find that the use of any other form of power is dependent upon the transmission and receipt of information. As Dorsey has perceptively pointed out, the energy potential of a human organization or social system depends upon its success in the processing of complex information ("An Information Energy Model"). In Deutsch's terms the transmission of information "can produce sometimes very large changes at the point of arrival . . . but these changes need in no way be proportionate to the amount of energy that carried the signal, much as the force of a gun shot need not be proportionate to the amount of pressure needed to set off the trigger (1963, p. 146).

Further exploration of the relation between information and energy may go far toward revealing some of the mysteries of social power. Unlike physical goods, the movement of more information from one place to another does not imply that there is less information at the place of origin. The only necessary losses are the information lost and the energy expended in the transmission process. But the previous supply of information, instead of merely being divided and redistributed, is now larger. Where one person had an idea, now a group of people have similar ideas. While this enlargement of the total supply of information may reduce the monopolistic value that may have resulted from previous scarcity, it may also greatly enhance the value of the shared information. This is particularly true when the shared information serves to mobilize new sources of energy to be used in reciprocal and cooperative action.

14. An illustration of the difference is provided by the fact that the second law of thermodynamics applies only to closed systems. Yet human organizations and social systems are open systems. Obviously the "same law" cannot automatically apply.

B. *Authority and Power*

AUTHORITY usually receives much more attention than power, not only in the more traditional currents of administrative thought but also in the everyday language of organizational life. Authority is more conspicuous; the head of an organization or unit is a man with authority. His power may not be so clear. In any case to talk about it openly may be regarded as indelicate. It is more decorous to discuss it in the language of authority.

One of the major clarifications in modern administrative thought is the differentiation between authority and power. Despite disputes on related matters, there seems to be a widespread consensus that authority is a source or form of power, but that power (or influence) cannot be understood in terms of authority alone. The significance of this distinction is perhaps most sharply illustrated by Follett's observation that administrators can confer authority on others, but power "is not a pre-existing thing which can be handed out to someone. . . ."[15]

1. AUTHORITY AS ACCEPTED RIGHT

In my judgment, the best way to capitalize upon the existing consensus is to use "authority" as referring to an "accepted right."

This usage is consistent with the normal understanding that a person with certain authority has the right to engage in a certain action. A driver's license gives one the right to drive the vehicle; without it, he is unauthorized to do so. A traffic policeman is authorized—has the right to—stop the driver and vehicle with a motion of his hand. He also has the right to speak with his superior officer. He may even have the right —depending upon the nature of the police organization—to speak when not spoken to, to make suggestions, or to influence his superior in various ways. But, except under the most unusual of circumstances, he will not have the right to give orders. His superior enjoys this right. This is part of his administrative authority, which may be regarded as the right to exercise power over certain people for certain purposes through the use of orders and other forms of influence.

In legal terminology we may properly say that a person or organization *has* a certain type of authority. We may even regard such authority as *vested* in the person or organization. While this form of discourse has

15. See "The Pioneers: New Beginnings," (Gross, *The Managing of Organizations,* Chapter 7).

its uses, it should not hide the fact that rights exist only because they are accepted by others. Hence, Barnard's dramatic statement that authority "does not reside in 'persons of authority' " but rather with the persons who accept such authority. Although Barnard refers specifically to subordinates who accept orders, his observation has wider validity. It applies not only to a superior's authority to give orders, but to a subordinate's right to make proposals. It applies to the authority of various "staff" officers and specialists to "intervene" in his business by requesting information and influencing his actions. In part, this "area of consent" or "zone of indifference" is determined by the general traditions and customs of an organization; in part, its boundaries are shaped by the individual relations that develop among people.

It is unduly confining, however, if we follow Barnard and Simon all the way and equate the acceptance of authority with the acceptance of any proposal made (or order given) by someone with authority. To do so suggests a dangerous return (at least in part) to the equation of authority with power or an equally dangerous equation of power with order-giving. An adviser's right to make proposals is not destroyed if his advice is sometimes accepted and, when accepted, modified. A superior's administrative authority is not negated if some of his suggestions to subordinates are not carried out (or even if his orders are somewhat changed, for better or worse, in the process of execution). The two elements come together only in the more extreme cases when the acceptance of a person's right to exercise administrative power is undermined by a demonstrated inability to use this right.

Let us now be more specific in pinning down the nature of authority in organizations. The authority of people in nonadministrative positions consists of rights to engage in certain actions which are required by their work or which neither violate the rules of the organization or impair the rights of others. The authority of administrators consists of the rights to engage in certain actions needed for the guidance of organizations or units thereof. These rights may be subdivided in various ways—such as rights to (a) receive, request, and transmit certain kinds of information, (b) make certain kinds of decisions, (c) initiate action through commands and other forms of activation, and (d) allot certain types of rewards and punishments. Some of these may be exclusively held, some may be shared jointly with others. All of them may be tied together in one bundle labelled "the right to exercise power in certain situations for the achievement of certain purposes." From this point of view administrative authority is like a hunting license. It legitimates, and sets certain limits upon, an administrator's search for power. It does not guarantee that he will find it.

2. AUTHORITY—LESS OR MORE THAN POWER

The crucial distinction between authority and power can best be understood by focusing on the two extreme cases of discrepancies between them

At one extreme, we find many situations in which people make little or no use of their rights. Those who enjoy accepted rights to speak or think freely may—through inertia, incapacity, or fear—neither speak nor think. Those who are authorized to drive cars or examine secret documents may do so only when the spirit moves them. In administrative posts within organizations this becomes more striking. Here we find many administrators who enjoy considerable authority but have little influence. Many of these make the mistake of equating formal or professional authority with influence. They fail to realize that significant power must be acquired through their own efforts in specific situations. Or else they limit their efforts in this direction to the acquisition of more formal authority, neglecting other sources of power. Among this group we find the "organizational figureheads" and "administrators in name only." They may be regarded as "reigning without ruling" or as having "abdicated" their tasks of leadership.

At the other extreme, we find situations in which power far exceeds authority. Some people in organizations exercise significant power over units—or perhaps even an entire organization—with little or no authority, or with authority acknowledged only by a minority in the organization. Many administrators exercise significant power far beyond the accepted borders of their authority. Among this group we find the *"eminences grises,"* the men with a "passion for anonymity," and the wirepullers behind the figureheads. As their power expands, protesting cries of usurpation are apt to be heard. Some among these will seek to legitimate their operations (and thereby strengthen their power base) by bolstering their authority. Over time, indeed, they may well succeed in achieving the accepted right to do what they have already been doing.[16]

Between these two extremes, some degree of authority is a necessary source of the power of administrators. Otherwise, their activities would be regarded as grossly "illegitimate." This is why the phrase "with varying degrees of authority" is an important part of the basic proposition dealing with administrators' power. The same proposition applies to the power of organizations as a whole. In order to get results, an organization must at least enjoy the right to exist and engage in a certain type of operations,

16. This is very close to the process whereby meaningful rights (as distinguished from mere "paper rights") are established in statutes and constitutions.

whether this right is formally stated in law or commonly taken for granted. The only exceptions to this rule are such "unauthorized organizations" as an organized group of criminals or an outlawed group of revolutionary conspirators. Yet even in these cases there is a good basis to assume that no such group can develop any significant power without some degree of at least tacit acceptance (if not active collaboration) from other individuals or groups in their own country or another country.

The use of the phrase "varying degrees of authority" may unwittingly suggest the possibility of a single element that can be precisely measured. Actually, any form of authority—and particularly administrative authority —is usually based upon a tangled web of unwritten and often unspoken understandings, precisely written statements that are relevant in only a minority of situations, and broad general statements that are subject to wide interpretation and interminable dispute. This tangled web is often perceived in different ways—and in the daily life of an organization even small differences in perception are important—by an administrator's subordinates, colleagues, superiors, and by external interveners in the organization's affairs.

3. SOURCES OF AUTHORITY

What are the sources of authority? What are the factors that lead people to accept the authority of administrators, particularly their special rights to engage in actions that are illegitimate for others to engage in?

One way to answer this question is to refer to custom or tradition. This answer will frequently be given in studies of the authority of a monarch in a feudal society or of fathers in a society with strong traditions of patriarchal family life. It may also be given with respect to any "boss" who has been around a long time. His authority is accepted now because it has "always" been accepted. The customs of the collectivity find their way into the habits of the members.

But reference to custom or habit merely pushes our inquiry further back into the past. We must now look for the earlier sources of the authority enjoyed by king, father, or boss. We must now ask what factors lead to the strengthening, weakening and changing of customs and habits with respect to authority.

Much of the accrued wisdom in this field (including the small portion supported by careful research) can be synthesized in the proposition that the sources of authority are to be found in (a) power itself, (b) social roles, and (c) the characteristics of the authority holders.

A. *Power.* The inclusion of power as a source of authority may seem to complicate matters, particularly since I have already referred to authority as a source of power. Yet the reciprocal relation between the two is an essential part of the power-authority-responsibility triangle. Difficulties arise only if one fails to keep in mind the definitions given above and falls back upon other usages which identify the two or make one a special case of the other.

The successful exercise of unauthorized power is itself a factor making for legitimacy; with the passage of enough time *de facto* may become *de jure*. It is in this sense that we must concede, whether we like it or not, that Might has often made Right. The process is more swift, as well as more acceptable, when authority is established through the softer forms of power.

A more subtle relation between the two occurs in the case of the authorized use of power. The usage of rights prevents the erosion that stems from nonusage; it contributes to the consolidation of rights. The legitimate use of rewards and punishments, finally, is an established method of preventing the erosion stemming from internal disaffection; it contributes to the maintenance of acceptance.

B. *Social role.* The most obvious form of authority in organizations is that which is embodied in the social role played by an individual or unit. A role as a whole consists of prescriptive expectations concerning future types of behavior. These expectations may be formulated in terms of authority and responsibility—that is, of actions that the role player has the right to engage in and of obligations to act in a certain way. Formal authority stems initially from those aspects of roles which are created by those who already have the authority to subdivide labor at lower levels. The act of formal subdivision creates patterns of formal authority, some manifest and some implied. These patterns are continually changed by subsequent "delegations" of authority and responsibility and by the steady accumulation of general rules and specific orders and requests.

The acceptance of formal authority within an organization is to a large extent grounded in the obvious need for a differentiation of rights. Just as the child learns to accept the authority of his parents, adults learn to accept the need for higher levels of authority in organizations. The complexities of organizational action make it essential for every member to accept a differentiation of rights. In fact, every organization member soon comes to rely upon the authority of others. Such reliance is an essential condition for the functioning of an organization.

Because it is essential, the acceptance of authority cannot be left to chance. It is bolstered by meaningful symbols—from uniforms and seals and crowns to titles, remuneration, and the material perquisites of office. The care taken in fitting such symbols accurately to an authority holder's position in a hierarchy will usually take precedence over efforts to delineate precisely what he is authorized or unauthorized to do. Similarly, elaborate rituals are used to enhance support for the higher levels of authority and concretize the legitimate transfer of authority to lower levels. But social roles—and the authority that comes with them—are not limited to those that are formally created within organizations. People may derive authority from their position in informal groups—as dealt with more explicitly in "People-in-Organizations: Informal Aspects" (Chapt. 10). They may derive authority from the "social position" to which they were born or which they have attained through personal achievement. To some extent such authority may carry over from general social relations to specific situations within organizations or from one type of organization to another. Thus the authority often enjoyed by an upper-class aristocrat or wealthy businessman in philanthropic or political organizations. Still another form of positional authority may be found in unusual situations. In times of crisis there will often be immediate acceptance of a person's right to take actions that would otherwise be regarded as entirely illegitimate. This may include breaking ordinary rules of behavior, the seizure or creation of a position of authority or even the removal of an incompetent authority holder—all of which is justified only by the critical nature of the situation. After the crisis has passed, as so dramatically illustrated by *The Caine Mutiny*, the situation may then be reviewed to determine whether or not the shift in the authority structure was justified.

c. *Characteristics of authority holders.* Another source of authority may be found in the personal characteristics of authority holders, apart from (or in addition to) their power and the formal or informal social roles they may occupy. Thus people of special or outstanding ability are customarily granted rights denied to others. People may win authority by acquiring special forms of knowledge. They may win it by the values they espouse or symbolize.

At one extreme these characteristics are combined in various ways to provide an authority base for gods. Divinity—and the divine right by which men have often ruled—is usually expressed in some combination of omnipotence, omniscience, and goodness. Midway between the gods and men are those supermen whose charisma—or gift of spiritual power— marks them as some form of hero, wise man, or saint. Further along on the continuum toward ordinary people we find the more bureaucratized charisma of those people who are not supermen but who are nevertheless superior because of some specialized form of ability, knowledge, or values. Here we find those administrators who have succeeded in adding personal authority to the authority accruing to them from the social role they occupy.

These considerations also apply to a unit or an organization as a whole. Thus a budget division, apart from the authority associated with its formal and informal functions, will enjoy more authority if it is perceived as able, knowledgeable, and well intentioned. The authority of a government agency will be similarly enhanced by widely perceived characteristics that win it admiration and respect.

To the three sources already listed, one might readily add consent. In the modern world, authority holders customarily justify their authority on the ground that it stems from clearly documented acts of consent by those over whom authority may be wielded. Thus, as elsewhere discussed in "The Dispersion of Authority in Organizations"[17] "ultimate authority" is found in stockholders of corporations, members of associations and electorates of nations. Formal authority at lower levels is strengthened by being derived from their acts of consent. But elections, plebiscites, and other means of formally recording consent are merely one way of winning generalized acceptance of rights under conditions when some are ready to accept and others are not. Acceptance of authority is rarely unanimous, particularly in a bureaucratic organization. There is a sense in which one might say that holders of formal authority are continually engaged in a campaign to win more extended acceptance of their authority from subordinates, colleagues, and superiors. Every operation in which they engage might be regarded as one in which a silent and unofficial form of voting takes place. The larger their majority, the greater the chances will usually be that minority opponents—except for those who find special advantage in the position of a hold-out minority opposition —will go along with the majority.

4. AUTHORITY NOT AUTHORITARIANISM

Studies of authoritarianism (such as Adorno *et al.*, *The Authoritarian Personality*) often seem to suggest that authoritarianism is rooted in a reliance on authority as opposed to reason, or force as opposed to persuasion. They have often led democratically-minded students of administration to regard authority as an antidemocratic phenomenon.

The consideration of this problem leads us back once again to the failure to distinguish between authority and power. When authoritarianism is studied as a brutal style of riding roughshod over others, the concept refers to a form of power. The authoritarian personality is characterized by the urge to dominate others and vent aggressions upon them.

Or else, it leads us to the identification of a particular form of author-

17. Gross, *The Managing of Organizations*, Chapter 3.

ity structure. In the authoritarian family, organization or state, we find a concentration of authority. Although the opponents of authoritarianism may orate against authority as a whole, what they really want is more authority for themselves—either by themselves replacing the present authority holders or by distributing authority somewhat more widely. As Rokeach has perceptively pointed out (1961, p. 234) "there is really nothing so ugly about authority." The ugliness arises in objectionable distributions and uses of authority.

Authoritarianism, moreover, can be fruitfully approached in terms of Rokeach's structural (rather than substantive) distinction between the open and the closed mind (1960). The authoritarian person has a "closed mind" approach to authority. In accepting the views of people with authority, he closes his mind to the cognitive correctness or consistency of what they are saying. In dealing with those subject to his own authority, he expects his position to be accepted apart from their rational consideration of it. In either case, the rewards and the punishments that accompany higher authority are expected to be decisive.[18]

The more open one's orientation to authority, the more attention will be paid both to information of a substantive nature and to information about the authority source itself. "The person has freedom to choose or not to choose to be influenced in a direction desired by the source, depending on his own assessment of both sets of information" (Rokeach, 1961, p. 235).

Thus, as Rokeach points out, a person may adhere to an ideology democratic in content, but his mode of adherence may be authoritarian.[19] This clearly applies to persons with administrative authority. But we may add that a person may also adhere to an ideology undemocratic in content, while his mode of adherence may be nonauthoritarian.

c. *Responsibility and Power*

THE CONCEPT of responsibility presents fewer initial difficulties than that of authority, since the terminological confusion with power does not exist. Moreover, there seems to be a common core of agreement that the term refers to some sort of obligation or duty. This usage may be concretized in the definition of responsibility as the *obligation to act in a certain way*.

18. This is surprisingly close to the Simon concept of authority in general.
19. A delightful illustration is provided by Phyllis McGinley's poem about "the angry man" for whom intolerance is "a state no tolerant man can tolerate."

The difficulties begin when, going further into the nature of responsibility, we analyze its relation to both power and authority. Here we find that—with certain conspicuous exceptions, such as Follett and Barnard—administrative theorists have given only passing attention to the subject. Too much of the literature of administration has dealt with authority. Power is now receiving greater attention. For a better understanding of the power-authority-responsibility triangle, much greater attention is needed to the third side.

There seems to be an emerging consensus, however, that responsibility is an obligation that has two dimensions. One dimension may be expressed as responsibility *for*, the other as responsibility *to* (Friedrich, 1941, p. 189). My analysis starts with this distinction.

1. RESPONSIBILITY FOR

Responsibility *for* is the obligation of a person, unit, or organization to perform certain services. These services may be referred to as duties, functions, or even responsibilities. Whether they are formally or informally prescribed, whether they are written in job descriptions and statements of function or simply taken for granted, they are an integral part of a person's or group's social role.

Since the concept of responsibility refers to all the activities in which a person, unit, or organization may engage, it is extremely broad in scope. A full statement of responsibilities will always be much more comprehensive than a statement of authority, which by its very nature is usually limited to a few specific types of actions that would otherwise be unauthorized. This, in itself, often tends to detract attention from *responsibility for*. Lists of functions, duties, and responsibilities tend to become hit-or-miss and over-long.

With respect to administrative responsibility (as distinguished from other kinds of responsibility) there are two special complications. First, while it is easy to define administrative responsibility in general as the responsibility for actions that help in the governance or guidance of organizations, it is much harder to spell out just what kinds of *specific* actions an administrator is responsible for. To do this requires the application to a specific situation of a general set of highly developed ideas concerning the actions to be expected from administrators. In many organizations very few people, including administrators themselves, have explicit and readily communicable ideas as to what the administrators at various levels are really supposed to do.

Second, there is a certain sense in which administrators are responsible not only for what they themselves do but for what others, particularly subordinates, do. They are responsible for getting things done by others. This brings us back to the question that arose in the discussion of the administrator's power—how to make the great jump between an administrator's contribution to an organization's activities and the performance of the organization. It is a jump that the administrator can himself make only by the exercise of power.

2. RESPONSIBILITY TO

An obligation is a social relation. It necessarily involves both an obliger (the person with responsibility) and an obligee or obligees (those to whom he is responsible). The latter, in turn, may be internalized in the form of conscience or personal values (in Freudian terms, superego). A person is responsible *for* certain actions *to* others and/or himself.

Thus a person in a simple nonadministrative position in an organization, in addition to being responsible for certain kinds of manual or mental services, is responsible for performing these services in a way which responds to the expectations of administrative superiors. He may be *held accountable* by all of them.

The difficulties inherent in this many-sided relationship become greater in the case of administrative responsibility. The administrator is usually responsible for a greater variety of actions and to a larger number of people and groups, including his subordinates as well as a possible host of interveners and controllers at higher levels of authority or outside the organization. As Barnard has pointed out, the predicament of the higher executive is that he will usually be responsible to conflicting interests and conflicting codes of behavior. Hence Barnard's emphasis upon moral creativity as an essential of responsible executive behavior.

Here again there is a complication. *Responsibility to* is essentially a two-dimensional concept. It may be thought of in terms of two vectors moving in opposite directions. The responsibility vector moving from obliger to obligee is a *sense of responsibility*. It is the human response to the human needs or desires of others, something that cannot be wholly imposed from without (Fromm, *The Art of Loving*, p. 28). The responsibility vector moving from obligee to obliger, on the other hand, is *holding someone responsible or accountable*. It is inevitably associated with checkup, supervision, control, and punishment. A certain amount of motion in this direction is undoubtedly necessary to prevent a sense of responsibility from being diverted or corroded. Too much action in this direction can often readily undermine a sense of responsibility and seriously impair the activities that a person or group is responsible for. That this often happens in organizations is probably due to the attraction of the *holding responsible* approach for those who use it as a way of giving expression to pent-up aggressions and getting rid of their own sense of guilt by pinning the blame upon others. "Whose fault is it?" is a "question that seems to obsess the Western world" and lead to denials, counteraccusations and an emotional atmosphere of doubt and despair (Gragg, 1964).

3. IRRESPONSIBLE AND RESPONSIBLE USES OF POWER

As political philosophers have warned for centuries, great power may be associated with an extremely low degree of responsibility. The power-wielder may frustrate the expectations of most people in order to serve the interests of a few. He may violate the deepest moral expectations of everyone. He may achieve only the lowest of his self-expectations. Those who might want to hold him responsible might be unable to do so or even afraid to make the effort. This is the element of truth in Lord Acton's oft-quoted quip: "Power tends to corrupt, and absolute power corrupts absolutely."

A great amount of power may also be associated with a high degree of responsibility. If we expect people to discharge their responsibility for great and difficult undertakings, we must expect them to acquire and use a large amount of power. A decline in power may make it impossible to act responsibly. Increments in power may lead to more responsibility. It is in this sense that power may ennoble as well as corrupt. This is the element of truth in Woodrow Wilson's seldom-quoted remarks concerning the public administrator: "The greater his power the less likely he is to abuse it, the more is he nerved and sobered and elevated by it. The less his power, the more safely obscure and unnoticed does he feel his position to be, and the more readily does he relapse into remissness" (1887, p. 197-222). Hence government, for Wilson, should become "a straightforward thing of simple method, single unstinted power, and clear responsibility" (1885, p. 332-333).

But we need not concern ourselves with absolutes in either power or responsibility. Absolute power is a myth. Power is always limited. It is bounded at its very base by the quantitative and qualitative limits of the various sources of power. It is held in check by the operations of competitors or opponents, the concessions that must be made to the opposition of those who are subject to it, and the inevitable frictions which accompany its use.

The "clear responsibility" of the Wilsonian dream, the situation in which the public executive commits himself to the discharge of precisely stated responsibilities representing the undivided expectations of a majority of the people—this is no less a myth. In a complex society responsibility is always blurred by the divergent and shifting expectations and interests of many different people and groups. Nor is it possible in complex organizations for obligees to hold obligers responsible through major reliance on direct sanctions.

Power, therefore, is a sword that can cut in any direction. Its use involves inescapable risks. It may frustrate the expectations of those who have legitimatized it. It may lead to the undoing of the power-wielders themselves.

On the other hand, power is indispensable to the attainment of desirable purposes. Without power, idealism by itself is a recipe for futility. Only through power can high and significant goals be achieved. It is in this sense that Follett says that "more power, not division of power, should always be our aim; more power for the best possible furtherance of that activity, whatever it may be, to which we are giving our life."

To this, I might add a less poetic but extremely practical note: The responsible use of power is one of the most effective ways to strengthen power. As already pointed out, one of the great sources of power lies in the motives, values, and allegiances of people and groups. Power users can develop power only by responding to such factors. As a practical matter, therefore, the administrator develops a special pattern of responsiveness. The more wisdom is exercised in doing this the greater the resulting power base.

The other side of the coin is revealed in the case of the administrator who fails to use the "license" given him by his position of formal authority. His abdication is itself a failure to discharge his responsibilities. It may be compensated for only by the action of someone else, hidden in the wings, who usurps power in order to see that the organization discharges its responsibilities.

D. *Authority and Responsibility*

ONE OF THE OLDEST MAXIMS of administration deals with the relation between authority and responsibility. Among writers on the subject this has been stated in many ways:

Authority is not to be conceived of apart from responsibility (Fayol, 1949, p. 22).

At all levels authority and responsibility should be coterminous and coequal (Urwick, 1943, p. 46).

In each responsibility is inherent an equivalent authority (Brown, 1947, p. 39).

Parity must exist between authority and responsibility (Koontz and O'Donnell, 1955, p. 296).

In everyday organizational life the maxim tends to be stated as a means of complaining about a lack of "parity" or justifying efforts to increase either authority or responsibility. The widest complaints seem to come from administrators who feel that they have not been given enough formal authority. For them the maxim may become a justification of a drive toward enlarged authority (and perhaps greater power) or of a decline in their feeling of responsibility.

On the other hand, those in higher positions of relative authority often complain that people in lower positions do not use their authority responsibly. Like Fayol, they feel that there is a tendency for people in an organization to seek authority and dodge responsibility. Like members of elected legislatures, they complain about the irresponsibility of the bureaucrats.

In addition to being rooted in the personal needs of people at various levels, the parity maxim expresses the inevitable connection between rights and obligations. One of the oldest and most deeply rooted human concepts is that the exercise of rights carries with it certain obligations and that those with obligations to perform must be allowed to do what may be required for such performance.

The prescriptive limitations of the maxim have been repeatedly pointed out in modern administrative thought. Simon, Smithburg, and Thompson have shown that in the interdependence of modern organizations no administrator can be given in advance, as a matter of right, all the resources, clearances, and other forms of cooperation that are needed for him to discharge his responsibilities (1950, p. 215-216). The inevitable administrative subdivision of authority is too great. Because of this, people can be expected to feel responsible for inquiring into problems that they themselves are not authorized to deal with (Newman, 1951, p. 176). They can be encouraged to feel responsible for making their contributions toward many larger accomplishments that are far beyond the individual authority of any of them (Follett). To these limitations may be added the observation that a goodly portion of administrative activity consists of involvement in "polyarchic relations" (Chapt. 9, D). In these, responsibility is usually high and authority rather low. As pointed out in previous sections, moreover, both authority and responsibility are extremely complex concepts that do not lend themselves readily to over-all "parity comparisons." It is more feasible to deal with specific and identifiable increments or decrements. These are dynamic factors in the life of organizations and their administrators. While they tend to move in the same direction, they also tend to do so at different rates, with a change in one contributing to a change in the other. Thus more authority may eventually result in more responsibility. More responsibility may lead to more authority. A decline in one may lead to a decline in the other.

But the connection is never one between these two factors alone. Both of them are always related in some way to the power base. The appropriate framework for appraising their interrelations is the power-authority-responsibility triangle.

Chapter 5

SOME EXPLODING FALLACIES

ONE OF THE ACHIEVEMENTS of administrative thought in recent decades has been the demolition of many administrative fallacies that were previously widely accepted. Although they may still have some advocates, these fallacies are at least no longer actively purveyed by the majority of thinkers, writers and teachers in the field.

In this chapter I shall discuss the following fallacies of this type:

> The manager is the man on top.
> Authority and power flow down from the top.
> Efficiency is the sole goal of administration.
> Technical skill equals good administration.
> Rank-and-file members of an organization should be
> free from outside pressures.
> Administrators should execute policy, not make it.
> In good administration things run smoothly and easily.
> Evading formal rules violates administrative theory.
> The principles of administration provide the answers
> to administrative problems.

By limiting myself to this area, I am thereby foregoing—or rather postponing until the next chapter—the pleasure of attacking "popular" fallacies. The delineation of these well-exploded fallacies is a form of stocktaking. It summarizes the extent to which the emerging consensus in administrative thought has contributed to the "unlearning process." It is a way of telling ourselves that the work of the pioneers in administrative thought, the developers of specific aspects and the contributors from other disciplines has not been in vain. It is a way of saying: "We've made a little progress."

The purpose of looking back, therefore, is merely to consolidate our intellectual resources in preparation for new intellectual disputes far beyond any area of consensus conceivable in the immediate future. It is to prepare ourselves for dealing with other fallacies that are more subtle and more dangerous.

We shall see a common pattern. We shall see that most of these are fallacies in which a part is mistaken for the whole. They are similar to such propositions as "A triangle is something with one side" or—at a higher level of sophistication—"A triangle is something with two sides." In every case, as we shall see, there have been understandable reasons why people failed to see, or preferred to close their eyes to, the existence of three sides. The reasons, however, are not to be accepted as justifications. Nor can the kernel of truth in each of them be tolerated as a basis of administrative instruction—any more than we would tolerate a geometry teacher telling his class that a triangle has two sides.

A. *The Manager Is the Man on Top*

THIS IS THE FALLACY of thinking that a manager or administrator can be adequately symbolized by the figure of a man standing at the top of a pyramid. Whether the pyramid represents a small unit or a vast conglomeration of units, the task of the manager is simply to guide or direct the activities of his "lower level" subordinates.

One root of this fallacy is "organization chart psychology": taking too seriously charts designed to spell out certain aspects of the division of labor and hierarchical subordination. The still deeper roots are found in the fact that "on top" symbolizes domination. The idea is thus extremely appealing to those with a strong urge to dominate or to be dominated.

Yet any man who gets to the top will be confronted with three sets of facts.

The first is that he will always find somebody "on top" of him. This may be his immediate hierarchical superior, a governing board, a control body of some sort, or all of these together. If he should be a prime minister, a president, or a chairman of a board of directors, these will be the representatives of his organized constituencies. No matter what his level, the manager may well spend much more time looking up than looking down.

Second, he will find that he is hemmed in and pressured on all sides. He must concern himself with colleagues and associates within the organization. These are people without whose cooperation he cannot perform his tasks; yet instead of being merely passive cooperators they in turn are often trying to get him to do things they want him to do. And further, the manager must deal with a large array of outsiders whom he must activate or resist.

Third, he finds that he is subjected to a constant bombardment from below. The people whom he is supposed to direct are constantly making requests that he must deal with, sending messages that he must study, and in many subtle ways trying to direct him.

Thus he finds that instead of being on top he is "the man in the middle," a term once reserved for the lowest level administrators or foremen (those in the midway position between the nonadministrators and the higher ranks of administration). He is not at the apex of a triangle, but at the center of a confused and whirling vortex of centripetal forces. To the extent that he puts substantial energy into his job, he not only is buffeted; he buffets. He is the center from which centrifugal forces also emerge and impinge upon other "men in the middle" inside and outside of his organization.

B. *Authority and Power Flow Down from the Top*

THIS IS THE IDEA that likens administrative authority and power to a water tank on the roof of a building. Once the plumbing has been properly installed, the administrator opens and closes the spigots in order to send the proper amounts of authority and power to the proper places.

Like the man-on-top fallacy, this one also is encouraged by overemphasis on organization charts. It is concretized in job descriptions which concentrate on hierarchical relationships instead of specifying the actual services to be performed.

This fallacy also appeals to those who feel a psychological need for an enlarged image of their own power, a need which probably varies directly with the degree of an administrator's internal feelings of weakness and insecurity.

The first defect in this conception, as Mary Follet pointed out long ago, is that many positions carry with them their own authority. Once the work to be done within an organization has been subdivided, a significant amount of formal authority has already been conferred. The director of a hospital does not give authority to a surgeon; the position of surgeon already contains authority. If the director gives more or less authority, he is expanding or contracting the position itself. This is an architectural change, not a mere matter of turning the water off or on at the spigot.

Second, it is not possible to delegate power beyond that small portion of power which is embodied in formal authority. The formal authority is merely a license an administrator can use in mobilizing the power he needs to do his job. He must prove himself by his own actions, and in so doing, he will need support from superiors. But such support is never indefinitely given, at least never in the necessary quantities; it must be won.

c. *Efficiency Is the Sole Goal of Administration*

THIS IS THE BELIEF that the one goal of administration, and the sole criterion by which administrative performance may be judged, is some relationship between input and output. One also comes perilously close to this fallacy when he states, with Gulick, that efficiency is "axiom number one on the value scale of administration" and then proceeds to ignore all other axioms.

The efficiency fallacy is rooted in the neutralistic "safe and sane" conception of administration. It is imbedded in the desire to find hard, objective facts that can be precisely measured, rather than in the acceptance of slippery intangibles. Above all, it has served as a point of unity between those people who, while disagreeing about other things, may find a common meeting ground in the goal of efficiency.

Few fallacies in administrative thought have been more repeatedly exposed.

First of all, apart from efficiency itself, there is the whole range of other major categories of organizational purpose. Among the goals of every organization, in addition to efficiency, are (1) the satisfaction of various interests, both external and internal, (2) the production of goods or services, (3) investing in the organization's viability, (4) mobilizing resources, (5) conforming with certain organizational codes, and (6) using the most rational techniques, both substantive and administrative, that can be developed. Any one of these purposes, or any combination, may under certain circumstances be more important to an organization than efficiency.

Second, upon more careful examination, the efficiency goal often declines in importance. It is relevant only to the extent that an objective scarcity of resources exists and that the members of an organization perceive this scarcity. It is measurable in precise terms only when it is possible to count units of both output and input. Here the great paradox of efficiency is that while efficiency is determined by the internal operations of an organization, it is precisely in the production of intermediate services within an organization that it is extremely difficult to find units of output that can be precisely counted. This is the reason why Simon reluctantly came to the conclusion that the efficiency criterion is applicable "largely to rather low level decisions."[1]

D. *Technical Skill Equals Good Administration*

THIS IS THE BELIEF that because a person reaches an acknowledged level of achievement in some technical field, he is therefore *ipso facto* qualified as an administrator.

This fallacy represents the phenomenon of "prestige transferance." People may believe that because a person is an outstanding theatrical performer, he is therefore uniquely qualified as a commentator on politics or a judge of the quality of cigarettes.

The fallacy is also rooted in the natural desire of every technician to have a superior who, by virtue of being a technician in the same field, will really understand him. It is grounded in the technician's equally natural desire to obtain the prestige and other emoluments associated with higher administrative posts without deserting his particular specialty.

If this fallacy has been given less attention in administrative writings than the previous fallacy of efficiency, it has been far more frequently exploded in administrative life itself. Almost every organization can show one or more examples of a good technician who has become a wretched administrator, an unhappy man, and a lost expert. Although technical skill is by no means a necessary obstacle to administrative success (and in some cases may in fact represent a partial prerequisite), it is by no means a sufficient condition. When the skilled technician becomes a good administrator, it is because he has learned certain additional skills not directly included within the area of his previous specialty.

The life of this fallacy, unfortunately, has been prolonged by schools of business and public administration where undue emphasis has been placed upon technical skills in such fields as methods analysis and production engineering, accounting and budgeting, and personnel manage-

1. See discussion in section D-2 of "The Pioneers: New Beginnings" (Gross, *The Managing of Organizations*, Chapter 7).

ment. In their justified enthusiasm for these important techniques, teachers have often tended to confuse these technical aids to administration with administration itself. The student has sometimes been allowed to graduate with the well-nourished illusion that his certified proficiency in one of these fields already qualifies him as an administrator. In contrast, the better schools channel the necessary enthusiasm for technique into an awareness of the problems of using techniques and technicians and of the place of each technique in the broader processes of administration.

E. *Rank-and-File Members of an Organization Should Be Free From Outside Pressures*

WHILE THE PREVIOUS FALLACIES can be stated interchangeably in terms of either "is" or "should be," this fallacy is invariably stated in terms of "should be" only. The reason is simple: Any flat statement that the rank-and-file members of organizations *are* free from outside pressures would represent a preposterous contradiction of readily observable facts. For the same reason, the "freedom from pressure" standard is usually applied only to the middle and lower levels of government organizations. Here it is used to voice resentment against "undue" pressure by outside politicians and outside pressure groups. Although historically rooted in the public service, this fallacy has also grown up in many private organizations whose top executives and directorates presume to arrogate to themselves the exclusive right of contact with outside forces.

The Achilles heel of this fallacy is that in a world where no organization can survive as an island unto itself, outside pressures make themselves felt throughout an organization. This is more or less obvious in a democratic society. It is less obvious, though just as true, in any dictatorship. No members of an organization can be, or should be, completely insulated from direct or indirect outside pressures.

Protective devices and procedures designed to cope with undesired pressures are, of course, essential. But any effort to handle the problem of protection by the complete denial of contact will, by itself, serve to weaken the defenses of an organization's members. The most delinquent children are sometimes those raised by over-strict parents. Like young girls in an environment of libidinous males, the rank-and-file members of an organization cannot learn to protect themselves unless they have contact with outside pressures. Only thus it is possible to learn the arts of passing the buck, postponing the issue, entrenched resistance, and —where this is required—justified acquiescence.

F. *Administrators Should Execute Policy, Not Make It*

THIS FALLACY is based on the narrow conception of administration as the mere effectuation of purposes determined by others. It was inherent in Taylor's sharp division between planning and execution and Goodnow's policy-administration dichotomy. In the field of the business corporation, this fallacy presents policy-making as the exclusive responsibility of boards of directors. In public administration this exclusive responsibility is regarded as the province of legislatures, chiefs of state, and cabinet members.

As with the belief in efficiency as the sole goal of administration, this fallacy is also rooted in the search for security. If administrators do not make policy, then they might be given full tenure of office irrespective of what changes in policy might be determined by the higher wielders of formal authority. They are also privileged to live on a tight little island of hard and objective fact instead of having to venture forth on the tempest-ridden sea of conflicting values.

The fatal defect in this belief is simply that the making and execution of policy are inseparately intertwined. Genuine policy—as distinguished from meaningless generalizations—comes into being through the activities of an entire organization. Purposes are given meaning and content by the people who cooperate in carrying them out. Purpose emanates from an entire organization in interaction with its environment. Those highest officials who may be vested with the formal authority for "policy formulation" often do little more than (a) legitimate the policies developed at the lower levels of the hierarchy, (b) make slight adjustments in some of the proposals submitted to them, or (c) make occasional choices between submitted alternatives. A large part of the work of people below the higher levels consists of preparing such policy proposals and interpreting them once they have been formally endorsed.

G. *In Good Administration Things Run Smoothly and Easily*

THIS FALLACY represents an administrative version of Utopia. It provides a vision of some glowing future in which purposes are unambiguously defined, the right people are always in the right places, and the organization moves forward without friction and in accordance with preordained procedures.

This fallacy is a form of escapism from the world of reality. It is a child-like fantasy indulged in by adults. At times it may serve as an ideal to guide people in the introduction of improvements. More frequently, it is a substitute for effective change, a standard which leads to organizational defeatism.

This fallacy has frequently been propagated—and probably will always continue to be—by a certain type of academic mind which delights in the inculcation of principles of action which have little or no connection with the realities of human action. The explanation of this phenomenon may perhaps be found in the attractiveness of Academia for people who are afraid of the harshness of the nonacademic world. But why is it that many students accept this fallacy so readily? Certainly this conception of organizational behavior does not conform with their own experiences in the family and the school, the two organizations with which they have had most contact. Is their readiness to accept the ideal of organizational Utopia itself a form of retreat from frustrations in family life and in school?

So long as motor vehicles are used, some people will always get hurt. Indeed, some will always get hurt badly. This is more reason, not less reason, to take action designed to reduce the accident rate.

The same is true in administration. Some people will always get hurt— and some very badly. This is why action is necessary to reduce the uncertainties, the friction and the tensions, the humiliations and the frustrations of administrative life. But no amount of well-intentioned action will ever eliminate them completely. To think that it will may indeed make it harder to reduce their incidence and easier for people to end up in the slough of disillusionment.

H. *Evading Formal Rules Violates Theoretical Principles*

THIS IS A MORE ESOTERIC FALLACY than the previous one. It consists of the belief so often voiced by practical administrators that whenever they break or evade the formal rules of an organization, they are thereby violating theoretical principles of administration. In its most virulent form it consists of the belief that by so doing they are also proving the impossibility of establishing theoretical administrative principles.

This fallacy has two roots. The first is the proliferation of premature, unjustified, and ill-formulated administrative principles. This has led to a rather unsophisticated revolt against the very idea of administrative theory or administrative principles, a revolt joined in by many academicians as well as practical administrators. Disdaining the extreme of blind acceptance of theoretical nonsense, the rebels have jumped to the other extreme of theoretical nihilism.

The second is the very wide-spread urge to break organizational rules. The existence of this urge is what accounts for a large amount of the informal relationships and procedures which always grow up along side formal structures and regulations. It also accounts for the inevitable degree of deviation which seems to be an indispensable prerequisite of any significant degree of conformity. The error, of course, enters in only when someone who sets himself the goal of breaking a theoretical rule thinks he has automatically done so when he succeeds in breaking an organizational rule. Very probably all that he has done is to deviate from some fallacious idea that has already been exposed. Modern administrative thought itself recognizes the limitations of formal organizational structure and the role played by informal operations. It is oriented more and more toward including, among other things, generalizations concerning people who break rules in organizations. Thus, the man who violates a procedural rule of his organization may well be operating in strict conformity with a theoretical law. He is not even an exception to the rule; his violation demonstrates his conformity.

I. *Principles of Administration Provide the Answers to Administrative Problems*

THIS CONSISTS of the belief that well-defined theoretical principles can by themselves—without the application of either skill or values—provide the answer to administrative problems.

As with the previous fallacy, this also has been rooted in the pretentious and premature work of earlier decades. It is also used by the "theoretical nihilists" who endeavor to prove the impossibility of administrative theory by assigning it an impossible function.

Today, however, among those acquainted with the current trends of modern administrative thought, there is wide-spread acceptance of these cogent ideas presented by Simon and his colleagues (1950, p. 20-21):

(1) Practical rules simply do not exist which can be applied in an automatic or mechanical fashion to actual organizational problems. . . .
(2) At the present stage of knowledge, administrative theory is of far

more practical use in diagnosing situations than prescribing suitable
courses of action. . . .

(3) The practice of administration involves skills—skills that have become
thoroughly incorporated in the administrator's personality—rather
than mere intellectual knowledge. . . .

(4) Practical recommendations for organization action always depend
upon the values of a person making the recommendations. . . .

Today it is generally recognized that valid principles of administration
must themselves deal with the limitations of both theory and theoreticians
in an administrative environment. It must deal with the components of
organizational action other than theory and knowledge. From this point
of view principles of administration are tools that administrators can use
in finding answers to administrative problems.

Part II

ENVIRONMENT

Chapter 6

THE IMMEDIATE ENVIRONMENT

*H*UMAN ORGANIZATIONS are "open" systems. They are rendered open by four phenomena that cut across organizational boundaries:

- *r* entries and exits, which transform outsiders into members and members into insiders;
- *r* multiple membership, which results in members' loyalties to outside groups;
- *r* resource exchange, which involves the absorption of inputs in the production process and the delivery of output produced; and
- *r* mutual or reciprocal influence on the part of both members and outsiders.

Some organizations go very far in limiting some of these interchanges. The most conspicuous examples are hospitals, jails, concentration camps, armies, ships or submarines at sea, monasteries, and communal settlements (Goffman, 1960). But the complete closure of any channel is improbable. The complete closure of all is impossible. No human organization is a closed system. The nature and extent of its "openness" is an important characteristic of all organizations.

The relations between organizations and the broad social environment are discussed in the next chapter. Here I shall concentrate upon the more immediate environment.

Any organization is usually surrounded by a complex array of people, units, organizations and opinions that interrelate with it on the basis of various roles. An oversimplified picture of this "encirclement" is provided by the following chart.

PUBLICS WITH OPINIONS

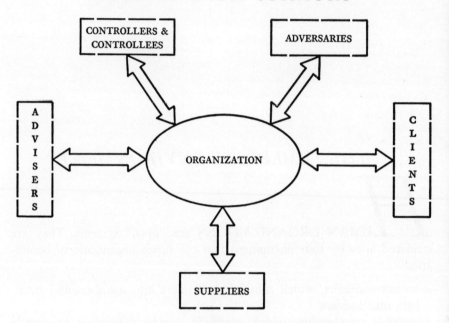

PUBLICS WITH OPINIONS

Any of these roles may be played by any type of organization, and many organizations play many of these roles at the same time. The less direct role of public opinion must also be recognized.

There is considerable variation in the visibility of the specific individuals and groups in these categories. Some of them, indeed, are well known to everyone in the organization; others are known to few organization members other than those who conduct dealings with them. Some operate in an open and above-board manner; others are behind-the-scenes operators. Many are still more intangible. Visibility, of course, is a relative matter. It depends upon the visual capacity of the seer as well as the characteristics of the seen.

But the mere identification of the various role facets, with their sub-facets, is not enough to indicate the texture of the organizational environment. I shall therefore identify some of these major strategies and the defensive or offensive strategies of the insiders. The external organizations and individuals playing these roles may be dispersed or clustered. Their interrelations with an organization may create a placid environment, a disturbed reactive environment, or a turbulent field (Emery and Trist, 1963). Their changing strategies of influence and intervention are a vital part of these various environments.

A. *The Clients*

THE CLIENTS of any organization or unit thereof are one of the most important elements in its immediate environment. Their importance derives from their role as *the receivers of the goods or services produced by the organization or unit.*

Here the word "clients" includes what is usually referred to by the word "consumers," but without the implication that consumption goods are exclusively involved rather than products used in production or investment. It also includes the idea of "customers," but without the implication that a direct monetary payment must necessarily be made. In this sense, the term cannot be used—as it has been by Gulick and Simon—to refer to the "people dealt with" by a government agency (who may indeed be the agency's adversaries) as distinguished from the "people served."

1. THE CLIENTELE NETWORK

To identify the clients of any organization, it is essential to recognize the chain of relations that may exist between the "direct" and the "ultimate" clients. The clients of a manufacturer include the consumer and the retailer as well as the wholesaler who buys all his goods. The clients of a trade school may include not only the students but also the future employers of the students. The clients of the man on one end of the assembly line are not only the workers at the lower end of the line but also the users of the final product.

The picture becomes more realistic if we think not merely of a clientele chain but of a "clientele network." The products produced by an individual, unit or organization usually fan out in many directions. The case of production for a single client is more the exception than the rule. Besides, the more varied the product mix, the more numerous the clients and the different types of clients. In fact, it is the differing needs of various clients that is a powerful factor in influencing the heterogeneity of an organization's "output mix."

2. THE INTERNAL CLIENTS

As already demonstrated, the clientele concept need not be limited, as it is in the terminology of marketing, to those who receive the products of an organization as a whole. The products of many units within an organization are produced to serve others within the organization rather than external clients directly. It is therefore helpful to use the concept of *internal clients*. This refers to those recipients of a unit's products who are external to the unit but within the organization as a whole. A full clientele network for any unit of an organization will start with such internal clients and then fan out into the organization's external clients.

Who are the various clients of the personnel department, the accountants, the purchasing officer, and the legal or economic adviser? Of the production gang and the man on the assembly line? Of this or that administrator?

From reading many official definitions of departmental functions and individual jobs, one gets the impression that the identification of clients is often subordinate to—or confused with—the identification of hierarchical relationships. A popular, but perverted, form of administrative philosophy holds that the job of subordinates is to serve their superiors. This might be justified psychologically, to a limited extent, on the ground that some superiors, perhaps the more immature, have a need for subservience.

But subservience by itself will not get goods or services produced, and under many circumstances it may interfere. Even to the extent that it might help, it would be a gross distortion to maintain that intermediate goods and services are produced at the lower levels of a hierarchy and move upward toward their consumers through the "chain of command" or the formal channels of communication. Any flow chart tracing the movement of intermediate products is infinitely more complex. The clients of intermediate products can be properly identified only by focusing upon the specific processes of production within an organization. When we do this, we will see that, broadly speaking, the major clients of the accounting division, for example, may include at least three groups: (a) supervisors of production units; (b) the heads of all units; and (c) the top executives. As indicated in Simon's study of controllers' departments, different types of information may be produced for each set of these internal clients (*Centralization vs. Decentralization in Organizing the Controller's Department*).

3. THE LESS VISIBLE CLIENTS

For any organization which sells its products the identification of direct clients is an automatic byproduct of the commercial transaction. In the case of agricultural departments, public schools, social welfare agencies, and any other organizations which come into direct contact with specified groups of clients, the absence of an easily identifiable cash nexus is not serious.

For many other organizations, however, the identification of clients and their interests is far from easy. Who are the ultimate clients of the army, the tax collector, and the government agency regulating the price of electricity? It would be a ludicrous mistake to answer this question by referring to the enemy, taxpayers, or the electric company. The ultimate clients, rather, are the people whose lives are presumably defended by the army, the people whose interest in a relatively stable unit of currency is served by the tax collector, and those whose interests would be impaired by uncontrolled prices for electricity. In all of these cases the clients themselves are a relatively large, amorphous, unorganized, and unvocal group. They include many people who do not know they are being served, as well as many who are not yet born. Their specific interests are hard to discover. They may, indeed, be expressed and articulated by the very agencies involved in serving them.

A similar lack of visibility is found in many areas of business enterprise. A broadcasting agency or a newspaper publisher may never really understand its audience. Although various market research techniques may provide a good idea of the size of the audience, they will rarely provide any deep understanding of the interests of the various people composing it. Under such circumstances it is only natural that more attention be paid to organized and highly vocal interests of advertisers to whom time on the air waves and space in the newspaper may be sold.

The same problem also arises within all organizations, both public and private. Many units and individuals seem to lose sight of—or never sight in the first place—their internal clients. This is particularly true of units and individuals whose product is to gather information or supply information or advice. Although the formal justification for their existence is to meet the needs of others in the organization, these needs may lack definition and the "needers"—particularly in the case of new types of informational or advisory services—may be antagonistic. Thus the producers of these internal services are faced with the simultaneous tasks of market development and product development. If these tasks are not recognized, the producers of these services may soon become preoccupied with self-serving activities and lose contact with the rest of the organization. One of the sad paradoxes of organizational life is that this is exactly what often happens to specialists assigned the formidable task of helping to improve organizational performance.

4. THE NUMBER OF CLIENTS

As discussed in the next chapter, the number of buyers whom any seller confronts is an important part of the market situation. Thus the economist's terms "monopsony," "oligopsony," and "polypsony" can be used to refer, respectively, to situations where there is a single buyer, a few buyers, or many buyers.

These terms may also be applied to internal clients and to external clients with whom there is no cash nexus. Their relevance is based upon the relation between numbers and power. When an organization or unit confronts only one client, its freedom of action is usually thereby restricted. The single client may call the tune. From this point of view there is little difference whether the single client (or monopsonist) is a private corporation, a government agency, or another unit within a private corporation or government agency. When the number of clients is larger, the supplying group has more opportunities for initiative and manoeuver. Thus a filing or purchasing unit which serves many divisions within an organization has more opportunities for independence, and the unit serving one division has more reason to be subservient. To gain more independence it may seek more clients.

5. THE STABILITY OF CLIENT DEMAND

One of the most delicate and all-pervasive aspects of an organization's environment is the stability of demand for its output.

In some fields of activity, seasonal fluctuations bring about regular routines and procedures for expansion and contraction. This may include the payment of extra-high wage rates while work is available—as in many parts of the construction industry. It may require a careful division between the "fixed" labor force, whose members are maintained on the payroll, and the "temporary" workers, who are taken on and dropped as the occasion demands. Where trade unions are dominated by the former group, special pains will be taken to see to it that not too many of the temporary workers are allowed to enter their privileged circle. In the development of political campaign organizations, during the months preceding an election, efforts will always be made to mobilize the largest possible number of unpaid volunteers, working under the direction of the smallest possible number of regular staff members. Special forms of compensation—such as badges, buttons, public declarations, membership on important committees, or meetings with prestigious political leaders—must be devised as a means of compensating the volunteers. In all circumstances, however, the successful operation of highly seasonal activities requires the preservation of a stable core over a considerable period of time.

In some countries the fear of declining demand and the rising unemployment is one of the dominant factors of organizational life. This usually leads to the rather well publicized efforts of workers to seek job security through featherbedding, resistance to the introduction of more efficient methods, and the insistence upon the protection of workers' rights through strict seniority rules and hiring and firing procedures. Somewhat less publicized is the effect this has upon the efforts of managers to build indestructible empires capable of withstanding the assault of economic contraction and to obtain comfortable social security arrangements for themselves.

While national policy can go a long way toward preventing, or adjusting to, cyclical economic fluctuations in demand, and organizations can often develop their own adjustments to seasonal fluctuations, technological change still remains as a major unsettling factor. The development of motorized transport, for example, almost wiped out the market for cavalry units (except for occasional use in mountain areas or parades), stage coaches, and horsedrawn carriages. Mass production machinery has meant the destruction of many organization and suborganizations specializing in the application of handicraft skills. The data-procesing revolution in office work threatens the stability of countless thousands of organizations and suborganizations now engaged in older, and slower, techniques of gathering, analyzing, storing, and distributing data. With the rapid advances in both substantive and administrative disciplines, the threat of technological obsolescence hangs like the sword of Damocles over the head of any administrator who cannot adapt himself to change. A large part of the daily life in every organization consists of the activities of those who conceive of adaptation as the building of barriers to technological change and of those who dedicate themselves to smashing through, or sneaking around, such barriers.

B. *The Suppliers*

No ORGANIZATION can be entirely self-sufficient. It must obtain resources, assistance, or support from groups and individuals in its environment.

In part, the dependence of an organization or unit upon its suppliers, associates, and supporters is determined by the objective situation. The supply situation is much more difficult in a have-not country or in time of shortages produced by war or inflation. Assistance is not worth very much when it comes from people who lack capacity or understanding. Neither assistance nor support are easy to get from those who are uninterested or hostile.

Yet relations with suppliers, associates, and supporters are never fixed entities. Even in the worst of circumstances they are directly affected by the ingenuity and imagination of administrators. Even in the best of circumstances the availability of resources, assistance and support, and the terms on which it is obtained, will depend on the interrelations between the organization and the suppliers.

1. RESOURCE SUPPLIERS

We shall use the term "resource supplier" (instead of simply "supplier" as in more colloquial usage) to refer to those who supply an organization with goods, services, or money. This includes all those to whom the organization or unit is itself a client. For an organization as a whole the suppliers may include sellers of land, equipment, materials, and services, lessors of land and equipment, lenders, and investors. It also includes those who supply tax-supported or other nonsold services. For a unit the suppliers are the others in the same organization who provide it with intermediate products and with the resources (personnel, space, materials, equipment, and money) without which it cannot make its own contribution to the production process.

In its relations with resource suppliers, the organization itself becomes the client. Accordingly, the previous discussion on the number of clients is here applicable. When the organization is the only client, its position is much stronger *vis-à-vis* resource suppliers. When it is only one among many clients, its position becomes weaker. This is why governments often set up central purchasing agencies to handle supply operations for many government organizations. This is also why farm and business organizations often establish associations or cooperatives to handle central procurement functions.

2. ASSOCIATES

The associates are those outsiders who work together cooperatively in the production of a jointly-produced product. They may be suppliers or clients also. But in their capacity as associates they do more than merely deliver or receive products. They participate directly in the processing of the products they deliver or the production of the products they receive.

Thus both the suppliers of fuel for a space ship and the agency involved in space travel send its people to work together with the builders of the space ship. Among government agencies producing complex intangible services, this type of cooperation is necessarily so intimate that it is often hard to tell who is assisting whom. Production often becomes a symbiotic process of mutual assistance. This is also true of many relations between units in all organizations. A large amount of intermediate products—from major policy down to some of the more routine services involved in recruitment and costing—are jointly-produced products.

When jointly-produced products are not recognized as such, the necessity for cooperation between organizations or units and their environmental assisters is not recognized. Thus a personnel or accounting unit may think that it alone can produce the recruitment or costing services that are needed. Schools may operate on the assumption that education is merely the result of what teachers do, hospitals on the assumption that recovery from disease results merely from what is done by doctors and nurses. Yet in all of these cases the clients are also associated in the production process.

3. SUPPORTERS

The supporters provide the influence or encouragement which an organization or unit needs to handle all of its relations with its environment. In the world of business such support is often provided by large lenders, investors or clients. For government agencies it may come from friendly centers of power in legislatures or associations. An interesting example of the importance of support from hierarchical superiors is provided by the Bureau of Lands Management in the U.S. Department of the Interior. From a graft-ridden, bumbling organization in previous decades, this agency became a relatively honest and effective agency by 1950. Yet the able executive who guided much of the transformation process could never have succeeded if he had not enjoyed the active support of the Secretary of the Interior and the President of the United States (Clawson, 1959).[1] On the other hand, many newly-established units and many groups of advisers or technicians brought in from other

1. In a personal letter to the author on October 26, 1960, this executive made the following comment: "During the early reorganizing days in BLM, I had splendid support from 'Cap' Krug [Secretary of the Interior]. He understood organizational matters, had quick perception, would make up his mind, and stay hitched! I was able to make personnel changes, including separation of incompetent political appointees. I said then that guts in your boss was the most important ingredient in making organizational changes. . . ."

countries often find themselves wandering helplessly in a barren organizational desert. Those who once wanted them seem to have forgotten them. The idea that "nobody wants us" may destroy their vitality.

There is always a tendency for the resource suppliers, associates, and supporters of an organization to exploit its dependence upon them by assuming the role of controller also. In some cases, this effort at control may be limited to obtaining a favored position with respect to a narrow range of an organization's activities—as with the awarding of contracts. In other cases the price of support is total subordination. In almost every country there are examples of some government agencies that can be metaphorically described as "owned and operated" by a group of contractors or by a clique of legislators or politicians who provide it with essential support. In the business world the effort to obtain freedom from external suppliers is a major factor in "vertical integration." Governments move in the same direction when they nationalize major sources of supply. But in neither case does this necessarily eliminate dependence on suppliers; it merely brings external suppliers within the loose boundaries of an enlarged organization.

c. *The Advisers*

THE ROLES OF ADVISERS are very similar in certain respects to those of suppliers. Advice may be a resource even more valuable than equipment, manpower, materials or money. It may be regarded as an important form of assistance or support.

But there are also important differences. The adviser *as adviser* mainly helps a unit or organization use the resources it already has (although the advice to be sure may be oriented toward getting more of such resources). *As adviser* he does not provide assistance or support in carrying out the advice that has been given.

The relation between an organization and an external adviser or consultant is inherently difficult. If an adviser's help is not solicited, it will usually be resented as an unwanted intrusion. If an adviser's help is solicited, the purpose is not necessarily to obtain advice. Other motives may be to (a) enjoy the prestige of relations with "high-powered" advisers, (b) obtain a rubber-stamp approval of a course of action already decided upon, or (c) obtain resources that would otherwise not be available (as when foreign economic assistance is coupled with advice by the assisters). When a major motive is to obtain advice, the presumed superiority of the adviser is likely to be resented by some members of the organization. "His mere existence," Bryson has pointed out, "is a mild slur on the competence of the men he is dealing with, and to whom he is giving the benefit of his superior knowledge" (1951). In the case of the "foreign adviser," the slur cuts deeper, for his presumed superiority implies the inferiority of the entire host nation. This sense of inferiority may be alleviated in part by rejecting his ideas on the ground that "they won't work here."

Advisers respond to the inevitable tensions of the adviser-advisee relationship by assuming varying roles. One set of role facets is found on the continuum between information processors and action proposers, another on that between detachment and involvement.

1. INFORMATION PROCESSORS AND ACTION PROPOSERS

The information processors "play it safe." They use their special skills in assembling and analyzing relevant information. This often leads to forecasts concerning future situations. It may even include the delineation of alternative future courses of action, thus opening up before the members of the organization a range of choice they may not have otherwise considered.

An additional step is to identify the advantages and disadvantages of the alternative courses. But then the information processors draw the line. They regard the task of weighing these competing considerations as—in Max Weber's words—"no longer a possible task for science, but for the man of action. . . ."

This limited advisory role is very close to that of the informal organization role of the Technique-Oriented, as discussed in "People-in-Organizations: Informal Aspects" (Chapt. 10). It is often accompanied by a greater interest in the improvement of analytic techniques and the approval of professional peers than in the problems of the client organization.

The action proposers go further. Whether responding to their own personal needs for self-expression or to the demands of their clients, they submit specific proposals and recommendations. In support of this role, Johr and Singer use the concept "the obligation to advise." In their discussion of the work of economic advisers, they maintain that because of his superior training and his freedom to spend more time on specific problems, "the scientist is undoubtedly better equipped to perform the task of weighing and to reach a conclusion. . . . The social scientist has not merely the *right* to evaluate . . . it is also his *duty*. He should not, therefore, withdraw from the task of himself providing a solution to a problem of economic policy" (1955, p. 71-72).

The presentation of proposals carries with it certain other obligations that may involve the adviser still more deeply in the affairs of an organization. One is to bring general proposals down to more specific and actionable steps. Another is to present the detailed analyses upon which the proposals are based. Still another is to defend their proposals against inevitable criticism. This last point is a delicate issue. It implies a willingness to engage in open advocacy and contentious debate. Johr and Singer support such a willingness on the ground that withdrawal from controversy might leave the debate to those who are less qualified to marshal the evidence (*Ibid.*, p. 73). Moreover, such advocacy is often the best testimony as to the depth of conviction that lies behind advice. As Chairman of President Truman's Council of Economic Advisers, Edwin G. Nourse proved willing to engage in internal advocacy of his own proposals, but unwilling to advocate Truman's proposals before the Congressional Joint Committee on the Economic Report. Although he rationalized his position in terms of abstract statement concerning executive-congressional relations, the basic, and understandable, reason for his reluctance to appear as a public advocate of the President's proposals to Congress was that they were not consistent with his own convictions (*Nourse*).

The fact that the administrators of an organization may want specific proposals, of course, does not commit them to any course of action when those proposals are received. The filing cabinets of corporations and government agencies are filled with detailed proposals that have been solicited from outside advisers and then unceremoniously ignored. At the other extreme, an adviser's proposals may be promptly seized upon, misinterpreted, and carried into action. The most that any action proposer can reasonably demand is attention and consideration.

2. THE DETACHED AND THE INVOLVED

The presumed detachment of an external adviser is one of his greatest sources of strength. This strength emanates from the presumption that he does not (at least in the beginning) have any personal interest in the structure of power within the organization. This is the reason why members of units are often highly antagonistic to advisers who are external to their own units but members of the same organization. Similarly, members of organizations often prefer foreign advisers. "A prophet is not without honor—save in his own country." In either case, the external adviser's strength is greatest as long as it is perfectly clear that his affiliation with an organization is temporary. If he should be recruited as a permanent member, or even prove interested in an indefinite relationship with the organization, the "honeymoon" is over.

Yet the very detachment which makes the adviser strong during the honeymoon period is also a source of weakness. Unless he develops close working relations with some members of the organization, he will be friendless. He needs allies within the organization to help him assemble and interpret the simplest facts. He must get further involved in the organization in order to understand its power structure and "personality." As this process of involvement proceeds, he will often find that some of the most constructive solutions to the organization's problems have already been developed by people at lower levels who cannot obtain attention or encouragement from their superiors. Like a steam-generating plant's "economizer," which takes hot gas generated down in the boiler and brings it up where it can be used at higher levels, his greatest contribution may be to open blocked channels of communication within the organization and provide moral support for the creative forces for change already active within the organization.

Sometimes the organization itself prefers the detached role. This is particularly true in those many cases where administrators see a detached role for themselves. As Tilles has pointed out in his study of small manufacturing companies, "too often the relationship is viewed as either an opportunity to buy the 'right answer' or to have a high and expensive authority provide both the insightful diagnosis and the sure cure" (1961).

The more skillful administrators, however, see the activities of external advisers as something which they themselves must take active steps to manage. This invariably requires the temporary involvement of the outsiders in joint efforts to define the problem on which advice is being given and to seek feasible solutions. Thus even when he does not dictate the advice he receives (whether he wants to or not), the recipient may in fact become a coproducer of the advice he receives. Under these circumstances the adviser's detachment yields to involvement.

Over-involvement by outsiders is prevented or offset in a number of ways. If an external adviser or advisory organization advises a large number of organizations, there is less chance that it will go too far in its relations with any one of them. Moreover, an advisory organization can reap the benefit of both roles by sending in a team of advisers, some of whom identify with the organization and its problems while the others will remain dispassionately neutral. The organization, on its part, can decide to build up a special group of advisers for itself and limit the outsiders' role to that of selecting or training the inside group. The maturation of such a group is often the best terminal point in the relationship between the organization and its external adviser (Lippitt, Watson, and Westley, 1958).

Any organization's reaction to the way in which an adviser handles the problem of detachment and involvement is inevitably affected by the adviser's prestige. Whatever his behavior is, it will be more acceptable if he enjoys a high enough social status. Impressive titles are unquestionably a help. Thus many recipients of foreign aid will not accept experts who are anything less than full professors. This situation is recognized by the process of "upgrading" people before they are sent abroad as foreign experts. In the United States foreign aid program many universities have given temporary professorships to people whom they would not accept as full-time professors on their own campuses. An historic precedent for this form of upgrading is found in the case of Captain von Steuben, the Prussian officer who became General George Washington's principal military adviser during America's War of Independence against the British. Benjamin Franklin and other Americans in Paris at that time "realized full well that no matter what accomplishments Steuben possessed as a staff officer, he would never attract attention if he reported in as merely a Prussian ex-captain." In recommending him to Washington, therefore, Franklin gave him the exalted but entirely fictitious title of lieutenant-general. "As a supposed technician of high rank Steuben was able to accomplish much for the American Army that otherwise, coming from a humble captain, would probably never have been listened to" (*Hittle*).

In many cultures, moreover, in order to be respected, the foreign expert must be a person "who is relatively older, more deliberate, quiet, understanding and restrained. He is seen as wise rather than brilliant. He is not necessarily seen as quick thinking, outgoing and highly expressive. These are qualities associated with the young and, therefore, are not status qualities in these cultures" (Gore, 1961).

D. *The Controllers and Controllees*

EVERY ORGANIZATION or unit is subjected to the influence of one or more actual or would-be controllers.

The multiple nature of such controls over units of organizations has already been touched upon in the discussion of multiple hierarchy in "People-in-Organizations: Formal Aspects" (Chapt. 9). Here we need merely add that all controls over the units of organizations do not necessarily channel through hierarchic superiors. Many external control agencies, particularly government regulatory organizations, deal directly with the subordinate units of the bodies they try to control.

The relation between controller and controllee is far less ambivalent than that between adviser and advisee. By the same token it is fraught with even more tensions. Neither organizations nor units like to be controlled. They will usually resent even those control activities which they know are unavoidable or necessary. They will often engage in open or hidden resistance.

1. GOVERNMENTAL AND NONGOVERNMENTAL

As might be expected, most external control organizations are governmental or quasigovernmental. Some are established merely to control "lower" organs of government. Some have broad control functions over narrowly defined sectors—as with those which regulate a particular industry. Others have narrowly defined functions with respect to broad sectors of society.

In the heat of controversy that usually surrounds the activities of such control agencies, one often hears the contention that the unique characteristic of government agencies is the extent to which they are subjected to external control. In fact, it is this subordination to public control that often defines the "public" nature of an organization in the more democratic societies. On the other hand, it must be remembered that even in such societies the government corporation has been specifically devised to obtain freedom from certain public controls. Hence the British quip, also applicable to many other countries: "This country contains a large number of privately owned industries which are subject to stringent government control and a small number of publicly owned industries which are subject to no control whatsoever" (*The Economist*, February 3, 1962, p. 399). There is little basis, however, for either form of generalization. The number of control agencies and the stringency of controls to which an organization is subjected can rarely be deduced from its legal status.

Nor should we assume that all external control organizations are necessarily governmental. Lenders and investors often exercise supervisory authority over organizations to whom they provide financial assistance. Associations, federations, and cartels often wield authoritative controls over the activities of their members. Holding companies control various aspects of the operations of their subsidiaries.

In none of these situations, however, can the formal relationship be *ipso facto* regarded as the actual one. There is no empirical evidence to sustain the old adage that the acceptance of public financial aid necessarily brings with it public control. Many private organizations have for decades succeeded in obtaining direct or indirect government subsidies while being subjected to nothing but the pretext of public control. There are private industries which, although formally controlled by public regulatory bodies, have succeeded in turning the tables and controlling the regulators. The controllers may become mouthpieces of the controllees (*Devons*, p. 51). We may presume they have also been capable of achieving a similar relationship with private control bodies. The nature and extent of external control over an organization must be determined by direct observation rather than by jumping to immediate conclusions on the basis of its legal status. As a guide to such observations we may enlarge the above-quoted quip from *The Economist* by adding at the end: ". . . and a number of privately and publicly owned industries which control the agencies that are supposed to control them."

In an increasingly interdependent world these efforts to control other organizations, it should be noted, increasingly vault over national boundaries. The most obvious cases are those of organizations with branches in many countries—such as many large corporations, international associations, and cartels, the Catholic Church and the international communist movement—and national states which control colonial territories, trusteeships or "satellites." Equally important, but somewhat harder to pin down, are the operations of national states as they "intervene" in the operations of many organizations in many other countries. The nature of this foreign intervention has been forcefully revealed by Cleveland, Mangone and Adams.

> At State Department press conferences and in formal diplomatic statements today, there is still much talk about "noninterference in the internal affairs of other nations." But when one examines the true nature of contemporary American overseas operations, this ancient and honorable principle does not describe the present reality. . . .
> Any powerful nation today deeply affects the internal affairs of its many less powerful neighbors . . . (1960, p. 6-7).

Although the authors did not make the point, it might be added that as a result of this situation, the less powerful make increasing efforts themselves to control various aspects of the operations of their more powerful neighbors.

2. THE CONTROL NETWORK

As with clients, the external controllers of an organization vary in the immediacy of their contact with it. They are distributed throughout a complex set of control chains that can best be described as the "control network."

The immediate controllers are those in direct contact with an organization. A government regulatory body is an immediate controller when it issues a price order to specific groups of sellers. So is a budget agency when it impounds the funds of a subordinate spending unit. A holding company, similarly, exercises immediate control over its direct subsidiaries. Homeowners who appear before a city council to seek the reversal of a land use ordinance are attempting immediate control.

When a central bank endeavors to decelerate economic expansion in industry by imposing reserve requirements and other controls on banks, it is engaged in the immediate control of a relatively small number of banks and remote control of a much larger number of industrial enterprises. Similarly, the representatives of the holders of ultimate authority—whether a government legislature or an association's convention—can rarely, if ever, engage in immediate control of any formally subordinate organization or unit. If it operates through legislation or some other form of written rule, it will need an intermediary (or a series of intermediaries) to interpret the rule and confront the regulatee directly.

Immediacy and remoteness in this sense should not be confused with the specificity or generality of what the controller would like to see done or with the methods of influence that he uses. Some of these aspects of control are discussed in detail in the sections on persuading, pressuring, and promoting self-activation in "Activating: Not By Commands Alone" (Chapt. 14). There is a connection, however, between these matters and the immediacy of control. Immediacy makes it easier to be more specific, while an effort to be very specific with remote control places a heavy burden on the communication system. Immediate control, moreover, even if "soft and sweet" methods of influence are used, is a more likely source of emotional tensions. The remote controllers are at least insulated from such shocks by their intermediaries.

To identify the major elements in any control network, it is not enough to look at the array of external controllers. Both immediate and remote control organizations frequently establish chains of control that penetrate the controllee organization.

Formal penetration is obtained by the official placement of members or representatives within the controllee organization in single positions. Both banks and government ministers will often appoint their representatives to serve on the board of directors of corporations they wish to control. Advisory committees are in widespread use as a vehicle for external bodies to make their views felt. A full-time liaison position may be established for the same purpose. Sometimes the controlling body will organize and staff a special control unit which will be formally accepted as a part of the controllee organization.

Informal penetration, which is probably more widespread, achieves the same purpose on an unofficial (and often *sub rosa*) basis. It is usually effected either by getting one's own people into strategic positions in the controllee organization or by winning the confidence or loyalty of people already there. Either approach is rendered easier when there is a common background of understanding and personal interest among members of the two organizations. At times the path may be greased by innocent favors or outright bribes.

The ubiquity of both formal and informal penetration stems from the ingenuity of the controllees as well as of the controllers. When some form of external penetration is inevitable, many organizations invite favored interveners at the expense of others. This may even go as far as opening the doors to a lesser enemy as protection against a more fearful enemy. Or else they may promote balanced penetration to play one group off against another. Penetration, moreover, may be merely a prelude to envelopment. Just as conquering armies have at times been enveloped and swallowed up in the course of time by the people they conquered, so the penetrators also may be converted into loyal members of the organization they were supposed to control. A classic example occurred in the U.S.A. during World War II when the Chairman of the War Production Board sent his chief aides into the military procurement agencies. Instead of serving as representatives of the central control agency, the "Nelson men" were soon won over by the agencies they had been sent to control.

E. *The Adversaries*

IN ADDITION to the burdens of dealing with clients, suppliers, advisers, and controllers, every organization must also cope with external adversaries. These may take the form of competitors, rivals, opponents, or enemies.

Each of these adversary roles, it must be repeated, may be superimposed on most of the other roles already discussed. This is particularly true of control roles. Those adversaries whose activities are most to be reckoned with are those who engage in immediate or remote control activities.

1. COMPETITORS

Competitors are those who produce the same or similar products. Economic literature is rich in discussions of the effects of different types of competitive situations upon the activities of a firm. A large number of competitors can compel an organization to make greater efforts to meet the needs of its clients. Such competition may become unhealthy and destructive if it prevents the building of organizations large enough to benefit from modern technology or if it is conducted in a manner which leads to the destruction of assets. If the competitive challenge is reduced— as in oligopolistic or monopolistic situations—it is easier for a firm to use resources wastefully, restrict output, skimp on quality, impede technological advance, or develop one or another form of organizational arteriosclerosis.

Similar considerations apply both to government organizations and to the internal competitive situation within any organization, including business firms. Some degree of competition inevitably creeps into both fields. Here again the same considerations that are traditionally regarded as applicable to business enterprises are applicable here—albeit on a smaller scale. Complete monopoly makes for rigidity; a certain degree of competition may contribute to the vigor of administrative leadership. An oversupply of competitors may lead to wastefulness. Here too, just as in the case of a business firm, the competitive situation cannot be measured purely in terms of the number of other organizations producing identical products. Like business firms, suborganizations also try to achieve more monopolistic positions through "product differentiation" and "quality competition." To the extent that they can produce something a little different from, or better than, that which might be obtained elsewhere, their position is stronger. Here, too, the major competitive threat is the existence of substitutes—as when a top executive may turn to his budget and accounting staff, his economic advisers, his technicians or his line officials for basic services in connection with the charting of long-range policy.

2. RIVALS

Rivals are those who produce entirely different products but compete for resources, assistance or support. In this sense all producers of consumers' goods are rivals for larger shares of consumer spending. The sellers of housing and automobiles compete with the sellers of food and recreation services. When government raises taxes this is an act of rivalry with all organizations that might otherwise obtain the tax increment in the form of sales revenue.

In the government sector the most bitter and unending form of conflict is that surrounding the allocation of funds among and within the various government agencies. Every budgetary increment for any one organization or unit withdraws funds that might otherwise be available for all others. If total government expenditures are stable or declining, this rivalry becomes particularly intense. Subordinate units in an organization are usually rivals for the attention and support of their superiors.

3. OPPONENTS AND ENEMIES

Opponent roles are played by external individuals and organizations who, although not necessarily competitors or rivals, nevertheless impede the operations of an organization or unit. The more passive opponents are those whose cooperation is needed, who have nothing to lose by cooperation, but see no reason to cooperate. Their interference is mainly a matter of inertia or disinterest. The more active opponents are those who see a conflict of interest. Thus a manufacturing enterprise that tries to build a plant in a residential area may be vigorously opposed by homeowners and their representatives. In the same way we may regard sellers as the opponents of government agencies that impose maximum price regulations upon them. In this case, as in that of regulatory activities of government, the clients are not the people with whom the government agency is most in contact, but the buyers whose interests are served by price control. Only when the price regulations are designed to serve the sellers, as is often the case with minimum price controls, can the regulatees be regarded as the clients. Similarly, taxpayers are the natural opponents of tax collectors.

Enemies are opponents whose opposition carries them into the more bitter forms of conflict. They are often competitors and rivals. They may also be found among clients, suppliers, advisers, or controllers. Wherever they may be, they are not interested merely in blocking those operations to which they are opposed. For them the perceived conflict of interest is so great that they want to curtail or destroy the power of the unit, organization or nation which they oppose. For a unit of an organization the most deadly enemy may well be found in another unit. For an organization as a whole the most deadly enemy is the one whose representatives have penetrated the organization. Such enemies are particularly dangerous because of their knowledge of the organization's inner operations, their access to confidential information, and their ability to work under cover.

F. *Publics with Opinions*

EVERY ORGANIZATION is surrounded by some vague, circumambient phenomenon often referred to as "public opinion." In its broadest sense, public opinion might be regarded as the workings of the value system of a particular society. It may also be a very specific part of the organization's immediate environment—as when an organization enjoys high esteem for its competence or suffers disrepute for its incompetence.

Yet the term "public opinion" is both misleading and dangerous if used to refer to some mythical organic entity that comprises the entire society, or to some artificial average that purports to represent all opinions in the society or at least outside the organization. Different opinions are inevitably held by different people. Under most circumstances, except for a few broadly stated issues during a period of national crisis, there will always be less than complete consensus in opinion. There will usually be at least two different opinions on a single question, and often many more. There may be any one of a varying number of patterns of dispersion among these various opinions. Hence any meaningful discussion of public opinion must start with a recognition of diversity. It is in this sense that people often talk about the opinions not of the public as a whole but of specific "publics." Indeed, there is nothing unusual in the same organization's being regarded as competent by one public and incompetent by another.

As soon as we start to identify the publics whose opinions are of greatest importance to an organization, we immediately come to the external roles of clients, suppliers, advisers, controllers and opponents. The leaders of the organizations that play these roles, in fact, are the "opinion leaders" whose opinions are always of greatest concern to the administrators of an organization.

But this does not exhaust the possibilities. There are two other types of publics. The first are those groups and organizations who do not at the moment play any of these roles but who *might do so* at some time in the future. Most business organizations and many government agencies are continuously looking for new clients. In more complex and interdependent societies almost any group of any significance may some day be a source of assistance or support, a passive obstacle to the winning of assistance or support or a direct competitor, rival, adversary, or even enemy. The opinions of these groups, while insignificant today, may become a force to reckon with tomorrow.

Second, there are the opinions of individuals who do not now play any of these roles and who do not belong to those organizations who may play a relevant role in the future. Such opinions, indeed, are at the outer reaches of an organization's immediate environment. Yet they may some day become the views of clients and suppliers. This potentiality is more significant because of the ever-present possibility that even unorganized opinion reflects interests that can be transmuted into power by the activities of new and existing organizations and coalitions.

Because of the importance of these various publics with opinions, the administrators of organizations are invariably engaged in some form of activity designed to influence such opinions. This, in turn, presupposes certain beliefs concerning the structure of existing opinions. To help provide an informational basis for such beliefs administrators try to keep "their fingers on the pulse of events," "their ear to the ground," or their "eyes on the situation."

Whether they use fingers, ears, eyes, or all together, administrators cannot readily discern, let alone measure, the opinions of either organized or unorganized publics. The same opinion will be expressed and felt by different people with varying degrees of intensity and stability. Many opinions are latent and unexpressed. Many expressed opinions serve to hide a welter of conflicting interests, emotions, and tendencies. Most people have no opinion on most subjects. As the techniques of modern opinion sampling have matured, many surveys have helped administrators come to grips with these problems. But in so doing, they have tended to concentrate on unorganized individual opinion. General surveys, as V. O. Key has pointed out for opinions on governmental activities, "tell us almost nothing about the dynamic relations between the upper layer of activists and mass opinion. The missing piece of our puzzle is this elite element of the opinion system" (1961, p. 536).

But to survey the opinions of group leaders creates even greater complications. Opinions felt most deeply may be repressed or else disguised to serve current leadership strategy. The firmly stated opinion of an organization leader may hide considerable dispersion of opinion among the members of the organization. Because of the high costs that are usually involved, specific surveys prepared to meet the use of individual organizations are usually limited to present and potential clients—as with the "deep analysis" methods of the "motivation research" opinion analysts used by various business organizations (Ferber and Wales, 1958). In fact, a specific and continuing opinion survey geared to the elite structure of all the key groups in an organization's environment has probably never been attempted. Such a survey would probably require a greater amount of time from an organization's administrators than they could spare. It would certainly require a greater amount of cooperation from many external organizations than is consistent with the major roles they play.

The administrators of units are concerned with the opinions not only of publics outside the organization but also of other units, informal groups and individuals inside the organization. Here the same considerations apply that have already been discussed. Here, too, formal survey techniques may be used. Thus far, however, their use has been generally limited to across-the-board analyses of opinion and morale. Few efforts have been made to undertake pinpoint surveys with respect to internal clients, suppliers, advisers, or controllers. Even when survey techniques applicable to such refined analyses have been developed (as they inevitably will be), this will remain a field in which opinions are informally identified and measured by administrators themselves in their daily give-and-take with the various units and people within an organization.

Chapter 7

THE GENERAL ENVIRONMENT

T HE TASK OF THIS CHAPTER is to deal with the broad social environment of organizations. This requires a discussion of the characteristics of societies themselves. By "societies" we refer to the large aggregations of all people and groups living within a defined geographical area.

Every society is unique, thereby providing a distinctive environment for the organizations which operate within it. It has a unique historical past and unique potentials for the future. In the present it constitutes a unique aggregation of individual and group behavior. Sometimes a society is merely a combination of sharply differing subsocieties. Like organizations, moreover, societies are also "open" systems and also affected by their environmental relations. The specific nature of the influence is determined by immigration and emigration, multiple loyalties (if not membership), the exchange of goods and services, and mutual influence.

Yet all societies are also similar. They are similar in the sense that men and women throughout the world have certain biological and psychological attributes in common. These similarities have been accentuated by contact between societies, the growth of similar technologies and methods of organizations, the facing of similar or common problems. In a sense, albeit a very limited one, it is even possible to speak of the "society of man" as a whole.

Any society is extremely difficult to describe. For the observer from within, certain aspects are so much taken for granted that they are not perceived. The outside observer will often exaggerate the importance of certain aspects and miss others entirely. Those who try to observe many societies will usually fail to go deeply into any one of them.

A casual look at various societies can be provided by establishing a set of "ideal types" or stereotypes. But like the remarks of a tourist guide, these can merely serve as an impressionistic introduction. Unless immediately supplemented by measures of dispersion, such indicators of central tendency can be grotesquely misleading.

A more intimate approach can be found by reducing all societies to a number of factors or elements that appear in various forms and combinations in every society. This makes it possible to identify the general environment of organizations in any single society and to identify differences with any other society. One way to do this is to divide a society into an economy, a polity, a culture or any other subsystem which our conceptual tools enable us to construct. This approach has the advantage of conforming with the traditional division of labor in academic organizations. We are then faced with the task of interweaving the subsystems, a task often neglected by those whose interest in society as a whole is limited by their preoccupation with a particular set of conceptual tools.

In this context it is advantageous to take a broader approach which provides for this interweaving at the outset by trying to deal with the total social structure at a high level of generality. One way of doing this is to apply the concepts used in analyzing the structure of organizations. Thus the structure of a society can be regarded as a *pattern of interrelated group roles*. Here also roles, hierarchy, polyarchy and codes are a composite of both the formal and the informal.

But the concepts used in analyzing organizational structure cannot be automatically transferred from one level of systems analysis to another. In a society the major actors can best be viewed as groups and organizations rather than individuals and units. A society is much more diffuse and complex than an organization. There is less reason to get bogged down, in a preliminary view, in all the intricacies of hierarchy, polyarchy and codes. There is much more reason to get the total picture into focus by trying to discern a society's power structure and value structure.

Here, moreover, it is no longer possible to postpone the discussion of the resources available to organizations. These are ultimately those that may be found in the organization's general environment. For this reason our discussion of social structure will be prefaced by a discussion of the resource base.

A. *Resources*

ONE OF THE MOST SIGNIFICANT of all differences among various societies is found in the popular distinction between "haves" and "have-nots." The gap between them is properly regarded as a source of international tension. The basic reason is that either the scarcity or abundance of resources creates serious problems for organizations and their administrators. To appreciate the significance of these matters we must consider just what it is that the haves have and the have-nots do not.

1. OUTPUT

The easiest measure of the difference between "rich" and "poor" societies appears in estimates of their current output of goods and services. In one of the most impressive efforts in this direction Rosenstein-Rodan (1961) shows the following picture:

| | *Population, 1961* | | *"Real" Gross National Product, in Dollars, 1961* | | |
	Millions	*Per Cent of World Total*	*Billions*	*Per Cent of World Total*	*Per Capita*
Developed Countries					
Western Europe	261	8.7	385	22.0	1,472
Oceania	16	0.5	24	1.4	1,513
United States	185	6.2	515	29.4	2,790
Canada	18	0.6	38	2.1	2,048
Japan	95	3.2	58	3.3	613
South Africa	15	0.5	9	0.5	598
	590	19.7	1,029	58.7	
Communist Bloc					
Soviet Union	215	7.2	212	12.1	986
Eastern Europe	100	3.3	82	4.7	825
China	694	23.2	116	6.6	167
North Korea	9	0.3	2	0.1	211
North Vietnam	17	0.6	3	0.2	199
	1,035	34.6	415	23.7	

Underdeveloped
Countries

Africa	206	6.9	34	1.9	164
Asia	780	26.1	89	5.1	425
Latin America	210	7.0	120	6.8	154
Europe	67	2.2	34	1.9	501
Middle East	106	3.5	29	1.7	257
	1,369	45.7	306	17.5	
Total	2,994	100.0	1,750	100.0	

These estimates point up some striking disparities. The United States with only about 6 per cent of the world's population produces about 30 per cent of the world's 1961 output. Per capita GNP in the U.S.A. is 17 or 18 times larger than in Africa, Latin America, or China. The variations are also large within each of the three groupings. In the communist bloc over 70 per cent of the output was produced by two areas, Russia and Eastern Europe, accounting for only a third of the bloc's population. These differences become still more vivid when pinned down to such specific product categories as food, clothing, housing, health services, education, recreation and cultural activities. One of the most meaningful of all such specific measures is the consumption of energy from mineral fuels and waterpower (the major sources of energy other than musclepower and woodburning). In 1950, for example, per capita energy consumption in the U.S.A. was about 10 times the same figure for Japan, 20 times that of Yugoslavia, 30 times that of Turkey, 40 times that of Peru, 50 times that of Egypt and 60 times that of India (Woytinsky and Woytinsky, 1953, p. 941).

2. WEALTH

Behind these differences in current output lie other disparities in the stock of such man-developed capital as

✓ farms and livestock
✓ buildings, roads, bridges, dams, and harbors,
✓ energy-producing facilities that can supplant the musclepower of people and animals,
✓ machinery and tools that use such energy in agriculture, manufacturing, transportation, and communication, and
✓ supplies of consumers' and producers' goods held for future use.

Although it is fantastically difficult to estimate the aggregate quantity of such stocks in any society, we know that the variations are substantial.

The capital provided by nature, no easier to quantify, is also unevenly distributed. Some societies—conspicuous among them the U.S.A.—have been blessed with a large variety, great amount, and high quality of soil, animal life, forests, vegetation, minerals, rivers, and rainfall. Some societies are rich in many categories but lacking in others. Others may be generally poor, with a sprinkling of isolated riches such as oil or copper. Still others have relatively little of anything.

But people themselves are the most important of all resources. It is people who produce the current output of goods and services. It is people who create and renew the accumulated stock of facilities, machinery, and tools. It is people who find or neglect natural resources, develop and use them or—as the case may be—deplete them. Only the energy and imagination of people can compensate for the lack of nature-provided resources by trading with others and the discovery of substitutes.

In a sense, therefore, the potentially richest societies might be thought of as those with the most people. But among all societies, even the most populous, there are wide disparities in health and acquired abilities. A society cannot escape the "have-not" level if a large part of its people are illiterate, ill fed, and ridden by preventable diseases. It cannot reach the "have" level without a labor force that includes a large proportion of skilled workers, technicians, specialists, professionals, intellectuals, and administrators. It cannot remain at the "have" level without a continual enlargement in the quality and quantity of people in these categories. This seems to necessitate also the continual enlargement of urban areas, which have thus far proved the only way of assembling the resources and external economies needed by large-scale organizations.

3. SCARCITY AND ABUNDANCE

In an environment characterized by low levels of output, capital, or human resources, sharp limits are placed on what an organization or an administrator can hope to do. In a "have" society, except for times of war or serious inflation, an administrator can have a telephone call made to a supplier of necessary materials, parts, or equipment. He can turn to the labor market to get people of such-and-such skills. In a nonindustrialized economy, however, it may take many months to get the needed supplies. The supplier himself may be nonexistent and, if existent, he may have no telephone. The shortages of skilled people will be just as acute. In many cases, there will simply be no conception of what a certain skill is—office secretary or cost accountant. Nor will there be highly developed government agencies capable of providing needed statistics. Even if there already exists a substratum of essential services in the field of health, public utilities, policing and transportation, the experienced administrator or expert technician from an industrialized country will often find himself at an utter loss in such a poverty-stricken environment. Unable to obtain reliable local information, to find understanding people to work with, or even to find a competent secretary, he may be as useless as the English aristocrats stranded on a desert island in Barrie's *The Admirable Crichton*. Here the most useful fellow may instead be someone who, while only a minor underling in "more civilized" society, at least can do better when forced to live by his wits.

An environment of abundance may create as many special difficulties as an environment of scarcity. Abundance leads to free and easy ways that cannot readily be modified. The interdependence essential to the creation of abundance may also create an overdependence on established ways. It is in this sense that a rich society runs the risk of becoming "soft." An abundance of natural resources or man-made capital removes the pressure (Galbraith might say "the need") for economizing on their use and conserving them for the future. As Galbraith has observed, "Wealth is the relentless enemy of understanding" (*The Affluent Society*, p. 1). Overproduction of goods or services—whether "over" relative to effective demand or in more absolute terms, whether general or concentrated in a few fields—leads to a drastic shakeup among the producing organizations, including the possible liquidation of many of them. An oversupply of people relative to suitable employment opportunities leads to an erosion of human resources. But surplus people cannot be stocked, as can surplus goods. Nor can they, short of emigration, famine, or war, be readily liquidated. If the number of unemployed is large, many of them will inevitably be employed in organizations that could get along without them. If the number grows, many will gravitate toward organizations that aim to produce drastic changes in the social structure.

At lower levels of economic development, underemployment of human resources—particularly in agriculture—is a concomitant of scarcity in output and man-developed resources. In the "have" societies unemployment often appears cyclically together with an "overproduction" in current output relative to effective demand. As the level of abundance rises in "have" societies rapidly changing technology continuously brings new skills into being and renders old skills obsolescent. Under such circumstances administrators can never escape the simultaneous problems of manpower scarcity and manpower surplus.

B. *Social Organization*

As POINTED OUT in "The Rise of the Administered Society,"[1] it is only through organization that people can convert resources into the

---

1. Gross, *The Managing of Organizations*, Chapter 2.

power to do significant things. Increasing power has been provided by the administrative revolution which has brought—and is still bringing—with it more organization, larger organizations, more bureaucracy, and more administrators.

Although the onward sweep of the administrative revolution is universal and unidirectional, there are tremendous variations not only in its rate of motion but also in the emergence in each society of a unique array of organizations and organizational roles. Every organization is inescapably affected by this aspect of its environment.

1. FAMILIES

Although families are to be found in all societies, there is a tremendous variation not only in their internal structure but also in their relation to other organizations in society. This relation can be dramatized by thinking of various societies in terms of their place on this three point "family role" continuum:

A - - - - - - - - - - - - - - - B - - - - - - - - - - - - - - C

Families or extended families as *the* organizations	Families as important units in larger organizations and constellations	Families as peripheral to larger organizations

At the limiting extreme of A, families or extended family organizations are the only organizations in society. The family itself, through its various combinations and subdivisions, carries on all organized activities. At and around B, many other organizations are active in society—particularly governments, armies, and churches, but also certain producing and trading organizations. But one family, or a small set of families, becomes the dominant factor in most organizations. Thus we have governmental dynasties, hereditary priesthoods and patrimonial business enterprises. The wave of the administrative revolution usually carries a society from the vicinity of B toward the vicinity of C. The area of family domination contracts as monarchies topple over and surviving dynasties tend to become ceremonial figureheads. The dynasts themselves find that family members cannot be relied upon to carry on the monarch's business and often establish merit systems. In business enterprise family activity lingers longer. Here the family serves a triple function as a source of capital, a reservoir of manpower that can be trusted and a motivator to build up family fortunes. The family firm and the paternalistic enterprise are often the prime movers in building new, large enterprises. Where the family is not large enough to supply the necessary capital and manpower, it may be enlarged. In Japan, the house of Mitsui maintained its dominant position in industry by expanding to include "eleven families plus cousins." Slowly and painfully, however, the requirements for skilled manpower force a retreat from family domination and nepotism. Except for such last strongholds as very small scale enterprises, family farms, and a scattering of family corporations, holding companies and foundations, the role of the family in large-scale organization is now peripheral (Harbison and Myers, 1952). Nor does the family hold its own even as the major producer of the traditionally "familial" services. A not inconsiderable portion of child care, sexual activity, recreation, eating, and laundry may be transferred elsewhere. Energies previously absorbed by the family are thereby released, often to be concentrated on the operations of other organizations.

Nevertheless, even at this point on our continuum the family still has an important influence upon administration. The family is still the first place where the human being acquires his attitude toward authority, social mobility, and cultural values, attitudes that determine a large part of his subsequent behavior in other organizations.

2. GOVERNMENT

All organizations in any society can be distributed on a continuum ranging from governmental through mixed to nongovernmental. Colloquially, we use the term "socialist" to refer to any society with a larger proportion of governmental or mixed organizations. A more discerning use of this scale necessitates a frequency distribution based upon a general classification of products or—in national accounting terms—the sectors of origin of national income. By this approach we can see that the "mixed economy" of many societies derives not only from mixed organizations but also from varying frequencies of governmental organizations in different sectors. Thus in India the relatively small areas of industry, transportation, and communication are predominantly governmental and the extremely large area of agricultural production is overwhelmingly nongovernmental.

Any picture provided by such a frequency distribution, however, must be modified by more qualitative considerations concerning the influence of governmental upon nongovernmental organizations. By regulation, control, assistance, and less direct forms of influence government organizations can become a dominant factor in the activities of nongovernmental organizations. Thus in the U.S.A. a Federal government generally regarded as "nonsocialist" wields much greater influence than the "socialist" government of India over private agriculture.

At this point we may note the limited usefulness of the frequent efforts to appraise the role of government in terms of government expenditures as a percentage of gross national product. This measure is useful only to calculate marginal changes within a given society or to compare societies which differ little in basic structure. If we should compare the U.S.A. with the U.S.S.R., the difference would be rather small in comparison with the vast difference in the nature of producing organizations. The reason is that the largest expenditures in both societies are those of households and individual consumers.

3. BUYERS AND SELLERS

One of the differentiating characteristics of organizations, as pointed out in Chapter 9, is whether or not they sell their end products. Sellers, however, imply buyers. The term "market" refers to some pattern of relations between buyers and sellers.

An important aspect of every society is simply the extent of buying-selling relations. First of all, many organizations produce goods or services for their own members only. In many nonindustrialized societies this is true of a large portion of family-produced agricultural products. This principle of "production for use by the producers" in all societies also applies to "household services" in general, and many of the services of "self-serving" associations. Second, there are many kinds of nonsale transactions with external clients. In certain primitive societies—as with the Trobriand islanders of Western Melanesia described by Malinowski—products flow circularly from one group to another, thus constituting an unplanned system of reciprocity (1926, p. 40-41). As societies grow wealthier philanthropic organizations distribute charity or "patronage" as a means of helping the needy, promoting the arts and protecting their own members against more vigorous redistribution activities by government. Nonetheless, the growth of government, particularly in the era of the administrative revolution, invariably brings with it a large volume of nonsold services distributed largely on the basis of administrative judgment and client pressure. The large-scale redistribution activities of government are made possible through governmental power to appropriate wealth through its powers of taxation and money-creation.

But the growth of nonmarketed government services should not lead us to an exaggerated dichotomy between markets and governmental activity. Governmental action itself has always been an indispensable factor in the growth of markets. In the nineteenth century "the road to the free market was opened and kept open by an enormous increase in continuous, centrally organized and controlled interventionism. . . .

Administrators had to be constantly on watch to ensure the free work-ings of the system. Thus even those who wished most ardently to free the state from all unnecessary duties . . . could not but entrust the self-same state with the new powers, organs and instruments required for the establishment of *laissez-faire*. . . . *Laissez-faire* was planned . . ." (Karl Polanyi, 1957, p. 140-141).

Specifically, governments have

* established the monetary and banking systems without which markets cannot develop very far beyond primitive barter,
* actively promoted both internal and foreign trade,
* provided the indispensable governmental services which protected property rights and contracts and afforded acceptable means of media-tion for market disputes,
* regulated markets in order to protect not only buyers and sellers but other groups whose interests would be jeopardized by uncontrolled market conflict, and
* entered many markets as important buyers, particularly in periods of war-inflated government purchasing.

Moreover, twentieth-century socialism—despite ideological leanings toward a utopian era in which everything would be freely distributed —has unquestionably produced a larger expansion in the volume of products marketed by governmental organizations. The fact that most prices in the Soviet Union and other communist-bloc countries are determined by government agencies merely means that the pattern of price determination is different from that in the so-called "capitalist" countries. It should not lead us to ignore the fact that in the former societies markets are also seen as an indispensable vehicle for controlling the distribution of goods and services (Bornstein, 1962).

The tremendous variety of market systems has rarely been analyzed empirically in any society. Yet we can readily distinguish the more important variables. One set of variables is provided by the simple dis-tinctions between the number of buyers or sellers. Thus any market can be characterized by its position in one of the nine cells in the following buyer-seller matrix.

		SELLERS		
		One (o)	*Few (f)*	*Many (m)*
B	One (o)	o,o	o,f	o,m
U				
Y	Few (f)	f,o	f,f	f,m
E				
R	Many (m)	m,o	m,f	m,m
S				

Thus, an m,m market represents the traditional idea of many buyers and sellers. On the same row we find not only the traditional monopoly (m,o) but also the oligopoly with many buyers (m,f). In the same column we find the monopsony with many sellers (o,m) and the oligopsony with many sellers (f,m). At the opposite end of the diagonal we find the market (o,o) in which one buyer confronts one seller. Other variables relate to the homogeneity, heterogeneity or uniqueness of the products involved; the supply situation; the extent of cooperation or organization among sellers or buyers; the extent and nature of government control; the availability of information on costs, output, and related matters; and the ease of entering the market as either buyer or seller. An extremely perceptive effort to group these variables into a set of generally discernible market types is provided by Wiles in his typology of (i) primitive higglers, (ii) price takers, (iii) full cost chargers, (iv) discontinuous producers, and (v) marginal cost chargers (1961, p. 4-5). To apply these distinctions to an entire economy would necessitate interweaving them into the matrix of organizations classified both by output (economic sectors) and governmental status.

4. ASSOCIATIONS

Another important aspect of any society is the role played by associations—that is, by organizations whose major members, apart from employed staff, are affiliates rather than employees.

In an advanced industrial society like the U.S.A. the number and aggregate membership of such associations is extremely high. The table on page 444 shows the distribution of over 11,000 associations in 1959.

Although comparable data are not available for other countries, there is enough evidence to indicate a luxuriant outgrowth of organizations in all highly industrialized societies. According to Finer, "Britain is more 'organized' than even the U.S.A., for long thought to be the home of 'joiners'" (1958, p. 5). In less developed societies the roles of associations are often usually more limited. They are performed rather by what Almond calls "nonassociational" and "anomic" interest groups. The former are "kinship and lineage groups, ethnic, religious, status and class groups which articulate interests informally, and intermittently, through individuals, cliques, family and religious heads, and the like." The latter are "more or less spontaneous breakthroughs into the political system from the society, such as riots and demonstrations" (1960, p. 33-38).

By cutting across membership in families and employment organizations, associations contribute to the "multiple membership" dimension of any society. They supplement the market by providing many unsold services for their own members. By bringing together many buyers or sellers with common interests, they also provide a channel for participating in or otherwise influencing specific markets. They provide facilities whereby competing or interdependent organizations can exchange information, mediate their differences, or coordinate their policies—as with community chests and trade associations (*Litwak* and *Hilton, 1962*).

Associations also play a major role in the activities of national and local government agencies, executive, legislative, and judicial. They provide the specialized personnel and skills required to collect and assess information on governmental operations and to influence the choice of governmental personnel, the organization of government, and the nature of government decisions. But the flow of information and influence is not unidirectional. Government organizations, in turn, often use such associations as means of collecting essential information and of extending their control over larger sectors of society than they could reach if left to their own devices.

NATIONAL ASSOCIATIONS IN THE UNITED STATES, 1959[a]

Type	Number of Organizations
1. Trade, business and commercial	2,462
2. Agricultural, including commodity exchanges	377
3. Governmental, public administration, military and legal	191
4. Scientific, engineering and technical	332
5. Educational and cultural	671
6. Social welfare	274
7. Health and medical	526
8. Public affairs	224
9. Religious	527
10. Fraternal, foreign interest, nationality and ethnic	460
11. Horticultural	74
12. Veteran, heritary and patriotic	135
13. Hobby and avocational	213
14. Athletic and sports	183
15. General (not elsewhere classified)	118
16. Labor unions	230
17. Chambers of commerce (international, binational, national, state, local)	4,155
18. Greek, letter societies (social, professional, honorary)	330
Total	11,482

a. National Organizations of the U.S., Vol. I of *Encyclopedia of Associations.*

5. POLITICAL PARTIES

Political parties are associations whose major activity is the effort to place their members in key positions in government. In societies where elections are not conducted they do this through intrigues, deals, coups d'etat or revolutions. Where elections are held, they do this by nominating candidates and trying to get them the votes required for election. The victorious candidates are always expected to appoint to office (or help get appointed) other party members—although the growth of civil service systems narrows the number of such appointments.

In order to win elections, negotiate deals or provide the support for coups d'etat or revolutions, all parties and party leaders are interested to at least some minimum extent in government policies and programs. In "personalist" parties where party leaders themselves clearly symbolize the interests of certain groups in society, or where they are merely engagd in rivalry to serve identical groups, the program approach of parties will not be highly articulated. Where parties serve a wide variety of interests, party programs will largely be a jumble of contradictions or when the communication system in a society allows the people "down river" to hear what party leaders say "up the river" a mass of generalities. Where parties represent fewer interest groups in society, they may differ very little from an ordinary association. In such cases a party can afford to be highly "ideological." If an ideological party of this type wins seats in a legislature, it will then have to make programmatic compromises if it wants to be very influential in the legislative process. If it joins a coalition cabinet, it will compromise its programs through the normal process of coalition building and coalition operation.

Party "systems" are often distinguished on the basis of the number of political parties in a society: one, two, or many. This is an acceptable starting point as long as a number of qualifying factors are promptly introduced.

First of all, some parties are of little or no consequence. They may operate merely to get publicity for a few people. If they actually run candidates in elections, they may never get enough votes to elect their own candidates or influence the fate of other candidates. With only a few exceptions, this has been the situation with minor parties in national elections in the United States. Hence the logic of referring to the United States as having a "two-party system." Similarly, there are many areas of the U.S.A. where the second party has been of practically no significance—and in fact has sometimes been merely an appendage of *the* party. Hence the frequent reference in the U.S.A. to "single-party" districts, towns, or even States.

Second, even where there are two or more substantial parties, it may well be that one party is firmly seated in control of the government and that rivals have no chance to dislodge it. In India the Congress Party has consistently won an overwhelming majority of the national legislature and of most state governments. In Israel the Mapai Party, although generally winning only a plurality of seats, has always been the organizer and kingpin of coalition governments. Although opposition parties in both countries are free to organize and campaign, it is difficult to see how any single party or coalition of parties could undermine the one-party hegemony of either the Congress Party or the Mapai. The same can be said about Mexico's Party of Revolutionary Institutions.

Third, a multitude of factions may often be found in one-party and two-party systems. "Insofar as factions develop freely inside a single party," Duverger points out, "this becomes simply a framework which limits political rivalries without destroying them; prohibited outside the single party, pluralism is reborn inside the party, and there it can play the same part. Thus the internal divisions in the Democratic Party in the southern states of America, where it is for all practical purposes in the position of a single party, are such that the party is nearer to classical democracy than to Fascism, thanks to the system of the primaries; as far as they are concerned it is possible to transpose the fundamental distinction between bipartism and multi-partism. . . . It is therefore conceivable that a single-party system may coincide with some kind of political democracy" (1954, p. 278).

In the United States the Democratic Party has long been sharply divided between its more liberal (mainly Northern) and more conservative (mainly Southern) wings. The Republicans have also been divided—somewhat less on liberal-conservative lines, somewhat more on foreign policy issues. Moreover, the electoral system of the U.S.A. is so constituted as to orient the Presidency and most Governorships somewhat more toward the voters in the larger metropolitan areas, and to orient the Congress (even when the majority of seats are held by the same party whose candidate has won the Presidency) more toward the rural areas. From this point of view a full-fledged two-party system can hardly be said to exist. This situation is reflected in the frequent calls for a stronger two-party system—one in which "the parties are able to bring forth programs to which they commit themselves . . . and possess sufficient internal strength to carry out their programs" (Committee on Political Parties, 1950, p. 17-18).

In analyzing party systems in developing countries, Esman has distinguished five types: (1) conservative oligarchies (Iran, Ethiopia,

Northern Nigeria, Afghanistan, and Peru); (2) competitive interest-oriented parties (Philippines, Brazil, Greece, Chile, Malaya, and Jamaica); (3) authoritarian military reformers (Pakistan, Burma, South Korea, Thailand, and the Sudan); (4) dominant mass parties (Mexico, India, Egypt, Algeria, Puerto Rico, Tanganyika, Tunis, and Guinea); and (5) communist totalitarians (China, Soviet Union, and the communist countries of Eastern Europe). "The dominant mass party regimes," he finds, "appear to combine the advantages of purposeful leadership, a developmentally oriented doctrine, the capacity both to mobilize and to discipline widespread support and participation, and the ability to deploy a variety of action and communication instruments. For these reasons, this type of regime seems to be particularly relevant to the needs of transitional societies undergoing rapid and radical transformation" (1963).

c. *The Power Structure*

As WITH SINGLE ORGANIZATIONS, the total structure of a society emerges from the role interrelations provided by hierarchy, polyarchy and codes of behavior.

To rise above the details of these relationships and obtain a perspective on the system as a whole, it is essential to consider the distribution of power within it. Who are the people who make which decisions? Where are the centers of power?

For the leaders of any important organization within a society these are the kind of questions which, precisely because they are so important, are hard to ask. Some sort of answers to them—no matter how limited —are part of the "tacit knowledge" of skillful administrators. But when experienced administrators become involved in more extensive relations within their own society, they are likely to find their previous answers less relevant. If they attempt relations with other societies, they may lose their bearings completely.

In previous chapters we have attacked the myths of central omnipotence by analyzing the factors that bring about a dispersion of intraorganizational power. We shall now concentrate upon interorganizational power—the distribution of power in a society as a whole.

Here also we find an inevitable dispersion of power. This does not deny the existence of extremely significant differences in the pattern of dispersion. These variations will be discussed in the subsequent sections on democratic and dictatorial patterns and on stratification.

1. THE DISPERSION OF INTERORGANIZATIONAL POWER

The underlying factor in the dispersion of power within any society is pluralism of interests. No matter what the degree of concentrated formal authority may be, this underlying pluralism makes itself felt in actions that are not totally subordinate to the authority wielders. To the extent that these dispersed interests are expressed by groups, organizations, cliques and coalitions they are transformed into significant power centers.

To the naïve observer, the primitive tribe—with its tribal chief and strong traditions from the past—might appear an exception to this rule. The anthropologists, however, have revealed the deep conflicts that are an inseparable part of tribal existence. An indication of the dispersion of power in a small tribe of about 17,000 people in Northern Rhodesia is provided by Turner (1957, p. 89-90):

> Beneath all other conflicts in Ndembu society is the concealed opposition between men and women over descent and the economic system. Influenced by this basic opposition, but possessing their own autonomy, sets of struggles arise within the social structure: conflicts between persons and between groups who invoke different principles of residential affiliation to support and justify their own specific interests, political, jural and economic; struggles between persons and groups couched in terms of a common norm which each party claims the other has broken; and conflicts between persons, united by a single principle of descent and residence, for positions of authority determined by that principle.

When societies become larger and more complex, other patterns of power dispersion develop. In feudal societies, dispersion is written into the system by the distribution of fiefs and the relative lack of horizontal interaction. The effort to establish greater control by a monarch brings him into direct conflict with the aristocratic nobility. The dispersion pattern is made more complicated by the entry into the fray of organized churchmen, merchants, artisans, and occasional "anomic" groups of peasants. Under such circumstances a large state or empire can be brought into being only by coming to terms with diversity. This is one of the central factors that made it possible for the Romans to build a much larger and longer-lasting empire than the Athenians. They were willing to give Roman citizenship to the people of conquered territories. In fact, a large part of Roman law was based on the recognition of greatly disparate interests throughout the Empire. The Athenians were a tighter "in-group." They felt that the "polis" which they loved would be destroyed by extending Athenian citizenship to others (Kitto, 1951). Instead they relied on semiprofessional military force to keep their empire together and were soon destroyed by the more professional and specialized military forces that rolled down from Macedonia.

With the development of large bureaucratic organizations, the pattern of power dispersion changes but the dispersion continues. Bureaucracies tend to become competing or countervailing sources of power. In the military forces this competition develops among the different branches and field commands. In the civilian government it is found among the different branches and the various agencies within each branch. A still greater dispersion is usually found among buying and selling organizations. As these organizations become larger, we usually see many "concentrations" of power in various sectors. Under such circumstances the pattern becomes one of the dispersion of power among giants rather than pygmies. At the same time new power centers usually arise with the emergence of different kinds of associations and political parties and factions.

But what happens when the giants get together?

The simplest way to get together is polyarchic relations among different organizations. As pointed out in Chapter 9, polyarchy may take the form of either dispersed or shared responsibility. In the first case, we see the kind of dispersion that takes place among negotiators and bargainers. In the second case, we see the more integrated form of dispersion that takes place within any collegial body. In both cases, it is possible for larger and larger concentrations of power to emerge through coalitions—formal or informal, fleeting or enduring—of different groups. In fact, the power to get things done in collegial bodies comes into being only through some type of coalition. But it is hardly possible—without a hierarchic umbrella—for any coalition to bring together all the significant sources of power in a society. Even if it were possible, it must be remembered that a coalition—whether a "holy" or "unholy" alliance among "natural" or "strange" bedfellows—represents a special pattern of power dispersion: ". . . group power can be extended through combinations only at a discount. While these discounts will vary in size, even when they seem comparatively small, they are an integral part of the power structure of a society" (*Gross*, p. 148-150).

The more ambitious way to develop a centralized pattern is to bring polyarchic relations within a framework of hierarchic subordination. This can be attempted on a truly extensive scale only by an organization capable of making legitimate use of force and violence, namely a government. The most ambitious effort to centralize social power in government is the totalitarian effort to convert society into one big organization. Although some of the organizers of the French Revolution envisioned a society of this type, their vision died with them on the guillotine. More than a century later, inspired in part by the spectacle of ever-larger organization by business corporations, this vision was reborn in the ideologies of the Italian Fascists, the German Nazis, and the Russian and Chinese communists.

But despite the ideological trappings of modern totalitarianism, large-scale organization in society as a whole is very much the same as in a single corporation or government agency. The only difference is that a society is usually more diffuse. Thus in a totalitarian society the dispersion of intraorganizational power is automatically transformed into the law of the dispersion of interorganizational power.

In a totalitarian society this dispersion is rooted in the highly specialized role differentiation. Here, the growth of bureaucracy to greater proportions than in any other society means a vast increase in the number of small, specialized domains of knowledge and power. These dispersed power centers can be brought together in part by polyarchic relations and by codes of behavior. But still greater reliance is placed upon the "hierarchic umbrella." Hierarchy can mature, however, only with substantial delegations of authority, which themselves become a springboard for dispersed power. Moreover, more complex hierarchic forms produce ever greater ambiguities and conflicts concerning the divisions of authority. They increasingly provide for not merely dual but multiple hierarchy. Within each military and civilian organization in the U.S.S.R., for example, the pattern of divided authority is as complex as in any large business or government organization in the U.S.A. Each such agency, in addition, is subjected to the authority of various agents of the Communist Party, the secret police, the State Bank, the Ministry of Finance, and the Ministry of State Control. In turn, the formal determinations of the structure of the state-society invariably give rise to a tremendous amount of informal roles, hierarchies, codes of behavior, and polyarchy. Whether more of these supplement the formal structure or more of them counteract it is not relevant to this discussion. In either case, they undoubtedly contribute to the dispersion of power within the Soviet society.

2. DEMOCRATIC AND DICTATORIAL POWER PATTERNS

If we have established the existence of a pattern of dispersed power in any totalitarian society, the classic case of centralized power, we have effectively destroyed the idea of central omnipotence as it applies to a society as a whole.

But we may at the same time have created the false impression that if power is dispersed in both totalitarian and democratic societies, there is no real difference between the two. To eliminate such an impression and to refine our discussion of the social environment within which organizations operate, we shall therefore distinguish between the dictatorial and the democratic patterns of power dispersion.

As with single organizations, the democratic nature of a society can best be measured by asking the question: *Who participates how deeply in what?* In Chapter 10 we discuss this question in terms of organizational democracy and dictatorship. Here we shall discuss it also in terms of political, economic, social, and individual democracy. These are additional ways of dealing with the "what" of our central question.

Political democracy entails a wide and deep participation in the great decisions concerning the top personnel of government and the general direction of government policy. In elections a substantial portion of adults are given an opportunity to choose between candidates of opposing parties or factions. Between elections it is possible to effectuate changes in policy through pressure, propaganda and negotiation by various organizations. In part, the extent of these democratic processes may be appraised by the nature of the electoral system and the freedom to organize and campaign (traditionally referred to as the freedoms of assembly, religion, petition, speech and press). But democratic forms and freedoms can be ignored by the people or exploited by dictators. The more important measure is the actual extent to which people take advantage of these rights.

In addition to political democracy there are four other modes of widespread participation in the various activities of a society. In each of these the *what* is somewhat further from the great global questions of statesmanship and politics but much closer to the daily lives of people. *Organizational democracy*, as pointed out in the previous chapter, makes it possible for more members of the organization to participate more deeply on matters that affect their personal work and the activity of their organization. *Economic democracy* provides people with opportunities for useful, satisfying, and remunerative employment, including the educational facilities that make it possible to take advantage of such opportunities. *Social democracy* provides guarantees that political and economic rights shall not be impaired because of a person's color, race, caste, religion, national origin, or sex. This is the area of democracy often referred to by the term "civil rights." Finally, *individual democracy* provides the individual with what Mosca called "juridical defense" against injustice at the hands of those who are stronger. Here we find the codes of "civil liberties," "due process," and the specialized organizations whose role it is to enforce such codes.

The interrelations between these five pillars of democracy are intimate.

None of them can be strong if the others are extremely weak. In the absence of social democracy political democracy may indeed exist—but as the privileged way of life for only a segment of the population. With the sustained impairment of economic or individual democracy it will crumble into dust. With a low level of political democracy, in turn, organizational democracy can scarcely develop in more than a spotty manner.

Nevertheless, the development of these five forms of democracy is always uneven. Society A will push ahead faster on political and individual democracy, B on economic democracy, C on social democracy. Many of the disputes as to which of the three is more democratic stem from confusion as to which form of democracy is being discussed. There is no doubt but that many of the democratic societies which boast the loudest concerning the quality of their democracy are seriously backward in two or more of these fields. There is also no doubt but that important aspects of democracy in some of these fields have developed within the framework of dictatorial regimes. Still more aspects of democracy have often developed in aristocratic societies. Political and individual democracy, in fact, were propably first born in the struggles between monarchs and aristocrats. The nobility and the gentry may act democratically in conducting their relations with others at the same level in society. The effort to win allies from lower levels may mean a cautious and limited extension of these privileges. Such extension becomes still more meaningful when it is used by people at lower levels as a springboard for breaking down the social barriers.

So-called "absolute monarchies" are the oldest forms of dictatorship. Here the Emperor, King, God-King, Tyrant, or Despot often wields the arbitrary power to kill, jail, punish, or promote anyone in the country. But the "absoluteness" of this power is counterbalanced by the narrow area in which it can be exerted. This is well illustrated in Riggs' analysis of the Siamese monarchy, one of the most "absolute" in world history. The King of Siam spent most of his time on elaborate religious ceremonies and court rituals. If he had tried to devote himself to national problems and policies instead, he would have been acting like a man instead of a god, thereby undermining the divine basis of his authority.

> But even if he were to devote himself in this way to administrative tasks, he would lack the machinery, the communications net, for transmitting policy to the country, and carrying it out in day-to-day affairs. . . . Local magnates—ranging from high patriots to parochial strong men—ran affairs much as they pleased. All deferred in awe to the sacred power of the king, but one reason for their willingness to recognize the court was its willingness to leave local questions and rules alone, provided traditional dues and services to the crown were forthcoming (1961, p. 75-76).

The modern authoritarian dictatorship covers a wider area. Its essential aspect is the suppression of political democracy by eliminating the legal means for the peaceful replacement of the top personnel of government. Opposition parties are allowed to operate only if they do so as "straw men." Otherwise they are liquidated by killing or jailing opposition leaders or forcing them into foreign exile or underground operations. To prevent the growth of new opposition centers, freedom of organization, speech, and the press is prevented or curtailed. This also leads to unpredictable infringements of whatever individual democracy may have existed in the past. The past levels of social democracy may or may not be impaired. Depending on the specific circumstances the level of economic democracy may change slightly for the better or for the worse.

The totalitarian dictatorship is a "horse of another color." Its leaders are driven by messianic visions of tremendous personal and national achievement. They are not satisfied with the curtailment of political democracy. They strike at social democracy by using various minority groups as scapegoats. They tear up whatever individual democracy has existed by making the ruling party or faction the sole source to which an individual can turn for defense. Through vigorous programs of economic expansion they may eliminate unemployment but often at the price of curtailing individual choice of employment opportunities. Above all, they attack organizational democracy at its roots by trying to integrate all significant forms of human organization into the one big organization of the state. This means bringing all trade unions, professional and scientific associations, and religious, age, sex, cultural, national, communal, and recreational organizations under the umbrella of the government and party hierarchy. Not even the family is exempt from this drive. In the heyday of Nazi and Bolshevik fervor children were not only encouraged to leave their families; they were encouraged to denounce their parents. In the "brainwashing" operations in the "thought" reform colleges in Communist China, it is reported that in the final confession which every student must submit before being reborn as a member of the Chinese Communist Community the "central feature is the denunciation of the father, both as a symbol of the exploiting classes, and as an individual" (Lifton, 1960, p. 488). All such efforts are accompanied by a thorough mobilization of the press, radio, television, schools, and arts for the ceaseless reiteration of the dominant ideology, goals, and myths and for the diversion of attention from internal problems to external enemies. In turn, this entails a serious effort to block off communications with people in other societies.

There is no doubt that the leaders of a totalitarian society can mobilize a tremendous amount of power through such efforts. They can divert more resources from consumption to investment than either a democracy or an authoritarian dictatorship. They can do much better than either in concentrating investment in carefully selected sectors. To the extent that they are successful in their various projects they can win over a substantial portion of the population to their style of doing things. But these potentialities are not unmixed blessings. They also serve to nourish the intrigues, cabals, plots, and counterplots that are warp and woof of the coalition of elite groups and power centers. In this situation the often-discussed struggle for power revolving around the position of top man is far less important than it may seem. What importance the struggle has derives more from its relation to the deeper struggles among the political lieutenants whom Neumann calls the "forgotten men in most discussions of the totalitarian state" (1942, p. 73). These are the hundreds of people who are locked in bitter struggle for the number two, three, and four positions in the government, secret police, armed services, industry, and educational and cultural institutions.

On top of all this, power is diffused ever more widely by the essential elements of large-scale organization—the division of labor, hierarchy, polyarchy and the codes that are required to protect the increasing plurality of interests. Whatever success the one big organization has in its ventures depends more and more upon an ever-more refined specialization of labor and the development of large fragmented elites of specialists, professionals and scientists. Multiple oligarchy becomes still more multiple. The old coalitions and clusters become more complex and fluid. A proportionately smaller number of issues can be settled or dodged by the gas chamber, the firing squad, the mock trial, imprisonment, or banishment. As a new generation of experts arises to take the place of the "old men" who established the totalitarian state, the old myths tend to become ritualistic verbiage. The old methods of mass indoctrination lead to tedium, withdrawal, or open or suppressed rebellion. To retain power, the old-timers try to broaden their base by using the techniques of a Khrushchev or Tito instead of a Stalin. But in the face of the assault by the new generation, there is no way of restoring the old ways without a new ideology or the crisis situation of international war. The first is unlikely without the second. The second threatens the very existence of the state-society. Thus sustained peace holds forth the possibility of conversion to an authoritarian dictatorship and the slow emergence of varying degrees of political, organizational, economic, social and individual democracy. The regime may survive but only at the price of internal change.

3. STRATIFICATION

What effect does stratification have on the power structure of society?

An extreme answer to this question is provided by Mosca's version of the myth of central omnipotence. In all societies, according to Mosca, "two classes appear—a class that rules and a class that is ruled. The first class, always the less numerous, performs all political functions, monopolizes power and enjoys the advantages that power brings . . . (1939, p. 50). Marx and Engels were more realistic. In dealing with earlier periods of history they recognized many classes in society. Although in dealing with the midnineteenth century they narrowed down to two great classes, the bourgeoisie and the proletariat, they recognized various substrata within cach. Above all, their theory of class conflict recognized the existence of a certain amount of proletarian power (as distinguished from formal authority) rather than a complete monopoly of power by the bourgeoisie. A Marxian analysis of the class structure of any society is in fact a tool for discovering its power structure.

Any analysis of social strata, however, must use far more tools than those provided by old-fashioned or modernized Marxism. It must recognize all the determinants of social status other than economic roles. It must deal with the full range of strata in society and with mobility within classes and from one class to another. It must be able to cope with the special type of class system found in India's four great *varnas*, the thousands of *jatis* or subcastes which compose the *varnas*, and the "outcastes."

Above all, in analyzing social strata we must take pains to recognize the new-style stratification ushered in by the administrative revolution. This is a stratification based largely on position within the formal hierarchy of organizations, modified by a ranking of various organizations and occupations. A person's salary or other income attached to any position is particularly important. As a common measure applicable to all organizations, it provides a quick first approximation that can then be modified in the light of other considerations. With an increasing number of fine gradations and distinctions, the old lines between "proletariat," the "bourgeoisie," and "nobility" become meaningless. The term "middle class" becomes vestigial verbiage.

In considering the effect of stratification on the diffusion of power, the first consideration is the extent of mobility that is possible from one stratum to a higher one. If people are frozen to one lower stratum by a class or caste to which they have been born, this is the greatest of all limitations on social democracy. It usually means a low level of economic and organizational democracy. At the same time, within the limits of their frozen position, they may enjoy a certain amount of individual democracy. They may even play a role in political democracy.

Similarly, when there is a high degree of mobility, stratification serves as a contribution to organizational, economic and social democracy—without necessarily impinging upon political or individual democracy. It is not easy to climb a ladder with elastic or invisible rungs. The hierarchies of large-scale organization often provide ladders and rungs that can be depended upon—or at least provide a healthy challenge to people with ability, energy and ambition.

Nor should it be thought that the existence of a top stratum implies a major concentration of power at the top. In India, for example, the highest castes are of the Brahmin *varna*. Historically, the Brahmins have supplied India with most of its intellectuals and top priests. The second category, the Kshatriyas or warriors, comprised those castes which legitimated their status as traditional kings and lesser rulers. In India and in all other countries there are many areas of decision-making that are handled almost entirely by people in the lower strata, and where higher strata people would not be either willing or able to intrude. It might also be added that the peculiar pattern of power diffusion provided by the Indian style of caste system is entirely inconsistent with the power pattern of modern totalitarianism. Strange as it may sound, the caste system in India is a barrier to both democracy *and* totalitarianism.

In considering the relation of stratification to power, however, we must remember that no social stratum—no matter how tight and clear its boundaries may be—is equivalent to a center of power. At the most, it represents a power potential based on an underlying communality of interests. This potential is not automatically realized. It must be exploited by leaders and organizers. Moreover, the communality of interests may also be interwoven with—and usually is—all sorts of divergent or conflicting interests. These too may be exploited through organized effort. The most that a class will do is drift aimlessly, respond haphazardly to stimuli from various directions, or follow in the wake of one or more centers of organized action. In any of these cases, power is mobilized not by classes or more specialized strata but rather by organized groups—whether political parties, government agencies, business organizations, associations or, religious groups—or clusters and constellations of such groups. Hence for the purpose of understanding social change, the analysis of social strata provides us merely with the essential background for the analysis of the actual array of organizations.

D. *The Value Structure*

THE VALUE STRUCTURE of a society is *a patterned set of general attitudes concerning what is desirable or undesirable.* It expresses the way in which the basic human interests of survival, commergence, differentiation and self-development have emerged in that society. At a higher level of generality than specific purposes, it indicates how people behave in trying to satisfy these interests.

No organization can escape the value structure of the society in which it operates. It is not merely something that affects the organization through its relations with the external environment. It enters the organization through the values of its members and is thus moulding the very "personality" of the organization itself.

Nor can the members of any organization—whether government agency, corporation, or union—escape a serious "culture shock" when they enter into intimate relations with organizations in other societies. Apart from the simpler difficulties resulting from differences in language, food, and climate, they are bound to receive a cumulative series of "sudden jolts" resulting from differences in basic values (Cleveland, Mangone and Adams, 1960, p. 26-45). This may easily lead to an exaggerated conception as to the nature of these differences.

There is probably no aspect of any society more difficult to analyze than its value structure. The "cultural relativity" approach of sociologists and anthropologists has tended to overemphasize the differences among societies. As Kluckhohn has pointed out, too little research has yet been done on the universal values that stem from the physiological, psychological, and social similarities of people in all societies (in Parsons and Shils, 1951, p. 395). In any society, moreover, values vary considerably in intensity, durability, and extensiveness throughout a population. Value conflicts and sharp deviations from both proclaimed and accepted values are inescapable. Values are rooted in allegiances to particular organizations and organizational roles. They are deeply affected by a great variety of beliefs and disbeliefs, both religious and secular. It is small wonder, therefore, that studies of values often lead to long lists ranging from high metaphysical abstractions to specific preferences, prescriptions and prohibitions.

For the purposes of our study, we shall concentrate upon a small number of elements that enter every value structure and have an unmistakable effect on organizational activity. By emphasizing the varying forms in which they appear we hope to avoid the traps awaiting those who use ready-made stereotypes of "national character."

1. NATIONALISM AND LOCALISM

Nationalism is a conspicuous element in the value structure of many societies. It provides the "sense of identity" which is as important for a society as it is for an individual. By emphasizing common national interests or traits, it meets human needs for commergence. By emphasizing national pride, honor, and power, it meets human needs for differentiation.

The common element in all nationalism is the consciousness or display of differences. This is expressed in terms of not only a special cultural heritage but also an innate sense of national superiority. The sons of Israel were not the only "chosen people." The native tribes of North and South America looked down on the invaders from Europe. The Africans and Malayans felt themselves superior in many ways to the traders and settlers from India and China. The Indians and Chinese know they are superior to the North Americans with respect to "things that really matter." People in the U.S.A. tend to regard the "American way of life" as the best in the world, to be at least admired, if not copied, by others.

Beyond this common core there are many differences. One of these can be expressed by the continuum between the polar extremes of what Williams calls "totalistic" and "pluralistic" nationalism (1960, p. 456-460). The former is a "100 per cent" attitude of fanatical devotion to some vague national myths. Externally, it is expressed in isolationist or autarchic attempts to withdraw from the world or expansionist efforts to dominate it. Internally, it is expressed in discriminatory attitudes toward minority groups, thus impeding the development of organizational, social, and individual democracy. "Pluralistic" nationalism, on the other hand, emphasizes such specific values as democracy, religious freedom, or higher living standards. In a more quiet and less flamboyant way, it may be no less a source of national pride and honor. Either form of nationalism, in turn, may well lead to the adjustment of organizational purposes to take into account the "national interest."

Another difference lies in the extent of subnationalism within a society. In a country like India, with at least fourteen linguistic areas and separable cultural backgrounds, local loyalties are so great as to hold forth the constant threat of separatist movements. Under such circumstances national values may be little more than a thin veneer. In countries where important local and regional values are represented in the national power structure, separatism is unthinkable. In fact, the conflict among local values may be an integrating rather than a divisive force. Similarly, the binational loyalties of Japanese-Americans, Irish-American and Italian-Americans—when not carried to an extreme point—may strengthen instead of weaken national spirit in the U.S.A. Nor need nationalism itself necessarily be an impediment to supranational values. With the growth of the European community the Frenchmen who consider themselves Europeans do not necessarily give up being Frenchmen. Multiple membership and multiple loyalties are social phenomena capable of covering international groupings as well as the family, workplace, church, and club.

2. INDIVIDUAL AND GROUP INTEREST

Another variable is the extent to which the people of any society are oriented toward the satisfaction of individual or group interests. For Parsons, this is the "pattern variable" of "self orientation" versus "collectivity orientation," for Kluckhohn the "self-other" dichotomy, and for countless others the continuum from individualism, freedom, or autonomy, to conformity, standardization, and control. The importance of this variable to the administration of organizations is obvious. It affects the purpose patterns of organizations, the extent of cooperation that can be expected, and the usefulness of alternative administrative practices.

Yet there are few social values as misleading or as hotly debated as this one. In human society self interest and group interest are always intertwined; neither can exist in isolation from the other. The various patterns of intertwining are exceedingly complex. Their nature, moreover, is frequently beclouded by proclaimed values which serve to embroider more dominant values. The more dominant values, in turn, may be sharply conflicting. Thus along with individual personality, equality, and freedom Williams lists external conformity as a dominant value in the U.S.A. (1960, p. 450-454). Thus the "classic" values of American democracy have been expressed in the ideas of the dignity of the individual, "rugged individualism," opposition to tyranny, impatience with hierarchical authority. At the same time America has traditionally been a "nation of joiners." The most rugged individualists were organization builders. The most vehement opponents of governmental hierarchy either are at or aspire to the upper levels of nongovernment hierarchies. The devotees of the "sacredness of the human personality" may themselves be "cheerful robots" carefully conforming to the standards of their organization or social stratum.

In part, these contradictions can be resolved by distinguishing between the values placed on different groups. In one society the self may be more closely identified with families, in another with private groups or associations. In one society government may be seen as a far-away or hostile entity, in another as an instrument for limited ends, in still another as more completely linked with self interest.

In part, they can be resolved by focussing on specific kinds of behavior. In some societies the value of the individual is illustrated by laws against suicide, while in others *hari-kari* or *suttee* may be permissible. In some societies the importance of protecting all individuals against injustice leads to universalistic regulations tempered by nondiscriminatory efforts at judicial equity proceedings. In other societies the approach is more particularistic in the first instance, with justice considered more in terms of each individual's social status.

Yet contradictions in this area cannot be avoided. Genuine conformity to group interests may be associated with a large amount of individual autonomy. It may, in fact, as Dalton has found, serve as protective coloration for covert "freewheeling" (*Dalton*, 1959). Or, as Williams has suggested, "the looser the package, the tighter the string—if the package is to hold together at all" (1960, p. 453).

3. ACCEPTANCE vs. ACTIVISM

A more clearly dichotomous variable is found in the continuum from acceptance to activism.

In some societies it seems natural and expedient to accept the world as it is or events as they develop. Whatever is, is by that token acceptable. Whatever happens would have happened anyway. The present order of human relations cannot be changed, so why try? It is not given to man to fathom the order in human nature. Anyone—other than a magician—who thinks he can read the future is a madman. Anyone who tries to do much to control it is a fool whom the gods will probably destroy. In such societies high value is placed upon leisure, inactivity, contemplation, and mysticism. Activism is reserved for a privileged few who must also make their obeisances to the unknown and the inscrutable.

In other societies, particularly those already hit by the ongoing wave of the administrative revolution, we find what Parsons refers to as "instrumental activism" (1951, p. 180-200). Here, in contrast, we find widespread acceptance of the idea of human progress based on a more orderly, predictable universe and on the power of human rationality as expressed in science and technology. At times this idea of progress will be expressed in grandiose messianic visions of Heaven on earth, of a world without poverty, despair, or unhappiness. At times it will be concretized by what the economists call the "demonstration effect" of the benefits that others have achieved through the more rational production and distribution of goods and services. This is the "revolution of rising expectations," expectations that are not limited to economics but are founded on the more general assumption that any aspect of the world can be changed by activism. Instead of thinking of the future in terms of the next few centuries, people tend to concentrate on four, five or six year plans. They divide up the future into scheduled activities. They develop and constantly refine conceptions of economy, efficiency and practicality. People are expected to "keep busy," "do something," and "get someplace in the world." In such societies the task of administering an organization is entirely different than in those where acceptance is still a dominant factor. Activity, speed, and technique become human values in their own right.

But here, too, although the differences are much greater than in the case of self and group interest, there are internal contradictions in every society. Where acceptance values have long been dominant, newer generations are bound to become activists and fight the older generations on this ground. Where activism has long been established, a growing number of people will start to wonder where they are really going.

4. THE "SPIRIT" AND MATERIALISM

In some societies the greatest values are placed on "things of the spirit." People and relations with them are deemed more important than goods or services. The mass of the people places great emphasis on ritual, custom, and ceremonies. The elite are interested in esthetic matters. The nonactivist elite are given over to a life of contemplation. Faith or mysticism are dominant elements of religion and philosophy.

In the more materialist society, material comforts—from the simplest necessities of life to the greatest of luxuries—rank at the top level of desirability. The hope of a higher level of consumption is the major motivator in economic growth. The promise of a higher level of consumption—apart from due attention to external threats—is the major promise of political leaders. "Conspicuous consumption" becomes a principle that shapes not only the dress, eating, housing, and locomotion of individuals and families, but also the buildings, furnishings and *décor* of corporations, associations, and government agencies. Nor is it limited to goods. Materialism also embraces the less tangible services provided by multitudinous adviser assistants or servants and by athletics, recreation, and entertainment. Tremendous energies are dedicated to the design, production and aggressive marketing of an increasing variety of all these material comforts.

This distinction has been used by Northrop (1946) in trying to define the difference between Eastern and Western civilizations. He finds the "highly ineffable and mystical quality of Oriental culture" rooted in concentrated attention "upon the nature of all things in their emotional and ethetic, purely empirical and positivist immediacy." Western civilization, in contrast, is oriented toward materialist conceptions of utility and economy. This leads to rational and nonmystical theory, science, and technology. The "reconciliation of the East and the West" can best be found, Northrop urges, by achieving a society which combines the orderly, scientific and systematic values of the West "with the compassion, the universal sensitivity to the beautiful, and the abiding equanimity and calm joy of the spirit which characterizes the sages and many of the humbler people of the Orient."

The two approaches, however, are in fact often combined under less impressive circumstances. Many of the "humble people of the Orient" have been thoroughly enslaved by the unavoidable, and ultramaterialistic, preoccupation with where, when, and how they and their children get their next meal. "Abiding equanimity" can be sharply disturbed by the intrusion of destitution and disease. The effort to introduce Western living standards and Western methods of attaining them has often led Easterners to a deeper and more thoroughgoing materialism than their most critical sages could possibly find and condemn in the West. On the other hand, many Westerners whose material appetites are easily satiated are mainly interested in things of the spirit. They may hide these interests behind the more publicly accepted façade of a drive for prestige, power or money. Behind this façade, freed from any concern with additional material comforts, they give themselves over to the life of learning, emotional and esthetic creativity and self-development.

5. COMMUNICATION

Other differences among societies are found in the varying values placed on alternative modes of communication. Organizational and administrative behavior in different cultures may be deeply affected by the balance between verbal and nonverbal communication, the pace of communication, the balance between honesty and deviousness, and the degree of indirection or directness. Hammond points out that indirection in communication is highly institutionalized in non-Western societies. In contrast, he finds (although without indicating that he has examined the American scene carefully enough) that it "is negatively sanctioned in American culture and must be relied upon covertly (1959). In his study of friction between Americans and Mexicans in Mexico, Fayerweather (1959, p. 25-27) reports that in Mexico indirection is used much more than in the United States as a means of avoiding tensions and conflicts. The formalities of etiquette, protocol, and organizational rituals, which differ extensively from country to country, are themselves often devices for channeling communication toward relief from tension and conflict. In some societies written communications also serve as a means of avoiding the possible tensions inherent in person-to-person relationships. In others they are often used as a mere convenience in facilitating person-to-person discussions, as with the case of discussion drafts. In still others this usage is rare; once it is written down a message acquires an aura of formal authority placing it beyond the realm of discussion.

But there is more to language than words alone. As Hall pointed out (1961), every culture has informal communication patterns. Some of these are found in the tone of voice or "superfix." Others are found in gestures, the contexts in which words are used, and even in the distance between two people who are talking with each other. The words alone express little more than the score of a Beethoven symphony. The specific culture of the society converts the formal notation into genuine music.

In all societies the basic network of communication is provided by face-to-face contacts. A major overlay is provided by the more impersonal communication networks of larger and more bureaucratic organizations. This overlay becomes deeper with the development of the administrative revolution. At the same time, a third layer comes into being with the development of the mass media organizations of the press, radio, television and cinema. This creates a complex communication system in which it is possible for increasingly large quantities of information to move with increasing speed through ever wider segments of the population. The very abundance of information enhances the role of interpreters and opinion leaders. Without them the top executives of large organizations—even more than ordinary people—would be helpless in the face of the growing information overload. This is an adaptation of "the two-step flow of communication" hypothesis set forth in Katz and Lazarsfeld (1955).

Part III

STRUCTURE

Chapter 8

THE HUMAN BEINGS

*T*HE BEHAVIOR OF PEOPLE, as stated in Chapter 2, is at the very heart of the administrative process. The study of administration depends upon, or is a part of, nothing less than the study of man. The acceptance of this idea is a prerequisite for any serious study of people in organizations and their guidance by administrators. The study of organizational purposes must start with an understanding of the purposeful behavior of human beings.

One way to achieve such an understanding is to flee the world of ordered, systematic thought and research and turn to art and literature. In the works of Shakespeare, Goethe, Dostoevski, and the countless unnamed authors of the Bible, the *Mahabhrata* and other national epics, we can undoubtedly find genuine insights into the nature of man. Here there stretches out before our eyes the vast spectrum of the human comedy.

Yet at one small spot on this spectrum we find a whirling cloud in which psychologists, psychiatrists, psychoanalysts, sociologists, anthropologists, and physiologists use different languages to express divergent views on the spectrum as a whole. And at a small spot behind this welter of words we can find something approaching consensus on a few fundamental propositions concerning the nature of man. Among these are the following:

1. The purposeful behavior of human beings is motivated by a multiplicity of interests.
2. Human beings are always part of some specific group environment.
3. Conflict is an inevitable part of human nature.
4. Human beings are unique personalities.
5. A large part of human behavior is irrational or nonrational.

In selecting these propositions I have not chosen all those ideas which students of psychology might agree upon or regard as most important. I have selected those which, in disposing of certain popular fallacies concerning human behavior, are particularly useful in the foundation of a general theory of administration. In elaborating upon them, moreover, I have found it necessary to do a certain amount of adaptation and remodelling. This may remove some of them from the area of consensus. Yet in my judgment it brings them closer to the insights of art and literature and the wisdom of experienced administrators. It moves them more fully into the area of immediate relevance to administrative practice and theory.

A. *The Multiplicity of Individual Interests*

THE PROPOSITION that "the purposeful behavior of human beings is motivated by a multiplicity of interests" stands in direct opposition to various fallacies of single motivation. It conflicts with any theory that focuses on economic gain, sex, or something else as *the* sole or determining object of human desire and that subordinates or ignores all other objects. A single motivation theory is acceptable only if one maintains a sharp distinction between real human beings and the economist's "economic man" or the "sex-driven man" appearing in popular misconceptions of Freud. It becomes dangerous only when one forgets this distinction and tries to force the variability of human behavior into the procrustean bed of a single-factor explanation.

As an easy alternative to single motivation theory, we can readily prepare long lists of instincts, urges, drives, interests, needs, and desires. Yet by so doing we would jump from the frying pan of oversimplification into the fire of utter confusion.

A more ordered, but still flexible, approach is provided by dividing human interests or needs into the four broad categories of survival, commergence[1] (or belonging), differentiation and self-development. This

1. For further explanation of this term, see page 174.

is merely a way of saying that people are interested in surviving, in being "a part" of something else, of being somewhat "apart" from others, and in developing their full potentialities.

To this extremely simple statement might be added the additional point that many actions satisfy all these interests at once, albeit in different proportions. Thus a person's work may provide him with the economic prerequisites of survival, the satisfaction of working with certain people, a certain amount of prestige, and an opportunity for developing his creative abilities. If you ask him today what his purpose is, he may answer that it is "to finish ABC, which is supposed to be completed by the end of the week." ABC may be an assembly job, a memorandum or an investigation. Whatever it is, if it is a goal to which he orients himself with a large amount of dedicated energy, we may be sure that in doing so he is probably motivated by a varied set of mutually-reinforcing personal interests.

The relation between various interests, however, is extremely complex. The motive power of any one interest may be greatly affected by the extent to which others are gratified or frustrated. Activities seen as relating to one type of interest may in fact serve as a substitute for action to meet another interest.

Above all, there is reason to suspect the operation of a certain hierarchy of interests. When survival interests are satisfied and there is a reasonable basis for confidence in their continued satisfaction, they are no longer powerful motivators. Commergence and differentiation interests may now become much more important. With greater faith in their continued satisfaction, the higher interests in self-development may emerge more fully. At this level a high degree of satisfaction is rarely possible, and so these higher interests may continue as powerful motivators. It is in this sense that A. H. Maslow holds that psychological health, instead of being the absence of disease, is essentially the gratification of ever-higher needs (1954, Chaps. 4, 5, and 8).

The following four categories of survival, commergence, differentiation, and self-development are an adaptation of Maslow's analysis.

1. SURVIVAL: PHYSIOLOGY, SAFETY, ACTIVITY

In order to survive, a person must provide a minimum degree of satisfaction for certain basic physiological interests.

Among the most obvious are the interests in food, drink, sleep, and sex. Less clear, but often directly reflected in the appetites, are the needs of the blood stream for certain proportions of water, salt, and sugar and the needs of the body for various minerals, hormones, and vitamins.

Closer to the safety needs are the physiological needs for protection against weather, injury, and disease, needs which are met through various forms of housing, clothing, and medical care.

Survival also requires protection against physical attack by animals or other human beings. These interests are usually met through weapons, the designation of special security forces, resistance to attack, and, on many occasions, preventive action designed to wipe out sources of potential aggression.

Other safety needs are related to the dangers of interference with the arrangements people have worked out to meet their physiological needs. Instability and unpredictability are threats to all orderly arrangements. Unemployment is a direct threat to the satisfaction of the needs for food, shelter, clothing, and medical care. Hence the deep-rooted human interest in economic security.

When a person perceives serious threats to the satisfaction of certain survival interests, these interests may become the most important things in life. Man does indeed not live by bread alone. But as Maslow maintains, the qualification of "Unless he has no bread" must be added.

> For the man who is extremely and dangerously hungry, no other interests exist but food. He dreams food, he remembers food, he thinks about food, he emotes only about food, he perceives only food, and he wants only food. The more subtle determinants that ordinarily fuse with the physiological drives in organizing even feeding, drinking, or sexual behavior, may now be so completely overwhelmed as to allow us to speak at this time (but only at this time) of pure hunger drive and behavior, with the one unqualified aim of relief (*Ibid.*, p. 82).

Similar statements can be made about other extreme deprivations or threats. This is why in time of great crisis—war, famine, pestilence and mass depression—the motivations of people tend to become more simple, similar, and predictable.

In periods of purely personal crisis, the frustration of survival interests other than food and sleep may lead to puzzling substitution phenomena. Thus serious threats to economic security may lead to a preoccupation with sex. The thwarting of sexual gratification may result in a preoccupation with food. When the young infant sees recurring threats to his very survival, the result may be a compulsive-obsessive neurosis during all his adult days. Drawing upon a wealth of psychiatric data, Maslow describes such cases as follows:

> Compulsive-obsessives try frantically to order and stabilize the world so that no unmanageable, unexpected or unfamiliar dangers will ever appear. They hedge themselves about with all sorts of ceremonials, rules and formulas so that every possible contingency may be provided for and

so that no new contingencies may appear. . . . If, through no fault of their own, something unexpected does occur, they go into a panic reaction. . . . The healthy taste for the novel or the unknown is missing or at a minimum in the average neurotic (*Ibid.*, p. 89).

One of the most elemental of all interests is the interest in continuing to live. "The only certainty that men have is that they must die. And yet," as Ferrero has pointed out, "they all live, until the arrival of death, as though they were immortal. . . . They fight against death until the very last moment" (1942, p. 311). Despite progress in extending life, this fight can be only temporarily successful. No matter how much people may deceive themselves, insecurity on this point is unavoidable. This explains the popularity of various substitute measures—from sexual reproduction and the construction of monuments to the religious belief in life after death.

Another elemental need is activity for its own sake. The human organism is not designed for complete idleness. Either body or mind, and usually both, must reach some minimum level of activity. Under special conditions induced by drugs, hypnosis, or perhaps extremely low temperatures, it may be possible to maintain human life for long periods with little or no activity. But under usual conditions, inactivity means decay, disintegration, and death. People simply must do *something*.

As one succeeds in meeting his physiological, safety, and activity interests, he attains a certain feeling of relief. But this relief may well be associated with emptiness. What seemed so important before attained is no longer of much importance. Although he may still take action to meet recurring survival needs and to strengthen his confidence in their continued gratification, they are no longer powerful motivators. Mere life and activity for their own sake alone seems useless.

We can thus appreciate the problem faced by all political parties which have developed their strength by action designed to meet people's interests in economic security. When people are no longer worried about economic insecurity, the old slogans and appeals lose much of their former magic. This is one of the reasons for the decline of the British Labor Party subsequent to its successes with its full employment program after World War II. It is one of the reasons why, after the economic reforms of the Roosevelt New Deal in the United States of America, the Democratic Party has never been able to get back to its peak of previous popular support. It is why a trade union which succeeds in achieving economic security for its members often needs the compulsion of a "check-off system" in order to keep its members in the union. It is why employers' efforts to motivate workers by economic rewards alone may often end in utter failure.

Problems such as these are at the root of the widespread question "After X, what?" Depending upon how the X is filled in, this question takes many forms. Among these are: "After peace . . . or security . . . or affluence . . . what?" Each of these questions implies that there are and must be some other purposes in life than merely satisfying basic survival interests

2. COMMERGENCE: BELONGING, CONFORMITY, AFFECTION

According to Maslow, once survival needs are fairly well gratified, "there will emerge the love and affection and belonging needs, and the whole cycle already described will repeat itself with this new center." "Submergence" would be an excellent word to express the common element of becoming a part of something larger than one's self rather than remaining a thing apart. However, since this word carries overtones of "submerged" in the sense of "exploited" or "drowned," "commergence" is used instead. Although a new word, it vividly expresses the ideas of closeness, togetherness, and identification.

The interest in belonging to some group or groups is very closely associated with safety needs. Few people are strong enough to stand against attack without support from others. But belonging and togetherness have value in themselves, apart from their clear contribution to security. People obtain gratification from merely being a member of a family, a work group, a nationality group, a political party. They obtain more direct satisfactions from belonging to someone or some group that will meet their needs "to be nursed, supported, sustained, surrounded, protected, loved, advised, guided, indulged, forgiven, consoled" (Murray et al., 1938, p. 182).

The usual price of belonging to some group is conformity with its accepted codes on patterns of behavior. In minor things, this means following the fad and the fashion with respect to clothes, demeanor, and speech—a phenomenon adults can best understand when viewing the behavior of children and adolescents. In more important matters, it means conforming with the customs and mores concerning sex, treatment of children and parents, communication methods, and the balancing of conflicting interests. The need for conformity, heightened by the normal processes of acculturation, is often so great that deviations from accepted codes will often lead to bitter self-punishment through an overwhelming sense of guilt. As the Freudians have demonstrated, this punishment may be at its deadliest when the sense of guilt is pushed into the preconscious and the unconscious mental processes.

Commergence can also mean affection, an emotional sense of attachment. A person's needs for affection can be at least partly met through the simple process of day-to-day interaction with a colleague—even a rival—at the place of work or in the office. In this sense commergence is a positive relief from loneliness. It should not, however, be confused with love; the word "love" is taken in vain more than the name of any deity. It is often said of an administrator that "he is in love with his organization." This often refers to the affection felt by one who is incapable of loving.

Like any other interests, commergence interests may be met in extreme ways. Belonging may be carried to the point of denying individuality. This is the horror envisioned in the literature of antiorganizational revolt.

Conformity may become utter submissiveness to authority or complete dependence on others. Affection may become a form of escape from the harshness of changing society. This is the defeatist picture presented by Matthew Arnold in "Dover Beach," in which the poet sees nothing but love as worth living for in a world of lost faith and armed might.

But as Erich Fromm has pointed out, the cry "Ah, love let us be true to one another" is, in this context, merely an effort to find "a refuge from an unbearable sense of loneliness . . . an alliance of two against the world . . . this egoism *à deux* is mistaken for love and intimacy" (1956, p. 88). In a more extreme form commergence becomes a mystic identification with the universe, a psychological release from the bonds of individual human existence (as with the negative aspects of the Indian *nirvana* and *moksha*), a complete joining with the world of nature through death and disintegration.

As a person achieves the satisfaction of commergence interests, he feels that he has arrived. He can now sink his roots. But so can a tree. This is usually not enough for a man or woman.

Thus here too we hear the question "After X, what?" Is belonging enough? Are togetherness and affection our highest goals?

3. DIFFERENTIATION: STATUS, RESPECT, POWER

The differentiation interests often appear to be merely the other side of the coin from commergence. The need to be the same as others is closely allied with the need to be at least a little different.

Yet differentiation tends to follow, rather than accompany, identification. One can usually afford to be different only when one already belongs. The obvious exception to this principle is the case of the ingrained outsider, the "isolate" or the rejected person who compensates for his apartness by conspicuous deviation.

The essence of all systems of status is that by ranking people in various orders they provide a clear system of differentiation. They meet the individual's need not only to have some place in the world, but a special place. Their effectiveness is based, among other things, on the fact that status differentiation can usually be depended upon irrespective of what a person might do. Except for the people at the very bottom of the totem pole, this assures at least a bare minimum of deference and perhaps some prestige along with it.

Respect is another matter. It is not given so readily, nor can it be automatically maintained. Genuine self-respect is probably harder to achieve and maintain than the respect of others. In either form, respect depends upon perceived performance or acknowledged status.

The sharpest form of differentiation is found in the wielding of personal power. The mover and the shaker clearly separates himself from the moved and the shaken, the dominator from the dominated, the aggressor from his victim. Economic, government, political, and religious organizations include many people—usually their most active members—whose needs for survival, belonging, status, and respect are well gratified. It is hard to explain their behavior except in terms of their deep-seated needs for more power and more secure power.

A person's interest in power may be expressed in many forms. For all those who yearn to shape great events, there are probably far more who feel an equally deep need to dominate just a few other people. In the case of a parent, it may be a need to dominate a helpless child—or an equally helpless mate. Or it may take the more positive form of nurturance needs, the needs "to give sympathy and gratify the needs of a helpless other: an infant or another that is weak, disabled, tired, inexperienced, infirm, defeated, humiliated, lonely, defected, sick, mentally confused. To assist another in danger. To feed, help, support, console, protect, comfort, nurse, heal" (Murray *et al.*, 1938, p. 182).

In any of their forms the differentiation interests are closely associated with the emergence of the ego and the sense of personal identity. As Maslow points out, these needs (which he prefers to call "esteem needs"), relatively neglected by Freud, were stressed by Adler and his followers and have since won widespread recognition among both psychoanalysts and clinical psychologists. There is general acknowledgment today that the "thwarting of these needs produces feelings of insecurity, of weakness and of helplessness. These feelings in turn give rise to either basic discouragement or else compensatory or neurotic trends." On the other hand, the satisfaction of these needs may lead to "feelings of self-confidence, worth, strength, capability and adequacy..." (1954, p. 90-91).

As a person achieves a certain level of satisfaction of his differentiation interests, he experiences a sense of elation interwoven with feelings of superiority. Yet this too pales. He may seek to restore the lost elation by straining for ever larger amounts of status, respect and power. If he succeeds, his victory may be counterbalanced by actions which, while necessary to make him stand more apart from others, have the indirect effect of making him less a part of anything else and even jeopardizing his personal survival. And the personal fruits of such a victory will be unquestionably diminished by the inexorable operation of the law of diminishing returns. He will be caught on the endless wheel of seeking more and more from life and, in fact, getting less and less.

So once again, we confront the question "After X, what?" What does it matter if we gain status, respect, and power and lose our souls in the effort?

4. SELF-DEVELOPMENT: LEARNING, CREATIVITY, LOVE

For many centuries mankind has been groping toward a common answer to this fundamental question. Philosophers, religious leaders, and poets have used different words to stress a common theme. In modern times the words themselves have sometimes tended to converge. For Erich Fromm, the highest goal in a world of sanity is man's freedom "to be himself, to be productive, to be fully awake" and to "respond to the world with our senses in a meaningful, skilled, productive, active and shared way" (1955, p. 347, 355). For Karen Horney, the goal is "spontaneity of feeling, an awareness and aliveness of feeling . . .the striving for wholeheartedness" in a context of mutual sharing and understanding (1955, p. 241-242). For Hans Selye, the endocrinologist, "man's ultimate aim is to express himself as fully as possible, according to his own lights" (1956, p. 299). Kurt Goldstein, the biologist and psychologist, finds the unifying concept needed to explain the diversity of human behavior in "the tendency of the organism to actualize itself. . . . The organism has definite potentialities and because it has them it has the need to actualize or realize them. The fulfillment of these needs represents the self-actualization of the organism" (1930, p. 203-204). Using Goldstein's term, Maslow elaborates the same theme in the following manner:

It [self-actualization] refers to a man's desire for self-fulfillment, namely to the tendency for him to become actualized in what he is potentially. This tendency might be phrased as the desire to become more and more what one is, to become everything that one is capable of becoming.

The specific form that these needs will take will of course vary greatly from one person to another. In one individual it may take the form of the desire to be an ideal mother, in another it may be expressed athletically, and in still another it may be expressed in painting pictures or in inventions (1954, p. 91-92).

The clear emergence of these needs, according to Maslow, depends upon prior satisfaction of the physiological, safety, belonging, and esteem needs. In fact, the steady gratification of these needs during one's early formative years can go a long way toward freeing a person from over-concentration on these needs in his later years. He can thus become more of an autonomous, self-actualizing person. In time of crisis he is also more capable of withstanding the frustration of any needs.

The difficulty with the term "self-actualization" is that it carries with it certain overtones of predestination, as though the self-actualizing person is working out some predetermined pattern. This same connotation attaches itself to the terms "self-fulfillment" and "self-realization." Another connotation is that self-actualization, self-fulfillment, or self-realization necessarily lead to some final state in which they have at last been achieved. In my judgment, "self-development" is a more adaptable term. Its use helps emphasize that at this point we are discussing action, never completely predetermined, to meet needs that can never be completely fulfilled. It helps stress the role of individual will and effort, as contrasted with an automatic process. It suggests an important relation between self-development and national development.

No matter which term is used, this basic idea has many facets. One of these is the interest in learning. Maslow divides this area into two parts. At a somewhat lower level he identifies the desire to know, as may be expressed in simple curiosity. At a somewhat higher level he finds that "after we know, we are impelled to know more and more minutely and microscopically on the one hand; and on the other, more and more extensively in the direction of a world philosophy, theology, etc. The facts that we acquire, if they are isolated or atomistic, inevitably get theorized about, and either analyzed or organized or both. This process has been phrased by some as the search for meaning. We shall then postulate a desire to understand, to systematize, or organize, to analyze, to look for revelations and meaning, to construct a system of values" (*Ibid.*, p. 96-97). At either level, knowing or understanding, learning is a process of growth, a process through which one becomes something more than one was before.

Another facet is the interest in self-expression. Actions to meet this need are often closely intertwined with actions of commergence, differentiation, or both. Yet in freer and more spontaneous forms these actions transcend the lower interests. The boy whistling in the fields, the girl singing to herself, the novelist or sculptor who really does not care what people think of his work—these are all meeting their needs for self-expression.

Self-development also involves the interest in creativity. Learning and self-expression are themselves creative activities. But the higher forms of creativity get somewhat beyond the self-involvement of both of these. Nor should creativity be thought of as something limited to the rarified atmosphere of the artist, the scientist and the intellectual. It can be much more humble. There can be creative shoemakers and carpenters—and creative foremen, division heads, top executives, and members of directorates. Maslow expresses this as follows:

> The creativeness of the self-actualized man seems rather to be kin to the naive and universal creativeness of unspoiled children. It seems to be more a fundamental characteristic of common human nature—a potentiality given to all human beings at birth. Most human beings lose this as they become enculturated, but some few individuals seem either to retain this fresh and naive, direct way of looking at life, or if they have lost it, as most people do, they later in life recover it. . . .
> If there were no choking-off forces, we might expect that every human being would show this special type of creativeness (*Ibid.*, p. 223-224).

While self-developing activity is rooted in actions that may serve to satisfy all one's interests, its most essential characteristic is that it enables one to transcend his interests. It is in this sense that self-development is on the borderline between motivated behavior and those forms of highly spontaneous behavior that lie beyond motivation. This, of course, is the essential characteristic of anything that can be called an ultimate aim. As an ultimate, it is purposeless. "The mystic experience, the experience of awe, of delight, of wonder, of mystery, and of admiration are all subjectively rich experiences that beat their way in upon the organism, flooding it as music does. These too are end experiences, ultimate rather than instrumental . . ." (*Ibid.*, p. 300). In this sense self-development is very close to the positive aspects of *nirvana* or *moksha;* it is a release from one's lower needs and a uniting with all mankind.

I doubt whether self-development can ever proceed very far if strictly ego-centered. True self-development involves an enlargement or broadening of the ego, an extension of the self so that it covers much more than self, a fusion or integration between the ego and others. In Selye's words, it involves a process which parallels the historic evolution of the single cell into intercellular altruism, the evolution of egotism into interpersonal altruism (1956, p. 282-283). This is self-development on behalf of interests broader than one's self.

At this level, self-development becomes a form of love. By "love"

I am not referring to the many things that masquerade under this much-abused term—not to sexual titillation, the accommodating exchange of favors and conveniences, the neurotic desire to dominate or be dominated, the idolatrous worshipping of a false image on a pedestal, and not the sentimental phantasies and daydreams so widely peddled by the cinema, radio and television, magazine "love" stories, and popular "love" songs. I am referring rather to love in the sense so brilliantly set forth by Erich Fromm (1956). This is love in the sense of a sustained activity of uniting with others. It may appear in the form of brotherly love, parental love, erotic love, self-love (quite different from selfishness), or the love of God in the sense that "God" is a symbol of all that is wonderful and beautiful in man and nature. It involves "the active concern for the life and growth of that which we love." It involves a responsibility for the psychic needs of others, a responsibility based upon knowledge. Above all, it means giving of one's self, loving rather than merely being loved. The giving and the receiving are inextricably interrelated. Neither the mother who wants only to give nor the beautiful girl who wants only to get is really capable of loving or being loved. If an exchange relationship is involved, this is not the exchange with which economists are accustomed to deal. Scarcity does not appear in the same form as in the market place. While love is a game involving many elements of conflict and tension, it is also one in which both sides may win at the same time. The more one gives, the more one may have left. The more one gets, the more the other may have. In its more physiological aspects, scarcity appears much sooner; sexual appetites may in most cases be quickly relieved. But love is far more than sex. In its fullest form it involves a deep mutuality and intertwining of human interests. (*Ibid.*, Chapt. 2, p. 7-82.)

The struggle for survival may wreck others. The pursuit of commergence and differentiation may prevent others from attaining similar ends. The pursuit of self-development in the sense of learning, creativity and love has none of these indirect results. In its more modest forms it is noninjurious to others. At its best it helps others meet their own needs.

While flouting the principles of economic scarcity, self-development interests also seem to transcend the otherwise inexorable law of diminishing returns. Here there is no easy satiation. One can never learn very much, let alone enough. One can never attain an ideal peak of creative achievement. There can never be enough love or too much love. Full satisfaction of these needs is simply unattainable. The process of pursuing the satisfaction of these as distinguished from other needs may thus be the most truly satisfying thing in life.

5. THE ROLE OF ECONOMIC GAIN

From the previous discussion one might get the false impression that since personal economic gain does not appear in any of the major headings, it has no role to play in the motivation of human beings. It is therefore desirable to correct such an impression by suggesting the specific nature of economic motivation.

First of all, some form of economic gain—particularly in an exchange economy—is a prerequisite for meeting man's survival needs. Food, drink, shelter, clothing, education: all these are dependent upon money. To a certain extent, the stability of sexual gratifications, even those associated with family life, is based upon money as well. Except in the case of those with accumulated economic means, full-time activity in any organization is therefore associated with some form of economic compensation.

Second, economic rewards are often recognized symbols of one's place in life. They may serve as a measure of the extent to which one has met the needs for both commergence and differentiation. Particularly in rapidly expanding market economies, they become general indicators of status, respect and power.

Third, in addition to being a measure of power, money is a direct source of power. It is an instrument of direct control over anything that money will buy. This is a power source of no small significance particularly since money can also indirectly enable one to get the things money cannot buy. Hence the phenomenon of many private business men who are "hell-bent" for enlarging their personal power but who justify their actions publicly only in terms of the pursuit of money.

Finally, as one of the most flexible instruments ever invented, money may also serve as a partial instrument in satisfying self-development interests and as a partial measure of progress in this direction. Many highly creative and self-expressive activities may take the form of the invention of new accounting devices or even of monetary manipulation. In the business world many of the most creative and even altruistic urges to develop new products, new technologies and new departures in basic science, are intertwined with—or disguised by—monetary calculations and rationalizations.

B. *The Individual-in-the-Group*

IN DISCUSSING COMMERGENCE needs I have already indicated the strength of the motives which impel individuals to participate in various groups.

It might also be added that in a world where isolated individuals can rarely cope with even their physiological needs, some minimum degree of participation is a stark necessity.

Yet even these observations understate the fact that no individual is "an island unto himself." Through no decision of his own, man is born into a family group. He grows up as a member of various groups and from time to time makes his own decisions about attachments to or affiliations with other groups. It may thus be confidently stated that "Human beings are always part of some specific group environment."

This proposition stands in opposition to the "Robinson Crusoe" theory of economic behavior or the Great Man theory of historical explanation. At their worst, these theories purport to explain human behavior in terms of pure individualism. At their best, they regard all other factors as "exogenous" or as part of a *ceteris paribus* to be examined by someone else; they then proceed to concentrate upon a thin and artificial segment of human behavior.

At this point it is pertinent to discuss groups in general, with special emphasis upon the relationships between the individual and groups. All of these relationships are equally pertinent to those groups which we call organizations.

1. MULTIPLE GROUP ATTACHMENT

Every individual is attached in some way or other to a number of groups. The most direct form of attachment is to a single membership group. But since most membership groups are composed of subgroups, many of them concentric, this form of attachment itself involves multiple membership. Thus in the family a young boy may belong both to the family as a whole and to the smaller group of children or young people. A post office clerk belongs not only to his unit, section, and division, but also to the postal service as a whole and to the civil service as a whole. A trade union member may belong not only to his local union and to a national union, but also to general labor federation and an international labor movement. This form of multiple membership is a direct function of the complex structure of groups and organizations.

The second form of multiple membership consists of membership in a multiplicity of groups. Rarely is any one individual wholly absorbed in the activities of any one organization and its subordinate parts. To the extent that this may be true, as with the housewife who lives only in and for her family or the executive who lives only in and for the organization, we are dealing with pathological cases. It is extremely rare that a healthy human being can find sufficient satisfaction for all his needs through one group alone. The only clear exception is the infant, whose early needs are met solely within the family. But the very process of acculturation by the family leads to the emergence of needs that can be met only outside the family. Thus the child joins one or more educational institutions. As an adult, his livelihood depends upon membership in some work group. During this process of growth he becomes a member of various play or study groups and may join one or another religious, neighborhood, political, national, or professional groups. This form of multiple membership results from the breadth of human needs as contrasted with the more narrow purposes of most groups and organizations.

Finally, one may be strongly attached to the values and objectives of a certain group without actually being a member. Among social psychologists such a group is usually called a "reference group." Thus many people may be followers or "fellow travellers" of a professional organization, a trade union or a political party without wanting to become a member. A reference group may also be one whose objectives are passionately accepted as a way of demonstrating his qualifications for future acceptance into membership. Thus the top executive group of a corporation may be a powerful reference group for an aspiring junior executive. For many people, however, the most influential reference groups are those who sit on certain pinnacles of prestige to which they themselves cannot realistically aspire.

2. THE INDIVIDUAL'S SOCIAL ROLE

As well defined by the Hartleys a "social role consists of the behaviors expected of individuals occupying certain positions in specific groups" (1952, p. 516). This is one of the most important concepts not only in social psychology but in social science as a whole.

It is these mutual expectations concerning the behavior of others—and, of course, conformance with them—that make it possible for the members of a group to achieve the necessary minimum of cooperation. Without such expectations group action would collapse under the weight of over-frequent experimentation and unpredictability.

When groups become more complex as a result of size, technology, and environmental pressures, social roles themselves become more complex. The reason is the growing interdependence of behavior between the members of the group, an interdependence which may require an elaborate meshing of individual roles. In the more firmly established organizations an effort is often made to define social roles through formal job definitions, an effort often thwarted by inadequate techniques of service definition and a neglect of essential interrelationships within an organization. In any case there are limits on the extent to which human expectations can be adequately expressed in writing, even if one should assume a static situation. The expectations that underlie any social role include the expectations of many different people, including not only associates and subordinates, but also different people at higher levels of responsibility. There are always bound to be certain conflicting expectations which cannot be quickly resolved except at considerable cost or certain expectations that one person will compensate for the deficiencies, physical or mental, of another. People prefer to leave expectations of this type ambiguous or unwritten, even though this may require a little time for a newcomer to learn his role.[2]

Over any significant period of time, moreover, the situation is never static. With new problems, products, personalities and technologies, new behaviors become essential. New expectations emerge. Old roles are shaken up. Moreover, the old structure of roles is always being shaken up by the new distribution of skills. Youngsters come along who know many things their elders never learned. The old timers must adapt, give way or fight a defensive action on behalf of their time-hallowed past behavior patterns. For the youngsters also the process may also be painful. The more they advance and the higher they go, the more they must abandon previous roles and learn the requirements of new ones, and the more they are in danger of rapidly becoming "oldsters."

At the same time, social role is never defined exclusively by others. Each individual himself contributes something to it. More forceful and creative personalities may through successful performance in flexible situations establish the major outlines of their own social role. Even in rigid situations the timid soul will contribute something to the role he enacts—much as even the mediocre actor of Hamlet's part will contribute something not specified either in Shakespeare's lines or the director's instructions.

The entire situation is complicated by unavoidable defects in the communication of expectations. Superior officers, for example, may take it for granted that a subordinate knows what is expected of him, thereby neglecting to explain. Or else explanation, when given, may be unclear. If clear, it may be misunderstood or misinterpreted.

3. THE INDIVIDUAL'S SOCIAL STATUS

The concept of status has already appeared in our discussion of the hierarchy of individual needs. Status is a concept fundamentally based

2. This subject is discussed in more detail in "Operating Goals" and "General Functions" in "Output: Operations and Functions" (Chapt. 15).

upon a group orientation. It exists in the eyes of others. One's own conception of status is mainly a reflection, whether clear or distorted, of the views of others.

In part, status has larger determinants than one's social role. A person's status may be ascribed to him because of attributes which are mainly unrelated to his personal performance—such as birth, family connections, race, sex, size, beauty, or age. In some societies, as emphasized in Parsons' list of cultural pattern variables, ascription is far more important than achievement (1951, p. 154).

In the era of the administrative revolution, however, increasing attention is given to achievement. Status is determined more and more by skill, knowledge, education, wealth, and power. In particular, it is determined by one's social role. Subject to only few exceptions, the hierarchy of social roles established within any group is the status system of the group. In organizations, as pointed out by Barnard, status is based both upon trade or occupation and upon formal positions of responsibility and authority, and is reinforced by various symbols and insignia (1948, p. 207-244).

But status is rarely limited to a single group; there is usually some carryover among roles in various organizations. The successful businessman and the political leader will often enjoy higher status in a fraternal organization, and occupy higher roles, than the unsuccessful businessman or the lowly political hack. Of course, status incongruence may occur—as when a person of higher education occupies a lower-skilled position or a person of some favored race or religion performs a social role usually assigned to members of a supposedly "inferior" race or religion (*Adams*). This is usually a source of dissatisfaction and anxiety to the persons involved, a factor that may in fact impel them into the leadership of powerful movements as a way of attaining the personal positions to which they see themselves as entitled. If the situation is reversed—as it may well be when someone succeeds in climbing beyond the status ascribed to him—the dissatisfaction will be felt by those who object to the shaking of established expectations by the "new arrivers."

4. DEGREES OF GROUP IDENTIFICATION AND LOYALTY

An inescapable consequence of multiple group attachment is differing degrees of identification with different groups and with the social roles one assumes within them. This is merely another way of saying that multiple loyalty is inevitable. Often, when one must make a choice between two different sets of expectations, multiple loyalty is transformed into divided loyalty.

In the family, multiplicity of identification is indicated by the extent to which a child identifies himself with the family's children, the parents, the grandparents or the family as a whole. In a large organization, a person faces a choice between his immediate work group and the many larger units of which the work group is a part. The natural tendency seems to be that the most deep-seated attachments develop within those groups whose members have the most frequent personal interactions. Homans formulates this tendency in his hypothesis that "the more frequently persons interact with one another when no one of them originates inter-action with much greater frequency than the others, the greater is their liking for one another and their feeling of ease in one another's presence" (1950, p. 243). This tendency is reinforced when people share common backgrounds and similar social values.

Identification, moreover, is a reciprocal relationship. Rejection by other members of the group will place a person in the position of an "isolate" or a "deviant." Acceptance must be earned through ascribed attributes or performance in accordance with the norms of the group.

No matter what the degree of actual or potential acceptance, one's degree of identification and loyalty to any group is also affected by one's level of aspiration. The person who orients himself toward higher status will usually identify himself somewhat less with his immediate work group. He will usually show greater loyalty to those reference groups whose judgments may affect his future roles.

The nature of certain roles—particularly administrative roles—is also a factor. The typical manager belongs to a number of overlapping sub-groups: his immediate subordinates, his immediate superiors and his im-mediate colleagues. If he identifies too closely with any one of these groups, he runs the risk of injuring his relationships with the others. Hence every manager is usually a "man in the middle," a person of necessarily divided loyalties and allegiances. Moreover, to the extent that an administrator sees his role as that of continuing initiation and thereby establishes a one-way interaction pattern, the degree to which he may be accepted within any one group will be small. This is one of the reasons why many people find loneliness and isolation in positions of administrative leadership.

The diversity of personal attachments and loyalties is compounded by one's membership in entirely different groups. Just as one must achieve some working balance between one's attachments to various parts of a given group, one must also achieve some working balance between attachments to family, work place, political party, and national or re-ligious group, to mention but a few. At the very least, these various groups compete for time and attention. Often, they demand different forms of behavior. Thus one's attitude toward various candidates for appointment to a vacant position will vary with the degree of one's loyalty to family, friends, political party or the perceived needs of one or another part of the organization. In policy decisions affecting large groups of people, the pressure of competing loyalties may be still stronger.

c. *The Individual's Conflicts*

ONE OF THE POPULAR FALLACIES concerning human nature is the concept of the Adjusted Man, the myth of the well-oiled personality who is perfectly adjusted to his environment and has risen above all inner conflicts. This is the individualistic version of the fallacy that in good administration things run smoothly and easily. It leads to unrealizable goals concerning personal behavior and unrealistic diagnoses of personal problems.

Conflict is an inherent part of an individual's life. One cannot rise above conflict. One can merely respond to it in varying ways. Hence the proposition that "Conflict is an inevitable part of human nature."

This is not to say that individual conflict in the abstract is either good or bad. Here too, as with organizational conflict, there is a double potential. Conflict can be destructive of human happiness and even of personality itself. Or it may motivate one to higher and higher levels of need gratification. In either case it is impossible to understand a person very well without learning something about his conflicts and reactions to them.

1. THE NATURE OF AN INDIVIDUAL'S CONFLICTS

As with organizations, individual conflict can be internal or external. Internal conflicts are derived, first and foremost, from the multiplicity of human purposes, social roles, and group attachments. It is only natural for people to want to do things which, if objectively compatible, are rendered conflicting by the shortage of time or which, if time is available, are inherently conflicting.

External conflicts develop as an individual's desires or actions are impeded by some natural obstacle, by one or more other individuals or by one or more groups. The very process of acculturation is one of conflict and tension between the individual and those who expect his behavior to conform to their desires. Many external conflicts, particularly those relating to multiple group attachments and multiple social roles, are internalized. They thus reappear in the form of sharply conflicting purposes and values. These are often the sharpest and most disturbing of all inner conflicts.

Apart from their source, an individual's conflicts vary in terms both of degree and of the interests to which they relate. A low degree conflict is that of a simple choice between alternative means—as when a woman chooses which dress to wear to a party. A more complex conflict arises in choosing among escorts. If there is an abundance of alternatives to choose from, the situation may be confusing but the conflict will not be intense. The conflict rises in degree if, in a society where the customs forbid it, she seriously considers having sexual relationships without marriage. The conflict becomes still more serious if two suitors or lovers decide to fight to the death for her hand. In every case a certain kind of action is impeded or frustrated. In the lower degree cases, the conflict can be settled by small modifications and shiftings. The highest degree cases are head-on collisions of the all-or-none variety in a situation characterized by a scarcity of alternatives.

Equally important as a determinant of intensity is the level of interests which are involved. Here it may be stated that the lower the interests on the hierarchy of individual motivation the more disturbing a conflict may be to an individual and the deeper the emotions that may be aroused. Thus a low degree conflict relating to one's physical survival is usually far more upsetting than one relating with respect to commergence, differentiation or self-development. It takes a very intense evocation of higher needs to lead one to the sacrifice of survival through martyrdom or suicide. The truly self-developing person, paradoxically, is the one most capable of standing up under the strain of acute frustration or giving up power, position and life itself on behalf of something larger than himself.

2. "NORMAL" RESOLUTIONS OF INDIVIDUAL CONFLICT

There is nothing that is more of a routine and every-day part of an individual's life than the way he handles his conflicts. Even unusual and unprecedented conflicts are usually handled in a "normal"—in the sense of healthy—manner.

Unfortunately, this aspect of normal behavior has been obscured by the lack of attention given to normal people by experimental psychologists and the inescapable emphasis of clinical psychologists on pathological cases. This overemphasis on the pathological handling of conflict is only partly counterbalanced by the tendency of the psychiatrist or psychoanalyst to go to the other extreme and find that everyone in the world (including the doctor) is neurotic. In discussing "normal" solutions to individual conflict, we are therefore venturing somewhat further into the area of hypothetical and the unverified than is necessary in the subsequent section.

Any such discussion, however, must be preceded by a qualification concerning the words "resolution" or "solution." Their use implies no aura of finality whatsoever. Every resolution or solution itself creates or leads to new conflicts. In fact, one of the most instructive ways of evaluating and ranking solutions is in terms of the character of the new conflicts emanating from them.

The first element in the normal reaction to conflict is delay. This is inherent in the very blockage which is the essence of conflict. This delay may involve a long period of time, while the parties to the conflict survey the terrain and search for solutions. At times, it may appear to be—or may actually be—interminable. Or else the delay may be momentary, while the tracks are cleared for some sort of action. In either case, the period of delay usually involves the piling up of additional conflicts related to the solution of the original conflict.

The second element is tension, or stress. This results both from the actual delay and from the anxieties involved in the prospect of further frustration. It inevitably carries with it a certain amount of painfulness. On the other hand, unless too acute, the tension itself usually stimulates a higher level of mental and physical energy and feelings of excitement which may be regarded as highly pleasurable. People who have become accustomed to working at high tension find it extremely difficult, therefore, to adjust to situations in which no serious conflicts need be faced.

The final element is some sort of resolution. Here as already outlined in section C of "The Conflict-Cooperation Nexus" (Chapt. 3), the pattern is extremely variable. It may include almost any conceivable combination of avoidance, deadlock, victory (or defeat), compromise and integration. Not only organizational conflicts but also the inner conflicts of individuals, it should be noted, can be resolved through integration. Here there is a reevaluation of personal interests, a systematic examination of the objective situation and the development of "the possibility of something better than either of two given alternatives," the possibility of both interests being met and neither frustrated. This is very close to a description of what is done in the best of modern psychotherapy.

Unfortunately, there is little or no research evidence which would indicate the extent to which the normal solutions to individual conflict are distributed among the categories of avoidance, deadlock, domination, compromise and integration. The tendency among practical people and cynics is to regard integration solutions as exceptional. My own hypothesis is that without underestimating the amount of pure compromise, one can regard integration of conflict as a normal part of the behavior of healthy people. The difficulty with psychotherapy is that the rituals of organized medicine and exaggerated analogies with physical disease have often prevented psychiatrists and psychoanalysts from giving enough attention to the inner conflicts arising from a complex and rapidly changing environment (Szasz, 1961).

No matter what the nature of the resolution, it is perfectly normal for people to react emotionally to conflict situations and to seek methods of expressing their emotion. These emotions may be expressed in acts of open aggression or hostility. They may be repressed and find their outlet in other areas through sublimation (the use of a substitute activity to gratify a frustrated motive), compensation (success in one area to make up for self-esteem lost in another area), displacement (the disguising of an uncomfortable goal by the use of a more acceptable one), or projection (the disguising of a source of conflict by attributing one's own motives to others). While these forms of reaction to conflict were initially discovered and dissected in the area of pathology, they are probably just as important to normal as to abnormal life. It is hard to conceive how people could handle their conflicts without the defense mechanisms which they provide.

3. "ABNORMAL" RESOLUTIONS OF INDIVIDUAL CONFLICT

Having reversed the usual process by first discussing normal conflict solution, I shall now return to the field of more usual concern to the psychologist: abnormal and pathological solutions to conflicts.

This is far more than an academic concern to the study of administration. There are at least some small bits or aspects of the abnormal or pathological in every individual. There are much more than small bits or aspects of neurotic behavior in most organizations. In some organizations examples may even be found of psychotic behavior.

Neurosis or psychoneurosis may be roughly defined as "a personality disorder, less severe than a psychosis, in which a person is unusually anxious, miserable, troublesome, or incapacitated in his work and relations with other people" (Morgan, 1956, p. 640). Whether we use this or another definition, the line between normality and neurosis is not easy to draw.

To some small degree, the distinction may be found in the nature of an individual's conflicts. Neurosis usually develops in connection with high-degree conflicts which frustrate the usual satisfactions of the most elemental needs for survival, commergence, and differentiation.

To a greater degree the distinction is found in the nature of individual behavior in reaction to conflicts. In neurotic behavior the normal reactions of hostility and aggression are expressed in a more extreme fashion. Or else, if repressed, sublimation, compensation, displacement, or projection are carried to greater lengths. In addition, more specifically neurotic forms of behavior may develop. These include fixation and compulsion, compliance and helplessness, withdrawal and isolation, sadism and masochism, hysteria, and highly idealized self images combined with deep-seated feelings of inferiority. In almost all cases the individual suffers acute and painful anxiety, although this may be interspersed with brief periods of joy and relief. In many cases, the neurosis is expressed in ailments of the digestive, nervous or respiratory systems and other types of psychosomatic disorders.

Finally, the neurotic reaction involves a lack of awareness concerning the underlying conflict or conflicts. The fatal process of repression, disguise, displacement, and false idealization is carried so far that the individual is even more removed from an adequate perception of reality than the ordinary limited human being. This is why many therapists emphasize "bringing the patient to a thorough understanding of his conflicts—their general effect on his personality and their specific responsibility for his symptoms" (Horney, 1955, p. 241-242).

In contrast with neurosis, psychosis may be defined as "a mental or personality disorder, more severe than a psychoneurosis, characterized by a bizarre, unrealistic behavior that is often so incompetent and dangerous that the person must be given custodial care" (Morgan, 1956, p. 640).

Here the flight from reality is more far-reaching. It takes the individual into an inner world of self-delusion. It removes him from contact with others through the normal devices and symbols of communication. It may lead to extremely severe states of depression, to delusions or hallucinations, or to one or another form of schizophrenia: simple, paranoid, catatonic, or hebephrenic.

It would be utopian to believe that the reaction of individual members of an organization to the conflict inherent in organizational and administrative activity is always to find normal solutions. On the one hand, organizational conflict often provides the final straw that moves a person across the border between normality and neurosis. On the other hand, certain forms of high organizational performance are often the result of obsessive and compulsive behavior. Organizational activity— and perhaps administrative activity in particular—often provides opportunities for people to channel and harness their neurotic impulses. The cost of such self-administered therapy can be measured only by the sacrifice of other aspects of organizational performance and the negative impact on the lives of other members of the organization. The fact that both of these costs may be substantial does not imply that they are not frequently incurred.

It is much less frequent for the psychotic person to function within an organization—at least at the lower levels. It seems that one can survive within an organization despite paranoia or schizophrenia only if one occupies an extremely high position in the directorate of a rapidly expanding organization—as with Hitler, Mussolini, and Stalin. By many relevant criteria such people, who if not fully psychotic were at least on the border between psychosis and neurosis, have proved effective organization leaders. In the case of the state organization in Germany, Italy, or Russia, the results of such leadership are to be measured in bloodshed and murder. In simpler organizations the results may appear in the debasement, humiliation and frustration of colleagues and underlings.

D. *The Individuality of Personality*

THE BELIEF in personality types or stereotypes is perhaps the most widespread of all popular fallacies concerning human nature. For many centuries people have made the grievous error of thinking that they have discovered the most important thing about someone else when they have identified his color, race, national origin, or religion. More pretentious but no less fallacious efforts have been made to establish personality types on the basis of astrology, phrenology, physiognomy, morphology, and endocrinology. Similar tendencies have been encouraged by specialists who, having developed scientific methods of measuring a few human traits, have unscientifically presented them as so-called "personality tests." Many people who should know better still paint crude pictures of a world peopled by introverts, other-directed people, executive types, and other stereotypes.

Although the study of human personality is a field in which divergence and disagreement are rampant, there is one point upon which most serious researchers and students are agreed: that the human personality is much more than any single trait or cluster of traits. Almost every theory of personality uses words like organization, system, structure and pattern to express the wholeness of human personality. When seen in their wholeness, rather than in terms of a few special aspects, it is then clear that human beings are unique personalities.

1. UNIQUENESS

The first determinant of personality is inherited characteristics. These are transmitted through the genes within the chromosomes. Biological investigation indicates that there are between 20,000 to 42,000 gene locations in the chromosomes. The theoretical number of possibilities in the offspring of any two people is more than twice as many. It may thus be concluded, as one biologist has put it, that "all human beings who have ever lived . . . have not scratched the surface of possible gene combinations in Homo sapiens" (LaBarre, 1954, p. 97).

Environmental factors are even more varied. In conjunction with hereditary factors, they produce a biological organism which is itself unique. Recent biochemical research has demonstrated tremendous variability among individuals with respect to almost every aspect of the structure and chemical composition of the human body. This undermines the old demarcation between the normal and the abnormal:

> If we consider the possibility that among the numerous measurable attributes that human beings possess there may be many which are not mathematically correlated, we are confronted with an idea which is opposed to the basic dichotomy of normal and abnormal. If 0.95 of the population is normal with respect to one measurable item, only 0.902 (0.95^2) would be normal with respect to two measurable items and 0.60 (0.95^{10}) and 0.0059 (0.95^{100}), respectively, would be normal with regard to 10 and 100 uncorrelated items.
>
> The existence in every human being of a vast array of attributes which are potentially measurable (whether by present methods or not), and probably often uncorrelated mathematically, makes quite tenable the hypothesis that practically every human being is a deviate in some respects (Roger Williams, 1956, p. 2-3).

Psychological variation, itself greatly affected by biological variation, is probably still greater. Every person grows up in a unique situation. His development is affected not only by the general cultural environment but also by the specific treatment he receives from parents, other family members, teachers, playmates, and other associates. In response to these environmental situations he develops various skills and abilities. He acquires certain attitudes and interests. He weaves himself into an intricate web of interpersonal relations and group affiliations. He develops a unique pattern of need satisfaction and need frustration.

This infinite variability does not imply that classification is impossible. On the contrary, classification of some sort is essential to any scientific effort to understand human personality. A large part of psychological research and analysis is based upon one of three classification systems. One emphasizes the stimulus aspect of personality—that is, how a person affects others. The second emphasizes the response aspect—that is, the pattern of response to defined stimuli. The third emphasizes the "inner organization of emotions, values and beliefs which determine a person's superficial responses (gestures and the like) and in turn determine his effectiveness with other people" (Stagner, 1960). Yet no classification system is scientifically valid if it purports to express the totality of any person's personality by identifying him as one or another type. The utility of classification systems, rather, is that, like the Bertillon system of fingerprinting classification, they provide a method of coping with the individual's uniqueness.

2. THE MANY FACES OF INDIVIDUALS

The preceding discussion is based on the oversimplified assumption that personality is a phenomenon that can be objectively observed. The full complexity of personality is understood only when we remember that personality, unlike such a simple matter as fingerprints, appears as something different to different observers.

Every man and woman has many different faces. To illustrate this simple fact of life, there is no need to use extreme cases of split personality. We need merely remember that the result of multiple group affiliation is multiple roles. This is why Mr. A is A_1 in the eyes of his subordinate and A_2 in the eyes of his superior. Nor does he appear as the identical Mr. A to both associates and clients. Likewise, he is not seen as the same person by his wife, his parents and his children. Appearance, moreover, should not be too quickly contrasted with reality. Mr. A appears different to different people not only because of their peculiar way of looking at him but also because he acts differently toward each of them. His multiple roles produce a multisided personality.

One of Mr. A's most significant faces is his own self-image. If this self-image is too dramatically at variance with the faces seen by others, Mr. A will probably be confined to a mental institution. But even the person who runs a mental health institution or commits others to it has a self-image quite different from the faces perceived by others. This too is a part of reality, and an extremely influential one at that. Even the most carefully observant psychologist, psychiatrist, or psychoanalyst may himself perceive only part of the series $A_1, A_2 \ldots \ldots A_n$. How can he confidently conclude that one of these, or one set of these, is correct and the others wrong?

But even if pinned down at a specific point in time, the personality is bound to change. While this process may be theoretically confined within certain limits, Mr. A of today is never the same as Mr. A of ten years ago. Under the impact of accumulated development, learning, and aging, each face inevitably changes its features.

E. *Normal Irrationality*

EVEN MORE MISLEADING and dangerous than the fallacies of the Economic Man, the Robinson Crusoe Man, the Adjusted Man and the Stereotype is the idea that people are—or could sometime become—creatures who always act rationally. This is the fallacy of the Rational Man. From this point of view, irrationality is the province of the uneducated, who must be taught, the unintelligent, who lack reasoning ability, and the abnormal, who should be cured.

This fallacy has had the great historic value of serving as a myth to justify the authority—if not to suggest the infallibility—of rulers and administrators. But the more successful rulers have known better. They have usually acted on the assumption that most other people are at least partly irrational. They have often succeeded in perceiving the irrationality of fellow rulers, rivals and—at times—themselves.

It is indeed true that neurotic and psychotic behavior is irrational and that the uneducated can never reach high levels of rationality. But normality and education do not imply strictly rational and logical behavior. There are many entirely normal forms of nonlogical behavior and educated irrationality. Hence the proposition that "a large part of human behavior is irrational or nonrational."

The nature of human rationality is discussed at greater length in Chapter 28. There a major distinction is made between the characteristics of rational action and the processes of calculation designed to help achieve rational action. Rational action is discussed in terms of three dimensions: desirability, feasibility, and consistency. A high degree of rationality in one of these dimensions, it is shown, may often be associated with a low degree of rationality on one or both of the others. Also, rational action, as measured by any dimension, is limited by environmental blocks, by individual and organizational limits on learning and by the self-imposed boundaries which are usually a prerequisite for scientific and technological analysis.

To these limits we must add those which bear upon the processes of calculation themselves. As pointed out in Simon's discussion of "bounded rationality," the human calculator usually suffers from imperfect information, limited computational ability and the lack of a complete and consistent preference ordering. We must add Barnard's profound observation concerning the possible irrelevance of rational techniques to certain materials that "cannot bear the weight of ponderous logic." We should recall his contention that in many situations the logical statement of a problem may change the situation that is being analyzed and thus render the formulation inaccurate. Thus rationality itself, in the more narrow sense, may turn out to be an irrational form of behavior.

Finally, both rational action and rational calculation are dependent upon three aspects of behavior which may lead to irrationality as well. First of all, emotions and feelings are the wellsprings of the very considerable energy needed for rational calculation. As Maslow has pointed out, there are few people more driven by the white heat of emotion than the scientist intent on finding an objective solution. Much of human action—rational, irrational and nonrational—is affected by love, hatred, resentment, anger, envy, and fear. Even when action is most fully premeditated, these emotions may determine more than anything else the nature of the information perceived, the computation system used and the purposes emphasized or sacrificed. Second, there is the area of automatic action. In part, particularly in the very young, this is based upon inherited instincts. In large part, it is the result of habit or imitation. In either case, premeditation and calculation are either absent or peripheral. Automatic action on many routine problems is essential to allow people to concentrate attention on those which are of a less routine nature. Third, there is the great area of unconscious and preconscious calculation. This area stands midway between automatic and premeditated action and often succeeds in dominating both. One need not accept Freud's special version of how the subconscious operates in order to recognize its tremendous importance. The subconscious may serve as a receptacle for conflicts which might otherwise obstruct rational calculation. Subconscious thought processes may themselves be capable of operating more rapidly and more successfully than their conscious counterparts.

Chapter 9

PEOPLE-IN-ORGANIZATIONS: FORMAL ASPECTS

*I*N THE PREVIOUS CHAPTER we looked at people apart from their roles in any specific organization. We saw that every person is a unique personality motivated by many interests, attached to many groups, affected by internal conflicts and acting nonrationally as well as rationally.

In this chapter we shall look at the structure of organizations. We shall focus upon their general characteristics and certain formal aspects of organizational structure.

In so doing, we cannot avoid using many terms that seem to take us very far from human beings. The word "structure," in particular, suggests something nonhuman and impersonal. One reason for this is that people often think of organizational structure in terms of the structure of buildings. This has given an architectural or engineering flavor to much of human thought, at both the common-sense and theoretical levels, about organizational structure.

But the relationships in human organizations are quite different from those among the parts of a building. They have meaning only in terms of the expectations and actions of human beings. When we talk about organizational structure, we refer to some pattern which joins the parts of an organization to the purposes of the organization as a whole. Any such pattern consists of some combination of roles for units and members and the relations established among them by hierarchy, polyarchy, and codes of behavior. These roles, relations, and codes have both their formal and informal aspects, sometimes referred to as the "formal structure" and the "informal structure." The difference between them is that the former are—and the latter are not—prescribed by the holders of formal authority.

While the informal aspects of organizational structure are more intimately related to the personality of individual members, this chapter will demonstrate that it would be a great mistake to regard the formal aspects as lacking in human qualities. They too are forms of human behavior. Instead of being fixed and unchanging like the walls and girders of a building, they are modified by a continual series of official changes. They are often embodied in oral decisions and requests; they can never be fully set forth in writing. Like their promulgators, they can never be free from internal inconsistencies and conflicts. As with all prescriptions for human behavior, they are never complied with completely.

The informal aspects of structures, particularly informal roles, are discussed in the next chapter. The broad subject of organizational codes, both formal and informal, is reserved for Chapter 19.

A. *An Overview*

BEFORE EXAMINING the internal structure of organizations, let us step back and take an overview of their general characteristics. In so doing, we shall see that entirely apart from its structure, every organization can be described in terms of output purposes, legal status, membership basis, production technology, and certain dimensions of size and time. The first three of these characteristics are often stated, at least partially, in formal charters—constitutions, by-laws, regulations, declarations of principle, agreements, contracts, covenants, and articles of incorporation or federation. All of them may have an important influence upon formal and informal structure.

Those characteristics which flow from an organization's immediate and general environment have already been discussed in Chapters 6 and 7.

1. OUTPUT ROLES

From the viewpoint of a society, polity or economy, the division of labor among organizations is made on the basis of—or evidenced by—the services or goods produced. The apostle's words, "By their fruits ye shall know them" (Matthew, 7:20), provide the most general basis for the identification and classification of organizations. The most obvious difference among political parties, churches, trade associations, fraternal societies, wholesalers, and railroads is that they provide different kinds of services for different clienteles. The most obvious difference among agricultural, mining, manufacturing, and construction organizations is that they produce different kinds of goods. (All of these organizations will be found in the census classifications of economic "sectors" or "activities," both of which are based upon distinctions among the major products produced.) Similarly, it is the output objectives of an organization more than anything else which define its distinctive role in society.

The fact that an organization is known by its output does not necessarily imply that its output is readily known. Some organizations are not quite sure what their fruits shall or should be. Few organizations produce just a single product. As explained in Chapter 14, their fruits may take the form of a highly variegated "output mix." As shown in Chapter 15, many services, particularly intangible ones, are extremely hard to identify.

Far easier to pin down is another important aspect of an organization's output—the basis on which its "fruits" are made available to clients. The term "business" or "firm" is usually reserved for an organization that sells its products to its clients. The sales revenue thus received is a major, if not the only, source of external revenue. (In the case of a bank, interest payments can be regarded as the cash payment for credit services.) This direct financial nexus between organization and clients makes it possible to place a monetary value upon output. The organization can thereby make a profitability calculation, which is the only generally feasible way of calculating output and input in the same units of measurement. In this sense, many government organizations, cooperatives, fee-charging hospitals, and schools—no matter how little profit they seek or attain—are business organizations.

On the other hand, there are those organizations (we might call them "nonbusiness") which transmit their goods or services to clients on some basis other than sales. The income of such organizations is obtained from government funds or nongovernment contributions. Although some or all of it may come from the clients of an organization, the route is circuitous rather than direct. Here we find legislatures, courts, armies, and governmental regulatory bodies—except in the borderline cases of mercenary troops and bribery.

Paradoxically enough, we must also include in the nonbusiness category most internal units in any business organization. Although they may be interested in contributing to the profit position of the organization as a whole (and this certainly distinguishes them from the units of a nonbusiness organization), there is no way of calculating a profit or a loss for themselves. The only clear exceptions are certain large subdivisions of those extremely large business organizations which have set up pricing systems for internal transactions. Another possible exception is in the case of some systems of piecework and incentive wages. Here the workers' position may be comparable to that of subcontractors who are directly paid for services rendered. Both internal pricing and piecework contracting, however, may exist within nonbusiness organizations.

2. LEGAL STATUS

The differentiation among organizations on the basis of legal status is a dangerous undertaking. Legalistic formulations have a hypnotic power. If one gazes upon them for a long enough time, one may end up being hypnotized into confusing form with substance and fiction with fact. Many a brilliant scholar has been carried off in a cloud of legalism, never to be heard of again in the world of reality.

Yet the legal aspects of organizations are themselves a part of reality. While they never reveal the whole story, they are always part of the story.

A. *Governmental or nongovernmental.* The most important legal distinction is that which may be used in placing all organizations somewhere on a continuum from governmental to nongovernmental. At one extreme, there are those clusters of organizations called "states" that exercise certain kinds of legitimate authority, or sovereignty, over all the people in a given geographical area. Each such cluster as a whole may back up this authority by using physical force of some sort, such force to be exercised by specialized organizations. National, as distinguished from local, states may also use such force or violence outside their geographical area.

At the other extreme, there are separate and clustered organizations that do not participate in any way in the sovereignty of states. Although they may try to extend their influence throughout the area of any state, their formal authority is limited to their members alone. Except for protective operations of a minor nature, they may not legitimately establish police forces or armed services.

In the middle stand a host of quasi-governmental organizations. These include (a) regional and international organizations formed by governments, but far from being federated governments, (b) mixed agencies formed by governmental and nongovernmental organizations, (c) government-established agencies that are instructed to operate as private bodies, (d) privately established agencies upon whom governmental authority is bestowed, and (e) those political parties that install—or try to install—their members in positions of power within governmental organizations.

B. *Corporate or noncorporate status.* In the sense that it may be thought of as having a personality of its own, every organization may be regarded as a corporate entity. In a legal sense, however, the corporate form allows an organization to enjoy certain rights that would otherwise have been denied it. The earliest of such rights was the right to hold property in perpetuity, apart from the death of the "natural persons" owning or controlling the organization. Among business organizations, the most important of such rights has become the freedom of stockholders from liability for the debts of the corporation. These and related "escape provisions" have enabled nongovernment organizations to mobilize and maintain larger aggregations of assets than would be technically possible through individual proprietorships, partnerships or nonincorporated syndicates, trusts or associations.

Among government organizations the corporate form has also served as an escape device. Here it has allowed government agencies to escape budgetary, accounting and personnel controls imposed upon "regular" government agencies, as well as formally sanctioned intervention by high state officials and legislative bodies.

There is a tremendous variety of corporate forms. Nongovernment corporations are set up in accordance with general laws in different states and countries and specific laws relating to certain types of enterprises such as banks, insurance companies and utilities. They may be stock or nonstock corporations. They may be mutual or cooperative corporations. Government corporations are usually created under individual laws. The diversity of these laws and the forms established under them is so great that many decades ago a skilled analyst observed that "the government corporation as a concept—as a definite and specialized form of administrative organization—is rapidly ceasing to exist" (Pritchett, 1941). Since then, with the development of more extensive controls over government agencies and consequently of still more varied patterns of escaping them, the diversity has become still greater. Moreover, the corporate form has become one of the major instruments for establishing private-public enterprise and blurring the line between government and nongovernment organizations. To the uninitiated, therefore, corporate law—both private and public—is indeed a jungle. Yet from this jungle have emerged forms of social innovation that have helped determine the nature and pace of the administrative and technological revolutions. As demonstrated by Sigmund Timberg's discussion of corporations as an instrument for inter-

national governmental cooperation on specific projects (1952), many new
and striking innovations may still be expected in this sphere.[1]

3. BASES FOR MEMBERSHIP

The boundary lines of organizations, like those of some countries,
are not always clear. Some people manage to stand astride them, with one
foot on each side. Some shift back and forth from one side to another.
Sometimes the boundary is a strip of "no man's land" peopled by those
who belong neither here nor there.

Nonetheless, boundaries there must be. These are determined by the
nature of membership and the conditions of entry and exit.

A. *Employment or affiliation.* There are two general bases for membership. The first is employment, which may be full-time or part-time,
permanent or temporary, paid or unpaid. Business and government organizations are mainly composed of full-time paid employees for whom
membership in the employing organization is a major part of their life.

The second is some act of affiliation or participation, as with associations, unions, professional societies, political parties, or churches. The
members of these organizations might be called "affiliates," to distinguish
them from the employed staff. In some organizations the higher officials
may be both employees and affiliates. In others, the employees are excluded from genuine membership and are regarded as mere "staff," "personnel," or "bureaucracy." In either case participation by the majority
of "affiliates" is apt to be casual, sporadic and tangential to their deeper
interests. The "activists" are generally limited to a few cliques that run
things, their rivals and the employees. In the case of some political parties
and churches, the term "member" is vaguely used to apply both to the
"organization" or "hierarchy" and to large, unstructured groups of followers or adherents.

A special and more limited form of membership is provided by those
cases, such as schools, hospitals, and jails, in which a service organization
and its primary clientele are joined together in a structured community.
Students, patients, and inmates are rarely directly involved in the production of educational, health, and custodial services; they are rather

1. In another penetrating article (1946) Timberg breaks down the so-called
"corporate fiction" into seventeen component fictions. Among these are the fictions that a corporation is governed by a "single group purpose," a "single group
will" or a "single group." Nonetheless, he believes that corporations "should be
regarded as not only the carriers of their own private interests, but instrumentalities for effectuating social and economic interests which the national and
international community regard as paramount."

the direct recipients. Yet they are much closer to the organizations producing these services than are the roomers in a hotel or apartment house. They may be regarded as client-members.

A distinction must also be made between individual and group membership. This is particularly important in associations and federations in which the nature of affiliation determines the location of ultimate authority among members. Many large associations are based entirely upon individual membership, with groups of members engaging in separate or local activities. Federations tend to be based upon group membership. Some organizations have a dual basis of participation, with separate voting privileges for both groups and individuals.

B. *Entry*. At one extreme, some affiliation organizations are wide open in the sense that anyone can join them by unilateral action on his own part. This may range from signing a piece of paper to making a dues payment. In some cases minor prerequisites may be required—such as a given occupational background or a recommendation by another member.

In all employment organizations, however, and in many associations entry is conditional. The new member must agree to accept certain obligations. Sometimes the prerequisites for entry are many and difficult. Organizations with an eye to the future tend to realize that a series of entry decisions will eventually determine the entire future composition of the organization. This leads to a series of openly stated entrance standards relating to ability, experience, and education. It may also mean equally stringent prerequisites—although harder to detect from the outside—with respect to sex, color, religion, age, special background, physical attributes, and personal compatibility. To offset some of these barriers, entry may be policed by government regulatory agencies. Additional barriers may be established by trade association blacklists and by trade union insistence on the hiring only of people who are already union members (the closed shop) or are willing to join the union (union shop).

At the other extreme, there are various organizations which people are forced to enter against their will and not allowed to leave. This includes large parts of many armies, organizations operating with "forced labor," some "closed shop" trade unions, and some political parties and trade associations. It also includes a large part of the "client members" of compulsory school systems, hospitals, and jails. If we want to regard families as organizations, we must keep in mind that although family entry through marriage may be voluntary, one's entry through birth is always involuntary.

c. *Exit*. In most organizations people have the right to leave when they so desire. Only in compulsory schools and such "closed institutions" as conscript armies, jails, mental hospitals, and concentration camps are people compelled to remain against their will.

Apart from compulsion, many barriers are erected to maintain membership. Most obvious are contractual obligations; more widespread are benefits such as pension plans, stock options, and seniority rights, which may be wholly or partially lost by leaving.

Still stronger barriers such as tenure and permanent status may be erected against an organization's effort to require members to leave. Even where these rights are not enjoyed, separation and expulsion actions are costly and nasty affairs. It is often easier to transfer a person to another unit in an organization or "kick him upstairs." In the case of the occupants of highest political office, removal may be impossible without a costly election campaign, a public program of vilification, impeachment proceedings, or the more violent extremes of coup d'etat or revolution.

4. PRODUCTION TECHNOLOGY

The development of modern organization is closely connected with the rising technology level.[2] Modern technology calls for more subdivision of labor, hierarchy and larger organizations; substitutes machinery and electrical energy for manual labor; promotes white collar workers, technicians and professional people; and tends to convert organizational work to intellectual rather than physical operations.

In the early days of "scientific management" there was a tendency to see administration mainly as a problem in engineering. Then the human relations school countered with the motto "People are not machines." Now there is ever-increasing realization that people in organizations, while not machines, are very directly affected by the nature of the production processes they use, including machines. As stated by one of the researchers in the field, it is becoming increasingly clear that "The technology of the plant—the way jobs are distributed and flow into one another and the nature of the division of labor—molds the type of work groups that evolve within the plant . . . the technological structure of the organization, in turn, exerts a major influence on the source of motivation and morale, the work group. This is the reason for the statement that the field of personnel relations has come the full circle to the point where engineering considerations are once again crucial" (Sayles, 1958, p. 4). The Tavistock analysts look at industrial organizations as "socio-technical systems" (*Trist et al.*, p. 196).

Thus, on an assembly line, a welder may have no direct contact with

2. See "The Rise of the Administered Society" (Gross, *The Managing of Organizations*, Chapter 2).

anyone in the plant except the man on his right and the man on his left, plus an occasional systems expert or quality controller who looks over his shoulder. In a small file room, six people may work closely together as members of a tightly knit group. In another situation workers may belong to a much larger department and may be divided into a number of smaller, informal groups working in competition one with the other. In many schools the accepted processes of education dictate that individual teachers work as lone wolves. Their main responsibility is "giving" a number of courses and for this purpose they need have no contact (except for somnolent faculty meetings) with their colleagues. These alternative patterns of production affect the extent of cooperation among individuals and units. They thus create many of the special problems of motivation and morale that are faced by administrators.

In a larger sense the production processes also determine the distribution of attention among material assets, people and ideas. There is a major difference between organizations in "primary industries," where attention must continually be focused on natural resources, and "secondary industries" with their attention focused on processed materials. There is a still greater difference between these and the "tertiary industries," dealing with services, particularly those services centering around relations between people and groups. In all of these sectors, there are major differences between the more "labor intensive" organizations and the more "capital intensive" ones with their problems of "hard goods" technology and long-range planning of expensive fixed investment.

Perhaps even more important is the rate at which new methods and processes are introduced. Technological change of any significance whatsoever is a threat, real or imagined, to the power or security of someone, often of many people in the organization. In its more obvious aspects, any technological change which enables the production of similar output with less labor threatens to reduce employment. But even where such an effect can be counterbalanced by expanded production or by transfers to other work, the change itself threatens established positions and expertise. It renders obsolete the accrued capital of knowledge in the hands and minds of those who operated in accordance with the previous processes. It may even suggest that the people responsible for the previous processes are inferior individuals, as compared with the wiser souls who promote the new processes. Furthermore, it may turn upside down the old world of established relationships and lead to a complete reorganization of work groups, tasks, responsibilities, and individual status. Similarly, rapidly changing technology is guaranteed to destroy organizational lethargy and routine. It places a higher premium upon administrators who are capable of adjusting quickly to new situations and of

Which Is Biggest?

	U.S. Dept. of Defense[a]	American Telephone and Telegraph[b]	CIO-AFL[c]	United Nations[d]
Members				
Employees	3.5 million civil & military	40,000 in central holding company	600 in national office	37,600 (including all U.N. programs and specialized agencies)
		729,000 in holding company and subsidiaries		
Affiliates (non-employed members)	476,000 in about 6,000 local national guard units	25 subsidiaries	132 unions 62,353 locals	110 member nations
		(over 2 million stockholders)[e]	15 million union members	(over 2 billion people)[e]
Material Assets		$24.6 billion		
Expenditures	$51 billion	$8.7 billion gross expenses	n.a.	$550 million
Output		$100 billion gross revenues		
Spatial Distribution	International, with operations in outer space	National, with foreign offices and operations in outer space	National, with foreign offices	International

a. United States Budget for fiscal year 1964. National Guard data from Encyclopaedia Britannica.
b. American Telephone and Telegraph *Annual Report* for 1961.
c. *Statistical Abstract of United States of America*, 1960. Table 298.
d. United Nations documents.
e. Included for background purposes, although they are "holders of ultimate authority" rather than members of the organization.

getting people to accept new rules and procedures to take the place of those that must be discarded.

5. SIZE

The size of an organization may be measured in five dimensions: (i) Number of members, with attention wherever appropriate to distinctions between employed, affiliate, client and individual-or-group membership; (ii) Material assets, such as land, buildings, equipment, machinery, inventories, credits, and cash. Often the most relevant measure is the quantity of a single type of strategic asset—such as hospital beds, classrooms, freight cars, or airplanes; (iii) Actual or budgeted expenditures. With government agencies and the internal units of all (including business) organizations, expenditures are widely used as a measure of output; (iv) Quantity of output. Monetary measures are possible only with business-type organizations. In other cases the quantity of different types of output cannot be directly aggregated; (v) Spatial distribution of members, assets, expenditures, or output.

Although a major increase in any one dimension may imply increases in some of the others, there is no necessary relationship between any two dimensions. This point is developed further in the discussion of organizational growth, particularly in "The law of disproportionality," in Chapter 17.

In considering the size of all organizations as a whole, or even of any large group of organizations, the most useful dimension is the number of members. First of all, the assets acquired, expenditures made and output produced by an organization are more measures of organizational action than of the organization. When we count members, we are coming closest to the organization itself, which essentially consists of the interactions among its members.

Second, membership size is the only dimension for which data are generally obtainable. Comparable data on the value of assets and output can usually be obtained only for business organizations; when obtained they are subject to serious problems of interpretation. Expenditure data for national labor federations are often kept secret. Spatial distribution cannot readily be quantified in comparable terms. This problem of comparability is illustrated in the table "Which Is Biggest?" Membership data provide the easiest basis for comparing the four giants: the United States Department of Defense, the American Telephone and Telegraph Corporation, the CIO-AF of L and the United Nations.

Once we go beyond employment figures, however, there are problems of comparability in membership data. By the number of affiliates, the CIO-AF of L, with its 15 million members, is certainly bigger than the United Nations. By the number of people represented, the United Nations is larger. By the number of people employed the United States Department of Defense is the largest of them all—and probably the largest single organization outside of the U.S.S.R. and China.

Despite these limitations, membership data provide a useful way of measuring the distribution of organizations by size groups. Thus an interesting comparison may be made between business, Federal Government and labor organizations in the U.S.A.:

PERCENTAGE DISTRIBUTION OF ORGANIZATIONS

Membership Size Group	Business, 1956[a]	Federal Government Agencies, 1960[b]	Trade Unions, 1958[c]
Under 1,000	99.0	41.5	7.5
1,000-10,000	.9	27.9	27.5
10,000-1,000,000	.1	29.7	64.0
Over 1,000,000	.0	1.9	1.0
Total	100.0	100.0	100.0

a. *Statistical Abstract of United States of America*, 1960. Table 625. Includes military employees and Coast Guard.

b. *Ibid.*, Table 502. Federal agencies only. Excludes Central Intelligence Agency and legislative and judicial branches. Executive Office of President regarded as one agency.

c. *Ibid.* Table 299.

Thus we see that while most business organizations have less than 1,000 employees, less than half of the Federal Government agencies fall in this group. (We may be sure that the proportion in this smallest category would rise considerably, if state and local government agencies were also included.) In contrast, almost two-thirds of the trade unions are in the 10,000 to one million category. By emphasizing the number of organizations, however, this table understates the importance of the larger organizations. A major shift to the higher categories is obtained by distributing the total number of members by the size of the organizations to which they belong:

PERCENTAGE DISTRIBUTION OF ORGANIZATION MEMBERSHIP

Membership Size Group	Business, 1956	Federal Government Agencies, 1960	Trade Unions, 1958
Under 1,000	65.0	.2	.1
1,000-10,000	17.6	1.0	1.3
10,000-1,000,000	17.4	25.0	85.0
Over 1,000,000	.0	74.0	13.6
Total	100.0	100.0	100.0

Sources: Same as in previous table.

If the available membership data on associations were compiled by government statistical agencies, it would be more appropriate to include trade unions together with other associations and to make a formal distinction between affiliates and employees, with an indication of the ratio of the one to another.

The effect of variations in group size has long been a subject of attention by social scientists. Thus Simmel stressed the difference between two-person and three-person groups. In a group of two "the social structure here rests immediately on the one and on the other of the two, and the secession of either would destroy the whole. . . . As soon, however, as there is an association of three, a group continues to exist even in case one of the members drops out." When a third member is added, he may combine with one of the others, become a mediator between them or follow a policy of divide and conquer (1950, p. 123, p. 145-169). It might be added that the third member may also become a "semioutsider" or a "sleeping partner."

As the small group becomes somewhat larger, cases of communication, attitudes of intimate sympathy and close identification may be lost. Smaller subgroups and factions are likely to develop. Leadership skills become a much greater factor in the creation of unity.[3]

As organizations become still larger, many relations become less personal (*Medalia*). There is even more specialization of function and more reliance on formal authority, rules and "antagonistic cooperation" (*Arensberg and MacGregor; Ellsworth*). With continued growth the organization faces increasingly serious problems of internal communication (*Burling et al.*), morale (*Worthy*), and absenteeism (*Covner*). These problems are heightened by geographical spread (*Kaufman*) and absentee ownership (*Warner and Low*). By the time it becomes a really large organization it loses much of the flexibility it enjoyed in earlier days. "Large organizations with different purposes seem to resemble each other more than small organizations with different purposes do. It is not too fanciful to think of a single organizational type toward which all giant organizations tend. An army, an industrial enterprise, a newspaper, a philanthropy, and a university all resemble each other, or, more exactly, they all approach a common type. Their small group prototypes, by contrast, do not resemble each other . . ." (Caplow).

In looking at large organizations, however, we must keep in mind Barnard's well-founded observation that nowhere in the world "can there be found a large organization that is not composed of small units"

3. This question has frequently been explored by the psychologists of group dynamics, but with more attention to discussion groups than to work groups. See particularly Hare (1953).

(1938, p. 110). Thus, many administrators within a very large organization are men and women responsible for the activities of small units. The differences between these units and "independent" organizations of similar size is merely that the former are part of a larger organization instead of merely some loose cooperative system. Without much more research on the matter, the implications of this difference are not so clear. Many small organizations—from bootblack stands and cigar stores to junk dealers and bricklaying firms—are probably as specialized as any "fractionated" unit in an industrial or government giant. Many small units in a large organization probably enjoy freedoms of action and initiative rarely approximated by the small entrepreneur. In any case, as will be discussed and elaborated upon in Chapters 10 and 17, the growth of organizations is followed by an inevitable dispersion of power. The deliberate cultivation and promotion of this dispersion may, indeed, be the result of conscious administrative action (*Kaufman; Chandler; Dill*).

6. TIME

There are also important time dimensions of any organization and its operations. Among these are the continuity, duration, and pace of its operations. Organizational age will be discussed in Chapter 17 in the context of survival or liquidation.

A. *Operational continuity*. Some organizations are involved in "continuous process" operations. Their members work—or must be ready to work—"around the clock." Among these are steel, chemical, and cement plants with ovens and other facilities that need day and night attention. In the case of hospitals, hotels, police forces, and armies it is the clients who need continuous attention or protection. In contrast with those that operate during the daytime only, these organizations require a high degree of scheduling and internal control. This degree is still higher for those that are expected to be ready for unexpected emergencies.

From a longer range viewpoint the activities of any organization fluctuate over a period of time. These fluctuations are sometimes violent. In agriculture these fluctuations are determined to a considerable extent by the cycle of the seasons and the biological attributes of specific crops. It is this assumed certainty of the agricultural production cycle which has throughout the centuries given rise to a certain common psychology among people involved directly in the cultivation of land. Both the cycle of the seasons and the inevitability of certain "acts of God" are taken for granted. It is only when modern technology enters the picture and disrupts the traditional cycle that new attitudes are developed and a new agricultural psychology comes into being. For military organizations these fluctuations are both more violent—since they involve a change from peace or "cold" war to "hot" war—and more unpredictable. Except for cases of clear aggression, no one is ever sure when war will break out. Thus military organizations spend most of their time getting ready for emergencies which may never materialize—or at least will not do so in any predictable manner.

B. *Operational duration.* Although the printing of a daily newspaper is a very quick operation, the production of printing presses takes much longer. The construction of a new building to house both the printing presses and the whole staff of the newspaper will take still longer. The newspaper announcement of the opening of a giant new dam or of the discovery of a new use for atomic energy will usually be the culmination of work which started many years ago.

The most obvious implication of a long drawn-out production process is the necessity for long-range advance planning. A little less obvious is the human problem which arises whenever people are expected to work hard on behalf of goals whose realization is far distinct in the future.

For military organizations the largest of all question marks is the assumption that should be made concerning the duration of "the next war." To plan for a long, drawn-out battle of attrition is one thing. To plan for participation in one tremendous holocaust which may last only a few days—or even a few hours—is something else entirely. The latter assumption wrecks all previous concepts of defense and attack, build-up, and mobilization. Under this assumption, the management of mass murder becomes a matter of split-second decisions made by an unbelievably small number of people whose identity cannot be fully determined in advance.

C. *Pace.* There is a great difference between the administration of a slow and leisurely operation and the administration of one which moves forward at a breakneck pace. In the former case more things can be done in accordance with rules and routine. Less conflicts will usually arise. Those which do can be mediated more readily. In the latter case, even in large and presumably inflexible organizations, routine will be swept aside in order to cope with crises. People will step on each other's toes and, when this happens, both sides will shout more wildly. The energies of both the managers and the managed will be drained. And yet—and this is one of the great glories of administration in times of crisis—both sides may get deep satisfaction from seeing that things are really accomplished and this sense of satisfaction may itself develop new resources of personal energy. This is why the fast-paced operation will usually attract people of more outstanding abilities and more audacious minds.

In military organizations there is an extremely sharp contrast between the leisurely pace of peacetime and the rapid pace of war. Officers best suited for one of these periods may be ill suited for the other. This is illustrated by the famous statement of a quartermaster-general (which probably appears in the lore of all armies): "My office was running splendidly until the war disrupted it." Efforts to maintain continuous "combat readiness" without the imminence of combat may easily become routinized and illusory.

B. *Roles and Functions*

AS WE LOOK INSIDE an organization, we find that its components or building blocks are its various units (or groups of members) and individual members. More specifically, the building blocks are the behavior expected of them and used as a standard to judge their performance. This is equivalent to the concept of social role presented in the previous chapter with respect to individuals and at the beginning of this chapter with respect to organizations as a whole. Here we concentrate on the social roles occupied by units and individuals. These are often referred to by the terms "function," "mission," "job," "task" or "duty"—used in either the singular or plural. The terms "position" and "office" are reserved for the social role occupied by individuals.[4]

1. OUTPUT, FUNCTIONS, WORK FLOW

The principle "By their fruits ye shall know them" is as applicable to the units of an organization as to an organization as a whole. The difference is that the role or function of a unit consists of intermediate rather than end products. Many units commonly have names which refer to the nature of their output such as personnel division, inspection section, tool-building shop, and legal department. If a unit's name is not fully descriptive (as with "the Administrative Office") this is often because it produces a varied output mix that cannot be aptly designated by one or two words. In any event a unit's output mix—and thereby its function in the organization—can be understood only by looking at the specific services it is expected to render.

4. A more detailed analysis of roles and functions, together with the extremely important distinction between operating goals and general functions, is presented in Chapter 15.

The only other bases of functional subdivision among units are location (as with field offices) and time (as with night shifts). Yet both location and time are subordinate to product. Any locational or temporal classification is superimposed upon product classification. A field office is an organization which is located in a certain place in order to produce certain products at that place. A night shift, day shift, or holiday shift produces certain products at a given place in time.

Proper attention to the importance of product classification as the basis of internal organization has been thwarted by the popular, but misleading, distinction between products, functions (in the sense of certain types of processes), and clients as different bases for organization. Actually, a "functional" or "process organization"—such as an engineering department or an electrolytic process division—is one which produces a specific type of service. A "client" organization—such as a ladies' dresses section of a department store or an adult education division of a university—is one which supplies certain products to specific categories of clients. In each case the use of terms relating to function, process and client is justified only to the extent that it aids in identifying the services or goods produced by a unit or in distinguishing between intermediate and final products.[5]

The output principle applies to individual roles also. The basis of every position or office is the bundle of services for which the occupant is responsible. The nature of these services is revealed both in the formal subdivision of labor among various positions and incurrent delegations and redelegations of responsibility. Many aspects of formal roles, apart from those that may be confidential or secret, can be only partly understood by outsiders or by organizations' members who do not interact frequently with the incumbents. Written job descriptions, as pointed out

---

5. In his classic "Note on the Theory of Organization" Gulick first suggested that a worker can be placed in a unit on the basis of one of these four considerations: the major *purpose* he is serving, the *process* he is using, the *persons* or *things* dealt with, or the *place* where he renders his service (1937, p. 15). Many other writers have taken up the same classification system. Business administration writers have often narrowed down the extremely broad term "purpose" to "product," and have broadened "process" to include professional functions, technical processes or the use of certain types of equipment. Simon has vigorously criticized the purpose-process-clientele-place differentiation by claiming that the only difference between purpose and process is that the former is at a higher level in the "means—and hierarchy" and that clientele and place "are really not separate from purpose, but a part of it" (1947, p. 28-33). Here he comes very close to recognizing the important distinction between final and intermediate products, but less close to the necessity of basing organizational classification squarely upon product classification or to the crucial distinction between output purposes and other organizational purposes.

in Chapter 15, tend to be out-of-date or to center on titles, financial rewards and the perquisites of office (which may range from a rug on the floor to a beautiful secretary). The loving care often given to the meticulous delineation of these matters is due in large part to their important contribution toward meeting the survival, commergence, differentiation, and even self-development needs of an organization's members.

Separate expectations concerning the output performance of units and individuals, in turn, are linked together by more general expectations concerning the "work flows" through which the various intermediate products contribute to the end products of the organization as a whole. A work flow that centers around the movement of raw materials (with or without processing) or identifiable documents (such as applications and purchase orders) can readily be visualized by administrators. It can be scientifically analyzed by production engineers.

Work flows centering around information and influence are harder to pin down. In large organizations they tend to be more significant. In organizations whose end products are intangible services they are "the works." Under such circumstances the work flow basis of unit and position functions may be rather vague. This vagueness is still greater in new and growing organizations, in which the end products themselves are unclear or changing (*Simon*, 1953; *Orzack*). With technological improvements in production processes the relation between established functions and actual work flow is often destroyed. At the same time new functions may be established whose relation to work flow and end product may be highly uncertain and sharply questioned within the organization. In any case, the total work flow in any complex organization is extremely difficult to understand. This difficulty is enhanced whenever organization charts, which are easy to prepare, serve to detract attention from work flow, which is almost impossible to chart or visualize in its entirety.[6]

2. FUNCTION COMBINATIONS

The output mix (or general functions) of any unit or position may be regarded as a combination or "bundle" of smaller, separable functions. With greater specialization, the processes of "cellular fission" usually lead to a large number and variety of positions and smaller units. This, in turn, leads to more complex patterns of combining positions and smaller

6. Many of the difficulties in developing techniques for the analysis of total work flow are shown in Chapple and Sayles (1961), which is based on the principle that "the technology or flow of work is the major criterion for designing the structure" of organizations.

units into larger units. Thus at both the highest and lowest levels of an organization administrators are continually faced with the question "How to combine functions?" Except for the first days of an entirely new organization, this question usually arises in the form of "Where to place a new function?" and "How to change the existing combination pattern?" Thus the search for any answer—even one calling for a drastic reorganization—is inevitably affected by the existing combination pattern. The answer itself is usually formulated—or justified—in terms of one or more of the following technical considerations: [7]

A. *Jointly produced output.* Positions or units performing dissimilar functions may be combined to cooperate in producing a similar set of intermediate products. Many of the largest units are based on this consideration. The "composite work group" provides a way of doing this with the smallest units (*Rice, 1958; Herbst*).

B. *Similar activities.* This consideration leads to the grouping together of specialists whose services may contribute to the production of a variety of dissimilar subsequent products—as with central units of lawyers or typists.

C. *Most use.* "The reception desk may be made a part of the purchasing department, sales department, or personnel department, depending upon which has the most callers and relies most frequently upon the receptionist to provide initial information and advice" (Newman, 1951, p. 137).

D. *Attention.* A new activity may be assigned to the administrator who will give it the desired form of attention—whether this means support, control or suppression. This may mean a "clean break" from its point of origin (Koontz and O'Donnell, 1955, p. 129-130).

E. *Independent check.* Care is often taken not to assign "policing" activities such as inspection, auditing, and investigations to those who are being "policed."

F. *Competition.* The development of similar combinations may provide "deadly parallels" whereby the performance of each may be judged competitively. The detachment of a subordinate unit may revitalize its former "parent" by providing stronger competition for budgetary allocations.

G. *Coordination.* The combination of dissimilar units may be necessary to keep competition within bounds and obtain more cooperation or better integration of divergent policies.

---

7. This list is derived, in part, from the acute observations embodied in Newman's "factors in grouping activities" (1951, p. 131-144) and Koontz and O'Donnell's "principles of association" (1955, p. 122-135).

H. *Costs.* Some combinations—particularly highly specialized similar activities—are conspicuously costly if a small volume of operations leads to idle time. This can be overcome by a broadening of the bundle. Costs resulting from red tape, inflexibility and personal aggrievement are harder to take into account.

The fact that these considerations may sharply conflict gives but a small indication of the difficulty of combining functions. Many changes in the fission-fusion pattern within an organization are far more than technical matters. They always have a direct bearing upon the personal satisfactions of the incumbents of positions and the members of units. They may have an important effect upon the distribution of power and status within the organization and upon relations with external groups. Whether so conceived or not, they may turn out to be ways of reshaping the objectives of the organization as a whole (*Simon*, 1953).

At the level of individual positions another consideration is the degree of monotony that may be created by narrow bundles of highly similar activities. This may result in a loss of work satisfactions and output (*Katz et al.*, 1950). This situation may be remedied through "job enlargement" (*Mann and Hoffman*, 1960; *Walker and Guest*, 1952). The broadening process usually requires more attention to training. Any more significant enlargement of the bundles also requires considerable freedom by incumbents in "switching" from one line of activity to another, or considerable looseness in the identification of activities. This freedom and looseness are greatest at the higher levels of administrative authority. Here also we frequently find "job enlargement" in the form of "multiple hat assignments," as when a person is assigned to two different positions or is given special ad hoc assignments in addition to his "regular" position.

3. SPECIALIST-ADMINISTRATOR COMBINATIONS

A built-in role conflict of increasingly serious proportions is often found in the combination of administrative and nonadministrative activities. The resulting mixture or compound is relatively stable when the nonadministrative or technical work involves no great difficulties and no great amount of personal commitment. But when such work is of a high order of technical complexity and can be properly performed only by the continuing investment of intellectual energy, a serious conflict may emerge.

The role conflict of the specialist-as-administrator often becomes particularly acute as he advances in his career and enters positions with increasing administrative responsibility.

In the first phase of a specialist's career, he has little or no administrative responsibility. In order to obtain more professional responsibility he must improve his professional ability. In the case of the "pusher," responsibility may grow more rapidly than ability. In the case of the "timid soul," ability may grow more rapidly than responsibility. But by and large the two elements move upward together at not too dissimilar rates.

In the second phase professional responsibility and ability both become greater, with the possibility that the latter may grow more slowly. This possibility is linked with the fact that at this phase the first major increment of administrative responsibility may enter the picture.

At this phase two aspects of the specialist-administrator role conflict may begin to emerge. First, it may become difficult to adjust to the addition of administrative responsibility, a responsibility for which the specialist has not been prepared, and perhaps not even warned about in the course of his professional training. If adjustment is slow, people will say that "he doesn't understand people" or "doesn't know how to get along with people." Second, administrative and specialist professional responsibilities compete for time and attention. "These administrative burdens," the specialist will complain, "keep me from getting down to work."

At the third stage the administrative burden rises sharply again. Professional responsibilities may increase also—but not necessarily. It may be increasingly possible to rely on the expertise of subordinates. It now becomes much more difficult to "keep abreast of things" in one's professional field. The conflicting time pressures now become more serious. The administrator may feel that he is being torn to pieces. Many years of training, his professional loyalties and ambitions, his intellectual predilections, all push him toward a continuation of the professional career which he has so arduously built up in his younger years. Yet in most cases this can be done only at the cost of sacrificing leisure, health, family life or administrative performance. The problem of coordinating the work of other specialists pulls him away from his own specialty. Moreover, organizational necessities, the peculiar structure of the ladder of advancement and his managerial ambitions impel him up the rocky road of administrative power and responsibility. For him personally this may produce an inner conflict with serious implications. For the organization it may mean—although not always—that a good scientist, doctor, or economist has been sacrificed to obtain a bad, a mediocre or an unhappy administrator.

At the fourth stage the chief engineer becomes a general manager, the doctor becomes a hospital administrator or head of the health department, the nursing supervisor becomes chief of nursing services, the dean becomes a university president, a field commander becomes a chief of staff. For all of these people, the increment to administrative responsibility is the largest in their careers. Their professional responsibilities inevitably decline—although the great variety of organizational, production, and staffing patterns make it impossible to generalize as to how steep this decline may be. At the time of this great "jump" no immediate loss of professional ability is involved. Yet now it becomes impossible for such people to give adequate attention to professional literature, conferences, writing, or research. Their "inside" work increasingly involves relations with other managers rather than specialists. In addition, there is an increasing preoccupation with "external" relations.

At either the third or fourth stage the conflict may be resolved by victory for the administrator in the individual's personality and withdrawal by the specialist. There may be deep regrets concerning the outcome; there may be elaborate pretenses that he is still an outstanding professional. Yet the die has been cast. Now that he is a full-fledged administrator, he will never go back to his "first love." His present love is a jealous mistress demanding all his devotion and attention.

Various efforts have been made to handle the problems of specialist-administrator role conflicts. One line of action has been to establish specialist roles which are as high in rank and prestige as, or even higher than, those of top administrative roles. No matter how much further action may be carried along this line, however, it could not appreciably affect the growing magnitude of the problem. In a technological age top administrative roles are more and more defined in terms of a compound of administrative and specialist responsibilities. Where this is not true, a specialist background—if not outstanding achievement—often enters as an informal prerequisite in connection with the prestige aspects of a position and the confidence which people must have in its incumbent.

Another line of action is found in educational programs—whether at pre-, mid-, or top career stages—designed to help specialists in the difficult process of learning to carry administrative responsibilities. Although these may be of great benefit to the organizations in which specialist-administrators play an important role, this does not mean that they will necessarily ease the acute personal conflicts of the individuals involved. The person who is pulled in two directions by a strong horse and a weak one is not necessarily better off if the weak one is strengthened.

4. INTERLOCKING FUNCTIONS

The combination of functions into bundles, however, is not as significant as the combination of actual activities into the work flows of an organization. This requires many points of interlocking action among both people and units. The very nature of the interlock will make it seem that functions are being duplicated. Thus the functions of a machinist will include certain services with respect to the care and maintenance of the machinery and tools he uses. But a special maintenance man may also be responsible for similar services. The line between their respective responsibilities can never be drawn so rigorously as to avoid an area of apparent overlapping. At a somewhat higher level there is a similar area of ambiguity and potential conflict, in the respective responsibilities of the foreman and the head of the maintenance department. This area may become still larger when we consider the respective roles of procurement, engineering, accounting and economic analysis personnel in determining when to replace old machinery with new. In one sense we can say that each deals with the same problem. In another it is clear that each deals with a different aspect of the same problem. Both of these viewpoints are correct. From the point of view of the organization as a whole it is clear that the various aspects are so inextricably interrelated that there are few places where one's responsibility clearly ends and the other's begins. The interlocking of functions requires some form of "overlapping" or apparent "duplication."

This is even more obvious in giant business organizations, large government departments and in the structure of government as a whole. Here one will even find scattered throughout the system people with the responsibility of considering similar aspects of problems, albeit from different viewpoints. Thus many units of the same systems will have their own analysts of the current economic outlook, their own Latin-American experts, their own nuclear fission scientists. Some of these may not only provide similar services; they may even compete for identical clients. Whether or not this is wasteful cannot be automatically deduced from evidence on overlapping or duplication. As one writer has put it, men would be pretty badly off if their shirt tails were not long enough to overlap with the top of their trousers. Nor does this observation sanction their reaching to one's ankles. It merely means that one cannot reach judgments about wastefulness without a careful analysis of the specific circumstances and alternatives. It also serves as a warning against the naïve aspiration—so often and so futilely voiced by alleged experts on administration and organization—for an organizational structure that will provide a crystal-clear picture of everyone's function and once and for all eliminate all duplications, overlappings and ambiguities. As a conspicuous case of an "oversell," this aproach may help "clinch the deal" in getting approval for a job analysis survey. It will also help those administrators who need expert assistance in "taking off" into a flight from reality.

c. *Hierarchy: Superiors and Subordinates*

HIERARCHY is the most conspicuous part of the formal structure of any organization. As such, it has frequently been falsely identified with the totality of formal structure. Still worse, the adjustment of hierarchic relationships has been falsely identified with the totality of the administrative process. This overemphasis is probably rooted in the psychological importance to many people of domination-submission relations and in a natural tendency to interpret organizational phenomena in terms of childhood experiences with superior parental authority.

In the field of administrative thought this overemphasis has led to a preoccupation with abstract prescriptive or normative principles on the "should be" side of the subject. Relatively little intensive research has been done on the "is" and "has been" of hierarchical relations.

1. THE ESSENCE OF HIERARCHY

The essence of hierarchy is the distinction between the role of "superior" (or "superordinate") and "subordinate." The person or group in the superior role is expected to exercise authority over the subordinate. The subordinate, in turn, is expected to accept the authority of his superior and be responsible to him.

We usually regard an organization as hierarchic, however, only when the superior-subordinate relation is carried further by making the first subordinate the superior of another subordinate. As an organization becomes more hierarchic, the number of subordinates who are also superiors becomes larger. We thus find authority and responsibility "flow" in an unbroken line from higher levels of authority to the lowliest subordinate. This line (traditionally called the "chain of command") may be referred to as the "line of authority." The various points on this line in different organizations are illustrated on page 221.

A large proportion of hierarchic relations are between a superior person or unit and a number of subordinates. The number of such subordinates may be referred to as the "span of authority" (the more traditional and limited term being "span of control"). The wider this span the more the lines of authority may branch out. The total number of people subordinate to the highest authority in the organization may be increased by widening the span, lengthening the line, or both.

Hierarchic level, it should be noted, does not by itself determine the grade or status of all positions or the personal rank of all incumbents. At each level we usually find a considerable range of positions and rank.

LINES OF AUTHORITY

Army	Government	Business	Catholic Church
Commander-in-Chief	Chief of State	Board Chairman	Pope Bishop
Army commander	Minister (or Secretary)	President	Priest
Corps commander	Service director	Vice-president	
Division commander	Office director	General manager	
Regimental commander	Bureau director	Production manager	
Battalion commander	Division director	General foreman	
Company commander	Section chief	Foreman	
Platoon leader	Unit chief	Group leader	
Squad leader	Group leader		
Private			

Thus a top administrator's direct personal assistant or secretary may have a much lower grade or rank than an administrator three or four levels below him on the line of authority.

In most cultures the concepts of "higher" and "lower"—and such related terms as "level," "top," "middle," "bottom," "above," "over," "under," and "below"—seem to be an ingrained part of man's perception of superior-subordinate relations. Historically, this has been explained by going back to the days of more primitive battle, when the military superiority of horsemen over footsoldiers was associated with their reaching a greater height. Divinity—particularly in the case of monotheism—is often thought of in connection with the heavens above. Man's superiority over woman may be symbolized by over- under- positions of sexual embrace. A more mundane explanation can be found in the frequent correlation, quickly learned by every infant, between height and strength.

Superior hierarchic authority is never absolute. At the lower levels it is always confined to a certain area of operations and limited by superior authority. At the peak of an organization it is always limited to the purposes of the organization, as well as being subjected to various external controls. Even in *The Leviathan*, where he proposed "absolute" monarchy as the ideal form of government, Hobbes placed reservations on the monarch's use of his "undivided sovereignty." Even in the Catholic Church, where the doctrine of "papal infallibility" has reigned since its formal proclamation in 1870, the Pope is infallible only on matters of faith and morals and not on administrative matters. Nor does the Pope have unquestioned authority to draw the dividing line between the "theological" and the "administrative."

Hierarchic centralization of authority, paradoxically, depends for its very existence upon a certain amount of decentralization. The centralizing effects of the line of authority are achieved mainly by grants of formal authority from those at the higher to those at the lower positions on the line. These grants may be spelled out, or be implicit in the formal positions that people occupy (Follett's "authority of the position"). Or they may take the form of current and accumulated delegations of specific authority from their superiors.

Moreover, higher authority is further limited by one of the great unwritten "laws" of formal hierarchy—namely, that the lines of authority serve as the formal channels of communication. The superior is expected to communicate with the "two downers" (and "three downers" and so on) through the formal line of authority, not directly. Although he preserves a residual or ultimate authority through his right to review the activities of his inferiors, he gives up—or at least substantially modifies —his right to exercise this authority through direct relationships at lower levels.

No organization can hold together without some pattern of hierarchy. In the words of Shakespeare's Ulysses (*Troilus and Cressida*, Act I, Scene 3), as he bewails the breakdown of hierarchic authority in the Grecian Army sprawled outside the walls of Troy:

> The heavens themselves, the planets and this centre,
> Observe degree, priority and place,
> Insisture, course, proportion, season, form,
> Office and custom in all line or order . . .
>
> Take but degree away, untune that string,
> And, hark, what discord follows!

The higher positions in any hierarchy provide a unifying symbolism of tremendous significance. Whether their legitimate occupants are revered, feared, loved, cursed, or sneered at (and all of this may occur together), they symbolize the purposes and values of the collectivity. They provide places where important decisions may be made or legitimated and where internal conflicts may be authoritatively settled. The entire hierarchic structure provides a foundation for confidence in the ability of an organization and its members to get things done. The lines of authority are the backbone of the internal communication system. They also serve as possible ladders for internal advancement, thus strengthening the identification of upward-aspiring individuals with the organization as a whole. Thus one need not regard hierarchy as the totality of organizational structure to agree with Ulysses that discord would follow should we "untune that string."

2. THE INVERTED PYRAMID

Hierarchic structure has been traditionally described in terms of a simple pyramid. This is based upon the idea that as we move from the higher to the lower levels of authority we find more and more people.

But this idea does not apply to the highest levels of formal authority. Here a comprehensive picture of hierarchic relations demands that we place an inverted pyramid on top of the traditional pyramid. This concept can be dramatized by the following illustration.

THE UPPER PYRAMID OF FORMAL AUTHORITY

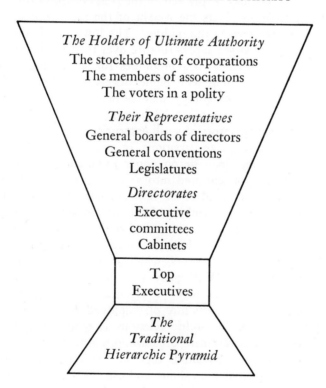

The Holders of Ultimate Authority
The stockholders of corporations
The members of associations
The voters in a polity

Their Representatives
General boards of directors
General conventions
Legislatures

Directorates
Executive
committees
Cabinets

Top
Executives

*The
Traditional
Hierarchic Pyramid*

At the highest level we find *the holders of ultimate authority*. For corporations these are the stockholders, for associations the total membership, and for a political community the voters. These may include hundreds, thousands, or even many millions of people. In organizations composed of other organizations—such as trade associations, general federations of labor, loose cartels, and weak federations of states—the holders of ultimate authority are the member organizations or states.

At the next subordinate level we find *the representatives of the holders of ultimate authority,* as they operate in legislatures, conventions, in general boards of directors. This group is much smaller, ranging from a dozen or two dozen people to a maximum of a few hundred.

Still lower on this inverted pyramid we find the *directorates.* These are the small executive committees, central committees, and cabinets. They usually range in size from two or three people to a maximum of one or two dozen.

Below the directorates are the *top executives.* From the viewpoint of the traditional pyramid they are the "men at the top." But no matter how firmly their feet may be planted on the peaks of the bottom pyramid, they carry on their shoulders the weight of the top pyramid. From this viewpoint they are "men in the middle." The lower-level administrators, in turn, have an even larger superstructure over their head, although they may have smaller individual responsibilities for supporting it. In either case the problem of dealing with higher levels of authority is often so onerous that little time or energy may be left for attending to subordinates. The only administrators who have no superstructure over their heads are the owner-operators of small enterprises.

There are interesting size variations. In some organizations—particularly the smallest—there may be no upper pyramid at all. In others all three levels may be concentrated into a small directorate. In a family-owned corporation the holders of ultimate authority may indeed be fewer in number than the members of the directorate—in which case we once again have a pyramid-type structure resting on its base rather than its apex. With universities and hospitals, likewise, there may be but two levels: a large board of governors, which holds the ultimate authority, and a smaller directorate. With many associations, the inverted pyramid at the top of the structure may be gigantic in comparison with the relatively small pyramidal structure of employed staff.

This general set of hierarchic relations is rendered more complex by multiple roles. In government organizations a minister standing at the top of the bureaucratic pyramid, together with his director general, may also be a member of the cabinet and the elected legislature, as well as a voter. In corporations stock ownership may be distributed in various ways among directorates, top executives and throughout the lower levels down to the workers. In a producer's cooperative the workers and bureaucrats as a whole are the owners, holders at ultimate authority. In associations and political parties built on the basis of "democratic centralism" the holders of formal authority are various groups of subordinates who elect their representatives and entrust them with formal authority.

3. MORE THAN PYRAMIDS

As we descend to a lower level of formal authority, however, we often find much larger numbers of people. This brings us back to the traditional hierarchic pyramid.

The tremendous potential of the pyramidal form for bringing large numbers of subordinates under central authority is suggested by establishing a model pyramid with nine levels of administrators and six subordinates for every person in the pyramid. This yields the following pattern:

```
            1
            6
          3 6
        2 1 6
      1, 2 9 6
      7, 7   7 6
     4 6,  6  5 6
    2 7 9,    9 3 6
  1,  6 7 9,  6 1 6
  _____
  2,  0 1 5,  5 3 9
```

A pattern of this kind would enable one top executive (or seven, if we include his immediate subordinates) to exercise formal authority over 2,015,539 people. A tenth level would bring the total to 12,093,234—and an eleventh to 72,559,404! Although with varying numbers of subordinates the arithmetic would also vary, this diagram suggests that organizations of huge size can be established hierarchically without more than eight to ten levels. This probably explains why I have found very few organizations with 10—and none with more than 12—hierarchic levels (as contrasted with the much greater number of levels often found on salary scales). Unfortunately, there has as yet been no systematic statistical research in this field.

If we look carefully at a large set of pyramidal hierarchies, we shall find a number of standard variations. The "fat" ones have wider—and the "thin" ones—narrower spans of authority. The "tall" ones have longer—and the "short" ones smaller—lines of authority. There is a tendency for the fat ones to be shorter and the thin ones to be taller. Within each pyramid we shall find major variations in the span of authority from one level and one unit to another. We shall find many short lines of authority that connect only two or three levels, with many fewer lines running from the very top to the very bottom. In fact, we shall find that the over-all pyramid is a cluster of smaller pyramids of varying sizes and shapes.

If we look still more closely, we shall find that factors such as these often destroy the pyramidal shape entirely. This is particularly true whenever there is a decline in the percentage of unskilled employees' positions at the lowest level and a proliferation of skilled and semiskilled positions at the middle. In his study of the U.S. armed forces (1960, p. 65-67), Janowitz has illustrated this change in the following tables:

Pyramid *Army Enlisted Personnel, 1935*		*Octagon* *Air Force Bomb Squadron, Post-Korea*	
	%		%
Master sergeant	.8	Master sergeant	7.0
First sergeant	.9	Technical sergeant	10.3
Technical sergeant	1.3	Staff sergeant	15.2
Staff sergeant	3.6	Airman first class	24.4
Sergeant	9.4	Airman second class	28.1
Corporal	9.0	Airman third class	13.5
Private first class	25.4	Basic airman	1.5
Private	49.5		
Total	100.0	Total	100.0

His data on the officer corps show the same kind of change in the higher ranks:

OFFICER CORPS, 1920-50, HIERARCHY OF RANKS

	Army		Air-Force			Navy	
	1920	1950	1950			1920	1950
	%	%	%			%	%
General	.4	.8	.5	Admiral		1.3	.8
Colonel	4.1	9.4	4.3	Captain		4.4	6.8
Lt. Col.	4.7	11.5	10.0	Commander		7.6	10.9
Major	14.9	20.7	17.8	Lt. Cmdr.		14.4	18.3
Captain	35.9	34.9	34.6	Lieutenant		32.8	28.8
First Lt.	32.6	13.9	26.4	Lt. (j.g.)		16.6	24.0
Second Lt.	7.4	8.8	6.5	Ensign		22.9	10.4
Total	100.0	100.0	100.0	Total		100.0	100.0

Janowitz's perceptive analysis of these trends is as follows:

This parallels the changing pattern of civilian social structure, where the upper middle class proliferates because of the expansion of new professional and skill groups. In part, this represents an effort to raise the status and income of the soldier. In part, it represents a tendency of organizations to grow internally. Basically, this expansion of the middle strata of ranks—officers and enlisted men—is a typical manifestation of organizations which have grown more complex.[8]

Similar data for other kinds of organizations would unquestionably reveal many hierarchic patterns far closer to octagons, pentagons or other shapes than to traditional pyramids.

4. THE LAW OF MULTIPLE HIERARCHY

The traditional hierarchic model is based upon the simplistic assumption that every subordinate has only one direct superior. This assumption is an excellent projection of the make-believe world that subordinates often concoct for themselves in an effort to escape the complexities of organizational life. It is rationalized by analogy with parental authority and the higher levels of authority. If one father, why not one boss? If one board of directors, one cabinet or one president, why not just one superior?

But just as the lines of authority may converge in their upward flow toward one spot at the top we usually find that in their downward flow two or more lines of authority—not just one—converge upon one subordinate. This is frequently, although not always, based upon a distinction between different kinds of authority. In the Federal Government of the U.S.A. and some other presidential systems the President is subject to the authority of, and responsible to, both the holders of formal authority (the voters) and to the legislature. Many subordinate officials of corporations and government agencies are subject to certain forms of authority formally exercised by committees of boards of directors and legislatures. In universities a department head may be directly subordinate to one dean and on other matters to another dean or to the rector, vice president or president.

This phenomenon of multiple subordination is even more widespread at the levels below the top executives. Here we find that various members of an organization may have "functional," "technical," or "professional" authority over other members who are subordinate to them only on certain types of problems or with respect to the enforcement of certain rules. Typical cases are found in the authority of budget, auditing and control personnel over everyone in an organization and of "staff" specialists over administrators in the "line" or the "field." In such cases we find many members of an organization who are subject to the authority of

8. It should be kept in mind that Janowitz's figures do not deal directly with hierarchic levels of organization. Many people with lower rank occupy subordinate positions in units at high levels in the military organization.

people of lower rank or grade, or at lower hierarchic levels. This is very close to what Simmel described as "the expediently distributed alternation of superordination and subordination" (1950, p. 286-291). Thus in one type of situation A may have direct authority over B and B over C, with X having no direct relation with any of them. But with varying situations the formally prescribed patterns may vary as follows:

Situation 1   *Situation 2*   *Situation 3*   *Situation 4*

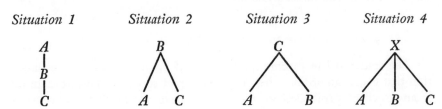

These shifting patterns are essential to operations under interlocking functions.

Another form of multiple hierarchy is found in appeal, grievance and suggestion systems, all of which are explicitly designed to provide additional lines of communication and authority. The very purpose of appeals systems is to allow subordinates to go over the heads of their superiors (*Evan*). Union-management grievance systems subject administrators at many levels to new "masters." Suggestions systems sidetrack them by providing additional channels of upward communication (Redfield, p. 140-158).

A special form of multiple hierarchy is found whenever groups of people belonging to different "classes" work together within the same organization. In most civil service systems there are various categories of civil servants, many of whom work together within a given organization. Military organizations usually have special career systems of their own; and in many military organizations civil servants work together with military officers. In the U.S. State Department various categories of civil servants work side by side with Foreign Service Officers, Foreign Service Reserve Officers, and Foreign Service Staff employees. In overseas establishments "alien clerks" are added to this heterogeneous mixture. Many of these special classes of employees are subject to the authority not only of their immediate hierarchic superiors but also of those who are formally responsible for the administration of the civil service and career systems.

Hence there is good basis for the Macmahon-Millett-Ogden finding, based upon their 1935-1941 analysis of the U.S. Works Progress Administration (1941, p. 266), that:

The theory of hierarchic decentralization should openly proclaim that lines of authority in the organization are frequently dual or even multiple, that the reaction of technology on administration is apt to increase the proportion of situations in which such conditions exist, and that the arrangement of structure and the training of personnel must provide for nicely divided loyalties.

The Macmahon-Millett-Ogden study, however, concentrated upon the dualistic distinction between "administrative authority" and "technical authority." More intensive studies of modern organizations would reveal more refined distinctions. They would probably also reveal that a large proportion of intra-organizational disputes result from divided loyalties and revolve—at least technically—around the boundaries between one form of authority and another.

Although the modern growth of specialization is a major factor in promoting a more complex interweaving of various types of authority, it should not be thought that multiple hierarchy—like Taylor's "functional foremanship"—is a recent invention that has grown up with the expansion of modern staff services. The formal hierarchies of ancient India, as described by Kautilya, and of the Byzantine Empire included special internal espionage or control systems directed by top rulers but operating at various levels. As far back as the twelfth and thirteenth century A.D. the formal structure of the Catholic Church provided for a separate hierarchy of papal legates—either a cardinal or a nuncio—who were authorized to by-pass the bishop and intervene in certain aspects of the affairs of both diocese and parish. The famous general staff system of the Prussians was based upon the concept of a "dual command function."[9] In each of these, the additional centers of authority served to strengthen central authority against the decentralizing tendencies inherent in large-scale organizations.

D. *Polyarchy: Coordinates*

EVEN WITH fully developed roles and rules, hierarchy itself is never enough to hold an organization together. It is essentially feudal in nature—albeit without fiefs and hereditary position. It deals with "vertical"

---

9. ". . . Scharnhorst began to bring into existence that peculiar Prussian device, the system of a command function jointly performed by the commander and the chief of staff. . . . The chief of the staff officers of a command was more than a coordinating subordinate; his status has been described with considerable accuracy as being that of 'junior partner' to the commander. Although the ultimate decision remained that of the commander, the chief of staff still shared in the results. Should a situation arise in which a commander disregarded the recommendations of the chief of staff, the latter . . . could insist on making his opinions a matter of record" (*Hittle*, 1949, p. 61).

relations alone, as with the line of authority from lord to vassal and sub-vassal. With the growth of specialization and economic interdependence, feudalism breaks down; horizontal and crisscrossing relations develop. In modern organizations such relations—which may be called "polyarchic" —fill in the otherwise bare and gaunt structure of formal hierarchy and round out a formal structure of much greater capacity and flexibility.

If hierarchy is a relationship between superior and subordinate, poly-archy may be defined as a coordinate relationship of responsibility. This does not mean that any two coordinates in this sense are at the same hierarchic level or of the same rank or grade. It merely means that their relationship is not one of superior-to-subordinate or that it takes place outside the sphere of their superior-to-subordinate relationship. Although polyarchy includes nonauthoritative relations among organizations, it will here be used only with reference to such relations within organizations.[10]

1. SHARED RESPONSIBILITY

One form of polyarchy is *shared responsibility*. This occurs when-ever coordinates share the responsibility for the same tasks or services. It is the fundamental relation between the members of any collegial body —whether it be a large assembly, such as a legislature or convention, or a smaller body such as a committee, board, council, commission, or panel.

The most conspicuous use of shared responsibility is in the upper pyramid of formal authority. Here the representatives of the holders of formal authority invariably interact on a polyarchic basis. The formal hierarchic elements in legislatures and conventions are limited mainly to the roles of those responsible for the scheduling of activities, the handling of committee work, and the internal direction of factions and parties. In the decisions of the legislature as a whole or of any of its committees all members have equal votes. The internal relationships are far more those of bargaining and power than those of formal authority. (Only in the relatively rare case of one-party systems with tight caucus control over all factions are internal relations on a formally hierarchic basis. Such a structure is far removed from the ordinary concept of a legis-lature.) Committees also play a major role. Their smaller size provides the basis for a division of labor within the legislature and other bodies representing the holders of ultimate authority. Appearing in the form of boards of directors, executive committees, cabinets, commissions,

10. This usage of "polyarchy" is not quite the same as that of Dahl and Lind-blom (1953), who concentrate on relations among organizations and regard hier-archy as "control of people by leaders" and polyarchy (or democracy) as "control of leaders by people."

councils and other collegial devices, they provide the typical organizational structure for directorates.

The most widespread use of committees, however, is at somewhat lower levels. Here they serve as one of the major methods of formally bringing together people from various points in the hierarchy. This is a representative function in many ways comparable to the representative functions of legislative assemblies. Although committee membership may be determined by hierarchical superiors, the representative pattern is crucial. When a problem cuts across the interests of many units in an organization, there is often no formal way to deal with it other than to establish a committee with representatives from each of these units. One alternative is to redefine the roles of these units so that the problem clearly belongs to one of them rather than to others; but this is a costly, time-consuming process of reorganization which may create more difficult situations with respect to other problems. Another alternative is to assign the problem in question to one unit in the regular hierarchy. But unless the roles of the other interested units are to be seriously impaired, these other units will usually have to be kept informed as to what is done or even asked for their advice. This, in turn, can often be done economically only by bringing representatives together in the form of a committee.

This representative function may be limited to one hierarchic level—as when a top executive sets up a "management committee" composed of his immediate subordinates. It may also span different levels in a hierarchy. Committees are often a formal instrumentality for enabling administrators to engage in systematic two-way communication with "two down'ers" and "three down'ers" without blatantly violating the hierarchic authority of intervening superiors.

Committees also play a major role in the adjudicatory processes within organizations. They provide a customary structural form for "internal courts" dealing with appeals, grievances and the application of stringent sanctions. They are used for the purposes of obtaining collective judgments on the qualifications of individuals considered for recruitment or promotion to important posts, on individual and group performance and on the merits and demerits of proposed courses of action. They provide an organizational framework for internal negotiation and for the reconciliation—and sometimes concealment—of the divergent views and interests. They are instrumentalities for mobilizing the power needed to obtain organizational action and for delaying, sidetracking or stopping organizational action.

For all these reasons large organizations are invariably given to the practice of establishing tremendous numbers of committees. These may be temporary or permanent, staffed or unstaffed, authorized to make decisions or only to offer advice and proposals. Their role may be narrow or broad, carefully defined or subject to the interpretation and initiative of committee members. They may be composed of the organization's members only, nonmembers only, or both.

Although all these committees, even the temporary ones, are part of the formal organizational structure, few organizations keep central records on the number, type and role of all their committees. Nor is the committee structure usually shown in formal organization charts. When occasional checks are made on the full use of committees, the results often produce a profound shock and sense of embarrassment. In any large government department, for example, it will usually be revealed that formal action has been taken to establish hundreds of committees. Many higher officials will be found to have formal membership in dozens of different committees.

One factor in the proliferation of committees is "committeeitis." Thus "let's set up a committee" becomes an automatic panacea for dealing with—or dodging—complex problems without exploiting the possibilities of using the existing hierarchic structure or without trying to integrate a new committee with it. Another factor is the anticommittee bias of "management experts" whose concept of formal structure is limited to simplistic models of formal hierarchy. If they give insufficient attention to the structural role of committees, their advice on organization and reorganization lacks realism. A new organization chart may be formally accepted within an organization and then just as formally negated by the decisions on the committee structure.

Trade unions may also provide an important—albeit sometimes unrecognized—part of an organization's formal structure. This is particularly true of union officers, union committees and management-union committees whose operations are based upon a formal agreement between the union and the organization. These individuals and committees will operate at various points in an organization's hierarchy but they are not subject to the hierarchic authority of the organization. Rather, they provide formalized opportunities for hierarchic subordinates to escape subordination and negotiate—directly or indirectly—with their erstwhile superiors on a formally equal basis. Although they may be closely linked with external labor bodies, they are also an integral part of the organization's structure. In fact, the union's internal structure and its tie-in with various levels of management will always have a major effect upon the distribution of authority and responsibility among administrative positions.

2. DISPERSED RESPONSIBILITY

Another form of intraorganizational polyarchy occurs among coordinates with *dispersed responsibility*. People responsible for different tasks or services are expected to attain certain common objectives by a process of mutual cooperation and adjustment.

The simplest case of dispersed responsibility is that of the relations between the different members of a single work group. A more complex case is that of the relations between the various administrators subject to the direct authority of an hierarchic superior. A still more complex case is the long series of coordinate relations that take place as materials or information in the production process weave their intricate path back and forth across unit boundaries.

Many of these relations are prescribed by those with formal authority. General rules sometimes include minute requirements for polyarchic relations. The most formalized example is provided by the rules governing an organization's budget-making process, which establish the framework for formalized bargaining among coordinates for their respective shares of scarce inputs. To the extent that they depart from hierarchic lines, clearance, consultation and "touch base" (or "keep them informed") procedures also deal with polyarchic relations. Production schedules set forth detailed work flow patterns among people and units with little regard to hierarchic levels. More important, polyarchic relations may be officially expected without any, or many, specific steps being formally prescribed. Role specifications often deal directly with cooperation and negotiation. Incumbents are selected in terms of their estimated ability to "get along" with coordinates. Coordinate subordinates are often instructed, or expected, "to work things out yourselves."

The extent of polyarchic relations in organizations is suggested by Landsberger's pioneering work in applying the Bales interaction analysis to the horizontal and vertical relations of production planning, production and sales personnel (1961). A simplified version of his findings in two plants follows.

	PER CENT OF HORIZONTAL INTERACTIONS ORIGINATED	
	Plant A	*Plant B*
Production planning and control	32	40
Production	17	41
Sales liaison	62	62

The horizontal interactions of sales liaison people are greater because "their job is mediating between the field sales force and the factory." A similar study has shown that "the purchasing agent's internal relationships (as opposed to his external relations with salesmen) are almost entirely lateral; they are with other functional departments of about the same rank in the organizational hierarchy—departments such as production scheduling, quality control, engineering, and the like" (*Straus*). These lateral relations are probably far more significant wherever mechanization reduces the need for supervision (*Simpson*) or, as in many government agencies, multitudinous clearances are essential to operations.[11]

To a certain extent, intraorganizational polyarchy of this type thrives only when covered by a hierarchic "umbrella." Higher hierarchic authority can be depended upon to legitimate agreements that would otherwise be unviable. It can be appealed to for the settlement of conflicts that would otherwise be irreconcilable. All this makes it much easier for coordinates to work things out among themselves on the basis of reciprocity, negotiation, bargaining, and mutual adjustment. Reciprocally, hierarchy depends upon polyarchy. The holders of superior authority can have time and energy for mediation, arbitration and legitimation on some matters only if a much larger amount of matters are handled through polyarchic relations alone.

In the actual processes of interaction polyarchic and hierarchic relations are closely blended. Hierarchic channels may be used as an instrument of polyarchic relations. Polyarchic relations may be used as channels of "fanning out" the orders of hierarchical superiors. In the full web of interrelations the distinctions between the two kinds of relations often fade away. This is particularly true when major attention is focused on the work to be done and the authority—in Follett's language—of each position. A suggestive hint as to how these interrelations might be analyzed has been provided by Stinchcombe's use of input-output matrices. Since a command or a bit of advice may travel through both hierarchic and polyarchic lines of communication, an input-output matrix may help indicate the nature of the tremendous variety of interrelations that take place through a complex communication net.[12]

11. In an overgenerous effort to explain Weber's neglect of this aspect of bureaucratic operations, Landsberger suggests that there may have been less "horizontal work flow" at the time when Weber wrote. Without getting into the question of how to measure "more" or "less," it seems more reasonable merely to assume that Weber simply did not see the horizontal relations that took place.

12. Stinchcombe (1961). A simpler technique is used in Weiss and Jacobson, (1955). It may be expected that much more refined techniques will eventually be developed. While Weiss and Katz use a simple matrix showing first-order relations, Stinchcombe attempts a "squared matrix" in order to show second-order relations also. It should be possible to go still further and, by applying an adapted form of the mathematical techniques used in input-output analyses for economies, deal with the sum of all internal relations and with external relations also.

E. *Centralization with Decentralization*

FEW ASPECTS of formal structure are more important than the pattern through which responsibility and authority are dispersed throughout an organization.

Few aspects are more difficult to pin down. Neither centralization nor decentralization are absolutes. An extreme of either one would destroy any organization. Not only do the two always appear together; they complement each other. The arteries of decentralization bring the life-blood of responsibility and authority to the various members, while the veins bring it back to the center. The decentralization of some functions is impossible without the centralization of others, and vice versa.

Nor can the nature of a centralization-decentralization pattern be detected by observing merely one aspect of formal structure. Role prescriptions and combinations are basic to the pattern. Hierarchy and codes of behavior, although they may appear to be centralizing forces only, are also techniques of decentralization. Polyarchy, despite its decentralizing aspects, is also an instrument of centralization.

To make it more difficult, centralization and decentralization must be thought of in terms of three dimensions: namely, the distribution of responsibility and authority by (i) vertical levels, (ii) horizontal levels and (iii) geographical location. The first of these is often thought of in terms of the extent of "delegation" of responsibility and authority. If this term is to be used, it must be kept in mind that delegation may be embodied in both the prescription of the function and in current requests by superior authority. Horizontal dispersion is affected to a large extent by the way in which functions are divided and combined. Thus the centralization of files, secretarial services, or purchasing takes certain functions away from certain spots and places them at others, but without necessarily raising them to a higher level of authority. The third is far more than a simple matter of geography. Dispersion in space affects the nature and reliability of communication systems, thereby forcing certain forms of decentralized action and centralized control.

The extent of decentralization at any one point can be appraised only with reference to specific functions. Unit heads may have more responsibility with respect to handling subordinates than in their dealings with outsiders, more responsibility in personnel than in financial matters, more leeway with current expenditures than with capital expenditures. The extent of decentralization with respect to any of these functions can be measured by (i) the type and number of decisions that can be made, (ii) the significance of these decisions in terms of their effect on costs, output and the number of people whose interests are affected, and (iii) the extent of freedom from review, reporting and consultation relations with superiors and others.[13] The extent of decentralization at any part of an organization cannot be regarded as an automatic indicator of the general pattern throughout the organization. Many divisions which have won a considerable degree of freedom from superior and horizontal control are run by "authority-hoarding" administrators who do their best to deny a similar degree of freedom to subordinate units. The administrators of tightly controlled subordinate units may react against what they regard as overcentralization by extensive delegation to subordinates of the small authority they enjoy.

Some of the factors making for centralization at the higher levels of an organization are obvious. A certain amount of centralization is essential to maintain a common pattern of accepted purposes, to coordinate many activities that may otherwise serve to defeat each other, and to provide a general framework for decentralized action. It is needed to prevent or counteract external efforts to weaken or destroy the organization through divisive action. It is needed to deal with external controllers— and in fact, may be demanded by them in order to see that control is effective. The larger an organization, the more important (and the more difficult) it is to develop central policies and controls that can hold it together. Less obvious, and much harder to pin down, is the drive of many top executives for larger amounts of personal authority as a means of satisfying their needs for status and respect. This factor may sometimes be associated with—and may often help to promote—a complementary interest of subordinates in escaping personal responsibility.

On the other side of the coin, the most objective factor in favor of decentralization is the advantage to be gained from the division and specialization of labor. So long as it is human beings instead of machines whose labor is divided and whose activities are specialized, some amount of responsibility and authority must inhere in both positions and units. Larger amounts may prevent or alleviate delays and congestion at higher levels and can lead to decisions that are not only swifter but more in tune with the facts of specific situations. They may lead to greater satisfaction and morale on the job, encourage initiative and ingenuity and

13. For purposes of job evaluation in connection with salary schedules, Jaques has attempted to measure responsibility in terms of the maximum time span during which an individual is expected to exercise discretion on his own account until his use of discretion is subjected to review (1956). Yet this method abstracts itself from the complex nature of interactions between the reviewer and the reviewed. The time spans used by Jaques seem to be imputed or "shadow" quantities rather than the results of direct observation.

promote the fuller development of individual capacities. The larger an organization and the more complex its operations, the more significant these advantages of decentralization (*Baker and France*). Yet these considerations must also be seen in the light of personal interests and motivations. Some people at lower levels are "authority hoarders" who favor decentralization for the same reasons that would-be despots at the top favor centralization. Others, as already suggested, fear decentralization because they lack the self-confidence in their ability to assume more responsibility or authority.

One of the many paradoxes of this subject is the fact that higher levels of competence must usually be reached before there can be more decentralization, while more decentralization is usually required in order to bring about the needed increase in the level of competence. Because of this "vicious circle" administrators always have an easy justification for not extending decentralization. When extensions are made, a price is usually paid in the form of inevitable errors and mistakes. This price can be kept within bounds only by "recentralization" or by new central functions—in the fields of training, communication, policy-making, or control—to buttress up the extension of decentralization. Another paradox appears in periods of emergency. At such times there are certain matters that can only be handled on the basis of far-reaching decentralization. When immediate action is needed, subordinates are usually not expected to wait until they get orders or clearance from superiors. Yet for other actions—and the ultimate case is the decision to unleash atomic missiles in response to a presumed attack—there is good reason to "pass the buck" to the top executive. Still another paradox appears in the conflicting effects of modern technology. More effective systems of automation and of information processing tend to promote and facilitate more centralization. The constant development of new skills, technologies and professions tends to promote and require more decentralization. One of the results of these built-in paradoxes is a continuous shifting back and forth in the pattern of centralization and decentralization. Not only are decentralizing measures usually accompanied by their centralizing supplements; but, in addition, they usually create problems that are solved by new measures of centralization with their decentralizing supplements.

Chapter 10

PEOPLE-IN-ORGANIZATIONS:
INFORMAL ASPECTS

*S*INCE THE PREVIOUS CHAPTER was limited to the more formal aspects of organizations, it could not possibly deal with the totality of organizational structure.

To obtain a total picture of any organization, we must also consider the informal structure. This is found in *those aspects of structure which, while not prescribed by formal authority, supplement or modify the formal structure.*

We shall initiate our probe of informal structure by noting the inevitability, as well as the variety, of informal roles, relationships, and rules.

We shall then set forth a large number of informal role facets—some general in nature, others applying only to administrators—that can be found in almost every organization. This will provide us with some rather vivid illustrations of the intertwining of individual personality with organizational role.

Finally, we shall chart the actual structure of internal power as manifested on various issues. This will bring us directly into such crucial matters as the dispersion of power within organizations and the nature of "organizational democracy."

A. *The Inevitability of Informal Structure*

MUCH OF THE INTUITIVE WISDOM of experienced administrators stems from their awareness of informal structure. Their "tacit knowledge" of their organization tells them that formal structure is merely the part of the iceberg that appears above the water. It often makes them inherently—although not necessarily coherently—skeptical of reorganization proposals that deal with the formal structure alone.

A coherent explanation of informal structure requires a recognition that roles, hierarchy, polyarchy, and codes each have their informal aura or penumbra *(Bakke)*. They may develop in fields untouched by formal structure, thereby supplementing or extending it. Or else they may combat, or even replace, the formal structure. In either case, they may subsequently become formalized.

As far as roles are concerned, the formal division of labor into units is only the starting point for group formation within the organization. Within any formally established unit informal subdivisions will usually come into being. Others will cut across divisional lines. Still others will cut across the organization's outer boundaries and include nonmembers. Such groups may be united on the basis of working relations with the organization, friendship cliques, specialist or professional skills, "old school ties," political party affiliations, national origin, religion, and other shared interests *(Argyris, 1954, 1959; Bloom; Burling et al.; Cumming* and *Cumming)*.

Administrators at all levels, furthermore, will often associate themselves with one or more informal groups of "buddies" from inside or outside the organization. As with the "kitchen cabinets" of many Presidents of the United States, these may be far more influential than the more visible and formally established cabinets and "executive committees" *(Gross,* p. 100-101). Their informal status makes it easier for their members to avoid publicity and attack and for their organizers to reorganize, replace or abolish them.

Similarly, the formally established position is only a starting point for the total role played by any incumbent. It is invariably overlaid by a series of less authoritative—although not necessarily less powerful—expectations. As a result of conflicting elements in the incumbent's personality and in the expectations of others, these may produce deep role conflicts. Some of these informal aspects may be minor or ephemeral. Others may become the dominant elements in the total role. Still others may become widespread and deeply felt expectations that are passed on from one generation to another. It is in this sense that we say that the various "strong" Presidents of the United States "enlarged the concept of the Presidency." After the example of the two Roosevelts, of Wilson, and of Truman, no American President—not even an Eisenhower—could be as passive as Buchanan or Coolidge.

The relationship between total role and individual personality is so close that it would be a misleading question to ask whether personality is a determinant or a resultant of total role. It is usually both. The total role of any President is unquestionably affected both by his own personality and that of various predecessors. On the other hand, there is a genuine basis for the common saying that "the office makes the man." When Thomas à Becket, King Henry II's Chancellor, was made Archbishop of Canterbury, he suddenly became a strong defender of the Church against the King. When a more or less ordinary man like Truman becomes President, he often becomes extraordinary. But in either case it is only because the expectations surrounding the new office awaken or develop potentialities formerly hidden in the depth of the incumbent's personality.

Because of this intertwining with personality, informal roles are extremely varied. The next two sections of this chapter are devoted to an identification of some of the elements underlying this variety.

Hierarchy also has its informal aspects. Informal patterns of authority —considerably affected by the presence of informal groups—emerge in every organization. People with no formal administrative roles will often achieve and exercise informal administrative authority (*Belknap; Grusky; Horstall and Arensburg; Stanton and Schwartz; Strauss and Sayles; Zaleznik*, 1956). These are the so-called "informal leaders," who at times may sit at the apex of elaborate informal hierarchies. People with formal authority will sometimes fail to exercise it; these are the "in name only" administrators or leaders (*James D. Thompson*). Others may exercise power far beyond the authority granted them. These are the people who are attacked by their opponents as "empire builders" or "usurpers of authority," and praised by their admirers as men who "enlarged the conception of the office."

Moreover, the formal lines of authority can never carry the entire burden of serving as channels of internal communication. They are therefore supplemented by an intricate network of informal communication channels (*Blau*, 1956, 1959; *Gardner; Whyte*). This network provides an important role for the informal groups referred to above. It also includes what is usually referred to as "the grapevine." An equally important part of the communication network is found in the various formal devices mainly, or ostensibly, established for other purposes.

"Suggestion box" systems encourage the free flow of innovating ideas around—or through—the barriers established by hierarchic superiors. Grievance committees, appeals procedures and "open door" policies by top executives are designed to allow complaints to move upward without being scotched by hierarchic superiors. House organs, general announcements, and general meetings are official devices for sending communications downward, and allowing a few to come up, without using the hierarchic channels.

Polyarchy is a natural hotbed of informal relations and practices. Whether based on disparate or shared authority, polyarchic relations are by their very nature extremely difficult to formalize. Since hierarchic relations may often produce serious interpersonal strain and since they often rely for their effectiveness upon an overuse of scarce sanctions, both superiors and subordinates often enter into a silent conspiracy transforming formally hierarchic into actually polyarchic relations. Thus a large department in a hospital, although formally headed by a famous doctor, may in fact be headed by a loose informal partnership composed of himself and the head nurse or a triumvirate which also includes a resident physician. The "boss," as already indicated, may share authority with an informal "kitchen cabinet." An "advisory committee" may give orders instead of advice. On the other hand, formally polyarchic relations are sometimes informally transformed into rigid hierarchy. The best example is the committee of "equals" thoroughly dominated by its chairman.

Informal rules and rituals are also an important part of any organization's codes of behavior. In many areas informal codes seem to precede formal ones—just as historically the common law seems to precede statutory law. But much of the common law of the organization defies codification and some of it—particularly in units with an *esprit de corps* of their own—defies the formal rules of the organization as a whole. In fact, formalization itself often seems to have the direct effect of promoting informal systems of action *(Babchuk; Belknap; Dalton,* 1950, 1955, 1959; *Lombard; Page; Weiss).* Together with informal roles and groups, these may be referred to as an "informal culture" *(Argyris,* 1959, 1960; *Dunham* and *Weinberg; Levinson et al.; Sykes; Turner; Zaleznik,* 1958).

One way of looking at formal structure is to note that formal roles, hierarchy, polyarchy and codes deal mainly with authority and responsibility. In contrast, the informal aspects of organization are more closely related to power. Only by looking at these informal aspects as well can we complete the authority-responsibility-power triangle and see an organization as a system of power.

We can now understand why many formal reorganizations seem to have little effect. They deal mainly with formal authority and responsibility and much less with the realities of power. Any potential effect upon the distribution of power may indeed be counterbalanced or negated by unsought or unnoticed changes in the informal structure. *Le plus ca change, le plus c'est la meme chose.*

We can also understand why it is that when we look at formal structure alone many organizations seem never or rarely to change. Thus one eminent commentator on the Federal Government of the United States has observed that "Except for the increase in size, the form of American Government is not very different today from that of Washington's first administration" (Blaisdell, 1948, p. ix). Insofar as one chooses to close one's eyes to the revolutionary changes in the informal structure since the days of Washington, this observation has some justification. But from a broader viewpoint we might point out that this is a case of *le plus ca parait la meme chose, le plus ca change.*

With the "discovery" of informal structure by some of the modern pioneers and researchers in the field of administration, some people have responded with the prescriptive principle that rational administrators should recognize informal aspects in order to eliminate them. If informal lines of communication exist, they should be used by administrators. When informal leaders develop, they should be appointed to positions of formal authority. Where informal rules are acceptable, they should be institutionalized. The "discrepancy," it is urged, can thereby be eliminated.

Yet unfortunately for this point of view the acts of elimination may themselves bring new informal aspects into being. New informal channels of communication, new informal leaders and new informal rules—these are the inevitable result of any effort to eradicate the informal aspects of organizational structure.

B. *Informal Role Facets: General*

AN INFORMAL ROLE is not merely *any* pattern of actual behavior; it is a pattern appearing in people's expectations. Nor are these expectations oriented merely toward what people *will* or *might* do; they are expectations concerning what people *should* do. As with formal roles, they are more a basis of evaluation than prediction. But informal role expectations are not limited to the authoritative statements of those with formal authority for the division of labor. They are therefore more varied in nature and more changeable. Although they are often a greater source of role conflict, they may also be much closer to actual behavior.

None of the role facets discussed below are total roles. If we call someone technique-oriented, the purpose is to identify one aspect of his total role rather than establish a stereotype. Nor does the use of pairs and triads mean that we are always talking about dichotomies or trichotomies. A person may be expected to serve as Nay-Sayer in some situations and Yea-Sayer in others.

1. THE TASK-ORIENTED, TECHNIQUE-ORIENTED, AND PEOPLE-ORIENTED

The Task-Oriented see their role as "getting the job done." They see the job to be done in terms of "output" and its uses by specified clients within or outside the organization. They want to be relied upon as people who "deliver the goods."

The Technique-Oriented see themselves as masters of procedure and method. With control officials, this may evidence itself in a ritualistic conformity with regulations. With specialists and professionals working in rapidly developing fields, it may sanction sacrifice of the organization's demands on the altar of professional pride or personal intellectual gratification. In either case the formal output goals are displaced. It is largely among the Technique-Oriented that we may find the "trained incapacity," "professional deformation," and "occupation psychosis" excoriated, respectively, by Veblen, Warnotte, and Dewey.

The People-Oriented, on the other hand, may play the role of patron saint and good samaritan to people in need. In the federal enforcement agency studied by Blau, "some officials lost sight of the generic objective of raising the standard of living of American workers in the course of dealing with particular underpaid (or unemployed) individuals. They were so concerned with the plight of the employees with whom they had contact that helping these specific persons became the major goal of their investigations and the main source of their work satisfaction. Thus one agent . . . said: 'You spread a little sunshine in this job. That's what I like'" *(Blau,* 1955, p. 191-192). Sunshine spreaders are also found in private organizations and in strictly managerial positions as well.

2. NAY-SAYERS AND YEA-SAYERS

Every organization needs Nay-Sayers. Unacceptable requests must be turned down. Yes Men must be counterbalanced. Utopian plans and proposals must be exploded. Role deviation must be countered. This may require not only a thick skin but also a high dexterity in the arts of saying "No" despite pressures to force a "Yes." More frequently, it may accentuate the "negative personality" of control or review officers who, irrespective of what the conditions may be, find deep pleasure in actions of reduction, rejection, and refusal. In the field of advice the Nay-Sayers can usually be depended upon to find weak points in any proposal and—when it is clear that their warnings will not be heeded—to magnify them with Cassandra-like prophecies of imminent doom.

The role of Yea-Sayer is always needed to balance the Nay-Sayers. In his simplest form the Yea-Sayer may be merely a "Yes Man" who sneezes when higher authority takes snuff. The more constructive Yea-Sayer is the one who, even though doubting whether a difficult job can really be done, will himself help to do it. He supports—or even originates —the proposals that are attacked by the Nay-Sayers and helps circumvent their opposition.

3. RULE-ENFORCERS, RULE-EVADERS, AND RULE-BLINKERS

In part, the Rule-Enforcers are Technique-Oriented Nay-Sayers. But they are also something more. They are "people of the book." The guidance found in the rule book takes precedence over the wishes or protestations of superiors, subordinates, colleagues, or outsiders. Where the book is not clear, their inner voice reveals the true meaning. Where neither is clear, they follow the unwritten rule: "When in doubt, don't."

Although the Rule-Enforcers conform more closely to the bureaucratic stereotype, many of the most successful bureaucrats are rule evaders. These are the "operators," the people who know how to get things done "irrespective." They are often adept at "riding the rules" and slipping through loopholes. They may be even more adept at evading or breaking the rules completely—and just as completely covering up their tracks. Some of the most successful Rule-Evaders for certain purposes are the very people who, for other purposes, are among the more conspicuous Rule-Enforcers.

The Rule-Blinkers are a still further departure from the bureaucratic stereotype. They are not against the rules; they just do not take them very seriously. In some cases they favor a general "indulgency pattern" as in the case of Gouldner's gypsum factory where the foremen were expected to close their eyes to infractions of the rules against workers' taking materials home for household repairs (*Gouldner*, 1954, p. 45-56). In other cases, eyeclosing is regarded as part of their role as an effective superior. "The toleration of illicit practices," reports Blau, "actually enhances the controlling powers of superiors, paradoxical as it may seem. By voluntarily relinquishing some of his prerogatives, the supervisor creates social obligation . . . the supervisor surrendered some of his immediate power in exchange for greater ultimate power" (1955, p. 169).

4. *THE INVOLVED AND THE DETACHED*

The Involved are those who are fully immersed in their work and the activities of the organization. In part, this is a matter of energy and dedication. It is also a matter of ego-involvement at the expense of other interests or as a substitute for less valued interests. Among manual workers, the Involved are often regarded as rate-busters and may have to pay the consequences. Among clerical and secretarial workers they include the many people who, having little else to go home to, take their work-time worries or pleasures home with them. The specialists and administrators among the Involved work long overtime hours and when they go home take along not only their worries but their work also.

Among the Detached, some are merely Slackers who "go along for the ride." They too may sometime be expected to pay the consequences. Others work in an energetic and devoted fashion, but are expected to "call it quits" at the end of regular hours. Thus in the federal regulatory agency studied by Blau "the practice of working overtime without compensation, to which some officials resorted who had trouble meeting the production quota, was generally disapproved. . . . This censure of working overtime can be considered a functional equivalent of restriction of output among manual workers which was compatible with the professional orientation of these white-collar workers" (1955, p. 146-147). As Blau suggests, the role of Detached can often best be assumed by the more skillful people who perform superior work with less effort than others.

At the higher administrative levels, where greater involvement and dedication is more customarily found, there is less approval or disapproval attached to one or the other. Here the difference is manifested less in the amount of energy actually expended than in the degree of psychological immersion. For the Involved a crisis in the organization is a personal crisis and an organizational defeat a personal defeat. Under similar circumstances the Detached can look at things from afar and have a good laugh at his own or the organization's expense. This role is facilitated by other interests and involvements. Like the "good executive" whom Clarence Randall contrasts with the "self-appointed overworked executive," the Detached often "spends a great deal of time with people who know nothing whatever about his business and who are not particularly impressed with his responsibilities. Many of them do not even know what he does, and care less. This helps him keep his own importance in perspective" (1959, p. 128).

5. REGULARS, DEVIANTS, AND ISOLATES

The role of Regular is defined by his relationship with his group. He accepts the values of others in the group and is accepted by them. He is "in." If the work of the group requires collective action, he is a Team Player. If the group is successful, it's "we did it." Many Regulars in a unit, however, may be Deviants from the point of view of the larger organization.

The Deviant's role departs from the values of the group or larger organization. Like Len, in Zaleznik's study of a factory group, the Deviant is not able to work out a comfortable relationship with other members of the group. He glories in his role as a "maverick." Essentially a lonely person, he is seen as a threat to the group. Or else, indeed, he may be created by the group itself as a scapegoat upon whom the aggressive feelings of its more disturbed members may be vented *(Zaleznik*, 1956, p. 80-91).

The Isolate is the true Lone Wolf. Standing further from the group than the Deviant, he is more an infidel than a heretic. Like Axel in the same Zaleznik study, he may be technically able, but socially incapable, of playing a highly differentiated leadership role. He therefore settles on "aloofness as a way of differentiating himself from the group." Because of his distance, he may be much less of a threat to the group than the Deviant *(Ibid.*, p. 91-95).

Many administrators try to play the role of Regular by becoming People-Oriented with respect to their subordinates or by organizing a "management team." Such efforts can be only partly successful. By the very nature of their "in-between" positions and divided loyalties administrators are always deviants in some of their group attachments. At the highest levels of power the administrator is always, at least in part, an isolate. After all the collective consultation has been engaged in, all the experts been heard, all the maneuvers been explored, the time comes when in the privacy of his heart and in the light of his own inner torments, he must make his own decision. This is what is referred to when people describe the "terrible isolation" of the American Presidency.

6. NEWCOMERS AND OLDTIMERS

The Newcomer to an organization is in some ways like a newborn infant. It is assumed that he knows little and must be taken care of by others. In some organizations he is expected to be "seen but not heard" for a considerable period of time. This situation may be formalized by novitiates, apprenticeships, and trial periods.

A particularly difficult Newcomer role is that of Successor. President Truman's job during his first year in office was unquestionably rendered more difficult by his unenviable role as successor to Franklin D. Roosevelt. In the case of lesser men, the passage of time may indeed brighten the predecessor's halo. Thus the new manager of Gouldner's gypsum factory suffered in comparison with the "Rebecca myth" that grew up around the memory of the man he succeeded *(Gouldner,* p. 79-83).

The Oldtimers, having been "around" a long time, "know the ropes" in a way that no Newcomer can possibly hope to learn them. They will often resolutely prevent any Newcomer from moving too fast unless he first pays them the attention and obeisance which they feel they have earned. By tacit agreement they may often see to it that "Newcomers" of five or ten years ago still feel like strangers, particularly when they are seen as potential threats to the Oldtimers.

More positively, the Oldtimers often achieve power far beyond what might easily be inferred from their formal positions. In organizations with a high degree of turnover unusual disparities may thus be created. In the state hospital studied by Belknap, the "hard core of senior attendants"— people at the bottom of the hierarchic totem pole—had the lowest turnover rate. Belknap reports that "The informal organization of the wards is maintained and transmitted in its essentials by a core of about 18% of the attendants" *(Belknap,* 1956). Other hospital studies report on cases where the organizational continuity has been provided by, and major power concentrated in, the hard core of nurses, nonprofessional administrative personnel, or even the chronically-ill patients *(Caudill,* 1958; *Cumming and Cumming).*

7. CLIMBERS AND STICKERS

The Climbers are expected to "get ahead." They are chosen not merely because of their assumed ability to handle their present positions, but because of their potentials. One or more paths of advancement are already laid out. Both their perspectives and their loyalties, therefore, will usually include the larger organization rather than the immediate work group.

The role of the Stickers is to "stay put." They are supposed to be satisfied with life and their position in it. The Stickers tend to cluster at the lowest levels of a hierarchy and at the top of various "career ladders." Unskilled, menial and low-status positions are filled by people who are expected to "know their place." Their mobility is blocked not only by the lack of opportunity but by their own lack of education, ability or experience. On the other hand, those who have already moved far have few places left to go. The top specialists may indeed seek to become top executives or even members of directorates. But when they have "arrived," the only mobility left is lateral and their basic role is one of survival. Since there is never enough "room at the top" for all who regard themselves as capable of filling the top roles, this often brings them into direct collision with those who are still Climbers. Some of the greatest tensions within organizations—and indeed in societies as a whole— stem from role conflicts between those who see themselves as Climbers and others who expect them to "stay put."

8. THE COSMOPOLITANS AND LOCALS

The Cosmopolitans in an organization are those who see themselves as members of a broader professional, cultural or political community. Within the organization, as Gouldner points out in his study of a college community, they may have the greatest prestige and may indeed become temporary "empire builders." But they are not committed to their local empires. They are Climbers interested in larger worlds to conquer *(Gouldner, 1957; Bennis et al., 1957; Carlson)*.

The Locals are less mobile. They are more rooted in the local community. They are more intimately wedded to the organization, where they probably reach comfortable middle-level positions. If they are still interested in climbing, they want to do it there. Since a larger number of them are Oldtimers, they are a force to be reckoned with. They are usually the most skillful both as Rule-Enforcers and Rule-Evaders.

c. *Informal Role Facets: Administrative*

As ALREADY INDICATED, each of the role facets discussed above may relate to either administrators or nonadministrators. We now come to roles that are more exclusively administrative or managerial in nature.

Almost any of these roles, however, may be assumed by people with no formal administrative position. When this happens it is merely another example of the extremely important role of informal leader, already referred to in the discussion of informal hierarchy in Section A of this chapter.

1. GENERALISTS: GENTLEMEN, MIDDLEMEN, INTEGRATORS

The role of generalist is a complex role rooted in various combinations of attitude, ability, and knowledge. The Gentlemen Generalists are those who are expected to demonstrate unswerving loyalty to the values of their class or caste. They are expected to conduct themselves like gentlemen among their peers and maintain the loyalty and respect of their inferiors. Their knowledge is supposed to derive from an education in matters regarded as important by the upper classes. It is usually founded upon early training in the revered classics of an earlier period, supplemented by "school of experience" knowledge concerning the problems faced by higher elites. Examples are the Confucian scholar-administrators, the earlier British and Indian Civil Services, educated Kings and Princes, and the crown princes of various business dynasties.

The Middlemen are the "uncommitted persons" who are expected to "make the deals" inside the organization. Apart from their concern with their own self-preservation and self-advancement, they are expected to place highest value upon organizational survival and growth. They are looked to for the ability to get things done through persuasion, negotiation and compromise without too much discrimination as to just what those "things" may be. They are expected to be experts in their knowledge of the organization's formal and informal structure.

The Integrators are the true generalists. They are expected to see the woods as well as the trees and to be motivated by interests broader than their own or even of their own organization. They are looked to for skills not only in communication and compromise but in the constructive integration of divergent interests. They are expected to understand the organization's broad environment as well as, or even more than, its internal workings. They are expected to know enough about relevant techniques to enable them to understand, evaluate, and coordinate the activities of many specialists and professionals.

2. BUILDERS AND CONSOLIDATORS

The Builders are those who are expected to establish new organizations, enlarge old ones, or initiate new programs. Difficulties stimulate them to greater efforts. In the earlier days of the administrative revolution the Builders were rugged individualists, robber barons, economic royalists, or flaming revolutionaries like Garibaldi, Mazzini, Lenin, and Trotsky. In the midtwentieth century they are more cultivated, operate on a larger scale and are probably more numerous. They are the innovating entrepreneurs and institution builders in the private sectors, in national governments and in international agencies. But when a great period of ebullient growth draws to an end, their part is finished. They may then be a heavy burden on the organization or else—like Trotsky—be pushed aside by a Consolidator.

The Consolidators are expected to "clean up the mess" left behind by great Builders. They are more adept at the arts of maintenance, routine, and slow and deliberate, rather than daring, growth. Many stereotypes of the Good Administrator have been built in the image of the Consolidators, with little attention to the less orderly Builders.

3. THINKERS AND DOERS

The Thinkers are traditionally expected to think of things for others to do. This is characteristically the role of specialists, experts and staff advisers. The Doers, in contrast, are those with the dread responsibility of translating thought into action. Their own thought deals more with "how" than "what" and with narrower aspects of "how." They pick up where the Thinkers leave off.

Some administrators perform both roles at the same time. In addition to being Doers, they are also responsible for originating major courses of action. But this is a rarity. Most administrators rely on others for original as well as detailed thinking. This combination is most successful when the Doer takes on the challenging task of integrating the detailed, original thought of large numbers of specialists.

4. GRANDSTAND PLAYERS AND BEHIND-THE-SCENE OPERATORS

The Grandstand Players are expected to play a conspicuously public role. They see themselves as "carrying the ball" on a huge field as thousands cheer them for their brilliance or courage. Whether Team Players or Lone Wolves, they thrive on publicity.

In exchange for the personal gratifications that may be involved, the Grandstand Players are often Expendables. They are expected to man difficult positions under sharp attack. Like soldiers before a battle, they think they may live forever. But after they have absorbed enough punishment of this type, their usefulness may be over. They may then be unceremoniously dropped, or else kicked upstairs.

The Behind-the-Scene Operators thrive on getting things done. By passing the ball to the Grandstand Players, they manage to be non-conspicuous. Here we find the *eminences grises*, the assistants "with a passion for anonymity" and the "faceless men." Occupying the more sheltered positions, they walk out on few limbs. They are willing to sacrifice publicity and public esteem for security. These are the Non-expendables of administration.

5. AUTHORITARIANS, LAISSEZ-FAIRES, AND DEMOCRATS

The Authoritarians are expected to dominate situations. The more genuine Authoritarians do this by detailed instructions to their sub-ordinates and close supervision over them. To achieve more through domination they may—like the "Leader" in the New England factory studied by Argyris—deal with subordinates separately, erect barriers between them and do everything possible "to prevent the barriers from being destroyed or overcome" *(Argyris,* 1953, p. 43-46). The same "divide and conquer" strategy may be applied to employees' efforts at self-organization through trade unions. The more superficial authoritar-ians are less interested in actual power and more concerned with defer-ence and the ceremonial recognition of their authority.

The Laissez-Faires are those who substantially withdraw from the use of their formal authority. They neither dominate subordinates directly nor try to influence them indirectly. Their permissiveness is not neces-sarily rooted in disinterest. It may stem from preoccupation with superiors, external affairs or other internal matters.

The Democrats are expected to encourage initiative by their sub-ordinates, participation in decision-making, and a more "free and easy" pattern of interpersonal communication than is possible with Authoritar-ians. They see themselves as sources of help and advice rather than a constant stream of orders. Thus the head of field engineering in one of the two electronic manufacturing companies studied by Barnes is quoted as follows: "I've tried to set up relations with the supervisors under me so that they can talk with me. For example, I don't try to make the technical decisions . . . but I do like to have them come up and use me as a sounding board . . . I'll make suggestions to them and sometimes I can help them from my own experience. Sometimes, too, I can refer Supervisor B and his project engineers to others in the company whom I know to be doing related work" *(Barnes,* p. 93-97).

Most administrators are all three together. Which of the three facets is predominant will, of course, be affected by the administrator's own personality needs. It will be affected by the personalities of his sub-ordinates, who may, as the case may be, crave domination or autonomy.

It will also vary from one situation to another. Times of crisis may require a leader to play a more dominant role on some matters and a laissez-faire role on others. As subordinates develop their capacities for more independent action, the democratic role is more in order. After spectacular success in pulling his plant "out of the red" and putting it firmly "in the black," the authoritarian leader described by Argyris shifted to a more democratic role *(Argyris,* 1953, p. 104).

6. IMPERSONALS, PERSONALS, AND CHARISMATICS

The Impersonals are close to the roles assigned by Weber to bureaucrats as a whole. They are not expected to reveal emotions or be conspicuously irrational. They are expected to think in terms of abstract categories of people rather than individuals. Many of them are Rule-Enforcers and Involved.

The Personals act more obviously like human beings. They demonstrate their interest in individuals. They show their enthusiasm or "blow their top" more readily. They may be either Authoritarian or Democratic.

The Charismatics are the inspirational leaders. As described by Weber, they have some indefinable "gift of grace." But Weber was wrong in thinking that the charismatic role has no place in large modern bureaucracies. Wartime inevitably produces charismatic leaders both in home-front organizations and in armies themselves, probably the most bureaucratic of all organizations. Even in less eventful times the Builders and the Grandstand Players often assume the Charismatic role. Yet those who succeed in doing this are not ordinary human beings. In fact, their extraordinary capacity invariably makes them somewhat inhuman. They can relate themselves intimately with people in general, even humanity as a whole, but not so readily with individuals.

7. THE FAMILY SUBSTITUTES

From time immemorial the heads of organizations have tended to assume the role of Father, Mother, or Sibling Substitute to their subordinates. In modern organizations, where old-fashioned "paternalism" is supposed to be on the wane, this tendency is nonetheless strong. It may also lead to the role of Husband or Wife Substitute. Members may find the outlet for their libidinous energies not only in deep intrapersonal relationships (or spiritual fusion with the Body Corporate) but in the comfort of a dependable relation with someone in higher authority. The paternal (or maternal) role is evidenced less by the harshness of disciplinary action, the sweetness of personal favors, or the security of social security measures. It is found mainly in the provision of emotional support, confidence and backing.

D. *The Power Structure*

WHO ARE THE PEOPLE who make the important decisions? Where are the centers of motive power within an organization?

If one tries to answer such questions by looking at the formal structure alone, it is hard to respond without using one of the myths of ultimate authority or central omnipotence. Although their validity may be "shattered," as demonstrated in *The Managing of Organizations*[1] their active propagation and widespread acceptance is probably an inevitable byproduct of the process of building and strengthening formal structure

Should one look only at various aspects of informal structure, however, the first impression may be one of chaos and confusion. One may quickly conclude that "no one decides anything" or even that "nothing is ever decided." This conclusion could be supported not only by the general principles of process and multiple causality but also by the observed interdependence of organizational roles.

The only way to bring order back into the picture is to focus it directly on the structure of internal power. This requires an examination of how people-in-an-organization are divided on various matters and how the power is distributed on various sides of the dividing lines. It also leads to a consideration of what is meant by "organizational democracy."

1. THE DISPERSION OF POWER

If we return to the "double pyramid of formal authority" (as set forth in section C-2 of Chapter 9), we may now ask what changes are needed in it to provide a general model for the distribution of organizational power.

Some of these changes are described in *Managing of Organizations*.[1] There we say that as an organization becomes larger and more powerful, there is a sharp decline in the importance of the two top strata of the inverted pyramid: the holders of ultimate authority and their representatives. The more important areas of power become the directorates, the top executives and the bureaucrats. When employees of the organiza-

---

1. Chap. 3, "The Dispersion of Power in Organizations."

tion organize into trade unions, a fourth center of power comes into being. We saw that, contrary to the "iron law of oligarchy," there can be no one all-powerful controlling group.

As we proceed further with this analysis, we then see that it is hardly possible to recreate the so-called "iron law" within any of these four centers. When the holders of ultimate authority are members of an organization, they are divided both formally and informally. When not members, they may be organized only through some representative system. Representative bodies are invariably arenas for the exercise of dispersed power. When this is not so, it is because power is exerted over them by directorates. At the level of the directorates, indeed, also of the top executives, there is a greater possibility of highly concentrated power for limited periods of time. Yet this is invariably counterbalanced by power centers at other parts of the organization. Among the bureaucrats the dispersion of power reaches its highest point. Here it is created by the very processes of formal specialization and delegation and augmented by the proliferation of informal groups, leaders, and lines of communication.

To all this must be added the pattern of external influences upon the organization. As pointed out in the following chapter, there is no sharp dividing line between power exercised from within and power exercised from outside. External power often operates through the members of an organization. Some of the strongest groups within an organization are those that operate on the basis of alliances and coalitions with outside groups.

As thus far discussed, however, these various areas or centers of power are merely unrelated sets of elements. They are rarely, if ever, arrayed on the field of interorganizational conflict in accordance with the pattern suggested by the double pyramid of formal organization.

To visualize the actual dispersion of power within an organization, we must start with a specific issue or cluster of issues. This may be a major appointment (and intraorganizational appointments are major matters for internal conflict and power plays, even within a so-called "merit system"), the issuance of a new regulation, or the installation of a new method of operation. Around this issue we then see an array of "forces," each one of which is a coalition of people or groups from different places in the organizational structure.

In the particular case here illustrated three of the four coalitions are headed by top executives. C_1, in contrast, is headed by two people at the next higher level of authority. They, in turn, are backed up by one bureaucrat, three holders of ultimate authority, and one from the trade union. From the vector's size, used to symbolize its effective power, it can be seen that C_1 is considerably stronger than C_3, which is composed of merely one top executive and one directorate member. C_2 has the same kind of top leadership as C_3 but also enjoys a certain amount of support from all other levels. C_4, likewise, draws support from all centers of power, but has more widespread and more tightly organized support among the bureaucrats. It is the strongest group on *this* issue.

A more careful analysis would require a number of refinements. The most important is the addition of outside individuals or groups to the various coalitions. Each element symbolized, moreover, might refer to an entire subset rather than a specific individual. Above all, the specific power of any given subset or individual would also have to be indicated. This would vary in terms of the leadership, composition and structure of each coalition and the specific nature of the issue at hand.

To analyze the total distribution of power within an organization, we must cover all issues or at least a fairly representative set of issues.

THE DISPERSION OF ORGANIZATIONAL POWER
ON A SPECIFIC ISSUE

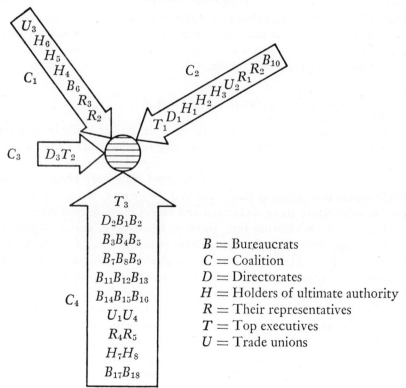

B = Bureaucrats
C = Coalition
D = Directorates
H = Holders of ultimate authority
R = Their representatives
T = Top executives
U = Trade unions

We must then rank these various issues in terms of their importance. Although this itself is a difficult and complex undertaking, it is what an experienced manager does on a rough-and-ready basis as he "learns the ropes" in an organization.

A number of hypotheses may now be set forth as to what analyses of this type may show.

First of all, on the most important issues—those that involve larger numbers of people and are hotly contested—the largest power will usually lie with a coalition of the C_4 type with substantial external support. Second, on issues involving two or more groups of the C_4 type, the amount of power on any one side will be decisively affected by relative leadership abilities displayed in each group. Third, on the issues that involve less people and are not contested, an extremely large amount of power will often be found in the hands of single individuals, pairs or small groups. Finally, there will be a general tendency for larger amounts of power to be exercised by people in higher positions of formal authority—most particularly from the directorates downward. In part, this is because formal authority is itself a source of power. One of the many reasons for this is that formal authority provides the authority holder with an excellent basis for the leadership of nonformal groups and coalitions. Another reason is that the prerequisites and awards that come with formal authority are themselves rewards and incentives that attract those people most capable of mobilizing power.

2. ORGANIZATIONAL DEMOCRACY

If central omnipotence is a myth, if actual power is always dispersed within an organization, then perhaps no organization can be run dictatorially. Perhaps every organization might be regarded as democratic.

Neither of these conclusions is warranted, however. There *is* validity in the distinction between dictatorial and democratic. Some organizations *are* unquestionably more dictatorial and others more democratic.

But the distinction has little merit if based upon voting, representation systems, and the other formalistic paraphernalia of democracy in political systems. These forms are applicable to organizations as a whole only when ultimate authority is in the hands of all members. Even when this is so, as with associations, cooperatives and collectives, the effect on the distribution of actual power within an organization is questionable.

A more fundamental approach to intraorganizational democracy is one which measures democracy in terms of *the members' participation in decisions concerning their own activities and the activities of the organization as a whole.* As Follett pointed out many years ago, participative democracy is much more meaningful than mere consent or acquiescence. Her judgment can be buttressed today by what we have learned concerning the way in which the heads of organizations and states have obtained consent or acquiescence by threats, propaganda, or manipulation. More positively her judgment can be supported by the fact that actual participation provides a greater opportunity for people to meet their needs for commergence, differentiation, and self-development. In fact, organizational democracy is one of the greatest factors in promoting the individual self-development of human beings. By participating in organizational decisions affecting his daily activities and those of many others, a person develops capacities that were hidden or stunted. He may not only meet his needs for belonging, status, and power; he may enjoy the endless satisfactions of intellectual or esthetic creation. In contrast, a person's entire self-development may be stultified, or even set back, if his organizational environment reduces him to acting as though he were a machine.

Participation, however, is a multifaceted concept. There can be no single measure of democracy in an organization—although for any particular purpose there may be value in concentrating upon a single facet alone. The three major facets can be identified by asking *who* participates, *how deeply*, and *on what?*

The most obvious participants are the administrators themselves and the "multiple oligarchies." In this sense the onward speed of specialization and the multiplication of administrative personnel is profoundly democratic. This democratic trend is carried still further when even the people at the lowest ranks or the lowest levels in the hierarchy—in Drucker's memorable words—are allowed or encouraged to participate in "the managerial vision." In the case of both administrators and nonadministrators the scope of participation is affected by the extent of internal conflict. Without the winds of conflict and the information borne upon them, many decisions are inevitably made in small and narrow circles. Mobility within the organization is another important factor in widening the circle of participants. With a greater proportion of Climbers to Stickers, there is a greater extent of interest in matters extending beyond one's individual position or unit.

The depth of anyone's participation is still harder to measure than the number of participants. At the one extreme, right at the edge of nonparticipation, is the mere sense of participation and the indirect or vicarious participation by one's elected, appointed or self-chosen representative. At the other extreme, there is the full participation in the form of direct and continuous activity at the work bench, desk or conference table. In some cases this may be isolated personal activity—as in the case of a worker repairing a special-purpose tool or a teacher in his classroom.

In others this may be personal participation in a group decision. The two may often be found together. Between the two extremes of a mere sense of participation and full participation, we find the more sporadic, illicit and fragmented participation of a group that is run by an authoritarian or dictatorial administrator. Here the actual participation of subordinates may still be great. The administrator may leave large elements of decision-making to his subordinates as he takes unto himself those which best satisfy his craving for self-expression and prestige. The subordinates may in fact retaliate through a long series of minor and scarcely visible decisions that are by and large beyond his control. But the extent of their participation will be impaired by the inhospitable atmosphere and the lack of a legitimate place for it in the organization as a whole.

The *on what* of participation must be understood within the general principle that *in organizations no one decides everything but every administrator—in fact, every member—may have an opportunity to help decide some things.* In a way this is similar to what happens in a democratic state at the time of a national election; every voter has a chance to help decide something. But there are a number of major differences. The voter in a national election makes a minor contribution to an occasional decision of great importance. The member of an organization makes a relatively larger contribution to a continuing series of decisions of lesser importance. The narrowness of organizational decision-making is compensated for by the multitude of decisions and the depth of participation in each. What is narrow from the viewpoint of the organization or of society as a whole, however, may be of transcendental importance to the individual. The decisions he helps to make in his organization may not shape the course of national policy or the future of the world but they may be much closer to matters directly affecting the largest number of waking hours in his own life. Moreover, the decisions in which he participates are inextricably intertwined with those of the High and the Mighty in the hierarchy of his organization. Their decisions are possible only because of large numbers of prior decisions by the Low and the Many in the same hierarchy. Moreover, whether they are carried out or reversed will depend upon the subsequent interpretation, reinterpretation and embellishment given them by the Low and the Many.

What is the relationship between intraorganizational democracy and strong leadership?

To answer this question, we must keep in mind that leadership strength has little relation to the brute, physical power expected of military leaders in the day of hand-to-hand battle. It has even less relationship to some of the characteristics often associated with allegedly powerful leaders: aggressiveness, an overbearing personality, stubbornness. Its only connection with force is the ability to draw upon vast reserves of personal energy.

Leadership strength in organizations comes from the use of personal energy to activate large numbers of people in achieving the goals of an organization. This strength can be measured only by such achievement, with due attention paid to the unavoidable obstacles and the physical resources available. Such achievement, in turn, is based to an important extent upon energetic participation by all the members of the organization. The strong leader, therefore, is often one who gains strength by promoting interorganizational democracy.

Part IV

PERFORMANCE

Chapter 11

THE MATRIX OF PURPOSES

*I*N APPROACHING the subject of organizational purposes, we are met by a striking paradox.

On the one hand, we find unanimous recognition of the central importance of purposes. Theorists are agreed that purposefulness is essential to any organization. Administrators spend considerable time in trying to achieve, clarify, change, or formulate purposes. Both will affirm that purposes are the heart of any plan of action, the guide to rational decision-making and a starting point for the rational evaluation of performance.

On the other hand, the question "What are your organization's purposes?" is invariably embarrassing. Most replies are incomplete or tortured, given with a feeling of obvious discomfort. An administrator's quick and easy answer is apt to be a glib evasion or glittering generality. Both the glitter and the generality rise to higher levels when a government leader is asked, "What are your nation's purposes?"

One reason for the embarrassment is that human purposefulness is too complex and intimate to be fully understood or openly described. The difficulty and delicacy of the subject can be illustrated by narrowing the question down and asking an administrator, "What are your personal purposes?" This very pertinent question will usually be regarded as brazen impertinence. The avowed purposes stated in any polite reply may have only a coincidental connection with actual purposes.

Another explanation is found in the rudimentary state of the study of purpose. For those who labor under the ultrapositivist injunction that nothing should be scientifically studied unless it can be directly observed and measured, the entire subject may be taboo. For others, the subject is oversimplified by single purpose models or by abstract approaches that avoid the substantive content of goal-oriented behavior. Hence, the ordinary language of organizational purpose is still immature. It is ill-adapted even for asking the right questions about purposes. It is still less suitable as an instrument to help experienced administrators in wrestling with purpose problems or expressing the intuitive wisdom they acquire in the process.

On the assumption that additional attention will be attracted to any subject that is formally labeled, I have coined the word "teletics" to refer to the study of purposes and purposefulness. The root of the word is "telos," the Greek word for "purpose." Teletics, it must be emphasized, is not teleology. It deals with the purposes of human beings in this world; it is not concerned with the grand purposes of a universe or deity. It is focused on human nature, not Nature. For all purposes included in teletic inquiry, there are human "purposers."

In this chapter I shall set forth what I regard as some of the elementary principles of teletic inquiry. These relate to:

- the time sequence concept of purposeful action,
- the multiplicity of organizational purposes,
- the patterns that bring order out of this multiplicity, and
- the balance between clarity and vagueness in purpose formulation.

Throughout this chapter, and the following ten chapters, two strands of inquiry and analysis are interwoven: purpose accounting and the analysis of purposefulness. The first is the conceptual analysis of the "global matrix" of purposes as provided through an elaboration of the "purpose categories" introduced in "The Management of Organizations" (Chapt. 2, section B-3). Just as the national accounts of the economists provide a conceptual system for formulating an economy's output, the global matrix provides all the concepts needed to formulate, although often in much less quantitative terms, the performance purposes of any organization. Here a set of principles is presented with a considerable degree of confidence. My contribution has been to synthesize concepts and generalizations already developed in disparate fields, bring them together into a teletic framework, and insert a certain amount of scaffolding and mortar in the gaps and interstices.

The second strand deals with the dynamics of purposefulness. This is the most difficult aspect of teletic inquiry, and the few principles here presented must be viewed with greater caution. The analysis of the emergence of purpose has long been impeded by overabstract approaches that failed to recognize the various components in the purpose matrix. This has put much of organizational theory in the position that macroeconomics would be in if economists had no concepts of national accounting. But purpose accounting by itself cannot explain how the purpose patterns of specific organizations come into being, any more than a good set of accounts by itself can explain why an economy or a business has grown or declined.

In this chapter much of the emphasis will be on the dynamics of purposefulness. In the subsequent chapters I aim at a balance between the two themes, an aim that will at times be frustrated by the necessity of special attention to conceptual clarification on the accounting side.

A. *Commitment to a Desired Future*

BEFORE DEALING either with the categories of purpose or the emergence of purposefulness, it is essential to spend a little time on the concept of purpose itself and the common characteristics of purposes and purposeful action.

A person may be said to have a purpose when *he is to some extent committed to action that may bring about a desired future situation.*

Thus the two key elements in purposefulness are *futurity* and *commitment*. Both of these are found in Tolman's analysis (1951) of human behavior in terms of action toward or away from a goal-object and in the Parsons-Shils conception (1951, p. 53) of people as capable of action "oriented to the attainment of ends or goals or other anticipated states of affairs." A full understanding of these elements requires a recognition of the importance of purpose sequences and the relativity of most means-ends distinctions.

1. FUTURITY

The futurity element of any purpose may appear in a variety of forms. A future situation may be a clear image, sharply perceived by a vivid and retentive imagination or represented by blueprints and verbal descriptions. It may be little more than a shadowy image "seen through a glass darkly" or barely sensed. In either case, it may fade from consciousness and operate at preconscious and unconscious levels or through habits and routines previously established.

This aspect of purposefulness is made more complicated—and more delightful—by the fact that purposeful behavior is always embedded in a substantial setting of nonpurposeful behavior. Many aspects of human growth and development proceed automatically in accordance with instincts, habits, and biochemical patterns. Many of the most valued aspects of human life are spontaneous rather than purposeful. Many of the most dreaded things in life are beyond the sphere of purposeful action; man cannot escape death merely by trying to live forever.

In conscious purposefulness the perception of futurity is inescapably rooted in man's perception of the past or present. This does not mean that man's vision of a desired future is necessarily limited to something that he has experienced in the past or that he has seen in the outer world. It does mean that the conceptual elements in any characterization of a desired future are inevitably obtained from past experience. It matters not at all that some experiences—such as ingestion, egestion, and sexual action—may have been originally initiated through the "genetic code" or instincts. The perception of any desired future situation will be based upon personal experience with past situations or personal observation of the actions of others. From these elements any image of a desired future is molded. It may be done rather mechanically—as when one's purpose is to do more or less what one has done in the past or to follow the example of others. It may be done with more imagination—as when one combines fleeting pieces of the past into a vision of something that has never before existed.

2. COMMITMENT

Without commitment, a perceived future situation is far from being a purpose. It may be only an anticipation or forecast of what is probable. If it is a desirable or desired situation, it is a little closer. But it may still be only a pleasant anticipation, even if the future situation is intensely desired. Purpose emerges only when there is some act of will, some actual effort to bring about the desired situation. This is what is meant by commitment.

The commitment element may vary greatly in intensity. At one extreme, a person may be a "man with a mission," passionately dedicated to bringing about a desired situation. Similar intensity is found when the desired future is negative in nature—namely, the avoidance of an extremely undesirable situation. The commitment to escape a known hell may be even deeper than the commitment to attain a known heaven. At the other extreme, the commitment may be casual and fleeting. The purpose of crossing a street involves much less will and effort than that of crossing a "color line" or status barrier.

At any point on this spectrum, emotions and feelings are always involved. As Arnold has pointed out (1960, p. 193-248), these may be "impulse emotions," positive ones such as love, liking, wanting, desire, delight, and joy, and negative ones such as hate, dislike, aversion, recoil, sorrow, and sadness. They may be "contending emotions," such as hope, daring, courage, and the anger of desperation, and the negative ones of hopelessness, despair, fear, and dejection. These emotions and feelings are exhibited as a prelude to avoidance or attainment action, during such actions and at any point of attainment or failure. The effort to suppress them by a cold outward appearance may make them far more significant in the life of the "purposer."

The source of commitment to desired futures is rooted in the great variety of human interests encompassed by the broad categories discussed in Chapter 8: survival interests, commergence interests, differentiation interests, and self-development interests. These various interests provide the motivations behind the commitment.

The relation between purposes and interests may be stated in two ways. Many desired future situations can be described as those in which interest satisfactions will be obtained or dissatisfactions avoided. All others can be described as instrumental ways of obtaining satisfactions or avoiding dissatisfactions.

It should be already clear from the discussion of interests in Chapter 8 that many purposes may be externally imposed rather than internally determined. Many purposes are commitments to future situations that are desired only because they are lesser evils—they are less undesirable than a highly probable alternative. It is in this sense that threats or promises may make people accept as serving their interests courses of action that they would otherwise regard as opposed to their interests.

3. PURPOSE SEQUENCES

Up to this point, I have referred to a desired future situation and to a purposer's commitment as though each were merely a point in time. This oversimplification must now be abandoned. The only realistic concept of purposefulness is that which is based on the idea of a sequence of purposes embedded in a sequence of events.

Let us suppose that my purpose is to go to Rome. I have decided to go by plane, and so must buy an airplane ticket. In order to get the ticket, I must make a reservation and pay out some money. Thus what may look like a single purpose from the viewpoint of the anticipated trip turns out, upon examination, to be a part of a *sequence of interrelated purposes*. This sequence may be symbolized by the line ABCD in the following diagram:

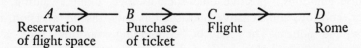

$$A \longrightarrow B \longrightarrow C \longrightarrow D$$

| Reservation of flight space | Purchase of ticket | Flight | Rome |

Now it turns out that in order to go to Rome, I suddenly find that I must cancel a number of prior arrangements. I feel I also need a new suit; since I do not trust my own judgment sufficient, I must convince my wife to go shopping with me. I then discover this will be easier to do if I help her get a new hat. So the straight-line set of interrelated purposes now becomes a *set of interrelated sequences*.

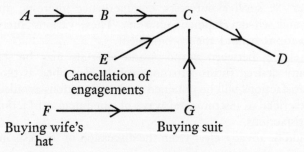

But what is the purpose of the trip to Rome?

The official reason is to explain a new policy to the manager of the Italian branch of my organization. But unknown to him, I'm also expected to report back on certain aspects of how the Italian branch is being run. If I succeed and submit a useful report, this will help the organization do its job better. It will also satisfy my superior's avowed purpose of putting the new policy into effect successfully and his not-so-openly avowed purpose of demonstrating that he is the best man for "that new top job."

There are some other purposes also. Not having been in Rome for many years, I want to visit there again. I am particularly interested in seeing some old associates who are living there now and whose views I want to obtain on some new ideas that I have not yet dared to broach in my own organization. In fact, this may even be why I proposed the Rome trip in the first place.

So the set of interrelated chains must now be extended further into the future:

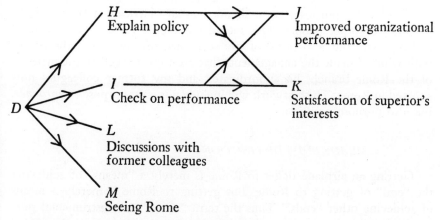

But this, too, is a great oversimplification.

Even in terms of my own purposes, there are other anticipated states or situations which have some connection with my trip.

Further away in the future, there are certain more *ultimate* purposes of my organization which my activities in Rome would be designed to further. These objectives include, but are not limited to, serving the national interests of my own country and, to a lesser extent, those of Italy. These purposes are more important in the sense that if it were not for them, I would probably not be going to Rome, nor would I even be a member of my organization. They are less important in the sense that they are rather vague and tenuous.

Closer to the present, there are many more *instrumental* purposes which must be achieved before I can get to Rome. To reserve flight space, I must get my secretary to call the airline. To buy the ticket, I must fill out, or have my secretary fill out, an elaborate form requesting a travel authorization. To take the flight, I must wake up early, bathe, shave, dress, eat, and drive to the airport—all in accordance with a tightly integrated schedule.

Thus the interrelated purpose sequences look more like this:

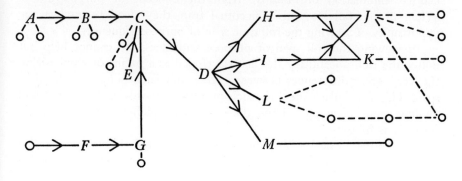

Finally, my purposes are embedded in any intricate network of the purposes of other people. This includes not only those of my superior and my wife but also those of my secretary, my associates, the people with whom I made the engagements that are to be cancelled, the manager of the Rome branch, his subordinates, and my former colleagues now situated in Rome. This network will include not only purpose *congruence*, but also purpose *conflicts*.

4. MEANS-ENDS DISTINCTIONS

Getting an airplane ticket to Rome is merely a "means" of achieving the "end" of getting to Rome. But getting to Rome is merely a means of achieving other "ends." Thus the term "means" (or instrumental purpose") refers to any state or situation which is *earlier* in time than some other state or situation. The term "ends" (or "ultimate purpose") refers to any state or situation which is *later* in a purpose chain or set of chains. The same state or situation may always be a means from one point of view and an ultimate objective from another.

In both practice and theory there are tendencies to exclude from purposeful activity an earlier or later part of the time continuum. When administrators lose sight of the later links, we are apt to see undue weight on rules and procedural devices which may produce little result except delight to their inventors and torture to their victims. This is what Sayre, in a discussion of civil service procedures, has referred to as "the triumph of technique over purpose" (1943, p. 134-141). Here Sayre uses purpose to refer to situations that appear later in the time sequence. When administrators neglect or forget the earlier stages in a purpose sequence, they are liable to end up with "utopian planning," a set of lovely objectives but no idea how to attain them.

In administrative action the exclusion of either end of the sequence—except for temporary concentration—can easily lead to the frustration of many purposes. In administrative thought the greater danger is the conceptual elimination of "means" from the concept of purposefulness. When people fall into this conceptual trap, they deny themselves the opportunity of viewing the full time span of purpose sequences.

In viewing the full span of purpose sequences, we cannot help but notice the rich vocabulary that has developed as a means of emphasizing the very great differences between earlier and later points on the time span. This vocabulary includes such impressive words as "strategy" and "policy" and "planning." Thus, the earlier-later dichotomy, in expanded form, is as follows:

The terms "strategy," "policy" and "planning," however, are also often used with reference to a full time span of purposes. It is in this sense that strategy is regarded as *including* tactics, that policies deal with *how* to achieve purposes (and in some organizations the term relates only to *how*) and planning deals with a time schedule starting with the present. Yet precisely *because* many people still think of these terms as oriented mainly toward the more distant future, increasing use is made of "program," "programming" and "program planning." The essential characteristic of a program is that it deals with a full time span, that the longer time span specifically includes the shorter. The term "function" is also used to refer to a later point on an action sequence. Here the reference may be to consequences in general or to the specific consequence of maintaining a system or organization. In either case the desirable consequence may be called "functional" and the undesirable "dysfunctional."[1]

Earlier	*Later*
Means	Ends
Instrumental purposes	Ultimate purposes
Tactics	Strategy, general strategy or grand strategy
Operating policy	Policy, high policy, or general policy
Execution	Plan, program

In making means-ends distinctions it is important to keep in mind Perry's observation that "the question of means and ends is never, in human life, a simple relation of a single means to a single end. The means to one end invariably affects other ends . . ." (1954, p. 124).[2]

5. INFERENCES

As already clear from the above discussion, purposes cannot be directly observed. We cannot see another person's desires. We cannot see his commitments. Even in introspection, the observation of purpose is

1. For a more extended analysis of the various meanings that have been attached to the term "function," and particularly for a stimulating critique of "structural-functional" analysis in the social sciences, see Nagel's "Functionalism in Social Science" (1961, p. 520-535).

2. Perry also goes on to elaborate a theme which is implicit in the multiplicity of human purposes: "If the end does not justify the means, what does justify it? The bare dictum that the end does not justify the means has no force whatever. At best it is a confused expression of several truths; that a means is ordinarily a means to many ends; that a given end does not justify its means regardless of other ends; that the means to a higher end overrules the means to a lower end; that a means is sometimes also an end" (1954, p. 125).

not easy. A person may readily identify a simple purpose of his own like crossing a street or eating a meal. But once he gets involved in more complex purposes, he faces serious difficulties—and the help of a psychoanalyst may be needed to bring about even a superficial understanding of his larger purposes in life.

We are therefore reduced to making inferences or imputations. In so doing we may be guided more by what we feel than what we think. By virtue of empathy we often put ourselves in another person's place and sense his purposes, even when he cannot or will not express them. We are impressed by our observation of emotions and feelings. We are guided by what people do as well as by what they say. We know that we ourselves never proclaim all our purposes and at times assume that this applies to others also. Like the young girl after relationships with a series of ardent suitors, we learn to distinguish between avowed, open, or manifest purposes and those that are actual, latent, or blatantly disguised. When we have reason to be unsure in our inferences, we look for recurring patterns of action. When we find them, we tend to interpret them as clear evidence of persistent commitment—even though we may not be sure as to the exact nature of the future situation which is desired. We are most sure of our interpretation when we see action that can have no explanation apart from certain inferred purposes.

The making of such inferences is in some ways similar to what physicists do in studying what goes on inside the atom. In both cases inferences are made from observed behavior. The existence of subatomic particles is inferred from certain activities that cannot otherwise be explained. One of the many differences is that in imputing purposes we operate on the assumption that people can make choices with respect to various points on a purpose sequence. While these choices may be sharply circumscribed by external power, imperfect information, and the habits and limited capacities of the purposer, we do not accept these constraints as reducing people to automata that follow some preordained script or program. On the basis of our own subjective feelings that we make choices, we impute choices to others also.

B. *Multiple Dimensions*

IF IT IS EMBARRASSING to ask someone what are his purposes or those of his organization, the question is nevertheless a legitimate one.

But to ask "What is *the* purpose?" is not legitimate. It is as much a trap as to ask a man when and why he stopped beating his wife. The very formulation of the question, if accepted by the respondent, guarantees an oversimplified and perhaps seriously misleading reply.

Anyone who *really* fixes upon a single purpose to the complete exclusion of all others has closed the door upon rational behavior. If he carries this approach very far in either private or organizational life, if he really achieves complete fixation on some single purpose, he can be regarded as insane.

In contrast, most single-purpose formulations are efforts to cope with the multiplicity of purposes. This is particularly true when army officers tell soldiers that their *single* purpose is to "get Hill 24," when economists maintain that the *single* purpose of business enterprise is to "maximize profits," or when civil servants say that their *single* purpose is to "serve the public." Single-purpose action doctrines usually aim at *including* other purposes (and thereby subordinating them) in a pattern whose capstone is the "single purpose." They rarely exclude intermediate or subsequent purposes. It is precisely because of the diversity of purpose that the emphasis on single purpose is so frequently regarded as necessary.

We have already noted the multiplicity that arises because of the sequential nature of purposes. Let us now probe more deeply into purpose multiplicity.

1. THE GLOBAL MATRIX

The major categories of organizational purposes have already been sketchily listed in "The Management of Organizations" (Chapt. 2, section B-3). These categories will be discussed, one after the other, in the following chapters. At this point, let us briefly summarize the entire set:

A. *Satisfaction of interests.* Organizations exist to satisfy the interests (or needs, desires, or wants) of various people, both members and outsiders. These interests are multiple, hard to identify, and overlapping. The satisfaction (or dissatisfaction) of these interests may vary by its intensity and by the location and number of people involved. This category of purposes is close to what is often referred to as *welfare, utility, benefit,* or *payoff.*

B. *Output of services or goods.* The output of an organization is composed of those products which it makes available for use by clients. These products may consist of services (tangible or nontangible) or goods. The quality and quantity of any product may sometimes be expressed in monetary as well as physical units. From the viewpoint of the organization as a whole, the output of any unit or individual is an intermediate or partial product rather than an end product.

C. *Efficiency or profitability.* When available inputs are perceived as scarce, attention is directed toward making efficient use of inputs relative to output. Since there are many ways of calculating input and output and of relating the two, there are many varieties of input-output objectives. Some of them are referred to as "efficiency" or "productivity." "Profitability" is applicable whenever output as well as input may be expressed in monetary terms.

D. *Investment in organizational viability.* In a minimal sense viability means the survival of an organization, without which no other purposes are feasible. In a fuller sense it refers to an organization's growth. In either sense viability requires the diversion of inputs from the production of output and their investment in physical, human and organizational assets.

E. *Mobilization of resources.* In order to produce services or goods and to invest in viability, an organization must mobilize resources that may be used as inputs. Because of the difficulties of obtaining scarce resources from the environment, "mobilization logic" may differ from "use logic."

F. *Observance of codes.* Codes include both the formal and informal rules developed by the organization and its various units and the pre- scribed behaviors imposed upon the organization by law, morality and professional ethics. These codes may be expressed in terms of what is expected or what is prohibited. In either case, code observance purposes are usually expressed in terms of tolerated margins of deviation.

G. *Rationality.* Rationality here refers to action patterns regarded as satisfactory in terms of desirability, feasibility, and consistency. *Technical* rationality involves use of the best methods developed by science and technology. *Administrative* rationality involves the use of the best methods of governing organizations.

Each of the above categories may be viewed as a separate dimension of organizational purpose. If we use the language of matrix algebra, we may think of these various dimensions as being brought together into a seven-row, single-column vector defining the desired future state of an organization. Yet each of these seven elements is itself a multidimensional matrix with its subelements themselves composed of multidimensional sub- matrices. Location in space and time are dimensions applicable to every element. Other dimensions are peculiar to each element. Thus output pur- poses may be expressed in terms of the quality and quantity of different types of products. For any one product there are many dimensions of both quality and quantity, each of which may be expressed in a variety of physical or monetary dimensions. In the following chapters these and other dimensions are spelled out in detail. The entire set of "nested" matrices may be referred to as the "global matrix."

When the full details have been supplied, it will become apparent that some combination of elements from the global matrix can define the performance purposes of any organization. Similarly, a series of such com- binations can express its changing purposes. At certain points it may be possible to use precise cardinal numbers as coefficients and reconcile different measures through weighting systems. At many others it may be possible to use nothing more than rough orders of magnitude or ordinal expressions as vague as "more" or "less." Sometimes, when the norms are noncommensurable, any weighting system would change, rather than reflect, the realities of purposefulness. Thus the global matrix provides an intellectual instrument for bringing together the quantitative and the nonquantitative, the measurable and the imponderable.

If at first glance it might seem that some actual organization purpose may not be expressed in any of these categories, closer examination will probably show that it falls within one or another subcategory or consists of a combination of subcategories. In any exceptional case where this might not be true, the exception would not "prove the rule." It would rather demonstrate the necessity of improving the rule by clarifying the terminology or restructuring some of the elements.

2. ACTION vs. ANALYTICAL HIERARCHIES

To understand the relations among the different categories of purpose, we must make a sharp distinction between action hierarchies and an analytical hierarchy.

An action hierarchy is one in which the relative importance of different purposes reflects the exigencies of a specific organization in a specific situation. At one moment, the highest priority purpose in an organization may be mobilizing resources, at another the satisfaction of dissatisfied clients. During one period the most important long-range objective may be organizational survival, during another period organizational growth. As one objective is achieved, new ones take their place. In the double sequence of events and purposes, people focus first on one action hierarchy and then on another.

The changing action hierarchies, moreover, rarely include all the elements in the global matrix. Through conscious selectivity, custom, taboo, oversight, or ignorance, many dimensions often receive the weight of zero. In fact, conscious commitment to the full sequence of all desired future situations would be impossible. Purposefulness is possible only when a significant portion of behavior is handled on the basis of habit and another portion handled on the basis of improvisation. In fact, purposefulness may be characterized as a clear interlude between routine, which makes it possible, and spontaneity, which may flow from it.

The situation is complicated by what might be called "purposeful nonpurposefulness." Many objectives can be obtained only if they are reduced to a subordinate position in an action hierarchy, as when we say that work satisfaction is a byproduct of the productive process rather than the basic aim. Those who place too much weight on efforts to obtain work satisfaction may easily defeat themselves—as may often happen in the frenetic pursuit of happiness, love or sexual pleasure. Thus people often learn to deemphasize those purposes which mean the most to them—not only as a protection against frustration, but also because some things can best be obtained without deliberate effort. Similarly, many learn that some obstacles can best be overcome and basic objectives achieved only through the very spontaneity that can be destroyed by overpurposefulness.

In contrast with changing action hierarchies, an analytical hierarchy expresses certain stable and all-pervasive relations. The global matrix is an analytical hierarchy in which all other purposes are subordinated to the satisfaction of human interests. The full pattern of subordination in this analytical hierarchy may be expressed in the following proposition:

Organizations aim at (1) satisfying human interests, of both members and nonmembers, by (2) producing services or goods with (3) an efficient use of scarce inputs, by (4) investing in their own viability, (5) mobilizing the resources needed as inputs, and doing all these things (6) in conformance with certain codes of behavior, and (7) in a rational manner.

In simplified form, these relations may be visualized as follows:

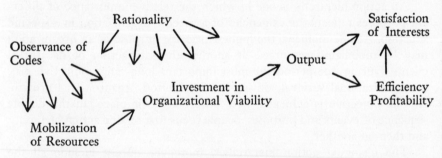

Thus organizations aim at bringing resources into the organization for strengthening it and for satisfying interests through the production of output. The observance of codes and rationality cannot be placed so well on a logical flow. As objectives of a more instrumental character, they are linked up with each of the other categories. In seeking to obtain other objectives the people in organizations may aim at being both "right" (in the sense of "correct" or "good") and "rational." The entire picture, however, must be loosened up by the qualification (explained in greater detail in the next chapter) that *any* of the other objectives may be regarded as a direct source of interest satisfaction of dissatisfaction. It is in this sense that we may regard the satisfaction of human interests as the "ultimate purpose" in the analytic hierarchy.

Although each of the categories has been formulated in terms that are particularly relevant to organizational purposes, it should be noted that they apply to individual purposes also. The purposeful behavior of any individual can also be described in terms of the satisfactions that he aims to obtain (or the dissatisfactions he seeks to avoid), the activities in which he wants to engage (service output), and his efforts to conserve on the use of scarce inputs. To do these things, individuals also must seek to maintain or strengthen their capacities, mobilize resources, observe various codes of behavior, and pursue objectives in a rational manner. The applicability of the global matrix to both individuals and organizations is no accident. If the same matrix were not applicable to both, it would deny the human basis of organizational behavior and would not be serviceable for dealing with the purposes of people in organizations.

When we drop the last two components, however, an interesting thing is revealed: the five-component matrix is now relevant to nonhuman systems. With a slight change in terminology we find that we are dealing with (a) inputs, (b) system maintenance, (c) output, (d) efficiency, and (e) function (in the sense of certain consequences outside the system). We now have a more general model which, with the inevitable adjustments always needed in moving from one system level to another, can be applied to the human brain, a single cell, a molecule, a solar system, a machine, or a man-machine system.

3. APPLICABILITY TO EVALUATION

While the previous point need not be pursued further in this context, it reveals something extremely relevant to our main line of inquiry: the applicability of the identical matrix to the actual performance of a system or organization. When we apply these categories to a single cell, we certainly are not referring to "commitments to desired future situations." Rather, we are using them to analyze action sequences.

If we now return to people in organizations (or to individuals alone), we find that the identical categories provide the language for describing, analyzing or even measuring actual performance. We might just as well have started in the first instance by establishing the global matrix as the set of concepts with which all aspects of action or performance can be described. The difference is that in one case we refer to various aspects of future situations or sequences, while in the other case we refer to past or present situations or sequences.

This analysis may now be rounded off by going one step further: the global matrix also includes within it all possible criteria that may be used for the evaluation of performance. The difference is that in evaluation these categories are used in the context of "the organization should" (or "should have") instead of "is" or "aims to."[3] From them one may select any "evaluation profile" with which to appraise the "effectiveness"[4] or "success" of an organization's performance.

In summary, *the identical set of concepts is applicable to the formulation of purposes, the analysis of performance, and the evaluation of performance.* The reason is that such concepts are ways of ordering, or structuring, complex information about performance—whether such performance takes place in the past, present, or future, and whether it may be regarded more or less desirable or undesirable. This is why some of the concepts set forth in subsequent chapters will often seem at first blush to be more applicable to the analysis of actual performance than to the formulation of purposes.

This three-way applicability of the global matrix may be illustrated by taking any organization at random and selecting one dimension from each of the seven submatrices, thereby listing seven identical prepositions that might be made by one person who states the organization's purposes, one who reports on its performance and one who sharply criticizes its performance. The only difference occurs in the two or three words used at the beginning:

	PURPOSE	PERFORMANCE	EVALUATION
	We aim to	*We do*	*You do not*
Satisfaction of interests	⟋ serve clients well		
Production	⟋ produce high quality products		
Efficiency	⟋ keep costs low		
Viability	⟋ build capacity to do more in the future		
Mobilization of resources	⟋ develop reliable supply lines		
Observance of codes	⟋ operate ethically		
Rationality	⟋ use modern methods of . . . (instrumentation, dysentery control, budgeting, operations research, etc.)		

With a little adjustment in the selection of dimensions, the same three-cornered discussion could center on any unit, any specific operation or mission, or any individual. With the introduction of more specific material, it could be the model for a three-cornered debate about a copper

3. It might be added that with appropriate adaptations the same matrix of concepts can be used in the esthetic evaluation of a poem, play, or painting.

4. The term "effectiveness" is sometimes used to express the extent of success achieved with respect to production objectives. In this context it seems more useful when used to apply to any and all aspects of performance.

mine, police department, research laboratory, political party, or even a judicial agency. Such a debate, in fact, would be more logical and less disjointed than many actual dialogues on good and bad administration. A popular tendency is for one person to criticize (or defend) on the basis of one objective and the other to retort with a defense (or criticism) on the basis of another objective. The multiplicity of purposes makes it easy for purpose declarations to be publicly formulated in one component of the matrix, reports on performance to be expressed in another and criticism and blame to be expressed in still another.

This does not mean that the purposer, the reporter on (or analyst of) performance, and the evaluator must all use the identical coefficients, weights and dimensions. The first may set a goal to keep net costs down to one dollar per unit. The reporter on performance may find that a net cost calculation is not feasible but that gross costs have been $1.20. The evaluator may use a different calculation of actual costs but may come to the conclusion that a big mistake has been made in reducing costs instead of improving quality and thereby providing more satisfactions for clients. Each may use the global matrix in the way that he is most accustomed to do so or, if a conscious effort is made to distinguish between these various categories, that is most appropriate to given situations.

In presenting this analysis I am not denying the difference between the realms of purpose, fact, and value. I am merely pointing out that these three realms are not unconnected. The bridge between them is provided by the concepts we use to describe actual, future, and desired performance.

The decision-maker or problem-solver walks across some bridge of this type. As he faces a set of alternative courses of action, he can make his choice only in terms of some desired future situation or sequence of interrelated situations. His choice may indeed be limited by his failure to note certain possible courses of action and by his inability to predict the probable consequences of any given course of action. It will also be influenced by his own habits, by established procedures and policies, and by pressures from others. But insofar as he *chooses*, his own decision-making action will be guided by his own purposes, the "facts" that he has concerning actual performance, and the evaluations that he has made of various actions. Any consciously rational choice will be articulated in terms of the concepts we have found within the global matrix.

4. PAST, OTHER, OR IDEAL

Any specific purpose may be formulated in terms of: (a) the past activity of an individual or organization, (b) the activity of another individual or organization, or (c) an ideal.

Similarly, when any type of purpose is used as a criterion of evaluation, we may evaluate by comparing actual performance with past performance, the performance of others or an ideal standard.

The past is always a fertile source of aspirations for the future. This does not occur only when one orients oneself toward a future replication of the past. It also occurs whenever one's purpose is to do better than before. This element is an inevitable part of purpose formulation. Also, the easiest form of evaluation is to compare present with past performance.

Anticipations of the future are also affected by one's perceptions of the activity of others who are engaged in similar activities. These perceptions may suggest how far we should aim to go beyond our past achievements. Other individuals, organizations and even entire countries and cultures often serve as models for imitation.

Yet the experience and achievements of others will rarely be completely comparable to the future situation faced by an individual or organization. The environmental conditions—as well as the people and organizations themselves—vary considerably. In order to cope with these specific conditions, it is essential to define purposes in terms of an ideal. Past achievements and the achievements of others will usually provide valuable and relevant information. But neither will be sufficient; the former is too restrictive and the latter too lacking in comparability. An ideal, on the other hand, is a creative act of imagination. As such it need suffer from neither of these restrictions.

Many ideals are often disguised in the trappings of empirical findings. Thus the objective of a 5 per cent annual growth rate may be justified by finding that we achieved that rate at one time in the past or that someone else is growing at that rate today. But no amount of statistical analysis can by itself lead to the conclusion that this rate or any other rate should be our goal. Goal formation of this type is a conscious act of desire and will.

Here it should be added that the experience of the past and of others, instead of leading toward any specific goal, usually offers tremendous latitude. Which point in the past should represent our future goal, or our basis of comparison? Which other organization (and at what point in time) should be our model? The data alone cannot provide a conclusive answer to these questions. In formulating an ideal, however, since we are limited by empirical facts, we can make these selections in accordance with our best judgment.

5. CONFLICT AND CHANGE

The inevitability of conflict within and among people and organizations has already been noted on a number of occasions. Here we need only add that there are many built-in conflicts within the global matrix itself. Many of these—such as the divergences between interest satisfactions for members and for nonmembers, between quantity and quality of output, between survival and growth, between mobilization logic and use logic, between small group and larger group codes, and between technical and administrative rationality—will be discussed in the chapters on each major purpose category. Others—such as conflicts between the short-run and the longrun aspects—apply to every category. Any of these conflicts may be mirrored or magnified in the specific purpose profiles of any individual or unit in an organization at any particular moment.

The entire situation is tremendously complicated by the processes of change. In part, this is a natural result of the sequence of events. With new, unpredicted and unpredictable situations, the old dimensions, co-efficients, weights, and permutations no longer become relevant. Let us return for a moment to my projected trip to Rome. Let us suppose that before the agreed-upon trip is taken, I learn of the possibility of getting "that new job" in a week or so. As a result, a new series of purpose sequences will start to unreel through my head. I may completely lose interest in my trip.

Changes of personnel can mean still greater changes. Suppose my superior should get his promotion and his assistant should temporarily take over his former position. His successor might want to cancel my trip and go to Rome instead. And I personally, at a time of such important personnel changes, might want to stay at home and "mend my fences." But if the trip does go through, there may then be many changes in the "objective situation." I might go a week later in order to handle a previous engagement which proved too difficult to cancel. I might find it imperative to engage in preparatory discussions with the manager of the Paris branch. When I get to Rome I might find a cable giving me a new assignment. Instead of staying two weeks, I may have to stay for four. And even with this prolongation there may be no time for me to see the sights or look up old colleagues, which had been part of my original purpose profile. By this time the policy I had set out to explain might itself be overturned for reasons that seem inexplicable to me. Whether I like it or not, whether I am well-prepared or ill-prepared for the shift, these changes in events inevitably change the structure of my purpose sequences.

In part, these changes may be a conscious adaptation to changing events. When you drive an automobile on a highway, you continually adjust both speed and direction in the light of the turns and traffic conditions that develop. You do your best to see what will develop a little bit ahead of time. If you are unfortunate enough to have to drive in a fog, you will have to adjust to conditions as they develop. In other human activities—particularly in large organizations and complex environment conditions—the fog will often last long and cover an immense area. Under such conditions people hesitate to commit themselves to long-range plans. If they do, they tend to leave wide room for interpretation, flexibility, and maneuver. This necessarily leads to still greater multiplicity in purpose profiles.

Alternative objectives, as Liddell Hart has pointed out (1954, p. 343-344), can be built directly into the essence of a plan: "In any problem where an opposing force exists, and cannot be regulated, one must foresee and provide for alternative courses. Adaptability is the law which governs survival in war as in life—war being but a concentrated form of the human struggle against enviromnent. . . . A plan, like a tree, must have branches—if it is to bear fruit. A plan with a single aim is apt to prove a barren pole."

The processes of change and adaptation are so fundamental that one may safely assume that any significant purpose—particularly any not in the immediate future—must be substantially changed in order to be attained. This is the great gap between human aim and achievement, between the vision and the reality.

c. *Purpose Patterns*

IN ALL THIS DIVERSITY, where is the unity?

With so many people in an organization having different and changing purposes, which purposes are the organization's purposes?

Some people answer this question by regarding as the purposes of the administrators the organization's purposes. They thereby leave out of consideration the purposes of all other members.

But even if we accept this narrow approach, we are still left with the problem of determining which purposes are those of the administrators. Here too we find a great variety of purposeful action.

The formal approach determines that we rule out all administrators except those at the highest level of formal authority and that at this level we confine ourselves to those purposes which are officially enunciated. By this time our answer will be in the form of glittering generalities that fail to express the unifying purposes that enable an organization to operate.

A more useful approach is suggested in the proposition (set forth in Chapter 10) that the unifying purposes of any organization are "constantly changing in response to new situations." As with a painting or a building, it is the pattern that provides the unity. With an organization however, the pattern is not merely something seen by external observers; it is a pattern that is accepted by the organization's members.

1. COHESIVENESS AND "PERSONALITY"

In an abstract sense, the various patterns of organization purposefulness can be analyzed in terms of cohesiveness. At one extreme we find a mutuality of interests and purposes. Here—whatever their specific purpose patterns may be—we find the organizations with a high sense of mission, *esprit de corps* and morale. The organization's product purposes are central elements in the work life of its members. Organizations of this type are able to remain united over a considerable period of time and in face of sharply changing circumstances. They can tolerate—and indeed benefit from—a high degree of internal diversity and conflict. The higher degrees of cohesion are usually associated with small membership and frequent possibilities of interaction among the members. It is thus found more among the units of large organizations than in large organizations as a whole. It is also more frequently found in organizations with high homogeneity of membership background (whether based upon family, education, common experiences or all of these together), selective ·standards for membership admission, a relatively small variety of end products, and ample opportunities for *quid pro quo* exchange.

At the other extreme are those organizations in which internal cohesion is based upon *quid pro quo* exchange alone. The dominant unifying element is the distribution of rewards, or incentives, rather than the sharing of mutual purposes. The major common purposes tend to be represented by the product mix and the observance of mutually advantageous rules. Under such circumstances internal conflicts may be far more disruptive than in a high cohesion organization.

In a more substantive sense, patterns of purposefulness can be thought of in terms of the "personality" or "character" of an organization. In this sense it is not enough to depict an organization as "more integrated" or "less integrated"—any more than the personality of an individual can be meaningfully described in such general terms. We must, rather, deal with those dominant traits that Selznick refers to as an organization's "distinctive competence of inadequacy" (1957, p. 42). In doing so, however, we are well advised to deal with tendencies and orientations toward the future rather than merely with descriptions of past behavior. In the case of individual personality, the role of purpose has been clearly emphasized by Gordon Allport: "What integrates our energies is the pursuit of some goal. When the goal is attained, the energy is dispersed. A person centered on becoming what he wants to become is far more integrated than one who has reached his goal—and has no place to go. To reach a goal we have to overcome distractions, discords, and obstacles. The effort involved is unity" (1961, p. 380). Similarly, in the case of an organization, we can do little better than look at the goals that integrate its activities. To do this systematically, we may turn to the global matrix and from it select whatever purpose profile is best suited to serve as the "personality profile" of a specific organization.

As with individuals, the personality of any organization is multi-dimensional and unique. The use of any oversimplified personality profile will lead to a stereotype. It may also lead to a mere aggregation that loses sight of the pattern as a whole. The great variety of possible patterns will become more evident as the following chapters expatiate upon the many dimensions in each category of the global matrix. As a preliminary illustration, however, it may be useful to indicate some of the purpose elements that often loom large in organizational personality:

Satisfaction of interests	Dedication to public interests
	Dedication to clientele interests
	Orientation toward interests of top management
	Orientation toward interests of all its members
Output	High quality output
	Fast work
Efficiency	Low costs in general
	Low labor costs
	High profits
Investment in viability	Permanence
	Empire-building
Mobilization of resources	Voraciousness
	Self-sufficiency
Observance of codes	Integrity
	Opportunism
	Discipline
Rationality	Technological progress
	Conservative management

The dominant personality characteristics of many organizations—as far as purposes are concerned—may be identified by combining a few facets of the type here listed. Thus to outsiders a bank's personality may be characterized by permanence, integrity, and conservative management. A corporation's personality may exhibit the qualities of dedication to clientele interests, fast work, high profits, and technological progress. The outstanding characteristics of a government agency, a hospital, or a school may be dedication to the interests of its clientele and of the public at large.

To members of the organization, however, the image may be somewhat different. In some cases, the difference will be merely the other side of the coin. Thus the very same characteristics which are seen by outsiders as low-cost production, fast work, or technological progress may be viewed by insiders as an overriding passion for penny-pinching, speedup or technological conservatism. In other cases, the dominant outward characteristics may be of an entirely different coin from the inner-perceived reality. Behind the impression of permanence may lie a chaotic empire-building operation which threatens the organization's survival. Behind the façade of conservative management that takes only carefully calculated risks may lie a reality of management so backward that it cannot discriminate between risk and certainty, let alone calculate degrees of risk. Behind a corporation's avowed concern for the interests of its clientele may lie a much greater concern for the power and prestige of its higher managerial group. Behind a government agency's loudly-proclaimed dedication to the public interest may lie a slavish devotion to the interests of a narrow group of clients, supporters, or controllers.

Even for an expert in the psychology of personality, the personality of any individual is extremely difficult to understand. As Gordon Allport has pointed out, "We have made some progress in manufacturing building blocks (traits) and in labelling them, but little progress in architecture. What determines the total form of personality we do not know" (1961, p. 386). The personality of an organization is still harder to pin down. It is rooted in a continuous interaction among the personalities both of its members and its component units. The multitudinous personality aspects of individuals are thereby considerably magnified. Moreover, the patterns of organizational personality are much less unified than those of individuals. Many organizations can operate effectively despite deep personality splits that in the case of an individual would lead to institutional confinement.

To achieve the minimum degree of necessary cohesiveness in the personality of an organization, its leaders must in some way affect the personality of its members. They must bring about a situation in which some of the purposes of the organization become a part of the purposefulness of members. This often leads to elaborate systems of disciplinary measures and indoctrination. At times it produces a high degree of conformance pattern of behavior, thought habits, dress, and speech.

At times the link between individuals and the organization is provided by the "official" personalities of organizational leaders, charismatic or otherwise. Whether these leaders be living people or dead and hallowed saints, their personal characteristics tend to express—in fact, even create—the shared characteristics of the organization as a whole. Members of the organization see such a leader not only as a family substitute but as a projection of their own hopes and unsatisfied desires. In their own fantasy world they live through him. His glory—perhaps even the high perquisites of office he may enjoy—is their achievement. Thus may organizational and individual personality be fused.

The personality of the leader is sometimes largely a fictitious creation. As with romantic love or a theatrical performance, illusion is an invaluable catalyst. It allows the followers themselves to participate in bringing into being a leadership myth which is freed from the earthly limitations of the leader himself. This is the kernel of truth in Thurman Arnold's rather extreme statement that institutional creeds "must be false to function effectively." If the extent of falsity is not widely apparent, this is because "the play is spoiled unless the machinery behind the scenes is carefully concealed" (1937, p. 356-357).

2. ASPIRATIONS AND CONSTRAINTS

In analyzing purpose patterns, it is helpful to use the concept of aspiration level. As developed by Lewin and his associates this concept refers to *the degree of difficulty in attaining the goal toward which a person is striving*. This difficulty is to be measured in relative terms—that is, with specific reference to the difficulty faced in attainment. Thus some schools, manufacturers, or national planning agencies may set themselves goals of unprecedented difficulty. Others may be less ambitious, orienting themselves toward a low level of aspiration.

Let us now consider in a preliminary fashion some of the factors affecting the aspiration level and its formulation.

One of the keystones of classical and neoclassical economics has been the hypothesis that the business entrepreneur aspires—or should aspire—to the highest possible level of profits. This idea was well expressed by the businessman who was quoted as saying, during a period of wartime shortages, "I'm out to get all the market will bear plus 10 per cent." This does not mean that the entrepreneur aims at maximizing output. If he produces too much, his profits might suffer. He seeks not *maximum* but *optimum* production. It is only when one is talking about utility or welfare itself that the maximum and the optimum are the same.

The idea of maximization and optimization have spilled over into many other fields. Public administration experts have often talked about the desirability of maximizing or optimizing efficiency, while political philosophers have often lamented what they saw as the efforts of politicians to maximize power. Freud's libido and id were undoubtedly would-be optimizers. Theoreticians on rational decision-making will often develop maximizing or optimizing equations at the drop of a hat. While they are not always clear whether the maximum-optimum hypothesis is to be regarded as descriptive or prescriptive, these theoreticians are generally agreed that maximization or optimization refers to some single type of purpose, preferably one that can be measured quantitatively.

Yet the difficulty with the high aspiration goals of "most" or "best" is that in real life they are *always* relative to the difficulties (or constraints) of any particular situation. Maximization is *always* "the most possible under the circumstances." Optimization is *always* "the best possible under the circumstances." If the circumstances include an opponent who may be seen as trying to inflict serious losses upon you, then you might play safe by adopting the "minimax" strategy. This means that instead of an all-out maximization effort you try to get the largest possible gains through action which is at the same time designed to minimize the risks you take.

An even greater modification of maximizing and optimizing behavior occurs when people decide to settle for anything that is "good enough." For Simon, this willingness to "satisfice" stems merely from people's lack of information, computational ability and a consistent preference ordering. For Boulding, it is more a result of trimming our sails to suit the wind. "We start by finding a wall between us and our desires; we end by bringing our desires to our own side of the wall. We start by trying to get what we want; we end by wanting what we get" (1960, p. 17).

But the Achilles' heel of the maximizing-optimizing hypothesis has been its almost exclusive relevance for single purpose situations artificially abstracted from the entire sequence of anticipated future situations. The fact that other future situations are also desired undercuts this approach to maximization far more seriously than the compromises rendered necessary by external circumstances. When it is recognized at the outset that purposes are always multiple, it then becomes obvious that any one purpose is a constraint on all others. "What then is the constraint and what is the maximand?" asks Boulding. "In terms of linear programming how do we identify in any particular problem what is the linear form to be maximized and what are the constraining inequalities? In more general terms do we maximize virtue subject to the constraints of satisfactory profits?" (*Ibid.*)

The full significance of Boulding's question can be appreciated only when we carry his line of reasoning a little further by adding still other objectives. What about the survival and growth of the organization? Do we maximize one or the other subject to the constraints of profits and morality? What about the power, prestige, or self-development of the managers? Do we maximize them subject to the constraints of viability, profit, and morality? What about service to consumers and the general public? What about the well-being or morale of the workers?

The growing recognition of multiple purposefulness has accelerated the retreat from single purpose maximization or optimization as an explanation of individual or group behavior. When we start from the very beginning, however, with the more realistic assumption of multiple purposefulness, we see that any one purpose is modified in the very first instance in order to fit into an anticipated chain of interrelated purposes or set of interrelated chains. As explained in Chapter 20, any pattern made up of such chains will be judged more or less satisfactory in terms of the desirability, feasibility, and consistency of various elements in it.

3. THE FEASIBILITY PARADOX

A satisfactory purpose pattern is not one dreamed up in an external tower; it is satisfactory in the light of all the internal and external obstacles and difficulties.

The recognition of these difficulties is embodied in judgments concerning the feasibility of a given purpose pattern—that is, the probability that it can be actually attained. Most judgments of feasibility are made on the basis of hunch and intuition. At a somewhat more rational level they may be made on the basis of reflection upon past or similar efforts and a conscious comparison between them and the contemplated course of action. A scientific approach to feasibility analysis is possible only through an effort to simulate in advance this contemplated course. If the simulation is realistic enough, then the major difficulties will be seen and may be analyzed.

In any appraisal of feasibility, whether intuitive or scientific, a paradoxical situation is faced.

On the one hand, if the aspiration level is set in terms of the patently impossible or even the wildly improbable, the result may soon become a devastating sense of frustration. This will lead either to a drastic reduction in the aspiration level or a blind and mechanical adherence to empty goals.

On the other hand, the difficulty, improbability, or even the perceived impossibility of goals set at an extremely high level of aspiration may themselves help summon up the energies which will make them more feasible. Hence the wisdom in the motto "Make no small plans," in the French leader's axiom: *"Toujours de l'audace,"* and in the Book of Proverbs' "Without vision the people perish." Nothing is more deadly than a dull and uninspiring plan than the timid refusal to take risks. The magnitude of the challenge created by a difficult plan may itself be a factor in determining the magnitude of the response to these difficulties. Hence the healthy effect on group morale that may be produced by such slogans as the one used in many military organizations during World War II: "The difficult we do at once: the impossible takes a little longer."

By the same token a purpose pattern which is geared to the *most probable* instead of the *best possible* tends to become a negation of purposefulness. The most feasible is the inevitable. When feasibility becomes the dominant criterion, people may be led to a passive acceptance of whatever the future may hold in store. Even when this extreme is not reached, an overfocusing on the difficulties may tend to enlarge their significance. The very process of analyzing them may itself detract from the feasibility of a contemplated course of action.

One way of escaping this dilemma is by developing a purpose pattern which combines many readily attainable goals with many supremely difficult ones. The small achievements prevent frustration while the dissatisfactions prevent self-satisfaction. Both together may serve to keep aspirations at a much higher level than would have been feasible by aiming at "good enough."

4. THE "OVER-AIM" AND THE "UNDER-AIM"

Considerations of strategy and tactics always have an important impact upon statements of avowed purpose. In traditional bargaining procedure, for example, a seller who wants to get fifteen dollars for a product may well ask twenty. This is his "asking price." The first offer, in response, may be ten dollars. Yet the purpose of buyer and seller in the first instance may well have been to settle for something around fourteen to sixteen dollars.

The same kind of strategy customarily enters into avowed statements of budgetary purpose. The organization that wants $15 million may ask for $20 million. To buttress this request, the overstated financial figure may well be accompanied by an overenlarged picture of the fine purposes that can be accomplished if this sum is granted. Sophisticated budgetary systems may indeed reduce the margin of overstatement. But since the budgetary process is inevitably based upon conflict and bargaining, this margin can never be eliminated. A large part of budgetary expertise consists of the ability to build up hidden reserves by asking for and getting more than is really needed.

Similar forms of deception enter into the "under-aim." The person who is seriously afraid of disappointment will often try to hide from himself the ambitious nature of his goals. He prefers the illusion of pleasant surprise to the shock of disappointment. In the same way workers and administrators will seek to have any official norms for themselves or their units set as low as possible. The officially promulgated "under-aim" will—when it turns out they have done much better—make their performance look much better and lead to higher rewards. This is one of the reasons for the traditional underestimates of tax collections as made by tax collecting bodies. It is one of the major considerations in the continuing struggle over norms and targets under an incentive wage system or a planned economy.

Similarly, administrators who are seeking approval of new developmental programs will tend to hide or understate their budgetary objectives. This is the strategy of "getting a foot into the doorway." Once money has been obtained for excavating ground and erecting the foundations of a building, it is easier to get additional funds for putting something on top of the foundations. By the time the project has progressed this far, not to proceed further would be conspicuous waste. But to have aimed to get all the funds at the outset would have resulted in getting nothing at all. The "under-aim" will also be used by those who believe that the avowal of ambitious objectives may provoke resentment and opposition. The behind-the-scene operators usually know that ambition is often most successful in the garb of modesty.

d. *The Clarity-Vagueness Balance*

IN POPULAR USAGE the two words "clarity" and "vagueness" are heavily laden with value judgments. Thus, clarity is seen as an unmitigated good. Purposes, it is said, must always be clear. The task of the good administrator is to define "crystal-clear goals." Vagueness, similarly, is regarded as an unmitigated evil. It is supposed to result from fuzzy thinking and bad administration.

In actual practice vagueness with respect to purposes is extremely widespread. Clarity with respect to one element in a purpose profile, or one stage in a purpose sequence, is usually counterbalanced by huge blobs of ambiguity at many other points.

Yet writers and theorists who recognize this fact often echo the popular call for clarity. This action does not imply that they think the goal of "crystal-clear goals" is really feasible, or even desirable. Their clarion call to war against ambiguity is often based on the tactic of fighting one extreme position by advocating another extreme position. It is much as though a doctor would advise total abstinence from food as a cure for overeating.

The goal of "crystal-clear goals" (apart from being itself unclear) greatly underestimates the complexity of purpose categories and human purposefulness. It implies that it is the administrator alone who defines purposes by his own acts of rational will, thereby ignoring the role of compromise and integration. It underestimates the very considerable virtues of vagueness. Above all, it thereby fails to define the administrator's problem of seeking a fruitful balance between clarity and vagueness.

1. THE USES AND LANGUAGE OF CLARITY

The intellectual values of precision in purpose formulation are rather obvious. Only when purposes are precisely stated can their logical interrelations be analyzed and developed. Precision is even more important in communication. When different groups of people must cooperate in carrying out interrelated sequences of action, precise formulations and schedules are essential. Otherwise, people who want to go in the same direction may find themselves going in different directions. Where an integration of divergent purposes is feasible, precision has the value— albeit a dangerous one—of uncovering conflicts of interest. As Follett has pointed out, this may be a prerequisite to their reevaluation and integration.

A demand for greater precision, moreover, is often a valuable way of filling serious gaps in purpose sequences. There is a tendency for some people to emphasize distant goals far off in a romanticized future and be delightfully vague with respect to the instrumental goals of the sordid present. There is also an opposite tendency for some people to spend so much time dealing with the present and the immediate future as to neglect completely longer-range objectives. In neither case more precision at one or another point will restore an appropriate balance.

The emotional values of precision—although not so well understood— are equally important. A precise goal, even though it may not be rationally justifiable, is much more dramatic than a vague one. Upon the United States entry into World War II, President Roosevelt enunciated a "victory program" for economic production. He set forth a goal of fifty-thousand airplanes, together with precisely stated figures for tanks and shipping. By the time the program got under way it became clear that the original numbers were not the best ones. But there was no doubt whatsoever about the galvanizing effect of using numbers. A few years later, when the period of reconversion from war to peace was approaching, the goal of full employment after the war was dramatized by calling for 60 million jobs. Greater retention, as well as attention, can be achieved by stating goals in this form.

Precision in the statement of purposes can also contribute to the building up of confidence in individuals and organizations. It suggests firmness, stability and strength. These are comforting values in a world of insecurity and confusion, particularly if people have reason to believe there is a sound foundation for the precision. When this belief exists, in fact, precisely stated goals may become reified, seeming to take on an independent existence of their own.

Ordinary language does not contribute to precision where precision is needed. The nature of this vagueness is illustrated by the large number of terms that are used to convey similar ideas concerning purpose—particularly objective, goal, norm, target, and standard. These words can be used more effectively if ranked on a scale of declining generality (or rising specificity). My own terminological preference, which is not consistent with ordinary usage, is to divide the labor among these words by the following arbitrary definitions:

A. Purpose —an all-inclusive term referring to any commitments to desired future situations or sequences of interrelated situations.

B. Objective —a specific category of purpose. Thus the major elements in the global matrix—satisfaction of interests, output, input-output relations, efficiency, mobilization of resources, investment in viability, observance of codes, and rationality—are organizational objectives.

C. Goal —an objective expressed in terms of one or more specific dimensions, such as the quantity or quality of production, or costs per unit of output.

D. Norm —a goal expressed with a cardinal or ordinal coefficient or a rough order of magnitude. Thus an efficiency goal of more units of output per labor input may be expressed as twenty units per manhour, man week. When used for purposes of evaluating performance, norms and targets may be called "standards." Because it is so specific, this might also be called a "target."

The following chapters will attempt to spell out a far more detailed language of individual and organizational purpose. This will be done by trying to define the major dimensions of each objective. This will identify the major problems involved in setting forth norms, targets and standards.

In the case of certain intangible goals precise norms are sometimes highly desirable. Under such circumstances it is often necessary to use one or more "purpose surrogates" to serve as the quantitative representative of, or substitutes for, goals that cannot themselves be quantified. In doing so, as brought out in a number of the subsequent chapters (particularly Chapters 12 and 15), it is helpful to survey the full range of possible surrogates. Above all, it is essential never to go so far in the exploitation of surrogates as to forget that they are only partial representatives and incomplete substitutes. They must be used, but they must never be taken too seriously.

2. THE USES AND LANGUAGE OF VAGUENESS

If all the points on a set of interrelated purpose chains were to be set forth with precise clarity, the result would be to destroy the subordination of one element to another which is essential to an operating purpose pattern. The proper focusing of attention on some goals for any particular moment or period in time means that other goals must be left vague. This is even more true for different periods of time. We must be very clear about many things we aim to do today and tomorrow. It might be dangerously misleading to seek similar clarity for our long-range goals.

Apart from its role in helping provide focus, vagueness in goal formation has many positive virtues. It leaves room for others to fill in the details and even modify the general pattern; overprecise goals stifle initiative. Vagueness may make it easier to adapt to changing conditions; ultraprecision can destroy flexibility. Vagueness may make it possible to work toward many goals that can only be attained by indirection. Some of the deepest personal satisfactions from work and cooperation come as by-products of other things. If pursued too directly, they may slip through one's fingers; the happiest people in the world are never those who set out to do the things that will make them happy. There is something inhuman and terrifying about ultrapurposeful action proceeding according to blueprint and schedule. Only vagueness can restore the precious element of humanity.

Above all, vagueness is an essential part of all agreements resulting from compromise. When a dispute is resolved, some degree of ambiguity enters into the terms of settlement. Hence the wide-open language often used in the final language of statutory law. Similar ambiguities are found in most constitutions, charters, declarations of purpose, policy manifestos, and collective bargaining agreements. Certain anticipated situations are always referred to in terms that mean different things to different people, and are valuable because of, not despite, this characteristic.

3. NUMBER MAGIC

Numbers provide the language of precision *par excellence*.

Yet numbers have always played a major role in the long annals of magic and superstition. Individual numbers—like three, six, seven, and many others—have been regarded as having special powers. Magical squares, triangles, and certain series of numbers have been vested with special qualities.

In modern times, when superstition parades around in fancier dress, number magic has not lost its ancient power. Statistics may not lie, but they certainly can bewitch—particularly in a culture which bestows high prestige on "hard" facts, "exact" sciences, and electronic computers. The users of statistics, moreover, may indeed engage in deception of themselves or others. They may merely fail to see or tell the whole truth concerning the background and limitations of their numbers. Or they may deliberately compile and organize their data in such a way as to show that output—or input also, for that matter—is what they want it to be.

General technical pitfalls in the use of figures—particularly those relating to averages, dispersions, base periods, sampling and tabular and graphic presentation—are covered in elementary texts on statistics. More specific warnings on sources of deception and self-deception with respect to the formulation of specific norms are provided in the subsequent chapters. Here we shall concentrate on four popular fallacies which are often serious impediments to the rational qualification of purposes and equally serious obstacles to the rational measurement and evaluation of performance.

A. *Premature quantification.* Perhaps the most dangerous form of number magic is premature quantification. "Primitive man probably devoted at least twenty thousand years to the task of recognizing the different sorts of stars in the heavens before it was possible to make measurements of their position and to express the times of their appearance with numbers. . . . Nothing but confusion has resulted, and can result, when mathematics is used before we are quite clear about the sort of things with which we are dealing and what sort of measurements it is useful to make" (Hogben, 1951, p. 224). Yet blind reverence for the quantitative achievements in any of the physical sciences often leads to a sacramental instead of an instrumental use of numbers. Modern man need not wait twenty thousand years before counting units of production. But he should at least give careful consideration to the definition of his units and their groupings before attempting quantification.

B. *Spurious accuracy.* The fallacy of spurious accuracy takes many forms. It is spurious accuracy to set a production goal of raising value production from 6,500 this week to 7,362 next week. The figure of 7,300 or the range of 7,300-7,400 would probably serve just as well. More precise figures could give a false impression concerning margins of error and the accuracy of advance planning.

It is spurious accuracy of a more vicious form when one spurns the use of all calculations that cannot be exactly stated or fully supported. An estimate may not be as precise as established fact but when nothing else can be obtained it is better than nothing (particularly if prepared and presented without any pretensions of accuracy). In fact, the impossibility of obtaining additional information may enhance the value of the less precise information we already have.

It is spurious accuracy to use cardinal numbers only and spurn the use of ordinal calculations. To know that A is larger than B and B is larger than C may be extremely significant even though we cannot determine the size of the interval between A and B or B and C. Much greater attention is needed to the relatively new field of scaling theory in the handling of social phenomena.

It is also spurious accuracy to use statistical data without indicating margins of error. Often, as painstakingly pointed out in Morgenstern's *On the Accuracy of Economic Observations*, the margins of error are exceedingly large—as in business accounting and national economic accounting. These errors may be due to such factors as the lack of designed experiments, the hiding of information, the lack of trained observers, defects in questionnaires, the accumulation of errors in mass observations, and the difficulty of dealing with unique phenomena. Yet data suffering from such errors are often presented as though they were error-free. "In the *physical sciences* it is customary to report data together with their carefully determined errors of observation and use them correspondingly. . . . In the *social sciences* such habits have not been developed" (1963, p. 8).

Finally, it is spurious accuracy, as Roy points out, when one allows numbers "to set aside, negate, and dominate the intangible elements, even when these are of overriding importance." This fallacy occurs whenever companies judge workers' performance in terms of quantitative output and neglect such qualitative factors as diligence, cooperation, punctuality, loyalty, and responsibility. It occurs when university officials carefully count the number of a teacher's publications and give insufficient attention to such less tangible factors as teaching ability, imagination, compatibility, interest in students, and devotion to the institution. Quantitative information should indeed be maximized, and made as precise as feasible. But in so doing one should give "due and proper weight to all other intangible, nonquantifiable factors" (Roy, 1958, p. 83-97).

c. *Missing definitions.* According to legend, Archimedes boasted that if he were only given a fulcrum on which to rest his lever, he could move the world. With much more justification any statistician worth his salt could validly claim that if only he were given the liberty of fixing his own definitions, he could make low production look high or vice versa.

Certainly any accountant who knows his business can, by using the "proper" definitions with respect to revenue, costs and time periods, convert a small loss into either a small profit or a larger loss.

In its grosser forms, this fallacy may involve the use of noncomparable data. Thus if we compare two companies whose net output is the same, but use net output only for Company A and gross output for Company B, the Company B's output will appear larger. At times we are forced into such a situation by the sheer unavailability of data, as in the following case:

	COMPANY A	COMPANY B
Net output	$230,000	unavailable
Gross output	unavailable	$250,000

Under such circumstances there are only two rational courses. One is to indicate frankly that there is no basis for a comparison. The other is to obtain one of the unavailable figures, either directly or through an informed estimate. If an estimate is used, it should be identified as such and its basis should be indicated.

In its more refined forms, this fallacy involves the use of comparable but highly selected data, without a clear indication of the precise nature of the data. Thus, an industry report might show that Company A produced a total output of $260,000 in contrast to $250,000 on the part of Company B. If no definitions are given, the fallacious nature of the conclusion will not be apparent. Yet the more precise picture might indicate that Company A's output value includes very high commissions to brokers and Company B's figures very low commissions. A full presentation of definitions might show the following situation:

	COMPANY A	COMPANY B
Net output (after commissions)	$230,000	$240,000
Gross output (before commissions)	260,000	250,000

Obviously, the conclusion one draws depends entirely upon which definition one uses.

In more general terms, it should be remembered that quantitative measurements of output—or of anything else—are no better than the definitions on which they are based. One cannot simply take numbers at their face value and assume that comparable and appropriate definitions have been used by the number-compilers. One must go behind the numbers to find out what they really mean.

D. *Single dimensions*. The previous illustration underscores the fact that the use of a single dimension may give a misleading impression. The choice between net and gross output, however, is only one of many choices. There are many other dimensions to be used in defining group boundaries, finding similar units and selecting time periods. In making a monetary evaluation of output we may choose between different aspects of value.[5]

It is fallacious, however, to believe that we must always select the "one best unit" and the "one best method." Actually, the use of a single dimension is warranted only when we are interested in a quick superficial picture. When our purpose calls for a deep analysis we must, rather, develop a carefully selected combination of many units and methods.

The world of purpose and performance confronts us with a bewildering variety of units and attributes. If we want to master it, we must attack it like jungle savages who have nothing but spears to use against a wild elephant that trumpets its defiance. We must throw as many spears as possible toward the largest number of vulnerable spots. Even then—although we may use detailed dimensions, many coefficients, a variety of weights, orders of magnitude as well as precise measurements, and where unblurred units are not available, all possible surrogates—we may not fully achieve our objective.

5. These and related dimensions of output are discussed in "Output: Services and Goods" (Chapt. 13).

Chapter 12

SATISFACTION OF INTERESTS

WHEN WE STATE that the satisfaction (or gratification) of human interests is the most important category of organizational purposes, we are on firm ground. People act together in organizations because by so doing they can satisfy interests that otherwise might not be satisfied as well or at all.

We may go a few steps further. We may indicate that these satisfaction objectives relate to the interests of both members and nonmembers. Most organizations are both "self-serving" and "other-serving." We may indicate that there are always differences of interests—both actual and perceived—among and between both members and nonmembers. There are always differences in the level and continuity of the satisfactions to which they aspire and to the provision of which an organization may commit itself.

Having gone this far, we find that we are still on high ground far removed from the dusty plain of purpose formation and emergence. If we descend with the men of theory and research, we find a number of paths that lead through the jungle of historic, and probably endless, debates. One path takes us to the controversies of philosophers and political scientists over special interests and the public interest. Another leads us to the work of psychologists in examining the interest basis of human motivation, the nature of satisfaction and morale, and the results of frustration. Still another takes us to the more disembodied satisfactions dealt with by economists and mathematicians under the name of welfare, utility, utiles, benefits, returns or (in the rather vulgar language of game theory) pay-offs. Among all these groups, moreover, there are those who share the conventional position of economists that the direct examination of human interests and their satisfaction is beyond their concern. This position is expressed in Boulding's delightful jingle (1958, p. 1):

> In modern thought (if not in fact)
> Nothing is that doesn't act,
> So that is reckoned wisdom which
> Describes the scratch but not the itch.[1]

This self-denying ordinance is supported by the large amount of nonsense in popular conceptions concerning the "itches" that impel men into scratching and other forms of observable behavior. It is adhered to by all those who deal with interest satisfaction in indirect or formalistic terms.

In the context of this book, there is no choice but to direct our attention to specific people and groups, their substantive "itches," and the satisfactions and dissatisfactions they may seek or obtain. This leads directly to the emergence of common interests, "public interests" as organizational objectives, and the surrogates of satisfaction and dissatisfaction.

A. *The Interested and Their Interests*

ORGANIZATIONS EXIST only because the actions of people in organizations are based upon commitments to satisfying the interests of various peoples and groups.

Yet there is a tendency for interest satisfaction objectives to appear in disembodied form, without the identification of any specific "interesteds."

1. This is close to the position of the welfare economists, as described by Little (1950, p. 51): "It is imagined that the mind is like a well of unknown depth, partly filled with water, the level of which could be altered by turning on various taps labelled economic, political, etc. Once the water is in the well there is no way of saying which tap it came from, and also it is impossible to say how much water there is in the well. One cannot therefore significantly ask how much economic welfare someone has; but one can say that the level of the water has risen or fallen as the result of turning the economic tap, if the other taps are not touched, i.e., one can say that economic welfare increased or decreased."

There is a similar tendency not to identify the interests themselves but to refer to them through the instruments of their satisfactions or vague abstractions.

To understand interest satisfaction objectives, therefore, we must often probe rather deeply behind the stated purposes of organizations. In so doing we come close to the intuitive probing of experienced administrators as they try to adjust their organizations' complex patterns of interest satisfaction objectives.

1. WHOSE INTERESTS?

Whose interests does an organization aim to satisfy?

This statement is sometimes answered by statements that an organization is exclusively dedicated to the interests of a single insider or outsider, or a small group of insiders or outsiders. Thus top executives may proudly affirm that a business organization is dedicated exclusively to satisfying the interests of the holders of ultimate authority, thereby establishing their allegiance to the cult of profitability as *summmum bonum*. The same proposition may be quickly agreed to by union leaders, for whom it is an indication that the interests of employees are not being given enough attention. Similarly, government officials may sometimes suggest that they serve the public interest alone. In such cases one may be pardoned for wondering how they manage to make a living. But here, as in most affirmations of single purpose, the real intent is to suggest priority for certain parties at interests rather than exclude the multiplicity of parties whose interests are to be served.

Any realistic answer to this question must be made in terms of a double array of individuals and groups. The first array is composed of all the members of an organization. Unless the members obtain some minimum satisfactions from participation in an organization, they may leave it. In compulsory organizations, such as conscripted armies and jails, this alternative may be forcefully foreclosed. In organizations whose exit doors are open, the unavailability of alternatives may itself keep people from leaving an organization—as in time of widespread unemployment. But in both of these cases, the provision of interest satisfactions—even if little more than the basic elements of survival—is essential to obtaining a minimum amount of participation. Where there are ample alternatives for obtaining satisfactions through participation in other organizations, a still higher level of satisfactions will be necessary in order to keep people from leaving.

If an organization were a closed system, there would be no need for going any further. But because complete closure is impossible, human organizations can never be entirely self-serving. Orientations toward the interests of outsiders are forced by the realities of resource exchange, mutual or reciprocal influence, multiple membership and entries and exits. Like individuals, organizations orient themselves toward the satisfaction of external interests both because this is necessary to satisfy their own interests (particularly in alliances and exchange relationships) and because they often identify their own interests with those of others. We must therefore deal with a second array composed of outsiders.

In the most immediate environment of an organization the people and groups in this second array are easy to identify: the direct clients, the suppliers, the advisers, and the controllers. Toward the outer reaches of a clientele network the identification of ultimate clients becomes more difficult. This difficulty is compounded in the case of the less visible and more intangible clients. Adversaries must also be included in this array whenever efforts are made to mollify them neutralize them or convert them into allies. This array becomes still longer when an organization appeals to the interests of more remote publics, whether organized or unorganized. It may, therefore, extend far beyond those individuals and groups who are the conscious actors, whether from inside or outside, in the life of an organization.

In the field of government the image of the juggler or tightrope walker has long been used to visualize the role of the high official or politician who tries to balance the pressures exerted by various external groups. In the field of business the "balancing act" image has more recently been applied to the activities of top executives in balancing the interests of investors, managers, workers, and consumers. This image may well be applied to all administrators at all levels in all organizations as they orient themselves toward the interests of different people and groups on the double array of insiders and outsiders.

Yet we can never accept the glib statements of those administrators who widen the myth of "one big happy family" to include outsiders as well as members, thereby coming up with the extravagant claim of "serving all interests alike." This appearance of fine impartiality glosses over the greater weights given to some individuals and groups at the expense of others. Some points on the double array are always more important than others—whether because of deeper interests, greater power or the ebb and flow of social conflict.

Nor can we deduce these relative weights from the charter or formal structure of an organization. Many private organizations seriously aim to serve a wide spectrum of "public" interests. Many "public" bodies give major attention to the interest of their members (or certain members) or certain small groups of "private" outsiders. True, many public agencies are involved in such a wide variety of conflicting interests that great allegiance to any one of them becomes unfeasible. Yet the extent to which this may be the case may be determined only by directly examining the activity of a specific public agency. Direct examination is even more important as a way of determining the attention given to the interests of members. There is nothing in the government-private distinction which suggests greater or lesser concern with the interests of employees. Even in the case of clubs, fraternal associations and other organizations set up to serve the interests of members only, we can never know—without looking—whose interests count the most.

Nor can we ever be sure how much the administrators themselves affect the varying weights given to different people and groups. They are merely one influence among many. The pattern as a whole is the product of an organization's past and present, of the pressures exerted by all the members, by many external forces in the immediate environment and by the social environment as a whole.

2. WHICH INTERESTS?

Interests are harder to identify than people or groups. They cannot be directly seen or counted. Like purposes, they can only be inferred. When we attempt to analyze them, we are brought willy-nilly into some of the deepest mysteries of human behavior.

A starting point for this analysis is found in the assumptions set forth in "The Human Beings" (Chapt. 8) concerning the interests of human beings. There we noted that despite their many differences modern psychologists seem agreed that individuals are motivated by a multiplicity of interests. We set forth, as a useful working hypothesis, the proposition that all human interests, or needs, interpreted as some permutation of interests in various forms of survival, commergence, differentiation and self-development. We also noted that (a) these interests stem in part from a person's relations with various groups, (b) many of these interests are conflicting, (c) the pursuit of these interests, is both rational and nonrational, and (d) each individual's peculiar pattern of interest, along with other factors, gives him a unique personality.

The application of these concepts in this context faces two major obstacles.

The first is that these interests can be understood—or enter into goal-oriented action—only in relation to some specific activities or things through which they may be satisfied. People rarely aim at survival in the abstract. They aim at something that may help them survive. This is a basic difference between interests and the desired future situations that may satisfy interests.

Let us pick at random any member of an organization—be he top executive, middle manager, or lowly clerk. A minimum level of financial remuneration and job security is necessary to meet his survival interests. His commergence interests call for certain relationships with his immediate work group. His differentiation interests call for some recognition of his special abilities, some differentiated status or some degree of respect, prestige or power. His self-development interests require opportunities to develop his full potentialities. All these things may be assumed.

But to understand the specific pattern of interests which motivate him, we must study *him*. To understand the balance of satisfactions and frustrations in his present situation, we must study *them*. To know what the organization's objectives may be with respect to the satisfaction of his interests, and of others like him, we must study *it*. We must look particularly at these specific activities of the organization which appear to have the closest relation to the satisfaction of his interests.

The specific interests of nonmembers may be approached in the same manner. All consumers' products can be directly or indirectly related to the basic human interests of survival, commergence, differentiation and self-development. In the case of many products, such as food, this interrelation can be set forth in a relatively simple product-interest matrix. Thus dairy products help meet certain physiological needs by providing various quantities of protein, calcium, butter fat and sugar. In the case of automobiles, the matrix becomes more indirect. Automobiles meet people's interests through a certain kind of transportation—presumably safe, quick, comfortable, and not too expensive. In a society that emphasizes mobility this, in turn, is often necessary to meet any other kinds of interests.

The second difficulty is that interests can never be automatically equated with stated claims, desires or demands. If a member demands more pay, he may be equally interested in more interesting work. If he demands more security, perhaps this is just a more acceptable verbal expression of other interests that are so overwhelmingly important—such as being respected—that he cannot talk about them. We must remember that his interests as a person are far broader than any satisfactions that the organization itself can provide, that his level of satisfactions will depend upon many things beyond the control of the organization.

Similarly, investors who seem to be interested in high dividend payments may actually be more interested in capital growth. Some may indeed prefer to see no dividends at all, just as long as the company behaves in a certain fashion. For certain private investors this may mean favoring certain other companies in business negotiations. For the custodians of government investments, this may mean the adoption of certain investment, price, or wage policies. Lenders who may seem to be mainly interested in prompt debt service may in fact be more interested in making larger and larger loans. Suppliers of parts may be more interested in an assured, expanding and long-term market than in maintaining their present prices. Members of control bodies may be more interested in deference than compliance, in matters of procedure rather than of substance, or in matters of little rather than major significance. Other members—and this probably happens in the control bodies of corporations and government executive agencies every bit as much as in the more publicized cases of legislative committees—may be mainly interested in personal booty. Some associates may be interested in far more intimate collaboration than they let be known. Others may be at least partly interested in opposition rather than cooperation. Rivals will usually be interested in at least some degree of collusion. Opponents will often be interested in some sort of a deal.

"Motivation researchers" have provided many striking demonstrations of what might be discovered by the careful probing of consumers' interests. Both dairy products and automobiles, for example, may meet many human interests that are rather remote from nutritional and transport interests. The manufacturers of these two product lines may also aim at meeting consumer needs that have no obvious relation to dairy products or motor cars. Their psychological advisers may prove that more ice cream will be sold if marketed in a manner that "symbolizes uninhibited over-indulgence or voluptuousness, via the mouth" (Packard, 1957, p. 86). More cars may be sold if they serve as status symbols, instruments for attaining a certain kind of personal power, or even as substitutes for wife or mistress. Ice cream may be packaged and automobiles designed, moreover, in ways that provide deep esthetic satisfaction. Since the automobile is a durable good that requires maintenance and repair, it may even provide a means whereby some people can meet their needs for learning and creative activity. Considerable attention has also been given to the satisfaction of sexual needs by consumers' products. Here the researchers maintain that fountain pens are seen as body images, automobiles as wife or mistresses, ladies' underwear as reassurance of feminity to women who have taken over functions traditionally limited to men, and cigars as symbols of masculinity and virility.[2]

2. A general review of "motivation research" may be found in Ferber and Wales, 1958. Here Dichter, one of the pioneers in the field, provides a general

Although this type of analysis of consumer interests has been thus far developed mainly in the sphere of marketed products, it is every bit as applicable to the products of government. The services produced by the modern "welfare state" are mainly designed to gratify the lower levels of human needs. This is the major explanation of why, under conditions of full employment and acceptable living standards, labor and reform governments lose their attractiveness to the electorate. The doctor is no longer needed when the patient is well. A gratified need is no longer a dominant motivator. The traditional statesmen of the welfare state can market their products successfully only when people are actually suffering, or fear they are about to suffer, from a failure to gratify their physiological and economic security needs. To the extent that these needs are met, they will be much less interested in public affairs (that is, the market for public services) unless the same or other statesmen find ways to meet their needs for commergence, differentiation and self-development.

The analysis of interests becomes still more difficult when we try not only to identify them but to appraise their importance, intensity, and duration. Such an appraisal is often an intuitive part of the process of forming objectives. In the case of one's own interests it is usually less articulate. Stronger interests tend to be reflected in stronger commitments—that is, stronger objectives. In the case of the interests of others the connection may be less intimate. The fact that consumers may desperately want cheaper prices and higher quality will not by itself determine the producer's commitment to the satisfaction of these wants. The intensity of these interests is less significant than the actual power which the "interesteds" may wield. Moreover, in the case of both "self interests" and "other interests," both internal and external interests, conflicting interests on the part of the "interesteds" must always be taken into account. An intense interest in one direction may always be partly negated by another interest in the opposite direction.

3. THE SURROGATES OF INTEREST

The concepts used in the preceding section are analytic terms whose use in the formation of interest satisfaction objectives is approximated only in the most sophisticated organizations. In actual practice there is

rationale for this approach (p. 21-31), Vicary an explanation of methods used (p. 31-36), Martineau a detailed application to the question "what automobiles mean to Americans" (p. 36-49), and Politz a critique to the effect that motivation research is really "hypothesis hunting, not hypothesis testing . . . preresearch, not research" (p. 50-64).

often considerable ambiguity as to whose interests are to be served and as to what level of satisfaction, with what accompanying degree of dissatisfaction, is sought. Above all, there is little explicit recognition of the basic human interests in survival, commergence, differentiation, and self-development. As stated above, "People rarely aim at survival in the abstract. They aim at something that may help them survive." This applies also to commergence, differentiation and self-development. These other somethings, in turn, become the concrete goals and norms. Although they are not themselves the interests to be satisfied, they serve as interest surrogates.

The goods and services produced by organizations are the most specific surrogates of interest. As instruments for satisfying the interests of various clients, they are often regarded as the actual embodiment of those interests. Thus we may very appropriately speak of people's interests in food, clothing, shelter, health services, transportation services and educational services. Although these are not ultimate human interests, they are often so regarded—and to the extent that specific types, amounts and qualities of such products are in fact essential to satisfy basic interests, this is an appropriate point of view.

It is also extremely convenient. These products are easier to identify, measure and appraise than are any of the basic human interests. Also, most of them serve a variety of interests. A woman's dress may contribute to survival interests by protecting against the elements, to commergence interests by indicating that she belongs to a certain social grouping, to differentiation interests by providing some distinctive characteristics, and to self-development interests by being a vehicle for artistic creation. But it is the dress itself which pulls all these interests together. The more interests may be satisfied by any product the more essential it is that the product itself be an objective of goal-oriented activity.

In the case of client interests the instrumental role of an organization's products is particularly clear. What may sometimes be less clear is that the same goods or services—or the process of producing them— are also instruments for satisfying the interests of the producers. In a minimal sense an individual, unit, or organization as a whole obtain financial rewards for their labor only by producing certain goods or services. By so doing they serve their own interests as well as those of their clients. Thus product objectives may readily become a surrogate of their interest in financial rewards. Beyond this, the processes of production may contribute to satisfying commergence needs through working together with other, differentiation needs by providing opportunities for prestige, respect and power, and self-development needs through creative activities. The pride of workmanship is not necessarily associated with an awareness of satisfactions provided to clients. It may also be based upon one's own personal satisfactions in doing a job and in the respect that may be won from other producers. Thus the products become the surrogates of the producers' interests also. The clients' interests in this or that type, amount or quality of product may thus be subordinated to the producers' interests in these matters. This subordination will usually be greater whenever the clients are unorganized or, if organized, are in a weak competitive position or are not sure exactly what they want.

A similar situation is found with respect to each of the remaining categories in the global matrix. The interests of both members and non-members of an organization may be satisfied through one or another form of input-output relation (efficiency, productivity or profitability), by investment in the organization, by the mobilization of resources, by the observance of certain codes of behavior and by technical or administrative rationality. In some cases interests will be satisfied (or frustrated) directly and immediately—as when hopes and aspirations are aimed at effectuating a certain economy, strengthening the organization's capacity, getting a new budget, enforcing a code, or obtaining a new technical or administrative improvement. In other cases more important interests may be satisfied by the contribution these achievements make to the production of goods and services. In either case, any such objective may be viewed as an instrument for serving human interests and serve as a surrogate for these interests themselves.

In any society with a market economy money is an instrument for the satisfaction of a broad array of interests. As pointed out in "The role of economic gain" in section A of "The Human Beings" (Chapt. 8), money is not only a prerequisite for meeting man's survival needs. It may also be a symbol of status and a measure of power. As such, it can indirectly help people attain many things that money itself cannot buy; it may even serve as a partial instrument in helping people on the pathway toward creative self-development. Accordingly, money has probably become the most universal surrogate of human interests. Like all surrogates, it is highly useful; we could not develop meaningful purpose patterns without it. But its very universality is its danger. Here more than in any other case people may readily mistake the instrument or surrogate for the human interests that they serve or represent.

4. THE SATISFACTION-DISSATISFACTION NEXUS

We must now elaborate somewhat upon the earlier statement that people act together in organizations in order to satisfy human interests. This baldly stated proposition may seem to suggest that the purpose of satisfying interests is completely disassociated from the dissatisfaction of interests.

The separation between the two is often suggested by lists such as the following:

Satisfactions	*Dissatisfactions*
Rewards	Punishments
Promises	Threats
Hopes	Fears

Thus satisfactions are rewards that are actually provided. When promised for the future, they stimulate hope. On the other hand, dissatisfactions are actual punishments. They are thus the basis of threats and fears concerning the future. While all this is well and good, it is too simple. The two columns tend to crisscross in obvious ways. A punishment may be merely a withdrawal of, or a reduction in, a reward. A reward may be merely a withdrawal of, or reduction in, a punishment. Hope may be oriented toward a reduction in dissatisfaction and fear toward a reduction in satisfaction.

The nexus between the two is still closer. Both play a role in self-motivation. Both are used in efforts to influence others. This close relation between the two becomes evident the moment we try to define our terms. Most psychologists would probably agree upon a set of definitions along the following lines:

Satisfaction:	The reduction of the tension created by the desire for some future situation.
Dissatisfaction:	The aggravation of such tension.

The existence of some degree of dissatisfaction may thus be seen as the basis for purposeful action to achieve satisfaction. The person who is satiated has no reason to commit himself to obtaining any future state—except in relation to an interest that is not satiated. A person who is more or less satisfied has no reason to strain himself too much to attain a somewhat better state. As Maslow has pointed out, (1954, p. 105), "a satisfied need is not a motivator." A state of future satisfaction can become a goal only if one suffers at present from the tensions of dissatisfaction rather than the apathy of self-satisfaction. These tensions themselves may be a very satisfying part of human existence—particularly when associated with partial attainments and satisfying forms of activity.

Yet "all interest has a forward reference in time; it is a striving after the not-yet-attained. The object attained is no longer desired; or, if enjoyed, its present existence does not suffice" (Perry, 1926, p. 250). This has been repeatedly remarked by poets, dramatists and novelists. Thus a universal note is sounded in Shakespeare's lines:

> For it so falls out,
> That what we have we prize not to the worth
> Whiles we enjoy it, but being lack'd and lost,
> Why, then we rack the value, then we find
> The virtue, that possession would not show us,
> Whilst it was ours.
> (*Much Ado About Nothing*, Act IV, Sc. 1.)[3]

In economics this phenomenon is referred to by the so-called "law of diminishing returns," which has become a major way of developing a working link between "use value" and "market value." While use value is determined by actual satisfactions, market value is regarded as relating more to the increment in satisfactions to be obtained by a small additional amount of a commodity. When a person's supply of a commodity increases and his interests or wants approach satiation, then the marginal value of every additional unit declines. When the commodity is scarce and interests become more and more unsatisfied, then the marginal value increases. This phenomenon may be expressed mathematically in sophisticated "indifference curves." The psychologists have added additional sophistication in their analysis of inhibitions. "Thwarted interests acquire a super added force from being 'pent up' and tend when the pressure is removed or reduced to react with a correspondingly greater intensity" (Perry, 1926, p. 553). Psychiatrists and psychoanalysts have indicated how repression and deprivation of certain interests may result in an accentuation of other —and seemingly unrelated—interests. Finally, as Robert Burns put it, "the best-laid schemes o' mice an' men gang aft agley." Small objectives, like crossing a street, may be readily attained. When objectives are more ambitious, there is always a "shortfall." In any ten tries, few people will hit the bullseye very often and many may miss the target completely.

The dissatisfaction-satisfaction nexus is made still tighter by the fact that people in organizations habitually create dissatisfactions for others. In part, this is a byproduct of conflicting interests; when A and B are eagerly seeking one position, A's attainment of this purpose means frustration for B. In part, it comes through the use of sanctions. After A becomes boss, he may use actual or threatened punishments as a way of influencing B's behavior. In neither of these cases can the objective of producing dissatisfaction be entirely ruled out of the sphere of purposeful behavior. In the first case, it is an obvious after-effect of a clear goal.

---

3. The phrase "rack the value" means to "strain it to its own pre-existing limit."

In the second case, it is a possible intermediate goal, the justification of which is found in its possible contribution to the attainment of other goals.

There are also situations in which individuals and groups purposefully set out to produce certain dissatisfactions for themselves. Highly neurotic people will often set up situations in which their existing frustrations are compounded; they are "failure prone." On the other hand, highly realistic (and nonneurotic) people—particularly the more mature and seasoned administrators—know that the good and bad always come together. They face up to immediate dissatisfactions in order to get a larger measure of satisfaction a little later. They know that any situation includes both dissatisfactions and satisfactions and are willing to settle for the most promising mixture rather than wait for some state of unadulterated well-being. The person who accepts an administrative position with his eyes open is one for whom the inevitable dissatisfactions are outweighed by the possibility of more highly valued satisfactions. He whose eyes are not yet open to the inevitability of dissatisfaction is due for a rude awakening.

Yet too much dissatisfaction can lead to demoralizing frustration, stress, and anxiety. If sustained for too long, it can lead to utter apathy. Repeated failures of sufficient magnitude will cause abandonment of any goal. Repeated punishments of any magnitude will inhibit—if not destroy—goal-seeking activity. "Interest implies hope as well as consummation. There can be no interest if there is no promise of success. This indispensable character of auspiciousness may attach to untried possibilities, and may reflect either youth and inexperience, or a wide or fertile imagination. ·It may reflect past successes, either the proved fruitfulness of certain specific means, or a general confidence begotten by the habit of success. It may reflect a condition of abounding vitality which may be temperamental or vary with health and emotional state. There is, in any case, a limiting point at which baffled interest passes over into despair and apathy" (Perry, 1926, p. 556).

Interest satisfaction objectives, therefore, are usually the product of some satisfaction-dissatisfaction combination. Gratification stops short of satiety, while dissatisfaction stops short of utter frustration. Thus a successive series of tensions is accompanied by a successive series of hopes.

The concept of a satisfaction-dissatisfaction combination should not be confused with the concept of equilibrium. A system of equilibrium, whether dynamic or static, is one in which any disturbance in the relation between the variables of a system will automatically result in a restoration of the previous relationship between those variables (Easton, 1956). The setting of interest satisfaction objectives, on the other hand, may involve the deliberate creation of a disequilibrium. This is implied in the concept of the hierarchy of individual motivation interests, as presented in Chapter 8. The satisfaction of survival needs usually leads to the sharper emergence of commergence needs and differentiation needs. If these do not emerge by themselves, external action may induce their emergence, thereby creating a disequilibrium. Self-development needs, moreover, can never be as fully met as others. The self-developing person is in a state of recurring, if not perpetual, disequilibrium.

Man's inner potentiality for disequilibrium is itself one of the reasons why external motivators may run the risk of providing ample gratification of survival needs. The thought that people will work hard only if motivated by the fear of losing their jobs is not much more advanced than the idea that the best motivator is the sword and the whip. In a world of personal and economic security man's higher interests can more readily come to the fore. In any society where people are not yet accustomed to having their basic interests met, some reassurance may be needed—and perhaps some help in stimulating hope, imagination or confidence.

B. *The Emergence of Common Interests*

IN THE PRECEDING PAGES we have emphasized the great variety of "interesteds" and of their interests and the many conflicts that inevitably exist among them.

But this should not be taken as a denial of common interests. There is nothing contradictory between the co-existence of common and conflicting interests. In fact, common interests usually emerge out of interest conflicts and give rise to new interest conflicts. It is these common interests which underlie the development of common purposefulness and organizational power.

1. THE ORGANIZATION OF INTERESTS

Many interests of people are rarely dreamed of and rarely perceived. This is particularly true of those higher personal interests which can hardly be taken seriously when people are engaged in a bitter struggle for mere existence. It is true of many interests which can be satisfied only through sequences of future action which depart so radically from the routines of past action that they cannot readily be imagined as feasible possibilities. "Organizers and leaders have their limitations. Many people with interests in common tend to be lethargic or concerned mainly with other problems. As a result, organized groups are usually but an imperfect organization of underlying interests" (*Gross*, p. 19). This may be referred to as the universal phenomenon of the imperfect organization of interests.

Unorganized interests have little power. They are merely a potential. "An interest by itself has neither eyes, voice, nor motive power. If, at a given moment, it should be to the immediate interest of domestic sugar producers to prevent the importation of Cuban sugar, the mere existence of that interest does not mean that anything will be done. Rather, it indicates a potentiality for the organization or operation of some group based upon the desire to restrict the importation of Cuban sugar. It provides an opportunity for private organizations, politicians and government officials to organize sugar growers and in one way or another to do something about their interest" (*Ibid.*, p. 18).

The development of purposefulness in the satisfaction of certain interests is the very essence of the process whereby a new organization comes into being or an existing organization changes its orientation. The organizers, initiators and leaders do not create these interests in the first place. But they exploit the opportunities created by their existence. They transform them into a source of power. Hence it is that "for almost every underlying interest of any (perceived) importance there are competing organizations seeking to build upon that interest, or competing organizers seeking to start a group of some sort. The more pronounced these interests and the more deeply they are felt, the greater is the probability that an organization may be built to represent a large portion of those who share the interest in common" (*Ibid.*, p. 19).

The very process of organizing interests and transforming them into a source of power creates limits upon the power thus brought into being. The satisfaction of certain interests through organized action may provide a direct incentive and example for the satisfaction of competing interests through countervailing organization. This has been one of the accelerating factors in the onward sweep of the administrative revolution. The same process operates within any large organization. The development of a complex subdivision of labor involves the creation of a large number of divergent interests within an organization. The organization of these many interests into separate units with power of their own is the basis of the dispersion of intraorganizational power.

The limits on power may be pushed back by extending the sphere of organization and by increased attention to organizational structure. Within the organization administrators may organize interests more effectively by making adjustments in formal and informal roles, relationships and codes of behavior. Where adjustments in existing structures are not sufficient, they establish new organizations or enter into alliances and coalitions with existing organizations. As already indicated, the creation of an organization is one of the basic ways of developing common or reciprocal interests. This principle applies not only to simple organizations but also to those whose basic services are the representation of, or mediation between, interests already organized. Thus at much broader levels interests may be organized by holding companies, federations, legislatures and political parties.

At lower levels of organization this process has sometimes been referred to as "the articulation of interests," while the function of political parties and other large representative organizations is described in general terms as "the aggregation of interests" (Almond and Coleman, 1960). My position, however, is that while individuals may "articulate" their interests, some degree of interest aggregation is indispensable to the formation of any organization. By itself, however, the concept of aggregation does not do justice to the many adjustments that are needed to bring interests together in either a small organization or a large national party. Hence I prefer the pair concept of "aggregation and integration."

2. THE PROMOTION OF NEW INTERESTS

Before approaching the subject of interest aggregation and integration more directly, it is essential to recognize the dynamic nature of interests and of the process of working with them. Interests are not merely "givens." They may be developed.

To appreciate the importance of this point let us return to the principle of the imperfect organization of interests. A corollary of this principle is the proposition that *the unorganized, less organized, and more latent interests, both internal and external, are any organization's greatest reservoir of potential power.*

The significance of this proposition is most obvious when an administrator aims at satisfying certain well-known interests with which his organization was not previously concerned. Thus, the executives of both employing organizations and trade unions have bid for the loyalty of employees and members by developing recreational programs. The workers need recreation, the reasoning goes. Why not satisfy this need by arranging for dances, picnics, and athletics? This reasoning has led to the proliferation of similar activities in the field of health, housing, and education. When carried to its logical extreme, it leads to the idea of meeting all human needs through the activities of one all-embracing organization. In Israel the General Federation of Labor has built unprecedented political power by going very far in this direction. In desolate or undeveloped areas large corporations have at times aimed to do this through company towns providing a full array of community services. More recently, they have pursued this objective through "welfare" and "employee service" programs. In some countries the Catholic Church has organized workers' movements whose aims may be expressed as follows:

> Our movement must embrace the whole person of the worker, the whole of the worker's life, the whole family of the worker, all workers' needs, and the whole working class. We want the working man and woman, youth and adult, in coming into our movement, *to find everything there* (Brijs, p. 10).

The deeper significance of this proposition, however, lies in its application not to obvious interests which are probably better met elsewhere but to *deeper human interests that lie far beneath the surface and can be met only through the regular work of the organization.* The interest in being part of a work group is probably far more powerful than that of joining a bowling club. The interest in winning respect and prestige on the basis of differentiated performance within the organization is at least as great, if not greater, than that of winning power by becoming a union officer. The interest in creative activity and self-development is one which for most people can reach some degree of satisfaction only through participation in the activities of the organization in whose service they spend most of their active waking hours.

Thus the more effective administrators are often those who bring to life the latent and previously unrecognized interests of members of the organization. In part, this may be done by the more passive process of satisfying survival interests. But there is no assurance that once survival interests are adequately met, other interests will vigorously emerge. Stimulus may also be needed in the form of excitement, irritation, and encouragement. In order to help people achieve higher and stronger satisfactions, the administrator often creates dissatisfaction by destroying self-satisfaction. In order to promote cohesion he often tries to awaken, or develop, common interests alongside of divergent interests.

A similar line of reasoning applies to external interests. For a manufacturer the easy path toward a broadening of clientele interests is to add a few additional products. If the basic product line is durable goods, he may then supplement his output of goods by supplying maintenance and repair services. But to go beyond the more obvious interest of his clients, he must make better products. He must think not only of what opinion analysis studies show that people say they want; he must think of what they could be brought to want if he himself took the pains to develop their critical faculties and taste.

The promotion of new interests is quite different from the ordinary arts of influence or persuasion. These are usually designed to appeal to *existing* interests: "the secret of effective propaganda is the ability to make a case in terms of the interests of those whom one wants to persuade. This means sensing what really interests people as contrasted with what someone thinks these 'true' interests are or should be" (*Gross*, p. 244-245). In contrast, the promotion of new interests is directed toward what, in the mind of the promoter, *should be.*

In the absence of enough empirical data on how this is done, we may turn to Perry's hypotheses concerning the means by which "interests may be generated, excited, modified, limited or negated" (1926). Perry finds four closely related methods:

A. *The presentation or representation of eligible objects of interest.*

The simplest method is to present the apple to the subject's sensory experience, so that he may feel and smell it, and thus receive effective stimuli to an interested response for which he is already predisposed (p. 525, 527-544).

B. *The presentation or representation of the act of interest.*

A second method is to manifest or stimulate an interest in the apple on my own part. I may gloat over it, express pleasure in it, or taste it, with unmistakable symptoms of satisfaction. In this case, I seek to arouse the interest not simply by affording it a suitable occasion, but by exhibiting the interest itself (p. 525-526, 544-548).

C. *Using the intrinsic effects of failure or success.*

Should these methods fail, I may resort to starvation. . . . I may remove the apple to a distance, or threaten to throw it away, or describe a prospective dearth of apples (p. 526, 549-564).

D. *Using the interaction of interests in the same subject.*

I may seek to gain my end indirectly through dealing with his other interests. . . . Through satisfying, or thwarting, or deadening his other interests by any of the first three methods, I may so affect his general state as to render him more susceptible to the interest which I am seeking to implant (p. 526, 564-588).

As Perry points out, the use of these methods differs with respect to recurrent and nonrecurrent (or progressive) interests. It might be added that in most cases (particularly in that of the fourth method) the users are usually guided by some working premises, inarticulate though they may be, concerning the various existing interests of those in whom new interests are to be aroused.

3. INTEREST AGGREGATORS AND INTEGRATORS

To a certain extent, common interests among different people and organizations emerge from the simple, uncoordinated processes of human interaction.

Yet organizational action requires much more than spontaneous co-operation. As indicated in Chapter 2, it requires conscious efforts to coordinate or integrate the activities of many people and groups. The administrators are those who have some degree of authority and responsibility for making such efforts. The power or influence which they may exercise depends upon their ability to aggregate or synthesize the interests of people. Only thus can people be motivated to exploit the power potentials of physical resources.

The relation between administrators and human interests is recognized in many separate contexts.

Thus when we look at an administrator's efforts to influence others, we think of the various rewards or punishments, promises or threats, incentives or disincentives that he may use. These are the most obvious ways of dealing with their interests. If this is too static a picture, we may then look at him as he tries to represent various people or groups—by voicing or symbolizing some of their interests. A still more dynamic picture of the administrator is one which shows him as a mediator between competing interests. This is a usual way of describing a politician or government leader. Stated in broad general terms, it is equally relevant to the interest balancing activities of administrators in any organization. At the lower levels in an organization, there are usually fewer interests to be handled. At the higher levels, there are often many more. In either case the complexity of the operation is affected by the extent and heterogeneity of external interests impinging upon the organization.

In previous chapters, mention has already been made of many of the methods used by administrators in aggregating and integrating interests. As pointed out in "The Conflict-Cooperation Nexus" (Chapt. 3), integration is one of the most effective ways of resolving interest conflicts. It is usually associated, however, with the other forms of conflict resolution: avoidance, deadlock, victory (or defeat), and compromise. In aggregating or integrating interests, however, administrators are rarely conscious of the differences between these various outcomes. Their attention, rather, is usually directed to such supremely practical matters as (a) trying to calculate their own interests, (b) trying to probe behind the words and actions of others in order to estimate the nature and intensity of their interests, a process in which empathy may be every bit as useful as intellectual analysis, and (c) trying to estimate how the interests of themselves and others may be affected by various courses of action. They usually learn from sad experience that considerable bitterness is usually involved in the process of pulling together the many interests of many people. If some interests may be satisfied, others must be frustrated, diverted, displaced or transformed. To paraphrase Abraham Lincoln's famous axiom about "fooling people," it may be possible to satisfy all interests of some of the interesteds a little bit of the time, a little bit of the interests of all the interesteds some of the time, but it is never possible to satisfy all interests of all the interesteds all the time. Seasoned administrators tend to develop thick and battle-scarred skins. They learn that to shape common purposes it is as essential to enter some conflicts as it is to dodge others. They learn that to survive and be effective on "the firing line" they must "dish it out" and "take it on the chin," that they must hurt and must be hurt.

The particular style that any individual administrator may use in aggregating and integrating interests may in large part be described in terms of his total organizational role. This will include his formal roles (as discussed in Chapter 9) and his informal roles (as discussed in Chapter 10). At this point we may add an extremely important point with respect to his personal characteristics. Both the roles that he is expected to perform and the quality of his performance in them will be greatly affected by three major factors: his knowledge, his abilities and his interests. No one of these three factors is enough, by itself, to qualify an administrator to handle his task. Each, in fact, is dependent upon the other. As will be developed in the chapters on administrative education in Part VI, "The Future," these are the crucial factors in the development of administrators. Anything that people may learn about administration—and any aids to learning that schools and teachers may provide through educational services and other methods—may be properly expressed only in terms of some knowledge-ability-interest combination.

Moreover, the performance of administrative roles and the appropriateness of any knowledge-ability-value combination is always determined by the specific situation. The power exercised in integrating or synthesizing interests, as indicated in Chapter 4, can be understood only with respect to specific power wielders, specific objects of power and specific environmental circumstances. Above all, as suggested at the end of Chapter 24, the perception of crisis by elites with power is often a precondition to the aggregation and synthesis of widely divergent interests. Without crisis perception the administrators will hardly be able to summon up the tremendous energies necessary for the remarkably complex—and painful—tasks that this process involves. Without crisis the various "interesteds" will be less willing to retreat from firmly-entrenched positions and less receptive to new interest patterns.

c. *Public Interests as Objectives*

COMMON INTERESTS emerge at many levels of organization—among the members of a small unit, within an organization, among organizations and throughout an entire society. As the number of "interesteds" becomes larger, these common interests may be referred to by a large variety of phrases produced by combining any adjective from the first column with any noun from the second:

Common	Interest(s)
Community	Welfare
Public	Good
General	
National	
International	

Perhaps the most widespread combinations of these terms are "general welfare" (which occupies a conspicuous place in the preamble to the Constitution of the U.S.A.) and "public interest."

Of all possible combinations, the most useful is provided by the phrase "public interests." The first of these two words is extremely flexible. It may be used with reference to any given public or groups of publics— from an organization to a community, a nation or the world itself. The second word is rather unusual in this context inasmuch as it appears in the plural rather than the singular form. This usage is consistent with the approach taken in previous chapters concerning the multiplicity of human interests and purposes. It conforms with the sage advice of Chester Barnard: "It will make much more sense to talk about 'Public Interests' than to approach the public with the subject in the singular."[4] It provides a convenient way of referring to the "common interdependent interests of many publics."

1. THE RISE OF PUBLIC INTERESTS AS OBJECTIVES

One of the outstanding characteristics of the twentieth century has been the increasing orientation of organizations toward the satisfaction of more interests of larger publics.

There is a growing concern in every country and throughout the world with these broader conceptions of interest. The executives of the large private corporation of the mid-twentieth century can no longer say—as did many of their nineteenth-century predecessors—"The public be damned." Today, the public must be wooed. Part of the wooing may be sweet words only, but another part must be some degree of purpose-fulness in serving public interests. The trend toward regulation of private organizations, both business and labor, and toward the nationalization of

4. Leys and Perry (1959 p. 27). But Barnard's was a still, small voice lost in the jangle of many scores of opinions presented to or summarized by Leys and Perry. Most of the others talked of interests in the singular or seemed to think of a single, undifferentiated public. A similar "singularity" is found in most of the ideas summarized in Schubert (1960) and Friedrich (1962).

economic enterprises is largely based on the desire to achieve this public interest orientation.

A similar concern may be detected in the sphere of government. Agencies that provide services to producers are criticized if they do not take into account the interests of the nation at large. Agencies whose policies are unduly dominated by certain small groups are criticized for neglecting larger interests. Considerable distress is created by government enterprises that seem to behave just like private enterprises; inefficiency may be tolerated, but not neglect of broader interests. At the same time— although unfortunately to a smaller degree—there is a growing feeling that no government can act solely in terms of national interests. There is a growing recognition that the interests of any one nation are inseparably intertwined with the interests of other nations. Public interest conceptions expand beyond national boundaries. They begin to take shape as "international interests" or the "welfare of mankind."

The growth of professionalism, moreover, has often brought with it —in degrees that vary from one occupation to another—an interest in public service. An important public service orientation, however imperfect, is found among the great established professions of medicine, law and engineering. It is found in the many emerging and quasiprofessions. It is found in schools, colleges, universities, and scientific laboratories throughout the world. It may be found in the lower, middle, and upper levels of almost any type of organization. In all these places the "still small voice of conscience" will every so often ask (in words comparable to those Justice Brandeis is said to have used whenever meeting his former law clerks), "What have you done recently to serve the people?"

Professionalization, however, is but one aspect of the ever-increasing specialization of labor brought with it by the onsweeping administrative revolution. Specialization creates interdependence and interpenetration of interests. One may not want to serve others, but one must. One may not want to be served by others, but one must be. In this age far more than in the day of John Donne, "no man is an island entire of itself." More important, no organization is an island entire of itself, it is rather "a piece of the continent, a part of the main," a part of a much larger system. When a piece of the "main" crumbles away, it diminishes the organization, for the organization is involved in mankind. In Donne's day there were many "mains." Today these are coming together into a world system which, like any society, can be described in terms of its resources, social structure, values and distribution of power. Today we must ask for whom the bell tolls; we know it tolls for part of us and we want to know which part.

There are tremendous differences, of course, in the extent to which various organizations orient themselves to the external world. An organization, like a person, may be other-oriented toward a few or toward many. Its self-orientation may be based upon varying degrees of self-identification with external interests. Apart from the ever-present influence of specific personalities and traditions, two general factors of considerable significance merit attention in this connection.

The first is the extent to which influential people in organizations succeed in achieving substantial satisfaction of their interests in survival, commergence and differentiation. When these interests are fairly well met and more attention is given to self-development, people can more readily transcend their own interests. It is at this stage that we may more readily find, as stated in Chapter 8, "self development on behalf of interests broader than one's self." Here the rugged individualist may become the genuine philanthropist, while his sons may turn to the public service. The successful politician may become the genuine statesman.

The second is the extent to which the administrators of organizations are brought face to face with a large variety of organized interests. The business executive who must deal with a host of suppliers, clients, and controllers as well as with the organization's internal units develops a much broader orientation to various interests than does the "inside executive." A still broader orientation may be usually developed by a creative trade association executive or by a banker who deals with many sectors of an economy. The public servant who deals with but a limited clientele can rarely develop a broad perspective and an understanding of the interests of many publics. When he faces a large array of vocal, active and conflicting publics, then the likelihood is much greater that he will become the prisoner of none and that he may be able to detect the great common interests that can be brought into being by aggregation and integration. Remove the pressure of organized external interests and much of the public interest orientation of many organizations will prove to consist in large part of smooth words fashioned by public relations experts. But *with* the pressure (which cannot in fact be removed) many of these words have—or quickly develop—genuine meaning.

The rise in public interest orientations, therefore, cannot be understood apart from interorganizational combat. Public interests become meaningful objectives as the result of various outcomes of conflict resolution. The processes of conflict themselves generate common interests among the contestants, interests in preventing conflict from going too far, in the rules of the game and the methods of bargaining and mediation, and even in the maintenance of conflicts whose disappearance might jeopardize the internal unity of the combatants.

2. THE MULTIPLICITY OF PUBLIC INTERESTS

Let us now return to the phrase "public interests," which is here used as a substitute for the more usual "public interest." The difficulty here, whether we have reference to a community, a nation or the world itself, is not the absence of any common interests. It is rather the profusion of common interests, a profusion so rich that it can never be expressed, without serious distortion, in any simple formula.

There are at least four reasons for the inevitable multiplicity of public interests. The first is that human interests are multiple. Human beings are interested in survival, commergence, differentiation, self-development, and in an infinite variety of activities and action sequences necessary to satisfy various permutations of these interests. Second, organizational interests are multiple. The common interests of any community cut across scores of actions of any organization in the community. Third, there are always many divergent and conflicting views on how common interests are to be brought together into patterns and how satisfactions (and the inevitable dissatisfactions) are to be distributed. Fourth, there can never be any one spokesman for all the common interests in a community. We may have a common interest in a good supply of drinking water, electricity, transportation, and food. Both the water department and the electric company serve common interests. But although the department uses electricity and the company personnel drinks water, each is oriented mainly to satisfying one, not both, of these interests. In the case of transportation and food there will be many different organizations providing different kinds of transport and different kinds of food. Each one has a special interest in serving one segment of the broad spectrum of public interests. If we now jump to the highest hierarchical point we can find, the chief of state, we will usually find—even in a completely socialist state—that at the most he can only be a symbol of all public interests. He can never take responsibility of directly serving all public interests. The most he can do—and the most any group of directorate members or top executives can do—is to serve a few selected interests of high urgency, such as defense against external attack, the mediation of internal disputes, or the maintenance of the system. Other public interests must be handled by a host of other organizations, whether they be governmental or nongovernmental. To assume that some one person or one organization can accept responsibility for serving all the interests that people have in common is tantamount to faith in an omnipotent deity or omnipresent church.

If we want to use the singular term "public interest," we should do so with the explicit understanding that we are hereby referring to some specific pattern of public interests. We hereby recognize the legitimacy of divergent and conflicting patterns of public interests. These patterns will vary in terms of (a) the identity of the "interesteds" who are included, (b) the nature of the specific interests for which satisfactions are to be provided, and (c) the distribution of satisfactions among both the interesteds and their interests.

Science, rationality, and their application through research may restrict, but never eliminate, the area of conflict between divergent public interest patterns. It always helps to get facts and analyze facts. Doing so will often prove that certain conflicts were only imaginary. Better yet, it will open up new avenues of integration. It will take people out of the realm of mere possibility by illuminating the more important realm of the probable and the feasible. But the pursuit of science and rationality does not lead people on one road alone. It opens up alternative roads. Experts—particularly if they are good ones—will almost always argue among themselves. They will inevitably be affected by their own pattern of interests in survival, commergence, differentiation and self-development.

Nor can public interests be conceived of only in the more obvious interests of various publics. A publisher of children's books or a producer of radio and television programs may demonstrate that millions of children are actively interested in cheap hair-raising tales of murder, villainy, rape, and mass carnage. An active distribution organization can always establish a mass market for one or another type of opiate. But the existence of these interests—and the ease with which they can be excited—does not establish the public interest character of action designed to nurture and satisfy them. Some of the noblest conceptions of the public interest are those which fly in the face of actively organized interests, even of interests which may temporarily win the tacit or verbal support of a demonstrable majority.

The term "welfare state" is often used to refer to national governments which aim to eliminate the major insecurities associated with the inability to obtain employment and a minimum standard of living. In this context the term "welfare" is much more narrow than when used in the broad concept of the "general welfare." It refers merely to that aspect of the general welfare which is promoted by helping satisfy certain basic human interests in survival. This kind of national government could be more aptly described as the "security state" or the "survival state." It is oriented toward meeting man's more obvious and elementary needs. A true "welfare state" would be one in which the goals of government included a wide variety of actions designed to stimulate and gratify the entire hierarchy of human interests.

3. THE INTERMEDIATE AND GRAND ABSTRACTIONS

Because of the multiplicity of public interests, many important abstractions are used to symbolize them.

As will be seen from the following list, each of them may readily be fitted into one of the major categories of the global matrix of purposes:

SYMBOLS OF PUBLIC INTEREST

	THE INTERMEDIATE ABSTRACTIONS	THE GRAND ABSTRACTIONS
Satisfaction of interests	Full employment Fair employment Equitable distribution of income Higher living standards	Peace, security Freedom, liberty, autonomy, self-determination Equality, tolerance Dignity, honor, prestige, pride Worth and dignity of individual Individual self-development, self-sacrifice, humility Culture, beauty, the arts Progress
Output	Growth in national output Output of specific services or goods Price stability	Abundance
Efficiency	Productivity Balanced budget	
Investment in viability	Investment Resource conservation Resource development Defense	Unity, national consciousness Expansion Saving free enterprise (or building socialism)
Mobilization of resources	External assistance Economic independence or self-sufficiency Favorable trade balance	
Observance of codes	Law enforcement Due process Fair procedures	Justice, equity Democracy Order, duty Obedience to god or gods
Rationality	Scientific or technological progress Good government or administration	Reason Wisdom

The Intermediate Abstractions are those which are the lifeblood of national debates on public policy. They enter into the language of controversy, planning negotiation and manouever in bureaucracies, legislatures and courts. The Grand Abstractions, on the other hand, provide the basic language for preambles to constitutions and manifestos and the perorations of orations. If the former are those for which people live, the latter are those for which they may be willing to die. For centuries on end, they have been the ideas that have stirred men's souls. They have become the symbol and inspiration of mass movements, wars and revolutions and the creation of new states. In declarations of independence and national purpose, in constitutions, charters and solemn covenants, they have become enshrined as national and international goals.

At times these terms become empty shells, devoid of meaning and content. At other times they become a shoddy façade to disguise tyranny, slavery, prejudice, exploitation, stagnation, or intellectual and moral bankruptcy. This can readily happen when Freedom is used to mean freedom for the strong to tyrannize the weak and freedom for the poor to starve, when Equality means equal rights for a few and the denial of unequal abilities, or when National Defense becomes a motto of supernationalist aggression. It happens when Economic Growth becomes an instrument in an armament race, Economic Stability a substitute for growth, or Dignity and Self-Fulfillment standardized phrases in empty orations.

The continuing strength of the Grand Abstractions lies in their recurring use to refer to some specific public interests. The idea of freedom, for example, has had power only when, in the context of a specific historical situation, it is clear that what is meant is freedom for certain large groups of people *from specific things*—freedom from tyranny, slavery, fear, monopolistic restrictions, discrimination, or poverty. Or else it is freedom for certain large groups of people *for specific things*—freedom of speech, thought, religion, educational opportunity, assembly, or organization. The Grand Abstractions are most powerful when rooted in the Intermediate Abstractions and, through them and along with them, in the deeply felt interests of people and well-organized groups. In turn, the Intermediate Abstractions attain greater power when they can be directly translated into Grand Abstractions. In the case of purposes relating to input-output relations (efficiency and profitability) and mobilization of resources, this translation is rarely made.

When any of them is given such a specific interpretation, it immediately becomes a way of describing action designed to serve the interests of human beings in survival, commergence, differentiation, and self-development on behalf of interests broader than one's self. The economic goals are basic to the satisfaction of survival needs and the emergence of all other needs. Independence, Honor, and Dignity, for example, are aspects of the differentiation needs. Cultural development and self-development are ultimates that can best be appreciated by those more fortunate people who, freed more than others from the shackles of lower needs, have reached the level of major emphasis on learning, expression and creativity. Certain types of specific freedom and certain aspects of equality are essential to any reasonable degree of gratification of all human interests.

These specifically interpreted ultimates have also appeared as strongly expressed demands in the form of natural rights. As such, they were justified on the ground that they were a part of "natural law." But with the more cynical enlightenment that followed the eighteenth-century Enlightenment, this foundation was shaken—at the same time that the asserted demands became increasingly recognized in legal rights. In my judgment, the foundation of man's rights in natural law can be rebuilt by the findings of social scientists as they devise principles, and eventually laws, that explain human nature. The rights of man are grounded on the needs of men and the common interests of mankind.

4. PUBLIC INTEREST MYTHS AND FALLACIES

In the case of single organizations, as explained in the previous chapter, the multiplicity of purposes has been one of the factors impelling people to use single purpose fictions in retreating from complexity or trying to bring order out of confusion.

In the case of larger systems, such as communities and states, the single purpose fiction creates many more difficulties.

On the one hand, the concept of a single public interest breeds fanaticism and intolerance. It suggests that the general welfare as a whole can be found in a single conception, program or ideology. Whether they are leaders of political parties, churchmen, or scientists, the "true believers" know that they have found the panacea. If others dispute their view of the public interest, this is merely a temporary imperfection in the state of the world. Their point of view will one day reveal itself, they feel, in a blaze of glory and command the same broad acceptance as the proposition that two plus two equals four. When advanced by utopians, such absolutist positions are harmless—or even entertaining; they may also be advanced, however, by powerful well organized groups eager to advance their own interests by loudly pretending concern with broader interests. Thus the Walrus, in *Alice in Wonderland*, led the oysters astray by expressing his friendship for them. As he devoured them avidly, he wept tears of sympathy. A more sophisticated version was presented by Adam

Smith's classic defense of the obviously self-serving industrial groups in
England of his day. Although the domestic manufacturer has no intention
"of promoting the public interest," he is nevertheless "led by an invisible
hand to promote an end which was no part of his intention" (*The Wealth
of Nations*, p. 423). The same convenient hand seems to appear in the
idea behind a statement attributed to an American businessman while
serving as head of a government department: "What's good for General
Motors is good for the United States." If such frankness had infected
some of his government colleagues at that time, they might have similarly
declared, "What's good for the United States is good for the world."[5]
Sentiments of this type, however, are usually expressed publicly in the
language of the Walrus. The colonial exploiter operates to "help the poor
heathen." The fifth columns and armies of the enslavers march under the
banners of liberation.

On the other hand, the concept of a single public interest may lead
to a sterile negativism or formalism. Thus those whose sensibilities are
offended by absolutist approaches and by Walrus-type deceptions may
go to the other extreme of concluding that this single public interest is
to be found in whatever results from the interplay of forces or whatever
some presumably qualified elite may determine it to be. This approach
leads rather directly to the proposition that it is "a general term without
content" (Thompson, 1950).

In contrast, those who use the concept more creatively invariably
assume—at least implicitly—that they are dealing, rather, with a multiplicity of common interests and alternative patterns of common interests.
This assumption underlies all efforts to handle controversial matters
through procedures that provide the opportunity for interests to be
identified and studied and for the interesteds to express their views on
satisfactions and dissatisfactions.

D. *The Surrogates of Satisfaction and Dissatisfaction*

THE SPECIFIC FORMULATION of satisfaction objectives requires something
more than the mere identification of people and their interests. If these
objectives are to be used in actual operations by being tested against performance, some way must be found to discriminate between degrees of
satisfaction.

5. Schubert suggests that this was a misquotation, or rather a partial quotation.
The full statement was ". . . for years I thought what was good for the country
was good for General Motors and vice versa" (1960, p. 5).

Yet human satisfactions—like interests themselves—are also locked within the minds and hearts of individuals. Even when we look into ourselves, it is hard to untangle our various interests and discriminate between degrees of greater or less satisfaction of each. When we look at others, the task is much harder. Here we cannot rely upon direct feelings and sensations, nor can we make direct comparisons.[6] Here, instead, we must use surrogates of satisfaction and dissatisfaction. These appear in the form of certain types of human behavior that are more readily observable: choices made, payments given on the basis of satisfactions received or anticipated, opinions expressed, and the subsequent results of satisfactions. Many of these types of behavior, particularly monetary payments, may be expressed in quantitative terms as specific norms or as measures of the extent to which a norm is attained.

1. CHOICES

The choices that people make are probably the most important indicators of satisfactions.

Where a person is confronted with a choice of stocks to invest in, beds to buy or doctors to use, the decision to select A instead of B is *prima facie* evidence that A is associated with a greater degree of satisfaction.

This surrogate is also intimately associated with the other three. The decision to pay a certain price usually represents the making of a choice, at least between buying and not buying, if not between different goods at different prices. A choice usually expresses one's real opinion more directly and openly than mere words can usually do. The choice of A rather than B may result from the consequences of the satisfactions previously given by A and B.

The great virtue of choices made as an indicator of satisfactions is that in the act of choosing, a magic common denominator is somehow or other found that cuts across all the pro's and con's, provides weights for all the various interests that are affected and cuts through the tangled skein of satisfaction and dissatisfaction. This is what happens when people vote for one political candidate instead of another, buy one car instead of another or stay in their old job instead of accepting a job offer elsewhere.

But like all other surrogates of human satisfaction, this too has its limitations. Choices are made in terms of present perceptions of past and

6. In the literature of economics this problem has been discussed as the problem of interpersonal utility comparisons. See particularly Appendix XI, "Measurability and Comparability of Utilities," Pigou (1952) and Little (1950).

anticipated satisfactions. Yet perceptions may be extremely misleading. Memories may be short. Future anticipations may be baseless. People habitually look backward or forward through glasses that are rosy-tinted or unduly black. Furthermore, many choices are made in terms of habit and custom. They may be made in sublime unawareness concerning the existence of any alternatives (in which case one could hardly say that a choice has occurred) or of certain alternatives that are not obvious at first glance. Finally, many choices are so difficult to make that the actual selection may be made on a devil-may-care or random "toss a coin" basis.

2. PAYMENTS

The second surrogate is the monetary price which people pay for goods or services. We may infer that when a person is willing to pay a higher price for Bed A than for Bed B or for the services of Doctor A as against those of Doctor B, the reason is that he has obtained—and/or expects to obtain—fuller satisfaction of his needs from Bed A and from Doctor A.

The great advantage of the monetary surrogate is that we are here dealing with ascertainable facts concerning aspects of behavior that can be precisely measured. We need only obtain data concerning the volume of sales and prices paid by types of buyers. We have left the troubled seas of human opinion and have reached the snug harbor of quantitative measurement. We can now gather in our statistics and use all the refined techniques of mathematical analysis in interpreting their meaning.

In the case of goods and services not available for sale, of course, this approach is not directly relevant. Where there is no price to be paid, as with the internal products of an organization and tax-supported services, client willingness to pay a price can hardly serve as an indicator of interest satisfaction. The most one can do, as explained in Chapter 21-C, is to use input value as imputed output value or try to establish an internal pricing system.

But even in the sphere of marketed goods, price and sales data may suffer from certain inherent limitations as indicators of client satisfaction. Most economists would accept Pigou's three observations in this connection (1952, p. 23-25). First of all, the relationship between satisfaction and a money measure "is mediated through desires and aversions" and "the money which a person is prepared to offer for a thing measures directly, not the satisfaction he will get from the thing, but the intensity of his desire for it." Second, "people's expectations as to the satisfaction they will derive from different commodities are often erroneous." This is a form of error which is nourished not only by client ignorance (which may be presumed to be substantial even without encouragement) but also by the widespread use of deception by the producers and distributors of goods and services. In this connection the division manager who uses bluff and personality tricks to give an exaggerated impression of the quality of his services is engaged in the same strategy as the high pressure salesman who bamboozles his customers through high pressure and misrepresentation. Third, "generally speaking, everybody prefers pleasure or satisfactions of given magnitude to future pleasures or satisfactions of equal magnitude, even when the latter are perfectly certain to occur. . . . Our telescopic faculty is defective . . . we, therefore, see future pleasures, as it were, on a diminished scale." The implication is that we are willing to pay for present satisfactions on an augmented scale.[7]

A fourth, and more serious, limitation is found in the widespread existence of imperfect competition and monopolistic pricing devices. The price paid can hardly be regarded as a valid indicator of relative consumer desire or satisfaction when monopolistic practices deny a free choice. Many purchases are made against the real desires of the purchaser—as in a shotgun wedding. Many prices are "agreed upon" in the same manner as one "agrees" to hand over one's purse to a stick-up man or a portion of one's income to a tax collector. The price paid may be more an indicator of power exerted than of desire felt or satisfaction predicted.

Finally, it should be kept in mind that the client judgment embodied in the payment of a given price is an overall judgment. To the extent that it can be genuinely related to interest satisfaction, it usually deals in a summary fashion with the satisfaction of all interests. This is a great advantage if one seeks an overall evaluation. It is a disadvantage if one seeks to infer the variable extent to which a product satisfies different interests. A more precise evaluation could be obtained only by confronting people with a variety of products each of which differs from the others in the extent to which they are presumed to deal with different interests; the willingness to pay might then be related to specific interest satisfactions. Yet this is a situation which is rarely approximated in real market situations. It could be properly developed only under laboratory conditions, in which case this approach would be transformed into the analysis of solicited opinion with monetary terms used as the basis of scaling the results.

7. One might carry this line of reasoning a little further and indicate that the relationship between desire and a money measure is mediated through actual consumer behavior and that the money paid by clients measures directly not client desire but client behavior.

3. OPINIONS

When a person says his interests have been satisfied, there is a common-sense basis for assuming that this is so. The reverse also seems self-evident. When someone complains bitterly, we may presume that he is dissatisfied.

Thus expressed opinion, whether unsolicited or solicited, is a major indication of genuine satisfaction. If most people say that a certain bed or a certain doctor is very good—and particularly if they keep on saying it over a long period of time—there is a *prima facie* case for agreeing with the popular verdict.

When opinions are unsolicited, however, they suffer from serious limitations. First of all, unsolicited opinions rarely, if ever, provide an accurate cross-section. Whether they appear in the negative form of complaints or in the positive form of testimonials, they are very much like letters-to-the-editor. They are submitted by the small minority who feel strongly about a subject or have a special axe to grind. Second, they are usually unstructured. They are usually based more upon general impressions and reactions than upon identified interests. Third, the satisfactions reported by different people are not directly comparable one with the other.

To some extent, these limitations can be overcome by a systematic collection of opinions. The proper selection of respondents can provide a representative sample. Careful formulation of questions, together with sound interviewing technique, can provide answers dealing directly with defined needs and other specified standards. Large-scale polling techniques that grapple with the direction, intensity and salience of opinions —particularly when they succeed in measuring the degree of each—can go far toward introducing a measure of comparability into the reported satisfactions of different people at specific points in time. Thus opinion polls are increasingly used by private and public agencies as a way of checking on client reactions to the quality of their products. Merit rating systems, designed to express judgments concerning the satisfactions given by the personal services of organization members, are often nothing but an orderly way of polling the opinions of a person's superiors and/or peers.

Yet solicitation itself may create other difficulties. No matter how technically efficient opinion polling may be, bias may creep in—or be put in—through a slanted selection of subject matter, the use of procedures that promise the desired results, the unfair or loaded phrasing of questions, or interpretation and presentation of the data in a manner that favors certain foregone conclusions. Direct incentives to bias are provided by the abundant possibilities of using the results of public opinion polls in propagandistic campaigns to influence public opinion. In commenting upon the opinion polls conducted for cigarette and dentifrice manufacturers, magazines, radio networks, and political groups, one student wryly observes that "it is remarkable how commonly the research conclusions support the sponsor's position and supply him with sales ammunition" (Kornhauser, 1947).[8]

Entirely apart from bias, another difficulty may be created through the very act of solicitation. The asking-answering situation is itself part of the opinion collection process. In such a situation there may often be quite a large gap between what people say and their actual degree of felt satisfactions. They may voice opinions, when they have none, merely because they think it is more becoming to do so. They may understate their true feelings because of restraints and inhibitions unknown to the interviewer. They may overstate their feelings as a way of "blowing off steam." Their interest in making an impression on the interviewer—or even on themselves—may introduce new shapes and contours into their own conceptions of their satisfactions. This problem of "question-answer distortion" cannot be solved merely by enlarging the statistical sample and assuming that deviations of this type will balance themselves out; the probability is that they will be reinforced instead. Nor can the validity of results be tested by comparisons with other polls. This all-too-prevalent fallacy is based on the unwarranted assumption that the other polls are themselves free from "question-answer distortion."

Moreover, whether solicited or unsolicited, expressed opinions may provide a misleading impression of the underlying state of satisfaction. Where satisfactions and dissatisfactions are intimately blended (as is often the case), any statement of opinion may be merely a haphazard statement concerning one facet of a complex situation. In some organizations bitter grumbling is an expected form of behavior. This is particularly true in armies, where complaints against higher officials often rise in direct proportion to the complainers' respect for their ability. The complaint itself, as a way of "blowing off steam," may even serve to enhance the satisfactions obtained by the complainers. Also, both plaudits and complaints may be ploys in the struggle for power within and among organizations. Thus the analysis of opinions will not by itself unlock the human mind and reveal the nature of human satisfactions. We must content ourselves with a framework of inference built from a number of surrogates.

8. It might be added that such research activity may also supply the research organization with the financial wherewithal to try its hand at less biased undertakings on its own account.

4. SUBSEQUENT RESULTS

Let us suppose we are formulating the objectives of clientele satisfaction for a bed manufacturer, a police department and a doctor. We may then say that in the first case the aim is that the people who use the beds sleep well. In the second case, we want a reduction in criminal acts and in the third case, quick recovery on the part of patients.

It is not easy to formulate specific standards concerning sleeping, crime or health and disease. Every one of these goals has many facets and the facts relevant to each are not easy to obtain. But if we obtain them, how can we use them? How can we relate verified consequences with the one factor we happen to be examining?

Let us assume that our sleeper has unquestionably slept long, well, and comfortably on our bed. How do we know that he slept well *because* of the bed? Maybe he would sleep just as well on any bed, or even on the floor. If we experiment with two different beds and he sleeps better on one of them, maybe the decisive factor is that in one case he was more free from worry than in the other.

Let us suppose that a patient dies after a serious operation. His family may immediately blame the doctor. What basis is there for this presumption? Perhaps the patient might have died in any case—and the only criticism of the doctor's services may be that they were superfluous?

The same problem is found in the case of intermediate services. Let us take the most universal of all intermediate services—the services of an administrator. Are we justified in concluding that a man is a bad administrator if his company loses money? Perhaps the conditions are such that it would lose money under any administrator. Perhaps the fact that it did not lose more money is an indication that his services were of a surpassingly high quality.

The controlled experiment provides the ideal method of appraising the connection between goods and services and the results of their use. This method can often be used in dealing with certain types of goods, particularly components and end products used in the production process. Its use becomes more costly in the case of consumers' goods. It is no simple matter to assemble two groups of consumers and insulate them from the effect of the many variables which influence human behavior. In the case of services, the model can hardly ever, if at all, be put to use. Here control groups are rarely feasible—although ready-made approximations may occasionally be found. The elimination of other variables is usually impossible. The precise identification of the variable we are interested in studying is itself a formidable task.

Hence in many cases the most we can do is "keep in mind the model of a controlled experiment, even if in practice we may have to deviate from an ideal model" (Stouffer, 1950).[9] By so doing we can be better aware of the logical gaps in our inferences concerning the presumed results of a given service. In the case of the patient who dies after the operation, for example, it is important to ask, "What would have happened if another doctor had operated on an identical patient?" In some cases the asking of this question may merely serve to underline our inability to judge the quality of the services which are being evaluated. In other cases, however, this question may provide the framework for reliable estimates. Thus, on the basis of detailed facts concerning the condition of the patient who died after the operation, a workable answer to the question can be formulated by (a) drawing upon an existing body of knowledge concerning the disease from which the patient was suffering, (b) obtaining relevant data concerning the condition of the patient before and after the operation, and (c) obtaining relevant facts concerning the operation itself, particularly the performance of the surgeon in question. The past record of the surgeon can also be taken into consideration—although any inference on the basis of past performance alone is necessarily shaky.

If we turn to the interests of members of organizations and look for the subsequent results, we may find a considerable variety of highly quantifiable satisfaction surrogates. Among the most obvious are the statistics on turnover, which relate to decisions to remain in the organization, and on output and absenteeism, which relate to the degree of devotion to the job. Yet such surrogates are to be handled with considerable caution. The technical difficulties in the handling of such data are considerable—as will be shown with respect to production in the following chapters on the quality and quantity of output. But far more difficult is the task of appraising the actual contribution of satisfactions received to the events described in turnover, output and absenteeism data.

9. Note similar discussion in Chapter 4, section A-2.

Chapter 13

OUTPUT:
SERVICES AND GOODS

*I*N OUTPUT OBJECTIVES, the second element in the global matrix, we find something much easier to deal with than the satisfaction of interests.

Here we may address ourselves to the "scratch" instead of the "itch." Instead of troubling ourselves with the identification of interests and "interesteds" and with the appraisal of satisfactions and dissatisfactions, we may center upon more tangible matters such as the quality and quantity of the services or goods to be produced by an organization.

But here, too, some of the problems may be formidable. Our output element is itself a complex matrix. Its complexity may well be illustrated by asking various administrators, "What are your organization's output objectives?" Although less embarrassing than a question dealing with all purposes, this question is also apt to create difficulties.

An engine manufacturer could promptly respond by giving the number of each type of engine to be produced in a specified period. He could supply an aggregate figure by estimating the total market value of all the various engines. It might not be so easy for him to distinguish between market value and value added by manufacture. If prices are rising rapidly, he would have still greater difficulty in comparing projected market or added value with output in previous years. Apart from price changes, he would find still greater complexities in dealing with the quality aspects of the engines. And all of these output facets would be more difficult to deal with if instead of being routinized products, his engines were designed for interplanetary space travel and hence subject to continuous redesigning.

A higher level of difficulty—and perhaps acute embarrassment—may be created if we address our question to the administrator of an organization producing intangible services. Just what is the output of an army, a tax collection office, and a government agency regulating electric companies? How can the output objectives of a school, a hospital, a trade union, or a trade association best be expressed? In many of these areas the first problem is not the calculation of quantity or quality. It is rather the elementary—but often baffling—task of identifying the specific services rendered. This problem also confronts the engine manufacturer when he looks inside the organization and asks such questions as "What is the output of the accounting department? The personnel unit? Or the research laboratory?" It confronts any administrator asked to answer the supremely relevant—but brazenly impertinent—question "What are *your* output purposes, sir?"

The major task of this chapter is to assist in the answering of such questions concerning output objectives. I shall approach this task by dealing with the role of output objectives, the services-goods concept of output, and some calculational problems involved in using monetary measures of output, handling time periods and determining the boundary lines of product groups.

This will provide a basis for dealing more directly in the next chapter with the formulation of goals for the quality and quantity of output.

The ever-perplexing problem of formulating output objectives for intangible services is reserved for treatment in Chapter 15.

A. *The Role of Output Objectives*

In chapter 11 I stated that "organizations aim at (1) satisfying human interests, of both members and nonmembers, by (2) producing services or goods [output]. . . ." The other elements in the global matrix followed in order. In that discussion the aim was to suggest a broad pattern of analytical relations among the major categories of purpose. We must now deal more directly with the role of output objectives.

In the daily work of any organization, unit or individual, the most regular aspect of operations—whether handled well or badly—is "getting the job done." When a new member enters an organization, the immediate question is "What is his job?" When a unit is being reorganized, the big question is "What are its new functions?" When a new unit is set up, the question is "What's it there for? What are its tasks?"

In all of these cases the central point of reference is the output of the organization, unit or individual. It does not matter much if output is referred to by such general terms as *job, functions,* or *tasks.* Once these have been pinned down to certain specific services or goods, it is then possible to work back and forth between them and other purpose elements.

The central role of output objectives derives, first of all, from the fact that only by producing certain services or goods can an organization or unit thereof satisfy human interests. This is more clear in the case of the interests of clients, direct and indirect, more visible and less visible. Output is the immediate link between them and the organization. Suppliers, supporters, and controllers may also have a direct interest in the kinds, qualities and quantities of output. In the case of other external interests the link may be more tenuous. Investors and creditors may not be so much concerned with the specific nature of the output, but some output there must be if their interests are not to be impaired. In the case of internal interests, as already indicated in Chapter 8, the entire spectrum of human interests may serve to influence the goals of behavior. But the output of the organization can never be divorced from the sequences of action necessary to achieve such goals. Security, money, comradeship, prestige, power, and self-development may combine in various ways in the purpose patterns of individuals. But for the member of an employment organization progress toward achieving such satisfactions—no matter how small—necessarily involves making some contribution to the output of the organization or at least of the unit in which he works. People and groups join associations and federations because of the services they may be able to obtain from them. Hence the output objectives of any organization provide a focal point for bringing together the diverse interests of both members and nonmembers. Although subject to change, they thus play a unifying and stabilizing role. The workers, foremen, technicians, managers, stockholders, suppliers and clients of an engine plant may disagree on many things; but they will all probably agree that it should aim to produce engines.

Moreover, goods or services may often serve as symbols of interest satisfaction. In the case of marketed products, as shown in the previous chapter, the monetary value of sold products serves as a satisfaction surrogate. It may also serve as a symbol of prestige or power. Similarly, the physical products themselves—entirely apart from its money value or the money received for it—may often symbolize the satisfactions they have been known to provide.

There are also many direct relations between output objectives and the other broad categories of organizational purposes. Unless output objectives can be formulated in some way, obviously, no calculation of efficiency, productivity, profitability or other input-output relations can be made. The major justification for efforts to maintain, expand, or strengthen an organization is to help it produce certain kinds of services or goods; this orientation is inherent in the term *productive* capacity. Resources are mobilized in order to provide the inputs without which output would not be possible. Codes of behavior deal to a considerable extent with the way in which people behave in the process of producing output. While rationality objectives relate to all categories of purpose, they often tend to focus mainly on output and input-output objectives. Thus output objectives tend to play a unifying role in the entire global matrix. This is why the formulation of specific quality and quantity goals is one of the major services of administrators.

But this does not mean that production purposes are uncontroversial. Quite the contrary! Because they are instrumental to the satisfaction of human interests, they are often a bitter bone of contention. In government agencies the determination of the services to be rendered is a political problem of the highest significance. Any proposal for significant changes—no matter what the political or economic system—sets off a complicated process of pressure and counterpressure. In organizations producing goods these matters are also significant. Workers, managers, stockholders and suppliers may agree that automobiles should be produced but may have different ideas as to types and quantities. A large measure of intraorganizational controversy centers around the product volume expected from various units and the changes in product type which result from new technology and design. In associations and federations the services to be rendered by the organization will be the central issue of any major policy controversies. Even if internal conflict is mainly a matter of personal rivalry among competing leaders, the more effective contenders will usually present themselves as crusaders to improve or change the services provided by the organization.

B. *The Services-Goods Concept of Output*

THE TERM "output" has already been consistently used herein to refer to the services provided or goods produced by an organization. The term "product" has been used to refer to both services and goods.[1] This usage

---

1. The term "commodity" is often used for "goods," but is usually limited to

is close to that of economists, for whom "national product" refers to the aggregate value of goods and services produced in a nation. It also allows the use of "produce," "producing," and "production" in referring to the process of providing services as well as goods. This usage has the great advantage of bringing the language of administration into contact with that of economists, engineers and general systems theorists. A minor disadvantage is that some people may mistakenly feel that these terms (including "output" itself) automatically carry with them a marketplace approach to the services of government or a production-engineering approach to the services of educational and research organizations. In such cases more acceptable synonyms may be found.

1. PRODUCTS AVAILABLE FOR USE

Output may now be more explicitly defined as *the goods or services that an organization, unit or individual makes or helps make available for use by clients.*

Availability for use does not mean that output is necessarily used by clients. In the case of goods use may be deferred; inventory accumulation may replace use. In the case of both goods and services the clients may not know about the output, may not want it or may even regard it as unfit for use. As we shall see later in the discussion of efficiency and productivity (Chapt. 16), the concept of output may be used broadly to refer not only to used output but also to waste—that is, those outputs than never reach the point of final usefulness.

This usage, moreover, rules out of the output concept a whole range of relations between an organization and its environment. It excludes from the output concept people who leave an organization—even those who may be "put out" by firing or expulsion. It excludes the subsequent output of clientele organizations. Thus airplanes are not the output of an engine plant, even though its engines may be used in making airplanes. Air travel cannot be regarded as the output of the airplane plant.

Above all, a clear distinction is here made between services and goods themselves and the satisfactions or dissatisfactions they may provide. The sickness that may be created by bad working conditions is an undesirable consequence, not a product. If the ejection of factory wastes into air or water creates air pollution, water pollution, or both, this may create dissatisfactions for many people. But neither the pollution nor the consequent dissatisfaction need be regarded as part of the factory's output.

---

goods sold on the market. I am using "goods" to include also those items produced for use within an organization rather than for immediate external sale. The distinction between goods and services is devolped more fully in Chapter 15.

2. END AND INTERMEDIATE PRODUCTS

The application of the output concept to units and individuals within an organization requires a distinction between end and intermediate products.

For the purposes of administrative analysis, the end (or final) products of an organization are those which, without any further action within the organization, are available for use by the organization's clients. Intermediate products (or parts, components, or interim products) are those which are made available by units or individuals within the organization and are ready to be used in the process of producing ·other intermediate products or the organization's end products themselves.

Thus iron ore is the end product for a mining company, but an interim product for the one that produces steel as well. Clearly, this is a relativistic distinction. It is unlike the more absolute distinctions used by economists in calculating a country's national product, for which purpose final products include only those purchased by consumers, government and investors and exclude both iron ore and steel.

Within any organization, there are various distinctions between those units which produce intermediate products alone and those more directly identified with the processing of end products. In part, this is close to the distinction between staff and auxiliary functions and line functions. Units with staff and auxiliary functions are mainly involved in the production of intermediate services. Units with certain line functions are often physically closer to the end products. But the intermediate end product distinction is much more farreaching. Both "functional" units such as engineering and legal divisions and "processing" units (usually regarded as "line") such as electroplating and heat treating are also involved in the production of intermediate products. By definition, most workers on a production line cannot be at the end of the line. As a result, many of them may find little meaning or satisfaction in their work. Instead of "producing a product," their purpose may be merely to align five parts of a part. The fractionation of work in large organizations places many professional workers in the same predicament.

The more removed any intermediate products may be from an organization's end products, the harder it is to get the units involved in their production to see the relation between their work and that of the organization as a whole. The tendency is for the members of such units to lose all sense of proportion—or even to lose heart. This is why some organizations try to establish a better perspective for the producers of intermediate products by stressing their contribution to end products. The U.S. Air Force, in fact, has attempted this approach with respect to its entire operations, which, from the viewpoint of the total national defense organization, represents mainly intermediate services. Thus the following statement appears in an Air Force booklet on administration (*The Management Process*):

> Operations in the Air Force are undertaken because they contribute to the over-all weapon system or to some subordinate weapon systems. From its role in building up and maintaining a weapon system, an activity or operation obtains its meaning. Hence, performance in any operation is performance directed toward achievement of some goal of the appropriate weapon system. Therefore, it must be judged by its contribution to that weapon system.

It is from this point of view that a battle may be a failure but may help to win the war.

In a fundamental sense the end products of an organization are usually cooperative products. When every unit or individual makes some contribution to the production of a product, it cannot be appropriately regarded as the output of any unit or individual. Similarly, many intermediate products can be brought into being only by cooperative activity among units. Many services provided by associations and federations can be brought into being only by joint activity among their member organizations.

3. CONTRIBUTED OUTPUT AND VALUE ADDED

The concept of *available output* has the great merit of focusing attention on the future potential of the services or goods provided by an organization, unit, or individual. It is particularly relevant to those concerned with the flow of output through the channels of subsequent processing or distribution. But it does not illuminate the specific contribution that has been made by the organization, unit or individual. It lumps together all the contributions of suppliers and associates. It provides no basis for comparing the output of the ore-mining company with that of the steel company.

In order to measure the output contributed by a business organization, economists and statisticians have developed the concept of "value added." This involves subtracting from the total value of output the value of all purchased services and goods. Through the use of this concept one can see clearly that while the output made available by a plant may decline, its contributed output may rise:

	Last Year	*This Year*
1. Value of sales	$8,000,000	$7,000,000
2. Value of purchased services and goods	6,000,000	4,000,000
3. Value added (1 minus 2)	2,000,000	3,000,000

Thus last year the plant may have done little more than assemble components bought from others. This year it has purchased less from others and produced more on its own.

From the viewpoint of an entire economy the added value concept is essential in order to aggregate output without having raw materials and processed parts appear again and again in all the products in which they are used. It is therefore a key tool in national accounting. For individual business organizations value added measurements provide a sensitive tool for revealing what a company has really done. This is why Drucker, in bewailing the lack of a good yardstick for productivity, suggests that the use of this concept (which he calls "contributed value") should "make possible, for the first time, the rational analysis of productivity and the setting of goals for its improvement" (1954, p. 71-72). Another business analyst has even suggested "modifications to the orthodox form of the accounting statement . . . which would result in a clear statement of the 'value created' and its distribution" (J. A. Scott, 1950, p. 44, 48-49).

Another potential in this approach is to narrow down "value added" to "value added to imports" or, in slightly different language, "the value added to goods and services purchased in foreign currency." This concept is of value in any country which regards itself as over-dependent upon imports or suffering from a shortage of foreign currency. It provides a sensitive and delicate instrument for measuring the contribution of any business undertaking to the development of local industry and the improvement of a country's balance of international payments. The techniques of using this instrument have been worked out in considerable detail in Israel, a country suffering from a serious excess of imports over exports. Yet they are fully applicable to any other countries facing the same problem. The essence of the calculation is to subtract from export-sales revenue all foreign currency costs. This must include not only the direct foreign currency costs paid by a company itself (including debt service on foreign loans) but also all hidden or indirect foreign currency costs. These include goods and services paid for in local currency by the company itself but in foreign currency by the company's suppliers. Once methods have been fashioned to measure the full import component, it is then possible to refine the concept still further. First of all, the total value added to imports can be divided into two parts: (a) "foreign currency earned by export" (or "value added by export"), and (b) "foreign currency saved by replacement of imports" (or "value added by replacement of imports"). Second, local currency costs can then be related to either of these two components. One can thus measure the cost in local currency of earning foreign currency by exports or saving foreign currency by replacing imports.

Such terms as value added, created value and contributed value, however, usually imply a monetary valuation of output. They are therefore not relevant to those many organizations that do not sell their products or even to the majority of units within business enterprises. Yet in these organizations and units also there may be a very important difference between the output made available to clients and their own contributions. There is no good reason why the concept of contributed output should be limited to marketed products. With more attention and ingenuity the contributed output concept may also be useful in setting goals for, and measuring performance by, organizations producing nonmarketed products. It can be helpful, for example, in indicating that an expansion in the services expected from an accounting or personnel division may be obtainable only through the expansion of the services such a division obtains from other units in the organization. It can show that a low output organization in an environment where relatively few external services and goods may be obtained has in fact produced much more than a high output organization which adds relatively little to the information and services obtained externally.

4. MARGINAL, OR INCREMENTAL, OUTPUT

Just as output may be seen in terms of either the products made available for consumers or of the contribution made by the organization, there are two ways of looking at the quality and quantity of products.

One way is to focus attention on the total product. Thus the administrators of the plant referred to under the discussion of added value may have set a goal of achieving an added value of $3 million this year.

Another way is to focus attention on the change that is desired— that is, on an increase from $2 million to $3 million. Thus, while the goal for total output may have been $3 million, the desired level of marginal or incremental output was $1 million.

Marginal or incremental calculations are particularly relevant to desired sequences of change. They concentrate attention upon the small steps that are usually necessary to effectuate major differences. Wherever cardinal number measurements may be possible, they facilitate the use of calculus and other advanced mathematical techniques. Only by focusing on marginal increments or decrements is it possible to formulate rates of change that can be used in comparisons between organizations and between economies. Marginal calculations, for example, are the basis of international comparisons of growth rates and of debates in various countries as to the desirability of, say, a 3 per cent, a 4 per cent, or an even higher annual increase in the national product.

Marginal formulations may be equally important in relating the quantity of output with satisfactions of clients and others. Satisfactions can be seriously impaired by "too little and too late" or by "too much and too soon." The problem of whether to use more or less input can often be best analyzed by relating marginal input to marginal output and marginal satisfaction.

Moreover, in many situations it may not be feasible to calculate the total quantity of output. This is particularly true of unsold products and intangible services. It may be much easier—and far more significant—to formulate goals with respect to specific increments that can be more readily identified. In this connection, let it be made clear that marginal calculations need not be made in cardinal numbers. They are also significant when made in terms of "a little more" or "a lot less." They are thus fully applicable not only to output quantity but also to any desired changes in the more intangible facets of output quality.

In some situations, however, a narrow margin approach to output goals may be very misleading. By focusing attention exclusively on an increment, it may divert attention from the total which is to be incremented. It may also serve to divert attention from overall comparisons between organizations and structural changes in output over long periods of time. These dangers may be avoided by a multidimensional approach that combines both total and marginal measures.

c. *Imputing the Value of Nonmarketed Products*

THE FORMULATION of output goals in physical measurements alone is very confining. Physical units provide no common denominator for entirely different types of products. They rarely supply a basis for comparing output with input through measures common to both. For these purposes we need a more refined and delicate instrument: monetary measurement. But can a monetary value be placed on goods or services not available for sale?

In the strictest sense the answer is No. The essence of a monetary evaluation of goods and services is that it is based upon the number of monetary units received from clients, or an appraisal of the money that would be paid by potential clients.

Yet this negative conclusion would leave us no means of quantification other than physical measurement. It would deny us the possibility of aggregating the total output of intermediate services produced by any unit within an organization. It would make it impossible to compare the output of different producers of nonmarketed products.

There are two ways of overcoming this difficulty.

1. INPUT VALUE

The first is to use some aspect of input value as imputed output value. The most common approach is to use aggregate costs. This is based upon the concept that value, after all, is "embodied cost." Or else certain costs which are beyond the control of a subunit might be subtracted. Sometimes labor costs will be the major or exclusive basis of the imputed output value. This is the device used internationally in calculating the contribution of government services to the national income. Although no one would defend the thesis that the output of two government agencies with identical budgets must necessarily have the same value to the country, there is simply no other basis of reaching a statistical imputation. When such calculations are made, they must be treated with considerable care in order to avoid becoming absurd. For example, it would not make any sense, in calculating the efficiency of an organization, to relate costs with value of output if total costs themselves are serving as surrogates of output value. There is thus an element of serious distortion whenever the efficiency or productivity of an economy is measured in terms of a relation between the labor force or man years of labor on the one hand, and the national income or product on the other. A truly meaningful relationship between labor input and total value of output can be developed only for the sector of marketed goods and services.

2. INTERNAL PRICING SYSTEMS

The second device, applicable only to intermediate, or internal, products, is to develop a system of internal pricing. This approach is highly developed in some large corporations which are divided into divisions that are expected to operate on a profit-and-loss basis. Thus when Division A buys goods or services from Division B it pays a "price." The total output of both divisions, even if most or all of it is "sold" internally, can thus be measured in units of monetary value. Even without the fiction of divisional profit-making, a similar system is at times used in supplying central staff services. Thus a charge is made to all units which come to the central office for economic, engineering, or legal advice or perhaps even for lesser services in the area of duplication and repairs.[2] This course can also be used within organizations which do not sell their final products.

2. It is interesting to speculate on what conclusions one might reach if one tried to apply such a charging system to the services supplied by top management. A basis for appraising the market value of top management services is provided by the operations of engineering and consulting firms which take over the management of companies on a contract basis.

When the "internal price" is fixed purely upon a cost basis, it amounts to nothing more than a specific method of using input value as imputed output value. Here the basic issue is whether to include overhead costs or to use only those costs for which the producing unit is itself responsible. A more mature system of internal pricing comes into being when the internal price is fixed for the purpose of making profits. Here an additional margin is added to costs. If this margin is not entirely arbitrary, it must be fixed with an eye on the market value of similar goods or services. In fact, it is possible to go so far as to knock down trade barriers with the outside world and put internal transactions on a wide-open competitive basis. Thus in the General Motors Corporation "No car division is under compulsion to buy from the accessory divisions, or under compulsion to pay the prices demanded by them. . . . Each accessory division must be able to meet the lowest prices of outside accessory manufacturers and to satisfy the quality and styling requirements of the car divisions" (Drucker, 1954, p. 68). Where this approach is used, internal prices are not "fixed" in the narrow sense of the word; they are rather determined by the interplay of market forces. The development of this approach to internal pricing, however, is feasible only in large organizations with highly sophisticated central accounting staffs. It is limited technically by the extent to which comparable products are available from outside sources. Furthermore, as Dean has pointed out, there are these four limitations on open-market transfer prices: (1) their applicability only to standard components, (2) quality differentials, (3) the possibility of price-cutting by outside suppliers to "get a foot in the door," and (4) the need to give business to internal supplying divisions with excess capacity (1951, p. 41-43). Dean also suggests that arbitrary transfer prices rule out "a policy of maximizing divisional profits" and thus "destroy a useful criterion for the value of vertical organizations."

Finally, there is good reason to support the conclusion of Simon and his associates that "a formal division of profit and loss statements probably justifies the cost of preparing it only when the company is so organized that a 'division' is a highly self-contained administrative unit, manufacturing and selling a well-defined product or group of products in relative independence from other units in the company. Where this condition is not satisfied, the benefits claimed for decentralized profit and loss accounting can largely be obtained more economically with less radical forms of responsibility accounting" (1954, p. 43).

The reason for this is that within the self-contained administrative unit itself, the various interim activities involve a large amount of cooperative activity and jointly produced products. Should too much attention be given to pricing the contribution of each unit to such cooperative activity, the cooperative relationship itself would be impaired. In fact, under such conditions the incentive would be to cooperate less in order to obtain a better profit and loss statement for each individual department. It would probably result in attempts both to charge higher prices for interdepartmental transfers of services and to cut down on the input factors channeled into the production of such services.

D. *Coping with Changing Monetary Units*

WHEN PRICES RISE and fall, the monetary unit changes in value. When these changes are small, they may be disregarded.[3] But when they are more substantial, adding up monetary units becomes more and more like adding eggs and elephants. A calculation of total value or value added for any one year may be a composite of "large dollars" and "small dollars." A financial statement showing output values over a period of years will be a jumble of "old dollars" and "new dollars."

The fact that this problem must be faced on the input as well as the output side does not make it easier. How can we deal with it?

1. "OSTRICH ACCOUNTING"

One answer is simply to thrust one's head into the sand, ostrich-like, and ignore the changes in monetary units.

In the accounting profession this ostrich posture has been consciously adopted, vigorously defended, and persistently maintained. Traditional accounting is based upon the fiction that the monetary unit is always of constant dimensions. "Although the assumption of a stable dollar is an assumption contrary to fact, to date the majority of accountants have

3. In passing, we might note that even when prices remain stable the collection of appropriate price information is not always a simple task. For example, the U.S. Government Agency responsible for price control during World War II found about seventy different ways of calculating price: "list, gross, net, maximum, opening, closing, spot, average, highest, lowest, contract, base, CIF, CI or CF, store door or delivered, f.o.b. (basing point, point of origin or destination), crated, boxed or wrapped, bare or stripped or with extras, quoted, accepted, actual or realized, trade, wholesale, preferred, special, leader, markdown, with service, advertised, mean, median, modal or typical, published, cost plus, sliding scale, breakeven, future, past period, over the counter, with commission, cost price, sales price, inventory price, ceiling price, weighted price, closing out, fire sale, damaged seconds, shopworn, sample, posted, negotiated, seasonal, cash, export, open, premium." Most of these prices represent different gradations on the long continuum from the lowest net price to the highest gross price (Neiswanger, 1956, p. 66-67).

felt no compulsion to modify accounting methods or procedures in an attempt to make allowance for such variation in the unit of measurement" (Finney and Miller, 1958, p. 167). The major explanation of this flight from reality is a pathetic desire to hold tight to hard "facts," even though their utility or even their "factfulness" is open to dispute.

> The accountant . . . has tried to eliminate the element of subjective judgment from the determination of income. He has tried to establish as nearly as possible hard and fast rules of calculation in order to eliminate the guesswork and to introduce precise measurements. But in a dynamic world subject to unforeseen changes of prices and business conditions, it is not possible to avoid guesswork in the determination of income. To the extent that the accountant can eliminate guesses, he is substituting something else for income (Alexander, 1958, p. 6-7).

The basic defense for this position is the contention that "users of accounting reports must assume the responsibility for interpreting financial data." The function of accountant is thus limited to recording transactions and events in mixed monetary units which "can be adjusted and modified by statement users if desired to serve their objectives and needs" (Finney and Miller, 1958, p. 627). Rigorous adherence to this approach would require two types of accountants—one to prepare accounting reports and another to interpret them. The movement toward "managerial accounting" is in fact a trend in this direction. Yet the accounting profession is itself moving slowly in the direction of recognizing the need for making adjustments to the changing value of monetary units. Committees of accounting associations periodically come to such conclusions as the following:

> The accounting effects of the changing value of the dollar should be made the subject of intensive research and experimentation; the specific significance of the basic problem should be determined with as much accuracy as possible; the means of its solution, if its significance warrants, should be thoroughly investigated (*Ibid*, p. 639).

In actual business practice, managers confronted with major price changes have usually felt the need for a common-price system of accounts.

> During the American Revolution some merchants kept their accounts in the stable currency of a former period as current prices often doubled in a period of a few months. During the surging German inflation of the early 1920's, various devices were used. Some firms translated their accounts into Swiss currency, which was relatively stable, and others stabilized their balance sheets at prices preceding the inflation (Hiram S. Davis, 1955, p. 103).

In modern times, even when price changes are not dramatic, a small but growing number of corporations publish supplementary statements with an adjustment of monetary values to price changes. Economists working on national economic accounts have increasingly learned to present their data in terms of stable monetary units.

The only logical answer to the problem of changing monetary units is to reduce them to stable monetary units. Moreover, this should usually be done as a matter of course. It is not something that can be introduced as an emergency measure in periods of sharp inflation or deflation and forgotten about at other times.

2. PHYSICAL INDICES

Another answer is to try to construct a physical output index. Thus, we may compute an index figure showing the percentage change in output of three standard engines from Year X to Year Y:

	Year X	Year Y	Output Index Year X = 100
Engine 1	1,000	800	80
Engine 2	200	400	200
Engine 3	400	400	100

Thus far we have avoided monetary evaluation. But the moment we try to establish an index figure for the change in output of all three engines together, monetary evaluation returns through the back door in whatever system of weights we use. If we perform no direct weighting calculations and arrive at a simple average of 126.6, we are therefore implicitly imputing equal monetary value to all units in each year. If we use actual prices, we are right back where we started from: the problem of coping with changing prices.

3. PRICE ADJUSTMENT

The process of price adjustment, however, is far from simple. Alternative methods—each one of which can be logically defended—will lead to significantly different results. Although the choice between these alternatives involves many complex questions of statistical technique, there are three strategic questions of a more managerial character.

The first is "where to place the base." In the field of price adjustment this is as important as Archimedes' question as to where to place his lever. One way is to convert all monetary units to those of a past year at the beginning of the period we are studying (often referred to as the "Laspeyres" system). Another is to use the latest year as the base (the "Paasche" system). The former often gives an upward bias, and the latter a downward bias. It is also possible to pick an interim year toward the middle of any period which is being studied. For any of these approaches the base period may also be a period longer than a year. Still a fourth method is the "chain system," that is revaluing each year in the prices of the preceding year. This facilitates the analysis of year-to-year changes. The revaluation can also be done at a fixed period longer than a year. Still another method is "the use of a fixed-base valuation, which is periodically moved forward with the passage of time, not on regular schedule but as events make desirable" (Hiram S. Davis, 1955, p. 44-53).

The second is simply "how to revalue." In times of inflation, the question is "what deflator to use." More broadly stated, the question is "What deflators or inflators to use?" One answer is to use the repricing technique—that is, to revalue specific quantities of output by the price changes for each item. However, this is an extremely laborious process. When a large number of items or companies are involved it is more feasible to use a price index—that is, a weighted average of specific prices chosen because of their representative character. Such indices may be prepared for the specific needs of any organization or group of organizations; or else use might be made of general price indices prepared by government agencies.

Apart from the multitudinous problems involved in the selection of the prices which enter into an index and the development of a proper weighing system, there is the broader problem of what kind of index is applicable. One point of view—which has the great advantage of simplicity—is that "the effects of price fluctuations upon financial reports should be measured in terms of the over-all purchasing power of the dollar—that is, changes in the general price level as measured by a GENERAL price index" (Finney and Miller, 1958, p. 639). A more logical position is expressed as follows:

> As capital operations are not affected by the same factors as revenue operations; as one capital operation is not affected by the same factors as another; and as one revenue operation is not affected by the same factors as another—it is clear that any attempt to use an over-all index would be abortive.
>
> Therefore, according to the circumstances an individual or group index must be employed which is constructed on a basis with which the particular capital or revenue operation whose money values are adjusted is compatible (Hiram S. Davis, p. 105).

This is the approach customarily used by economists (though not without considerable controversy on the choice of specific indices) in making fixed-price calculations of national income and national product. It may be expected that accountants also, as they begin to accept with better grace the challenge of changing prices, will follow in the footsteps of the economists.

In addition to these two strategic questions of how to select base periods and deflators (or inflators), we might also mention the question of changing quality characteristics. Price increases provide the best common denominator for measuring increases in product quality. But if a price deflator takes no account of quality improvements it will understate the level of output and overstate the amount of price increases.[4] Yet this brings us to the subject of the reconciliation of quantity with quality, a subject which will be discussed in detail at a later point.

4. INTERNATIONAL MONETARY ADJUSTMENTS

Still more difficult problems of adjustment must be faced whenever we want to compare the national output goals or performance of different countries. Here we are faced not merely with changing prices within a country but also with different systems of monetary evaluation.

The simplest form of adjustment is to convert value figures of different countries into the currency of one country by using official exchange rates. This is the method that has traditionally been followed in international comparisons. Yet this method could avoid serious distortion only if the exchange rates used were the same as the average relationship of the internal purchasing power of the various currencies involved. Because of exchange rate controls, tariffs, indirect taxes, and the production of many products that never enter into international exchange, this condition could hardly ever be expected to exist in the modern world.

A more accurate system of international adjustment, therefore, is to calculate the purchasing power equivalents of different currencies with respect to specific categories of goods. While this is a much more laborious task than the use of one simple exchange rate, it is the only realistic method. The use of this method by the O.E.E.C., for example, shows a markedly different relationship between the national output of the United States and that of European countries than that which is obtained by the

4. This is a perennial criticism of the deflators used in dealing with national economic accounts. Thus Richard Ruggles (1959, p. 94), in reviewing the methodology of the U.S. national accounts, maintains that there is "an upward bias in the price indices for almost every category of expenditure. For commodities it exists because quality changes and the introduction of new products cannot be integrated adequately into the price data. For services it exists because by and large the value of services is assumed not to increase, although there is strong evidence that it does."

use of exchange rates. Thus, an exchange rate adjustment showed that in 1950 the combined national product of the United Kingdom, France, Germany, and Italy amounted to only 35 per cent of the national product of the United States. The use of internal purchasing power equivalents showed that the exchange rates undervalued the output of these countries and that the combined product should be 50 per cent instead of 35 per cent.[5]

E. *Handling Time Periods*

No OBSERVATION concerning quantity can have meaning unless related to some period of time. Did the steel plant produce 100,000 tons of steel? We must immediately ask how long it took. Did two workers each grind 100 valves? Until we look at the time involved, we might think that their quantity of output has been identical. The time dimension might show that one spent four hours in grinding 100 valves and the other six hours.

1. ALLOCATING VALUE TO TIME PERIODS

When the quantity of ouput is measured in physical units, products or components are usually regarded as having been produced at the time of completion.

When monetary units are used, the situation is more complex. Strictly speaking, we cannot say that monetary value has been created just because a product has been produced. We must rather deal directly with the revenue received from its sale (apart from adjustments for changes in inventory, a point discussed in the previous section).

Here we face two broad choices. One is to allocate the revenue to the period, or periods, when the actual cash is collected. This is usually called the "cash system" of accounting. Under this system, expenses are likewise allocated to the period when they are actually paid.

In contrast, under an "accrual system" revenue is allocated to the period in which sales are made or services rendered, regardless of when

5. Gilbert and Kravis, 1953, p. 13-28. The authors maintain, however, that although "measures of the real internal purchasing power of European currencies in terms of dollars show these currencies to be worth more than the value, indicated by prevailing exchange rates . . . it can, nonetheless, hardly be concluded that those currencies are undervalued relative to the dollar for the purpose of exchange equilibrium" (*Ibid.*, p. 17).

payment is made. Similarly, expenses are allocated to the period in which they are incurred, without reference to when the expenses are actually paid. In government accounting, the expenses are sometimes allocated on an "obligation" basis—that is, to the period in which the decision is made to use money for a specific purchase. This is somewhat closer to an accrual than to a cash system.

The cash system has the virtue of simplicity. It automatically provides a picture of an organization's cash position. It eliminates the necessity of depreciation allowances, since the entire cost of a fixed asset is allocated to the period in which money is laid out for its purchase. It avoids complicated adjustments for bad debts and advance payments. Because of these advantages it is widely used by small businessmen, professional men who deal almost exclusively in personal services and by national and local government agencies.

The accrual system, however, is the accepted basis both of formal business accounting and of national income accounting. When an organization's operations involve a significant amount of material inventories and capital equipment and production processes that stretch over a considerable period of time, it is the only method of achieving a proper matching of revenues and expenses by periods. It is a prerequisite to any rational effort at cost accounting or performance budgeting. Thus government reformers have periodically advocated the accrual system as the basis of government accounting.[6]

2. THE CHOICE OF TIME UNITS

In choosing the time units to be used, one may theoretically select any division or multiple of the day as measured by the astronomer. The arbitrary and relativistic nature of these units, which are based upon the rotation of the earth in relation to some presumably fixed star, need not usually concern us in ordinary calculations. This becomes a problem mainly when dealing with transport services which involve the rotation of a plane or ship around the rotating earth. This problem will become much more acute, of course, if and when time units must be established for interplanetary travel and/or (let us be really imaginative) for interplanetary. output comparisons.

In the meantime the important considerations are the production

6. See "Commission on the Organization of the Executive Branch of the Government," *Budgeting and Accounting*. Burkhead, however, points out that "where the bulk of an agency's expenditure is composed of wage and salary payments, the difference between cash and accrual measurements will not be of sufficient importance to invalidate the cash basis for the purpose of performance budgeting" (1956, p. 152).

process which is being studied and the purpose of the measurement. We could hardly conceive of measuring battleships produced per hour or years spent on producing a pin. When dealing with the total output of organizations, years or months are customary units of time. Smaller units are often more suitable for small subunits and for individuals. In time and motion studies it has often been found that the second does not provide a small enough subdivision of an hour. Thus the ordinary stopwatch used in time study divides the minute into 100 divisions. The decimal hour type of stop watch allows measurements down to units of 0.0001 (one ten-thousandth) of an hour.

But there are two aspects to the time dimension of quantity. We can only measure output per hour if we locate the specific hour. If we are measuring the amount of time used in producing a valve, are we talking about the morning hours of work, the noon hour, a period approaching quitting time, or an average of them all? Both people and organizations have "peak" periods and "trough" periods. These may be the result of fatigue, improper organization of work, the peculiar nature of the production process, or cyclical or secular changes in market demand. If we set standards for a peak period and measure performance during a trough period, the results will be nonsense. If both are based on peak periods, the results will be one-sided. If both are based on long periods which span the fluctuations, the results will be meaningful but will lack the detail necessary for genuine understanding of the relation of output to time. The most accurate approach is to use a time series for both the formulation of standards and the measurement of performance.

In fashioning a time series expressed in terms of index numbers or percentages, we face the problem of where to place the base. If one chooses a period of low output as a base, the picture given will be a relatively rosy one; if one chooses a high output period, the impression will be more dismal. One method of avoiding this "base period effect" is to set an ideal standard of output for each period of time and use this moving standard (instead of some past period) as the base.

3. TIME AS VARIABLE OR CONSTANT

In calculating the time dimension of output, one can use time as either the numerator or the denominator.

In the first case the formulation is $\frac{T}{Q}$ (where $T =$ Time and $Q =$ Quantity of output). Thus, we can fix a unit of a given valve or number of valves and measure the varying amount of time spent by different workers.

Or else we can turn the formula upside down: $\frac{Q}{T}$. This allows us to fix a given unit of time and then measure the varying amounts of output produced by different individuals or an organization.

For measurements of internal output within a narrow scope, it makes no great difference which approach is used. For broader measurements, however, particularly when we are interested in interorganizational comparisons, it is usually more convenient to use a time unit as the denominator and to regard quantity of output as the variable.

F. *Resolving Boundary Problems*

WHENEVER SIMILAR UNITS are conceptually brought together for the purposes of quantification, there are apt to be boundary line problems. Just as when the political map drawers argue about the territory of a disputed area, decisions must be made on where the boundary line shall be placed. Sometimes these decisions may have a major effect on the number of output units that are included.

1. INTERMEDIATE AND SEMIFINISHED PRODUCTS

There is always something arbitrary about the imposition of time periods upon the seamless web of human action. Whatever cutoff date we use—whether it be the end of an hour, month, or year—the web is ruptured. There are always many goods or services that are partially completed and still in the process of production. There are often overlapping production processes, each with an inherently different time span. The same can be said for the imposition of initial dates. Similar ruptures are created when the man-made boundary lines of types and subtypes are imposed upon nonidentical discrete units. For purposes of statistical neatness the loose threads that are created must be woven back into the fabric. How one goes about this repair mission provides wide room for statistical maneuver.

When physical units of output are used, a typical boundary problem relates to the distinction between the output of completed units and the output of intermediate products which serve to build up inventories. Thus, "if the production of cement is taken to mean finished cement, the amount of actual production engaged in by the mill may be greatly understated because the quarry, the raw grind and the burning departments may have produced large quantities of clinker for inventory while the finishing department was operating on a reduced scale. In this situation the output of finished cement per man hour would fluctuate erratically because of changes in production for clinker inventory. . . . To overcome this difficulty the cement industry has devised, by empirical means, a statistical unit by which production is measured. It is called 'equivalent cement.' In the computation of equivalent production, consideration is given to the production of both clinker and finished cement" (Neiswanger, 1956, p. 67).

2. PRODUCTION vs. SALE

When monetary units are used, a similar problem is presented. Here, however, instead of looking back upon incompleted production from the viewpoint of completed production, one looks back upon production from the vantage point of sale. Thus for two different years the production and sales figures of a shoe factory may look as follows:

	VALUE OF OUTPUT DOLLARS	
	This Year	*Next Year*
Production	500,000	400,000
Sales	400,000	500,000

The difference between production and sales is the addition to, or the withdrawal from, inventory. But is the key output norm for next year 400,000 or 500,000?

The answer, of course, is a matter of definition. One can define output in production terms alone in order to stand foursquare with physical measurements of output. But this means that one imputes a value figure on the basis of an estimate on what sales returns would have been if all the output had been sold. One can define output produced but not sold or sold on the basis of withdrawals from inventory. Or else one can combine the two in somewhat the same manner that clinker cement and finished cement are merged into synthetic physical units of equivalent cement. Here the synthetic unit would usually be the total value of sales plus or minus the value of additions to, or withdrawals from, inventories.

3. GROSS OR NET

Whether one deals with physical or monetary units, there are a number of choices as to where the boundary line is to be drawn. The terms "gross" and "net" are usually used to indicate inclusion or exclusion of borderline units. In the measurement of housing space the difference between the two is the width of the borders themselves, in this case the walls (and if cubic measurements are used, the width of floors, ceilings, and roofs as well). In the measurement of the national product of an economy, the difference between gross and net is the estimated value of capital consumption. In manufacturing, the boundary units may include delivery, waste products, defective and returned goods, packaging, and the value of rebates, commissions, discounts, consumers' services and sales taxes. Where there is more than one relevant consideration of this type, precision can be achieved only by a full statement of what is included in net or gross. Sometimes it is desirable to distinguish between a number of different boundaries which can be used for varying purposes.

Chapter 14

OUTPUT:
QUALITY AND QUANTITY

WHAT ARE YOUR GOALS for the quality and quantity of output?"

This is a recurring question faced by every administrator. It is one of the most important questions any administrator can ask himself. An organization's output is one of its most distinctive features. Its output goals provide an essential amalgam for holding it together. Attempts to clarify them are of strategic importance whenever there are significant changes or pressures for changes in the quality or quantity of output.

In answering this question, as shown in the preceding chapter, significant distinctions may be made between end and intermediate products, contributed and available output, and marginal and total output. It is also necessary at times to handle the problems of imputing value to nonmarket products, coping with changing monetary units, allocating output to time periods, and defining group boundaries.

But apart from these conceptual problems, there are more fundamental issues to be faced. In fact, the over-all question concerning output goals breaks down into three separate questions: What kind? How good? And how much? The third question involves some of the basic human conflicts over the level of output.

In addressing ourselves to these questions we shall see that each has many dimensions. We shall see that any answer may run headlong into a number of built-in conflicts. We shall also note that all three questions may often involve us in a consideration of the conflicts between quality and quantity.

A. *The Primacy of Quality*

THE RELATION between quality and quantity has always posed one of the most fundamental questions for philosophy, mathematics, and all the sciences. At one extreme, there have been those who declare, in the words of Seneca, "It is quality rather than quantity that matters" (*Epistles* 45:1). At the other extreme, there have been those who maintain, with Lord Kelvin, that "when you cannot express it in numbers, your knowledge is of a meagre and unsatisfactory kind." In reviewing this historical controversy, one writer points out that "the dialectical juxtaposition of quality and quantity, of uniqueness and repetition, of abstract theory and concrete description, has from far back been the *leitmotif* of the running methodological controversy in social science" (Leontief, 1961, p. 117).

The progress of science can in large part be described as a movement from qualitative to quantitative statements. "The entire history of physics is essentially a history of quantified 'qualities.' Temperature, elasticity, viscosity, luminosity, color, energy, are all examples. The history of chemistry is not too different. The backbone of chemistry is the atomic theory, which is essentially a quantification of quality based on the discovery that innumerably 'qualitatively different' substances can be described as combinations in strict quantitative proportions of comparatively few (less than 100) basic substances, the elements" (Rapoport, 1954, p. 158). Psychologists, sociologists, and economists have gone so far in this direction that anyone impatient with carefully compiled statistics or unfamiliar with mathematical techniques can no longer hope to understand much of the modern work in these fields.

The trend toward quantification has also been accelerated by an extension of measurement beyond the simple process of counting. Modern quantification also deals with relations of rank order (noninterval scales), direction (vectors), and structures and patterns (matrices). Much of modern mathematics gets along without numbers at all or introduces them only at advanced stages of dealing with a problem (Kemeny, 1961).

Many aspects of quality can thus be more readily dealt with in quantitative and mathematical terms.

But the great contribution of these trends is not the *replacement* of quality. It is the *addition* of quantity. The qualitative base still remains. In fact, any progress in quantification rests upon prior progress in the field of quality. True, the effort at quantification often forces a sharpening of conceptual qualitative tools. The reason is that only through such sharpening is improved quantification possible.

The primacy of quality becomes more clear when a distinction is made between two closely related meanings of the term "quality." By the first meaning any question concerning quality asks "What kind?" This question is answered by classification. Various phenomena are grouped on the basis of certain similarities into categories, classes, groups or sets.

The question "How much?" can never be answered without some preceding answer to the question "What kind?" Some form of classification underlies all forms of quantification. Enumeration is simply the *process of counting the units within a category*. Other forms of quantification are *processes of establishing relationships between categories*. In either case some implicit or explicit identification must be made of the phenomenon whose units are counted or relationships analyzed. Statements of identification require qualitative analysis. This is a matter of conceptual clarity and refinement in the definition of categories and their boundaries. Here quantification may be of direct or indirect help. But it is rarely sufficient. We thus arrive at one of the major principles of human knowledge: *quantification depends upon identification of kind*. The more exact depends upon the less exact. Mathematics can deal with some aspects of any phenomena in the real world. But it can leave the realm of pure theory and come into contact with quantifiable data only by crossing the bridge provided by qualitative concepts.

When the second meaning is used, a question concerning quality deals with "How good?" rather than "What kind?" In this sense quality refers to *the extent to which a product conforms to certain product specifications*. Statements answering the question "How good?" may be regarded as *quality judgments*. The relationship between statements of identification and quality judgments is rather close. As will be shown later in this chapter, identification is always done by selecting one or another facet of product specification. Quality judgment is merely a more intensive form of identification.

Once we answer the question "What kind?" we often rush immediately to deal with "How much?" Thus, when an economist measures the long-range changes in the output of consumers' durable goods, he rarely concerns himself with whether or not the successive models of refrigerators and washing machines are better or worse than the preceding ones. He pushes the question "How good?" to one side. He justifies this action by the absence of reliable data on changes in goodness. He assumes that such quality changes are not significant or that the costs of obtaining data on them outweigh the benefits to be reaped. In many cases, however, even in the absence of data on the subject there is reason to believe that the changes may indeed be significant. When we continue to ignore the question "How good?" we should then realize that we may be sacrificing one form of precision for another. We should recognize that we may be winding up "with a system of quantitatively well-defined relationship between qualitatively ill-defined variables . . ." (Leontief, 1961, p. 128).

B. *What Kind?*

IN PREVIOUS CHAPTERS I have pointed out that a "multiple facet" rather than "pigeon role" approach to classification provides the most useful method of distinguishing among different kinds of organizations. Thus, while organizations might be classified by legal status, size and other general characteristics, different purpose patterns should also be taken into account (Chapt. 2). By stating the principle "by your fruits shall ye know them" (Chapt. 9), I have also highlighted the key role of product purposes in organizational classification.

The task of this section is to deal more directly with the kind of fruits that might be known. This will be done by dealing with the concept of output mix, the degree of product variety, and the balance between standardized and unique products.

1. THE OUTPUT MIX

The listing of output types is the essential starting point for any specifications or measurements with respect to the desired or actual quality or quantity of output. The term "output mix" (or "product mix") provides a convenient way of referring to such a list. Engineers first used this term with respect to the goods produced by factories. Subsequently, it has been applied to other business organizations—sometimes in the variant of "sales mix." The concept is also applicable to all types of services and to every level of organizational activity.

If we should start with a nation as a whole and then go down to individual members of organizations, we shall find output mixes appearing in such forms as the following:

LEVELS	FORM OF OUTPUT MIX
A nation	National income by sectors of origin; gross national product by categories of expenditure
A factory	Production schedule
An airline	Flight schedule
A mail order house	Catalogue
A restaurant	Menu
A school	Curriculum
A government agency	Statement of functions
A unit within any of the above	Statement of functions
A member of any unit	Statement of functions

A quick glance at the table on page 566 on "output mix" of a national economy indicates that the breakdown of national income differs from that of the gross national product.

Both of these classifications, it should be emphasized, are based upon products. Any sector or area of economic activity is distinguished from other sectors by the similarities among the products it produces. The subdivisions of the gross national product are also based upon various kinds of goods and services. The difference is that in the first case the output mix emphasizes the source of the output and in the second case the use of the output. By the first we can measure the extent to which an economy's output mix shifts from agricultural and mineral products to manufactured goods and services. By the second we can measure the changing pattern of consumption and investment.

In this particular respect calculations of national output do not differ from the output mix of most single organizations. To understand the output of a single organization, different bases of classification—albeit less detailed—may also be needed. The output of a shoe factory may be classified by materials used (leather, rubber, felt), kinds of use (sport, work, regular and dress), and types of users (men, women and children). An airline's flight schedule may be classified by origin and destination, scheduled and unscheduled, first class and economy, passenger and freight. A restaurant's menu may be classified both by entire dinners and by an individual listing of *à la carte* orders. A school's curriculum may be classified both by the departments in which they originate and by various programs that cut across departmental lines.

In each case also the output mix is the starting point for tracing the internal interrelations that result in the final products. For an economy as a whole this may be done through an input-output matrix showing

NATIONAL INCOME BY SECTORS OF ORIGIN[a]	GROSS NATIONAL PRODUCT[b]
	Private Consumption
1. Agriculture, forestry, hunting, and fishing	1. Food
2. Mining and quarrying	2. Beverages
3. Manufacturing	3. Tobacco
4. Construction	4. Clothing and other personal effects
5. Electricity, gas, water, and sanitary services	5. Rent, rates, and water charges
6. Transportation, storage, and communication	6. Fuel and light
7. Wholesale and retail trade	7. Furniture, furnishing, and household equipment
8. Banking, insurance, and real estate	8. Household operation
9. Ownership of dwellings	9. Personal care and health expenses
10. Public administration and defense	10. Transportation and communication
11. Services	11. Recreation and entertainment
	12. Miscellaneous

Government Consumption

1. General administration
2. Defense
3. Justice and police
4. Education and research
5. Special welfare services
6. Health services
7. Transport and communication facilities
8. Other services

Investment

1. Fixed capital formation
2. Increase in stocks

a. The United Nations, *A System of National Accounts and Supporting Tables.* Although this classification is proposed as a model for international use in the interests of international statistical comparability, it is based upon the classification systems actually in use in many countries. It is also very close to the one set out in the U.N.'s *International Standard Industrial Classification of all Economic Activities.*

b. The United Nations, *A System of National Accounts and Supporting Tables.*

the extent to which the output of every sector is used as an input in other sectors (Leontief, 1941). A similar technique may also be used for individual organizations. In an elementary form this is what is done by "flow charts" that trace the movement of certain intermediate products through an organization. It may also be done by statements of function and performance budgets that say something significant about the output of units within an organization.

In all cases, moreover, unless some detailed classifications are used, serious mistakes may be made about the nature of output. Let us assume that there are two personnel offices in different organizations, each with approximately the same budget or the same number of staff. If we ask what types of services are provided by each, the answers might show the following mixtures:

Personnel Services	*Personnel Office "A"*	*Personnel Office "B"*
Personnel records	Yes	Yes
Recruitment	Yes	Yes
Transfers	Yes	Yes
Promotions	Yes	Yes
Job analysis	Yes	No
Job evaluation	Yes	No
Merit rating	Yes	No
Negotiations with unions	No	Yes
Training	No	Yes
Personnel counseling	No	Yes

Let us now assume that there is a third personnel office. "A^1," which provides the same set of seven services which is provided by "A." This does not mean that their output is identical. "A" may concentrate the bulk of its attention on recruitment and personnel records. "A^1" may make a "big thing" out of job analysis and merit rating.

In the case of organizations producing marketed products, the relation between volume and output mix changes is even more tricky. Let us now take the case of two engine plants that each achieve a total sales value of $2 million in the same year. Judged by dollars received, it appears that their output is identical. Yet when we look into the product mix of the two plants, we may draw a number of additional conclusions.

	VALUE OF SALES ($)	
	Factory A	*Factory B*
Engine 1	1,000,000	—
Engine 2	600,000	800,000
Engine 3	400,000	700,000
Repair services	—	500,000
Total	$2,000,000	$2,000,000

From the viewpoint of total engine production, the output of Factory A is 25 per cent larger. In terms of engines 2 and 3, the output of Factory

B is 33 per cent larger. With respect to Engine 1 and Repair services, there is little basis for comparison.

Let us now suppose that in the following year, with no change whatsoever in the total number of engines produced by Factory A, the total value of Factory A's output rises to $2.4 million. One may jump to the hasty conclusion that prices must have risen. But an examination of the product mix might show the following picture:

| | YEAR X | | YEAR Y | |
	Number	*Value ($)*	*Number*	*Value ($)*
Engine 1	1,000	1,000,000	800	800,000
Engine 2	200	600,000	400	1,200,000
Engine 3	400	400,000	400	400,000
Total	1,600	2,000,000	1,600	2,400,000

Thus, with no changes whatsoever in the total number of engines or in prices, the factory had merely reduced the output of one of its low-priced engines and doubled the output of its high-priced engine. Similarly, dramatic changes in sales value could be obtained by changes in prices without any changes in the quantity of the various types. In real life, of course, product types, volume, and prices all change at the same time. Under such circumstances a sophisticated approach to product mix formulation is required both for stating objectives and understanding what has actually happened.

Finally, formal output mix statements rarely identify all kinds of output. The national accounts habitually exclude housekeeping services by housewives, although those by hired servants are included. They also provide little or no place for the activities of political parties and many other associations whose activities may have an important impact on the economy as well as society. Similarly, in most organizations there are peripheral outputs that may not appear in formal statements: a factory's repair or maintenance services, certain made-to-order products, a bank's advisory services for customers, an airline's liquor sales to passengers, a school's guidance services. In the case of individual output, as discussed in the next chapter, people are sometimes expected to provide services that cannot be approximately referred to in written statements of function. Sometimes, in the case of organizations and units producing intangible services the entire output mix may be unclear. This is particularly true with services which are not sold to clients and therefore need not be specifically identified at the time of sale. Under such circumstances, unless special efforts are made to define production purposes, most members of the organization are apt to see a product "hash" instead of a product mix. This subject will be dealt with again in the next chapter.

2. THE DIMENSIONS OF OUTPUT VARIETY

The degree of variety in the output mix of an organization has a major effect on the capacity of output objectives to serve as socially meaningful goals.

Output variety may be measured by three dimensions. The first is simply the number of product lines. Thus a cement plant and a home-building company are usually one-product organizations. But most organizations have a multiproduct output mix. Hospitals, besides providing health services, usually engage in training and research activities as well. Universities, in addition to educational services, usually place major emphasis on research also—with minor attention to student guidance and placement. Many manufacturers produce and many wholesalers and retailers distribute a tremendous variety of products.

The second dimension is the number of types of each product. Cement plants usually produce different grades of cement and homebuilders different kinds of houses. The health services of a hospital may include such fields as obstetrics, pediatrics, general medicine, mental diseases, special diseases such as tuberculosis or infantile paralysis, and surgery. In many of these fields, there is an important distinction between in-patient and out-patient services. In all of these fields the hospital may include in its product mix varying amounts of diagnostic, therapeutic, or preventive services. The educational services of a university may include training in the arts, humanities, sciences, and professions, with many hundreds of different courses (at the undergraduate, graduate, or postgraduate level) offered by scores of departments or centers grouped together in up to a dozen different colleges, schools, faculties or institutes. A hardware manufacturer may produce scores of different sizes and grades of every item in his catalogue.

The third dimension is the similarity or dissimilarity among the various products. This may be expressed by the Simon-Smithburg-Thompson distinction between a "unitary" and a "federal" (or holding company) organization (1950, p. 269-272). Any single-product organization is unitary. A multiproduct organization may be unitary if the various products lines and product types are closely related one with another. A vertically integrated steel company is unitary, since the many intermediate products from ore mining on are unified by their contribution to the final output of sheets, plates and shapes. A horizontally integrated company that manufactures many different kinds of steel products from wire and hardware to tools is federal. Some large corporations are holding companies for separate branches with little in common except top executives, certain central services and a presumed interest in money making. Some large departments of government are holding companies for large bureaus and offices with little in common except top executives, certain central services and a presumed interest in certain aspects of certain public interests. In the United States the Department of Health, Education, and Welfare is a sprawling agency of this type. There is no common output mix for the Public Health Service, the Social Security Administration, the Office of Education, the Food and Drug Administration, and other units. In any large university the gulf may be even greater between the teachers in various departments, faculties and colleges. A vague common interest in education may be readily counterbalanced by tremendous differences among students, teachers, and subject matter, and by the lack of widespread interaction among teachers in the basic processes of instruction.

A rapid growth in the variety of both end products and intermediate products seems to be a major characteristic of the onsweeping administrative revolution. In societies that are predominantly agricultural the major element in the national output mix is a limited variety of agricultural products. In industrial societies the economy produces a greater variety of such products and an ever-increasing proportion of other goods and services. In the more advanced industrial societies tremendous ingenuity is usually exerted in developing new products. These include not only new and more varied types of consumers' and producers' goods but also an ever-growing and ever more varied (and presumably improving) array of public and social services. At the intermediate level this process is paralleled—and accelerated—by the equally rapid growth of specialization. The proliferation of specialized areas of expertise means a rapidly growing variety in intermediate services. Together, new end products and new intermediate services tend to develop hand-in-hand with the expansion of organizational size. The large organization is better able to afford the costs of a growing variety of internal services. A growing variety in end products is often one of the best ways to compete with other organizations, appeal to more clientele interests and expand and enhance an organization's power. As this occurs, large organizations become more and more federal in character, with "federalism" extending below the top levels and reaching many of the lower units also. One of the reasons for the widespread dispersion of power in many large organizations is the fact that only at the lower levels is there a unitary product mix capable of mobilizing the interests and loyalties of members.

3. THE STANDARDIZED AND THE UNIQUE

Another facet of every output mix is the balance between standardized and unique products. The term "standardization" refers to the repetitive production of substantially similar products. If an organization installs a "simplification" program (that is, reduced output variety), this does not necessarily imply standardization. Multiple products may be standardized. An organization with a single product line may operate by meeting the unique specifications of every single client.

At one extreme, some products are completely standardized. Every day millions of substantially identical nails, shirts, pens, and other products are produced throughout the world. Any differences between the products are the result of defective production and control processes rather than of intention. Even in the field of services, particularly those involving manual labor, there is often a considerable degree of standardization.

With organizations producing standardized products, administration involves major emphasis on fixed schedules and procedures. Evaluation and control may be handled in quantitative terms. Operations tend to be routinized, whether or not mechanized.

At the other extreme, many organizations concentrate upon producing more or less unique goods: custom-tailored clothes, special-purpose machinery, or houses designed to fit the buyer's taste and the landscapes on which they are located. Most intangible, end product services—particularly in teaching, medicine, law and other professional fields—are modeled to fit not only the needs of particular consumers but also the psychological inclinations of the producers themselves. Administration itself is a service which, if it is any good, is usually designed to meet the special needs of unique and changing situations, organizations, and individuals.

In organizations producing unique products, the scope of routinized action is much smaller. Here fixed schedules and procedures have less relevance to the central tasks of the organization. If the effort is made to emphasize them, they will be openly or surreptitiously evaded. Mechanistic approaches will smother the initiative and flexibility needed for successful performance. Evaluation and control will tend to be more qualitative than quantitative and to be less based on preordained standards.

Most organizations will probably be found somewhere between these two extremes. Unique products are often assembled from standardized parts and components. The specifications of standardized products often change considerably over periods of time. Finally, the standardization of various intermediate products is often regarded as necessary to release organizational energies for concentration on the production of unique products.

c. *How Good?*

As ALREADY POINTED OUT, quality judgments answer the question "How good?"

In this sense quality may be defined as *the extent to which output conforms to certain specifications.*

Although the term "specification" sounds like something hard and fast, a specification is merely *a human expectation concerning one or more attributes(or facets) of goods or services.* Do we want to specify the attributes or properties of Engine 2 in the product mix of the engine plant? Or of Personal Division A's services with respect to personnel records? Then we look for those attributes which certain people—producers, clients, or outside experts—expect to find in each. The fact that these attributes might be recorded in blueprints or in written statements of function cannot deprive them of their human origin.

1. THE THEORY OF OUTPUT SPECIFICATION

Despite the subjectivity, infinite variety and frequent ambiguity of output specifications, it is possible to establish a theoretical framework for dealing with all such specifications. This framework is based on the simple proposition that an organization or unit thereof (a) takes certain input factors, (b) combines them through a production process and thus obtains (c) products with the characteristics that will (d) satisfy the interests of specified clients.

We thus obtain a four-rung ladder, or hierarchy, of output specification:

Client satisfactions

Product characteristics

Production processes

Inputs

The use of all four levels of output specification is not essential under all circumstances. For some purposes partial specification is sufficient. This is what is usually done in statements of identification. The answer to "What kind?" is usually given by selecting one or a few specification facets.

For other purposes, particularly for the setting of quality norms by producers, all four levels are required. Only thus is it possible to limit oneself to surface specifications dealing only with one or two facets. More careful study will always reveal almost endless possibilities for exploring each of these levels more fully.

The art of output specification consists of determining in each specific situation just what degree of comprehensiveness and intensity is desirable. To make such *ad hoc* judgments and to carry them into practice require, in turn, some understanding of what is involved at each of the four levels.

2. CLIENT SATISFACTIONS

The highest level of quality specification ties in directly with our previous discussion of interest satisfaction. The quality of beds, automobiles, and medical services can best be judged in terms of their contribution to sleep, transportation, health, or other results that people may expect from these products. The quality of administrative services is best judged in terms of their actual contribution to the success of an organization.

Previously we saw that each of these questions usually breaks down into a complex set of interrelated interests. We must now add the principle that a product's performance in satisfying various interests or needs should be seen in the light of specified conditions. In the case of goods these conditions may relate to methods of use or maintenance. Food cannot be expected to be nutritious if allowed to spoil before it is eaten. An electric refrigerator cannot be expected to keep food cold if the electric current is shut off or the refrigerator door is left open. While such things may be taken for granted, other situations demand explicit specification. It would be ridiculous, for example, to specify performance standards of an airplane, or measure its actual performance, without carefully pinning down such factors as the payload, weather conditions (particularly the strength and direction of windcurrents), the flight route, and the composition and ability of the crew.

In the case of a service, the nature of the conditions specified is somewhat different. While the possibility of varying conditions in the future need not be taken into account, the conditions extant during and before the provision of the service are broader in nature. If we are dealing with the battlefield performance of any army officer, we must take into account the amount and quality of the manpower and equipment resources at his disposal, the nature of the terrain, and the strength and ability of the opposing forces and the support given him by other units. The conditions also include a less tangible, but perhaps even equally decisive factor: the nature of his relationship with his superior officer. If we are dealing with the performance of individual soldiers, the relationship with both comrades and officers is an integral part of the conditions of performance.

3. PRODUCT CHARACTERISTICS

Because product performance in satisfying interests is so hard to specify at the outset or verify subsequently, there is a tendency to give greater emphasis to product characteristics. This tendency is particularly obvious in industrial quality control where attention is often focused almost exclusively on conformance with or deviations from precisely measured lengths or weights. This approach is highly justified whenever the specified length or weight is itself the best way of satisfying certain defined interests. It makes less sense when great efforts are exerted to see to it that walls, for example, have a load-carrying capacity far in excess of any actual load that could ever be placed on them and far in excess of any rational safety factor.

Here, too, we find a multiplicity of possible standards. Once we recognize the difference between goods (which are things) and services (which are the activities of people), we find that product characteristics can be set forth in any one, or all, of the following categories:

Goods	*Services*
Location in space and time	Location in space and time
Age	Duration
Durability	Speed
Physical characteristics:	Affective characteristics:
volume, weight, color,	emotions, attitudes, etc.
hardness, texture, etc.	
Design: shape, arrangement	Style: sequence of activities,
of parts, balance, etc.	balance, etc.

An illustration of the precision which is possible in specifying the physical characteristics of goods is provided by the following set of standards for blue spring steel strip, as developed by the Radio Corporation of America (Ireson and Grant, 1955, p. 640):

The materials shall conform to the following requirements as to temper:
   (a) Material over 0.020 inch in thickness shall be tested for hardness only. The hardness shall be 66 to 70, inclusive, Rockwell 30 N Scale.
   (b) Material 0.020 inch and under in thickness shall be tested for bending properties only. Strip of any width shall be bent 180 degrees between the jaws of a vice or testing machine, around pins of diameters specified. . . . The material shall either fracture transversely or remain intact. . . .

The specifications then go on to indicate for each of many thicknesses of steel strip the range within which the strip must be able to be bent without fracturing. This range is defined in terms of the diameter of the pin around which the strip is bent. Thinner strips are expected to bend around pins of a smaller diameter; for thicker strips pins of a larger diameter are allowed.

These performance standards are supplemented by detailed standards with respect to thickness and chemical composition. Wherever refined units of measurement are used, a range—or tolerance—is given. Thus a thickness of 0.020 inch and under may have a plus or minus variance of .0005. The carbon content of the steel is allowed to range from 0.85 per cent to 1.05 per cent. Other characteristics are identified without numbers, but in detailed descriptive terms:

> The steel shall be uniform, clean, blue and smooth. It shall be free from rust, dirt, pits, seams, spots, cracks, slivers and other imperfections, in accordance with good commercial practice.
>
> Edges shall be free from burrs, unless the order specifies that slit edges are acceptable.

It may be assumed that these standards with respect to performance characteristics and chemical input are based upon a careful appraisal of the needs which are to be met by various types of steel strips. This assumption is particularly justified in the case of a company which, like the American manufacturer referred to, uses the strips as components in manufacturing its own products or sells them to other companies that can afford to analyze product characteristics in such detail. In the case of goods sold to unorganized consumers, the relation between product characteristics and client interests is rarely appraised with comparable intensity.

4. PRODUCTION PROCESSES

In order to satisfy certain interests or to achieve certain product characteristics, it is often essential to produce a product in a certain way. It is thus relevant to set forth standards for the production process itself.

Thus when manufacturers order parts from suppliers, they may often specify that these parts must be produced in a certain manner and under certain conditions. The parts manufacturer will go still further in prescribing his own standards of operation at each stage of the production process. His production engineers may not only prescribe certain basic bodily movements for workers but may also establish detailed systems for the flow of materials and paper work through the organization.

Operations research specialists may devise standardized patterns for solving various repetitive problems relating to inventories of materials and the replacement of machinery. In the same way the nurses in an operating room and the musicians in an orchestra develop advanced technical standards for the performance of their precise roles in delicately timed activities.

Here also there is a tendency for quality standards to stray away from the higher goals of interest satisfaction. This can happen just as readily with an over-zealous production engineer as with a musician whose zest for technical skill overbalances his interest in the esthetic qualities of the music he may happen to be playing.

5. INPUT FACTORS

Finally, quality standards may be set forth in terms of input factors used in making a product, either the labor, materials, or machinery to be used, or the monetary costs of all these inputs together.

Thus, clothing manufacturers stress the quality of the materials from which their suits or dresses are made. If these are "handmade," they are supposed to be even better. An American dairy firm once advertised that its milk came from contented cows (although reference was not made to the contentment of the dairy maids or farmers). Airlines boast that they offer "jet flights." The quality of a school's educational services is often inferred from the academic degrees and professional publications of its teachers. One of the most up-to-date studies on nursing services sets forth quality standards dealing with the composition of the professional and nonprofessional staff, the architecture of the nursing unit and the arrangement of working facilities (American Hospital Association, 1960).

At any given stage of technology, a specific combination of input factors may be the prerequisite for product performance which meets the needs of specific clients. The setting forth of input goals and norms, therefore, is often essential as a way of guiding an organization's activities toward the output of products with the characteristics required to satisfy defined interests.

Yet this does not mean that input standards are a sufficient condition for achieving the desired performance. Ugly clothes can be produced from the best cloth, poor milk from contented cows, delayed flights by jet engines, and mediocre instruction by teachers with high degrees. Nor does it justify the use of costs as though they directly measure performance in the satisfaction of interests. There is a good presumption that very low expenditures on public education and national defense will not lead to high quality educational or military services. But high quality can in neither case be equated with a high level of expenditure.

6. THE WEIGHTING OF QUALITY FACETS

In a world in which everyone could seriously aim at utter perfection on every aspect of quality, the multiplicity of quality facets would not create a serious problem at the stage of goal formulation.

But in the real world organizations, units and individuals are always aiming at something less. Their ideas of perfection itself are subject to constant change. The level of actual achievement varies from one facet to another. Above all, it seems that high quality with respect to some facets often requires a sacrifice of quality with respect to others.

It therefore becomes essential to find some way of interrelating a variety of specific quality goals or norms. From the evaluation side, this means the interrelating of standards or criteria.

This interrelating is always handled through some form of weighting, either unsystematic or systematic.

Most weighting is handled unsystematically. The simplest form of unsystematic weighting is the exclusion of most quality facets from attention and concentration upon a few. The act of exclusion is not a conscious one. It is based on custom, habit, ignorance, prejudice or mere lack of awareness. The problem of reconciling the remaining facets still remains. It may be ignored—as when an automobile manufacturer aims to increase engine power and comfort without paying much attention to safety or durability. Or it may be handled on a rough-and-ready intuitive basis.

The higher forms of unsystematic weighting are based upon an acute, though but partially verbalized, awareness of patterns. Here choices are made through intuitive judgments based on careful observation and long experience.

Through systematic weighting people may bring some degree of order and comparability into the on-going flow of unsystematic weighting. The simplest system consists of merely identifying some pattern that can be clearly perceived and using it as a model for imitation.

A more systematic approach is to identify a number of quality facets and assign a numerical weight to each. This will allow a quantitative balancing of greater quality with respect to one facet against lower quality with respect to another.

This does not mean that a low score on any point can always be counterbalanced by higher scores on other points. Some quality goals must sometimes be regarded as prerequisites; anything less means total disqualification. Thus, in the case of the steel strip referred to in subsection 3, above, perfection itself with respect to thickness, cleanliness, smoothness and hardness could never compensate for inability to bend without fracturing. This is an aspect of weighting which, while never neglected in experienced intuitional judgment, may sometimes be lost sight of in formalized systems.

Obviously, even the best formal weighting system cannot eliminate subjective judgments. The results will be predetermined by the weights assigned to each facet. But if the assigned weights have some relation to the actual weights, this approach may go a long way toward making subjective judgments more comparable. It can thus facilitate the communication process with respect to goal adjustment and appraisals of actual performance.

A still more formal approach may be provided by the creation of quality grades. Thus we may decide that Grade A shirts will be made of specified materials, colors and design. Grade B shirts will be made with the same colors and design but with cheaper materials. Grade C shirts will be those shirts which because of certain defects beyond the allowable margin of error are not accepted into the A or B class. We have now simplified matters by reducing the more difficult question "How good?" into the simpler question "What kind?"

But how has this transformation been accomplished? Why three grades instead of two or four? What is the distance between the grades? How do we decide upon the boundary lines of each grade?

In part, the answer is that in establishing grades we do nothing but formalize our unsystematic or systematic weighting system.

There is something more to be said, however. In establishing quality grades we somehow or other distinguish between different levels of clientele satisfaction. These levels may be thought of or expressed in any one or more of the satisfaction surrogates: choices made, payments given, expressed opinions, or subsequent results. Thus, in determining the facet patterns for each of the three grades of shirts, the aim will usually be to make perfectly sure that certain potential clients would agree that A is generally more desirable than B, would actually choose it in preference to B or would be willing to pay more for it.

An interesting use of a satisfaction surrogate is found in the efforts of research laboratories to measure the quality of scientific work. While the number of published scientific papers has long been used as a measure of the quantity of research output, it gives no direct indication of the quality or significance of research output. Nor can the substantive evaluation of single papers be readily based on a uniform grading system. Accordingly, techniques have been devised for counting the number of instances that each single paper may be cited (Westbrook, 1960). This may be done on a net basis that eliminates self-citations (one of the minor sins of the academic world) and in-house citations. The net number of citations thus helps identify high quality papers, scientists, and research laboratories. The justification lies in the hypothesis that widespread citation of paper by other scientists may be regarded as an expression of positive opinion concerning its scientific quality. Moreover, a high number of citations might also be regarded as a goal of scientific work—a goal to be sought by efforts to produce high quality research. However, since citations may also be affected by vigorous dissemination programs, by adherence to current fads and fashions of research, or by tacit understandings concerning reciprocal citation, high performance by this standard must sometimes be heavily discounted.

D. *How Much?*

In chapter 13 and the previous sections of this chapter the major emphasis has been upon the concepts needed to express output objectives or calculate output performance. While this has meant less attention to the dynamics of purposefulness, it has anticipated the discussion of quantity objectives by already presenting the major concepts needed in expressing an answer to "How much?"

We are now therefore able to address ourselves to this question without getting bogged down in such matters as contributed value, changing prices, kinds of products classification systems, and methods of judging quality. We may now shift our attention to the emergence of purposefulness with respect to the quantity of output.

One way to do this would be to start with the highly developed body of economic theory on output determination by business firms. One might then broaden this body of theory to cover nonmarketed as well as marketed products. However, this would involve two major difficulties: (a) a major expansion in the direction of recognizing multiple, interrelating goals, and (b) a switch from the prescriptive rationality of most economic theory to empirical analysis of what actually happens.

I prefer to start with a broader and more flexible approach applicable to all organizations and founded *ab initio* on purpose multiplicity and an interest in explanation rather than prescription.

1. CAPACITY AND CONFLICTING PRESSURES

The level of output may be regarded as the resultant of three dynamic and interrelated variables: productive capacity, external demand, and producers' desires. When we focus upon any one of these, the other two may then be seen as limits or constraints upon the influence of this one factor. Yet it would be an error to regard any of them as a mere passive restriction. Their constraining function, rather, stems from their actual or potential influence upon the level of output.

The productive capacity of an organization or unit thereof will be discussed in more detail in "Investment in Organizational Viability" (Chapt. 17). Here it will suffice to point out that an organization's capacity is based upon both the resources available to it and its ability to use such resources.

External demand may come from various sources. For a unit a higher authority's demand for more output may be counterbalanced by the insistence of various members upon output restriction. For an organization, various external groups may press inconsistent demands. For many business organizations, potential buyers may want different quantities of different products. In times of depression and low purchasing power, their demands may be ineffective—even though their needs may be great. In periods of prosperity, when purchasing power and available supplies are both high, demand may be ineffective for lack of underlying needs that cry out to be satisfied.

According to the neoclassical economists' theory of "consumer sovereignty," the output of marketed products is decided upon entirely by consumers. "Neither the capitalists nor the entrepreneurs nor the farmers determine what has to be produced. . . . The consumers are the sovereign people. The capitalists, the entrepreneurs and the farmers are the people's mandatories. If they do not obey, if they fail to produce, at the lowest possible cost, what the consumers are asking for, they lose their office . . . profit and loss are the instruments by means of which the consumers keep a tight rein on all business activities" (Von Mises, 1962, p. 20-22). The most obvious defect in the theory of consumer sovereignty is the assumption of perfect competition. In this respect it may be regarded as another "myth of ultimate authority," to be added to those referred to previously. By exaggerating the power of consumers, it has often served as a means of obscuring the power of large producers. Less obvious, but equally significant, is the assumption of total acquiescence *within* the producing organization to the profit-maximizing desires of the entrepreneurs. In this respect it is based upon the "myths of central omnipotence."

The third factor is producers' desires. As a constraint, this factor is every bit as important as capacity. The limits people and organizations impose on the volume of their output may not readily be disregarded. As a dynamic influence, they are capable of shaping each of the other two factors. When people and organizations desire to produce more, they can take steps to expand capacity. They may often do so even though existing capacity is sufficient. Above all, they can promote external demands. This may be done by alliances or coalitions and by direct negotiations with clients and other groups. It may also be done by large-scale efforts to cater to existing interests of clients or bring into being wants that did not previously exist. Much of business advertising and salesmanship is directed toward these ends. Hence, consumer demand, rather than being the ruling sovereign is itself, at least in part, created by producers. As Galbraith has put it, "That wants are, in fact, the fruit of production, will now be denied by few serious scholars . . . the production of goods creates the wants that the goods are presumed to satisfy" (1958, p. 154-155). This observation may also be extended to the sphere of government services. If the modern state produces an increasing volume of services per citizen, the sole explanation cannot be found in an automatic response to citizen demands. The desire of government organizations to provide more services, and their ingenuity in promoting demand for them, must also be recognized.

2. PRODUCERS' PROPENSITIES
TO CONTRACT OR EXPAND

In considering the effect of producers' desires upon total output, it would be a serious mistake to assume a vigorous urge to expansion on the part of all government agencies, business firms, or other organizations. Many such organizations often look askance at the idea of higher levels of output. Some may even prefer contraction.

It would be an even more serious mistake to assume that individual members or small units within an organization are inherently interested in restricting output. Although this assumption was made by Frederick Taylor and may still serve as a major premise for some administrators, it is scarcely relevant to the activities of specialists and professionals. Nor can it any longer be accepted as a guide to the understanding of workers' activities.

Whether we are considering an organization, a unit thereof, or a single member, it is much more realistic to start with the assumption that any producer may exhibit propensities toward either the contraction or expansion of output or even toward both at the same time.

To some extent, these propensities are influenced by productive capacity and external demand. When capacity has been strained in the past, is being conserved for future use or is running down through obsolescence, there will usually be less desire to expand output. When people are convinced they cannot do much more, there is little chance that they will try. On the other hand, unused capacity exerts a pressure toward its utilization. In the case of unused physical resources this pressure appears in the form of the costs of nonuse. In the case of unused human capacities the costs of nonuse may be dramatized by active protest.

Similarly, an interest in contraction on the part of producers may result from a situation where there is no external interest, let alone demand or encouragement, or where conflicting demands create deep uncertainties and intolerable internal conflicts. When external pressures toward expansion whether by hierarchial superiors or by pressure groups, fail to take into account the interests of producers, they are apt to be met with open or hidden resistance. On the other hand, external demands may serve to awaken and reinforce producers' interests in more output.

Apart from the influence of capacity and external demand, producers' desires are also influenced by cultural and personal factors. Some cultures —and some people in all cultures—place a higher value upon leisure or upon a leisurely form of work than upon the extra efforts, whether mental or physical, that might be needed to produce more. This orientation may be buttressed by the uninspiring nature of a particular organization's output and the uncertainty of clear rewards resulting for an output increase.

In many situations, indeed, producers see increased output as a possible cause of sharp dissatisfactions. One such dissatisfaction may be falling prices. Businessmen and farmers will often curtail output in order to bolster prices and income. Another such dissatisfaction may be unemployment. Workers will often restrict output in an effort to keep their jobs. All types of producers may work against expansionary efforts that threaten their existing security, their positions of authority, or established ways of conducting affairs. This is one of the reasons for traditionalist opposition in underdeveloped societies to industrial development and the accompanying economic expansion. In industrially developed societies it is one of the factors militating against efforts to promote sustained economic growth.

On the other hand, high levels of output may beckon toward greater satisfactions. For some people, increasing output serves as a means of self-development. It may also—particularly in competitive situations— serve as a path toward the maintenance or enlargement of security, prestige or power. Businessmen may prefer the larger total profits that come from mass production even though prices and unit profits may dwindle. The leaders of other organizations may prefer the excitement and stimulus of large-scale operations, even though this may mean less attention to the quality of services or goods provided.

There was a time when psychological researchers thought that propensities toward high or expanded levels of output could be neatly correlated with some form of external demand—particularly supervisory style—or with high levels of personal satisfaction. Subsequent research demonstrated that the effect of supervisory style upon output depends upon the personality needs of workers (*Lewin, Lippitt, and White; Baumgartel,* 1957). It also demonstrated that high output may also be associated with certain types of dissatisfaction (*Zaleznik, Christensen, and Roethlisberger*). More recently, attention has been given to the close relationship between capacity or ability and the desire to produce (*French; Maier*). It may be expected that future research will relate output propensities directly to both capacity and external demands, to the entire hierarchy of human interests (as discussed in Chapter 8) and to the satisfaction-dissatisfaction nexus (as discussed in Chapter 12). It is to be hoped that such research will not be confined to workers and technicians but will be directed as well to the propensities of administrators and entire organizations.

E. *Quality-Quantity Conflicts*

Does large-scale output necessarily mean a reduction in quality? Does high quality necessitate a reduction in volume?

Often, indeed, quantity and quality seem either incompatible or incommensurate. Sometimes they seem to be both.

The difficulty of this problem may lead people to seek an easy way out by focusing exclusively on either quantity or quality. Yet whichever of these two aspects of output is ignored, it tends to worm its way back toward the center of attention—at which point people may then concentrate upon it and forget the other one. Sooner or later, however, it becomes difficult to avoid direct attention to the subject.

1. THE "NONCOMPATIBLES"

The problem of incompatibility flows from the conflict between large quantity and high quality. This conflict is expressed in the widespread belief that high quality is possible only with a small quantity of output or—as stated another way—that large-scale output makes high quality impossible.

There are many roots for this belief in the basic incompatibility between large quantity and high quality.

First of all, high quality output often requires far more inputs per unit than low quality output. When the supply of these inputs is limited, the attempt to distribute them over a large number of units will reduce the quality of every unit.

Second, an increasing supply of anything tends to reduce human awareness of the satisfactions it supplies. Under certain circumstances scarcity may enhance the quality of anything. This proposition—one of the historic foundations of economics—is particularly evident in the case of monetary value. But it also has wider applicability. In a nation of blondes, the rare brunette is more attractive—and in a nation of brunettes, the rare blonde is more highly prized. The rareness of an object enjoyed may itself rub off on the enjoyer—and thus contribute to the satisfaction, and stimulation, of his differentiation needs. Status and prestige are inextricably associated with scarcity rather than abundance.

Third, these conflicts between high quality and large quantity are paralleled—and probably reinforced—by the social conflict between the elite and the mass. With the growth of modern industry the aristocrats of the old order have always seen the quality of everything they enjoyed threatened by large numbers of *nouveau riche* and newly-enfranchised poor. The intellectual elite of the administered society often see mass production—whether in goods, communication, education or culture—as a degradation of quality.

Yet none of these factors is as powerful as it may sometimes seem.

On the input side, there are many areas in which large quantity is a *prerequisite* of high quality output. There are many high quality goods which can be produced only through the use of expensive machinery which is economically justifiable only when its cost is distributed over an extremely large quantity of output. Some forms of quality control, likewise, are feasible only in mass production operations.

On the supply side, a large quantity of output does not conflict with absolute, as distinguished from relative, value. It may even help promote rising standards of value. Thus, in the early 1950's in the United States the high-fidelity phonograph was a relatively rare instrument. By the early 1960's, as many more of these instruments were produced, their quality rose appreciably in absolute terms. Their price and their prestige value fell concurrently. But as more and more people came to expect a higher quality of musical reproduction, new techniques were developed. With the advent of stereophonic phonographs, mere "hi-fi" has fallen substantially on the relative scale of quality evaluation. Once stereophonic instruments are available in large quantities, we may expect that the same cycle will repeat itself and that absolute standards will be pushed still higher.

Nor does large-scale production necessarily mean standardization, with a consequent loss of the quality elements associated with differentiation. The standardization required for economical mass production may be limited to intermediate products. These, in turn, may be assembled in a great variety of patterns and embellished with made-to-order parts of components.

As far as aristocracy is concerned, the true aristocracy of intellect is based neither upon the deprivation of the masses nor the maintenance of some "old order." It is based upon the always-rare ability of a few to pioneer in establishing new standards of value. The true aristocrats are oriented toward raising absolute standards of quality in everything and for everyone. Their power stems from the common interests of human beings not merely in survival and commergence but in differentiation and self-development. They are agitators and organizers in the modern revolution of rising expectations.

The existence of a conflict between the goal of high quality and the goal of large quantity cannot be denied. There are almost always obstacles to the simultaneous achievement of both of these goals. But this does not mean that they are necessarily incompatible. An integration can often be made without compromising on either large quantity or high quality. In many situations it is only by aiming at such an integration that the two can be achieved with only a small degree of compromise.

2. THE "NONCOMMENSURABLES"

The problem of the noncommensurability of quality and quantity measures is not as fundamental or profound as the incompatibility problem. It is more of a technical problem. But it is also more widespread. It may also throw a cloud of confusion over any discussion of large quantity vs. high quality.

Let us temporarily assume a single measure that answers the question "How good?" and a single measure to answer "How much?" Let us then explore the possible patterns of divergence between these over-simplified formulations of quality and quantity goals.

For any particular point in time we may thus face the following choice among three products of varying quality and quantity:

	Product 1	*Product 2*	*Product 3*
Quantity	1,000	1,100	1,200
Grade	A	B	C

Which is to be preferred—a larger quantity of the lower grade product, or a smaller quantity of the higher grade product?

The problem is more complicated if we face a choice between alternative product mixes. This, indeed, is the typical problem in formulating the output goals of any organization or unit. It may be schematized as follows:

	Product Mix 1	Product Mix 2	Product Mix 3
Quantity			
Grade A	100	200	300
Grade B	800	400	200
Grade C	100	400	500
Total	1,000	1,000	1,000

To make this problem seem simpler than it ever really is, we have here assumed fixed inputs, a fixed total quantity of output, a reliable grading system, and only three out of an infinite set of possible divergences. Which product mix is to be preferred?

Let us now look at two periods of time instead of one and concentrate upon the change that takes place between the first and the second. Our problem is now made somewhat easier if (a) there is a change in only quality or quantity, (b) both change in the same direction, or (c) there is no change at all. These alternatives may be illustrated as follows:

	(a)	(b)	(c)	
Quantity	+ − 0 0	+ −	0	+ = increase
				− = decrease
Quality	0 0 + −	+ −	0	0 = no change
Result	+ − + −	+ −	0	

In these patterns of divergence, we have no problem in identifying the nature of any change. In pattern (a) we still face the problem of determining the magnitude of the change in either quality or quantity. In pattern (b) we face the more complex problem of finding a common denominator for two magnitudes.

A fourth pattern, (d), occurs when quality and quantity move in opposite directions:

(d)

Quantity	+	−
Quality	−	+
Result	?	?

This usually occurs in a movement—either prospective or actual—

from one product mix to another. One of its most complicated forms is represented by a choice between future product mixes in which the quantities of various grades vary in both absolute and percentage terms:

	PRESENT		FUTURE					
			Product Mix 1		Product Mix 2		Product Mix 3	
Quantity	No.	%	No.	%	No.	%	No.	%
Grade A	100	10	200	25	120	10	70	5
Grade B	800	80	400	50	480	40	910	65
Grade C	100	10	200	25	600	50	420	30
Total	1,000	100	800	100	1,200	100	1,400	100

Which of these prospective situations is more desirable?

The problem is made still more realistic if instead of dealing on the quality side with "How good?" only, we add "What kind?" Each product mix is thus converted into a set of different types of products, with some sets divided into quality grades and others merely into subtypes. The present mix, moreover, is always tarnished by defects in observation and measurement. Any future mix is beclouded by some inevitable degree of uncertainty. Finally, the whole situation is made more complicated by the multiplicity of quality and quantity facets for each type of product.

As with the divergencies between the various facets of quality itself, the problem of commensurability cannot be solved by more precise measurements. The problem arises from the differences in the units of measurement. It can be solved only by some form of weighting—that is, by translating units of one into units of the other or finding some common units for both.

This is often done through "negative weighting," the conscious or unconscious disregarding of either of the two aspects of output. In the case of intangible services, where it may be impossible to identify units of output, let alone count them, quality may be the sole focus of attention. Wherever there are units that can be counted, however, we are likely to see a most widespread form in the concentration upon quantity without judgments of quality. In national economic accounting, for example, calculations of the changing national product are usually made with little attention to quality changes. In the administration of universities and colleges the research output of academic personnel is often measured exclusively by the number of published articles and books. This may be justified on the shaky ground that publication itself is an indication of a quality evaluation made by publishers and editorial boards. A firmer ground for justification is the fact there can be no argument over the number of published documents or pages, while there can rarely be any end to arguments over their comparative value. When statistical or quality aspects are compiled (as through the counting of citations), the problem of reconciliation still remains.

An endless series of additional examples can be found of situations in which the spotlight is turned on quantitative measures and quality is left shrouded in the shadows. Some of these are probably not too different from Anatole France's story of the trial of General Pyrot in *Penguin Island* (p. 204-205). In presenting his evidence against Pyrot (who, like Dreyfus, is accused of treason), General Panther, the Chief of Staff, summarizes his evidence as follows: "I have in my archives seven hundred and thirty-two square yards of them [proofs] which at five hundred pounds each makes three hundred and sixty thousand pounds weight. . . . The smallest is less than the hundredth part of a square inch, the largest measures seventy yards long by ninety yards broad."

In the case of marketed products it is sometimes possible to use monetary value as a means of dealing with quality as well as quantity. Figures on sales revenue will often reflect differences in quality. Higher grade merchandise usually commands a higher price, while people usually pay less for lower grade goods. Moreover, net value figures can take into account the costs involved in substandard merchandise, spoilage, rework costs and losses in returned goods.

Nevertheless, market prices are not always directly responsive to gradations in actual quality. Consumers may be ignorant concerning the quality of the goods they buy. They may be misled by deceptive advertising or packaging. In times of serious shortage they may be willing to pay high prices regardless of quality.

In order to escape complete reliance upon prices, it is possible to develop arbitrary rating systems to translate quality differences into quantity differences. In incentive wage systems this is often done by assigning points for certain differences in quality and using these points to modify calculations of quantity. Thus, if three different types or grades of a product are produced, Grade A items can be assigned 1 point apiece, and Grade B and C items .7 and .3 points apiece.

		PRESENT		FUTURE	
Types of Products	Points Per Item	No. of Products	No. of Points	No. of Products	No. of Points
A	1.0	1,000	1,000	1,200	1,200
B	.7	100	70	600	420
C	.3	100	30	600	180
		1,200	1,100	2,400	1,800

Thus, without looking at the differences between the various items, it would appear that output had risen from 1,200 to 2,400, and increase of 100 per cent. But the point system indicates an increase from 1,100 to 1,800, an increase of only 64 per cent.

Any such rating system, however, must be handled with kid gloves. Its value depends entirely upon the selection of the quality facets that are taken into account and the manner in which points are assigned. The difficulty of the required computations will usually lead to selection not on the basis of significance but of ease in quantification and handling. The number magic resulting from precise quantification will mislead many people into seeing in such rating systems a significance far greater than would be attributed to them even by their proud inventors.

Chapter 15

OUTPUT:
OPERATIONS AND FUNCTIONS

*I*N DEALING with the output of organizations, administrative thought has often revealed a lack of balance with respect to the distinction between services and goods.

On the one hand, much of the language of business administration seems based on the ridiculous assumption that goods are the only form of output. This is a legacy from the goods-oriented engineers and industrialists who have contributed so much to administrative thought in the realm of production engineering. On the other hand, in the field of public administration most thinkers have dodged the problem of dealing directly with the output of government organizations. Knowing that they are not dealing with organizations that produce goods as end products but lacking a clear service concept of output, they have often tended to overemphasize the input side and the procedural aspects of the production process.

In both fields, however, specialists working in intellectual isolation one from another have devised various administrative techniques to help formulate service objectives and appraise service performance. Personnel specialists have developed job description, job specification, job evaluation, and performance (or merit) rating. Organization specialists have concentrated upon ways of describing the functions or missions of units. Budget specialists have worked on performance budgeting. Operations researchers have analyzed various types of operations. Yet because these specialists have not worked within a common conceptual framework, there has been little appreciation of the simple fact that all of these tools and techniques—whether they use the term job, function, mission, or operation—involve identifying or measuring the quality or quantity of service output.

In the previous two chapters, in order to simplify the task of clarifying general concepts of output, I have often ignored the special problems of service objectives. The ground is now prepared for tackling them directly.

After tracing the background of certain deep-rooted prejudices against services, I shall analyze the distinguishing characteristics of services and their critical role in organizational action, particularly in the production of goods. I shall then examine the various surrogates available for measuring the quality and quantity of intangible services. Against this background, I shall then discuss each of the major administrative techniques relating to the formulation of service objectives and the appraisal of service performance.

A. *The Prejudice Against Services*

THE PREJUDICE against services has deep historical roots. It stems in part from the French physiocrats, Adam Smith, and Karl Marx—all of whom attacked services as "unproductive."

In the mid-eighteenth century Quesnay and other French physiocrats maintained that agriculture was the only "truly productive occupation." Expressing the views and interests of the large landowners, the physiocrats regarded artisans, merchants and manufacturers as sterile and unproductive members of society. This approach was associated with the definition of national income and wealth as "an aggregate of consumer commodities only."

Writing somewhat later in the eighteenth century, Adam Smith took over from the physiocrats the distinction between "productive" and "unproductive" labor. But favoring the expansion of industry, he could not tolerate the exclusive emphasis upon agriculture. He, therefore, expanded "productive" to embrace all labor engaged in the production of material goods, or commodities. The epithet "unproductive" was reserved for services:

> The labour of some of the most respectable orders in the society is, like that of menial servants, unproductive of any value. . . . The sovereign,

for example, with all the officers both of justice and war, who serve under him, the whole army and navy, are unproductive labourers. They are the servants of the public and are maintained by a part of the annual produce of the industry of other people. . . . The protection, security, and defense of the commonwealth, the effect of their labour last year, will not purchase its protection, security, and defense for the year to come. In the same class must be ranked, some both of the gravest and most important, and some of the most frivolous professions: churchmen, lawyers, physicians, men of letters of all kinds: players, buffoons, musicians, opera-singers, opera-dancers, etc. . . . Like the declamation of the actor, the harangue of the orator, or the tune of the musician, the work of all of them perishes in the very instant of its production (*The Wealth of Nations*, p. 315).

In transforming Ricardo's labour theory of value into the theory of "surplus value," Marx conceived national product and income as founded upon goods alone.[1] Thus, in Russia and other Communist countries which follow the strict Marxian tradition, national income estimates have often been largely based upon the "material production concept of national income." In the non-Communist countries, on the other hand, this concept has been thoroughly routed by the "'comprehensive concept" developed in detail by a long and distinguished line of economists and statisticians. In these countries, national income accounts include all the services that Adam Smith had tried to exorcise.[2] In the words which Alfred Marshall used to counter Adam Smith's distinction between durable and nondurable utilities, national income includes "every service rendered, every fresh utility brought about . . . the services of the domestic servant who makes

1. It is interesting to note that in his earlier writings Marx directly attacked Smith's idea that services are necessarily unproductive. He held that "Chefs and waiters, for instance, are productive laborers in the sense that their labor is converted into capital for their employer . . . the result has its origin not in the content, nor in the produce of the labor, but in its determined social form" (*Theories of Surplus Value,* written by Marx in 1860, newly translated and appearing in *A History of Economic Theories,* p. 200-224). In his later writings, however, Marx found that by concentrating upon commodities alone and disregarding his earlier comments on the role of services, he could more easily fashion his theory on the materialization of surplus value into capital. It might also be noted that Adam Smith, in the very chapter attacking all services as unproductive, recognizes that some services are "useful." At another point, he uses "useful" as equivalent to "productive." Let us not expect too much consistency from great men!

2. Studenski, 1959, p. 11-26. Studenski points out that to the extent that the Marxian concept of material production is actually carried out in statistical practices (without allowing services to creep in through the back door), the Communist figures are understated in comparison with those of other countries. On the other hand, when rates of national economic growth are computed upon goods alone, in an economy where the growth of services is restricted, the result may be an overestimate of growth in comparison with countries using the comprehensive concept of national income and enjoying an expansion of services.

or mends or cleans a carpet or a dress, as well as the results of the work of the upholsterer, the milliner and the dyer."[3] This is clearly broad enough to include sovereigns, the officers of war and any others heavily involved in guiding organizations.

Yet the Quesnay-Smith-Marx emphasis upon goods still reverberates in the air. Indirect labor is generally regarded as less "productive" than direct labor, that is, labor in more direct contact with goods. In organizations it is referred to as "overhead" or "burden," the implication being that services are a burden upon more productive activities. Economists still operate in terms of definitions that formally exclude research and education from the measurement of investment. Although there is more and more recognition that research and education can be among the most productive forms of investment, economists have not yet been able to break away fully from the traditional idea that investment must be in hard goods and that services must be classified as current consumption.

While this hidden prejudice against services is powerful, there is a more open form of prejudice which is more clearly associated with group interests and social struggle. As Galbraith has vigorously pointed out (1958), this prejudice is based upon the fact that in the industrially developed countries the larger vistas for the expansion of services are in the public sector. Efforts to expand public services inevitably conflict with the interests of those business firms that are oriented toward selling consumers on the consumption of more and more privately produced goods. Thus goods tend to be rated more highly in some circles, with services often looked upon as a necessary evil. As Galbraith puts it with reference to the United States, "We set great store by the increase in private wealth but regret the added outlays for the police force by which it is protected. . . . On ancient and traditional grounds we relegate one important class of production to second class citizenship" (*Ibid*, p. 134, 137).

B. *The Intangible Nature of Services*

THE PREJUDICE against services is reinforced by the fact that these "second class" products are often intangible. In contrast, the greater tangibility

3. Alfred Marshall, 1909, p. 52-53. In his best-known work Marshall comes to the defense of distributive services, pointing out that the work of the sailor or railway man in carrying coal above ground is just as "productive" as that of the miner who carries it underground. He also maintains that man cannot "produce" material things: he can only change "the form or arrangement of matter to adapt it better for the satisfaction of wants." The only things he can "produce" are "new ideas" (1920, p. 63).

of goods seems to confer upon those who produce or handle goods directly a more recognizable form of status and role. At times, in fact, it seems that the producers of goods are "hardnosed," "grounded upon reality" and "practical." The producers of services, in contrast, run the risk of being "soft," "unrealistic" and "impractical."

To some extent, these connotations stem from some very real differences between services and goods. While these differences might be summed up by stating that services are less tangible than goods, they can be better understood by a more careful probe into the nature of this intangibility.

1. ACTIVITIES INSTEAD OF THINGS

The essential difference between the two forms of output is that services are *activities* and goods are *things*.

As things, such goods as milk, magnesium, motors, and correspondence can be directly seen, felt, counted, weighed, and measured. They are also static, in comparison with services. They do not *act* by themselves; they may *react*.

Services, on the other hand, are less concrete and more dynamic. They are the activities of people—of teachers, doctors, accountants, physicists, machine operators, stenographers, soldiers and administrators. The terms "operation" or "mission" are sometimes used to refer to some identifiable sequence of such activities. The terms "function" or "task" are often used to refer to certain types of such activities.

A service may itself consist of moving people or things from one location to another. But after the service has been rendered, it cannot itself be moved. While it is being given, it can be inspected. Once it has been given, it cannot be sent to a laboratory for examination; one must content oneself with an observation of aftereffects and reactions. A service cannot be stored or stockpiled—although the storing or stockpiling of goods is itself a service. One cannot invest in accumulated services, as one can invest in raw materials, machinery and real estate—although one can invest in people and facilities that have a service-giving potential.

Certain activities are much more tangible than others. This is the case with all services that involve the movement or storage of things or people. Transportation services can be pinned down in terms of the number of passengers or crates, passenger miles, and ton miles. Warehousing services can be identified in terms of the volume or weight of what is stored and the duration of storage.

But when services involve the processing or dissemination of information, they reach a high degree of intangibility. Under such circumstances it becomes harder to develop a well-rounded hierarchy of organizational purposes. Output purposes, being hazier, tend to fade. Undue prominence tends to be given to other purposes. Similarly, it becomes extremely difficult to measure output performance. Although the components assembled by workers on the assembly line can be counted precisely, it is difficult to reach even a rough approximation of the quantity of services rendered by a doctor, engineer, budget officer, or personnel technician. When as a result of this difficulty there is little or no information on the output side, it thus becomes impossible—no matter how much information may be obtained on the input side—to devise very meaningful measures of efficiency.

In the case of services that are both intangible and intermediate, these difficulties are compounded. Here there is a natural tendency for the members of the organization to establish substitute goals by grasping any tangible products that they can find. This tendency is particularly pronounced in the case of organizations which deal, process, and/or store substantial amounts of information. In all such organizations, there are records of some sort—whether they take the form of letters, memoranda, tables, charts, forms, microfilms, or electronic tape. In a vast sea of less tangible personal services these records stand forth as precious islands of tangibility. They can be counted, touched, seen, and stored. The producers of these records may thus lose sight of their purpose as a vehicle for the transmission of information. The accountant may think of his job exclusively as "keeping the books," the file clerk as "building the file." The adviser may concentrate upon "producing a report"—and will usually take care to see that it is handsomely bound. They and countless others will prepare forms—and insist that people fill them out—calling for more information than is necessary to transmit to any potential user. Thus it is that an intermediate product, because it is tangible, can become enshrined as the be-all and end-all of an organization. Thus it is that in the production of paperwork "means" may triumph over "ends."

In the sense that goods also are designed to satisfy certain needs, it may be said that they also "serve." The economist may hold, with Pigou, that the national output "is composed in the last respect of a number of objective services, some of which are embodied in commodities, while others are rendered direct. These things are most conveniently described as goods—whether immediately perishable or durable—and services . . ." (1952, p. 31). Thus we may refer to goods as embodied services or even—if we so desire—to services as disembodied goods. Yet despite the word-play, the fundamental distinction between things and activities is clear.

This does not mean that the application of the distinction is always clear. Although we may like to think of them in other terms, books, documents, and phonograph records are goods. Although they do not resemble more material things, oxygen and other gaseous products are as much goods as the tanks in which they are stored. Batteries, generating plants and wires are goods, but the electric power which they generate or distribute is a service. Confusion on this point is one of the reasons that criminal codes prohibiting the theft of goods alone do not always cover the theft of electricity through the tapping of power lines.

2. EPHEMERAL INSTEAD OF DURABLE

Whether perishable or durable, all goods have some existence in time *after* they have been produced. They can thus be stored or moved from place to place.

But services, once produced, immediately vanish. They are more ephemeral than the shortlived butterfly. A service may be given over a period of time, even a long period of time, but once given, it is consumed immediately. Although it may be said to "live" in memory or in the impact it has had, it no longer exists. Although a similar, perhaps identical, service can be performed again, the predecessor has disappeared.

Despite the ephemeral character of activities, time takes on a special importance with respect to services. As Parsons points out in his theory of action, "Any act is always a process in time. The time category is basic to the scheme." He emphasizes that an act or activity "always implies a future reference to a state which is either not yet in existence, and which would not come into existence if something were not done about it by the actor, or, if already existent, would not remain unchanged" (1949, p. 45). In other words, the futurity-orientation of services is sharper than that of goods. Precisely because of their ephemerality the life span of services, while they are being simultaneously produced and provided, may be even more critical a dimension than the durability of goods.

A special time dimension is provided by what might be called "contingent" or "assurance" services. The services performed by military forces during war may be all too tangible, and readily pinned down in both time and space. But military forces may also provide a service during peace time, the service of assuring people that they are capable of destructive efforts against aggressors. The difficulty of defining these services stems from the fact that the contingencies of their future use may never be known in advance, except to the initiators of aggressive action. Other contingent services may be more specific—such as the telephone lines available for use when needed or the automobile waiting in the courtyard. In all of these cases the knowledge that such a service is available may itself be a service. In Milton's words "They also serve who only stand and wait" ("Sonnet on His Blindness").

3. RELATION TO CLIENTS

Because of its ephemeral character a service cannot exist in splendid isolation. It must have some form of contact with some recipient or beneficiary, with some client whose needs it meets. If there is not a client who is served by it—as in the case of a teacher in an empty classroom or a heater burning away on an uninhabited desert island—then it is not a service.

As already noted, goods may be regarded as a form of congealed or embodied service. If they do not meet the needs of clients at once, they can do so later. With services, the needs must be met at the very time when an activity is performed. Otherwise, it is wasted activity—comparable to the breakage and scrap that may occur in the output of goods.

This does not mean that there must be a direct contact between a service and identified clients. As pointed out in "Satisfaction of Interests" (Chapt. 12), many organizations produce services for nonvisible, remote clienteles.

Some products, of course, are produced exclusively for the use of the producers themselves. The classical case is that of agricultural goods in a pre-exchange economy where on-the-farm consumption is the general rule. With the development of exchange economies, the distinction between the producers of goods and the clients or consumers of these goods becomes highly marked.

In the field of services, however, the distinction is often less clear. There are many basic services which everyone—except the ultrarich and indolent who are waited on hand and foot by servants and valets—must perform for himself. But even in performing services for others, there is a very fundamental sense in which the producer himself becomes a client. The service which is involved in any form of human labor, whether manual or mental, skilled or unskilled, satisfies certain physiological or psychological needs of the person who performs the service. If these needs are not sufficiently met, it is highly doubtful if the production process can be effective or efficient. If they are given undue stress, the service producer becomes self-serving. Thus we find the government official whose main concern is his use of power, the teacher whose main delight is hearing his own voice and the social worker whose chief purpose is meeting the needs of his own personality rather than of his clients.

4. BLURRED BOUNDARIES

All goods have clearly defined spatial boundaries. It is easy to tell where one unit ends and another begins.

With many services the boundary lines are much harder to find. As activities, they are often continuous processes, with no clear beginning or end. The end of a violin concert may mark the end of a particular service by a concert violinist. But the service of an accountant, a general or a secretary is rarely terminated at the end of a fiscal year, a battle or a meeting. The end of a given time period may find the service half-completed and the completion of one phase of a service may lead imperceptibly into many others. Many related services are often inextricably intermingled.

Moreover, since services are activities, the dividing line between input and output is often much less clear than in the case of goods. When a teacher appears before his students, his activity is at the one and the same time his labor input and a teaching service. Which it is depends upon the vantage point from which one looks at it. When the teacher writes a textbook, however, the input in the form of labor vanishes as soon as it occurs. He, himself, will probably remember the labor input, but the reader sees only the "good."

The consumers and suppliers of bread may argue vigorously as to whether a loaf of bread has the desired weight, flavor, degree of cleanliness or number of calories. But at least they know they are talking about bread and not butter.

In the case of services, one may dispute the very identity of the product. What are the services of a personnel officer, a planning expert, an economic adviser? Different people within an organization may have entirely different—even sharply clashing—conceptions of these services. Their needs differ, and so do their demands with respect to the services which may contribute to the satisfaction of these needs. These differences may relate not only to the substantive content of the activity performed, but also to the degree of administrative authority and responsibility to be exercised. In the interest of internal peace the organization may prefer ambivalence with respect to the nature of these services.

Government agencies serve the ends not only of entire communities but also of specific groups within a community. Many of these groups have conflicting interests. Thus when we ask what are the precise services to be rendered by government agencies dealing with education, health, police and economic affairs, we immediately enter the field of major clashes between interest groups and political parties. Here political advantages are often found in ambiguities and compromises which may make it extremely difficult to determine just what service is being performed.

c. *The Service Basis of Production*

ONE WAY TO appreciate the importance of services is to look at their role in the total national product and income of various countries. In almost all countries of the world the service sectors add up to at least one-third of the national income. In the richer countries the proportion tends to reach one-half. In the United States of America, despite Galbraith's attack on the relative overexpansion of goods, the proportion of services to goods is unquestionably the highest in the world. Moreover, the general tendency in the highly industrialized countries is toward a relative expansion in the service sectors. Galbraith's position is merely that this trend should move still faster and should provide still greater emphasis upon certain publicly produced services.

In a deeper sense, however, services play a still more critical role, no matter what the balance may be between different components of national product and income. This role stems from the fact that services are the basis of *all* production processes.

When we say that a factory produces an icebox or a worker produces a valve, we are correct only in the sense that we are using the concept of *available output*. The statement is acceptable from the point of view of the wholesaler who receives the iceboxes from the factory and the assembly operator who places the valves in the icebox.

But the statement is incorrect as a representation of what the factory or worker have done. For this, we need the *contributed output* concept. Neither factory nor worker made the metal. They merely added certain services. Nor did the supplier of the original metal produce the metal. The metal came from the ground in the first instance. All the so-called processes of "production" consisted merely of various services applied to the hard goods obtained from the ground or from processors who had already applied certain services. Goods are not created by man's production processes. They are material inputs that are obtained externally and processed through various productive services.

Production processes in general, whether the output consists of goods or services, may be regarded as consisting of two types of services: (1) holding and moving, and (2) dividing and uniting. These services may be applied to inputs of things or information or to people who, like the railroad's passengers or the hospital's patients, are the direct clients of the services provided. In organizations the successful provision of these services is dependent upon administration, an intermediate service composed of various facets of these two major types.

1. UNITING AND DIVIDING

By uniting I refer to the various production processes usually referred to as assembly, joining or synthesis, and by dividing to separation, reduction, and shaping. The transformation of goods through manufacture always results from some combination of these services. Yet even when there are no goods to be transformed, it is these same services which produce service end products.

A. *Uniting*. In the case of goods, processed parts may be united by mere assembly. Such materials as metal, plastic, cloth, or wood may be pressed together through welds, screws, nails, glues, and other joining methods. With chemicals the joining process takes place through the synthesis of molecular components.

People also are brought together through physical means—although here pressure takes entirely different forms. It may be actually applied, as with rewards and punishments; it can be made effective through the perceived possibility of future application, as with promises and threats. But here a new factor enters the picture, persuasion. People, in contradistinction to things, can be brought together by persuasive appeals.

The assembly of ideas or feelings is basically an intellectual or artistic process. It may take place at the level of routine collection and eclecticism or at the highest level of creative synthesis.

B. *Dividing*. Here various materials are cut into pieces, trimmed down to size, or as in the case of petroleum refining, reduced to a large number of components.

People are only rarely subjected to the reduction process—as in the borderline cases of dental extractions, surgical extractions, and amputations, and hair and nail trimming. If reduction is carried too far, it leads to extermination. Short of this, groups of people may be divided by the use of pressure or persuasion to separate what has previously been brought together.

The division of ideas into their component parts is one of the major intellectual processes. In its highest form, it is based upon the fairly well developed technologies of deductive logic and pure mathematics.

2. MOVING AND HOLDING

By "moving" I am referring not only to the transportation of things and people but to the communication of information, by "holding" to the storage not only of goods on shelves but also of information in memory systems.

A. *Moving*. In the process of uniting or dividing a certain amount of movement is always required. This may consist of a continuous, one-direction movement, as in a classical assembly line, or a straight-line chemical reduction process. Or it may involve a complex choreography which moves materials back and forth between a large variety of organizational units specializing upon specific types of assembly or reduction services.

Perhaps the greatest technological developments in the field of movement have taken place in the field of services. Thus things and people, which were previously moved by camel, horse, or automobile, can now be propelled through the air at speeds far in excess of the speed of sound and over distances that will eventually make interplanetary travel a feasible operation.

A closely related but much more complex technology is found in the field of communication of ideas and feelings. With or without assembly and reduction, these may be moved within a vast network of interpersonal relations through a growing variety of communication mechanisms.

ʙ. *Holding.* In the case of things holding is a relatively passive operation. In its simplest form it involves nothing more than supplying a resting place in shelves, warehouses and filing cabinets. In its more active form it involves little more than protective action to prevent degeneration processes (whether rust, decay, mold, or melting) or the use of pressure to prevent movement, as in the case of materials held under the bit of a lathe.

In the case of people, the holding process has two aspects. A minor aspect is found in those services which involve the holding of people. Here perhaps the only pure holding operation is that which takes place, through the combined use of pressure and persuasion, in keeping people in prisons, mental hospitals and other closed institutions.

The second, and more important, aspect is found in those services which aim at getting people to hold on to information through the processes of memory, habituation, and learning. Special technologies aimed at achieving this objective have been developed in connection with both educational and therapeutic processes.

In this case we see a phenomenon which is a distinctive characteristic of many services: the recipient may take an active part in the production process. In the production of goods this cannot happen. The wood and slate which serve as the materials in the production of a teacher's blackboard react in accordance with physical or chemical laws; they will not act on their own. But in the production of teaching services—whether they involve the assembly, reduction, movement or holding of ideas and feelings—some students can be expected to initiate action on their own part. They may even become partners in the production process. Thus it may be said while systems of goods production are closed, production systems in the field of services are often open to the possibility of active client participation. This possibility is particularly apparent in the case of services produced by teachers, doctors, advisers, and—above all—administrators.

3. THE PRODUCTIVE NATURE OF ADMINISTRATION

Of all services, administration more than any other has borne the brunt of accumulated prejudices. The costs of administration are usually lumped together with other things into "burden" and "overhead" costs, with a still stronger presumption that they are "unproductive." This point of view is reinforced by the natural resentment of subordinates against their administrative superiors. In crude terms this is expressed in the quasi-Marxist stereotype *"we* do all the work while *they* just reap the benefits." It is expressed in the more sophisticated, but no less hollow, fiction that the successful administrator is somebody who gets everything done by others and may therefore sit idly at an empty, uncluttered desk doing nothing at all. Finally, the view that administration is unproductive is buttressed by the internal distress of many administrators themselves. As an intermediate service, administration often seems far removed from the end products of an organization. As an intangible service, it is hard to pin down. Many administrators suffer from a queasy feeling that they are not sure what they are doing or why.

Yet some types and amounts of administrative activity are essential to the production of any goods or services by an organization. Mere spontaneous cooperation as already pointed out in Chapter 2, is not sufficient to assure the sustained coordination of the various changing types of uniting, dividing, moving and holding services. In other words, administrators make it possible for people to produce. In this sense, *administration itself is one of the most productive of all human activities.*

This fact need not prevent us from branding as "unproductive" any end products that we do not like or value. It does not keep us from finding that in any particular organization there may be more administrative activity than is needed. It need not interfere with our attacking as "unproductive" any particular administrator who seems to get little accomplished or to prevent others from accomplishing anything.

D. *Surrogates for Intangible Services*

How CAN WE APPRAISE the quality of services rendered by a school, a research department or a ministry or department of foreign affairs?

How can we calculate their quantity?

These questions are not rendered much easier by a willingness to forego cardinal numbers and interval scales. In the case of such intangible services it is difficult enough to find a basis for rough orders of magnitude or ordinal ranking.

The first step in trying to answer such questions is, as indicated in Chapter 14, to deal with the logically prior question, "What kind?" The services rendered by most schools, research departments and foreign ministries are usually, indeed, a complex output mix. Rather than try to deal with the entire mix in some overall fashion, it makes more sense to deal separately with each major component in the mix.

But any single component may itself be extremely hard to pin down. This is well illustrated when we try to appraise the quality and quantity of a teacher's services in a specific course or a researcher's work on a specific inquiry. Here we have no choice but to look for various surrogates that can be used as substitutes.

In the most fundamental sense, the entire appraisal of quality rests upon the use of surrogates. Clientele satisfaction, as pointed out in the previous chapter, provides the highest level of quality specification. Yet the appraisal of human satisfactions, whether of clients or anyone else, can be done only through the use of surrogates. As pointed out in Chapter 12. the surrogates of satisfaction or dissatisfaction are (a) choices made, (b) payments given, (c) opinions expressed, and (d) subsequent results. The other levels of product specification may also be used: product characteristics, production processes, and input factors. In the case of services, however, each of these may itself be extremely hard to pin down. When they are precise—as with the use of approved techniques or the academic degrees obtained by personnel—they are apt to be rough indicators only and subject to serious misinterpretation.

The quantity of intangible services is still harder to pin down. Here the basic problem is the identification of activities that can be counted or measured in terms of greater or lesser volume. Where discrete activities cannot be identified, we have no choice but to use one or more quantity surrogates.

1. NUMBER OF CLIENTS

The first quantity surrogate is the number of clients served. Thus the output volume of schools, hospitals, and social workers is often measured by the numbers of students, patients and, social work cases. In their function as service surrogates, such clients may be classified by the subjects taught, the ailments treated, and the nature of personal and family difficulties. They may also be classified in stages of service rendered. Thus the number of college students may be counted for each year in a three- or four-year program. Patients may be divided into pre-operation, post-operation and convalescent. Social work cases may be divided into active, inactive and closed cases.

Even in the case of unseen and indirect clients, it may be possible with enough effort to count the clients who are served. The classic example is that of the radio broadcasting station. As a basic test of its effectiveness it must make some survey of the number of listeners. It is also possible for government administrators to estimate the number of people who, as members of groups affected by particular decisions or activities, are served by them.

2. DURATION OF SERVICE

Of all the characteristics of services, duration is the most suitable as a surrogate—and one of the most widely used. Thus the quantity of teaching services is often measured by their duration. In fact, "semester hours," "annual hours," and "weekly hours" are the building blocks from which teaching curricula and students' educational programs are built. They are flexible and convenient units. They can be divided by subject matter—French, philosophy, physics, and administration. They can be subdivided by types and processes—graduate, undergraduate, seminar, laboratory, exercises, review. They can be added up into the work load of teachers and the minimum requirements of students.

Duration surrogates are particularly useful when combined with clients into the double surrogate of client-duration. Thus instead of counting students or teaching hours alone, we may count student hours. The resulting figures, properly subdivided by subjects and levels, will come much closer than either surrogate separately to an approximation of the quantity of teaching services. Similar computations can be made for patient days (sometimes referred to more abstractly as bed days) and case work hours.

Here again it must be emphasized that a surrogate, even a double one, is not the service itself. A measurement of one hundred student hours is no direct indication of what has been done, either by teacher or student, within the time period under consideration. Part of the time may be content-thin. Part may be pure waste. A more effective teacher might be able to provide the same amount of teaching services in half the time.

3. INTERMEDIATE OR SUBSEQUENT PRODUCTS

Where tangible end products cannot be found, it may nonetheless be possible to find many intermediate products that are very tangible and can easily be counted. In office work one can readily count committee meetings, conferences, telephone calls, interviews, and inspection trips. One can count lectures, quizzes, and examinations in teaching. One can count the number of injections given and bed pans emptied by nurses. The most universal of tangible intermediate services is the preparation, transmission, reading, or storage of letters, memoranda, and reports. Such written documents can readily be seen, counted, or even weighed.

There is not always a clear relationship, however, between the quantity of end and intermediate products. In fact, the very act of focusing strong attention on tangible intermediate products may result in diverting attention from, and reducing the quantity of, the end products.

Tangible units may also be found by focusing on a subsequent stage of the production process. Thus the output of a valve grinding unit may be calculated not in terms of grinding services but in terms of valves passed on to the polishers. The polishers, in turn, may count their output not by polishing services but by the number of valves passed on to the next stage. Essentially, this is the available output concept once again. When contributed output is intangible, available output may serve as a quantity surrogate.

4. INPUT FACTORS

Here again, just as with interest satisfactions, input factors may serve as surrogates.

Labor is perhaps the input factor most widely used for this purpose. Its use is promoted by the fact that with many services labor seems to be equivalent, or almost equivalent, to the full service itself. This phenomenon is particularly evident when we measure labor in terms of time. Thus ten hours of a teacher's work or a nurse's work might seem to be equivalent to ten hours of teaching or nursing services. Actually, the difference may be very great—as when a teacher spends three to four hours of preparation before every one hour of actual teaching.

Another limitation on the use of labor as a service surrogate is that many services require inputs of materials, facilities, and equipment. This limitation can be overcome by using aggregate costs (that is, the monetary sum of all commonly counted input factors) as a surrogate for output value. As pointed out in Chapter 13, this is one of the ways to impute the value of nonmarketed goods.

A more basic difficulty with any form of surrogate in terms of labor inputs or aggregate costs is that, as with the use of duration units, it may interfere with the calculation of efficiency. An output-input relationship cannot very well be established if the same input factor is itself used as a measurement of both.

E. *Service Goals and Administrative Techniques*

THERE IS a deep and little-recognized ambiguity in much of the literature and practice with respect to service goals. This ambiguity is rooted in the use—or misuse—of the techniques of job description, job specification and job evaluation. It spills over into, and exercises a disorganizing effect upon, the use of other administrative techniques.

This ambiguity centers around the fact that the terms "functions," "jobs," "tasks," or "duties" can be used in both a specific and a general sense.

In the more specific sense the functions of an organization, unit or individual consist of a detailed output mix. They are defined by answering the three basic questions: What kind? How good? and How much?

In the more general sense the functions may be usually stated by answering the first question only: What kind? This requires a little more than a simple list of the kinds of output. In the case of individuals, these functions may be associated with a *job* (or *position* or *office*) instead of an individual. Thus in a large construction organization the job of construction engineer could be held by many different people at the same time—some working on houses, some on bridges, and some on roads.

For the sake of clarity I shall refer to the former as *operational goals* and the latter as *general functions*. After explaining each of these concepts and the relation between them, I shall then turn to the closely related fields of performance rating and performance budgeting.

1. OPERATING GOALS

The existence of operational goals is a *sine qua non* of organizational activity. All members and units of an organization have some idea—however fuzzy or mistaken it may be—of what they are trying to do, of what is expected from them. Except in highly repetitive and highly routinized undertakings, these operation goals are subject to constant flux. Administrators try to see to it that the goals of individuals and groups fit together, to guide the process of goal change and adaptation, and to cope with the more serious goal conflicts.

As already indicated, a full set of operational goals may be regarded as a detailed output mix dealing with the kind, quality and quantity of services to be rendered. Thus, in accordance with the theory of product specification (as set forth in Chapter 14) questions of kind and quality break down into the following specific questions:

Client satisfactions	Who are the clients?
	What interests or needs of these clients are to be satisfied?
Product characteristics	What are the specific activities to be performed?
	Where, when, how fast and for how long?
	What are the other distinguishing characteristics?
Production processes	What methods are to be used?
	What particular sequences or styles of action?
Input factors	What manpower inputs?
	What material inputs?
	What inputs of machinery, equipment and other facilities?

The question of quantity may be answered in part by the specifications concerning speed and duration. But this itself requires a pinning down of specific activities. Where this is not possible, as shown in the previous section, there is no choice but to use one or more quantity surrogates: number of clients, duration, intermediate or subsequent products, or input factors.

In preparing for unique or unprecedented operations it is usually customary to spell out all or most of these various facets of output. A typical case is the operational goals required for the construction of a house. More dramatic examples may be found in military operations. In both cases considerable effort will be spent in spelling out the input factors, the methods to be used and the activities to be undertaken. With respect to client satisfaction, somewhat more attention will probably be given to the internal clientele, that is, to the services to be rendered by carpenters in preparing the way for the painters or by the artillery in preparing the way for the infantry. The builders may give much less thought to the satisfactions to be obtained by the people who will live in the house. Many military officers may not even be able to imagine the role of this specific battle in the grand strategy (if any) of national conflict.

Another circumstance favoring the spelling out of operational goals is the need for closely integrated activity on the part of entirely different units or organizations. When people are formally subdivided into special units, the subdivision may enter their inner life. It is the formal and publicized framework for their individual status and group identification. They are members of an accounting division, a sociology department, a stamping department, a research unit, an artillery platoon. This is the point at which they receive their financial remuneration and from which they may aspire to move to a better or higher position. Whatever cooperation may actually take place with people from other compartments as an essential part of operations tends to be dimly perceived, or else seen as unwarranted interference in *their* work. Thus the stamping operation in a metalworking "production unit" may well be an operation which calls for as much integration as that needed between the pilots, artillerymen, and infantrymen trying to capture an enemy post. But the maintenance men, methods analysts, safety inspectors, and quality controllers may often be seen as nonproductive interlopers who are intervening in the operations of the machine operators.

Thus methods are needed to combat this tendency toward psychological isolation and to promote common efforts on behalf of a coordinated operation. The customary device in military organizations is to provide a special name—such as Operation Overlord or Operation Bolero—and detailed descriptions for specific operations. The fact that Operation Overlord was a code name should not lead us to think that military secrecy was the reason for giving the operation such a label. On the contrary, naming it made it harder to keep it a secret from the enemy. But it also made it easier to develop the widespread cooperative effort needed to make the operation feasible.

In civilian organizations, apart from occasional use of the military device of giving special names to specific operations, many other devices have been used for similar purposes. Special operations may be put into the hands of "task forces." More repetitive and routinized operations may be turned over to standing interdepartmental committees. In many universities research operations cutting across interdepartmental boundaries are often turned over to special institutes or centers which draw upon different departments for their personnel. Yet in these situations it is much rarer for specific operations to be separately labeled or separately specified. There is a much greater tendency for the edges of operations to be loose and fuzzy—with one operation mixing in with another so that it is extremely difficult to tell where one begins and another ends.

In all complex operations, whether civilian or military, there is a tendency for the more tangible, comprehensible, or familiar operations to attract a disproportionate amount of attention. This tendency becomes most pronounced in the case of concrete, intermediate services—such as report writing, bookkeeping, or inspection—within a broader operation which is undefined. Under such circumstances, one can hardly blame the report writer and bookkeeper for developing a report-writing or bookkeeping mentality. When it is hard to see the woods (and even the higher executives might not have made the effort), one can hardly expect technicians or specialists to see anything but their own favorite trees. One of the great paradoxes of administrative action is that rational efforts to clarify output objectives at any one point—by focusing major attention on that one point—may make it still harder for anyone to see the woods.

One might think that on something so fundamental as an organization's daily operations, the problem of the clarity-vagueness balance (as discussed in Chapter 11) might be a minor one. Certainly, this is a field in which a high degree of clarity is both feasible and essential. No airline could operate without its flight schedule, no battle without its battle plan. Even in the case of less tangible activities clearly defined sequences of action are indispensable to establish the roles of individuals and units, to provide for communication and cooperation between them, and to provide criteria for judging success or failure.

Yet there are many things that operational specifications cannot do. They cannot lay out all possible lines of desired action. They cannot cope with the unexpected. They cannot take the place of initiative and discretion. In short, they cannot do more than lay out certain broad boundaries for human activity.

The dilemmas of specificity become particularly acute with respect to formal documentation. In any operation of even moderate complexity there is a mass of detail that cannot be handled unless reduced to writing. The written word is essential to the assembly, storage, analysis and dissemination of information. It also has tremendous symbolic value. "In the Beginning was the Word," wrote the Apostle (John, 1:1). Written words are often the authoritative signals or guides for the beginning of organizational operations. When they come forth from electronic computers, they are still more authoritative.

In the theatre a script is needed to guide the operations. But a professional performance of *Hamlet* could never be achieved merely by relying on Shakespeare's script alone. Good actors usually change the script in many ways. They always add to it many elements of style, voice, meaning, and "stage business" that Shakespeare would never have tried to write down. The director, above all, provides the stimulus and the coordination required to undertake the activities that could never have been frozen in writing in advance.

In administration, also, "the play's the thing" and not the script. Many aspects of even the simplest operation can never be expressed in writing. They must be sensed and felt. Others can simply never be written down in official documents; they deal with delicate relations that had better be left at the level of informal understanding and subliminal awareness.

In administration, moreover, there are many more changes in the plot. With changes in the clientele network and in the satisfaction-dissatisfaction nexus of both outsiders and members, changes must always take place in the end product mix and in the internal product flow. The pace of this change often precludes any painstaking process of continuous amendment of current operating plans. Daily action is the key channel of operational definition. In supplying cues and suggestions, in voicing praise and blame, in issuing verbal instructions, administrators define or clarify operational goals in real life. If written plans are seen as the major instruments for clarifying output objectives, they are nothing but a snare and a delusion—and a pathetic way of wasting the money of an organization and the time of its members. They can be no substitute for the action definitions which, because they are expressed in life instead of petty legalisms, give the members of an organization an ingrained feeling and understanding of common objectives.

2. GENERAL FUNCTIONS

In order to carry on their operations, organizations develop various conceptions of general functions (in the sense defined above). These functions are determined both formally and informally. They include not only the written word but also the unwritten and the unwriteable. They are major factors defining the social role of every organization, unit and member.

The general functions of an organization as a whole are proclaimed in any list of the items in its output mix. Business organizations habitually prepare lists of some sorts in order to attract customers. Organizations producing nonmarketed products customarily include such listings in oral and written statements used to mobilize resources, win support, and report to members or controllers. With some organizations—as with the General Motors Corporation or a mental health hospital—the major functions may be suggested by the name itself. Often they may be indicated by listing the major units of the organization, many of which will carry the names of a general product line.

At the level of units within an organization, with names becoming more descriptive of operations, specific statements of function tend to become more remote from them. One reason is the tendency to root such statements in the division of labor only—with little attention to the operating interaction among what has been divided. This tendency is supported by the fact that such statements are usually generated as part of internal competition for status and resources. In the case of units producing intangible services, moreover, there is a tendency for individual units to define their own functions less in terms of what they do and more in terms of what they would like to do if they could.

At the level of the individual, there are many purposes to be served by detailed statements of general functions. As shown below, various techniques have been developed to serve these purposes:

GENERAL STATEMENTS OF INDIVIDUAL FUNCTIONS

Purposes	*Technique*
To help in recruitment	Occupational analysis of the labor force, or major sectors thereof
To help establish positions (jobs or offices)	Job description (also referred to as position classification)
To serve as a guide in recruitment, promotion and training	Job specification
To assist in the determination of pay scales	Job evaluation

Although the personnel experts in this field would like to develop standardized terminology for other people's jobs, they have not yet done so for their own. Hence the various terms in the right-hand column are often used interchangeably. Job analysis may be used to refer to any one of them or to the process of obtaining data for all of them.

Most of these techniques purport to be rooted in operations—in the services that people are expected to provide. Yet there is a general tendency for job description and specification to lose contact with operations. This phenomenon has been recognized by one of the ablest technicians in the field, Carroll Shartle: "The statement of work performed is the heart of job analysis. It is probably also the phase which is likely to be the least well done" (1955, p. 134).

The major reason that "the statement of work performed . . . is likely to be the least well done" is not the difficulty of pinning down intangible services. Nor is it even the lack of conceptual sophistication in dealing with the kind, quality and quantity of service output. It is rather that other elements in such statements often attract the lion's share of attention. These include:

Hierarchical location
Grade and salary
Title of job or position
Qualifications of incumbents (including education, experience, and other personal capacities)
Rank with respect to common characteristics of all positions (such as qualifications, effort, responsibility, initiative, judgment and working conditions)

The first three of these factors involve the social status of every incumbent. As such, they tend to draw attention away from the output aspects of social role. Thus the most precise parts of job descriptions are those statements identifying those *to whom* (and *for whom*) an incumbent is responsible, and specifying grade, salary, and title. They are also the most reliable. Information on *for what* he is responsible will usually be nondescriptive (particularly in nonroutine jobs) and out-of-date. It will often be designed mainly to justify the hierarchical location, salary, and title.

The title of a job or position, like the name of a unit or organization, may often suggest the types of services to be rendered. Indeed, with increasing specialization and professionalization, there is a tendency toward occupational distinctions that convey meaningful information. There are many types of welders and many types of doctors. At the administrative level, however, titles tend to become meaningless. One can never tell the kinds of things a person is supposed to do from such titles as assistant director, deputy director, executive or administrative assistant, or vice president. More important, there is a widespread tendency to flatter employees by giving them high-sounding titles. One of the oldest jokes in business (applicable to any other organization as well) is: "Give a man a new title to avoid giving him a raise." A fancy title may also impress clients and other external individuals and groups. Thus the title of "salesman" is rapidly being replaced by "sales engineer," "regional manager," and "territory manager." As with Operation Overlord, the name itself does not suggest what activities are to be undertaken. It is not the label that counts, but the information behind it.

Information on the "qualifications of incumbents" defines a set of services in terms of the quality of one input factor, manpower. As such, it is relevant to service specification, but at the lowest level of the hierarchy of product definition (Chapt. 14). It is easy for the link to be lost (or, in fact, never to have existed) between the qualifications used as criteria for recruitment or promotion and the kinds of activities actually expected of incumbents.

Information on such factors as the degree of effort, responsibility, judgment and initiative is at a higher level of product specification; it deals directly with product characteristics. But in job evaluation the purpose is to rank jobs within a salary structure. Such ranking must be made in terms of common characteristics. The distinguishing facets of the kinds of work performed vanish from sight. If available, they might have been used in preparing the raw materials for evaluation. But job evaluators will rarely, if ever, go to the trouble of starting their work by preparing job descriptions based upon the hard core of service output.

In an open rank system, such as is used in the British and Indian civil service and in most military and foreign services, it is often said that job descriptions are not used. Here a person's salary, status, and hierarchical position are determined by his "personal rank," not by the particular job he happens to occupy at a given time. Here, too, formal job descriptions often come into being as generalized descriptions of the kinds of services usually expected from, let us say, artillery captains and first secretaries of embassies. Here too, even more than in many other organizations, people are expected to "know their job"—that is, know their specific output goals in one post as distinguished from what they were in a previous post. The use of personal rank systems for the purposes of salary classification, promotion and recruitment does not detract one iota from the overriding importance of individual output goals. It detracts only in part from the use of statements of general functions. Whether written or unwritten, concepts of general function are essential for purposes of recruitment, training and promotion.

In this respect, the major difference between "personal rank" and "job classification" systems is that in the former the concepts of general function may tend toward an extreme of informality. (as in the British and Indian civil services) and in the latter toward the other extreme of documentary formalism (as in the U.S. Federal civil service). In either case, and even in the ideal case of the happy medium between the two, general functions are never as important as operating goals. An incumbent who knows only his job description is still a long way from knowing his job. To state the point more technically, it is the more concrete and ever-changing operating goals (upon which any meaningful statements of general functions must be based) that embody the purposefulness of organizations.

3. PERFORMANCE RATING

The question "How well did he—or they—do?" relates logically to the quality and quantity of services rendered.

One might suppose, therefore, that in systems specially established to rationalize the evaluation of performance, concentrated attention would be given to the comparison of observed performance with operating goals for the quality and quantity of output. Indeed, we find just this in the methods often used by military staffs in evaluating military operations, by airlines in evaluating the performance of pilots, and by a few other agencies dealing with operations that have been systematically analyzed if not routinized.

But we find something quite different—and rather depressing—in many of the formal systems appearing under the name of performance rating, merit rating, service rating or efficiency rating. Most of these systems have not been devised to serve the needs of those responsible for organizational performance. They often come into being, rather, as instruments of *superministration* by higher control agencies that want to see if the workers "down there" do their work efficiently. Or else they are approached in the framework of *subministration*. They provide information for use not in the guidance of performance but in handling promotions, occasional decisions on terminations, and disciplinary action. In industry, one of the pressures toward merit rating has come from incentive pay schemes which have made it possible for workers in routinized operations to earn more money than their supervisors. Merit rating holds forth the promise of overcoming such disparities by providing a basis for increasing supervisory pay also.

Few such systems use as their starting point a person's specific goals for the quality and quantity of output during a specific period. Most of them are devised by staff specialists who are not very familiar with or interested in operations. When administrators and employees do not have a sense of purposefulness, the staff specialist will rarely have the insight and courage to point out that the clarification of output objectives is the prerequisite for rational evaluation. Rather, "general qualities such as cooperativeness, tact, initiative and resourcefulness tend to be weighted out of proportion to the performance requirements of particular types of job responsibilities." Moreover, there is a widespread tendency to use the same rating system for a variety of purposes other than the performance in a specific job: "appraisal of growth potential, training needed, fitness for promotion or suitable next assignment."[4] To make matters worse, the rating process is often excessively quantified—with precise numbers and weights used for each criterion and provision for aggregating the numbers so that every rated employee comes out with a number or label attached to his name. Finally, all this is embedded in an elaborate framework of review, consultation, and other reinforcing rituals.

Under such conditions performance rating may fan interpersonal tensions in an unnecessary manner and result in a considerable loss of time and energy in maneuvering, informal bargaining, and formal appeals for revision. These tensions and losses will become even greater if an effort is made to keep the ratings secret. Although designed to help improve performance, performance rating may thus contribute to its deterioration.

When a performance rating system interferes with their work instead of helping them, many administrators will take the easy way out. They will "ride with the system" by filling out the forms in some standardized fashion that will not create trouble and that has very little connection

---

4. Both these quotations are from the Committee on Foreign Affairs Personnel, 1963, p. 92-93. Although these findings refer specifically to rating practices in the U.S. Foreign Service, they are applicable to the majority of performance rating systems.

with their real evaluations. They can thus transform the system from a major impediment into a minor nuisance at the cost of just a little more waste in paperwork.

Because of the widespread dissatisfaction with performance rating, a search for more useful approaches has come into being. These include such methods as the encouragement of self-rating, the divorce of rating from disciplinary matters, and the abandonment of over-all numerical evaluations.[5] The most fruitful approach to the evaluation of individual performance is one that centers around a person's own formulation of his output goals. The prerequisite for this, obviously, is that he have output goals. This, in turn, is possible only if the goals formulated for him by the organization be internalized by a process of integration (or compromise) with his personal goals. Under these circumstances his administrative superior enters the picture less as a stern deity who decides *ex post facto* whether he goes to heaven or hell, but more as an aide, adviser or catalyst in the integration of personal with organizational goals. The rating process and the control process can thus become an inherent part of individual performance. The administrator's contribution to performance rating is thus part of his basic task of guiding the activities of his unit or organization.

4. PERFORMANCE BUDGETING

Another approach to the specification of operations and missions is found in the increasing efforts by government agencies to develop "performance" or "program" budgets. Traditional government budgeting has usually consisted of lists of specific inputs—manpower, equipment, and materials—and their costs, grouped in accordance with the organization and units receiving budgetary allocations and using inputs. Such input lists cannot by themselves give much of an idea as to the nature of the output expected to result.

One of the first proposals aimed at dealing more clearly with the output side as well was contained in a report of the first Hoover Commission:

> We recommend that the whole budgetary concept of the Federal Government should be refashioned by the adoption of a budget based on functions, activities and projects: this we designate a "performance budget" (U.S. Commission on the Organization of the Executive Branch of the Government, 1949, p. 8).

5. For a critical review of customary performance rating practices, together with a discussion of more positive approaches, see Douglas McGregor, 1957 and 1960.

A more sophisticated presentation is found in Mosher's proposal for program budgeting by defense agencies in the U. S. A.:

> The changes which we have come to associate with performance budgeting, such as simplifications, and others, important as they are, are only a part of the concept. Underlying them is a notion which represents a quite radical departure from previous practice and previous ways of thinking. It is simply that when we budget and authorize funds we are providing for things to be *done* rather than for things to be *bought*. Moneys are furnished for activities and functions rather than for purchases and payments. . . . In a sense this amounts to substituting ends for means as the focal points of financial planning and control (1954, p. 81).

Many writers and practitioners have followed the example of Burkhead and distinguished between a *performance budget*, which deals with a narrower form of operation, and a *program budget*, which "embraces a number of performance units" (1956, p. 139).

The high expectations aroused by the campaign to establish performance and program budgets have only been partly fulfilled. In fact, a campaign originally designed to give increased clarity and precision to government budgets has itself led to an abundance of obfuscation. One reason, as explained in Chapter 18, is that the budget-making is inevitably a process of sharp conflict among groups and within groups. The maneuvering and tactical plays of the budgetary conflict require a certain amount of smoke-screen operations. Thus many executive officials of government supported performance budgeting because they thought it would weaken Congressional control—particularly if it could replace previous forms of input accounting. Many taxpayers' organizations and members of Congress saw it as a way to supplement traditional forms and strengthen Congressional control. They approached performance budgeting in the framework of what might be called *superministrative* budgeting, the process of supervising or checking on what someone else administered. Less attention was given to performance budgeting as an internal tool, as an element in the "use logic" of an organization's activities.

In addition, discussions of the subject have suffered from terminological sloppiness. The Hoover Commission's words "functions, activities, and projects," cover a lot of different ideas. The same can be said for "things to be done." Nor does it help to say that such a budget emphasizes "purpose"; we have already seen what a variety of concepts may be included within the idea of "organizational purpose."

The key concept in the consideration of performance budgeting is that of *output*. A performance budget is one which first identifies the output of an organization or unit thereof, provides the most relevant and feasible information on its quality and quantity, and then relates input to output. In so doing, it is essential to focus upon the end products of the organization or unit. In budgets for such concrete things as public buildings and roads, insofar as construction specifications have been available, we have always had a clear basis for performance budgeting. One need only identify specific buildings or specific road sections and then allocate to them all the costs relevant to their construction.[6] This is one of the reasons it is ridiculous to imply that performance budgeting requires a *complete* refashioning of government budgets. Actually, it requires nothing more than a special effort to do for intangible services what has often been done or approximated in budgets for organizations producing tangible products. In short, a performance budget is any set of output goals (as defined in this chapter), to which is added a calculation of the inputs required to achieve them.

6. The process of allocation may be somewhat difficult when such costs are spread over a number of budget years or when the costs of different buildings or roads are lumped together. Also, when the output is composed of unique products, over-all cost comparisons are not very relevant, and meaningful cost analysis may be possible only by concentrating attention upon more standardized intermediate units of output.

Chapter 16

EFFICIENCY OR PROFITABILITY

*F*OR DECADES efficiency, economy, productivity, and profitability have been sacred cows of administration. A quasireligious fervor has often been aroused by the Gulick maxim that "in the science of administration, whether private or public, the basic good is efficiency." Others have used "economy" with equal enthusiasm. "Virtually the whole world has within our time," Parsons observed, "come to assign to economic productivity a very high value indeed" (1960, p. 100). Among many economic theorists and some businessmen, "profitability" is often acclaimed as an ultimate aim.

Although all these terms have different referents and each has many variants, they have something in common beyond the fact that their proponents often evidence more fervor than clarity. The common element is that each deals with an input-output relation. Whether physical or monetary terms are used, the aim is to reduce input in relation to output or increase output in relation to input.

The task of this chapter is to help clarify the nature of input-output objectives as a whole. This will place them in an appropriate perspective as important—although sometimes subordinate or forgotten—elements in the matrix of organizational purposes.

I shall start by discussing the role of input-output objectives, with particular attention to their instrumental character and the limitations on their use. I shall then deal with inputs and cost, taking a quick look at some of the mysteries of cost calculation.

Against this background I shall then survey the broad array of alternative input-output measures: the "partial" ratios, the "broad" relation of profitability, and other "broad" relations. In addition to shedding some light on the alternative uses of each concept, this discussion will reveal some of the paths that are taken in the effort to attain greater efficiency, economy, productivity, or profitability.

A. *The Role of Input-Output Objectives*

INPUT-OUTPUT OBJECTIVES are still more complex than the output objectives discussed in the previous three chapters. In addition to the output side, they also include two additional elements: some measure of input and some relation between the two.

Yet they are by no means as significant as output objectives. As will soon be explained, their role depends mainly upon the perception of resource scarcity. Moreover, their usefulness is impeded by serious practical difficulties.

1. THEIR INSTRUMENTAL ROLE

When input-output objectives are viewed in the context of the global matrix of organizational purposes, it becomes clear that in an analytic sense none of them can be regarded as "ultimate" or "overriding." Hence special attention is needed to their inherently instrumental nature.

First of all, a certain minimum relation between output and input is essential for the survival of any organization. Just as staggering losses (negative profits) will doom a business organization, wanton wastefulness in the use of inputs will threaten the continued existence of any organization.

Second, output objectives are often inextricably associated with tacit assumptions concerning relations with input. When output objectives are raised, it is often taken for granted—even though input measures may not be explicitly used—that certain inputs will not rise proportionately. This latent role of input-output relations is fostered by the variety of input measures that may be implicit in the situation.

Third, more desirable input-output relations may make it easier for an organization to achieve other goals. Improvements in productivity are a classic way of easing the tensions that arise from sharp inequalities. When it is possible to increase the size of the pie, it is somewhat easier to satisfy interests that would otherwise require a redistribution of a smaller pie. When the pie is bigger, it may also be easier to achieve a higher quality or better composition of output, to mobilize external resources, to observe prescribed codes of conduct and to improve technical and administrative rationality. Above all, input-output objectives are habitually seen as instruments of satisfying human interests. If output is the vehicle for satisfying certain interests, the costs of input are seen as providing dissatisfaction for other interests. Thus input reduction or output increase is seen as a direct way of improving the satisfaction-dissatisfaction nexus.

It is precisely because there may be so many favorable consequences resulting from increased efficiency, economy, productivity, or profitability, that administrators may try to dramatize input-output objectives by single-purpose fictions that distract attention from the desired consequences.

2. THEIR PLACE IN GOAL CONFLICTS

The "nonultimate" nature of input-output objectives is also revealed by the apparently inevitable conflicts that arise between them and other deeply valued organizational goals.

First of all, when displayed by the forces of evil, efficiency and productivity are scarcely desiderata. One of the deadliest aspects of the Nazi genocide campaign against the Jews of Europe was the deadly efficiency of their gas-chamber operations. The instruments of modern warfare will become still more appalling when more efficient weapon systems will make it possible to destroy human life without wasting resources in the simultaneous destruction of physical facilities and when "doomsday machines" will be cheap enough for every nation to build its own stockpile. The same principle applies in less strenuous forms of conflict. The built-in inefficiencies within the administrative system of many governments are not attributable only to accident or to the irrationality of politicians and public bureaucrats. The preservation of inefficiency in government is one of the best guarantees against the sustained expansion of public enterprise or regulation. Thus, in the United States of America there have at times been powerful interests that opposed improvements in government efficiency on the grounds that this would lead to an extension of governmental functions.

Within a single organization the conflict of objectives is even more apparent. Large increases in efficiency, economy, productivity, or profitability may be possible only at the cost of dissatisfactions to some members and external groups, curtailments in output quality, dissipation of organizational assets and violation of certain codes of behavior. In any event large increases have often been sought with inadequate attention or deliberate efforts to conceal the undesirable consequences. This is why efficiency experts and economy drives are often met with suspicion and resistance. This is why profit-seeking may be regarded as an hostile act. In some cultures, indeed, a deep interest in efficiency or profitability may be regarded as somewhat improper, if not downright immoral. Above all, efforts to raise the quantity of output may require a reduction in efficiency, profitability or both. In a period of all-out war production, when capacity is strained and marginal resources have to be brought into use, increased production has often meant decreased efficiency and higher costs per unit of output.

Improved productivity at one point in an organization may be directly associated with lower productivity for the organization as a whole. Efficiency experts have often succeeded in getting less people to produce more reports that are not needed and that, in fact, burden the organization. The same phenomenon has occurred under "transfer pricing" systems, with divisions of a company enhancing their own profit position at the expense of the company as a whole. Similarly, a reduction of inputs per unit does not imply that enough units will be produced. Some of the most efficient work ever done has been done by people who do very little but do it at amazing speed. Thus the lazy man or woman may achieve top efficiency in terms of unit output at a low level of total output.

Finally, the terms "efficiency" or "economy" are often used with explicit reference to a desired reduction in certain inputs, or costs, but without reference to what may happen to output. In some cases the actual purpose—strongly felt and fairly well hidden—is to eliminate or curtail certain forms of undesired output. Under these circumstances the "purposers" may well prefer a lower level of output with less efficiency as against more efficiency with a higher level of output. It may be easier to attain this objective under the banner of "efficiency" or "economy" than by a frontal attack on the undesired output. In other situations, the output side of the relation may be tacitly assumed. This occurs when budget-cutters take the position that if some of the inevitable "fat" is cut output will take care of itself. There may be good justification for this position when the knife is applied directly to the fat. But when an across-the-board cut is made and the knife is thereby passed down the line to those who are not thinking of the organization as a whole, the people and operations with the greatest potential for raising the level of productivity will often be the first to be cut. Here again the efficiency drive may readily result in reduced efficiency.

3. DEPENDENCE ON PERCEIVED SCARCITY

The instrumental nature of input-output relations is underscored even more when it is realized that concern with economizing on inputs arises only when there is a perceived scarcity of resources that can be used as inputs. If resources are so abundant that they cost nothing, people will drop any concern with the input side. All that will be left are output objectives. The same will be true when—as may often happen—resource scarcities are not seen or, if seen, little understood. One of the purposes of budgeting is to create scarcities among the units of an organization and to heighten the perception of scarcity among the personnel.

Resource scarcity, however, is usually a matter of degree. There are few resources which may be available in any quantity that may be desired. The typical situation is one of comparative scarcity. Thus, when an army has vast reserves of manpower, it will tend to be wasteful of "manpower inputs"—and particularly if it is short on other resources. If it has untold reserves of ammunition and little manpower, it will tend to conserve the latter but not the former. As an organization or a society becomes more affluent, interest in economizing is bound to decline. ". . . If the things produced are not of great urgency, it follows that the efficiency of the process by which they are produced ceases to be an overriding consideration" (Galbraith, 1958, p. 287).

Scarcity and abundance, moreover, are relative rather than absolute dimensions. In noncritical battles military leaders will tend to conserve their inputs. In a strategic battle that may mean the difference between a nation's survival or destruction, military leaders will often move ahead with little regard to the cost in lives, equipment, or "scorched earth." Scarcity and abundance are also relative to the possibility of efforts to obtain additional resources. For a university president who heads an outstanding fund raising organization, there is rarely a shortage of funds for any worthwhile project. In times of national crisis organizations can learn to make good use of labor, equipment and materials that they would ordinarily brand "marginal" or "substandard." In almost every organization there are untold potentials of manpower and brainpower that are rarely galvanized into action.

A negative illustration of the principle of perceived scarcity is provided by areas or societies suffering from large-scale unemployment and underemployment. Here there is a perceived abundance of manpower—or at least certain types of manpower. Under such circumstances there can be little serious interest in economizing on the use of manpower. John Lewis has pointed this out in his study of the Indian economy: "It is almost impossible to inject a psychology of efficiency of the importance of good work, of time-saving, into an organization so long as the inputs of human time itself are not regarded as valuable and scarce" (1962, p. 135). Under such circumstances the objective, rather, will often be to use the largest possible amount of manpower in relation to output.

At first blush it might seem that information inputs are exempt from the principle of perceived scarcity. Unlike labor equipment and materials, the transfer of information from Point A to Point B does not render it unavailable for alternative uses. It may still exist at Point B. Yet the scarcity factor enters the picture with respect to the energy and absorption capacities of the information users. It is the very abundance of information and the ever present danger of an information overload within an organization that makes it essential to economize on information inputs. The success of such economizing, however, will depend among other things upon the perception of the scarcity of capacity to absorb and utilize information.

4. PRACTICAL LIMITATIONS

Apart from goal conflicts and perceived scarcity, there are three serious limitations on the use of output-input objectives.

The first is simply getting the necessary information. Most of the trouble occurs on the output side. The rough-and-ready concepts used to deal with the quantity of intangible services often become less useful when an attempt is made to establish a relation with inputs. The use of output surrogates can be extremely misleading. In the case of nonmarket products the absence of an established monetary value for output usually rules out any use of the profitability concept. Hence Simon's belated recognition that "the absence of a common numerator . . . makes the criterion of efficiency applicable largely to rather low-level decisions" (*Administrative Behavior*, 1957 ed., p. xxxv). Moreover, even when relevant units of output quantity are available, a sophisticated accounting system is required in order to identify input measures that can appropriately be related to the same output units. The costs of obtaining such data may sometimes outweigh the benefits obtained.

The second is terminological. Although "productivity" and "profitability" are usually used to refer to output-input relations, "efficiency" is an all-purpose term that is widely used to refer to a multitude of ideas. In popular discourse "efficient" and "inefficient" are often used merely as a means of expressing approval or disapproval—as synonyms for "good" or "bad." They are used to indicate whether or not "the job is done"— that is, to refer to output objectives alone, without reference to inputs. They are also used to refer to the degree of rationality that is used; here the emphasis may be placed on methods with little or no attention to the output-input situation that might result from such methods.

Economists often use "efficiency" in a more sophisticated—but no less troublesome—sense. In welfare economics, particularly, the term expresses a relation between inputs and the total welfare or utility presumed to result from the use of such inputs. This might be regarded as a diffuse form of output-input relation. The output itself is subordinated to the presumed interest satisfactions resulting from the use of such output. These satisfactions are calculated by the single surrogate of monetary value of output. Other indicators of output quality and quantity are excluded from consideration. Barnard carries the usage of the welfare economists one step further by defining efficiency itself as the extent to which the satisfactions to the participants in an organization—for Barnard, both insiders and immediate outsiders—exceed the dissatisfactions associated with their contributions to it. This concept is based more squarely on interest satisfaction than that of the welfare economists, since the satisfactions of all organization members are also included. With this broadening, however, the monetary value of output cannot be used as a measure, and Barnard turns to sheer survival as the indicator of efficiency.

Another source of confusion may arise from the idea of an "input-output matrix" in macroeconomics. This is a mathematical technique for dealing with the interdependence of industries in an economy (Leontief, 1941). This interdependence arises from the fact that a typical industry uses as inputs outputs from other industries and through them makes indirect use of its own outputs. Thus steel is used to make the railroad cars used to transport the coal used to make steel. As suggested in Chapter 9, this technique may also be used in analyzing complex interrelations within a single organization. As usually used in macroeconomics, however, input-output analysis is based on the assumption of fixed proportions of input to output. It is therefore not directly relevant to the possibility of varying relations between input and output, which is the concept dealt with in this chapter.

The third difficulty is the tremendous variety of input-output relations—a variety too vast to be covered by such terms as efficiency, economy, productivity, and profitability. As indicated in the previous three chapters, the output side may be expressed in anything ranging from a broad product mix down to a single type of output. Production objectives for any single output type may be expressed in terms of contributed or available output. On the input side one may deal with total inputs or with any conceivable input factor. In the case of both output and input, there are usually broad choices with respect to physical or monetary units, the use of marginal increments, averages or totals, and the resolution of "border conflicts."

Whatever methods are used to express output and input, there are also many different relations that can be established between them. In some cases a simple ratio may be used with output serving as the numerator and input the denominator—as with output units per man-hours. In other cases these roles are reversed—as with machine time per output unit. In profitability relations the total input value is usually subtracted from total output value; the difference may then be related to output value or some dimension of financial assets. Or else output and input may be assumed to be equal, with attention focused on the margin between total output (or input) and that portion which is usable or used. This margin may then be used as the numerator in a ratio with total output.

To cope with the endless number of permutations that are possible, I have found it desirable to distinguish between two broad groups of output-input relations. The first comprises the partial relations, in which the input side is represented by a single type of input. The second comprises the *broad* relations, in which all or most inputs are aggregated.

In subsequent sections of this chapter, after the nature of inputs has been discussed, the major types of input-output relations within each of these groups will be explored. This will illustrate the desirability of using a multiplicity of concepts in both stating objectives and appraising performance.

B. *Input Quantity and Quality*

OUR USE of a services-goods concept of output requires that we use a services-goods concept on the input side also. It provides us in advance with basic concepts and dimensions that are as applicable to services and goods on the input side as they are on the output side. It identifies basic problems that appear on both sides—such as price adjustments and allocations to time periods. In fact, the problem of quality-quantity conflicts is often more acute on the input side. The need to obtain firm quantitative input data that can be related to output often diverts attention entirely from the quality of inputs, particularly when input quality and input quantity seem noncommensurable.

While the unique aspect of output is its intimate association with the satisfaction of clientele interests, the unique aspect of input is its intimate association with costs and assets. Further, there is more quantitative information available on the input side than on the output side. Thus, we can add up the salaries of people producing nonmarketed services—whether in government agencies, the units of a business firm or the central office of a professional association or political party. We can keep records on the use of materials and equipment. This wealth of information on the input side often detracts attention from the output side. Moreover, it can become so complex as to defy comprehension. The process of defiance is facilitated by the proliferation of advanced accounting techniques and the tendency of many professional accountants to augment their power by wrapping their calculations in a cloud of presumed objectivity and impenetrable mystery.

1. FROM ASSETS TO INPUTS TO COSTS

Inputs may be defined as *services or goods used by an organization, unit or individual in the production of output.*

Since output is also composed of services and goods, it is clear from this definition that the distinction between input and output, lies in their chronological position in the production process. Input comes first, output later.

In using this concept, care must be taken to distinguish between direct and remote inputs. Just as there is not much sense in regarding air travel as the output of an engine plant, there is no sense in regarding the jet engine as the output of the mining company that provided the ore from which the engine's metal was obtained. There is sense, however, for any organization to look backward at the vast network of product flows from which its inputs must be obtained and forward to the complex clientele network through which its output may flow as input. This perspective provides administrators with a basis for formulating objectives on the mobilization of resources, the satisfaction of clientele interests and the scheduling of production.

Inputs stand midway between assets and costs. The association is so close that any one, indeed, is often used as a surrogate for one of the others. This sometimes leads to a confusion among all three.

The assets of an organization, as explained in greater detail in Chapter 17, are its physical and human resources. But these assets are merely potential inputs. *Assets become inputs only when and as used in the production of output.* A new machine may be "put into" the organization, but there is no "machine input" until the machine is actually used. Similarly, it is not the members of an organization that are inputs but rather the services they provide. In this connection it should be pointed out that services or goods may be used as inputs without first being formally regarded as assets in the financial accounting sense. A formal accounting of assets is rarely made for such things as incoming documents or oral information—even though these may unquestionably add to the existing stock of documents and information.

While inputs comprise the full flow of services and goods into the production process, costs are ways of thinking about those inputs, or input aspects, that involve some sacrifice or expenditure. The total flow of inputs never enters into any formal system of cost calculation. Any cost calculation, whether formal or informal, is made from the viewpoint of some "cost bearer." The same input within the same organization may be cost in one set of accounts, may not appear in another calculation and in a third may be a benefit instead.

2. THE MULTIPLICITY OF COST CONCEPTS

When we consider the various ways in which some inputs are looked upon as costs, our attention is struck by the multiplicity of cost concepts.

A. *Monetary and nonmonetary costs.* It is often assumed that costs must necessarily be expressed in monetary terms. In fact, the rest of this discussion will center largely around monetary concepts. It is important at the outset, however, to emphasize that monetary cost values are merely ways of quantifying the underlying physical costs—in the same way that the monetary evaluation of output may serve as a surrogate of interest satisfaction. They may understate or overstate the physical costs, depending upon the circumstances affecting the determination of price. Moreover, in the nonmarket transactions within an organization or between an organization and a government agency, substantial time and energy may be expended in obtaining "free" inputs. The burdens imposed upon a unit or member by engaging in a difficult operation can never be calculated—or even understood—merely in terms of the monetary costs of the operation.

B. *Outlay or opportunity costs.* Outlay costs are the traditional cost figures that accountants record on their books. They are measured by looking at money spent. They may also be measured in nonmonetary terms, as with the strain, heartache or "psychic costs" of a particular action.

Opportunity costs—often referred to as economic, differential, or incremental costs—are less obvious in nature, but more important. They are the costs of sacrificing other opportunities for using the same inputs. They are measured by considering what else might have been done. "Whenever the problem allows an opportunity to buy all input factors for cash, outlay cost is the correct concept to use" (Dean, 1951, p. 259).

Under these circumstances outlay cost is itself a measure of what else might have been done. Thus a ten-dollar outlay on ball point pens means the loss of the opportunity to obtain ten dollars' worth of other resources. But if we widen our perspective to include a day in the life of an administrator (including the time spent in making notes with his pen), the specific outlays for salary, equipment, assistance, and other items down to the pen he uses are not so important. Far more important is the comparison between just what he was doing with his time and what else he might have been doing with his time. Similarly, "the cost of getting a college education is not confined to the outlays on tuition and books, but also includes the earnings that are foregone by not working full time. . . . The cost of sending bombers on a particular mission is not the price of the gasoline and ammunition but, rather, the damage that they would have done the enemy had they been sent on a substitute mission" (*Ibid.*, p. 260). In business enterprises opportunity costs may be calculated by comparing the profitability of alternative courses of action. In all types of organizations and situations the analysis of opportunity costs is fraught with dangers. It requires an identification of feasible alternatives and an estimation of probable cost elements under each. As Anthony points out (1960, p. 489-492), this process may be simplified by concentrating attention only on those costs which are different rather than looking at the total array of costs. But unless the total array is looked at, important cost elements may be overlooked. Moveover, "The longer the time span of the proposal, the more items of cost are differential. In the very long run, all costs are differential" (*Ibid.*, p. 492).

c. *Actual, expected and standard costs.* Another distinction may be made between *actual, expected* (or *budgeted*) and *standard* costs. The first are those costs that actually occur. The term "actual" should not be taken too seriously, however. If actual costs are to be prepared in time to be used (rather than merely become "archeological costs" in the historical records of an organization), they can be calculated only on the basis of rough estimates. Expected costs are those estimates made in advance and embodied in formal budgets of future expenditures. Standard costs are costs expected on the basis of technical estimates of what the costs should be for specific outputs. Cost "variances" are the difference between the standard and actual costs. They may be broken down into the various factors accounting for the difference—such as time and rate variances for labor and usage and price variances for materials.

d. *The variability of costs.* Another distinction may be made between *variable, semivariable* and *fixed* costs. The difference between these lies in the nature of their relation to the volume of output. Variable costs vary directly and proportionately with volume; these may include power, direct labor, and supplies. Semivariable costs—which may include indirect labor, maintenance, and clerical costs—vary directly but less than proportionately with volume. Fixed costs—such as building depreciation, property taxes, supervisory salaries, and occupancy costs—do not vary with volume, at least within certain limits of volume changes. (In this context, the term "fixed," of course, does not imply that such costs cannot be changed or controlled. It is the nonvariation of fixed costs as volume increases which yields the lower total unit costs of expanded operations. The category often includes many relatively useless and readily dispensable input items—such as office luxuries.) Nor can any specific input items be automatically regarded as variable, semivariable or fixed regardless of the circumstances. The proper classification depends upon a direct look at any specific situation and the additional inputs that may be required by various types of volume changes. Over the "long run" all costs behave as variable costs.

E. *Costs by organizational units.* Costs are also grouped—particularly in budgetary statements—by the various organizational units that "incur" them (that is, use the input factors to which the costs refer). This way of classifying costs is essential for both internal administration and external control. In those cases in which a particular organizational unit is responsible for a specific intermediate product, this classification may be identical with that of direct costs by unit of output. Such a classification by itself, however, can never provide an allocation of overhead costs or reveal the costs of products produced jointly by two or more units.

The classification of costs by organizational units provides a basis for the development of "responsibility centers." This is one of the more recent ideas in the field of managerial cost control. As indicated by Anthony (1960, p. 321-323), this goes one step beyond the old idea of "cost center." It can even be carried as far as "profit center" or "investment center." The application of the idea requires a rather clear identification of those costs for which the head of an organizational unit may be properly held responsible. This may also require special attention to controllable or escapable costs as contrasted with those costs that are noncontrollable.

F. *Costs of specific input factors.* The foundation for all calculations of monetary costs is some system of keeping track of specific input factors. Often, this is done on the basis of the expenditures made for their acquisition by the organization, without specific reference to when and how they are used.

In government organizations these input factors are often listed as "objects of expenditure." This is a somewhat ambiguous term if one thinks of "object" as the "objective" (or output) which the expenditure—

and the inputs acquired through the expenditure—is supposed to help achieve. Rather, the "objects" are the inputs, or sources of inputs, themselves—such as personal services, equipment, transportation, communication, office supplies, printing, fuel and light, etc. In some governments, capital expenditures are lumped together with all other expenditures, while in others a firm distinction is made between operating and capital expenditures.

In business organizations the various objects of expenditure are grouped somewhat differently. Manufacturers usually distinguish between (a) production costs (or cost of sales), which include direct materials, direct labor and manufacturing overhead, and (b) period costs, which include selling, administration, and such general expenses as insurance, depreciation, interest and taxes. Dividends may occasionally be regarded as the cost of invested capital. Capital expenditures are usually handled in a separate budget, with only interest payments and depreciation reflected in the current budget.

G. *Unit costs.* Unit costs are obtained by allocating to specific output units the costs of some or all of the relevant input factors. This may be done both for intermediate products (at "responsibility centers") and end products. Job costing collects the costs for an identifiable batch of products as they are produced. Process costing provides the costs for all relatively homogeneous products as they are produced during a given period of time. Performance budgeting, as already pointed out in Chapter 15, is a way of identifying certain units of output to which costs may be assigned. Direct costs are the easiest to obtain. Here all that is needed is to allocate such direct costs as labor and materials to specific units; this is easier with respect to process costing than job costing. Even this may be extremely difficult, however, when people are working on different products or—as in the case of intangible services—none of the products can be clearly identified.

To get the total costs per unit it is also necessary to allocate to each type of unit some proportion of indirect costs and overhead expenditures. The allocation of such costs can always be done in a variety of ways. In the case of overhead expenses for which some identifiable services are rendered, such as maintenance and repair, the allocation may be made on the basis of time spent, or a fixed set of charges for services rendered. In the case of other overhead expenses, such as light and heat it may not be worthwhile to keep track of specific services rendered. In the case of general administration and research and advisory services it may not be possible. Hence allocation may be done arbitrarily on the basis of one or another aspect of direct costs themselves—such as number of people, hours worked or payroll.

3. THE ARTS OF "COST CREATION"

From most books on accounting one gets the impression that cost calculations are hard facts and that cost calculation is an objective process of reporting on these facts.

Experienced accountants, however, know full well that cost calculation is a creative process. Without violating any codes of professional accounting, any competent costs accountant can produce a wide variety of acceptable cost data to describe a single operation. Which data he arrives at will depend largely upon his artistic skill in adjusting the available data to the specific purposes of the calculation. The nature of this artistry, however, is rarely revealed in the literature of accounting.

The opportunity for the exercise of creative judgment arises directly from the many different ways of looking at the same facts concerning input costs. At times this latitude may be exploited for purposes of deception, as an organization uses different sets of books to conceal the purloining or misuse of funds or to evade legal controls. At other times the deception may not involve law-breaking at all, as in taking advantage of "loopholes" in tax laws or "putting the best foot forward" in interpreting facts to investors and controllers. On these occasions, so long as consistent cost classifications are used within a given presentation, no ethical codes need be broken. On still other occasions, it is essential to look at a problem from many different viewpoints, each of which may require a different approach to costs. This may even involve a multiple set of accounts, each for a separate purpose. Although this may seem as nefarious as "double bookkeeping," it may be merely an application of Dean's wise comment that "different combinations of cost ingredients are appropriate for various kinds of management problems" (1951, p. 258-259).

There are four major areas for discretionary judgment with respect to costs, and a host of minor opportunities as well. These will now be discussed seriatim.

A. *Allocation of common costs.* I have already mentioned the problem of allocating indirect and overhead expenditures. There can be no one, all-purpose method of doing this. If such costs are to be allocated, an arbitrary choice of method must be made. Equally indeterminate are the direct costs of joint products. The classic example is the variety of end products—the hide, the many different cuts of meat, and so on that are made from a pig. "There is no way of knowing how much of its cost belongs to the hide and how much to the bacon" (Anthony, 1960, p. 382). The problem is just a little easier in the case of alternative products—that is, when the proportions in the end product mix may be deliberately changed. "The cost of an alternative product can always be computed in terms of the foregone profits from the other product, where the cost of a joint product (as distinguished from the product package) is essentially indeterminate" (Dean, 1951, p. 319). With nonmarketed products, particularly intermediate services, the problem is no easier. Whenever there are a number of products being produced, the assignment of direct costs requires burdensome records. This burden is often avoided by the use of standard or estimated costs in place of actual costs. The creative judgment enters into the fixing of the standard or calculation of the estimate (or "guesstimate").

B. *Allocations to current or capital expenditures.* Whenever an organization keeps a capital account, it is essential to determine what types of expenditures are to be capitalized (in which case the costs will be spread over a period of years) and what types are to be regarded as current expenditures. Repairs and maintenance work are properly charged to current expenditures—*unless* they involve the replacement of wornout parts, rehabilitation, remodeling or any form of betterment. In actual practice the *unless* line may be extremely unclear. In many cases repair and maintenance necessarily involve some degree of replacement, if not betterment as a whole. The opportunities for choice are also great in the case of intangible assets—such as patents, trademarks, copyrights, and good will. They are still greater with respect to the costs of research and development, the training and education of organization members and improvements in organization and administration.

c. *Depreciation costs.* The allocation of capital costs over a period of time raises still greater problems. Any calculation of depreciation costs invariably starts with two assumptions as to (1) how long an asset will last and (2) what its residual value will be at the end of its life. These are factors that can never really be known in advance—particularly in an age of rapid and unpredictable technological obsolescence. Yet the assumptions used are rarely carefully calculated probability statements. They are rather arbitrary starting points determined in terms of the accepted conventions in a particular field or on the basis of the desirability of the result they will yield. In addition, the calculation of depreciation requires (3) a choice between various methods of allocating depreciation costs over the assumed period. This may involve use of the "straight line" method, "accelerated" methods which allocate more depreciation in the earlier years or methods of allocating on the basis of actual use.

Still greater problems, however, are involved in (4) determining whether to base depreciation estimates on original cost or replacement value. The decision on this point, as on previous ones, may well depend upon the purpose for which depreciation is calculated. One such purpose is the computation (that is, reduction) of tax liability. For this purpose relevant tax laws and regulations will prescribe certain broad limits. But these limits need not be adhered to for other purposes. As stated in Bradshaw and Hull (1950, p. 83), "it is not necessary to conform to tax laws and regulations in establishing the policies to be followed in book accounting or in the preparation of financial statements." Another purpose is to determine policy with respect to the building up of savings and reserves; in this case replacement value is unquestionably the best guide. Still another purpose is to make decisions on the replacement of old equipment. In this case, from the viewpoint of managerial analysis, "The depreciation charges on the books . . . have no significance for the replacement decision" (Dean, 1951, p. 604). They are sunk costs; the only relevant costs are those bearing on future alternatives.

D. *Costs of withdrawals from inventories.* In calculating the cost of materials taken from inventories, complications are introduced by changing prices of materials bought. In times of sharp price fluctuations, this can be an extremely confusing factor. At least seven alternative ways of coping with this problem have been devised. Among these two of the best known are the highly divergent FIFO and LIFO systems. FIFO—or first-in, first-out pricing—requires that materials withdrawn from inventory be priced at the price of their original purchase. At a time of rising prices, this system tends to yield lower costs (particularly if large inventories have been accumulated over a long period) and higher profits. LIFO—or last-in, first-out pricing—charges current production with material costs which most nearly correspond to the prices paid currently to replace the materials consumed. This tends to show higher costs and smaller profits. As with depreciation costs, tax liability may be a major factor in determining which method is used. But whatever system is used for tax purposes need not be used in determining costs in connection with cost-plus contracts or with negotiations on prices.

E. *Miscellaneous.* In addition to the wide discretion in the matters listed above, there are a host of minor cost questions that can be handled with considerable latitude in judgment. Some of these have already been discussed in the chapters on output calculations. Thus different cost figures may be obtained by choosing between marginal, average or total calculations, by various methods of adjusting to price changes, and by the handling of "boundary problems." Expenses as well as revenues must be allocated to time periods on either an accrual or cash basis. Whichever system is used, there is often considerable leeway in charging costs against one month or another (but more so in an accrual system) and in the selection of the particular short-range or long-range time period for which costs are to be calculated.

There are several conclusions to be drawn from this panoramic picture of different ways of "creating" costs. One is that the costs figures provided by traditional financial accounting—whether in business, government or other organizations—are not necessarily relevant to all administrative problems. The second is that different problems require different kinds of costs. "These special-purpose costs differ from 'actual costs' in content as well as viewpoint. Different combinations of cost ingredients are appropriate for various kinds of management problems. Disparities arise from deletions, from additions, from recombination of elements, from price-level adjustments, and from the introduction of measurements which do not appear anywhere in the accounting records" (Dean, 1951, p. 258-259).

4. COSTS OUTSIDE AN ORGANIZATION'S ACCOUNTS

Despite the ingenuity that has been used in perfecting accounting techniques, the formal accounts of an organization can never show the costs of all the inputs used by it.

First of all, there are many internal inputs that are not reflected in an organization's accounts. In the case of wear and tear on equipment and machinery, the postponement of maintenance and repairs may postpone the accounting record until a later date. In the case of wear and tear upon members of the organization, the costs may be shifted entirely to the people themselves. Workmen's compensation and insurance programs have tended to bring some of these costs back from individual members to the organization itself. But no methods have yet been devised that will allow an organization to cover the costs to its members—particularly those involved in difficult problems of conflict and adjustment—of the strains and tensions that may be an integral part of both normal operation and recurrent reorganization. No system of "payment by results" compensates all the members—particularly administrators—for extra efforts made on the job. No system of extra pay for overtime can compensate people for—let alone record—the hours spent pondering on organizational problems after official working hours. These nonrecorded and unpaid inputs might be regarded as surplus value, as a measure of the exploitation of man by the organization. If this interpretation has Marxian connotations, it is Marx turned upside-down; for in these cases it is usually the manager and not the working man who is most exploited.

Another major cost which is practically never reflected both fully and in an organization's accounts is the cost of unemployed labor. When machinery is not used, the fixed costs of interest and depreciation (or rental payments, if it is leased) continue. Thus idle capacity may be immediately seen as a major burden on the organization. But when people are laid off during business fluctuations, the picture is quite different. The labor costs in an organization's accounts immediately decline, as might be expected of variable costs. But from a broader viewpoint, as John M. Clark pointed out in his classic *Studies in the Economics of Overhead Costs,* labor can also be regarded as a fixed overhead cost: "Whenever a laborer has invested time and money in specialized training, the result is, in a certain sense, fixed capital which is useful in one occupation and in no other, and which must earn whatever return it can, because the investment cannot be withdrawn and moved into some other line of business" (1923, p. 15). The overhead costs of unemployed labor need not be confined to workers with special training. The minimum costs of the laborer's health and working capacity must be borne by someone whether the laborer works or not: "If it is not borne, if the maintenance is not forthcoming, the community suffers a loss through the deterioration of its working power which is at least equivalent to the cost of maintaining the laborer. Thus the burden is there in any case; it cannot be avoided. From this point of view it appears that a large part of the cost originally counted as wages represents an overhead cost which the laborer is responsible for covering as best he can, just as the employer is responsible for covering the overhead cost on account of capital. However, if the laborer fails to cover it, the community does not escape the burden, and it is ultimately borne by industry in the shape of reduced productive power and damaged morale. And thus it comes back to the employer in any case . . ." (1923, p. 16). This cost also comes back to the employer in the form of contributions to unemployment compensation, termination payments and pressures to keep unneeded workers on the payroll; these may be directly reflected in the accounts. But the accounts will never show—although they will be affected by—the costs arising from instability and insecurity among the workers and the consequent reduction in the organization's productive capacities.

As the above discussion reveals, there may also be many external inputs not reflected in an organization's accounts. These are the services or goods provided outside the organization either gratis or on the basis of incomplete compensation. The most obvious inputs of this type are direct government subsidies to individual organizations or indirect subsidies in the form of tax exemptions, tariff import quotas, and direct or guaranteed loans. Somewhat more general in scope are the government's expenditures with respect to unemployment compensation, social security and—still more important—the education and training of the labor force.

Even more important is the assistance to be obtained from a general environment which has a full supply of the various inputs an organization may need. As indicated in the "resources" section of "The General Environment" (Chapt. 7), every organization needs external sources of services and goods. If these cannot be obtained from the outside, the organization may have to take on the job—and the much larger costs—of supplying them. Perhaps the most important external economy is the availability of high-quality information in an environment distinguished by large numbers of organizations and people engaged in creative action, thought and research. The desire to exploit such inputs is one of the major reasons for the mushrooming of metropolitan and megalopolitan areas.

Another form of "cost" outside an organization's accounts is often provided by the secondary consequences of its activities. In *The Social Costs of Private Enterprise* (1950, p. 228-229), Kapp points out that "private production activities tend to give rise to a wide variety of social losses not reflected in entrepreneurial outlays." He illustrates this theme by documenting the extensive costs involved in industrial accidents, occupational disease, woman and child labor, air and water pollution, the depletion of exhaustible natural resources, excessive distribution channels, and above all the social costs of economic depressions. He includes both those costs which "are ultimately reflected in monetary losses and public expenditure" and those which "are of a less tangible character and can only be estimated in terms other than market values."

But the phenomenon which Kapp depicts is by no means limited to private enterprise. Cost shifting is a universal phenomenon. Public bodies also shift costs one to the other. Thus the operations of a public resource development may require additional expenditures by other public bodies dealing with public works, exploration, statistics, and business regulation. The external costs of military programs—in the sense of services provided to military agencies from "civilian budgets"—are notoriously large. Nor is the shifting necessarily limited to other government bodies. The external costs of government agencies can also be passed on to private enterprises and consumers.

In Kapp's discussion, however, no distinction is made between those "social costs" which reflect inputs into the productive process and those which reflect consequences of an organization's activities and therefore stem from the output side. It might be more helpful to regard the former as unpaid inputs and the latter as resultant dissatisfactions (in contrast to the satisfactions presumably resulting from its output) for which no compensation is provided. This subject will be returned to later in this chapter in the discussion of social efficiency.

c. *Partial Productivity or Efficiency Ratios*

PARTIAL INPUT-OUTPUT RELATIONS are those most customarily employed in calculations of both productivity and efficiency. These are developed in the form of ratios relating some specific input factor to total or contributed output. When a single unit of input is used, it will serve as the denominator—as in

$$\frac{\text{Output}}{\text{Unit of Input factor}}.$$

This is the most usual form. When a single unit of output is focused upon, it will serve as denominator—as in

$$\frac{\text{Units of Input factor}}{\text{Output unit}}.$$

The usefulness of any partial ratio is usually limited to those circumstances when there are no significant changes in other input factors. Even when this condition is satisfied, the use of a partial ratio may lead to serious misunderstandings concerning the relative contribution of various input factors.

1. LABOR INPUTS

Of all partial input-output ratios the most widespread have been those dealing with labor inputs. Information on labor inputs is easier to obtain than on other input factors. For those concerned with the output capacities and propensities of workers, it has often seemed the most relevant information.

The production engineers have developed careful techniques for measuring "labor productivity" or "labor efficiency." They concentrate on specific operations yielding tangible output units that can readily be counted. They keep a careful eye on output quality, so that output increases are not attained by sacrificing output quality. Above all, they give attention to a whole series of methods for reducing the labor-output ratio. These include improvements in product design, the machinery and materials used, the processes of production and the provision of training and incentives for workers. Most of these are beyond the direct control of individual workers. Targets for labor output are, ideally, to be set only *after* improvements in these methods. Under these circumstances labor-output ratios have considerable significance. Short-term increases in physical output or decreases in direct labor time may be reasonably attributed to the skill, persistence or effort of individual workers.[1]

1. An excellent presentation of these many considerations, along with the basic

This cannot be said for the general level of output per worker at any one time or for increases over a long period. Methods improvements usually require an increment in indirect labor. This increment is not taken into account by any measure of direct labor. Indeed, indirect labor costs are extremely hard to estimate, since they fall in the troublesome category of general costs that have to be arbitrarily allocated. Moreover, the most dramatic and continuous output increases are likely to result from the substitution of machinery for labor or better machinery for obsolescent machinery. This may be illustrated by the following figures:

	Mainly hand labor	*Mechanization*	*Improved Mechanization*
Manhours per 100 output units	5	2	1
Machine hours per 100 output units	1	2	1

If we look at manpower alone, we may get the impression that the decline in labor time may have resulted from something done *by* the workers. What has really happened, however, has happened *to* them: replacement. Thus labor productivity and efficiency ratios can be very misleading when used as major concepts in setting goals for an organization or an economy or in comparing the performance of different organizations or different economies. In this context they lose the utility they had for the measurement of small changes during short periods at given points in a production process. Instead, they become a loose and potentially misleading way of referring to the rate of labor replacement.

Let us now look directly at some of the alternative labor-output ratios that may be used within a single organization. Both labor and output may be expressed in either physical or monetary terms. The labor calculation may be based on direct labor only or total labor. The period covered may extend from an hour to a year. The output may be either available output (total value), or contributed output (value added). With these variables kept in mind, let us look at the changes that have taken place in a specific factory between last year and this year. Let us ask the simple question, "What happened to labor productivity or efficiency?"

The table on page 640 shows that there is no simple answer. Although only some of all the possible labor-output ratios have been listed, there

principles of method study and work measurement, may be found in the International Labor Office's *Introduction to Work Study*.

is a great variety of answers from which to choose. The two ratios based on manhours show a 10 per cent increase. The ratio of total output value to manyear shows a 19 per cent increase. This, indeed seems excellent.

But there was also a sharp reduction in the number of hours per week. This led to a reduction of 4 per cent in output per manweek. With an increase in the number of weeks, output per manyear underwent no change at all. In short, increased output per manhour was balanced off by less manhours.

When we look at the other ratios, we find reason to question the significance of the dramatic 19 per cent increase in total output value per manyear. Although wages rose, the increased direct labor costs were counterbalanced by the increased output per hour. So far so good. But indirect labor costs also rose—and were not counterbalanced. As a result total labor costs per output unit rose by 15 per cent (recorded in the table as a 15 per cent decline in efficiency). When we look at the monetary side of output, we find that more components were bought. This is one of the basic reasons for the 19 per cent increase in total output value per manyear. The value added per manyear, in contrast, fell by 10 per cent. The value added per dollar of total labor cost, fell by 29 per cent!

2. CAPITAL INPUTS

The limitations of labor-output ratios immediately suggest looking at capital-output ratios instead. When we do so, we find once again the same problems that confronted us before. At the level of an individual machine, its "rated capacity" tells us how much output we should expect from it under proper working conditions. But unless the machine has worn out or been damaged any lower level of output is merely a rough and ready indication that other factors have interfered with its level of output. If we look at land instead of machinery, we may then measure agricultural output per unit of land. This is one of the most dramatic ways of measuring the tremendous impact upon agricultural production of the combined use of agricultural machinery, fertilizers, improved seeds, crop rotation, and, in some areas, irrigation. Similarly, we may focus upon any other form of physical capital—such as the amount of office space or the tons of steel in inventory—in which we may be interested at a given moment and construct an appropriate ratio to guide its conservation through better use of other input factors.

If we go beyond these specific physical forms of capital, we then face the problem of calculating capital inputs in monetary terms. This is far more difficult than calculating total labor costs. It necessarily involves

What Happened to Labor Productivity or Efficiency?

PARTIAL RELATIONS: LABOR INPUT			CHANGE IN PRODUCTIVITY OR EFFICIENCY	
Physical I: Physical O	*Last Year*	*This Year*	*Increase*	*Decrease*
Output unit per manhour	1	1.1	+ 10%	
Manhours per output unit	1	.9	+ 10%	
Output units per manweek	40 (40 hours per week)	38.5 (35 hours per week)		− 4%
Output units per manyear	1,920 (48 weeks)	1,920 (50 weeks)	0	0
Monetary I: Physical O				
Direct labor cost per output unit	$2 ($2 per manhour)	$2 ($2.20 per man-hour)	0	0
Total labor cost per output unit	$2.50 ($.50 indirect cost per manhour)	$2.88 ($1 indirect cost per manhour)		− 15%
Physical I: Monetary O				
Total output value per manyear	$9,600 ($5 per unit)	$11,420 ($6 per unit)	+ 19%	
Value added per manyear	$7,000	$6,300 (with more components bought)		− 10%
Monetary I: Monetary O				
Total annual output value per dollar of total labor cost	$2.23	$2.06		− 6%
Total annual value added per dollar of total labor cost	$1.63	$1.15		− 29%

a choice among various methods of depreciation and inventory evaluation. Because of the difficulties involved, it is often easier to use instead the value of new investment. This is particularly pertinent in trying to judge the output or income that may be expected or sought from a specific capital increment. Businessmen will often establish a rule-of-thumb ratio to the effect that a new machine must pay for itself in three to five years. Economic planners will use equally rough rules of thumb based on capital-output ratios or "capital coefficients" ranging from two to five. Thus with a capital-output ratio of two, it is presumed that a new investment of 100 million monetary units (usually calculated in net terms) will result in an annual increment of 50 million in national income. Neither of these calculations has much utility unless approached within a framework that deals specifically with the other major factors affecting output. The crucial question is the degree of capacity utilization expected from both existing capital and the proposed increment. In the case of the businessman this is blanketed in by his estimate of future profits. In the case of the economic planner, this factor—along with the crucial questions of the quality of the capital and its management—is more frequently overlooked.

3. OTHER INPUTS

While labor and capital inputs are the ones most frequently used in partial ratios, other input factors may also be used.

In discrete production operations, use is often made of material-output ratios. These may help in efforts either to reduce the proportion of a given material or to keep track of and reduce the amount of wasted materials. In the latter case, they may tie in with efforts to make better use of scrap. The calculation of fuel-output ratios may help in efforts to conserve on fuel expenditures.

Another important ratio is that of electric power to output. For modern industry and modern civilization as a whole one of the most dramatic changes has been the vast expansion in inputs of electrical energy. This is closely associated with, but not limited to, the replacement of manpower by electricity-driven machinery. The use of electricity inputs can help appraise any machine's capacity to transform electricity into machine operations. It can also serve as a way of aggregating capital inputs without getting bogged down in the morass of capital valuation.

In certain operations it might also be helpful to attempt a calculation of information inputs, or even the marginal cost of additional information, and relate the resulting input element to output. The key problem is to find some way to deal with the quality of information, not merely quantity.

Similarly, if the qualitative aspects of administration (a special form of labor service) could be sufficiently specified, it might be possible to attempt some experimental calculations with respect to administration-output ratios. Yet the dispersion of administrative functions makes it extremely difficult even to count the number of administrators in an organization. Counting the hours someone spends in administrative activities may be misleading for a single person and an unspeakable burden for an organization as a whole. Until these difficulties are overcome, the position affirmed in the previous chapter on the essentially productive nature of administrative activities (as distinguished from frequent aberrations) must be based mainly upon deduction, intuitive interpretations of experience, and faith.

D. *Profitability*

WHENEVER we may express output value in money units, either through market prices or an internal pricing system, we may escape the disadvantages of narrow input-output relations and measure both sides by the common denominator of monetary value. This is profitability, a broad input-output relation of tremendous usefulness in formulating goals and appraising performance.

Profitability is also the most controversial of all input-output relations. Divergent ideas of what profits are or should be enter into continuing controversies over the allocation of organizational income, government programs of taxation and regulation, the distribution of power and resources in a society, and alternative forms of corporate and social organization. Technical disputes between economists and accountants have been so sharp that "accountants have made an energetic effort in recent years to discard the word for their purposes and to refer to the conventional concept as 'business income,' a neutral term that avoids any overlap with economy theory" (Dean, 1951, p. 12).[2]

This is also an area in which the arts of deception have been highly developed. As can readily be inferred from the previous discussion of "cost creation," any self-respecting accountant can turn a large profit into a modest profit or a modest profit into a small loss. With enough input of legal skill and just a little strain on publicly stated norms, the "profit

2. Note that in preparing financial statements business accountants generally use the terms "income statement," "statement of earnings," or "statement of operations," instead of "profit and loss statement."

juggling" margin can become quite large. This margin may be exploited for "tax avoidance" (that is, the reduction of tax liability within the law rather than illegal "tax evasion"). It may be used to hide profits from regulatory agencies and unions or justify public loans or subsidies, practices widely indulged in by government corporations (even in "socialist" economies) as well as private enterprises. It may be used to show a more favorable picture to potential investors.

1. THE MULTIPLICITY OF PROFIT GOALS

Behind much of the popular polemics on profits lie some fundamental ambiguities concerning the referent of "profit." Thus the term has been used to refer to

- any personal satisfaction, utility, gain or advantage, with "loss" referring to any form of dissatisfaction,
- certain forms of income from property, such as dividends, interest or rent,
- funds accumulated in reserves, or
- the surplus of revenues over expenses, with loss entering the picture when the former is less than the latter.

The last of these meanings is the net income or net margin concept of profit and loss. This is the general concept used in income-earning organizations of both the "profit seeking" and "nonprofit" variety and in both "capitalist" and "socialist" countries. It is from this surplus, when it exists, that funds may be taken for dividends, investments, the building up of reserves and other uses.[3]

As already pointed out, different conceptions of cost and different accounting methods may yield a multiplicity of profit figures from the identical situation. Indeed, entirely apart from efforts at deception, it is often necessary to look at the same situation in terms of different profit calculations. Thus profits after taxes are more appropriate for some purposes (such as the consideration of dividend policy) and profits before taxes more appropriate for others (such as judging organizational performance apart from uncontrollable increases in tax rates). In some situations of unused capacity it is sound to calculate the profitability of additional output in terms of out-of-pocket costs only, thereby dodging all the choices with respect to capital costs. The conduct of a company's

---

3. The relation between profits and value added can be seen from the following equation: Value added equals cost of services and goods supplied by an organization plus its profits (or minus losses).

regular operations may be appraised by its operating profit. Yet only by looking at its real net profits—after the effect of such nonoperating activities as the sale of a factory building or the way in which reserves are invested—can one appraise the financial effect of its total activities.

But the multiplicity of profit goals stems from much more than the variety of cost conceptions and analytical techniques. Even *within* any fixed set of definitions and accounting methods and apart from the question of aspiration level, there are at least five divergent ways of formulating profit goals.

A. *Short range* or *long range*. If one took seriously the profit-maximizations assumptions of the old-fashioned economists, one might think that business managers invariably leap at every opportunity to obtain an extra drop of profit. Yet to do so may often interfere with future profitability or even lead to future losses. Apart from external market problems, this choice is always to be faced in internal operations. Current costs can always be reduced, and current profits thereby raised, by skimping on repairs, maintenance or product quality. Except in the case of "fly by night" concerns, attention is usually given to longer range considerations. But there is no general period of time for which profitability is habitually calculated. The "life" of new equipment is computed in terms of arbitrary conventions. Where long-term budgets are established for specific periods, profit goals tend to be *a priori* general considerations that help bring together a host of much more specific subsidiary goals. At times, they are merely *a posteriori* objectives empirically determined in the light of current feasibilities (Chamberlain, 1962, p. 52-55).

B. *Product and product mix.* "What I make on the peanuts I lose on the bananas." The fact that this oft-quoted street vendor can calculate the profitability of a single product line attests to his sophistication. To look at total profitability alone may mean the continuation of product lines that detract from total profits. Yet the fact that the street vendor may still continue to sell bananas may indicate a still more sophisticated awareness of the need for multiple profit concepts. A product line that loses money in the short run may make money in the long run. It may even contribute to product mix profitability in the short run by serving as a "loss leader" or using capacity that would otherwise lie idle. Similarly, divisions that increase their profits under internal pricing systems may do so at the expense of the firm's total profitability. A full-bodied approach requires analysis in terms of both the product and the product mix, the individual unit and the organization as a whole.

C. *Unit and total profits.* When we focus upon a single product line, we face the classic choice between higher unit profits with a smaller sales volume and the possibility of a higher sales volume with lower unit profits. In underdeveloped countries business traditions often favor relatively high unit profits. With the coming of mass production methods the tendency, rather, is to exploit the economies of scale and obtain larger total profits through the production and sale of a larger volume of lower priced units. The transitional period holds forth difficulties. Even when higher total profits are very attractive, higher unit profits often seem more consistent with established ways of doing business or with the maintenance of quality traditions. Even in industrialized societies, they are often regarded as a more reliable guide to acceptable total profits. The possibility that a larger volume may result from lower prices is often fraught with considerable risk and uncertainty. It often requires a much longer time perspective than some companies can reasonably afford.

D. *Profit on sales or investment.* Absolute profit figures are not very useful in comparing profits from one period to another or from one company or unit to another. For these purposes it is customary to express profits as a per cent of sales or investment. The difference between the two is considerable. The same absolute figure may seem very high as a per cent of one and very low as a per cent of the other, as with the following two companies:

		PROFIT AS A PER CENT OF	
	Absolute Profit	*Sales*	*Investment*
Company A	$1,000,000	20%	2%
Company B	1,000,000	2	20

Company A is probably one with expensive equipment and a low investment turnover (that is, a low ratio of sales to investment). Company B probably has a much lower investment base and/or a high turnover.

The weight of economic and business logic seems to be against too much emphasis on a per cent of sales. Pursuit of higher ratios of profit to sales has often resulted in lower absolute profits. Moreover, the percentage of investment approach provides a more rational common denominator for companies with changing or different investment bases. It is more responsive to the investors' interest in a return on capital.

But the weight of actual practice, particularly among the large number of smaller firms, is probably on the side of profits as a percentage of sales. Chamberlain reports that this "is probably the most commonly encountered" (1962, p. 55). McNair and May (1957) have bewailed the widespread tendency among retailers to think almost exclusively of profits as percentages of sales. One reason for this tendency is that both the profit and the sales figures can be taken directly from a company's income statement. This facilitates simple calculations for either planning or control. The use of investment data involves dipping into the greater complexities of the balance sheet. Moreover, as one controller has put it, "The relation of profit to sales comes nearer to being a comparison of like to like. . . . Assets, however, are conventionally expressed in an unraveled tangle of anachronistic and absolete dollars" (quoted in Chamberlain, 1962, p. 55-56).

E. *Profits on assets or net worth.* One of the complications involved in calculating profits as a return on investment is the necessity of choosing between different measures of investment. Thus investment may be calculated in terms of original cost, book value after depreciation or estimated replacement value. In any of these cases current liabilities may be subtracted. A still greater choice must be made between using total assets or net worth, sometimes referred to as owners' or stockholders' equity (that is, total assets less all current liabilities, debts and reserves for specific purposes). How great the difference is may be seen by going back to Company B:

	PROFIT AS A PER CENT OF	
Absolute Profit	*Total Assets*	*Net Worth*
$1,000,000	10%	20%

We now see that the 20 per cent figure applies only to net worth. If we look at the company's profits as a return on total assets, the figure is only 10 per cent. In this case, obviously, the net worth is half the total assets. Where net worth is a smaller proportion of total assets, a shift to profits as a percentage of total assets makes the resulting figure seem still smaller. Where net worth is larger, the change is not so dramatic. In either case, the use of total assets makes profits seem less conspicuous. Whether or not this is a sufficient reason, many business executives explain their use of the total asset base on the ground that it provides a way of measuring total performance without reference to the sources of capital. Others make it clear that they regard the financial claims of depersonalized ownership as merely an incidental part of financial management rather than the dominant factor it was in the days before the separation between business ownership and managerial power. Against all these considerations it is unlikely that the preference of most economists for a net worth base will be very influential.[4]

In accordance with the last three sets of choices, we may now see that a multidimensional set of profit goals might look as follows:

4. A 1960 survey showed that 89 companies used some version of total assets as against 50 employing the net worth approach (Chamberlain 1962, p. 58).

	This Year	*Next Year*	*Change*
Profits per unit	$1	$.90	− 10%
Total profits	$1,000,000	$1,100,000	+ 10
Profits as % of			
Sales	2%	1.8%	− 10%
Assets	10	12	+ 10
Net worth	20	18	− 10

The goal of less profits per unit and per sales is part of the strategy of obtaining a higher volume of sales and total profits. The goal of less profits on net worth is associated with a program of increasing equity capital and reducing the proportion of loan capital. If calculations were made for a longer time period and different product lines, the number of profit dimensions would increase correspondingly.

2. THE LEVEL OF PROFIT ASPIRATION

Still another dimension of profit goals is the level of aspiration. Do businessmen always aim at maximizing profits, or do they often seek merely a satisfactory or "fair" profit?

In answering these questions it is hard to escape the influence of two conflicting pressures. On the one hand, there are economists whose technical skills revolve around the assumption of profit maximization as the guiding principle of business undertakings. In the effort to prevent serious losses on their intellectual investment in obsolescent theory, they stress profit maximization so strenuously as to provoke a counterreaction that may understate the power of profit goals. On the other hand, business spokesmen—in the public as well as the private sectors—increasingly court public favor by stressing their desire to balance profit goals with the interests of labor, consumers, and the nation. Their utterances for public consumption are often so drippingly pious that one is led to suspect them as disguises of a savage drive for profit.

The question itself needs careful examination. In the light of the previous discussion we now see that a maximum profit can never be any single, undifferentiated figure. It is rather a multidimensional goal applicable to an arbitrarily defined and somewhat indefinite period of time. Further, in the light of the discussion on "aspirations and constraints" in Chapter 11, we see that profit objectives are invariably modified by other objectives in the purpose matrix. The recognition of these other objectives is one of the reasons for the "growing realization by theorists that many firms, and particularly the big ones, do not operate on the principle of profit-maximizing in terms of marginal costs and revenues" (Dean, 1951, p. 28). Drucker carries the logical analysis one step further by identifying profit as a "limiting factor" and describing profit goals as minimum goals. Thus businessmen aim not at maximum profit but at the minimum profit necessary to cover the costs and risks of staying in business and to insure a supply of future capital through retained earnings or external funds. Profit is also a minimal test of business performance (1954, p. 36, 76-81). This is in keeping with Barnard's report, based on many years of business experience, that "effort to prevent loss is many times as important as the effort to secure profit" (1948, p. 16).

The better part of wisdom is to assume that the level of profit aspiration in business enterprises varies considerably. The factors that influence this level in the case of any single business organization appear in each of the purpose categories other than input-output relations. They include both personal dispositions and influences exerted by other organization members and external forces. Some of the more frequent factors serving to reduce the level of profit aspiration are as follows:

Satisfaction of Interests	Remuneration of top executives by salaries and "extras," counterbalanced only in part by stock participation and other links with profits.
	Weak power position of stockholders interested in profits as basis for larger dividends.
	Interest of executives and/or stockholders in greater security than in larger financial returns.
	Interests of executives in power, prestige, creativity or other goals that may be attained without more profit or at the expense of profits.
	Nonacceptance of profit goals, or opposition to them, by various organization members, particularly professional people, workers, or union.
	Adaptation to constraints exercised by competitors, suppliers, and controllers.
Output	Production of nonprofitable products because of tradition or public service.
	Maintenance of quality standards at the expense of higher profits.
Investment in Organizational Viability	Building a larger organization at the expense of profits. Maintaining a more comfortable asset structure at the expense of profits.
Mobilization of Resources	Mobilizing more resources than can be profitably used.

Observance of Codes	Refusal to violate ethical, legal, or professional codes in order to raise profits.
Rationality	Use of technical or administrative methods that do not make the most of profit opportunities.

In listing these factors, I am not suggesting that, apart from the specific circumstances, any one of them should be looked upon with general approval or disapproval. In some situations public interests may be better served by a government corporation that actively seeks profits instead of merely trying to "break even." The interests of a private corporation can often be better served by aiming at less profits instead of more. The appropriate level for profit goals can best be judged in terms of a specific organization, a specific environment and the global matrix of organizational purposes.

3. WHAT DO PROFITS MEASURE?

What is the significance of any particular increase in profits?

It is merely that there has been a change in the relation between some calculation of output value and some calculation of input costs. If the question refers to an increase in a profit percentage, the change may include—or be limited to—a decrease in sales volume, asset value or net worth.

Such changes can never be automatically attributed to any single causal factor. For one thing, the increase may be conceptual only. It may have resulted from a shift from one set of definitions or calculating methods to another. Apart from such matters, the change may have resulted from any factor or factors that tended to raise output value, decrease output costs or both. Output value may have risen as a result of larger volume or higher prices. These may have resulted from improved quality, more aggressive marketing or advertising, the use of monopolistic or quasi-monopolistic power, influence with large buyers, rising demand, or sudden shortages. Costs may have decreased as a result of improved production methods, lower quality, larger scale operations, greater use of capacity, lower wages, lower prices on purchased products, higher morale among some employees, pushing some employees to their utmost, the deferral of maintenance, repair, research and training activities, or special assistance in the form of a protective tariff, tax exemption, low-interest loan, or direct subsidy. Many a company in many a country has raised profits not by production efficiency in the traditional sense but by more efficient methods of building monopoly power, bribing purchasing agents, hypnotizing consumers, undermining a union or getting public subsidy.

Nor is it possible, from the narrow facts on a particular profit increase, to infer any future consequences. The increase may contribute to or detract from various basic interests of the organization and its component parts, including their interest in future profits. It may contribute to or detract from the interests of any particular external group or the entire network of public interests as a whole.

Thus profitability is no automatic, all-purpose indicator that signals when things are going well or badly. It is rather a complex set of indicators that can be understood only in the context of looking at the organization in its environment. Its great value is that by virtue of being a resultant of so many factors, profitability provides a way of exploring the total context.

By the same token, one may presume a certain significance in any organization's record of a sustained profit pattern over a considerable period of time. On the assumption of acceptable and consistent definitions, one may presume that output has been worth more than input. Nor is this merely an abstract evaluation by some appraiser called in for the purpose. It is a summation of the real-life appraisals made by all the clients of the organization's products. Conversely, the existence of sustained losses suggests that the output has been worth less (at least to the clients) than the input. The implication is that the continued existence of the organization is in jeopardy unless output value is raised, input costs are lowered or the deficit is covered by others who are willing and able to do so. In the case of publicly subsidized enterprises, the loss or deficit serves as a rough-and-ready indicator of what it costs (whether or not everyone will agree that the cost is worth paying) to keep the enterprise going.

The broad sweep of history during the last century has unquestionably contracted the relative area of marketed products. With the expansion of free public services and of large business corporations whose internal transactions take place on a nonmarket basis, this trend will certainly continue.

Yet this trend does not imply the end of profitability as goal or standard. More and more organizations are interested in developing internal pricing systems that allow the setting of profit goals for their component units. Government corporations are increasingly expected not merely to break even but to make enough profit to finance at least part of their future investment programs. Indeed, the profit standard has been formally taken over by socialist planners. Thus only a few years after the 1917 revolution, the USSR officially accepted the profit standard as applicable to state-owned plants. "The 12th Congress of the Communist Party [1923] resolved that 'a country's industry can be victorious only if it yields more than it absorbs. . . .' It was decided that all plants should work on lines of 'business accountability,' operate without loss, and achieve a profit" (Bienstock, Schwarz and Yugow, 1944, p. 81). In successive waves of reform this decision has been reaffirmed and translated into increasingly specific measures of accounting and control. Neither in Russia nor in other socialist countries has it been found too difficult to reconcile profit-seeking with socialist principles. In fact, high profits in socialist countries often serve the function of indirect or hidden taxes and are maintained at levels that, under capitalism, would be sharply attacked as excessive.

E. *Other Broad Input-Output Relations*

IN ADDITION TO PROFITABILITY, there are other input-output relations that are also free from the limitation of focusing upon only a single factor. Although none of them are as useful as profits, all of them are useful in supplementing profit measures or, when profits cannot be calculated, in "holding the fort." Of these, cost accounting is the only one that has been developed in a sophisticated fashion. "Total productivity" calculations are still in their infancy. Calculations of thermodynamic and social efficiency of organizations may never be susceptible of precise quantification.

1. COST ACCOUNTING GOALS

Where it is not possible to place a monetary value upon output, it may still be possible to identify output—whether final or intermediate, whether services or goods—and estimate the costs associated with its production. This is what is done in cost accounting, as explained earlier in this chapter in "The multiplicity of cost concepts." As explained in Chapter 15, the essence of "performance budgeting" is the identification of operations to which costs may be assigned. In either case, cost goals are established either as targets for cost reduction or as maxims to which adherence is expected and by which performance may be judged.

The great virtue of cost accounting goals is that they can be used in almost every type of operation. The defect of this very virtue lies in the fact that the output side is expressed in units or operations only. Thus there is an inevitable tendency for the detailed quantification on the input side to detract attention from those aspects that may be no less important, although less quantifiable—namely, the quality of output and its contribution to the satisfaction of clientele interests.

2. *"TOTAL" PRODUCTIVITY*

For many decades economists have measured the productivity of national economies, regions, and specific industries by partial productivity ratios. The input factor most widely used has been manpower, since information on the labor force and employment is usually easier to obtain than information on capital.

In his monumental *Productivity in the United States*, Kendrick points out that "partial productivity ratios, while useful for measuring the saving in particular inputs achieved over time, do not measure overall changes in productive efficiency, since they are affected by changes in the composition of input, i.e., by factor substitutions" (1961, p. 6). In an effort to measure "overall changes," Kendrick has calculated *total productivity* for the U.S. economy as a whole and thirty major industries. A brief summation of his overall findings for a period of more than sixty years may be presented as follows:

AVERAGE ANNUAL PERCENTAGE RATES OF CHANGE
FOR THE PRIVATE DOMESTIC ECONOMY

REAL GROSS PRODUCT PER UNIT OF

	1	2	3	4	5
			Total Factor Input		*"Real*
	Labor	*Capital*	*(weighted average*	*Real Gross*	*Productivity"*
	Input	*Input*	*of 1 and 2)*	*Product*	*(4 minus 3)*
1889-1957	2.0	1.0	1.7	3.5	1.8
1889-1919	1.6	0.5	1.3	3.9	1.6
1919-1957	2.3	1.3	2.1	3.1	1.0

Labor input is measured by work done, with higher paid work given a higher weight. If manhours are used by themselves, the labor input declines (as a result of the declining workweek) and a higher partial productivity ratio is produced. Capital is measured in terms of tangible capital available (that is, the estimated real net capital stock, weighted by base period rates of return), as calculated from information on capital formation. The concept is limited to tangible capital: land, farms, and forests; structures; equipment; inventories; and net foreign assets. If an addition were to be made for intangible capital, such as investments in education, research and development, the partial productivity ratio would decline. On the other hand, no account has been taken of varying degrees of utilization of capacity. If Kendrick's figures could be adjusted to capital actually used, the capital input would decline and the partial productivity ratio would rise.

By computing the increase in real product per "total factor input" Kendrick gets away from the problems created by the partial ratios. He knows that of the total annual output increase of 3.5 per cent, "about half of the growth in output was accounted for by additions to real capital and labor inputs, and half was contributed by increases in the efficiency with which the inputs were utilized, i.e., in productivity" (1961, p. 60). Thus the figures on the difference between the annual increase in real product and the annual increase in real product per unit of total output are the "real productivity" increases. Similar calculations by Denison are more comprehensive in their handling of labor and capital inputs. For the period from 1909 to 1958 they show real national income increasing at 2.89 per cent a year, total inputs at 2.20 per cent and national output in relation to "total input" at 0.67 per cent (1962, p. 146-148).

The further development of this type of an analysis is bound to be significant. For one thing, it can be much more enlightening than partial productivity ratios in comparing various industries throughout the world. It can also provide a valuable instrument for comparing the performance of individual companies without directly using their confidential data on costs and profits.

3. *"THERMODYNAMIC" EFFICIENCY*

For the engineer efficiency is measured by the ratio of used output to total input. Thus when an engine uses fuel containing 100 units of energy and provides 85 units of used energy, efficiency is 85 per cent. The remaining 15 units of energy input come out in the form of heat or smoke. This, also, is output—but in an unused form. If the unused output, or waste, can be reduced to 10 per cent, then the efficiency of the engine will be raised to 90 per cent.

It will be noted, however, that total output includes both the used energy and the unused energy which escapes in the form of heat or smoke. Total output is, and must necessarily be, equal to total input. For total output to be either more or less than total input would contradict the law of the conservation of energy. Thus the maximum goal is 100 per cent efficiency. But this maximum is never wholly attainable. Some amount of waste or leakage is always inevitable.

A great advantage of applying the thermodynamic concept to organizational performance is that it expresses the sound, common-sense principle that "You can't get something for nothing." If you get an increase in output quantity, output quality, or both, there must be an additional input someplace—even though it may not be reflected in the cost figures of an organization's accounts. It may be an additional input of energy, or—as more likely—of needed information or skill. The obvious disadvantage of this concept is that in the case of an organization, unlike an engine, there are no physical units that can readily be applied to both the output and the input side. In ordinary monetary terms the thermodynamic concept of equality between input and output is easy to determine, but not particularly relevant. Thus if we regard profit as the cost of management, then in a business organization the cost of input will equal the cost of output. But this adds nothing more than a semantic twist to ordinary profit calculations. Similarly, the national income summarizes the cost of input factors. When we add indirect taxes and depreciation (which may be regarded as costs of government and capital), the sum equals the gross national product.

A more useful approach—and one more strictly thermodynamic—is to identify waste in any form. Once we know that certain inputs or outputs are not used, we know that this is an indication of inefficiency. The problem, of course, is to distinguish between unavoidable or tolerable waste and avoidable or intolerable degrees of waste. This can sometimes be done without calculating total output or input—as when we see large amounts of idle manpower, unused machinery or "dead inventory."

A more meaningful approach to waste is to start by estimating the optimum output capacity of an organization. This can be regarded as the best and largest product mix that can be obtained with optimum use of the skill and energy of all members and the optimum use of sources of external support. The input side can be left out of the calculation. One need merely compare actual output with potential output. The difference can be regarded as the waste which results from the failure to utilize internal and external resources. This is the same analysis that economists make for an entire economy when they estimate its "full employment level of output" and subtract from it the actual output under conditions of unused resources. The "gap" or "deficit" between potential and actual output is a measure of national waste.[5]

This concept of efficiency as reducing the gap between the actual and potential is one of the most important concepts to be operationally developed in the coming stages of administrative practice and theory. It can provide an instrument for unleashing the tremendous untapped po-

5. Thus in the U.S.A. the "gap" in the first quarter of 1963 was estimated at $30 billion, *Economic Report of the President*, January 1964, p. 37.

tentials within almost every organization. Its successful use depends, of course, on increasingly sensitive ways of estimating potentials.

4. SOCIAL EFFICIENCY

The formal accounts of an organization, as shown in this chapter's earlier discussion of "Costs outside an organization's accounts," never include as costs the many inputs received from its members and from the external environment. Nor can the monetary value of output, when available, possibly reflect all the many satisfactions and dissatisfactions that may be engendered by its output. On the other hand, the concept of social efficiency takes into account all costs, those borne by others as well as by the organization, and all aspects of output value. It includes imponderables as well as quantifiables.

In a narrow sense, the concept of social efficiency is used merely as a way of calling attention to a single aspect of input or output that might be overlooked. Thus if an organization from Megalopolis sets up a field office in a country without educational facilities, it will not regard the field office as less efficient if its ratio of training personnel to total staff is higher than in Megalopolis. In a country with a serious shortage of foreign exchange, the import component in the output of a highly profitable factory may be so great that the factory is losing instead of earning foreign currency. Although its high profits suggest internal efficiency, its low "value added to imports" (see "Contributed Output and Value Added" in Chapter 13) may lead government officials to regard it as socially inefficient.

In a broader sense, the idea of social efficiency may be used to do much more than attract attention to a single factor that might otherwise be neglected. It may be used to provide a comprehensive evaluation of all factors relevant to input-output relations. In an intuitive way many experienced administrators think in terms of rather broad social efficiency concepts. A major reason for this is the ever-present possibility that unpaid costs may suddenly turn up as costs that must be paid, as with overtime pay, contribution to workmen's compensation insurance or tax increments to support public services. Similarly dissatisfactions may "come home to roost" in the long run. This may happen to business firms in the form of lower sales, government agencies in the form of reduced appropriations, associations in the form of declining membership and any of these in the form of public regulation. Public control agencies, in turn, can rarely regard the accounts of an organization as *prima facie* evidence of social efficiency or inefficiency. They must try to look further. To anticipate their actions, the regulated organizations are themselves often forced—whether they like it or not—to broaden their perspectives.

On the other hand, the growing size and complexity of the public infrastructure (or social overhead) of the modern economy creates tremendous opportunities for individual organizations, private and public, to expand their output on the basis of unpaid external inputs. Under such circumstances the accounts of single organizations mean less and less. What seems to be efficiency, economy, productivity or profitability may, indeed, be the result of the ability to amass and exploit a vast amount of unpaid inputs. However, the complications involved in making a full social accounting are enormous. They include dealing not only with interest satisfactions, output and input but with each of the other categories in the global matrix of human purposes. Above all, while this matrix provides an abstract framework within which to start to initiate an analysis, any meaningful appraisal of social efficiency requires the development within this matrix of a specific profile of social goals. Only then could one specify the direct measures and indirect surrogates to be regarded as essential information. It is conceivable that the techniques required for doing this may yet be developed as national economic planning matures into national social planning of a more coherent and self-conscious nature than may now be found. If so, it may be predicted that such techniques will have only minor relevance to ordinary organizations. Their major relevance, rather, will be the examination of major new ventures or the periodic appraisal of the performance of certain large organizations or of society as a whole.

Chapter 17

INVESTMENT IN
ORGANIZATIONAL VIABILITY

*V*IABILITY, the fourth element in the global matrix, concerns the maintenance of the organization itself.

In a minimal sense, viability means concern with *survival*. This has been referred to by theorists and researchers as the "preservation of equilibrium," "system maintenance," "conservation," or "stabilization." In the daily language of administration it may be expressed as "keeping our heads above water," "staving off reorganization," or "staying in business."

At a higher level of aspiration, the viability objective takes the form of *growth*. This may be expressed in terms of an increase in resources or productive capacity, in size or health. It may be referred to as "fulfilling our real responsibilities," "enlarging our place in the sun," or "being of greater service." In a pejorative sense the same objective may be referred to as "empire building" or "bureaucratic aggrandizement."

The division between the minimal and the higher levels of viability is not always so sharp. Major attention to one may be a prerequisite of serious orientation toward the other. Both of them require the investment of time, energy, and resources in the strengthening of the organization's capacities.

Viability objectives play such a major role in the life of all organizations and administrators that they often seem to divert attention from other objectives. The extent to which this may be so is remarkably hard to determine, however, since viability objectives arc closely intertwined with all the others. I shall discuss the nature of this relationship at the bebinning of this chapter.

This discussion leads to a separate analysis of the forms and measures of both survival and growth and the roads taken towards their attainment.

The concluding section deals with the strengthening of the capacity of organizations. This discussion requires the presentation of a managerial approach to investment in the replacement, expansion, conservation and development of human as well as material assets.

A. *The Role of Viability Objectives*

VIABILITY OBJECTIVES are often hard to talk about in terms deemed appropriate for external consumption. Since they deal with the organization and its members, they are necessarily self-oriented, if not self-seeking. Internal commitment to them is so strong that explicit goal formulation may not be as essential as with respect to input, output and the satisfaction of external interests.

1. THE IRON LAW OF SURVIVAL

In the hierarchy of personal interests, as pointed out in Chapter 8, survival is the most basic consideration. Without personal survival no other personal interests may be met. Without some minimum degree of security with respect to survival, other interests will be relatively weak. If survival may be taken for granted, however, it loses its power as a motivating factor.

At the level of the organization or unit thereof, survival occupies a similar position. The unwritten law of every organization is that its survival is an absolute prerequisite for its serving any interests whatsoever. "Survival, self-perpetuation," Writes Wiles in describing economic organizations, "these are motives that can be absolutely relied on . . ." (1961, p. 202). In describing other organizations Michels found that the efforts of leaders to achieve "self-perpetuation" were at the top of oligarchical tendencies. If the principle he enunciated is to be restated as "the iron law of multiple oligarchy," we may place alongside it "the iron law of survival." If administrative opportunism is the willingness to sacrifice principles to achieve an jective, there are few objectives other than survival for which this sacrifice will be more willingly or quickly made.

In stating this principle, we must beware against letting any metaphorical comparison with personal survival run away with us. The two kinds of survival are by no means identical. When an organization dies, people who belonged to it may still live, although their fortunes may decline. When people liquidate an organization, the result is not as tragic as suicide. The death of an organization does not necessarily mean that the interests served by it will no longer be satisfied. They may be satisfied just as well by individual action or by another or new organization. Organizational death merely means that the organization which previously existed will no longer be a vehicle of either satisfaction or dissatisfactions. Organizational survival, on the other hand, does not guarantee the personal survival of its members, some of whom will also leave the organization by separation or death. It is merely a simple and obvious prerequisite for the satisfaction of other human interests, both of members and nonmembers, through its activities.

Another difference is that with the differentiation of functions within an organization, most members need not be personally concerned with the organization's survival. Except in time of acute crisis, survival problems are handled by administrators. Others may thus take survival for granted. They may even enjoy the luxury of activities that threaten survival, since others may be relied upon to undo the damage. Or else the administrators of units within the organization may concentrate their attention upon unit survival, come what may for the organization as a whole. This damage may be harder to undo.

2. THE BROADER BASE

The scope of viability objectives includes more than just maintaining an organization in existence. "Mere existence is no life." When survival seems assured, viability goals become less minimal. Administrators and members seek to prevent organizational decline (apart from threats to survival), maintain organizational stability or increase organizational size or capacity. These goals, in turn, are deeply rooted in their potential contribution to other objectives. Thus a growing organization may provide deeper satisfactions for more interests of more people and groups. It may be able to produce more and better quality products, be more economical in the use of scarce inputs, be more effective in mobilizing resources, more willing and able to conform with behavioral codes, and more capable of acting rationally. An organization which is stable, even though not growing, may be able to attain these objectives better than one which is declining or contracting. In some situations, indeed, the hope of organizational survival may depend upon aggressive efforts to achieve the higher goal of organizational growth. In many cultures bigness is a symbol of all that is most admired (and envied), growth a measure of vitality, stability an indication of stodginess and contraction a proof of decay.

The actual weights that may be placed upon the various objectives served by organizational growth are never easy to determine. The most effective justification of an organization's growth is its contribution to satisfying the interests of large or powerful groups in the external environment. Within the organization the most effective justification of a unit's growth is its contribution to the top executives, or whoever else may have the power to promote or impede the growth of the unit. Yet in both cases the driving force behind the growth process may be a deep commitment to satisfying the personal interests of key members. Although it may, this need not mean that the justifications are false. The key to the satisfaction of much broader interests is, indeed, often the kind of organizational growth which provides higher personal satisfactions to growth-minded leaders. It is this fusion of self-interest and other-interest that provides a solid interest base for growth objectives. If the builders and consolidators are strengthening their own position, how can we be sure that they are not advancing the interests of others also? History is full of occasions when human needs were inadequately met because there were not enough leaders who sought to satisfy their own needs by activities that opponents would criticize as "empire building." Whether there is justification for using this critical epithet, or others even stronger, depends upon what the observer sees concerning the balance between self-interests and other-interest. For the more penetrating observer it also depends upon the nature of the self-interests involved. The base of growth objectives is best protected against inevitable criticism when the self-interest of the Builders involves "self development on behalf of interests broader than one's self," rather than mere accretions of status, respect and power.

B. *Survival or Liquidation*

THE CONCEPT OF SURVIVAL is simple. An organization survives if it stays in existence. The alternative is liquidation.

Let us now look at the various measures of organizational survival, the conditions under which survival takes place, and the significance of survival or liquidation.

1. MORTALITY AND AGE

"Dust thou art and unto dust shalt thou return" (Genesis 3:19). No matter how strong man's "life instinct" may be, mortality is his greatest certainty. If there is a "death instinct," as Freud claimed, it is merely oriented toward the acceleration of the inevitable. Human institutions are predicated upon this inevitability. The human organism has, in the words of Isaiah, "a covenant with death" (28:19).

One way of understanding human mortality is to view the human individual as an organization with limited possibilities for the replacement of worn-out parts. While skin and blood cells are replaced rapidly, the rate of natural replacement in the cells of basic organs and, above all, the nervous system, is low or nil. Artificial replacement of worn-down, injured, or severed parts has thus far been limited to teeth, skin, pieces of bone structure, limbs, sightless eyes, and parts of rudimentary organs. Until scientists can stimulate more thoroughgoing natural replacement or devise more farreaching means of artificial replacement, immortality is impossible for the human organism. The closest man can get to immortality is to produce other mortals through sexual reproduction and artifacts that may outlive both himself and immediate progeny.

In contrast, an organization as a group of individuals has no "covenant with death." Centuries ago, without the help of science, organizations learned how to replace *any* part, the higher as well as the lesser organs. Many of the most dramatic episodes in political and organizational history consist of experimentation with artificial or forced replacement. So long as other people are available to serve as replacements, it is possible for this kind of organization to live forever—not in some noncorporeal "afterworld" but bodily in this world. Thus, the organized group is a human artifact through which man can seek a vicarious immortality beyond that provided by monuments or works of art.[1] The Pyramids and the Parthenon may survive forever—but only as messages of wisdom and beauty to people who receive, interpret, and value them. Only in a metaphorical sense can we say they "live." The Catholic Church, as a continuing organization of living people, is alive in a direct sense.

1. This statement does not apply to individual family units, which have only a limited life. Once children achieve independence, usually to establish new family units, they cannot be replaced. The replacement of either parent is only a temporary expedient. Clans and dynasties may last for many generations, but the individual family can rarely last for much more than a few decades. This is the root of the personal tragedy of parents, particularly women, who may become overcommitted to their family functions and develop no others on which to base a satisfying life. On the other hand, as a type of social organization, the family is unquestionably the longest lived in human history.

Although the replacement of worndown parts is a necessary condition of survival, it is not a sufficient condition. It merely creates the *possibility* of immortality. As with individuals, a *probable* outcome is determined not only by the organization's internal structure but also by its environment. With both individuals and organizations, the environment is a source of sustenance and deprivation. Both individuals and organizations need a certain minimum amount of resources, support, and challenge from outside. Both may be liquidated by external attack. In both, external difficulties may upset the conflict-cooperation nexus and bring on liquidation through internal dissension. Both need special mechanisms of defense, immunization and counterattack. Here again the organized group has a potential advantage over the individual organism. Unlimited by any genetic code governing its morphology, the organization can establish any new organs that might prove useful in the strategic process of resisting and dividing opponents, winning over neutrals and nurturing supporters.

In the case of individuals, statistical probabilities of survival can be calculated on the basis of vital statistics on such matters as births, deaths (from various causes), age distribution, and disease. These data are assiduously collected to serve the needs of organizations involved in military mobilization, the protection of law and order, public health services, life and accident insurance, and market analysis. In the case of organizations, the data available on numbers, mortality, and age are mainly byproducts of regulation, tax collection, and debtor-creditor disputes with respect to business enterprises. Academic research in organizational demography and ecology has been sporadic and superficial. "In Marshall's day biology was the queen of the sciences, and analogies from her were freely drawn by philosophers and economists. Now that physics is the queen of the sciences, economists neglect to study firms as a population with an age structure" (Wiles, 1961, p. 229). Nor have political scientists yet taken on the relatively easier task (easier because of the relatively small number of units) of studying government organizations in ecological terms.

Nevertheless, three rather firm conclusions may be drawn from the incomplete analysis of imperfect data. The first is that "the first five years are the hardest." A study of business mortality among U. S. business firms (Kinnard and Malinowski, 1960, p. 22), shows the following concentration of liquidation among the youngest firms:

Percentage closing within:	*1844–1926*	*1926–1954*
1 year of opening	24	29
2 years of opening	37	47
5 years of opening	63	69

The new business is particularly subject to economic fluctuations, strong competition, and unforeseen technological changes. Organizations capable of facing these conditions can rarely be built quickly—particularly if their organizers lack administrative capacity, financial resources, and external backing. Similarly, the first years of a new government agency are the most dangerous ones. This is one of the reasons that new functions are sometimes assigned to old agencies. The possibility of a new unit being treated like a stepchild in an old organization may be less terrifying than the prospect of its fending for itself as an independent organization. When the Roosevelt administration took this latter course in setting up emergency agencies during World War II, every new agency was engulfed in a bewildering sequence of reorganization and liquidation.

The second conclusion is that larger organizations seem to last longer than smaller ones. The small firm's expectation of life is astoundingly short. The business mortality rate seems to rise sharply (and life expectancy decline) for firms with fewer employees and small net worth. Most older firms are of intermediate if not large size. Corporations, which are generally larger, survive longer than nonincorporated enterprises, which are generally smaller.

The third conclusion is an unquestionable tendency toward organizational longevity. Gulick was on firm ground in his wry comment concerning government agencies: "Next to the church they are in all civilizations the most vigorous embodiment of immortality. A government unit is by nature a monopoly. It does not have a profit and loss record; its balance sheet is buoyed up by 'good will,' its deficits are met from taxes, loans and hope. Under these conditions a governmental unit can continue for many years after its utility has passed, or its form of organization or program have become obsolete" ("Notes on the Theory of Organization," 1937, p. 43). To Gulick's list of reasons might be added that government birth processes are more selective. Business firms, particularly in the distribution and service fields, may often be set up at the whim of a few people with small capital and little ability. Government agencies are established after careful deliberation by many people and groups and are usually staffed by people with tested experience in the arts of organizational survival. We must also add a warning against taking too seriously Gulick's assumption that a large organization with a "profit and loss record" and "balance sheet" may be a less vigorous embodiment of immortality. The practice of entering "good will" on the asset side of a balance sheet originated on the basis of the assumed continuity of the enterprise. "Obviously, a concern which expected to 'fold up' the next month, the next year, or even perhaps the next decade, could not expect its bankers or stockholders to take seriously a financial appraisal of projected earning power (capitalized into the form of a continuing asset). There could be no 'good will' without continuity" (Cole, 1961, p. 77).

Larger business organizations, moreover, have often enjoyed "womb to no tomb" protection. Protective tariffs and import quotas, often enacted in the first instance to protect "infant industry" may continue long beyond infancy. Bankruptcy proceedings have developed as a way to safeguard continuity of business enterprises—albeit under new management.

> If ... railroads may be kept running despite financial embarrassment in the treasurer's office, if manufacturing establishments can persist in the employment of personnel and the production of goods despite the need of red ink in the controllers' reports, the business world is spared the repercussions which a break in the pre-existing skein of business relationships would otherwise have caused, the extent of the disturbance varying, of course, with the size of the enterprise that had gotten itself into difficulties. The series of repercussions which a sudden closing of the doors of General Motors or General Electric would touch off is almost inconceivable; but the damage to the whole country would surely be tremendous. . . . There has been an increase in the body of men and women, dispersed more widely over the country, who have stood ready to take over concerns that have faltered financially under previous management. . . . Even apart from the "trust movement," as usually conceived, there has been the added element that, over the last half century or more, prosperous enterprises were glad to become larger by the absorption of competing or ancillary firms that were heading for financial difficulties. . . . (Cole, 1961, p. 82-83).

Finally, direct government assistance can often be obtained—particularly in time of depression—to tide over large enterprises whose survival affects the livelihood of thousands of people. All these factors help explain why "No large United States corporation, which is also large in its industry, has failed or been seriously in danger of insolvency in many years" (Galbraith, 1958, p. 113).

The death of smaller organizations is not necessarily tragic. Some organizations are set up for special shorttime purposes and then swiftly liquidated. Temporary citizens' committees and associations are often set up under the protective wing of established organizations seeking new ways of mobilizing popular action for political or legislative campaigns. Business subsidiaries are often set up to take on special risks, or to incur losses needed for the purpose of tax exemption; when the task is done, the protective wing is withdrawn. Among cultural and fraternal associations, as with small business enterprises, new organizations come and go. The death of one and the birth of another may signify a change in relationships among the same people or a new pattern of leadership. A new organization, even though doomed to an evanescent existence, has the virtue of allowing its organizer or organizers to strut the stage in the mantle of authority. In personalistic politics, whether on a local or national basis, campaigns for elective office are conducted by small organizations centering around the candidate and his friends, organizations that will pass out of existence whether he wins or loses. From a broader historical viewpoint, we may even find an important social function formed by organizational mortality. Trailblazing is a risky affair. Hundreds of the industrial pioneers in the late nineteenth and early twentieth centuries went bankrupt in the effort. The wreckage of the first automobile companies was part of the process that led to the General Motors Corporation and the other "immortals" that now bestride the automobile industry in the U.S.A. In this case some of the earlier companies rose from the grave of bankruptcy and through merger or consolidation returned again to the heights of administrative power. In the international field, the United Nations was built out of the wreckage of the League of Nations. It still remains to be seen whether the United Nations will evolve into a stronger international organization or whether the history of its predecessor will be repeated.

2. HIBERNATION

Many bears last through a bitter winter by crawling into a snug den and hibernating. Similarly, an organization or unit can avoid the wintry blasts of opposition by snuggling into a well-worn routine. In doing this great care may be taken to maintain the proper state of lethargy. The full completion of any program (as shown in the *Mahabhrata*'s fable of the cat who was turned out the moment he killed the mouse in the lion's cave) may lead someone to suggest liquidation. Any swift action, any precipitate decision, any new burst of initiative, any taking of avoidable risks, might attract attention and criticism. Government agencies can do better than bears in this respect. When they enjoy the protection of an external interest group and the tradition of long acceptance, they may be able to maintain a dormant or semidormant state for decades. After World War II it was discovered that a U.S. battle monuments commission set up eighty years earlier at the end of the Civil War was still in existence. Some of the holdover units from World War II might well last another eighty years. Similarly, smaller units in larger organizations, both private and public, often approximate the functionless immortality of the appendix in the human body.

The dormant type of survival is often facilitated by high liquidation costs. In the direct sense, such costs may include termination payments and relocation efforts for employees, the disposition of property and time-consuming investigation and negotiation with respect to outstanding liabilities. The indirect dissatisfactions may be still higher. They may include psychic insecurity among other units that fear similar liquidation and substantial losses to supporting organizations. They may involve a substantial diversion from more attractive tasks and a commitment to tangle with opponents whose strength might prove greater than originally apparent. Hence, rather than attempt the liquidation of the useless, it is often judged better to "let sleeping dogs lie."

3. ADAPTATION

Hibernation may be regarded as a minimal type of adaptation to the environment, an adaptation characterized by withdrawal. It is probably much more of a limiting case than a general tendency. In general, changing environmental conditions dictate a much more active form of adaptation. The price an organization pays for the privilege of remaining in existence in the future is usually continual changes that prevent it from remaining what it was in the past.

The most sustained environmental changes in the modern world are technological. An organization that got underway in the "horse and buggy" days must make adaptations to the era of automation, the electronic computer, the jet plane, and mass communications. The tempo of work, the equipment used and the methods of operation must all be changed. This process of adaptation is endless. In some industries, particularly those where technological innovation is fostered by defense and outer-space programs, it moves forward at a breathtaking pace. Whatever is already in operation is *ipso facto* obsolete. The up-to-date technology is that which is now at the research and development stage, already being blueprinted as a basis of operations three years later. Three years later, by the same principle, it too will be obsolete. Even where the pace is less hectic, organizations must somehow or other manage to keep up with the technology of competitors and opponents. This necessarily involves continual changes in the clientele network, the output mix, inputs, resource mobilization, codes of behavior, and technical and administrative methods.

Equally dramatic are those environmental changes which consist of ups-and-downs in economic conditions and shifts in political and social structure. Business firms must adjust to economic fluctuations or perish. The most adept learn to "ride the business cycle" by building up reserves in good times, developing price policies that may allow them to break even in bad times, or using bad times as an opportunity to squeeze out competitors and tighten their organizational structures. Organizations that may be threatened by political and social change often develop friends and allies among the major contestants in the national power struggle. In this way they may be assured of "protection," or at least better treatment, in the event of a sudden change. The most well-known examples are the large business corporations that provide financial support to more than one political party. This is not entirely different from the posture of those civil servants under formal merit systems whose loyalty is pledged in advance to any political party that comes to power.

Less dramatic but often overwhelming in its impact may be an organization's success in achieving a given objective. Civic reform groups often fall to pieces once they have won a successful campaign. The Townsend movement mushroomed rapidly in the 1930's on the wave of a campaign to obtain liberal old-age pensions. It was unable to adjust to the situation created when modest old-age insurance payments began to be made under the U.S. Government's new Social Security program. Labor unions which grow rapidly in periods of acute distress among workers are apt to lose their vitality when they have succeeded in winning better conditions. Adaptation requires new output goals to meet new needs. The National Foundation for Infantile Paralysis was confronted by such a situation as it became clear that with new vaccines infantile paralysis could be conquered (*Sills*, p. 268-271). By developing a broad set of goals which included the promotion of medical research in many fields, it laid the foundation for subsequent adjustment of its product mix. In many liberated colonies, such as Egypt and Burma, army organizations formed to achieve liberation have transformed themselves into a combination of general-purpose career service and political party in order to run civilian government activities.

The process of adaptation is never smooth, steady and painless. Since it is continually met with resistance by those who fear change, it tends to be jerky, tumultuous, and painful. Two steps forward are often followed by three steps backward. Three steps forward are often suddenly taken after protracted refusal to move more than an inch. The Catholic Church did not adapt to the post-Renaissance world until after the world-shaking Reformation. From the Counter-Reformation onward, it has provided an unprecedented example of adaptation to modern science and social and political revolutions, a process facilitated by the high degree of autonomy enjoyed by its bishops. It has even reached a *modus vivendi* with the dominant interests in some communist countries. The impressive outward façade of immutable dogma has probably facilitated the pace of intraorganizational mutation.

No matter how objective the terms used to describe adaptation by organizations, the process is fundamentally one of human adaptation. Over the long run, as indicated by the previous discussion concerning replacement, organizational adaptation involves a change *of* people. But too many people can never be replaced at the same time. If the attempt were made, the continuity of the organization would be impaired. If an entire army unit is wiped out in battle, it can never be rebuilt. If a new unit is formed to take its place, it will be—despite similarities in mission and structure—a *new* unit. In the short run, the most important form of adaptation is change *in* people. In turn, the changing *of* people usually results, willy-nilly, in many changes *in* people. When a respected administrator leaves, his former associates and subordinates may fondly hope that under his successor "things will be the same." They won't be. Nor will they themselves remain the same. Sooner or later they will adapt in some way to the personality, style, and interests of the successor.

Adaptation cannot be thought of in terms of *any* change in the behavior of people in organizations. Some change is nonadaptive or even misadaptive. There are limits to the extent to which people can adapt to new situations. There are conditions under which they will degenerate instead of develop. A dramatic example of degeneration is found in Captain Queeg's response to the vicissitudes of the storm in *The Caine Mutiny*. In a positive sense, adaptation boils down to human maturation and learning. Maturation is the under-the-surface process of developing new and better responses to problems. Learning is the more active process of acquiring new knowledge, new abilities, or new interests. One of the major tests of the level of maturation and learning of administrators is the extent to which they directly address themselves to the process of promoting changes *in* people within their organizations. The Catholic Church has been outstanding in this respect for centuries. As the founder of the first universities in the West, it has consistently prepared a steady stream of younger people for service in the church hierarchy and—probably to a lesser extent—encouraged certain areas for learning among the older members of the establishment. Military and foreign service career groups have encouraged the latter through the practice of rotating assignments. The military agencies have traditionally exploited periods of peace for the continuous training of officer personnel in formal educational organizations and simulated combat. The recent boom in executive development programs, both within organizations and at educational institutions, represents an extension of these traditions to business and government. The initiation of such programs provides top executives with the satisfaction of feeling that while they themselves may be mortal, they are planning for the immortality of their organizations.

4. PERMANENT REORGANIZATION

A more significant contribution to immortality may be provided by the constant changes that take place in the formal and informal organizational structure. In every organization, there is a continuing accrual of small structural changes consisting of adaptation to the shifting spectrum of personalities, interests, and methods. Rapid technological advance produces a host of more obvious organizational changes. It requires new skills, new subdivisions of labor, new patterns of hierarchic and polyarchic relations among units, and new rules and rituals. It renders obsolete or obsolescent people and units rooted in an older technology. It usually intensifies the anxieties of those who may lose their past positions of prestige and leadership, while creating opportunities for new elites eager to rise to the top. Also significant, although less obvious, is the impact on organizational structure that may result from changing economic, social, and political conditions. Chandler has shown that changing market conditions have been "of overwhelming importance to the changing structure and strategy of American industrial enterprise" (*Chandler*, p. 382). Any sharp decline in economic activity or sharp increase in competition is also important. Either one may presage an organizational "shakeup" in business firms. In both business and government, shifts in the social and political environment often result in organizational changes bringing to the fore those better able to deal with the new conditions. Sometimes the newly arrived political leaders will themselves intervene in an effort to dictate the nature of these changes.

As a result of all these factors there is reason to formulate the "principle of permanent reorganization." This principle has two variants, descriptive and prescriptive. The descriptive principle tells us that there is a tendency toward continuous change in the structure of all organizations. During any one period of time these changes may be small or large, planned or unplanned. Many of them are part of the web of internal and external conflicts in which every organization is enmeshed. All of them illustrate the more general concept of structure as merely the more stabilized aspect, or the limiting case, of process (Chapt. 2).

The prescriptive principle of permanent reorganization is followed by administrators who are committed to the continual use of reorganization in the conduct of affairs. Reorganization may often seem the best way to change the power structure and purpose pattern of an organization. What the reorganizers themselves may publicly announce is less important. "Many arguments about form and structure are really rationalizations or concealments of arguments about substance" (Simon, Smithburg and Thompson, 1950, p. 44). Whether the justification is increased efficiency or abstract principles of administrative rationality, reorganization may also be used as a substitute for substantive action. Charlton Ogburn illustrates this in his vivid picture of a military unit in the Pacific during World War II: "We trained hard, but it seemed that every time we were beginning to form up into teams we would be reorganized. . . . I was to learn later in life that, perhaps because we are so good at organizing, we tend as a nation to meet any new situation by reorganizing; and a wonderful method it can be for creating the illusion of progress while producing confusion, inefficiency and demoralization" (1957, p. 29-44). Although Ogburn's criticism may have been justified in this case, one can hardly accept at face value an over-all judgment by one of the "suffering reorganized."

In many situations administrators must choose betweeen the "change-over costs" and temporary dissatisfactions involved in reorganization and the greater losses that might be incurred by maintaining an inadequate organization. In military services, furthermore, tight organization and routinization may easily undermine the initiative of officers and bring on a hardening of the organizational arteries. Recurrent shakeups may keep people on the *qui vive*, thereby providing better preparation for the uncertainties of battle. In the Israeli Defense Forces, one of the best small armies in the world, the prescriptive "principle of permanent reorganization" leads to a thoroughgoing structural change, with the replacement of the highest officers every two or three years. As explained to me by a member of the Israeli General Staff, this is not reorganization for the sake of a better structure. Nor is it reorganization "for its own sake." Rather, it is reorganization for the sake of the enlivening effect that recurrent shifts in roles and relations have upon the adaptive behavior of officers and soldiers.

5. WHAT DOES SURVIVAL INDICATE?

The survival of an organization is one of the easy things to measure. So long as we can find out when it first came into being and so long as its boundaries are not blurred by merger or reconstruction, its age provides a clear, quantitative measure. What does such a measure indicate?

The fact of advanced organizational age unquestionably indicates that an organization has continued to satisfy certain human interests. More specifically, it indicates that sustained satisfactions have been provided both for members and nonmembers, although not necessarily all of either. On the other hand, victory in the struggle for survival does not indicate that the victor is the "fittest" by all standards. As Marshall pointed out, the law of the "survival of the fittest" merely states that "those organisms tend to survive which are best fitted for their own purposes. Those that utilize the environment most, often turn out to be those that benefit those around them most; but sometimes they are injurious" (1949, p. 242). Survival through the hibernation route merely indicates that the survivor has been exceptionally fit to devise ways of lying dormant and unnoticed.

With people, old age means a low life expectancy. Beyond a certain point (which varies enormously with individuals and with progress in medical science) it means decreased energy and vitality. Before that point has clearly arrived, it may result in cautiousness, stability, dignity, and fear of sudden change. These characteristics tend to be dominant attributes of older organizations dominated by older people. A large group of Oldtimers in strategic positions throughout an organization can weight the scales in favor of tradition instead of innovation, routinization instead of creativity.

Yet it would be a serious mistake to allow biological analogies to run away with us. There is a major difference between the age of an organization and the age structure of its members. Although an old organization may have a disproportionate number of elderly members, as with the U.S. railroads during the 1950's and early 1960's, it need not. It may be better equipped than other organizations to provide for early retirement and for recruitment of younger members at various levels. Moreover, the age structure of an organization is a tricky thing. The existence of elderly people in senior positions usually holds forth the promise of advancement for those who might hope to replace them. A large proportion of very young men in the senior positions, although it may temporarily provide the "vitality of youth" at the top, usually restricts the avenues of future advancement. Unless a good proportion of them can be pried loose before they are old, this can lead to a premature debility throughout the middle and lower levels. The chronologically young sometimes turn out to be timid souls who serve as focal points for the spread of organizational arteriosclerosis.

The frequent statement that "an organization has a life of its own" is a way of indicating that it is the product rather than the sum of its parts. What it does can never be fully predicted by anyone, including its leaders. Its actions are the result of many interactions, both within it and between it and its environment. As its members are replaced, continuity is provided by those who remain and by external expectations. But the biological analogy is carried too far if the idea of "a life of its own" implies a life apart from the people in it. Every organization is embodied in its members and their interrelations. It exists only as part of their life. If all the members of an organization should suddenly be wiped out of existence by epidemic, murder, or war, the organization also is wiped out. No matter how durable may be the physical assets left behind it in the form of buildings, files or machinery, the "life of its own" is over.

It follows that the biological concept of an organism that passes through infancy, maturation and inevitable decline cannot be automatically applied to human organizations. The truly old organizations, those that have lasted more than a century and have weathered major social and technological changes, are the most likely candidates for immortality. On much the same basis works of art and literature are regarded as immortal classics only after passing the "test of history." Hasty acclaim of a new drama or painting will bring the retort "Only time can tell." What time tells—and nothing else can—is that an unchanged work of art has brought deep esthetic satisfaction to changing generations of people. When an organization has passed the test of history by continual adaptation to new conditions, there is reason to believe that it may have the capacity to provide sustained satisfactions in the future.

c. *Growth or Decline*

IN ACTION, as distinguished from analysis, it is difficult to separate the survival of organizations from their growth. Some form of growth—and also of decline—is usually associated with the adaptation process that makes survival possible.

Growth and decline, in turn, are more complex and dynamic than survival and liquidation. Since growth of various parts tends to be disproportional, it is difficult to formulate growth objectives covering all dimensions and parts of an organization. Since growth tends to take place at changing rates, it is difficult to formulate growth objectives for an extended period of time. It is still more difficult to adjust to the implications of growth.

1. THE LAW OF DISPROPORTIONALITY

The first complicating factor is that the dimensions and parts of organizations tend to grow or decline at disproportionate rates. This tendency is so universal that it may well be labeled, albeit with some trepidation, "the law of disproportionality."

The dimensions of organizational size, as pointed out in Chapter 9, are number of employees, spatial coverage, volume or value of material assets, expenses, and actual or potential output. In periods of growth one or two of these spurt forward at different rates, followed more slowly by the others. Some may decline, as expenses per unit of output. In periods of decline, the lead will usually be taken by actual output. When decline leads to liquidation, this will never take place after the fashion of the mythical "one-horse shay," all of which dissolved into dust at one moment. At the very moment of dismemberment or reorganization, many of these dimensions will be far above zero. Nor is there any fixed relationship between these various dimensions such as the square cube law in the physical world, which holds that the surface of an object equals the square, and its volume the cube, of its linear dimensions.

Moreover, absolute and relative size rarely move proportionately. To do so, no matter what dimension be used, would require an identical growth (or decline) rate on the part of all comparable organizations or units. In a market growing at 10 per cent a year, an organization which increases its sales by 5 per cent is falling behind in terms of "market penetration." Under such circumstances, like the Duchess in *Alice in Wonderland*, it must "run faster in order to stand still."

Above all, the growth of an organization as a whole is invariably based upon different rates of growth for its various units. The process of increasing specialization, or functional differentiation, often means the creation of new units which start small and then grow for a while more rapidly than the organization as a whole. One careful study (*Baker and Davis*, 1954)[2] suggests that in certain industrial organizations some of these—such as inspection, maintenance, engineering, tool design and toolmaking—have grown faster than direct employment. The number of employees involved in supervision, purchasing, tool handling, personnel, accounting, time and motion study, and production control seems to have grown in proportion to the increase in direct employment. On the other hand, the number of top executives and employees involved in shipping, receiving, and plant protection seems to have grown more slowly. Moreover, the process of replacing labor with machinery means a relative, if not an absolute, decline in the number of machine operators and machine tenders, with a corresponding increase in indirect, white collar, or clerical employment. The introduction of electronic computers, in turn, has often meant a sharp decline in the number of clerical employees. The number of administrators may rise (*Terrien and Mills*) or decline (*Loken and Thake; Anderson and Warkov*) with the size of

2. Since the study dealt with 211 manufacturing companies during one period of time, its conclusions concerning growth rates are merely inferences from the relative size of units in different-size firms.

an organization or vary with organizational complexity (*Anderson and Warkov*). A large part of reorganization and structural adaptation consists of adding or subtracting a unit or a number of positions at selected spots or of making more massive changes through new combinations. Accordingly, the internal growth processes of an organization are characterized by a combination of both growth and decline. The objective of relative growth for one part of an organization inevitably implies a relative decline in many other parts and may imply an absolute decline in some. The perception of these implications, in turn, affects the goal formulation and action of those whose decline may thereby be rendered imminent.

A number of crude efforts have been made to formulate stable relations between the varying growth rates within organizations. Thus Ralph C. Davis at one time suggested that "staff personnel tend to increase in geometric progression as line personnel increase in arithmetic progression up to a point of optimum organization" (1951, p. 528). A few years later, however, he himself participated in an empirical study (quoted above) which showed that "the rate of growth of various staff groups differ" (*Baker and Davis*, p. 59). A more fanciful effort was made in Haire's effort to apply the square-cube law to four companies of various sizes. With considerable ingenuity he equated "surface" with the number of employees "having to do primarily with things outside the firm" and "volume" with the number involved in "internal" work. With an increase by the former to the power of two, the latter seemed to grow by the power of three (*Haire*). The main value of this exercise, however, is to illustrate lines of empirical research that might be undertaken with tighter definitions, a larger array of data and mathematical tools of increasing sophistication. Until this is done, it is unlikely that we shall find any stable relations underlying the disproportionality of organizational growth.

2. THE LAW OF CHANGING RATES

Another complicating factor is that whatever dimensions are used to measure the changing size of an organization or unit, change tends to be characterized by changing rates. This tendency is so universal that it may be called "the law of changing rates."

The most obvious illustration of this tendency is provided by analogies with biological organisms. The young blade of grass, the human infant and the elephant start out by growing at exponential rates. Then after rapidly doubling in size and weight they slow down and eventually stop growing entirely. If they were to continue for just a little while longer at their earliest rates, the blade of grass would soon weigh more than a man, the baby would be bigger than an elephant, and the elephant's trunk would touch the clouds. If they were to continue growing throughout their lives, even though very slowly, they would exceed the average optimum size for the species. In one important respect this analogy is applicable. In human organizations rapid rates of growth—particularly exponential rates—cannot be maintained forever either. A slowdown is inevitable. Moreover, rapid *rates* of growth, as distinguished from large absolute increases, are probably more frequent among smaller than among larger organizations.

Yet there are at least three points at which the greater complexity of human organization renders the biological model inapplicable. First of all, few human organizations start out with exponential growth rates. Many, as evidenced by the considerable number of business enterprises with less than ten employees, remain exceedingly small for their entire life. Many, as illustrated by three of the four enterprises studied by Haire, remain very small for quite a few years before starting to grow rapidly. Like the traditional economies in Rostow's description (1960), many preconditions must be met before they are ready for the "take-off" into long-range steady growth.

Second, the growth curves of organizations are less smooth and regular than those of biological organisms. Growth often comes in jerky spurts. Period of growth may be alternated with periods of decline or stability. Internal motivations, technical and administrative abilities, and environmental conditions, rather than a genetic code, are the determining factors.

Third, there is no absolute size maximum which can be derived from an identification of the "species" of an organization. Many organizations, particularly the larger "immortals," seem apparently capable of an endless series of growth spurts. In this respect also they are more like the highly industrialized economies which, although they may be beset by recurring periods of stagnation or decline, are unquestionably capable of endless growth in total output and output per capita.

There are constraining factors, however, which are similar to, although not identical with, those that limit the size of living organisms. Boulding points out (1953, p. 22-25): "as an organism grows it absorbs more and more of its environment, and eventually it uses up the more favorable parts of its environment, and the environment turns increasingly less favorable." He finds that while this factor does not operate so strongly at the level of the biological individual, as distinguished from populations, it does operate strongly for a single organization. A new sect or a labor union can expand up to the point where it exhausts potential sympathizers.

A business enterprise can grow up to the point where it is stopped by competition and declining demand. A government agency faces increasing difficulty in getting appropriations. It might be added that the process of growth itself, particularly by large and powerful organizations, tends to create a certain amount of external jealousy, resentment, and antagonism which serve as obstacles to further growth.

Yet all of these limits can be extended. Organizing drives, advertising campaigns, and public relations activities can expand the potential circle of members or customers. The limits imposed by competition may be hurdled by getting together with competitors and developing various forms of cooperation or integration. The limits imposed by the demand for an existing product can be sidestepped, as so many U.S. industrial companies have done since World War II, by product differentiation and territorial expansion. More resources can be obtained and opposition can be more effectively overcome by the development of external allies and supporters. All of this is more feasible when the general environment, instead of being a fixed quantity, is itself expanding in terms of population growth and economic activity.

Up to a certain point, moreover, an environment that appears unfavorable—in the sense that it provides resistance and opposition—may be conducive to growth. Here we may find a physiological analogy in D'Arcy Thompson's findings that "strain, the result of a stress, is a direct stimulus to growth itself . . . the living cells are 'stimulated' by pressure, or by what we call 'exercise,' to increase and multiply" (1961, p. 238). Some of the considerations applicable to this phenomenon in organizations are mentioned in the previous discussion of the positive effects of conflict (Chapt. 4). In addition, the challenge aspects of resistance should be mentioned. Growth-minded administrators are often motivated to more prodigious efforts by the very difficulties involved in action and expansion. Slowdown or decline often set in at the time when the challenge fades and there seems to be "no new worlds to conquer."

A stronger limit on growth is provided by what Boulding terms "the principle of increasingly unfavorable internal structure." As the size of an organization or organism increases, it is impossible to maintain the proportional structure of the organism intact. Thus a flea (which can jump a distance many times its own length) could not jump at all if it were the size of a man. Its slender legs would break down under such a weight. An insect, which breathes through the skin, cannot grow very much; beyond a few inches, it would need lungs to serve a larger area with oxygen. A one-celled organism cannot be much larger than an amoeba, for if it grew much larger its lack of a specialized nervous system would jeopardize its communication with the environment. Similarly, "as an organization increases in size beyond a certain point, it becomes more and more difficult to maintain an adequate system of communication. . . . The major executives are of necessity insulated from the direct environment of the organization they govern. . . . Information coming up the line may be lost or may reach him as misinformation; instructions going down the line may also be lost or may result in misunderstanding" (Boulding, 1953, p. 22-26). Modern technologies of transportation, communication, and information processing cannot by themselves solve this problem. By moving men and messages more rapidly, they tend to lead executives from the frying pan of too little information to the fire of an information overload.

The major difference between an organization and most organisms is that the former can change its structure. Nor is an organization, like the caterpillar-butterfly, limited to one metamorphosis. It can continually adapt to the requirements of size by developing new roles and functions, new hierarchical and polyarchic relations, and new codes of behavior. It is this ability which makes it possible for organizations to use modern information technology in the development of improved communication systems.

3. THE "NONLAWS" OF RETURNS TO SCALE

Economists have often formulated the so-called "law of augmenting returns to scale," whereby an increase in the size of an organization yields greater returns, and the "law of diminishing returns to scale," whereby increased size means less returns. The two laws may be represented by a simple curve that rises and falls. The highest point in the curve (the lowest point if costs are used), after which increased size would mean less returns, represents the "optimum" size.

Such "laws" are not intended to explain what actually happens to organizations, or even to business enterprises. Even economists would probably agree that the actual growth of organizations is the result of the motivations and actions of its members, their technical and administrative capacities, and environmental conditions. This pair of opposing "laws" is formulated, rather, as prescriptions, to help indicate when managers should expand, stop, or contract. But there is little basis for calling them prescriptive, since they do not indicate just when it is that the first law passes out and the second takes over. This indication can be provided only for specific organizations in specific situations and environments, although the process of making such a special calculation may be considerably helped by information concerning the implications of size changes for similar organizations.

At this point, however, the primary question immediately becomes, What do we mean by "returns"? The idea of an optimum implies a goal by which the best is judged. Are our goals (or returns) to be thought of in terms of some measure of profitability, the test used by classical and neoclassical economists? Or shall we think mainly about unit costs? This is the approach of E. A. G. Robinson, who defines the optimum firm as one "operating at that scale at which, in existing conditions of technique and organizing ability it has the lowest average cost of production per unit, when all those costs which must be covered in the long run are included" (1957, p. 11). Or should we look at both of these, and survival as well, as does P. J. D. Wiles in coming to the conclusion that "the doctrine of the optimum size of the firm must be abolished. . . . In no even remotely possible circumstance is there any *a priori* argument for diminishing returns as a single firm expands" (1961, p. 223, 215).

As we extend the range of goals or criteria, we immediately find ourselves faced with different optima. A certain size may seem ideal for the purpose of getting more personal power or of producing a larger volume of output. A still larger size may be optimum for the purpose of building reserves against future emergencies. A much smaller size may be optimum from the viewpoint of creating working conditions of pleasurable and human intimacy among the organization's members. Still a new dimension is included if we explicitly relate size to various strongly held goals concerning social structure. As Wiles suggests, for many economists the law of diminishing returns is seen as coming quickly into effect in order to "exorcize that appalling threat to the classical theory of competition, indefinitely increasing returns to scale" (1961, p. 230).

There is no particular reason why all of these optima should coincide. Some, indeed, will always be widely divergent. Nor is there any reason why, through a combination of circumstances, a curve of diminishing returns at one stage of growth may not change its direction and rise at a later stage. The more realistic consideration of the implications of size, growth and decline requires a breadth of approach capable of dealing with the multiplicity of organizational purposes and multicausal relations. From this point of view, the larger-sized organization enjoys certain advantages and suffers certain "defects of its virtues." The same may be said for the smaller-sized organization. As an organization grows larger or smaller, there are invariably various changes in this pattern of opportunities and problems. The kinds of changes that *may* take place are illustrated as follows:

POSSIBLE IMPLICATIONS OF

	Larger Size	*Smaller Size*
Satisfactions	More opportunities for advancement and creative work. More power and prestige. Possibility of satisfying more clients.	More intimacy in interpersonal relations. Easier for the fewer people to reach the top. Possibility of providing deeper satisfactions for less clients.
Output	Opportunity for greater end product variety. Opportunity for greater specialization in intermediate services.	Possibility of more attention to quality. Possibility of greater speed in a smaller range of operations.
Input-Output Relations	Lower unit costs in many circumstances. Higher profits in many circumstances.	Lower unit costs in some circumstances. Higher benefits in some circumstances.
Investment in Organizational Viability	More capable of ability to build larger strategic reserves. Ability to adapt more thoroughly to major environmental changes.	Greater opportunity for future growth. Ability to hibernate. Ability to adapt more quickly to some environmental changes.
Mobilization of Resources	Opportunity to get more money on better terms.	Ability to mobilize marginal resources.
Observance of Codes	Greater ability to change external codes. Greater opportunity to develop internal codes.	Greater opportunity to evade external codes. Greater flexibility with internal codes.
Rationality Technical	Ability to invest broadly in research and development. Ability to meet technical minimum on size.	Ability to make major innovations in narrow area.
Administrative	More complex administrative problems. Impossibility of close control over many activities.	Simpler administrative problems. Possibility of closer control over more activities.

Since some of these considerations have already been discussed and others will be taken up subsequently, I shall here touch upon two aspects only: input-output relations and rationality. With respect to both costs and profits the potential of increasing returns from larger size is quite clear. The large organization can take greater advantage of the benefits flowing from specialization, standardization, large-scale buying, cheaper financing, and certain technical operations (like a continuous rolling mill) that can be only handled on a large scale. Where there is unused capacity, a high volume of operations will reduce unit costs by spreading fixed costs over a large number of units. Reasons such as these explain the fact that empirical data on unit costs by size of firm seem to show more L-shaped than U-shaped curves. Sixty per cent of the examples assembled by Wiles show costs declining with size and then flattening out at the bottom of the L. "Another 31 per cent show a slight increase of costs in the largest size class. But sharply increasing costs with size are practically unknown. Most—but by no means all—of these slight increases are well within the expected margin of error that any empirical correlation should show." On the other hand, profitability "sometimes shows a distinctly U-shaped correlation with size, although the largest firms are never so unprofitable as the smallest." Also, there is "greater dispersal in the profitability of small firms" (1961, p. 213, 255-257). It would seem that the managers of larger firms are not equally capable of exploiting their opportunities for lower costs and even less equally capable of doing so with respect to profits.

The implications for technical rationality are also clear. On the one hand, a small organization—by virtue of greater flexibility—may be in a better position to make a major innovation in some area or put to use an innovation pioneered by others. On the other hand, only largescale organizations are capable of pioneering technical innovation on a large scale.

> In industries where firms are few and comparatively large—oil, metallurgy, automobiles, chemicals, rubber, heavy engineering—the investment in technological advance is considerable. . . . But in many industries where the firms are numerous and small—coal mining, home construction, clothing manufacture, the natural fiber textile industry, the service industries—the investment in innovation is negligible. No firm is large enough to afford it on an appreciable scale; there is a real question as to whether it is worthwhile for such firms (Galbraith, 1958, p. 126).

In the areas of agricultural, military and space technology, major technological advances have often been made by small universities, laboratories, and enterprises—but under the wing of mammoth research programs organized and financed by large governmental bureaucracies. Moreover, while the technical base of a given operation may establish a minimum scale, it "contributes hardly, if at all, to the fixing of a maximum scale beyond which growth will lead to progressively increasing cost per unit." The organization can avoid any technical diseconomies by reduplicating the process—that is, achieving larger size through a large number of operations of the desired scale. Any difficulties resulting from this kind of growth will be created not by technical considerations but by the greater burdens imposed upon administrators (Robinson, 1957, p. 31-49).

This brings us to administrative rationality, where the implications of size are also very clear. With growth the problems faced by adminis-trators usually undergo radical changes. The nature of some of these changes is illustrated in Dale's analysis of major organizational problems in seven enterprises at various stages of growth (1952, p. 22):

Stage of Growth	Size When Problem May First Arise (By number of employees)	Organizational Problem and its Possible Consequences
I	Any size	Formulation of objectives: Division of work
II	10	Delegation of responsibility: The accommodation of personalities
III	50-100	Delegation of more management functions: The span of control
IV	50-300	Reducing the executive's burden: The staff assistant
V	100-400	Establishing a new function (functionalization): The staff specialist
VI	100-500	Coordination of management functions: Group decision making
VII	Over 500	Determining the degree of delega-tion: Decentralization

In associations and federations, growth brings a twin set of organiza-tional problems: these associated with the growing number of employees (for which Dale's analysis is relevant) and those associated with the growing number of affiliates. These nonemployed members may include individuals, organizations or both. Here, larger numbers raise new prob-lems concerning the adequacy of representative bodies and the handling of action conflicts, factions, and separatist movements.

The common denominator in all large organizations, no matter what their membership basis or their formal ideology, is the impossibility of close central control over many activities. This is the bedrock basis of the tendency toward dispersion of intraorganizational power in large organizations, as already discussed in Chapters 9 and 10. It is this tend-ency which, if not offset by a high order of administrative adaptability, will result in "decreasing returns" from scale.

4. THE LAW OF DELAYED ADAPTATION

The growth process is always complicated by a universal tendency toward delayed adaptation to the new problems created by organizational growth. This may be called "the law of delayed adaptation."

A vivid illustration of delayed adaptation is provided by Chandler's case studies of changes in the formal structure of DuPont, General Motors, Standard Oil (New Jersey), and Sears, Roebuck (*Chandler*). During these companies' first period of growth loose alliances of manufacturing or marketing firms were consolidated into a single consolidated organization with a central headquarters. The emphasis was mainly on the accumulation of resources. In their eagerness for expansion the empire builders often "collected more facilities and personnel than were really necessary to meet the existing demand." Structure was "often slow to follow strategy, particularly in periods of rapid expansion" (*Ibid.*, p. 16). Only later was the effort made to organize these resources through a centralized, functionally departmentalized structure with defined lines of authority and communication. The next period of growth, based upon product differentiation and territorial expansion, once again emphasized resource accumulation. Eventually, to rationalize the use of resources, each company moved to a decentralized system of autonomous divisions held together by a central office limited to general planning and control. "Rarely did the building of the necessary structure come immediately. Its construction called for time, thought and energy" (*Ibid.*, p. 283).

One reason for the delay in adaptation is the sheer difficulty of finding out what to do. An adaptive response involves much more than automatic application or imitation. It involves the painful application of accepted generalities to special circumstances. This was what was done during the first period of adaptation referred to in Chandler's case studies. At that time, most administrative theory—particularly "scientific management"—centered more around the factory floor than the large organization. Moreover, the administrative tools of budgeting, inventory control, personnel management, and cost accounting were still in their infancy and considerable time had to be spent in nurturing and developing them. A still more difficult form of adaptive response is creative innovation. As Chandler demonstrates, the creation of the multidivisional decentralized structure was a social innovation of major proportions. It went far beyond the bounds of existing business practice. It required a far greater sophistication in the development and use of administrative tools. The tremendous difficulties involved in this kind of adaptation are well illustrated by Chandler's story concerning the elaborate 1930 report of the Frazer committee at Sears, Roebuck. While formulating admirable recommendations for cost cutting, the Frazer committee lost sight of the more important goal of a higher sales volume. The committee members seemed oblivious of the very relevant experience at General Motors and DuPont. In 1947 a second group of consultants went to the other extreme of "making too many general comparisons with the decentralized model as worked out at General Motors and DuPont without taking sufficiently into account the differences between Sears' needs and those of the multi-industry automobile and chemical industries" (*Ibid.*, p. 242-261, 321-323).

No matter what degree of creativity is needed, the process of adaptation depends upon the presence at the right time and place of creative individuals. The supply of such people is usually limited, or else their energies are attracted by technical rather than administrative problems. In Chandler's four case studies the innovating pioneers of the new decentralized structures were generally "younger executives, who had only recently entered top management, but who had had experience in the company's general business, and whose careers had not been wholly confined to work with that one firm" (*Ibid.*, p. 320).

A still more fundamental reason for delayed adaption is the inevitable inertia or resistance that confronts the proponents of structural adaptation. "Men long accustomed to handling administrative matters in one way," Chandler reports, "had difficulty in devising new administrative structures" (p. 323). They had less difficulty in slowing down the innovators. At DuPont "Irenee DuPont strongly resisted the recommendations for a new structure." At General Motors and Standard Oil "Durant and Teagle remained unconcerned about the inadequacies of their existing organizations and the suggestions for their structural improvement." General Wood at Sears delayed reorganization from 1932 to 1948 (p. 279). In all of these cases it took a sizeable crisis to bring action. In fact, Chandler's broader survey of scores of other companies further suggests that "the essential reshaping of administrative structure nearly always had to wait for a change in the top command" (p. 380).[3]

According to Chandler, "one of the primary reasons structure was slow to follow strategy was that the existing management was unable to change its ways. . . . The psychological hazards of adjusting to new ways, new tempos and new duties seem to have been a more significant block to structural change than a concern for diminished power and prestige" (p. 320). Yet as Chandler himself concedes, his analysis was based on attitudes toward top level formal organization as revealed in company records. If he had found ways to penetrate behind the written documents,

---

3. In the scientific community, also, Thomas Kuhn has demonstrated, major changes in ways of looking at the world come about only after crises created by the breakdown of older "paradigms" or conceptual frameworks and after the "lifelong resistance" of the previous top command is overcome. Kuhn quotes Max Planck to the effect that "a new scientific truth does not triumph by convincing its opponents and making them see the light, but rather because its opponents eventually die, and a new generation grows up that is familiar with it" (1962, p. 150).

if he had gone further down the hierarchy where so many stumbling blocks to organizational change can easily be placed, if he had looked at the informal as well as the formal aspects of structure, his analysis might have been different. Organization adaptation inevitably means major changes in the pattern of power and prestige. The innovators themselves are usually people whose innovating energies are inextricably embedded in their personal drives for higher positions and greater opportunities for self-fulfillment. This inevitably means a complex and delicately shifting struggle between advocates of different viewpoints and between competing aspirants for the comfortable position of successful mediator.

Usually delayed, adaptation is also always incomplete. Resistance makes total adaptation impossible. Even the most drastic shakeup will turn out, under close examination, to contain many elements of compromise and to be but the opening stage in a series of adaptations. By the time the series is completed, new problems will create the need for further adaptation. Moreover, apart from resistance and further change, the law of disproportionality affects even the creative impulse underlying the adaptation process. The most significant innovations tend to be responses to those aspects of growth which are perceived as a source of imminent and acute crisis. The innovators concentrate their shots, instead of scattering them. In order to shake tradition on such matters as the role of a central office and the degree of autonomy to be enjoyed by divisions, they usually become staunch defenders of tradition and routine on many other matters, such as government regulation or relations with trade unions. Those who innovate in these areas, in turn, tend toward passivity on internal structure.

The most monumental examples of delayed adaptation may be seen in those countries where the network of government organizations has grown rapidly through the nationalization of private enterprises or the initiation or expansion of public enterprises. In Russia, where the central government assumed tasks of economic administration unprecedented in world history, the process has been both long and bloody. It took at least thirty years of painful struggle and experimentation before the centralized, functionally departmentalized model (patterned after large capitalistic enterprises) was formally abandoned and a serious search was begun for more decentralized methods. In England the Labor Party based its 1945-51 nationalization program on a large number of quasi-autonomous public corporations (themselves highly centralized) and never got around to attempting coordination through an over-all plan.

D. *Investment in Assets*

No ORGANIZATION would long be viable if the energies of its members and administrators were devoted exclusively to satisfying interests through current output and input-output performance. The process of adjustment to changed conditions requires efforts to improve the organization's capacity for future performance while at the same time utilizing its capacity to tolerate the delays and errors in the adjustment process. This involves the use of resources for investment in new assets or for the conservation or development of existing assets. Accordingly, investment, conservation and development goals are often the most strategic of all viability objectives.

Here once again, as with intangible services, we see the natural tendency for tangible goals which can be more readily quantified to take precedence over intangible goals which may be more important. Explicit and highly sophisticated concepts and measures have been worked out with respect to the accumulation, protection, use and evaluation of land, machinery, inventories, cash and credits. Human and social assets, without which these material assets would have neither capacity nor value, are thought of in less explicit and more intuitive ways. Although they may be regarded as more important in times of crisis, they are often neglected in the ordinary course of affairs.

1. REPLACEMENT AND EXPANSION

Most economists and accountants would probably accept John W. Kendrick's definition of investment as "the application of resources and the incurrence of costs in the current period with the objective of increasing productive capacity and income in future periods" (1961, p. 104). By using "value" in place of "income" we can make this definition applicable to organizations and units producing nonmarketed output. This usage, it should be noted, refers to current investments, or increases in assets or capital. It is different from the use of "investment" to refer to the total stock of existing assets or capital (as in "profits on total investment") and more narrowly to refer to investment in securities.

Without a certain amount of attention to investment, the material assets of any organization may quickly be dissipated. Machines wear down or become out of date. Inventories are used up. Reserves of cash and credit run dry. To avoid stagnation, decline, or liquidation, some kind of replacement is needed. To engage in different or more varied operations, new kinds of machinery and supplies are needed. To grow, or even to maintain relative size, investment must be large enough to increase total capacity and assets. In organizations whose operations require little more than a structure and minor equipment—as with associations, some service agencies and the smallest business enterprises—these investment needs may be handled on a sporadic basis. When expensive new buildings are needed, as with churches, schools and government agencies, more time is needed to develop construction plans and mobilize the necessary funds. Still more time and energy are needed to formulate specific goals for the replacement and expansion of the expensive and complicated equipment used by the larger enterprises engaged in agriculture, mining, manufacture, construction, transportation, communication, and information processing. Engineers, scientists, economists, mathematicians, accountants, finance experts, and administrators may work together in formulating the details of long-range "capital budgets" (or "development budgets") and building an image of the desired future asset structure. The potentialities of such an asset structure may be spelled out by sophisticated projections of future income statements and balance sheets.

Are the concepts of investment and capital applicable to human assets also?

Adam Smith answered affirmatively by including in his definition of fixed capital "the acquired and useful abilities of all the inhabitants or members of the society." He justified this inclusion with an explanation long neglected by economists:

> The acquisition of such talents, by the maintenance of the acquirer during his education, study or apprenticeship, always costs a real expense, which is a capital fixed and realized, as it were, in his person. Those talents, as they make a part of his fortune, so do they likewise of that of the society to which he belongs. The improved dexterity of a workman may be considered in the same light as a machine or instrument of trade which facilitates and abridges labour, and which though it costs a certain expense, repays that expense with profit (*The Wealth of Nations*, Bk. II, Chapt. 1).

The great majority of economists abandoned this approach in favor of the material asset concept of investment. Although Marshall recognized the incontestable logic of a more comprehensive view, he felt that it was impractical because of the difficulty of assigning money values to investment in human assets (*Principles of Economics*, Appendix E).[4] Marshall's

---

4. This position was not quite consistent with Marshall's attack on the material production concept of national income. (See discussion under "The Prejudice against Services" in Chapter 15.) Yet it must be conceded that the problem

view has become the basis of the sharp distinction between investment and consumption in national economic accounts throughout the world.

More recently, however, many economists have shaken the structure of national accounting by proposing to recognize investment in human assets. Theodore Schultz charges that economists have misunderstood the nature of economic growth by failing "to take account of human capital and the important part that it plays in production in a modern economy." He proposes attention to five major categories of human investment: (1) health facilities and services, (2) on-the-job training, (3) formally organized education, (4) study programs, and (5) migration to adjust to changing job opportunities (1961, p. 1-17). He estimates that from 1900 to 1956 in the U.S. annual investment in formally organized education rose from one-tenth to one-third of all investments in physical assets (1960, p. 571-583).

A still broader approach is taken by Kendrick. In applying the definition of investment quoted above, he states that it includes two forms of "hidden investment." The first is "investment in persons," which includes education and health expenditures, items traditionally classified as consumption outlays. The second is "intangible investment by business and government." Of these, the most important types are "expenditures for training and other ways of improving the efficiency of employees, and research and development outlays for the purpose of devising new equipment, processes, and procedures for increasing efficiency generally (1961, p. 104-110).

Business accountants have made some small steps in this direction by providing for "intangible assets" in balance sheets. These may include goodwill, patents (or other rights such as copyrights, trademarks, leases, and franchises), developmental research and "organization expenses." The initial rationale for intangible assets was carefully restricted. Thus the sum beside "goodwill" in a balance sheet does not represent an appraisal of what the company's name and reputation are worth. "Goodwill appears in the accounts of the company only when the company has *purchased* some intangible and valuable property rights. A common case is when one company buys another company and pays more than the fair value of the tangible assets owned by that company. The amount by which the purchase price exceeds the value of the tangible assets may be called goodwill, representing the value of the name, the reputation, the location, or other intangible possessions of the purchased company" (Anthony, 1960, p. 32). Similarly, patents were first included only when acquired

---

of identifying investments in human assets and calculating their quantity is even more formidable than that of quantifying intangible services.

by purchase. The growth of large research departments that develop patentable processes and devices has undermined this limitation. Many companies now include the value of patents obtained as a result of their own activities rather than purchase from others. This, in turn, has sometimes led to the classification as capital expenditures of general research and development outlays (along the lines of the Kendrick definition quoted above), whether or not they result in the acquisition of patents. This practice is as debatable among accountants as is the Schultz concept of human capital among economists. Still more debatable among accountants is the question of "organization expenses." This term, it must be noted, refers to the *initial* expenses involved in setting up a new organization. "The traditional attitude of accountants toward organization expenses is that they are a sheer loss," Finney and Miller points out. "It is doubtful whether the profession will accept the theory that organization expenses are an intangible asset" (1958, p. 416). Theoretical objections, however, may quickly be overcome when the inclusion of these expenses as current costs guarantees that a new company starts out "in the red." Classifying them as intangible assets allows a company to break even or show a profit. In support of this position, Finney and Miller suggest that initial organization expenses may be regarded as continuing assets that need not be "written down" throughout the whole life of an organization (*Ibid.*).

It is highly unlikely, however, that either accountants or economists will ever develop formal accounting systems capable of dealing quantitatively with the full range of human and intangible assets. In fact, the effort to go further in this direction will often lead to major oversimplifications, particularly through lack of attention to qualitative aspects. Administrators, fortunately, need not depend on formal accounting systems. They can use the data derived from such systems as informational starting points for managerial analysis.

Managerial analysis, in my judgment, is frequently based on a large measure of intuitive wisdom concerning investment in three types of human or intangible assets. The first is investment in the organization itself. Initial organization activities are merely the most obvious form of net investment. No matter what the accountants may record in their books, administrators always invest time and energy in organization and reorganization. The investment nature of these activities is not challenged by the fact that they are apt to come in spurts and bunches or may often be ill-advised or unbalanced. In fact, this stems in part from their being seen as a diversion from the more immediate tasks of current output, which is an essential aspect of most investments.

The second is investment in people themselves, as distinguished from the relations between them. However different the formal rationale may be in different organizations, on-the-job training has developed because administrators have seen it as an investment in human skills. Research and development activities have been sponsored not only to provide new forms of machinery but to develop new forms of human "know-how." For centuries, long before the modern concepts of human relations, administrators have sought various ways to obtain and keep the goodwill of their colleagues and subordinates.

The third is investment in the external environment. Far more has been spent to gain the goodwill of clients, suppliers, controllers and adversaries than has ever entered into the balance sheets through the purchase of other companies. In recent decades much of this investment has taken the form of advertising to increase the value of trademarks and brand names and public relations to build the "institutional image." A more fundamental form of environmental investment, although less tangible, is investment in the maintenance of friendly relations with powerful external groups, the winning over of neutrals and the dividing of opponents. The diversion of resources to investments of this type may not only make future operations more effective. It may also be the essential prerequisite for achieving an organization's goals for the replacement or expansion of material assets.

2. CONSERVATION AND DEVELOPMENT

In a passive sense, conservation involves the maintenance of reserves. The most obvious reserves are those appearing in the form of inventories, cash, unused credits, or land taken out of production to facilitate soil replenishment. Reserve capacity is also important—as when machinery is operated at slower speeds or for shorter periods than is technically possible. Estimates of machine capacity, in fact, are often optimum figures obtained by deducting a desirable degree of under-utilization from the technical maximum. This is one of the reasons why actual production in peak periods may sometimes exceed the "rated" capacity.

In a more active sense, conservation involves the maintenance of assets through proper use, handling, and repair. In agricultural programs, this means the application of advanced skill in plowing, seeding, planting, and animal husbandry. In forestry it requires skillful methods of cutting and replanting. In all fields where machinery is used it means considerable attention to techniques of operation and repair. Preventive maintenance programs emphasize regular checkups and scheduled improvements in advance of breakdown or deterioration.

Development is the other side of the conservation coin. If carried too far, the maintenance of reserves can lead to the dissipation of assets. Land that lies fallow too long becomes barren. Materials in inventories may spoil or rust. Idle machinery, even if protected against rust, may degenerate. In the passive sense, then, development means avoiding excessive underutilization. In the more active sense, development activities are those that provide for constant improvements in quality.

Like material assets, human assets also need conservation and development. Rest periods and vacations and steady operations are instruments of both passive and active conservation. Development is provided not only by formal programs for human development but by difficult operations which, although unsuccessful by other standards, may have the merit of providing valuable experience for the organization. Losing a battle may help develop the capacity for winning the war. Most administrators realize that reservoirs of goodwill—particularly among colleagues and powerful external groups—must be carefully nurtured. This is why careful administrators are often reluctant to exploit "good connections" too frequently; a reservoir may run dry. This is why they spend considerable time in "fence building," both internal and external.

The fact that administrators may orient themselves toward the conservation and development of human assets does not mean that these goals are given the same emphasis as goals for material assets. Farm managers have traditionally been more concerned with the health and housing of livestock than of farm workers. Factory managers have traditionally given more attention to the proper care of machinery than of machine operators. As Rensis Likert has pointed out, traditional management information systems tend to accentuate this lack of balance. In analyzing a series of studies and experiments with different styles of administering clerical work (*Morse and Reimer*), he has shown that authoritarian methods of supervision "can yield substantial immediate increases in productivity . . . at a cost to the human assets of the organization. . . . Under present management practices companies are encouraging their managers, by the facts used in promotions and by the formulas used to compensate them, to press unduly for immediate production, cost reduction and similar goals, and thereby profit personally by reducing the value of the company's investment in the human organization." Similarly, Likert reports that companies' investments in consumer goodwill are liquidated by actions that reduce the quality of output and substantially increase current earnings (1961, p. 73-75). What Likert does not mention is the corroding effect of unemployment. "Human capital deteriorates when it is idle because unemployment impairs the skills that workers have acquired" (Schultz, 1961, p. 13). Moreover, the fear of unemployment will often create situations in which people will deliberately refuse to use or improve the skills they have. Single organizations can do little or nothing to combat the existence of this fear, but they must nonetheless pay the price in the form of serious underutilization and erosion of human skills.

Furthermore, there is often a goal conflict between conservation and development. One of the reasons administrators hesitate to develop improved organizational structures is their feeling that it may be wiser to conserve existing relationships that have worked well in the past. Many people in organizations are interested in conserving their own energies while making optimum use of the energies of others. Many administrators regard executive development programs as excellent for their subordinates but inapplicable to themselves.

3. THE MANAGERIAL BALANCE SHEET

Where financial balance sheets are used, they can provide administrators with useful information on the structure of an organization's material assets and of the various claims against them. This information may be used both in setting goals and in appraising performance. In business organizations, whose balance sheets usually include property accounts and owners' equity, goals and criteria are both often formulated in terms of ratios dealing with assets, claims (liabilities) and their interrelations. Among these the most frequently used are the following:

Assets
Inventory to working capital
Receivables to sales
Inventory to sales (inventory turnover)

Claims
Net worth to total equity (or capital/liability ratio)
Current debt to net worth
Total debt to net worth
Profit on total equity
Profit on net worth
Bond, profit and stock ratios

Assets-Claims
Current assets to current liabilities (current ratio)
Cash and receivables to current liabilities (acid test)
Current liabilities to inventory
Funded debt to working capital

In organizations without property accounts and owners' equity, balance sheet information centers around a variety of separate funds and the charges against them. Here the critical relations center around the amount of new revenues obtained (equivalent to the net income or profit of a business) and the changing volume of surplus, that is, unappropriated funds.

In their raw form, however, balance sheet data are not immediately useful in helping to formulate goals with respect to the maintenance, expansion, and use of physical assets. Where financial reports are prepared mainly to give an accounting to external controllers, as with most government agencies, they are rarely useful for internal administration. Even when prepared to meet the timetable and the needs of administrators, the financial reports need considerable adjustment and amplification. Managerial accounting and managerial economics have developed as methods of processing and interpreting the raw data in financial accounts. Managerial accountants and managerial economists are able to provide administrators with better overall figures on physical assets and their use—particularly figures that are more relevant to future decisions. Engineers, technicians and financial experts are able to go behind these overall figures and provide valuable information on the specific assets and claims reflected by them.

But the capacity of an organization can never be appraised merely by getting better information on material assets. Even the changes in balance sheet data cannot be understood on this basis. The output of an organization is the product not of physical assets alone but of the total structure of human and physical assets. Changes in financial balance sheets are merely shadowy reflections, "seen through a glass darkly," of this larger structure. In this sense, neither managerial accounting nor managerial economics are truly "managerial."

In analyzing the neglect of human assets by business organizations, Rensis Likert suggests that administrators would be better able to see the whole picture if they had "accounting procedures showing the investment in the human organization." Although he illustrates the usefulness in varying circumstances of at least seventeen kinds of data on motivation, morale, attitudes and supervisory methods, Likert does not follow up directly on his idea of a broader system of accounting (1961, p. 71-73, 192-221). It is a moot question, as suggested earlier, whether formal accounting systems could ever be established to include both human and material assets. Certainly, any attempt to carry out Likert's implied suggestion would be doomed to quixotic triviality if it were undertaken on the assumption that one could obtain sharp quantities that could be readily aggregated in commensurable terms.

Nevertheless, if Likert's methods of uncovering attitudes and thought patterns were applied to administrators on a wide scale, we would probably find a rather widespread use of concepts approximating a comprehensive managerial balance sheet. This has already been suggested in the previous discussion concerning managerial attention to investment, conservation and development goals for human assets. Moreover, a key balance sheet concept with rather broad implications is the dual nature of assets: for every asset, there must be a claim; for every increase in what an organization has, there is an increase in what it owes (in the form of debt or owners' equity); every increase in debt means an increase in assets; and for every appropriation there must be a source of funds. These concepts have meaningful counterparts in managerial approaches to the assets represented by organization, people and external support. If a given pattern of relations between positions is an asset to the organization, the other side of the coin is the claims that incumbents have upon the organization. The maintenance of the organization involves the maintenance of these claims. The claim side is enlarged when an organization builds up its reputation, the goodwill it enjoys and sources of external support; all of these involve inescapable obligations. Sometimes, these nonmaterial elements are intimately wrapped up with the material ones. Thus the expansion of material liabilities through loans or investment often provides a commitment by the claimants which is a powerful source of support. A business enterprise is sometimes saved by creditors who could not afford to have it fail. The United States Government in its earliest days, under the leadership of Alexander Hamilton, rapidly expanded its debt in order to enjoy the intangible assets represented by strong vested interests in its survival and growth.

Chapter 18

MOBILIZATION OF RESOURCES

*J*UST AS INTEREST SATISFACTION is dependent upon output,
so an organization's output is dependent upon input. While certain
interests may be satisfied by things other than output, the output of
services or goods is impossible without input. Hence goal-oriented activity in organizations always includes efforts to obtain the resources
from which inputs are obtained.

For any organization as a whole, resource mobilization is a crucial
part of its relation with its general environment and, most particularly,
with its suppliers. For any unit within an organization, it is a crucial part
of its relation with other units and with the organization's administrators.
For both, the exigencies of the mobilization process often lead to a high
degree of secrecy, or even deception, concerning purpose sequences.
This degree is heightened—or at least preserved—by the conventional
terminology of accountants and budgeteers.

In modern administrative thought Newman and Parsons have suggested lifting these matters above the level of technical detail and dealing
with resource mobilization in more general terms. Newman lists as one
of the basic administrative processes (together with the old standbys of
planning, organization, directing, and controlling) "assembling resources—
that is, obtaining for the use of the enterprise the executive personnel,
capital, facilities, and other things needed to execute the plans" (1950,
p. 4). Parsons finds "two main foci" of a manager's external responsibility. One is mediating between the organization and its clients; the
other is procurement. Like Newman's "assembling resources," this means

490

"procuring the resources necessary for carrying out the technical functions (i.e., financial resources, personnel and physical facilities)" (1960, p. 62). Both Newman and Parsons then proceed to concentrate on the assembling of personnel. Newman justifies this narrow focus by the "variety of specialized problems" involved in obtaining money, physical facilities and materials (1950, p. 317).

This chapter attempts to deal with resource mobilization in terms applicable to all resources. I shall start by analyzing the reasons for the inevitability of a struggle for resources. I shall then concentrate upon two complementary—and often conflicting—aspects of purpose formation in this area, "mobilization logic" and "use logic," and upon their combination in the more unpleasant subjection of "demobilization." This will require the identification of certain common elements in the "tool subjects" dealing with the mobilization of money (accounting, budgeting, finance), people (personnel management), and physical facilities and materials (procurement). This may contribute to the development of a more "managerial" approach to these extremely important technologies.

A. *The Necessity of Mobilizing Resources*

WHY SHOULD ORGANIZATIONS and their administrators worry about "assembling" or "mobilizing" resources? Why can they not confine themselves to making the best possible use of whatever resources they already have?

The answers to these questions indicate that every organization is involved to at least some degree in a struggle for resources. The nature of this struggle, along with the technical requirements of its operations, provides the setting for the formulation of its resource objectives.

1. THE "RESOURCE FLOW" DAYDREAM

The human infant is *given* the milk on which his survival depends. Only after many years of nurture in the bosom of his family does he learn to obtain sustenance by his own efforts. If he fails to learn this, his behavior is properly regarded as infantile.

In the bosom of the organization many members are given many of the resources they need to do their work. The clerical worker will get desk, chair, paper, office machinery, and an in-basket to bring documents to be processed. The manual worker will get workplace, materials, machinery, and tools.

The fondest dream of many an administrator is that he too may enjoy a painless, automatic flow of resources. With resources given to him and his group he can then dedicate his energies to the difficult enough task of putting them to use.

This daydream is buttressed by the thought that if he uses available resources to produce a high enough quality or quantity of output, virtue will be rewarded by a sustained flow of the resources needed for continued success. It is induced by the feelings of frustration when virtue is not rewarded on earth, by the stringencies of becoming indebted, and by the unpleasant connotations associated with the image of the huckster, beggar, con man, and professional fundraiser. Its theoretical analogue is found in the perfection competition model of "classical" and "neoclassical" economists, in which the "factors of production" are seen as automatically flowing to wherever they can be used most profitably. Another theoretical justification is embodied in the concept of "resource allocation." This concept is based on the premise that high in every organizational hierarchy there sits a Resource Allocator who considers "claims" and acts upon them through the inscrutable processes of "rational calculation and control."

In the real world, as distinguished from the realm of daydreams and unworldly models, an organization's resources are, on the whole, obtained through goal-oriented effort. Those that seem to fall from the sky like manna may indeed arrive only because they were actively sought. Those resources that may be obtained effortlessly are rarely sufficient. They must be supplemented through active efforts. Nor is it enough if these efforts take the form of a simple claim or prayer. Resources do not come, like obedient slaves, when called. They must be mobilized.

The necessity of mobilizing resources is founded upon their scarcity. When there is an overabundance, or surfeit, of any resource, mobilization efforts are not needed. But a surfeit of all resources is a rarity. Any organization usually faces a situation where it will suffer a shortage of certain desired resources—in terms of quality, quantity, or both—unless active steps are taken to obtain them. An acceptable supply, moreover, is a temporary situation. Materials are used up in the process of production. Machinery wears down through use or is made obsolescent by technological progress. People grow old and die, or else leave the organization for other reasons. Continuous replacement, if not expansion, is essential. The initial shortage of resources, moreover, is enlarged by obstacles to their immobility. The fact that people, machinery, or materials may be available some place does not bring them into being at the specific place and time where they are needed. There are many ingrained resistances to movement—particularly in the case of people. In fact, customs, preju-dices, and institutional policies may affect not only the decisions of people as to where they will work, but of suppliers as to whom they will provide with machinery or materials. In the case of all resources, above all, there are terms that must be met. These terms usually become more difficult to meet when there is serious competition among resource users.

As an authorized claim against all resources that can be bought or hired, money is the most general form of resource. In any society where money is used as an instrument of exchange, it is kept in short supply as a matter of technical necessity. The shortage of money thus becomes the most generalized form of resource shortage, the competition for money the most generalized form of resource conflict. If the money supply is seriously expanded, this will usually increase the competition for physical and human resources. The reduced scarcity of money will be counterbalanced by the increased scarcity of various forms of serv-ices and goods.[1]

Accordingly, all organizations are engaged in a continuing struggle for certain qualities and quantities of resources. The worker has re-sources given to him only because other members of the organization—and particularly the higher administrators—spent energies in mobilizing them.

2. THE UNIVERSAL BUDGET BATTLE

Within every organization there are always intermittent skirmishes for scarce resources—for office space, parking space, new machines, or the best secretaries. These skirmishes may become very bitter.

But the most sustained and detailed internal battles are those surround-ing an organization's budget. Although there may be great differences in the way in which organizations' funds are obtained (and these differ-ences indubitably affect the nature of the battle), there is a very real sense in which internal budgeting makes all organizations akin. The various units within organizations (with but minor exceptions) state their resource goals in "budget requests." These move "upward" through the hierarchical channels of communication, and hierarchic decisions are made

1. The complete abolition of monetary scarcity could occur only in the ex-treme limiting case of all-out inflation. Under such circumstances money would be useless as an instrument of exchange and resource mobilization would be effectuated through various forms of barter.

at regular intervals on the money allocated to each unit. These "allocations" are often the formal ratification of distribution patterns determined
through the polyarchic processes of negotiation and bargaining. These
processes are structured by (a) formal categories for classifying the
inputs to be obtained through the use of resources, (b) accepted patterns
for justifying budget requests, and (c) elaborate procedures for reviewing
requests, appealing decisions, and obtaining information on resource use.

All this requires specialized personnel. In the first instance budget
specialists are hired to help top executives in the allocation process
vis-à-vis units at lower hierarchic levels. This requires more manpower—
and eventually specialized positions—to help the units at the lower levels
in their campaigns to get their desired share of the "pie." Both sets of
specialists may at times join forces in helping the top executives in their
campaigns to enlarge the total pie.

The cyclical aspects of the budgetary battle should not obscure its
continuous nature. The preparation of a budget request for any year
(whether fiscal or calendar) must usually begin at least a year, and often
much longer, before the first day of such year. The preparatory stage
is followed by the various stages of decision at various levels of formal
authority. At any moment in the cycle action may be initiated to change
past decisions through new interpretations or new allocations. Thus administrators and budget specialists are usually involved in two annual
budgets at once—the current year's and the coming year's. In the case
of longer term programs a much larger period may be involved. Where
operations cut across organizational subdivisions or funds are obtained
from many external sources, different sets of budgetary categories and
procedures may be built into the process. Detailed budgets may be required on strategic types of resources—such as personnel, new machinery
and cash.

The costs of the budgetary battle are not easy to calculate. Nor is
the enthusiasm of budget specialists for determining other costs customarily applied to the costs of budgeting. These costs involve far more
than the work of budgetary personnel. They include the time devoted
to the budgetary battle by many others, including most administrators;
this means the substantial opportunity costs of time that might otherwise
be devoted to resource utilization. In addition, there are the psychic costs
of "battle fatigue" (*Argyris*, 1952).

If the costs are high, the benefits may also be very high. The internal
budgetary battle may bring to the inner depths of an organization an
awareness of the resource scarcities that confront the organization as a
whole. The increased perception of scarcity—and allocation decisions
distribute scarcity as well as resources—may create a deeper interest in

efficiency. Above all, the outcome of the budgetary battle at its best is to strengthen the organization's capacity both to mobilize external resources and to utilize them effectively.[2] To what extent these benefits may outweigh the costs is a question that can be answered only in terms of specific organizations in specific circumstances.

3. THE STRUGGLE FOR EXTERNAL RESOURCES

In seeking the resources that are distributed through the budgetary battle, few organizations depend upon obtaining resources from their members alone. The key examples of such internal orientation are trade unions, trade associations, federations, and clubs whose monetary resources are derived mainly from dues payments by members. In many such organizations—particularly trade unions and trade associations—a major objective is to strengthen the financial position of its members; activities in this direction may be regarded as external resource mobilization by indirect means. In business enterprises that sell securities or products to their members, the money thus received is itself often merely a supplement to funds obtained externally. Even where all or most money is raised internally, as with a cultural or recreational club, the money is usually used to seek external resources. By and large, most organizations direct major efforts at resource mobilization from the external environment.

In the most primitive societies resources have historically been obtained by the simple processes of foraging, gathering, hunting, and fishing. This has usually been associated with the seizure of others' resources through conquest and theft—practices that have persisted in one form or another throughout the centuries.

One of the outstanding achievements of the administrative revolution has been continuous innovation in institutionalized techniques of large-scale resource mobilization. Without the use of these techniques the growth of large-scale organizations, large-scale operations and modern machine technology would have been impossible. The major techniques are listed in the following table.

---

2. This might be regarded as the modern budgeter's restatement of Machiavelli's observations that "In our times we have seen nothing great done except by those who have been esteemed niggardly. . . . A prince must care little for his reputation of being a miser . . . ; this niggardliness is one of those vices which enable him to reign. . . . There is nothing which destroys itself so much as liberality, for by using it you lose the power of using it. . . ." (*The Prince*, p. 8-59).

TECHNIQUES OF MOBILIZING

	Money	*Physical and Human Resources*
Government organizations	Taxation Money creation	Commandeering Drafting of people Expropriation of property Rationing of goods

All organizations (including government)	Borrowing
	Sale of services, goods or securities
	Lease of property
	Contributions
	  Appropriations
	  Gifts and legacies
	  Subsidies
	  Dues
		Borrowing
		Purchase of services or goods
		Rental of property
		Contributions
		  Gifts and legacies
		  Volunteer services

		Barter

The most highly developed techniques and institutional arrangements are those relating to the mobilization of money. Each of the techniques on the left column are embedded in vast accumulations of knowledge, knowhow, tradition, theoretical debate, and social conflict. Taxation is one of the central and distinctive functions of any government (in the sense of an aggregation of government agencies) at any level. Money creation is a distinctive function of any national government (albeit often shared with private banks). An important part of the history of modern government—and of any particular government—can be written in terms of the evolution of governmental authority, power, and practice in taxation and money creation. There has usually been less public dramaturgy involved in money mobilization through these techniques available to all organizations. There is rarely any high visibility in an organization's efforts to borrow funds through bank loans or supplier credit, a university's campaign to obtain legacies from the estates of the deceased rich, or a business enterprise's exploitation of the manifold opportunities for hidden or open subsidies from government. Occasional attention is attracted by occasional "high pressure" operations in the sale of securities. Government agencies will often "go to the public" in an effort to obtain a large appropriation or borrowing authorization from a legislature or executive agency. Nonprofit organizations organize large-scale, recurrent and professionally directed campaigns for voluntary contributions.[3] The peak in visibility (and audibility) is probably reached in the sales campaigns that business organizations conduct through all the various chan-

3. An intensive trail-blazing analysis of a MOPS campaign (Mass, Operational Periodic and Secular—in the terminology of the authors) is to be found in *Seeley et al.* (1957).

nels of mass communication and personal contact. Yet in each of these instances—including the collection of dues from people who are "members in name only"—the use of these techniques is more than a technical matter in the narrow sense. Or to put it in another way, the intricate techniques of securities registration, amortization tables and inheritance laws are embedded in—and in action terms can only be understood as part of—the broader techniques and strategies of fund raising.

Like internal budgeting, external fund raising costs money. The more direct and obvious costs are usually concretized in expenses of tax collectors, interest, and dividends, fees to investment houses and rental agents, budgets for sales forces and advertising, and the salaries of professional fund raisers. As with internal budgeting, the indirect and intangible costs may add substantial increments to such figures.

An intangible cost of considerable importance is embodied in what may be called "the money illusion." The unavoidable dedication of vast energies to the external mobilization and internal distribution of money often diverts attention from the resources against which money is a claim. The instrument of exchange comes to be taken for the services or goods exchanged; the surrogate is seen as the reality.

When people become accustomed to the idea that money provides the purchasing power to obtain any and all resources, money mobilization becomes a high status function. The skills involved in using the mobilized funds are placed lower on the status ladder. Witness the differential position in organizations and society of financiers, controllers, and budget officers as opposed to that of procurement and recruitment officers.

Moreover, when physical or human resources are in short supply, the process of adjustment to the necessity of seeing resources in real as well as monetary terms is often a slow one. During World War II, when the U.S. suffered a serious shortage of natural rubber, a warehouse fire destroyed part of the country's scarce rubber stocks. When questioned at a press conference, a high government official stated that there was nothing to worry about: "the total loss was covered by fire insurance." In the same period many defense agencies and defense contractors presumed that large-scale appropriations of national funds gave them the wherewithal for armaments production. It took quite a while before they learned, under the stringencies of war mobilization, that money merely gave them a "hunting license" to seek needed resources. In the case of machinery, materials and components it proved easier to brush the money illusion aside. With respect to manpower, this process was much slower. In the early days of the U.S.A.'s program for the exploration of outer space history started to repeat itself. Huge sums of money were obtained from the Congress by government agencies and from the government agencies by private contractors—with but little realization of the bottle-neck created by the short supply of scientific, technical and managerial manpower.

External resource mobilization also has its international aspects. The growth of modern industry has been associated with world-wide searches for raw materials—particularly oil and minerals. This search has often been associated with political and economic imperialism and the subjugation of colonial peoples. A liberated colony, in turn, such as the U.S.A. after the revolution of 1776, has usually needed large amounts of external resources in the form of capital investment and manpower. In the mid-twentieth century the efforts of liberated colonies, and other "developing countries," to achieve a rapid rate of economic development had necessitated a sustained excess of imports over exports. An important element of success has been the extent to which they deliberately oriented themselves toward the goal not of short-term economic independence, but of the sustained flow of machinery, goods, and highly skilled manpower from the more developed countries.

B. *Mobilization Logic*

IN A WORLD of perfect rationality and orderly action an organization's efforts to mobilize resources would be squarely based entirely upon its plans for their utilization.

In the real world the formulation of resource objectives is also rooted in the exigencies of the budgetary battle and the struggle for external resources.

Moreover, the acquisition of additional resources is closer in time than the period of their utilization. It is easier to peer into the near future than the far future. Long-range planning often develops in the first instance as a short-range technique of resource mobilization. One of the great values of an ambitious long-term plan is its use in winning the support of investors, lenders, budget allocators, and contracting agencies. At the level of a nation as a whole, a national economic plan—particularly in its early stages—may be more useful in mobilizing the energies of key elites than in guiding the use of resources.

At a high level of abstraction the strategy and tactics of resource mobilization are no different than those used in any form of social combat. At the other extreme they are intertwined with the special problems involved in specific types of resources, mobilization techniques and environmental situations. In this section I shall seek a middle ground by identifying a general "mobilization logic" that seems to guide the formulation of objectives in the budget battle and the struggle for resources.

1. THE MOST POSSIBLE ON THE BEST TERMS

In "The Matrix of Purposes" (Chapt. 11), reference is made to the "over-aim" and the "under-aim." In the budgetary battle and the struggle for external resources these often take the form of overestimates of current costs and underestimates of capital costs. The former derives from the desire for leeway in bargaining and from widespread expectations that budget demands provide room for allocators to exercise their prerogative of budget cutting.[4] The latter derives from the desire to obtain approval for programs that might otherwise be objected to on account of their high cost. This modesty on the side of costs may be accompanied by extravagant optimism with respect to performance. Thus in submitting research and development proposals to defense agencies in the U.S.A., business concerns have widely engaged in "competitive optimism" concerning the results to be obtained in any given period of time (Peck and Sherer, 1962, p. 412-424).

The more fundamental strategic question, however, is the aspiration level itself. The use of deception in the course of the struggle is of less importance than the quantity and quality of resources that are actually sought. In a society where high value is placed upon achievements, the more successful organizations are usually those that aim high in seeking external resources. In an organization with high standards of achievement, the internal units aim high—and fight hard—in the budget battle. In both cases the mobilization of resources is seen as a means of satisfying external and internal interests, sustaining more or better output and helping build a strong and growing organization.

The vigorous mobilizers—even though they may make life difficult for their competitors—contribute the most to the economic growth of a country and to the vitality and dynamism of an organization. Hence the great value to any country of the "rugged collectivism" of those private or public organizations that push forward to expand their own programs "at all costs." Hence the great value of those units in an organization which, instead of being content with the budgets they can easily get, are constantly straining for more. It is hard for a manager to

---

4. "In this kind of game," writes Moore in his analysis of large private corporations, "the honest man is a fool. The reduction of excess claims by an across-the-board cut rewards the least moral contestant, the one who makes the most inflated demand" (1962, p. 119).

respect any unit head who is perfectly satisfied with the amount and quality of people, equipment, and materials already available to him. Satisfaction with the status quo—as distinguished from enforced acquiescence as an outcome of the budget conflict—usually indicates an absence of interest in improved performance. Success in getting increases that may not really be needed is, within any organization, "a reward for well-doing, a mark of approval" (Moore, 1962, p. 119).

Nor is there reason to think disdainfully of resource mobilization objectives that are not fully backed by utilization objectives. It often makes sense to get resources first and decide how to use them later. In the case of long-lived resources, particularly machinery and people, most projected use patterns will often change radically in the course of changing conditions. The presumption that one can foresee the details of their future use may be both pretentious and stultifying. Often, the particular pattern of resources obtained will itself determine how they are used. This is particularly true in the case of administrative manpower. The good administrator is not merely someone who can be hired to do a preordained job. He will himself help determine the nature of the job. Similarly, in planning a national educational system, educators cannot adjust educational programs to future manpower requirements deduced from a projection of the future structure of an economy. The composition of studies in an educational system will itself be a major factor in determining the structure of future economic activity.

The vigorous mobilization of resources has a double bearing on resource scarcity. On the one hand, it is the basis of resource scarcity. Resources are scarce only if and when people want them and to the extent that their efforts to get them threaten the success of similar efforts of others. Resource mobilization and resource value are thus two sides of the same coin.

On the other hand, the pressure on resources may itself be a major factor in expanding the total quantity of resources. Working estimates of resource supply are often understatements geared to the allocators' necessity of appearing, and being, niggardly. Under pressure from active mobilizers, supply may be expanded by drawing down upon internal safety margins and reserves, without necessarily withdrawing resources from other uses. Supply calculations, moreover, are usually based upon routines, habits, and traditions with respect to both physical and human resources. The calculators will habitually ignore the potentialities of low-grade materials, less shiny or unconventional equipment. They will consistently underestimate the potentialities of women, of members of racial, religious and national minorities, and of people who are physically handicapped, "too old," or "too young." Yet just as scarcity is created by active demand, so the usefulness of resources is created by the ability to arrange for their fruitful utilization. Many resources are regarded as "marginal" merely because of an institutional incapacity to use them or a biased desire not to do so. At times, indeed, the expansion of supply through the use of marginal resources is a costly process, as with the extraction of minerals from low-content ores. But no generalization can be made with respect to marginal resources as a whole. In some cases, the only additional cost is that of changing prejudices and routines.

In agricultural countries seeking rapid industrial development, it is easy to reach the limits of domestically available resources. Under such circumstances the acceptance of the existing supply situation dooms the country to slow progress or to the minor acceleration that can be achieved by dictatorial methods of expanding investment through forceful restraints on consumption. The key to rapid growth is action to escape the constraints of domestic supply by vigorous mobilization of external resources in the form of investment, loans, subsidies, and migration from other countries. The possible results of such efforts are illustrated by the cases of Puerto Rico and Israel, two countries with remarkable rates of economic growth during the post-World War II period. In both these countries economic growth was sustained by a huge volume of capital inflow from abroad. In both, although official policy statements talked about economic independence in the near future, the operational aim was to obtain the largest possible volume of foreign assistance for the longest possible period on the best possible terms. Thus the "ultimate" objective of economic independence was subordinated to a long-range policy of sustained economic dependence.[5]

The "terms," of course, are always a modifying factor. As economists delight in pointing out, the costs of acquiring additional resources (whether expressed in terms of prices, salaries, wages, interest rates, or repayment periods) serve to modify the demand for them. High or rising costs usually mean lower or trimmed-down objectives.

The terms, however, are not limited to financial costs of exchange relationships. They also include the costs of mobilization efforts and the conditions that may be imposed by those from whom resources are obtained. Attractive financial terms will often be rejected because of the "strings" attached by lenders or investors; these may include restrictions of resource use or various forms of intervention in the operations of the

5. The phrase "economic dependence" (or independence) is here used with reference to the magnitude of a country's deficit in the balance of international payments on current account or the extent to which it is dependent on foreign aid as distinguished from local sources of investment. It is not used to suggest any form of political dependence.

recipient. Even subsidies, legacies, and voluntary contributions may be regarded as too costly if the "strings" are too binding.

Only in rare circumstances are the terms a given and unchangeable datum. They are usually a variable that can be adjusted—if only to a small degree—by negotiation or "shopping around" for alternative sources of supply or alternative resources. Even after acceptance, they are subject to adjustment through interpretation or negotiation; this is the typical way of handling restraints imposed by carefully-defined budgetary allocations. Thus "the most favorable terms" are themselves a key objective in the budget battle and the struggle for external resources.

2. SOURCES AND SUPPLY LINES

Mobilization logic also requires attention to sources of supply. In the most general sense, this involves discovery of the best sources, the maintenance of supply lines and—where there is no choice—the development of new sources. Objectives in this area add realism to those concerning the quantity and quality of resources to be mobilized. They may even transcend them at times, as when efforts to strengthen supply sources determine the nature of the supplies sought.

A widespread strategic problem is that of attaining a favorable balance between supply sources inside and those outside the organization. In the case of money, the choices are usually rather restricted. For the organization as a whole, choice exists only for those organizations that obtain money from members through dues, loans, or sale of securities. For units, choice exists only when—in addition to the organization's budget system—money can also be obtained from other units or directly from supplementary external sources. Within universities these choices become great when government agencies and foundations allocate research funds directly to individual departments. Under such circumstances any large-scale mobilization of external funds will increase the autonomy of the department. It may also threaten the unified operations of the university as a whole.

In the case of goods, this strategic problem arises in the form of the question "To make or to buy?" Here the realistic opportunities of using internal sources are rather restricted. Most organizations are dependent on the external environment for most of the goods they may need—and this applies even more to the units of organizations. This dependence can be substantially modified only through large-scale expansion in the direction of vertical integration. Even then, the giant enterprise which extracts minerals from the ground and carries them to the final stage of processing faces major "make or buy" questions with respect to machinery and supplementary materials. It can never go too far in the direction of "make" without overextending its operations and losing the benefits of large-scale production.

In the case of personal services, the problem takes two different forms. In the first the question is: "To rely entirely on the services of members or to seek services from outsiders?" In the interest of reliable and sustained performance on an organization's central tasks, the great weight is usually on the side of the members. The external services of consultants and advisers are usually sought under special and unusual circumstances (as when a person goes to a doctor) or when the expertise needed cannot be found within the organization. When such services are needed on a regular basis, it may be possible to buy them through contractual relationships with other organizations. This has often proved feasible with respect to research and development services. Many government agencies in the United States have found it more useful to promote the creation of external research agencies for such purposes than to establish similar divisions within the government structure. The "contracting out"—as opposed to the "in-house"—strategy allows higher salaries to be paid to the contractor's employees, helps protect them from political influence, and helps protect the government agency from criticism that it is enlarging its own staff.

In the second form the problem relates directly to the sources of personnel for the organization itself: "How to strike a balance between recruitment (and promotion) from within the organization and from outside." On the one hand, the organization itself is the most immediate training ground for its own people. The possibility of advancement within the organization can be a major incentive to individual performance and self development. The potentialities of many people within the organization, although repressed by routines and hidden by preconceived roles, may be much greater than those of outsiders whose defects may be hidden and whose achievements in other situations may be exaggerated or irrelevant. On the other hand, complete reliance on those who come up through the ranks may lead to an "ingrown" organization. This is the danger faced by an elite career service which does not provide for "lateral entry." External recruitment is often essential to obtain personnel with a wide variety of skills, background, and experience. The *possibility* of external recruitment is always essential to modify the more automatic operation of seniority rules and create a healthy degree of competitive tension among upward-oriented members of the organization.

The most complex problems of mobilization strategy are those involving choices among external sources of supply. Here we find the ever-present choice between reliance on a stable supplier and a search for new and better suppliers. The former course can develop reliability and mutual understanding, but at the cost of developing complacency and a degree of monopoly power. The latter course can develop healthy competition, but at the cost of instability in lines of supply. Nor is it always possible to obtain a competitive situation. Suppliers may openly fix their prices and terms, or do it *sub rosa* through rigged bids. When genuine competition is obtained, its results may not be conclusive. The lowest bidder may be of doubtful reliability. It is thus rather dangerous for any organization, private or public, to get into a situation where it *must* accept the lowest bid. Similarly, in competitive examinations for entrance into civil service systems, devices are usually found to allow consideration of factors other than grades—such as interview boards, as in the Indian Civil Service, or the possibility of choosing one candidate from those with the three highest grades, as in many parts of the United States.

In a much broader sense choices among alternative sources of supply are also part of any organization's power politics. From a negative point of view, any government organization can be weakened by a "spoils system" governing the hiring of employees or awarding of contracts in accordance with external political influence. Private organizations face the same danger when undue pressures on appointments, purchases and banking arrangements are exerted by board members or stockholders who seek to advance their own interests or that of other firms with which they are connected. Defenses may be provided by merit systems, competitive bidding, conflict-of-interest codes, and review or investigation procedures.

From a more positive point of view, the ability to choose among alternative supply sources allows an organization to use resource mobilization as an instrument in the development of power. Supply is inseparably connected with support. Purchasing builds lines of credit. Borrowing creates a vested interest on the part of the lender. Debts, particularly when large, become social assets. Hence creditors will often protect themselves by providing further assistance to their debtors. The careful handling of purchases and appointments can build good will and "mend fences" without necessarily compromising on terms or quality. A merit system can be used in such a way as to select only the qualified people from a favored political party or the protegees of friendly groups. Similarly, competitive bidding can be used as a way of seeing to it that one's friends and supporters keep their prices down. The instruments of protection against undesired external influence may help an organization "play politics" on its own terms.

Resource mobilization may also be used to undermine the power of competitors, rivals, adversaries and enemies. In warfare, a high principle in the strategy of the indirect approach has been "a logistical military move directed against an economic target—the source of supply of either the opposing state or army" (Liddell Hart, 1954, p. 163-164). Lines of supply and communication can be cut not only by direct attack but also, closer to the source, by preclusive buying. Similarly, in nonmilitary situations many organizations will grab people, goods, patents, and even entire companies, mainly to prevent their utilization by others.

3. JUSTIFICATIONS

Sources of power and sources of supply tend to fuse together in the purpose patterns of an organization. The reason is that the relation between them is reciprocal. While resource mobilization provides an instrument for developing organization's power, the development of power is also a prerequisite for mobilizing resources. Resource mobilization, therefore, inevitably involves the development of strategies aimed at building a network of support. This involves the rather thoroughgoing use of the arts of direct and indirect persuasion and pressure.

In the budget battle, the arts of persuasion are habitually centered on justifying specific requests. Here it is possible to identify a number of universal arguments used in "building one's case." Thus, a proposed increase in any unit's budget will usually be justified on one or more of the following grounds:

A. *It would add little, if anything, to past expenditures.* The budget allocation for the immediate past is always the starting point for considering that of the immediate future. In this "past plus" formula, what is past is usually sacred. Disputes—and justifications—usually center around the plus. Its size will seem less terrifying when interpreted as the continuation of established trends or the carrying out of past commitments. It may seem like nothing at all when attention is concentrated on one dimension that has not increased—such as maintaining the same number of employees (after wages have risen) or replacing old equipment with the same number of equipment items (at higher unit costs).

B. *It is needed to "keep up."* Here the argument is made that unless the increment is given, the unit will "fall behind" in comparison with similar units in other organizations. The criteria for "keeping up" may be established in terms of new techniques or machinery; "we too must have the latest and best." The criteria are particularly powerful when concretized in minimum input ratios—such as one personnel man per 1,000 employees or 4 per cent of revenues for advertising—established by professional associations or "impartial experts."

C. *It can be afforded*. To prove that the increment can be afforded, it is helpful not only to play down its size but also to indicate how the additional money can be obtained. Suggesting a diversion of funds from other units is a dangerous course; it risks head-on internecine conflict. Wherever possible, therefore, units try to "earmark" certain kinds of revenue for their own use. In government operations, earmarking provisions are often written into tax laws. As in the case of gasoline taxes earmarked for highway expenditures, they are also useful in justifying tax increments.

D. *The cost of not granting the increase would be too high*. This is the argument that "we can't afford *not* to do it." To deny the increase would be another case of "too little too late." It would be equivalent to throwing a ten-foot rope to a man drowning twenty feet from shore. If the budget allocators are to behave rationally, they have no choice but to grant the increase.

E. *It would pay for itself*. This is the positive side of the previous argument. To approve the increase will be to save at least as much money—if not more—in other expenditures. In a unit that does not sell its output (as is true of most units, even those in business enterprises), this favorable outcome cannot be demonstrated in the unit's own accounts. The argument, therefore, always points to savings in other places. Government agencies habitually justify increases by claiming that they will produce large savings for citizens and nongovernment organizations.

F. *It would serve the interests of all*. Here the previous argument is broadened to cover all categories of resultant benefits. The increase will help the unit advance the interests of the organization as a whole or help the organization serve the public interest. Within a business organization this general interest may be specified in terms of an alleged contribution to the company's profits or general financial strength. In government—as is consistently done with respect to parks, weather reports, and health services—it may be justified in terms of its contribution to the national defense. In either case, the difficulty of pinning down the specific contribution and comparing it with that of other proposed expenditures rarely interferes with the vigorous use of the argument.

In the struggle for external resources, justifications are much more varied. The objects of persuasion are a more diverse group. Different styles of persuasion—as well as different media and channels—will be used with various types of clients, lenders, investors, and suppliers.

Nevertheless, there are a number of unifying elements that underlie all such efforts, and are applicable to the budget battle as well. The first is found in the proposition that "the secret of effective propaganda is the ability to make a case in terms of the interests of those whom one wants to persuade" (*Gross*, p. 244). This means starting with what people perceive their interests to be, rather than what one thinks they should be. It also means trying to determine the extent of latent, unperceived or hidden interests.

Another is found in the principle that the most persuasive case is made by actual demonstration. The propaganda of the deed is worth far more than the propaganda of the word. The strongest element in persuasion is the well-based report on actual performance. Thus an established reputation for the successful use of resources is a major weapon in the mobilization of resources.

Finally, as in most instances of social conflict, persuasion is generally accompanied by some form or degree of pressure. Resources are not obtained through justifications alone. Rewards and punishments are always involved. If something is to be obtained, something must be given. This means that some things must be promised and others, at times, threatened. Among businesses, this is referred to as simply "trading" or "making a deal." Within legislatures, often with less approbation, it is called "logrolling." Within both business and government agencies, pressures may be exerted—and the basis for a deal created—by the strategy of spending money as rapidly as possible. In the case of highly valued services the exhaustion of funds may create a crisis that can be relieved only by their rapid replenishment. In other cases it at least proves that last year's budget was not too high; hence the frequent bursts of business and government spending in the last month of every budgetary year. Whatever the form may be, pressure is the very lifeblood of efforts to obtain budget allocations and mobilize external resources.

In deals concerning the future use of resources (as distinguished from the financial terms of payment or repayment), the propagandistic element is often hard to distinguish from the substantive. This is particularly true whenever specific conditions are established concerning the use to which a money increment is put. Money from a budget allocation, loan, or gift may be specifically earmarked for a specific use. But if the organization already had funds for this purpose, the receipt of the increment will merely release funds for other purposes. Under such circumstances we have an instance of what might be called "propagandistic earmarking." Thus a university gives a rich donor the honor of having his name attached to a library that it was going to build anyway; his funds make it possible to do many other things. A plaque near a new bridge in Persia indicates it was built with funds from the U.S. Government. But any one of dozens of other activities might also have been selected; the plaque is easier to pin down than the use of a resource so flexible and fluid as money. In neither case would genuine earmarking have been possible except in the framework of a total allocation of all funds available to the university or the Persian government.

c. *Use Logic*

"MOBILIZATION LOGIC" by itself is a dangerous guide. The objectives it brings into being can lead to profitless conflict, the accumulation of unneeded resources, and the erosion of external confidence and support.

"Use logic" is more sober. It means the formulation of objectives in terms of an anticipated pattern of using the resources sought. While it too requires an imaginative probing of the future, the imagination is here applied to the more restricted area of the organization's (or unit's) future operations.

By itself, it too is dangerous—particularly when applied by specialists or administrators with little awareness of the crudities of the resource and power struggle. It can lead to static objectives that stifle initiative in the actual use of resources. It requires supplementation by mobilization logic.

Mobilization logic is usually taught in the hard school of experience. It is thus learned quickly and deeply, albeit at a low level of articulation. Yet mobilization logic may itself lead to the development of use logic. This is particularly true when budget allocators, lenders, and investors insist on something more than fancy justifications and start checking on resource use. This external pressure is supplemented within the organization by those who, under the pressures of scarcity or of professional orientations, are mainly concerned with resource use. It thus becomes necessary to learn use logic also—not only to "get a job done" but also to keep on getting resources.

1. THE "REQUIREMENTS"

The use logic of resource mobilization is oriented toward answering the question of what resources are really "required" or "needed."

In a certain sense, this question can never be objectively answered. The term "requirements" (like "needs") merely provides a more impressive garb for "desires," "wants" or "demands." These are essentially subjective. They are rooted in whatever objectives or goals an organization or unit may establish for the satisfaction of the interests of members and nonmembers. Any statement of the requirements of an organization or unit is an indirect way of talking about how it works to obtain its highest values. It can thus be judged only in terms of such values, which are themselves subjective. Thus any disputes on requirements are in large part not on what is needed to produce an agreed-upon set of products but disputes rather on what products are to be produced, what the future of the organization is to be, and what interests it should aim to serve. It is in this sense that V. O. Key (1940) points out that there is no budgetary theory that can determine whether X dollars should be allocated to Activity A rather than activity B. Or, as Wildavsky has put it (1961), budget-making "represents conflict over whose preferences shall prevail. . . ."

On the other hand, a more objective basis for "requirements" may exist *if* specific objectives for an organization's product mix and asset structure are already taken as given. This is the essence of use logic.

2. RELATION TO PRODUCT AND ASSET OBJECTIVES

In developing a use logic approach to resource objectives, three types of calculations are involved.

The first deals with the product mix. In the more sophisticated forms of use logic this is done by identifying the quantity and quality of end products, including intangible services, to be produced over specified periods of time. This also includes a resolution of "make or buy" (or in more general terms "produce or get") problems.

The second deals with the desired asset structure. Because of inevitable changes in the product mix, unpredicted difficulties with the inputs obtained, and unpredictable occurrences in the production process, use logic demands reserves. The higher the degree of uncertainty, the greater these reserves must be. Mobilization logic and use logic often coincide at the point, since the very essence of a reserve is that its use is not specified beforehand. The main difference is that mobilization logic usually aims at the largest possible reserve (subject to the costs of getting and maintaining it) under the guise of a specified use. Use logic is more aboveboard, with more attention to the costs of reserves.

The building of reserves is already a step removed from the production process and the product mix. Its mention carries us forward into the broader category of investing resources in building the assets of the organization. Thus the desired asset structure as a whole takes its place, along with the desired product mix, as a datum from which resource requirements can be deduced. The two forms of "givens" are brought together by the fact that an organization's human and physical assets, as discussed in Chapter 17, determine in large part its capacity to produce some desired form of product mix. They diverge to the extent that the organization's survival and growth are not necessarily linked to any given product mix.

Third, on the basis of the desired product mix and the desired increments to the existing asset structure, it is then possible to derive the desired flow of inputs into and through the organization. Ideally, the "input mix" is calculated in terms of quantity and quality, real and monetary units, and specified periods of time.

In this more austere framework the problem may now be regarded from the viewpoint of production rationality. Many of the most sophisticated techniques of economics and engineering may be relevant. Their full use will even point out the desirability of adjusting the composition or level of the product mix or asset structure.

But even when use logic can be protected from the intrusion of other questions (and when it is not used merely to rationalize other objectives), it does not always lead to rationally determinate solutions. Production technology in the modern world is always in a state of flux. The inputs used in the past are merely starting points in considering what inputs may be needed to produce similar products in the future. New materials, new machinery, and new human skills are always coming along to complicate the picture. New input combinations are always possible. Nor, as shown in the discussion of inputs and costs in Chapter 16, is it always possible for reasonable people—even reasonable technological experts—to agree on which of two production methods is to be regarded as the cheaper.

D. *Demobilization*

THE INGESTION OF RESOURCES is always counterbalanced in part by more or less automatic forms of egestion. Materials leave an organization in the form of goods produced. Paper spews forth in a continuous stream of letters and reports. Waste products leave via the wastepaper baskets and junk heaps. Equipment that breaks down is disposed of or rebuilt. Through the normal processes of attrition (death, retirement, and voluntary separation), a portion of the members leave every year.

Nevertheless, the mobilization of resources and the production of output invariably leads to the accumulation of *surplus resources*—that is more resources than are needed to produce the desired product mix and build the desired asset structure. This accumulation may take place through: (a) excess mobilization, stemming from exuberant mobilization logic or defective use logic; (b) changes in use patterns, resulting from new ideas concerning product mix and asset structure; (c) technological obsolescence, resulting from new technologies to which existing personnel, machinery, facilities, or material stocks cannot be adapted; or (d) deterioration of physical or human resources through age, wear-and-tear, spoilage, overuse, or disuse.

Where there is little or no cost involved in their maintenance, surplus resources are a good thing to have. Even though not of the best quality, at least they are something to fall back upon in time of emergency. They can be a second set of reserves, a contribution to the organization's efforts to conquer scarcity.

But the costs are often considerable. Surplus materials and equipment take up space, require at least elementary forms of maintenance, and freeze capital that could be used more fruitfully elsewhere. Unneeded people, apart from the space they occupy, clog the channels of communication and deaden the pace of activity. The costs represented by out-of-pocket outlays are small compared to those resulting from organizational congestion and obesity. Even the accumulation of money can become over-costly, as when an excess of cash on hand denies the benefits that would be obtained by using it to reduce debt, earn interest or dividends, or assemble real resources.

Use logic, therefore, inevitably demands more forceful methods of egestion. These may take such forms as the termination of supply contracts, the reduction of inventories, the dismantling or replacement of machinery and facilities, temporary layoffs of personnel, or compulsory separations. All of these—together with the more automatic processes referred to above—may be subsumed under the term "demobilization."

The formulation of demobilization objectives involves some prickly problems.

1. DETERMINATION OF "NONREQUIREMENTS"

The most prickly of all demobilization problems—and the most fundamental—is the determination of what should really be regarded as surplus. To the extent that demobilization logic is use logic in reverse; the "nonrequirements" as well as the requirements are derived from calculations concerning product mix, asset structure and input flow. But demobilization logic is also rooted in the struggle for power and resources. On one hand, it is influenced by the prestige and power that may come from hoarding or empire building, entirely apart from the future use of the resources amassed. On the other hand, demobilization objectives may be instruments to "trim the wings" or even liquidate internal comcompetitors or adversaries.

The determination of manpower "nonrequirements" is often extremely hazy. The abilities and characteristics of people cannot be pinned down as readily as those of machinery and materials. The actual and potential performance of people is largely dependent upon social situations whose analysis is both difficult and controversial. Manpower input requirements cannot be determined solely on the basis of unit costs. As shown in Chapter 16, they also depend upon goals concerning the total number of units. These difficulties are compounded by the tremendous labor-displacing implications of modern technology and by the continuous struggle as to who should bear the social costs of both "transitional" and "permanent" unemployment.

Above all, the initiative in determining manpower "nonrequirements" is often in the hands of administrators and specialists who have failed to keep up with the pace of accelerating and uneven changes in technology, administration and the organization's environment. It is particularly hard for such people to face the possibility that they themselves are rapidly obsolescing and may soon become surplus. They are often in the most strategic position of all to resist replacement, transfer, or significant reconditioning.

2. PRESENT OR RECONDITIONED FORM

Resources that are surplus in their present form may—with a certain amount of reconditioning—prove useful in the same unit. If not, reconditioning may facilitate the process of internal transfer or full separation.

While the techniques of reconditioning, retooling, or reconstruction are well-developed with respect to machinery and buildings, they are little developed with respect to people. The educational techniques that have been developed are themselves often regarded as "surplus baggage" by oldfashioned administrators. Programs of education and retraining are apt to be so costly that only the largest organizations can afford them. Where they are installed and prove effective, they may also develop more ability than the organization can absorb and contribute to voluntary separations on the part of people the organization can least spare.

3. FULL SEPARATION OR INTERNAL TRANSFER

A person or a machine not needed in one unit of an organization may prove useful in another unit. Full separation from the organization makes no sense unless such possibilities are surveyed.

In the demobilization of the members of an organization, the choice between the two approaches becomes particularly prickly. Full separation may mean a personal tragedy for the person separated and for members of his family. It may produce undue fears and instability among other members of the organization. In some circumstances it can be handled properly only by the costly process of finding the person a position in another organization. In a period of recession or depression this may not be possible.

Internal transfers also have their costs. "Downgrading" is hard to effect and, when effected, may also be tragic. A horizontal movement with no loss of status and pay may be met with resistance in other units. Transfers by "kicking the fellow upstairs" may weaken the administration of the entire organization—unless "upstairs" includes some nominal or honorary positions where surplus people can do no harm.

4. SLOW DEMOBILIZATION OR SUDDEN PURGES

Surplus resources accumulate through a combined process of slow accretion and of sudden spurts resulting from new products and technologies. Similarly, the demobilization process in most organizations usually consists of both continuing "dis-accretions" (as with the routine decisions of business organizations on inventory control and machine replacement) and major purges. In part, the latter result from sudden changes in conditions—as when peace, depression, or a technological revolution bring on, respectively, demobilization of an army, mass payoffs by business, or the junking of existing machinery. In part, sudden purges also result from the slow development of demobilization logic, resistances to demobilization, and the frequent difficulty of overcoming these resistances through anything other than drastic action.

In the case of people, there is a tendency for both continual demobilization and sudden purges to operate at odds with use logic. Death, marriage, disenchantment, the reaching of retirement age and the other factors affecting normal attrition can be relied upon as a way of reducing personnel. But they are less reliable as selectors of the "unrequired." The difficulty with large layoffs is not that they unsettle the organization; this can be handled. Rather, those who are laid off often include the most capable or promising people. Those who remain are those with the most power to maintain their position. Both slow and sudden demobilization may be countered by large-scale resistance. Either a single separation notice or a big layoff may be met by a strike, slowdown, sabotage or the less noticeable but more deadly weapons of apathy and noncooperation. Society as a whole and even government agencies may punish an organization that does not relieve an unemployment situation by maintaining unneeded people on its payroll.

Considerable resistance is usually exerted against the disposition of surplus documents. Here there is no one to speak for the documents, and the burning of a memorandum can hardly be regarded as an act of cruelty. But the memoranda, letters, forms, and cancelled checks in the files of an organization are, in fact, the most tangible products produced by many people—particularly by administrators. For many, they are the only footprints left in the sands of time. To destroy them is like destroying one's children. Even if the organization's future is in doubt, the viability of the records may be assured. In the United States, laws often require approval of an archivist before records may be disposed of or destroyed. Under this protection the cubic feet of stored records grew from 4 to 18.5 million from 1932 to 1948 (Millett, 1954, p. 386-387). The increase has probably been exponential since then. There is reason to suspect this phenomenon is more or less universal.

Chapter 19

OBSERVANCE OF CODES

OR THE YOUNG CHILD, life is a continual process of discovering one rule after another. When he begins to join formal organizations, rules become even more important. He finds many codes that bear on the behavior of members, units and organizations as a whole. Some of these are the internalization of external codes: laws and regulations, moral and ethical precepts, and professional principles. Others are brought into being by the organization itself or by its various formal and informal units. Many are hallowed by custom and tradition. All represent "the right ways" to do things.

Although code observance by organizations and their units is partly a matter of habit and routine, a large amount of conscious, goal-oriented activity is continually required. The most conspicuous forms of this activity are enforcement operations aimed at keeping inevitable deviations within tolerable bounds. In addition to the use of sanctions and indoctrination, this involves explaining, clarifying, interpreting, reconciling, and adjusting various codes. It involves devising new rules and procedures to meet new situations. Less conspicuous but still more widespread are the continuous efforts to subordinate or modify other aims to conform with "the right way." Often, attention to code observance objectives becomes so great that organizations and their administrators are sharply criticized for allowing "higher" ends to be displaced by "means" or "instrumental purposes." In terms of the analytical hierarchy of purposes, code observance—like rationality—is indeed among the lower and more instrumental of all purposes. But the action hierarchy is more fluid. At times the vicissitudes of a situation require high priority for code observance, with other purposes temporarily subordinated. For some administrators, moreover, doing things the "right" way may itself be perceived as a higher goal—just as walking in the path of righteousness may for some people be more important than any destination to which the path may lead.

It is often easier to think of code observance objectives as constraints upon purposeful activity rather than as direct objects of goal-oriented action. This is a matter of emphasis. Whenever administrators focus sharply upon one category of purpose, all other purpose elements appear as constraints. Thus the necessity of making profits may appear as a constraint to the businessman who is set on building an ever-expanding organization, while the necessity of maintaining the organization may appear as a constraint to the one more interested in making larger profits. Similarly, a code prohibition is a negative restraint for the person whose actions are prohibited; for the code enforcers, observance is a positive goal. In any case, an element regarded as a constraint is not thereby expunged from an organization's purpose pattern. It is rather placed in a certain perspective within it.

In discussing code observance objectives, this chapter starts by identifying their role in relation to other objectives.

An effort is then made to deal substantively with an "inner core" which is to be found in almost all organizations. This is followed by a discussion of the major variants that emerge in specific situations.

The chapter concludes by discussing the problems involved in the handling of code deviations.

A. *The Role of Code Observance*

As EXPLAINED in "People-in-Organizations: Formal Aspects" (Chapt. 9), an organization's structure is not completed by the specification of roles and of hierarchic and polyarchic relations. Codes of behavior provide the mortar that holds these elements together. Observance may take the form of conformity based upon habit or desire or of compliance under the compulsion of open or hidden sanctions. In either case, a basic minimum of code observance is an inherent part of the purpose pattern of every organization.

1. RULES

It is never easy to discover all the rules in an organization. Many formally established rules are never written down. The written ones may defy understanding save by long experience. The informal rules are usually shadowy and evanescent, crystallizing—like any form of common law—in the face of clear violations. Some rules are so fully taken for granted that to express them openly would itself violate the rules of common courtesy or suggest the possibility of unthinkable exceptions. Thus as Moore has pointed out, "a company can scarcely affect indifference to the fact that a boss has killed his secretary in a fit of rage over a misspelled word, even though there may be no company rule expressly forbidding the killing of secretaries having more than two years of service with the employer" (1962, p. 54). All rules are subject to imperceptible changes and unpredictable interpretations. Often the only sure criterion is embodied in the principle that "the rules are what the rule enforcers say they are."

Moreover, the rules are extremely varied in nature. At one extreme there are the prescriptions, those telling you what you *must* do. At the other extreme there are the proscriptions, which tell you what you must *not* do. In between there is a vaguer middle area. Certain preferences tell you what kind of behavior is *desired* under certain conditions, even though not required. Certain permissions tell you what is *allowed* under certain conditions, although not necessarily desired.[1]

The distinction between rule enforcement and goal attainment in general is made difficult by the fact that in a certain sense we may say that an organization's code deals with the satisfaction of certain interests by producing certain outputs, economizing on scarce resources, maintaining the organization's viability, and mobilizing the resources needed to do all these things. More narrowly, however, the codes dealt with here are a residual category; they deal only with the right ways of seeking to attain other objectives.

Even in this narrow sense, the distinction is rendered difficult by the fact that the instrumental rules are often indispensable steps toward interest satisfaction, output production, efficient operations, viability, and resource mobilization. Many external interests may be satisfied only by conformance with general codes of behavior, particularly laws, regulations and ethical prescriptions. The interests of members are always bound

---

1. The prescription-preference-permission-proscription continuum is taken from Merton's discussion of cultural goals and institutional norms (1957, p. 133).

up in the rules. The rules may provide a common bond that differentiates an organization or unit from other groups (*Davies; Dornbusch; Page*). They may also go far—or too far—in meeting the needs of the rule enforcers for prestige and power. They invariably provide some basic minimum of security for all members.

Many of the rules in every organization deal with the myriad details of output and resource economy. They structure the complex processes of work, work methods, work flow, and the calculation of the quality and quantity of inputs used and outputs produced. They put order into the myriad interrelations involved in the complex processes of making decisions. They help unify the organization by channeling and limiting the budgetary battle and other internal conflicts and guiding behavior in the struggle for external resources and other environmental conflicts. Together with established roles and role relationships, the rules provide every member with the indispensable degree of confidence as to how the other members will operate. They provide the foundation for the predictability and order which makes it possible for members to cope with the unpredicted, the unpredictable and the random. Like habit, custom, and tradition in the life of an individual, they give structure to the on-going process of organizational activity. Hence, it is more important for an organization to have *some* rules—sometimes almost *any* rules—than to have *good* rules. The very red tape against which members and clients may vociferously complain may itself be indispensable to meeting the needs of the complainants.[2]

The link between rule observance and rationality is quite complex. Many of the rules are the direct products of technical or administrative rationality. Thus rules concerning work methods and the handling of machinery and materials may be the outcome of scientific or technological investigation. Rules relating to the coordination of operations and the hiring, compensation, and promotion of personnel may result from careful administrative study. The very fact that some decisions may be avoided by routinely following the rules makes it possible to free administrators' attention for dealing with nonroutine problems. Yet the presumed rationality of a rule may be open to serious question. The investigation or study on which a rule has been based may have been merely a form of self-justification. If sincere, it may have been conducted on an irrational basis—as happens with innumerable administrative studies. Above all, rules that once had a good rationale tend to persist long after

2. Complaints against red tape are themselves identified as a phenomena to be examined by researchers in Gouldner's perceptive "Red Tape as a Social Problem" (1952).

the rationale itself has disappeared. Almost every organization follows certain procedures for the simple reason "it's always been done that way." The pressure to obey the rules often operates strongly against those who want to "use their heads," and against recognizing the existence of non-routine problems. Following "the book" may mean the blindest irrationality.

The codes of organizations, as has often been noted, invariably reflect broader social codes. Ethical and moral values of the society and community in which an organization operates are carried into the organization by its members, who are also members of the society and community. The codes of professional groups may be brought into an organization by members who also belong to professional associations. Some external rules and regulations are always taken over and internalized.

Less attention has been paid to the active social role of organizational codes as sources, rather than reflections, of broader social values. Thurman Arnold has pointed out that "creeds and theories develop automatically from organizations" (1937, p. 178). The same may be said concerning people's ideas and sentiments concerning "the right ways" of doing anything at all. The family is not the only locus of the socialization process. The methods of thought, conduct and behavior that are learned in formal organizations are inevitably carried over into the full lifestream of members. This need not mean that an official who insists on three carbon copies of all documents will expect carbons of birthday cards accompanying presents from his children. It does mean that his general attitudes toward rule observance, rule breaking, loyalty, rational procedures, and similar matters will be a part of the environment in which his children grow up. It does not mean that if he is utterly ruthless in dealing with people at work, he may not be gentle with his children and an inveterate churchgoer. But his attitudes toward people will become part of inhuman or antihuman attitudes in his community; and if he takes part in church affairs, he will probably be as ruthless an operator in church politics as he is at work. Similarly, to the extent that organizations breed a spirit of conformity among their members, there is no doubt that this spirit spreads to other activities as well. If much of "traditional morality has been authoritarian" (Edel, 1955, p. 328), this may well be a reflection of the authoritarian ways of life and thought that have developed in many organizations over the centuries.

2. RITUALS

In the study of primitive societies anthropologists have analyzed the many rituals which help hold savage groups together. It is somewhat harder for "civilized" observers to note the ritualistic elements in their own lives. Rituals may be more obvious in religious organizations and in fraternal associations with elaborate ceremonies of initiation. It is less obvious in the case of the large, modern, and highly rationalized government agency or business corporation. In fact, the absence of ritual from administration seems implicitly assumed by Fortes and Evans-Pritchard (1940, p. 19) in their question concerning the need for ritual to promote the solidarity of African tribes: "Why is an all-embracing administrative machinery or a wide-flung lineage system insufficient to achieve this (i.e. solidarity)?"

The reason that rituals, rites, and ceremonies are less visible in modern organizations of all types is that we take them for granted. We have the same difficulty in detecting the familiar that seafish would have in measuring the salinity of the water in which they swim. This is one of the reasons why the rituals of African tribes seem so strange to civilized observers. It is also one of the reasons why experienced administrators from one culture may be so shocked by administrative practices in another culture; they are unprepared for the different forms of ritualistic and ceremonial rules.

Yet if we examine the rules of administered organizations in the light of our knowledge of primitive ritual, we shall find many similar elements which, while not necessarily religious in nature, are not rational in the narrow sense of technical or scientific rationality. We shall find a wide-spread use of symbols which not only identify individual roles but also evoke emotional perceptions of the purposes of an organization and the common values of its members. These may appear in the form of official seals, special names, insignia, flags, mottoes, slogans, jargon, uniforms, or even distinctive stationery. We shall also find a large number of ceremonies, rites, and ritualistic practices. Many of these may be regarded as *rites of passage*. These include the various ceremonies associated with a member's acceptance into an organization: inauguration, "swearing in," and periods of trial. They include the ceremonial practices relating to promotion, departure, and death. Many of the "hazing" rituals in fraternal organizations and the elaborate procedures for academic promotion in universities are truly *cults of affliction*. The honor is more profound, and group solidarity greater, by virtue of the trials and anguish of those who successfully "run the gauntlet." *Rites of intensification* serve to reemphasize the common purposes of the organization. These are found not only in ceremonies of laying cornerstones for new buildings, opening new projects, citations for exceptional performance. They are also found in conventions, regular meetings of all members or employees, office parties, and other social festivities. They are found in procedures that reconcile conflicting ideals of members or help reconcile ideals with practical necessities (Thurman Arnold, 1937, p. 358-366). *Rites of divination* are found in the elaborate procedures whereby many organizations try to peer into the future by having accepted seers transmute past trends into official forecasts. *Rites of sanctification* are often found in voting procedures, meetings of governing boards, and the preparation and elaboration of written documents. All of these, apart from intrinsic uses, may also be used to provide greater legitimacy to decisions already made or actions already taken.

The above comments are liable to serious misinterpretation. They might be mistakenly construed as an exposé of vestigial remnants of primitive irrationality in modern organizations. They might be regarded as based upon a tacit assumption that rational administration requires the purging of ritualistic elements from formal rules.

The point here being made, however, is simply that some degree and form of ritual is inherent in organizational rules. Ritual is as much needed to hold a modern organization together as it is to overcome the interminable conflicts among the members of a primitive tribe. To try to eradicate it might be as irrational as to suppose that it does not exist. The frequent failure of intellectuals as administrators is often due to their overemphasis upon "rigorous dialectic and the so-called intellectual skills" at times when more attention should be given to rites, ceremonies and symbols (*Ibid.*, 1937, p. 385-393).

3. CONFLICTS

Although the inevitability of internal conflicts has already been discussed in "The Conflict-Cooperation Nexus" (Chapt. 3), it might appear that by virtue of their unifying functions, an organization's codes stand outside the conflict area. Particularly when codes serve to channel and settle conflicts, it might be assumed that the codes themselves are above the conflict.

Yet such an appearance may easily be illusory and such an assumption unfounded. As Barnard has pointed out, code conflicts are a normal part of organizational life. The more obvious forms of conflict occur between the codes of different groups in an organization, or between formal and informal codes. Some of the sharpest and subtlest conflicts are between different codes, whether formal or informal, held strongly by the same group. Thus as we shall see somewhat later, the code of telling the truth may be inconsistent with the code of order. The suppression or distortion of information may be required in the interests of discipline. Also, many codes are based upon a builtin double standard. One code is used with some people and a second code wtih others. In broader areas this has been illustrated by the old jingle:

> The law locks up both man and woman
> Who steals the goose from off the common
> But lets the greater felon loose
> Who steals the common from the goose.

In organizations, similarly, there often seems to be a code which flatly states that different kinds of behavior are expected from people at different levels. This differentiation may indeed be inherent in the differential privileges which invariably accompany hierarchical stratification.

Finally, any behavioral code may readily conflict with the attainment of "higher" organizational goals. Thus at times obeying laws may be sacrificed to profitmaking, loyalty to the public interest, justice to viability, and established procedures to efficiency. Often the conflict is much more complicated, involving a large array of desirable objectives. This is one of the major causes of willful or unwitting deviation.

B. *The Inner Core*

AT THE CENTER of every organization's vast web of behavioral codes, there is always a hard inner core[3] of prescriptions, preferences, permissions, and proscriptions. This inner core is founded on the elementary requirements of human cooperation in organizations. In one form or another—and the forms indeed vary—it is found in every organization in every culture. These codes relate to such fundamental matters as order, loyalty, honesty, justice, secrecy, and opportunism. If these are persistent elements in the moral fabric of all societies (and the first four seem to have universally open acceptance, with the fifth and sixth universally accepted in practice), at least a partial explanation may be found in the thought patterns developed through participation in formal organizations.

In presuming to specify a universal inner core of organizational morality, however, I am not suggesting a higher measure of observance than for any other codes. Deviation strikes indiscriminately, affecting both universals and variants in organizational codes.

---

3. Although stated in empirical terms and limited to the organizational context, the concept of the "inner core" is close to the "valuational base" concept set forth by Edel as "a standpoint for evaluation, providing moorings to which a morality may be fastened (1955, p. 297).

1. ORDER

No society can function properly without the maintenance of some minimum degree of "law and order." The maintenance of law and order is thus the most elementary responsibility of governing a society.

In single organizations, breakdown and dissolution occur much more frequently. Unlawfulness and disorder are a still greater threat, orderliness a still greater good. The requirements for cooperation and predictability are more minute and precise.

In a narrow sense, the maintenance of order is seen as relating to the structure of an organization. As an objective, order involves general acceptance of established roles, hierarchic and polyarchic relations and rules and rituals. The code of order prescribes a minimum amount of internal discipline, proscribes large-scale deviations and permits the use of rewards and punishments as enforcement measures.

In a somewhat broader sense, the code of order often demands adjustments in the codes wherever this is needed to maintain order. A legalization of the previously illegal is preferable to a breakdown in discipline. Codes governing intraorganizational conflict are preferable to the persistence of disorderly internal conflict.

In a still broader sense, the code of order expresses a general preference for predictability in human behavior. Entirely apart from roles and codes, people are expected to preserve a certain continuity between yesterday, today and tomorrow. Innovators may introduce drastic change, but not too often and not in too many places at once. In fact, creativity and innovation in one aspect of an organization's work—be it structure or technology—may be expected to be associated with conservatism and tradition in other aspects. Reliability, a great virtue in any cooperative endeavor, is not seen as only the capacity to get things done. It is also the capacity to do things in a way that will not cause undue surprise or consternation.

Above all, the code of order requires a basic minimum of honesty in relations among the members of an organization, of loyalty to the organization, and of justice in the distribution of rewards and punishments among members. The three codes dealing with these matters—each of which has had a profound effect on ethical principles in general—will now be discussed separately.

2. HONESTY

The code of honesty is so much taken for granted within organizations that to put it in writing would be ridiculous. For an administrator to voice it orally would usually be regarded as insulting. Nevertheless, three separable elements in this code can be distinguished.

The first is "Tell the truth (or something close to the truth) most of the time in internal communications." In negative terms it is "Don't lie or deceive unless it is a 'white' lie for the clear good of the organization." The foundation of this rule lies in the necessity of reliable communications within an organization. If internal lying or deception should become widespread in an organization, all communications would be suspect. The organization's viability would be seriously threatened.

In countries entering the first stages of industrialization, the importance of this code is not automatically appreciated. People whose background lies in the "primitive higgling" of small-scale agriculture and trade will often bring with them into larger-scale organizations old habits of deceit, guile and trickery. This would not be so great a handicap if these methods were used only with outsiders and if truth-telling guided relations with colleagues and subordinates. But the idea that there must be "honor even among thieves" is not so quickly appreciated. When it is, it is not easy to draw the line between internal and external communications. Lying to outsiders can readily become a source of confusion to insiders also. It was probably on such grounds that Jeremy Bentham commented "that, if there were no such thing as honesty, it would be a good speculation to invent it, as a means of making one's fortune" (1931, p. 64).

The second facet of organizational honesty is "Keep your word (or promise or agreement)." The idea of contract is not limited to the market and interorganizational agreements. All sorts of implied and quasi-contracts are made within organizations. These may relate to work assignments, job conditions, promotions, or the exchange of information or favors. The failure to carry out threats of punishment may impair morale even more than reneging on promised rewards. The deterrent effect of a sanction often lies less in its severity than in its inevitability. In the area of operations, moreover, people must frequently act on the basis of what someone says he *will* do. If he does not in fact do it, the effectiveness of operations is threatened. In the case of very complex operations involving a high degree of coordination, the result of "word breaking" may be disaster.

Third, the code of honesty provides that "You shall not steal anything substantial from the organization." This precept also is based upon rigorous necessity. If the physical or monetary resources of the organization are purloined by its members, the organization is threatened. Hence the growth of large-scale organizations has invariably been accompanied by sustained action to protect these resources against serious thefts by members. This has led to extensive systems of accounting and control, internal investigation and espionage, and protection by public law. These efforts have been backed up by external agencies, particularly investors and public appropriating bodies with a stake in the resources of organizations. One of the results has been the proliferation of accounting and control systems so fully oriented toward the prevention or detection of theft that they impede the collection of accounting data needed for internal decision-making. Also, much of the red tape that prevents speedy action by large-scale organizations, particularly government agencies, derives from procedures based on the assumption that without continual double checking an organization's resources may be appropriated by its members.

3. LOYALTY

The code of loyalty derives from the requirements of an individual's membership in a group. With membership comes a sense of obligation to support the organization in some way, by thought if not in deed. It is often reduced to a bare minimum by the fact that the member's participation may be marginal—as with many associations in which the payment of dues provides for little more than a fictional form of membership. Above all, even when membership is based on genuine interaction, loyalty to the organization may be diluted by conflicts between personal interests and those of the organization, between external interests and those of the organization, and between conflicting interests within the organization.

With respect to the first of these conflicts the "inner core" code of loyalty deals with two extreme cases. In situations of dire need, when the organization is seriously threatened, the code of loyalty says "subordinate personal interests to those of the group." As Stouffer and his associates have demonstrated, this code played a major part in preserving the solidarity of American army troops in combat (*Stouffer et al.*). In more negative terms the loyalty code proscribes the acceptance of bribes and other corrupt practices that might benefit the individual but injure the organization.

Greater complications arise when an individual's action against the interests of his organization serve not only his own interests but the interests of another organization or group to which he belongs. Loyalty to a political organization has often led high government officials to appoint incompetents to government posts. Loyalty to family and friends has had similar results in business. Loyalty to other business enterprises has led business officials to favor certain suppliers over others. Loyalty to outsiders (apart from personal rewards that may be obtained) has often led the members of organizations to provide secret information to competitors or enemies or to serve as saboteurs or provocateurs. Most actions of this type are clear violations of the loyalty code of the disadvantaged organization or country.

But the "inner core" loyalty code is extremely broad. It merely proscribes actions that would seriously subordinate the interests of an organization to those of another group. Interminable efforts are undertaken to develop and enforce more specific rules. Among these the most widespread seem to be rules and procedures providing that:

a. people be hired only after some demonstration that they are reasonably well qualified. Merit systems, it should be noted, cannot eliminate the influence of political affiliations, friendship, and family connections. But they can go a long way in seeing that jobs are given only to properly qualified party members, friends, and relatives.

b. contracts, licenses, and other benefits be given only after an objective analysis of the interests of the grantor organization. Within these limits the grantee organization with "inside connections" will usually win out. But this need not disadvantage the grantor.

c. limits be placed upon the external connections of members—in terms of membership, ownership, investments, or employment. In some instances, particularly when organization officials are expected to be, like Caesar's wife, above suspicion, constraints may be applied upon those with whom a person may associate. "Guilt by association" is bound to develop whenever someone associates regularly with opponents or enemies of his organization.

d. the external connections of various members be made a matter of official or even (as in the case of some government agencies) public record.

Still greater complications arise with respect to conflicts between loyalty to the organization as a whole and loyalty to a formal unit or informal group within it. Here we find that most members feel the strongest loyalty to their intimate associates rather than the organization as a whole. The minority of serious aspirants to higher administrative ranks tends to be more loyal to the larger organization they hope some day to lead. Top executives tend to stress personal loyalty to themselves. Many serious analysts of government, such as Don K. Price, advocate a much higher and broader sense of loyalty, one which may curtail loyalty to their immediate groups or superiors:

> The first loyalty of the subordinate in the United States is not to his superiors in the executive hierarchy. It is not to the service as a body, except perhaps for a few members of the military and foreign services. It is certainly not to the Congress or to any political party. All these loyalties are secondary, even though they may be powerful and generally

binding. The primary loyalty is to the Constitution of the United States, under which only the people are the ultimate power, and the individual official must sometimes judge for himself his relative obligations to the branches of the government and to the various levels of officialdom (1954, p. 138-139).

If the Price precept were to be applied to other organizations, it would require that the highest loyalty be given to an organization's charter and through it to the interests of such holders of ultimate authority as the stockholders of corporations and the members of associations. It would also obligate individuals to be prepared, on occasion, to use their own best judgment and conscience in determining the nature of these interests.

4. DISTRIBUTIVE JUSTICE

"If it is the business of injustice to engender hatred whenever it is found," asks Socrates, "will it not, when it springs up either among free men or slaves, cause them to hate and be at strife with one another, and make them incapable of effective action in common?" A little later, he answers the question by stating that "utter rascals completely unjust are completely incapable of effective action" (Plato, *Republic*, Book 1). The inner code of justice is based upon the requirements of effective action in common. All members of organizations desire or expect some degree of fair treatment by the organization and its administrators. This involves some minimum attention to the interests of individual members and groups. It involves some limit on the extent of favoritism, discrimination or "pull." It requires the use of judgment by administrators rather than random or chance decisions. It thus tends to reduce the area of uncontrolled action and bolster the role of rules. At the same time, justice goes beyond the provisions of the rules—just as courts of equity go beyond, and are not limited to, statutory or common law.

Justice, or fairness, applies to the distribution of both punishments and rewards. On the punishment side, the inner code embodies the general expectations of members that

- the punishment more or less fit the crime,
- some degree of mercy be at least occasionally shown,
- serious or repeated offenders be "brought to justice," and
- favored persons should not be exempted.

On the reward side, the inner code embodies expectations that positions, salaries, titles, privileges, and other rewards have some relation to members' contributions. An active sense of felt injustice may arise whenever people feel that their rewards are seriously out of line with what they are "entitled to" by reason of the work they do, or their age, seniority, sex, ethnic or caste background, or education (*Zaleznik et al.*, 1958). With respect to both punishments and rewards, the sense of injustice "almost always involves specific examples of what is felt to be unjust favoritism towards others" (Parsons, 1954, p. 30).[4] It is because distributive justice involves the detailed comparison of such examples, that there is so little firm ground between the vague, abstract rules of justice and the "just way" of distributing specific punishments or rewards. Moreover, the sense of what is fair or unfair varies vastly among cultures. Differentials that might seem eminently fair in Thailand, where there are sharper distinctions among people on the basis of social status, might seem monstrous violations of justice in a more egalitarian society (Riggs, 1961, p. 130-131).

5. SECRECY

The administrative revolution has brought with it a tremendous growth in generally available information concerning organizations. The searchlight of publicity has been turned upon public and private organizations by public hearings, public investigations, the collection of increasingly sophisticated statistics, and the dissemination of "news" by the media of mass communication. Governments are sometimes expected, in the Wilsonian phrase, to make "open covenants openly arrived at." Government agencies are expected to live in a "goldfish bowl" of public scrutiny. Private organizations are expected to render a frank accounting to their stockholders, private associations to their members.

The continuation of this trend, however, is limited by the universal inner core code of organizational secrecy. Like any individual, every organization has its secrets. Some of these derive from conflict relations with external groups. A sovereign state cannot afford to allow potential enemies to learn of its plans for defensive or offensive operations. A police agency must preserve the secrecy of the steps it is taking to seize suspected criminals. A business must keep the details of new products or new technological processes from its competitors.

Secrecy is also indispensable to the preservation of internal unity. Shared information is one of the bonds that hold people together. By

---

4. In this essay Parsons relates sensitivity concerning injustice to the growing child's perception of discriminatory treatment in the family. He also points out that aggressive behavior may serve as an outlet for expression of resentment against such treatment. In formal organizations, similarly, feelings of injustice at the hands of superiors may lead to aggressive action against associates.

differentiating one organization from another, it helps identify the group —much in the same way that the maintenance of a strictly private life contributes to the process of individualization (Simmel, 1950, p. 330-338). Some of this information consists of secrets that cannot be told: shared experience which can only be felt and cannot be explicitly conveyed. Some of it can be betrayed. In gangster organizations the basic code is "no ratting" and the penalty for deviance is usually death (Tyler, 1962, p. 232). In other organizations the penalty may be weaker but the proscription, albeit more politely expressed, is not much different. The strongest proscriptions, in fact, often apply to the secrets of units and groups within organizations. To the extent that information is a source of power, the careful guarding and hoarding of information may be vital to the maintenance and expansion of power. This requires defensive operations against the information-gathering activities of controllers, inspectors, investigators, liaison men, and "inside dopesters." Some information will always be given freely. Some will be given in exchange for other information. Some will be given in tremendous floods in order to bury the recipients in an unmanageable flood of data; this is what has often been called "the old Army game." Many public reports are part of the coverup operations of internal groups. Many systems of keeping "confidential" or "secret" information from outsiders can be fully understood only when seen in the light of desires to keep such data from various insiders as well.

As Friedrich has pointed out, there are many human relations in organizations that would be rendered much more difficult if their details were widely known. "A supervisor reporting on his men should be able to speak with complete frankness; but if his views are not kept confidential, he will not be able to do so, since he has to continue satisfactory working relationships with the men (1941, p. 56). To this observation we may add the probability that the supervisor's men may have already succeeded in keeping part of their actions secret from him and that his superior undoubtedly rations out to him very carefully "higher-level information" on the plans and problems of the upper levels of the hierarchy. In the light of these considerations, we may expect that he too will keep certain information from his superior rather than "speak with complete frankness." This is why it is impossible for any top executive or anyone else in the organization to "know everything" about the organization. The distribution and flow of information in organizations is highly structured. If all information could go anywhere at any time—even within the organization's boundaries—the organizational structure would be destroyed.

6. OPPORTUNISM

One of the great paradoxes of organizational behavior is found in the inner code of opportunism. This code permits some degree of compromise and exception with respect to all other codes, both the inner core and the outer layers. It permits some degree of subordination of all such codes to the purposes of interest satisfaction, output quality and quantity, efficiency, viability, resource mobilization and rationality. It recognizes the need for continuous adjustment among these many objectives if they are to be brought together into an accepted pattern. In the colloquial language of administration this code is expressed in many ways. Administrators are expected to "face up to the unpleasant facts," "do what has to be done," and "cut through red tape." This latter prescription, of course, does not mean "eliminate all red tape." It means, "get things done despite the unavoidable and necessary rules," whether by knowing the rules so well that one can "ride them" by finding "loopholes" or by partially ignoring some of them. This is *not* the equivalent of "be unscrupulous" or "anything goes—the sky's the limit." Nor is it merely the expression of the informal codes of informal groups. The formal role structure itself recognizes the necessity for compromise by providing widespread authority to exercise varying degrees of discretion in applying rules to specific circumstances and special cases. Thus empirical research has provided countless illustrations of authorized and unauthorized use of such discretion by white collar workers (*Francis and Stone*), foremen (*Roethlisberger and Dickson*), supervisors (*Blau*), middle-level officials (*Turner*), and higher executives (*Dalton; Gouldner, 1954*).

The importance of opportunism is easier to recognize at the higher levels of authority. Simon, Smithburg, and Thompson point out that opportunism "renders the executive more flexible and adjustable; it enables him to see the importance of, and to act on the principle of, doing a little wrong to do a great right" (1950, p. 396-397).[5] In one way or another, however, the code touches all members of an organization. In the early days of the twentieth century the Industrial Workers of the World learned that production could be brought to a halt in factories by a firm insistence on the part of workers that they would conform to all estab-

---

5. In Barnard's terminology, by contrast, opportunism appears as "the antithesis of the moral element" (1938, p. 201). The possibility of doing "a great right" would seem to be denied. Yet this is a terminological difference only, one which flows from a narrow definition of opportunism in the first instance. In a broader context, Barnard sees compromise as an exemplification of moral responsibility (*Ibid.*, p. 272-282).

lished rules and procedures, without any exceptions whatsoever. "Working to rule" has since become a well-recognized technique of "slowdown." Less objectionable than a strike and less costly to the workers, this weapon has been used very effectively by French customs officials and British postal employees. There is no case on record in which any form of "working to rule" has been combatted by amending the rules in the effort to make them more workable. If such an effort were to be made, the very act of amendment, promulgation and explanation would divert energies from regular operations. Once the new roles were fully understood and clarified, their uncompromising application would probably once again result in a slowdown—unless the changes consisted of leaving most decisions to on-the-spot discretion.

One of the paradoxical aspects of the law of opportunism, in addition to the fact that it is a prerequisite of code observance, is that its formal enunciation might tend to undermine confidence in the rules themselves. This danger was exhibited in the U.S. Navy's handling of a "rulebook" lieutenant who insisted "upon following regulations to the letter as finance officer of the San Francisco Navy Dispensary." For example, he refused to certify a time card for an employee who have been given permission by an officer to referee a football game. Because of his refusal to sign reports that would have regularized such minor irregularities, a physical evaluation board of the Navy found that the uncomprising lieutenant was suffering from "a mild case of paranoia" and "unfit for duty in his rank." Four months later the Secretary of the Navy set aside the board's findings and ordered the lieutenant returned to duty. Although the sanctity of the rules in general was thus upheld, the rulebook officer, who in any case had only eight more months before retirement, was moved to another assignment (Associated Press dispatch, September 22, 1960).

c. *The Outer Layers*

THE INNER CORE of codes common to all organizations is usually only a small part of the codes in any organization. This core is usually surrounded by many outer layers of greatly varying codes. Some of these are extensions of the minimum codes of order, honesty, loyalty, justice, secrecy, and opportunism. Many take the form of policies, regulations, or procedures governing an organization's operations, the movements of people, materials and information and the maintenance of records. These highly specialized codes are largely determined by the output mix, technology, and traditions of specific organizations. In addition, there are other codes whose nature can be expressed in terms of varying degrees and combinations of conformity and individualism, impersonality and particularism, dubious and due process, and the internalization and inversion of external codes.

1. CONFORMITY AND INDIVIDUALISM

A certain degree of conformity by members is itself required by the inner core code of order. No organization can operate if its members' interactions are governed by pure individualism.

Beyond this minimum the extent of expected conformity varies with the depth and scope of an organization's rules. In organizations that are small, are rapidly expanding or declining, are engaged in nonrepetitive operations, or are subject to a rapidly changing technology, rules are usually less detailed and cover a more limited area. Extremely detailed rules are usually found in organizations that are very large, are engaged in routinized operations or in nonroutinized operations demanding clocklike coordination. Where successful performance may require unusual patterns of thought and action and the elimination of external loyalties, the rules may be extended to include the major aspects of members' total behavior. Thus armies, espionage organizations, conspiratorial political parties, and messianic reform movements usually dominate the private lives of their members. Highly compulsive administrators of other organizations may, in working out their personal problems, seek similar objectives. In any of these cases the pressure for conformity may result in faceless men, automated personalities and all the indignities exposed by the literature of antiorganizational revolt. Entirely apart from the special characteristics of an organization and its administrators, the degree of conformity is also affected by the cultural values of its members and the society in which it operates (*Richardson*).

Yet all the conformity that may be found in organizations cannot be regarded as observance of codes. Much of it often goes far beyond what is formally or informally expected. As illustrated by Blau's study of a state employment agency, literal compliance with rules may result from lack of personal security. "The instances of overconformity and resistance to change observed in the state agency were motivated by anxious concern with the attitudes and opinions of superiors (*Blau*, 1956, p. 188). While superior officials themselves may create considerable anxiety of this type, it would be an oversimplification to find the source of all such anxiety within the organization itself. Many people come to formal organizations with deep insecurities rooted in early family experiences and in present home life. Identification with organizations and overconformity with its rules provide balancing factors in lives that might otherwise be seriously unbalanced.

On the other hand, a considerable amount of apparent conformity may hide various forms of individualism. Dalton gives many examples of middle managers who use conformity as "protective mimicry." Individualists privately and conformists publicly, they pretend to conform as a means of carrying out their individual desires within the organizations. In other cases, genuine conformity on some matters is used to compensate for—and possibly cover up—nonconformity on other matters (*Dalton,* 1959, p. 100, 244, 268-270). Conformity itself may be individualistic in nature. In reporting on his experiences with training groups, Dr. James Mann (1962) has identified "the exceedingly intense competitive aspects of conformity—the paradox of individualistic ends underlying surface conformities. . . ." Truly individualistic feelings, he points out, "are often so deep that they express themselves in endless ways of moulding organizations to meet individual needs."

The codes of informal groups within an organization have long been recognized as "strategies of independence" (Bendix, 1956, p. 536) as, counters to overconformity with the rules of the organization as a whole. Many studies have indicated the strength of such codes in resisting pressure toward conformity with official production goals (*Roethlisberger and Dickson; Donald*) and technological innovations (*Ronken and Lawrence*). Professional workers and middle managers often form close knit informal groups whose code is to introduce certain innovations despite the official hostility of their superiors. "In one instance five junior men from different departments, meeting together in express disobedience of their superiors' orders in an obscure corner of an employee locker room, made plans that ultimately led to successful teamwork among their departments in the development of a new product" (*Learned,* p. 140). In the Federal Government of the U.S. informal groups of intellectuals from various departments, working in cooperation with members of Congress and private "pressure groups," have often been the centers of initiative in developing major "new products" in the field of government services. The possibility of organizing or participating in such freewheeling groups has provided many officials who might seem to be dyed-in-the-wool conformists to bureaucratic tradition with countless opportunities for individual initiative and enterprise.

What is not always recognized is that compliance with formal codes and commands may itself require a considerable amount of individualism or initiative. This is particularly true whenever the members of organizations are officially expected to handle problems whose solutions are not automatically or easily provided by the organization's established policies,

rules and procedures. In such cases the code says "think for yourself."
For many in the organization this may be "an unsought freedom that
imposes suffering" (*Dalton*, 1959, p. 243). For others it is a stimulating
challenge. The nature of this challenge has been well illustrated in a
modern British novel (Cruttwell, 1962, p. 58):

> The Chief Civil Servant recognized with delight the keenest pleasure
> he knew; the engaging with a problem insoluble to others, but to himself
> only almost insoluble. What some find in making love he found in this;
> with the confidence that is born of a thousand past successes, he could
> play with it and delay it and be amused by it, certain that the end desired
> would be perfectly attained. . . .

As with painting, poetry, and music, individual achievement may reach
creativity and high peak when operating within the constraints of given
rules. Creative individualism is usually found not so much in wanton
nonconformity as in the fruitful exploitation of existing rules.

Judgment and initiative may also be formally required—albeit to a
less obvious extent—at the lower levels of organizations. Even in factory
production, as Bendix has pointed out, the coordination between materials,
machines and production schedules "depends to some extent on the
good judgment of each worker in his every act of complying with rules
and order. . . . The importance of such 'good judgment' is naturally much
greater in the case of the skilled worker than in the case of the unskilled,
but it is neither absent nor negligible in the case of the latter." This is
illustrated by the case of "inmates of Nazi concentration camps, who were
employed in factories during the war and who sabotaged the production
effort by consistently asking for detailed instructions on what to do next."
This withdrawal of initiative and individual judgment is said to have
reduced output up to 80 per cent" (1956, p. 204). Thus "working to
instructions" may be as devastating as "working to rule."

2. IMPERSONALITY AND PARTICULARISM

In bureaucratic organizations, according to Weber, people act in
accordance with "a spirit of formalistic impersonality, *sine ira et studio*,
without hatred or passion, and hence without affection or enthusiasm.
The dominant norms are concepts of straightforward duty without
regard to personal considerations" (1947, p. 340). Merton carries this
point further by observing that "Since functionaries minimize personal
relations and resort to categorization, the peculiarities of individual cases
are often ignored" (1957, p. 202). This impersonality is close to what
Parsons refers to as universalism in contrast with particularism. The
universalistic norm, according to Parsons, requires that "in qualifications

for membership and decisions for differential treatment, priority will be given to standards defined in completely generalized terms . . ." (Parsons and Shils, 1951, p. 82). The literature of antiorganizational revolt carries this theme further by revealing the decline in human warmth and the growth of alienation in many organizations.

If we desert the make-believe world of ideal types, we must regard impersonality and universalism as pattern variables rather than norms of unchanging significance. To a certain extent these norms are themselves embodied in the inner core code of order. Beyond this minimum the degree of variation among organizations is extremely great. Furthermore, within a single organization a certain amount of impersonality may co-exist with a considerable amount of hatred and passion, affection and enthusiasm. Universalism and particularism may exist side by side. Bureaucratic decisions are always influenced to some extent by personal and subjective motives. Bureaucratic controversies play upon, and are fed by, the entire gamut of human emotions.

The most obvious antidote to impersonality and universalism is provided by informal groups and informal codes. The informal group is often a place where warm, human relationships are developed. Sometimes these may be the most meaningful relations in people's lives—particularly in the case of those with warped family relationships. Sometimes the scope of informal group activities extends far beyond the context of the organization and provides for personal interaction in other organizations and in less structured personal behavior.

The formal organization itself may contribute to such tendencies in two ways. First, formally established committees may promote a certain amount of human give-and-take among the members. The diffused responsibility inherent in this form of polyarchic structure requires interpersonal relations quite different than those emanating from hierarchical structures. There is nothing impersonal, distant, and remote about the relations among the members of a management team, professional task force, or autonomous work group (*Rice*, 1958; *Herbst*). Where these groups are fairly successful, the dominant norm may be accomplishing a group task on the basis of mutual respect, reciprocal accommodation, affectionate rivalry, and sustained enthusiasm.

Second, a thorough-going application of universalism leads to a certain form of particularism. Categorization is meaningless unless broad categories are broken down into more refined ones. Only by so doing is it possible to apply general rules to specific cases. The continuing process of refinement may thus lead to the definition of individual classes or even —where enough pressure is exerted—to the identification of individual cases that are *sui generis*. It is this orientation toward particularism which introduces labyrinthine complexity into any well developed body of rules and regulations.

3. DUBIOUS AND DUE PROCESS

The inner core code of justice is a bare minimum prescribing only the most elementary protection for the members of organizations. It may exist side by side with open or suppressed resentment against felt injustice. It does not itself apply to outsiders. There are undoubtedly many thousands of organizations whose codes and practices with respect to the just treatment of members, outsiders, or both are—to put it mildly—rather dubious.

At the same time there has also been a great flowering of codes of "due process" extending far beyond the bare minimum. These protect members or outsiders against arbitrary, capricious, unfair or biased actions by public or private organizations. They do this by providing individuals with such rights as

- the right of advance notice, or subsequent appeal, or both, with respect to action that might damage them,
- the right to be heard orally during a hearing or appeal, to present and rebut evidence, to examine the other side and to have expert assistance, and
- the right to obtain a statement of the facts and reasons on which any adverse decision may be based.

The greatest progress in this direction is found in the public sector. Here due process is usually made available by provisions for judicial review of various government agency decisions, appeal procedures within the agencies themselves, and special procedures that must be followed in taking action seriously jeopardizing the interests of external individuals or organizations. Where merit systems are established, they usually provide avenues of appeal for employees with grievances and even advance hearings in the case of terminations or serious disciplinary actions. Many military organizations have elaborate machinery for appeals by subordinates against the decisions of superiors (*Evan*). As in totalitarian societies, there is a tendency for the suppression of individual rights in many areas to be counterbalanced by fastidious attention (at least on paper) to protective codes in other, and often less important, areas.

In the private sector the greatest progress toward due process has been made through collective bargaining. Grievance procedure operations have often become one of the most important forms of union-management relations. They serve to protect workers against reprisals for appealing management decisions and to provide appellants with expert assistance at no personal cost. Beyond the area of collective bargaining, emerging codes of personnel administration provide due process protection for unorganized workers, professionals and managerial personnel. The ever-present threat of government regulation on behalf of consumer interest, combined with tendencies toward the professionalization of administration, has often led to what Selznick calls a "corporate conscience." This is "the internally accepted system of fair dealing, of respect for personal rights, of authority constituted and justified by rational necessity in the light of public ends. In a phrase, it is corporate 'due process'" (1963).

In both sectors the expansion of due process rights may serve to curtail the effectiveness of an organization's operations. Much of the steam behind the Administrative Procedures Act of 1946, for example, came from business organizations that objected more to government regulations themselves than to the way in which regulatees were handled. Much of the inefficiency of government agencies has often been attributed to the procedural protection of civil servants against dismissals. These objections have most validity whenever due process provisions are intensively used or lead to intervention by external judicial agencies. The greatest contribution of due process, however, is that the existence of the right to appeal often serves to prevent the occurrence of injustice in the first place. Excessive use of appeal systems is rare. Moreover, time-consuming intervention by external agencies can often be avoided by more flexible use of the established hierarchy itself as the vehicle for upward appeals. This is often possible only because external alternatives serve as a threat to loosen up the attitudes of superiors who might otherwise regard appeals as intolerable acts of insubordination.

It should also be recognized that due process codes may contribute to the overall effectiveness of an organization. By counteracting certain aspects of personal insecurity, they may help develop personal contributions based upon more significant motives than fear. "In the absence of a clearly understood channel of appeal, substandard decisions can be made by subordinate managers which produce a widespread sense of grievance. This can suddenly burst forth in the form of serious disturbance and conflict," writes Wilfred Brown in explaining the management of the Glacier Metal Company. "An appeal is very much like a safety valve of a steam boiler" (*Brown*, p. 272-273). Moreover, due process may help break down the isolation of top executives by providing them with more information about important events at lower levels. Brown points out that in administering an appeals system "one comes face to face with some unexpected and sometimes unpleasant result of one's own policy, and comes to realize that it was too little considered before being introduced. This is always a salutary experience." Similar observations might be made concerning the salutary effect of private executives learning more about the grievances of consumers, suppliers, and other outsiders who may presently have little recourse against the unjust operations of large private organizations.

4. EXTERNAL CODES: INTERNALIZED OR INVERTED

External codes always have a significant impact on the full network of codes within an organization. The most direct impact occurs when these external codes are themselves internalized. Almost every organization takes over—and makes its own—certain rules or rituals that originate in its social or immediate environment. In organizations that accept the general social structure, the scope of this internalization (which may be compared with the socialization process in the life of individuals) is rather wide.

In organizations openly in conflict with major social institutions, internalization still operates—but more selectively. Gangster organizations, although rejecting the constraints of the criminal code, tend to internalize the traditional business codes of merciless, unrestricted competition and then, as they mature, to adopt the more highly developed codes of structured competition (Tyler, 1962, p. 227-237). The Russian Bolsheviks, in their fight to overthrow previous Russian governments, rejected "bourgeois morality" and reliance on lawful means, but they took over the operating codes of the Tsarist secret police. In fact, most revolutionary organizations are tied by common codes to the regime against which they fight. The American revolutionaries, in their struggle for independence from England, were essentially Englishmen acting in accordance with the highest traditions of English liberty. Many of the key leaders in the successful anticolonial battles of the mid-twentieth century were educated in a "parent" country whose moral and intellectual codes themselves provided an impetus to the struggle for freedom.

As these illustrations suggest, the internalization of some external codes may be accompanied by the rejection of others. Nor is rejection limited to the extreme cases of flagrant lawbreakers. In one form or another it is found in all organizations. The important point, however, is not mere deviation. It is rather the development of "counter codes" transforming virtue into vice or vice into virtue. If the "outsiders" dictate that it is wrong to do X, then doing X becomes the right thing to do. If they favor a certain method of action, its pursuit becomes an act of disloyalty to the organization. "Resistance to tyrants is obedience to God." In contrast with internalization, this form of indirect impact by external codes may be called "code inversion."

Code inversion stems from many sources. The most obvious are direct conflicts of interests. When business organizations are subjected to external regulations that threaten profits or market penetration, when government agencies are subjected to rules limiting their use of money and personnel, resistance is to be expected. This resistance may reach the point of code inversion whenever the external codes are seen as illegitimate or going "too far." This point may be reached very quickly in the case of new codes that call for sudden changes in established ways of doing things. In his study of business opposition to government regulation in the fields of trade practices, wages and hours and labor relations, Lane has shown that the psychological changes may be the most important. Regulations in these fields

- challenged the businessman's belief system, profaned his idols and deprecated his myths,
- denigrated the businessman himself, lowered his status in the community, and allocated to him a role subordinate to the one he has enjoyed,
- frustrated men by depriving them of choices to which they had become accustomed, and
- aroused new anxieties and developed uncertainties in a time already tense with doubt and foreboding.

All of this together "exacted a toll of anxiety, frustration, and dejection beyond all relation to the economic cost" (1954, p. 19-20). A similar study on the extremely widespread violations of price control and rationing regulations during World War II indicated a widespread feeling among business concerns that "it was all right to violate the law if one could get away with it. This explanation of illegal activities was held by many not only with reference to the black market but in relation to other laws as well" (Clinard, 1952, p. 338). The possibility of code inversion is also inherent whenever external groups attempt to impose a new code of conduct without prior consultation or without providing the affected organization a chance to participate in code formulation. Under such situations quick acceptance might threaten the internal morale of the organization or the power position of its administrators. By asserting the organization's "autonomy," resistance can serve to strengthen both.

The forms of code inversion are also multiple. Open deviation is probably the rarest variety, disguised deviation the most common. Another variant is avoidance, the carefully calculated exploitation of loopholes in the code. Thus a large part of the work of tax lawyers and tax accountants consists of helping large organizations handle their affairs in such a manner as to reduce their tax liability. Since this can be done without breaking the tax laws, tax avoidance—as distinguished from tax evasion—is entirely legal. The same principle applies to any other form of regulation, including the internal regulations of public and private organizations. Finally, code inversion may authorize or prescribe far-reaching action to have the code changed. Apart from requests or appeals for revocation or amendment, this may take the form of direct or hidden attacks upon the code's proponents and enforcers or of over-compliance as a *reductio ad absurdum*.

D. *Strategies of Contained Deviation*

MENTION has already been made of deviations from organizational codes in the form of inevitable code conflicts and irrepressible tendencies toward nonconformity. To this, we might add the deviations sought or sanctioned by the code enforcers themselves. The Rule Enforcers, as pointed out in Chapter 16, may be themselves the most successful Rule Evaders. If not above the law, they may be at least beyond the grasp of any other enforcers. Then again, for some administrators, a rule-blinking indulgency pattern may be helpful in attaining other objectives. Moreover, deviations tend to be self-multiplying. We need not accept Moore's principle of "the least moral determinant," according to which the actual standards of conduct are set by the least observant participant (1962, p. 266-267), in order to realize that successful deviation often provokes imitation. For all these reasons, in addition to the evidence that one may obtain from looking at or living with an organization, we may hypothesize a universal law of inevitable deviation or imperfect compliance.

Hence the formulation of organizational objectives with respect to rules and rituals is rarely limited to specification of the "right ways" of behavior. It usually includes instrumental objectives aimed at preventing misbehavior. At times unknowing administrators may set themselves the goal of perfect compliance. When this happens, unless counterbalanced by other administrators more aware of the law of inevitable deviation, they will usually provoke greater noncompliance than might otherwise be the case. Most experienced administrators appreciate what Merton calls "the social function of permissiveness." Although they might find it indiscreet to state this publicly, their actual behavior recognizes that "the function of some measure of small delinquencies remaining unobserved or if observed, unacknowledged, is that of enabling the social structure to operate without undue strain" (1957, p. 344). In effect, this means that code observance objectives are transformed into goals of containing deviations within tolerable limits. In this perspective the compulsive enforcer may unwittingly play a helpful role. By pressing for perfect compliance, he may at times serve to make small deviations more acceptable to nonconformists.

There are three major strategies for seeking contained deviation: external control, internal control, and code adjustment. The strategy of external control is based on the proposition that few codes may be entirely self-enforcing. It involves special systems of surveillance, punishment, and reward. It may call for elaborate activities of explanation and persuasion. Its weakness lies in the fact that watchmen can never see enough of what is going on and the more they see the more resistance they may provoke.

The strategy of internal control is based on the proposition that self-enforcement, where feasible, is the most effective and economical. It involves widespread participation in the formulation of codes as well as their enforcement. It may call for special actions to develop a stronger sense of common purposefulness, and a higher degree of loyalty, among the members of the organization. It relies on the most terrible of all punishments, man's sense of guilt. Its weakness lies in the fact that if not prodded from time to time man's conscience often slumbers. When awake, it may be silenced. "Your conscience must be your guide," a legislator has said to newly elected members. "But you can almost always subdue your conscience, you can always educate your conscience" (Quoted in *Gross*, p. 94). With but little adaptation, this comment is applicable to the members of other organizations also.

The strategy of adjustment is based on the proposition that code changes may be a prerequisite for improved observance. It may involve anything from a minor amendment to total reconstruction. Apart from the containment of deviation, it may lead to significant improvements in the codes themselves. Its weakness lies in the fact that too much adjustment may make the codes incomprehensible.

The three strategies tend to be complementary, the strong points of one counterbalancing the weak points of the others. This does not mean that they are always pursued concurrently and with equal emphasis. The tendency rather is for organizations to run through various cycles of "heads must roll," sweetness and light, and code innovation, of code observance, code nonobservance, and code rewriting. Under the stimulus of the environmental situation and the total pattern of purposes, these various strategies tend to follow one upon another in irregular pulsebeats.

Chapter 20

RATIONALITY: SATISFACTORY
ACTION PATTERNS

*T*HE FINAL CATEGORY of organizational purpose is the objective of doing things rationally. This means trying to formulate and achieve purpose patterns that are more, rather than less, satisfactory.

The inclusion of rationality in the matrix of organizational purposes is a way of saying that people in organizations seek to behave rationally. In this sense an organization may be described as an instrument for both technical and administrative rationally. The administrator's role may be regarded as requiring a constant search for present rational action and the capacity to behave rationally in the future.

The acceptance of rationality as a purpose category does not require that we close our eyes to man's irrationality. With rationality, as with all other human objectives, neither the desire nor the search are guarantees of attainment. In organizational as well as individual action whatever rationality is attained is invariably intertwined with irrationality. The inseparability of this connection will be made evident by our analysis of rationality.

A. *The Action Concept of Rationality*

A POPULAR WAY to look at human rationality is to concentrate upon the deliberate processes of decision-making and choice. The emphasis is placed upon highly articulate processes of cognition and logic. Through computer simulation and direct observation much is being learned about how these processes actually work. How they *should* work is the sphere of prescriptive (or normative) rationality. Here many decision theorists aim at developing "a complete set of rules of behavior in all conceivable situations" (Von Neumann and Morgenstern, 1953, p. 33).

Another—and more inclusive—approach is to look at action itself. This approach recognizes the tremendous contribution of deliberate decision making to rational action. Yet it also recognizes that many rational actions may be subconscious, instinctive, or habitual rather than the product of deliberate calculation. It recognizes that in certain situations an attempt at deliberate calculation might be highly irrational. It recognizes that irrationality may stem from interest conflicts and lack of abilities, as well as from defective knowledge and calculation. It sees rationality as grounded in emotions, instincts, and interests as well as cognition. Above all, it places the emphasis upon the action dimensions which calculators aim to achieve. It distinguishes between rationality and irrationality on the basis of these action dimensions.

There are three fundamental dimensions of rational and irrational action: desirability, feasibility and consistency. The extent to which a purpose pattern is satisfactory (or "satisfices") is usually determined in the light of all three.

1. DESIRABILITY

Desirability is the highest test of rationality. As one philosopher has put it, "Action—at least of the sort called rational and sensible—is for the sake of realizing something to which positive value is ascribed, or of avoiding something to which disvalue is ascribed" (Lewis, 1946, p. 366). In the game theory of prescriptive decision-making, the "postulate of rational behavior" holds that "of two alternatives which give rise to outcomes, a player will choose the one which yields the more preferred outcome" (Luce and Raiffa, 1957, p. 50).

The highest test of desirability is the extent to which a given course of action satisfies human interests. In extreme cases this test may readily be applied. Thus the depths of irrationality are reached by people who consistently frustrate their own basic interests. Habitual self-frustration of this type is usually found only among psychotic individuals. The logical processes of calculation aim at achieving more rational patterns of interest satisfaction whenever they help reveal (a) genuine as distinguished from illusory interests, (b) common interests that might be obscured by divergent interests, and (c) long-range dissatisfactions that might be the unforeseen consequence of short-range satisfactions. Calculations of this type are extremely difficult. As shown in Chapter 12, they involve the question of "whose interests" as well as "which interests." To judge the extent of satisfaction, we must resign ourselves to the use of various surrogates.

Human interests may also be served by every other category of organizational action or purpose. Hence there is an important element of rationality in action to produce services or goods, economize on scarce resources, invest in the viability of an organization, mobilize resources, observe codes of behavior, and help achieve rational action. Each of these elements in the global matrix contributes to a desirable purpose pattern. The measures applicable to any elements may serve as surrogates of human interests and indicators of rationality.

2. FEASIBILITY

The test of feasibility deals with the adaptation of means to given ends. By this test rational action takes place when the means—the intermediate steps—actually contribute toward achieving a given end. It is highly irrational to seek to produce goods, raise efficiency, strengthen an organization, or mobilize capital by muttering a prayer or incantation—although these might be rational means of achieving such other objectives as quieting insecurity or conforming to behavioral codes. Other things being equal, it is highly irrational to seek an objective by the least feasible instead of the most feasible path. The great contribution of science and technology to rationality is that by dealing with cause-effect relations they indicate feasible ways of doing many things that could otherwise not be accomplished. The most rational action sequences are those in which every step has a high probability of leading to desired objectives—although false starts and repeated experiments may be needed in order to learn how to do this. Many analysts of rational calculation prefer to concentrate on the feasibility dimensions. By so doing, they avoid many of the greater uncertainties involved in dealing with desirability.

3. CONSISTENCY

The final test of rationality is consistency. In processes of calculation this is indeed a major test; consistency is one of the major aims of mathematics and deductive logic. Similarly, it is nonrational to seek two objectives which are noncompatible. It is rational to reconcile such inconsistencies. In many cases, however, it will be found that inconsistent action may lead to undesirable consequences or embody means that are not feasible.

If rationality were to be construed only in terms of strict feasibility, it would be the lowest, or most instrumental, element in the analytic hierarchy of organizational purposes. It would be expressed only in terms of the means of achieving some pattern of interest satisfaction, output, economizing, viability, resource mobilization, and rationality. Yet serious attention to feasibility invariably leads, as Simon has pointed out in his discussion of "satisficing," to a modification of the ends themselves. Desires are modified to meet the demands of feasibility. When desirability is brought fully within the scope of rationality, we then see that rationality becomes expressed not merely in certain limited methods but in the entire array of ends as well. *Rationality is an attribute of the entire purpose pattern.*

Accordingly, rationality is a multidimensional attribute. This is why it is so easy for reasonable people to disagree violently on the extent to which past or future action is satisfactory or unsatisfactory. A desirable course of action may be unfeasible. A feasible course of action may be inconsistent with another objective. Two consistent objectives may be undesirable. Few lines of action will be regarded as achieving optimum desirability, feasibility, and consistency. Different people and groups, both inside and outside the organization, may have divergent views on the extent of each. Overall rationality, therefore, usually consists of an acceptable, or satisfactory, pattern of limited desirability, feasibility, and consistency. This is why organizational action is always a splendid hunting ground for critics. Without much effort, one can always find something to criticize as undesirable, unfeasible or inconsistent. Much greater effort is needed to evaluate an entire action pattern.

B. *The Learning Base*

THE CAPACITY for rational action is rooted in the learning process. Because they cannot learn enough, animals cannot achieve a very high level of rationality. Computing machines will become more rational only insofar as they are endowed with greater learning capacity. Only by additional learning can a person act more rationally on his own.

Learning processes, however, are much broader than the cognitive processes that result in the acquisition and use of knowledge. The objects of learning include abilities and interests as well. The questions "What can he learn?" or "What has he learned?" can be answered fully only in terms of some combination of knowledge, abilities, and interests.[1]

1. KNOWLEDGE

Simple facts are at the lowest level of knowledge. They are given shape and form by the concepts that help us perceive and distinguish them. These concepts, in turn, are usually brought together into rules of thumb or tacit generalizations. At the highest level they are interrelated through explicit theories. When these theories are sufficiently rooted in data (rather than being abstracted from data, as in the case of mathematical and logical theories), they mature into sciences.

2. ABILITIES

The ability to use knowledge looms high in the ultraintellectualist theories of rationality, often with exclusive attention to analytic ability at the expense of synthetic ability and with insufficient attention to the ability to imagine new action sequences and purpose patterns. There are also many other abilities, in the field of sensory perception, motor action, and communication, that go beyond mere intellectual ability.

At a certain level of adequacy any ability can be regarded as a skill. At a much higher level of performance a skill becomes an art. In art—whether it is the art of administration, bridge building, or statistical interpretation—we find a greater degree of the ability to evaluate the relative importance of factors that cannot be precisely measured, an ability often referred to as "judgment." Wisdom goes beyond art and includes a higher level of judgment. It consists of the ability to select and use those types of knowledge and abilities that are most relevant to any particular time-sequence of interconnected acts.

3. INTERESTS

The acquisition of new, different, or broader interests is probably the most important aspect of learning. Human interests, we have already seen, are the motivating factors in purposeful behavior. They provide the emotional drives necessary for sustained effort of rational calculation.

1. The specific knowledge-ability-interest combinations relevant to the learning processes of administrators are discussed in "What Should Administrators Learn?" (Chapt. 27). The distinction between these three products of learning stems largely from the knowledge-attitude-ability trichotomy in Summer's *Factors in Effective Administration* (1956).

Their multiplicity and changeability lie at the root of multiple and changing purposes. Total fixation upon one single interest and the subordination of all other acts to its satisfaction, while often the model for ultraintellectual models of rationality, is indeed a more accurate model of psychopathic irrationality. Human rationality involves flexibility in the sphere of interests and thereby of purposes, objectives and goals.

In this context we can fully understand the tremendous contribution to rationality that may be obtained through human organization. Weber long ago stressed the increased rationality made possible by using many specialists and experts. But this is only a part of the picture. The interplay of interests within an organization and between it and its environment provide a fertile ground for the acquisition of new interests. The combination of many people provides remarkable opportunities to harness many abilities and many sources of knowledge.

This context also throws more light on the sources of power. If power is the ability to cause desired actions, or the causation of action by action, we then see that it is based upon rationality. Both are thoroughly embedded in sequences of action that are desirable, feasible, and consistent. From this point of view intended rationality is, indeed, intended power. The search for acceptable purpose patterns by organizations and their administrators is part and parcel of their efforts to develop, maintain and use power or influence. Hence it is entirely correct to regard knowledge—as is often done—as a source of power. It is still more meaningful, however, to recognize knowledge-ability-interest combinations. From this viewpoint the power of organizations and administrators is rooted in their capacity to learn.

c. *The Limits on Rationality*

SINCE THE RENAISSANCE and the Enlightenment one of the greatest articles of man's faith has been the idea of ever-expanding areas of rational action. This faith has been rooted in the replacement of magic by science and in the vast development of technology. It has been supported by repeated demonstrations that organizations are capable of rational action far beyond the puny powers of mere individuals.

Although faith in expanding rationality may serve as a spur to more ambitious action, it may also blind people to the fundamental limits on rationality. First of all, there are internal limits to the learning process. Many people learn very slowly indeed. Often they learn the wrong things, and have great difficulty in unlearning them. Eventually, the processes of individual learning seem to slow down—or sometimes, long before death, stop entirely. These limits affect each of the three dimensions of learning. The acquisition of knowledge is limited by man's cognitive abilities. No one can come anywhere close to omniscience. The acquisition of abilities is also limited. As general purpose organisms, men can rarely develop truly outstanding abilities in any one field of action. When this is done, it is usually at the expense of other types of abilities. The acquisition of interests may be stifled by insecurity, deprivation, and frustration. If people do not know what they want, if they are hampered by the lack of a complete and consistent preference ordering, this is because they are motivated by conflicting and changing interests.

True, by building formal organizations it is possible to extend these limits. Those who learn more may guide the actions of those who learn less. People who stop learning may be replaced. Human abilities may be supplemented by the abilities of machinery—not only in the movement, analysis, and synthesis of things but also, with the great advances in computers, in the transmission, analysis, and synthesis of information. Yet the very act of extending the limits on rationality at some points may contract them at others. This is particularly true in any organization whose administrators are themselves uninterested in learning.

Moreover, the environmental situation itself sets serious limits on the rationality of any organization. The interests, abilities, and knowledge of an organization cannot develop in a vacuum, since the organization's members are themselves drawn from the environment and subjected to continuous external influences. Above all, the controllers, suppliers, and adversaries of an organization may serve to frustrate the formulation or achievement of an acceptable purpose pattern. When blockage is provided by nature only, then greater rationality may overcome it. When blockage is provided by people and other organizations, then greater rationality by the blockers will negate the rationality of the organization that is blocked.

d. *Narrow and Broad Rationality*

THE LIMITS just referred to are those which are inherent in human action. One way to escape these inherent limits is to impose additional limits on the kinds of information taken into consideration. Such additional limits make it possible to be more rational in certain respects within a more narrow pattern of action sequences.

The most narrow pattern of action sequences is represented by the mental activities of abstract mathematicians. The most relevant dimension in erecting a mathematical system is its consistency. The accumulation of data is not relevant; it could not prove a theorem right or wrong. In science and other empirically based fields of thought data are important, but careful limits are placed on the kinds of data that are relevant. These data are organized by specialized concepts and theories. Any effort to deal with broader models, more types of action, and longer time spans means less precision, certainty, and consistency. In this sense the social sciences—since they deal with more inclusive systems—and many more variables—operate in a broader area of rationality.[2] A still broader area is occupied by the more normative fields of activity, such as government, ethics, and administration. To the extent that these focus on the larger questions of what is desirable for people, groups and societies, they deal with broader rationality at the expense of narrow rationality.

A rough indication of possible points of differentiation between the narrow and the broad rationality may be provided as follows:

	Narrow Rationality	*Broad Rationality*
Scope	Shorter time span	Longer time span
	Fewer types or aspects of action	More types or aspects of action
	Greater need for analytic abilities	Greater need for synthetic abilities
	Dealing with fewer interests and "interesteds"	Dealing with more interests and "interesteds"
Rationality dimensions	Desirability largely given or assumed	More attention to desirability
	Greater attention to feasibility	Greater risks and uncertainties
	More emphasis on consistency	Less emphasis on consistency
Learning dimensions	More specialized approach to knowledge	Less specialized approach to knowledge
	Working within given model or with tighter model	Working without given model or with looser model

We must also recognize the possibility of a greater irrationality that may come into being whenever efforts at rational action are kept within

2. Social phenomena, in contrast, are but a small part of the physical universe. In this sense they are but a narrow slice of physical phenomena. But in the sense that it grapples with many more interrelating variables, any social science is broader than physics.

sharply confined limits. Thus, to approach a complex problem of human motivation and conflicting interests with the techniques of production scheduling, or to use zero sum, two-player game theory in analyzing a conflict-cooperation situation with many participants, is to achieve the higher irrationality. Here we might add Barnard's profound observation concerning the possible irrelevance of rational scientific techniques to certain materials that "cannot bear the weight of ponderous logic." We must recall his contention that in many situations the logical statement of a problem may change the situation that is being analyzed and thus render the formulation inaccurate. Thus rationality itself, in the more narrow sense, may turn out to be an irrational form of behavior. The peak of irrationality is reached in any international situation in which it is rational for many nations to engage in an arms race which may end with the destruction of all nations. Whether man can escape this highly rationalized form of insanity is beyond our present ability to calculate.[3]

E. *Technical and Administrative Rationality*

RATIONALITY may also be divided into two closely related and partially overlapping forms, technical and administrative.

Technical rationality is based upon the use of the world's great and growing fund of science, technology and simple know-how. It is used in building mathematical theories, developing production systems and designing new machinery or services. It is embedded in the less tangible technologies of lawyers, economists, statisticians, and psychoanalysts. It includes the humbler techniques of handling a computer, power press, or typewriter.

Administrative rationality is based upon the best possible methods of guiding organizations. It refers to the world's great fund of know-how and of amorphous, premature, incomplete, or currently useful concepts and generalizations concerning organizational and administrative action. It includes all the techniques of getting people in organizations to work together in trying to satisfy interests, produce services or goods, economize on scarce resources, maintain or strengthen an organization, observe codes of behavior, or improve the rationality of their actions.

3. The concept of narrow rationality is somewhat similar to Weber's "formal rationality" used to refer to means-ends calculations within an organization, and Mannheim's "functional rationality," which applies to feasibility calculations in general. The concept of broader rationality is similar to Weber's "substantive" and Mannheim's "substantial" rationality.

Because of the limits on rational action, both technical and administrative rationality always include a lot of nonsense. Technology, for example, is historically rooted in the practices of witch doctors, shamans, conjurors, astrologers, and seers. As some of their techniques worked better than others, the interest in getting things done led to the more intensive development of more desirable, feasible, and consistent behavior sequences. The history of science and technology is the progressive development of such sequences at the expense of magic. Yet in all technology some degree of magic still exists, whether in the form of unexamined assumptions, pure guesswork, accepted ritual, or simply blind hope and faith. In fact, as we open up new areas of exploration, the urge to act before we know everything often impels us to enlarge our use of the causally unrelated or unrelatable. Many laymen would be petrified if they should ever hear the frank confessions (usually made among themselves alone) of doctors, engineers, and accountants concerning the hocus-pocus and bluff-and-nonsense which they often feel impelled to use.

Yet there *is* a difference. The difference is that in administration the proportion of magic and ritual is higher than in most other fields. The boss's "final decision" on a question of basic policy may have as little relation to the problems toward whose solution the policy is directed or to the actual policy which is carried out as does a rainmaker's prayer to the thunderstorm which may or may not follow. The cock may feel that his crowing produces the sunrise. The administrator who proudly uses human relations techniques to achieve a production increase may, in fact, be keeping production from rising further. In purely technical fields, the tremendous investments that have been made in research and development insure accelerating progress. In this sense technical rationality may be regarded as having reached a higher degree of development.

Both technical and administrative rationality, moreover, may vary in their scope. Some aspects of technical rationality are broader than others. Some aspects of administrative rationality, particularly those dealing with certain extremely detailed processes or small units, are very narrow. In general, however, the higher developments in technical rationality are achieved at the cost of ever-greater narrowness in scope. The looseness of administrative rationality, in turn, is often a result of its breadth. Administrative rationality cannot operate within any tight model. It must build bridges between models and reality. It must take into account a full pattern of divergent and reciprocally constraining objectives. It requires consideration of the whole situation in which an organization finds itself and a long-term perspective toward its objectives. In a certain sense, indeed, it encompasses technical rationality. Particularly at the higher levels of authority and responsibility, it includes the weaving together of the activities of many technicians. It includes measures to promote greater technical rationality on the part of the organization that is administered. This involves the direct promotion of the very proliferation of specialization that makes administrative rationality more difficult.

What about the administrator who tries to be "scientific" in dealing with administrative problems?

The answer to this question depends upon what is meant by "scientific." If the term refers to the calculating methods and heuristics used by scientists, then the use of a strictly scientific approach would be as unwise and irrational as a biologist's treating his own children like rats in a laboratory. Scientists operate on the basis of various calculational norms aimed at the expansion of credible knowledge and theory. Among these may be special attention to such considerations as semantic clarity and distinctness for their own sake, the compatibility of ends-means relationships with principles of formal logic, and compatibility of the definition of a situation with scientific knowledge (Schutz, 1943). Yet these considerations, in fact, "occur as stable properties of actions and as sanctionable ideals only in the case of actions governed by the attitude of scientific theorizing. By contrast, actions governed by the attitude of daily life are marked by the absence of these rationalities either as stable properties or as sanctionable ideals. . . . Any attempt to stabilize these properties or to enforce conformity to them in the conduct of everyday affairs will magnify the senseless character of a person's behavioral environment and multiply the anomic features of the system of interaction" (Garfinkel, 1960). It is eminently rational for administrators to promote scientific inquiry and to use its results (including those obtained from efforts to study administration scientifically). But it is irrational to think that an administrator can conduct his affairs in the same manner that a scientist can conduct research. The broader rationality of the administrator can never be as narrowly focused upon methods of calculation; it must always be oriented much more toward satisfactory action patterns.

A final word on the narrowness versus the breadth of administrative rationality. Because of its multidimensionality, there are few administrators capable of considering the rationality of an organization's entire purpose pattern. The subdivision of labor provided by organizational structure limits most administrators to certain aspects of a few elements from the global matrix. Moreover, no matter what elements they may be concerned with, most administrators develop a personal style of comparative weighting among desirability, feasibility, and consistency. Some will adapt the role of creating new concepts of what is desirable to seek, apart from considerations of immediate feasibility. Some will concentrate upon devising more feasible ways of achieving what is generally recognized as desirable. Some will give major attention to the rationality of what is currently feasible. Others—including those of a legalistic or academic bent—will become the proponents of consistency. When there are enough administrators in an organization to provide complementary representation for these various dimensions of rationality, the conditions are ripe for the synthesis of these limited approaches into a broader pattern of rational action. Such a synthesis usually comes, it may be added, not in technical documents or in policy conferences but in the heat of action itself.

At a higher level of complexity the same phenomenon occurs in the interaction among a group of organizations in an economic sector or in a society as a whole. An action pattern which is narrowly rational for a single organization may interfere with the efforts of others to achieve desirable, feasible, or consistent action. Broader rationality may be obtained through supraorganization or cooperative relationships of various sorts. But the broader pattern thereby resulting will usually contain still more elements of unplanned and spontaneous action. There will usually be far more room for rational men to differ profoundly on the desirability, feasibility, or consistency of any element or of the action pattern as a whole.

Part V

ADMINISTRATIVE PROCESSES

ADMINISTRATIVE RATIONALITY—or at least its knowledge dimensions—has been the subject of most of the preceding chapters. The task of this chapter is to round out the presentation by focusing directly upon the broad processes of decision-making and communicating and the "seamless web" of planning, activating, and evaluating. Each of these processes makes an important contribution to the formulation and achievement of satisfactory action patterns.

There was a time when any serious discussion of administration might start, and perhaps even end, with a discussion of these and similar processes. In contrast, it is a major contention of this book that processes can best be understood in the light of purposes and that purposes can best be understood after an identification of major "purposers," that is, people-in-organizations-in-environments. Hence the environment, structure, performance sequence.

None of these processes, it must be stressed, is peculiar to organizational and administrative behavior. Each is also relevant to technical as well as administrative rationality. The analysis of such processes, in fact, is often relevant also to the study of action in any system, not merely formal organizations. Some of the outstanding developments in other fields—particularly in communicating and decision-making—have taken place in the analysis of machine systems, cells, individuals, and small, ephemeral groups. In this context, naturally, we shall concentrate upon the role of these processes in formal organizations and the problems they present to administrators and other members.

These five processes, it should be noted, provide an excellent entry into the identification and analysis of many other processes. "Controlling," for example, in the sense of a corrective check on action, is a combination of evaluating and activating. The technical administrative processes are all specialized instruments of planning, activating or evaluating. "Organizing," in the sense of creating or changing an organizational structure, is an activity that may be the object of planning, activating and evaluating.[1]

1. The major problems faced in the process of organizing are already set forth in Chapters 9, 10, and 17.

Chapter 21

THE DECISION-MAKING STRUGGLE

*D*ECISION-MAKING is one of the major activities through which administrators seek to achieve rational action by organizations. If it has at times been regarded as the most important administrative activity, this is because it enters into all other administrative processes. Decisions must always be made concerning the nature of communications, planning, activating, and evaluating. Decisions on other matters are themselves crucial information to be communicated, vital elements in plans, bases of activation, and objects of evaluation.

Most of the vast literature of decision-making has centered around normative models of individual or technical decision-making developed by economists or mathematicians. The distance of such models from actual decision-making has been discussed or documented by Banfield, Hirschman, Lindblom, Neustadt, Pfiffner, and Simon. As a result of their work, it is now feasible to set forth a realistic model of actual decision-making. On the basis of the evidence now available, it would seem reasonable to do this by slicing the decision-making process into three interrelated phases or subprocesses: defining problems, choosing courses of action, and justifying the choices.

Each of these phases is itself a process of struggle. The inner logic of decision-making involves all decision makers in a struggle among conflicting calculations. These become intertwined also with the inevitable conflicts within the organization and between the organization and its environment. Even a purely technical decision (itself a result of conflicting considerations of desirability, feasibility and consistency) may prove highly irrational unless support can be mobilized for it through the strategy or tactics of conflict resolution.

In a very significant sense, administrative decision-making has been the continuing subject of most of the previous chapters. Administrative, as opposed to technical, decisions relate to the structure (and environmental relations) of an organization and its members' performance in satisfying various human interests by mobilizing resources, investing some in the organization, using the rest in the output of services or goods and doing all this efficiently, rationally and in accordance with behavioral codes. By reviewing the major considerations in both structure and performance, we have already dealt with the major types of problems calling for decision by administrators. We are now prepared to analyze the decision-making process itself in more abstract terms.

A. WHAT IS THE PROBLEM?

Although decision-making centers around the handling of problems, the nature of the problem itself can rarely be taken as entirely given. "Detecting the problem is as important as finding the answer" (Hilgard, 1959). Understanding its nature is even more important, since this may go a long way toward indicating how an answer may be found or whether, indeed, any answer is possible at all. As Drucker has wisely observed, "the most common source of mistakes in management decision is the emphasis on finding the right answer rather than the right question. . . . The first job in decision making is therefore to find the real problem and to define it" (1954, p. 351-354).[2]

"What really is the problem?" This is one of the most challenging questions any administrator can ask himself. It is one of the most constructive questions to ask when members of an organization consult together on future action. But in the first case, if not immediately brushed aside, the question is apt to lead to acute internal discomfort. In the latter, it may promptly throw a meeting into an uproar. To probe into the nature of a problem, particularly when people are busily trying to solve it, may create as much embarrassment as the question "What are your purposes?"

2. Drucker goes on to state that finding the right questions is specifically characteristic of managerial decision-making, whereas problem solving is the major focus in "the unimportant, the routine, the tactical decision." Yet it is clear that even in the latter instances problem defining is crucial. No problem is unimportant, routine or tactical unless someone defines it as such.

The difficulty of dealing with "What is the problem?" stems from the very nature of problems themselves. As suggested by Johnson's analysis of thought processes (1955), a problem exists for a person or organization *when, and only when, the person or organization perceives some blockage of purposeful activity.*[3] Thus the elements in any problem are people, purposes, and blockage. Remove any one of these three and the problem disappears, "Stated thus, a problem is a personal thing," Johnson points out. "It is not a characteristic of a situation. It is had by a person, or an animal, in a certain situation, and to call a situation a problem situation is to assume that the subject of the discussion is motivated toward some goal in the situation that he will not attain on the first try" (Johnson, 1955). The first try need not be actually made. The perception of future blockage—as when the ultrabashful suitor is afraid to ask for or steal a kiss—is enough to create a problem. In organizations, however, many problems and problem situations come to the fore only when a blockage has persisted after many tries by many people.

Thus "What is the problem?" resolves itself into three closely related questions: Who is involved? What are their purposes? What is the blockage? In any complex situation, moreover, there are many different people with different purposes and different perceptions of blockage. This means, in effect, that most problems in organizations—and all really important problems—are huge clusters of closely related problems. It is only to be expected, therefore, that each participant will have his personal version of what the problem "really is."

Let us suppose that a manufacturing plant suffers from recurrent breakdowns of machinery. As shown by the table on p. 762, different people will have entirely different views of "the same" problem. From the foreman's point of view, the problem may be identified as one of "proper machine care by workers." This, indeed, is what it is for him. to get the workers to have such a problem. Similarly, the maintenance man and the foreman would agree on the purpose but not on the blockage. For the latter the problem is the foreman's lack of cooperation. The accountant, the engineer, and the salesman, in turn, each have a different perspective on the "same" problem.

The existence of problem clusters of this type is to be taken for granted as an inevitable part of organizational life. Although any particular cluster may be colored by unique personality constellations, this is not a mere matter of personality differences. The allocation of different

---

3. This is a restatement of the definition in Johnson, 1955, p. 63: "A person may be said to have a problem if he is motivated toward a goal and his first goal-directed response is unrewarding.

DIFFERENT VIEWS OF "MACHINE BREAKDOWN PROBLEMS"

People	Purposes	Blockages
Foreman	High output Operations without breakdowns Proper machine care by workers	Machine breakdown Improper machine care by workers Disinterest of workers in output
Workers	High output Higher wages Better jobs	Bad machines Management wage policies Few opportunities
Maintenance Man	Proper machine care Controlling maintenance activities of workers	Interference from foreman Insufficient authority
Accountant	Proper allocation of repair expenses Lower production costs	Current or capital account? Machine breakdowns
Engineer	Better products Technological advance	Bad machines Inadequate capital budgeting
Salesman	Higher sales Lower prices	Lower prices Higher production costs

roles among the organization's members decrees differing purpose patterns and blockages. Each member, therefore, gets and develops his personal "agenda" of problems. Even when an identical problem appears on two agendas, the priorities will usually vary. Thus, if the maintenance man's and the foreman's views of the problem should begin to coincide, the former may regard it as urgent. The latter may see it as subordinate to a dozen more urgent problems, including breaking in some new workers, handling complaints that might otherwise lead to a strike, and meeting a production quota by the end of the week.

With administrators, from the foreman up through the factory manager to the company's president, the handling of personal agendas is itself a major problem. The positive purpose of getting something accomplished and the negative purpose of obtaining respite from intolerable pressures are blocked by the tremendous variety of matters demanding attention. In many cases this blockage is increased by an administrator's accepting as his problems the problems brought to him by others. In other cases it may be decreased by dodging his responsibilities and "passing the buck" to others. Effective delegation, as a middle course between these two extremes, can never be obtained merely by following a formal set of role specifications set up in advance. The "authority of the position" is too general to deal with the nuances of sequential decision-making. Any constructive contribution that the administration may make to the participation of others in decision-making depends upon how he helps break down a problem cluster into specifics that may be handled by different people. Thus, if the factory manager makes the foreman's problem his problem, he will undermine the foreman's authority and overload his own agenda. If he pushes the problem off his agenda, he may risk greater trouble at a later date. These extremes will be avoided if, by taking a distinctly "managerial" view, he sees his problem in terms of how he can help the foreman and the maintenance man handle *their* problems more effectively. When formulated in this way, a new problem has been created for addition to the total cluster. If this process of creation is carried a little further, it may lead to a triple set of problems:

People	*Purposes*	*Blockage*
Factory manager	Promotion of cooperative action by foreman and maintenance man	Tensions between them Factory manager's lack of time to deal with matter.
	Review of output schedules and production methods	Engineer's commitment to present schedules and methods
	Review of possibility of replacing machines	Insufficient information on other machinery

By this new formulation, what may have been originally seen as a problem of machine breakdown now becomes a three-headed problem of cooperative relationships, production scheduling, and machine replacement. Categorization along these lines immediately suggests further ways of analyzing the blockage. For one who is familiar with the processes of cooperation, production scheduling, and machine replacement, it immediately suggests where to look for alternative solutions. It suggests what kinds of facts and opinions might help find them.

Above all, the new formulation—if acted upon at all by the factory manager—changes the old problem cluster. Additional problems of potentially greater significance are added. Some of the old problems may lose their urgency or change their shape. In analyzing creative thought processes generally, Rokeach has placed major emphasis on the formulation of questions that have significant "implications or consequences for the ideas, products, feelings and welfare of other human beings" (1962). When an administrator approaches problem formulation creatively, he invariably creates new and significant problems for himself and others in the organization.

B. *WHICH ALTERNATIVE TO CHOOSE?*

Any conscious decision is a choice among alternatives. The decision-maker may choose among various formulations of the problem, as just discussed, or go further and choose among alternative ways of dealing more directly with the blockage. In either case the choosing is a process of resolving conflicts among conflicting considerations, people, or groups.

When we talk about important decisions, we rarely refer to single acts of choice among alternatives. An important decision, rather, is invariably a huge cluster of sequential choices in which the earlier choices help determine the alternatives available. At one point the actual choice may represent one of the more negative outcomes of conflict resolution: avoidance or deadlock. At other points the outcomes may be more positive and dramatic in nature: victory-defeat, compromise, or integration. At no single point do the available alternatives provide for more than small and rather marginal changes in the existing situation. The simplistic choice among grand alternatives is usually a daydream of those who are disconnected from real-life problems. Or else it may come into being as decision-makers launch trial balloons or attempt to divert attention from the genuine alternatives with which they are concerned.

What then is the great decision, the strategic choice, the decisive turning point?

There are only three possibilties. First, it may be a symbolic act which ratifies decision sequences already completed or promotes commitment to future sequences. Second, if truly a single act, such as an executive's final approval of an important policy, it is a choice which has genuine significance only insofar as it represents a commitment to future sequences of action and may limit or determine the nature of future alternatives. The long-range decision is something that always takes place in the present. Third, if truly a major decision, it is a shorthand way of talking about a sequence of choice among sequences of ever-shifting alternatives.

Since any alternative actually chosen is embedded in a sequence of alternatives and choices, choice involves some assumptions concerning prior and subsequent events. Most of these assumptions are usually taken for granted on the basis of previous experience. Some of them may be worked out on the basis of sophisticated efforts to calculate the probable consequences of future action. Such calculations are more reliable when limited to relatively short sequences and repeated at frequent intervals. Preoccupation with estimating the probability of future consequences, however, often diverts attention from the more mundane task of estimating what is probably going on in the present. When this occurs, any calculation of future consequences may be vitiated by the lack of understanding of the earlier elements in the sequence.

The most obvious alternatives whose consequences might be analyzed are those that are "given" by the situation. They are the courses of action that are customary. They are embodied in the expectations of others. They are formulated in the proposals of the various participants. It often takes considerable skill—even art and judgment—to select those alternatives whose consequences are worthy of serious consideration. It may take even more skill to weave these alternatives together into an action pattern that is acceptable on grounds of desirability, feasibility, and consistency.

Creative decision-making goes much further. In addition to formulating significant questions, it creates new and significant alternatives. The formulation of such alternatives, particularly when many members of the organization participate in the process, may be far more important than the act of choice. Since the process itself is sequential and may stretch over a considerable period, formulation and choice may blend together in a wondrous and imperceptible fashion. Considerable art and judgment—even wisdom—may be put to use in creatively devising and selecting new and significant ways of avoiding issues, getting victories or deadlocks instead of defeats, or fashioning compromises instead of deadlocks. Still greater wisdom is required in the analysis and synthesis of the more obvious alternatives in order to achieve an integration of conflicting interests.

The administrator, however, is not necessarily the person who formulates new and original alternatives. If he does too much of this, he may cast too large a shadow over his associates and subordinates. His contribution, rather, is to foster a creative and innovative spirit in the organization, to create the strains and tensions that can best be relieved by significant breaks from mere routine and custom. His distinctive creativity is embodied in the ability to recognize creative alternatives and add the touch of feasibility needed to carry them into action.

C. HOW TO JUSTIFY THE CHOICE?

In his theory of "cognitive dissonance," Festinger deals with the behavior of individuals who, disturbed by inconsistent (or dissonant) information, try to render them more consistent (or consonant). Thus a decision maker may reduce the dissonance between his actual choice and the rejected alternative in two ways:

> He can persuade himself that the attractive features of the rejected alternative are not really so attractive as he had originally thought, and

that the unattractive features of the chosen alternative are not really unattractive. He can also provide additional justification for his choice by exaggerating the attractive features of the chosen alternative and the unattractive features of the rejected alternative (1962, p. 95).

In organizations the resonance of dissonance may easily create a serious threat to any form of action. Any rejected alternative has more than attractive features. It has advocates who may not readily accept rejection and who may stubbornly, though not necessarily openly, press for a reversal of the decision. There are not only weak points in the armor of any accepted alternative; there are opponents eager to exploit them. Thus the dissonance may readily reverberate throughout the organization. If the dissonance problem is dealt with merely by changing the course of action, the nature of the dissonance may change but its volume may continue unabated.

Accordingly, to enhance the feasibility of any chosen alternative, administrators often try to make it seem more desirable than it really is. This tendency has been well summarized in Pfiffner's report on an analysis by Nicolaidis of 332 administrative decisions:

> The administrative decision maker tries to please as many persons as possible, including himself, thus adding a strong political tinge to the decision process. But he also *clothes his decisions with reason.* The politics of the situation requires him to abandon a simple "engineering solution," but he saves face by supporting his decision with reasons which possess face validity . . . (Pfiffner, 1960, p. 128).

The acceptance of justification as an essential phase of decision making should not be looked upon as an act of cynicism. Administrators have often started highly commendable activities which could not be continued without a well-reasoned justification. Sometimes they cannot even start unless opposition is first overcome by such a justification. If the opposition is embedded in their own fallacious ideas of administration, the role of administrative justification may then be to support and strengthen their better instincts. Moreover, the justification of decisions the administrator already wants to make is rarely the end of the road. It may be a fruitful pathway toward opening up new roads of action through new diagnoses, new programs and—above all—by creating new syntheses of interests.

> The result of rationalization is often to create a new end which is distinguished by its integrative character or by the fact that it is confluent with many interests, drawing them together, embodying them, satisfying them, and engaging them jointly. . . . The function of apologetic reasoning is to enable a man or a nation or mankind . . . to find some common ground for harmonious and united action. If apologetic reasoning when so

interpreted is to be called by the name of "rationalization," then that name must acquire new associations and come to mean the use rather than the abuse. For the thing itself is a normal and effective condition of all personal and social life, and in the exercise of its true function is as much bound to honesty and truth as is any other mode of reasoning (Perry, 1926, p. 386-389).

There are a number of typical difficulties affecting both the use and abuse of justifications. The first is the problem of competing rationalizations. To make a course of action attractive to people with different points of view, it may be necessary to develop a number of divergent justifications. Thus, as indicated in Chapter 3, it may be necessary to have the same compromise seen as "a great victory" by some people and as "meaningless" by others. If the communications go astray, this may lead to a new form of dissonance. The second is the problem of room for retreat. As Pfiffner also points out, an administrative decision should "contain a built-in justification which will furnish an excuse, and possibly an avenue of retreat, in case results are not anticipated" (Pfiffner, 1960, p. 129). If the justification renders the rejected alternatives too unattractive, this may unduly restrict possible avenues of retreat. The third is the ever-present possibility that rationalization may triumph over rationality. Preoccupation with the "good reasons" that may be supplied to others may easily lead to neglect of the "real reasons" for the choice. In the complex communication system of a large-scale organization the former may even come to be confused with the latter. Specialists hired to justify authority already achieved or actions taken on other grounds may even refuse to cooperate unless decisions are sometimes actually made on the basis of the rationalizations they devise.

Hence there are opportunities for outstanding administrative creativity in justifying choices as well as in formulating problems and choosing among alternatives. Routine justifications require little knowledge or ability. Only genuine understanding, wisdom, and breadth of interests can give birth to a truly creative justification. Many of the great myths, philosophies and traditions of nations and institutions have emerged in this way.

Chapter 22

COMMUNICATING:
THE RECURRENT MIRACLE

*U*NLESS IT CAN BE COMMUNICATED to others, an administrator's decision has no value. In fact, without the ongoing process of communication, the decision could not have been made in the first place. Only by communicating information is it possible for the members of an organization to act together in an organization or exert any influence upon people and groups in their human environment. Hence an organization may be viewed not only as a decision-making system but as a communication system also. The organization's formal and informal structure, as the embodiment of this system, provides the channels through which internal communications are sent and received.

In computers, servo-mechanisms and biological processes (such as the transmission of the "genetic code" by chromosomes), communication is relatively simple. Within and among organizations, and particularly among administrators and others, it becomes much more complicated, with blockages at many points. When we consider the seriousness of these blockages, it seems nothing sort of miraculous that people sometimes understand what administrators are trying to tell them. Because administrators have learned rational ways of using or improving communications systems, the miracle is a recurring one.

A. *THE BARRIERS*

Communication may be viewed as a process in which senders transmit messages by sending symbols (or signals or signs) through channels to receivers. Feedback may be provided by return messages from receivers to senders. Difficulties usually arise at each point in the system. These are a widespread source of open or suppressed dissatisfaction (*Caudill; Davis and St. Germain; Jackman; Jacques*, 1951).

1. Senders. A person is a sender only by virtue of his having a message that he wants to convey to one or more recipients. The sender may also want to influence the subsequent behavior of the recipient. Any such influence, however, is possible only to the extent that the more immediate purpose of the communications effort is successful.

The first barriers to communication are found in the behavior of message senders. Many senders are more interested in self-expression than in communication with others. Many are not quite sure to whom they are communicating. Some send messages haphazardly. Some administrators send contradictory messages without realizing it. Still others may be more interested in influencing subsequent acts of the recipient than in the essential intermediate step of successful communication. They may be so much interested in communicating *to* others that they lose interest in receiving communications *from* others, even those messages that might convey information concerning the success of the original communication. In some communications the sender's main purpose is to "build a record," that is, to communicate something about how good he is to superiors, investigators or historians who may someday examine his actions (*Read*). Finally, many potential senders simply do not want to communicate.

2. Messages. The information in a message need not be limited to ideas and thoughts. It may also include feelings, emotions and attitudes. The contents of a message may thus be said to be equivalent to the contents of—or images in—the sender's state of mind, plus those that may soon be forgotten or tucked away in memory. A message is a way of summing up or aggregating a series of such states or images.

Many barriers to communication stem from the nature of the messages themselves. New and complex ideas may defy the understanding of either senders or receivers or both. More understandable subject matter may suffer from clumsy structure and *non sequiturs*. Most messages have a latent as well as a manifest content; the former may be much more difficult to understand. A perfectly clear message—such as a sharp criticism or threat—may be exceedingly unpleasant, thereby leading the sender to veil it in ambiguity. A totally clear message may exceed the bounds imposed by the code of secrecy. If the sender censors part of it, the remainder may be disjointed or unintelligible. Above all, almost every organization suffers from an "information overload." The plethora of messages and other information makes it extremely difficult for either sender or receiver to give adequate attention to many of them. Thus, before the Japanese attack on Pearl Harbor in 1941, the American officers at Pearl Harbor received many messages suggesting the danger of attack. In addition to being ambiguous, these messages "were always accompanied by competing or contradictory signals, by all sorts of information useless for anticipating this particular disaster" (*Wohlstetter*, p. 3).

3. Symbols. A state of mind or image cannot be directly transferred from one person to another. The transference process can be accomplished only by having the message expressed in some set of symbols. The most obvious symbols are provided by language, both verbal and mathematical. Any other form of observable act may also convey a message. There may be high symbolic content in tone of voice, rate of speech, nonverbal sounds, facial expression, motions of the hands, bodily stance, bodily contact, and physical distance or proximity. The single word "No," or "Yes," when accompanied by enough of these supraverbal symbols, may have dozens of different meanings. Silence itself may speak volumes. The message that a person has no future in an organization may sometimes be vigorously communicated by not inviting him to a meeting.

Many colloquial words are extremely ambiguous. To reduce ambiguity, many organizations develop a technical jargon of their own. This often results in heavy "bureaucratese" which interferes with communication by making messages dull and uninteresting.[1] With the growth of scientific and professional groups in any organization, technical terms from the various sciences and disciplines are necessary. While this will facilitate communication among experts, it may seriously impede communication among different experts and between the experts and the administrators. Instead of bringing some common tongue into this tower of Babel, administrators may clothe their own messages in the symbols of hierarchic authority, thereby detracting attention from the message symbols themselves.

4. Channels. The most direct channel is face-to-face communication, in which the continuous interchange of messages takes place through

1. Before the Battle of Trafalgar, Nelson is recorded as having said to his fighting men "England expects every man to do his duty." In "bureaucratese" this moving message might have been rendered as follows: "England anticipates that as regards the present emergency, personnel will face up to the issues and exercise appropriately the functions allocated to their respective occupational grades."

both auditory and visual means. This interchange is usually more intensive and free moving in small groups, more limited and formalized in large groups. When people do not meet face to face, indirect channels may be provided by personal intermediaries (with each intermediary becoming both a receiver and a sender), written documents, and such mechanical transmission instruments as the telephone, loudspeaker systems, and television.

In organizations with the opportunities for face-to-face communication in small groups severely limited, extensive use is made of intermediaries. The formal lines of hierarchic authority provide a network of such intermediaries. As pointed out in Chapter 10, such lines can never carry the entire burden of serving as channels of internal communication. Administrators use other formal devices—such as polyarchic relations, house organs, general announcements, and general meetings—to send messages downward. To get more messages coming upward they may use suggestion systems, grievance committees, and "open door" policies. To do both, they may try to exploit the informal aspects of organizational structure. "In most organizations," as pointed out by Simon, Smithburg, and Thompson, "the greater part of the information that is used in decision-making is informally transmitted" (1950, p. 226). If nonhierarchic channels are used too extensively, however, this may seriously undermine the hierarchic structure. The authority and self-respect of hierarchic superiors depend upon some privileged position athwart the channels of communication. Even when a reasonable balance has been obtained between those various channels, there is always serious resistance to the upward flow of messages. In sending messages upward subordinates tend to sugar-coat their messages, censoring information that may reflect unfavorably upon themselves. Moreover, with every intermediary there is a distinct possibility that some part of the original message may be diluted. When messages are sent through a long line of intermediaries, the result may be a serious loss not only of time but of content and clarity. If the purpose is to restrict the number of recipients, as with confidential or secret messages, the result may be "leaks" whose source cannot be detected.

Even when special units are set up to gather information and serve as message centers, major blockages may undermine their operations. Two days before the Japanese attack on Pearl Harbor three intelligence officers interpreted intercepted Japanese codes as indicating "attack on an American installation in the Pacific by one P.M. on December 7, 1941. But their efforts were unsuccessful because of the poor repute associated with Intelligence, inferior rank, and the province of the specialist or longhair. General Gerow, head of the Army's War Plans Division, for example, felt that 'enemy information of such grave moment would be brought to my attention . . . by the Assistant Chief of Staff, G-2, and not by a Signal Corps Officer' " (*Wohlstetter*, p. 310-312). In fact, the intelligence officers might have been able to arrive at this interpretation earlier if they had pooled their data instead of holding each other at arm's length. They might have been impelled to cooperate more closely if they had been kept better informed concerning the progress of diplomatic negotiations. Most of their information "on State Department Policy came from the decoded material sent to Tokyo by the Japanese ambassadors in Washington" (*Ibid.*, p. 295).

5. *Receivers*. A person is a receiver only by virtue of his perceiving and interpreting symbols sent by some sender. If he finds symbolic content in dark thunderclouds, he is not participating in the communication process—unless we want to posit some supernatural being who has sent the cloud as a warning. He is not participating in the communication process if he pays no attention whatsoever to a message someone has tried to send him. On the other hand, by intercepting messages sent to someone else, he may be a receiver whose participation was unwanted or unpredicted by the original sender.

A major obstacle to communication at the reception end is provided by a potential receiver's disinterest in receiving messages. Attention to messages is an active art that draws upon a person's energies. If there are too many messages, the receiver has no choice but to withdraw attention completely from some and give but partial attention to others. Thus many communiqués will lie unread in the pile of documents in an administrator's "in box." Others will not be read; they will be "scanned." In face-to-face communication many people—perhaps administrators more than others—are interested only in having others listen to them. They may listen only to snatches of what others say to them. No matter what the channel, they may reject messages that they do not like or forget them immediately.

Finally, the accuracy with which any message is received is influenced by all the many factors that may tend to distort human perception. Psychologists have long pointed out that the end product of perception is usually the result not only of what is perceived but also of influences within the perceiver and the situation at the time of the perception. Some typical distortions are often referred to under the rubric of stereotyping, halo effect, projection and perceptual defense (as spelled out in Zalkind and Costello, "Perception: Some Recent Research and Implications for Administration"). The most significant internal influence is the receiver's "frame of reference," through which messages are filtered. Thus, symbols will always be interpreted from the viewpoint of the receiver's past experience with the same symbols. The strongest filters are probably provided by expectations and beliefs. At Pearl Harbor, before the Japanese attack, prevailing military belief held that the major threat was internal sabotage by the Japanese population of Hawaii rather than external attack. Warnings that related to external attack were filtered through this prevailing belief (Wohlstetter, p. 393).

As a result, there may be very little correspondence between the images originally in the sender's mind and those produced in the receiver's mind. The only direct way for either one to check the effectiveness of the communication is to ask for some form of restatement or reformulation of the message. Any attempt at verification, however, is itself an effort at communication. It too may be seriously impeded by the obstacles that arise at every stage in the process—the sender, the message, the symbols, the channels, and the receiver.

B. *THE AIDS*

A tremendous number of techniques have been developed whereby administrators may remove or dodge the blockage at each point in the communication process. The major techniques of this type may be broadly classified as follows in terms of the types of blockage they may serve to remedy:

Sender blockage	Special positions or units with function of disseminating information inside or outside the organizations
	Formal and informal reporting systems.
Message blockage	Standards for the preparation of reports
	Summarization of long or complex messages
Symbol blockage	Improved style
	Training in use of special terms
	Visual aids
Channel blockage	Liaison officers and special intermediaries
	Routing, screening and clearance procedures
	Reeducation of hierarchic levels and number of intermediaries
	Exploitation of informal channels and polyarchic relations
Receiver blockage	More use of face-to-face communication
	Indoctrination in common frame of reference

The use of such techniques is, by itself, no guarantee of improved communication. Any one of them may, in helping cope with one source of blockage, bring another kind of blockage into being. If many of them together should result in much more communication, the result could be a serious increase in the information overload. Or else they might bring more things out in the open than the members of the organization are prepared to tolerate. A certain amount of communication blockage is often needed not only to help people concentrate on specialized roles but to blur conflicting interests that might otherwise "blow the lid" off the organization.

The appropriate use of well-known techniques and the invention of new ones is rooted in the broader rationality of administrators who have acquired an interest in the communication process, an understanding of a communication system, and the ability to communicate. The administrator with an interest in communication is one who, instead of taking communication for granted, is always aware of the possibility of blockage that might occur at any point. He is interested in the selective distribution of information throughout the organization. Above all, he is intimately concerned with the substantive content of the information he sends and receives. "You can't write writing"; and you can't communicate communication.

Effective administrators also learn to understand the communication system in their organization. They become familiar with the strengths and weaknesses as communication channels of the formal and the informal relations in the organization's structure. They recognize that "the complex personal judgments of values, the meanings which individuals attach to certain facts, and the self-enforcing group attitudes, are all of prime importance" to the context of effective communication (*Learned*, p. 104). They are aware of the possibility that at any time they themselves, by virtue of their higher authority and status, may readily serve as an impediment to the flow of communication between themselves and subordinates.

Even mediocre administrators often develop certain obvious skills of oral or written presentation. The more successful administrators, develop the skills of listening also, thereby facilitating their entry into two-way communication interchanges. Both types of skill reach the level of art only when the administrator as sender-receiver is able to "empathize" with *others* at various points in a communication network— that is to sense *their* feelings and ideas and glimpse what messages look like through *their* frame of reference.

Chapter 23

PLANNING:
DEVELOPING PURPOSEFULNESS

A PLAN OR A PROGRAM is a sequence of future actions to which a person, unit or organization is committed. In its simplest form planning is the process of making, changing, or coordinating such plans. Planning by administrators is a process of promoting planning by people, units, and organizations and weaving various plans together into a common purpose pattern. In essence, therefore, administrative planning is purposeful action to develop purposefulness.

As a more structured form of administrative decision-making, planning is the subject of many preceding chapters and all sections of this chapter. Thus the global matrix of organizational purposes is merely a way of setting forth in an analytical hierarchy the various performance purposes that enter into plans. The previous discussions have dealt with the conceptual and dynamic aspects of each category separately. The task of this section is to deal with the process through which these various purposes are woven together into action sequences.

Many concepts of planning, unfortunately, are little more than special forms of the fallacy that "in good administration everything runs smoothly and easily," liberally seasoned with myths of central omnipotence. Many planners see themselves enthroned on a divine chair high in a hierarchical heaven, with the rules of reason (as they expound them) carried out by lesser people. If, in their ignorance, politicians, workers, and "line administrators" do not cooperate, they must be "educated." And if they will not be educated, this goes to show the depths of man's ignorance and the perversity of the world.

In actual practice planning is much more complicated. A combination of decision-making and communication, it is bedevilled by all the difficulties of both. The first element in the planning-activation-evaluation circle, planning may largely determine the effectiveness of the other two. It often yields plans that can never be activated or that serve as obstacles to—or even substitutes for—action. Underplanning and neglect of planning may readily be replaced by utopian planning or overplanning. The best laid schemes of men as well as mice "gang aft agley." Those succeeding today may create the rigid routines that prevent rational planning tomorrow.

Let us now define planning more specifically as the process through which (a) some people, who may be called the "planners," (b) commit themselves or others to (c) some representation of future action. Each of these phases confronts administrators with serious problems.

A. THE PLANNERS

In a very fundamental sense the only nonplanner in an organization is the mythical person who operates entirely in accordance with plans laid down by others, ingrained habits and—when neither plan nor habit dictate his acts—total spontaneity. Even assembly-line workers moving in accordance with the choreography of time-and-motion engineers have a minor leeway in planning their movements (and may indeed develop anti-plans to frustrate the engineers). In a much larger sense all skilled workers and technical and professional employees, and administrators do some planning—even though it may be very short range—for the use of their own time. All administrators and many technical and professional employees do some planning for the activities of other people. The potentially most important planners in any organization are its top executives and upper-level bureaucrats. As Cleveland has pointed out in connection with foreign affairs planning, "The most usable end product of planning is not a paper, but a person thoroughly immersed in the subject—a person whose mind is trained to act, having taken everything into account, on the spur of the moment. And that is why the ultimate decision maker must himself participate in the planning exercise. A busy boxer, training for the bout of his life, cannot afford to let his sparring partners do all his daily calisthenics for him" (1963, p. 4).

The administrator, however, is often so pressed by immediate problems that he has little time to invest in longer-range planning. Besides, he will usually lack the technical abilities and knowledge necessary for many aspects of planning. The typical solution to this problem is to establish specialized planning positions or planning units. This step may long be deferred by ignorance or resistance. When taken, it may readily lead to a number of typical "planner problems."

First, the planning specialist or planning unit may readily become seriously disengaged from the operations of the organization. This is particularly likely in the case of highly professional planning personnel whose professional "lingo" separates them from the rest of the organization and whose major aspiration is recognition by professional peers outside the organization. Under such circumstances the specialized planning unit may serve as little more than a symbolic substitute for long-range planning or a rationalization for the failure to develop long-term plans (*Banfield,* 1952).

Second, when the planning specialists try to come to grips with realities, they are apt to meet serious resistance from "line" administrators (*Devons; Gold; Hammond; Thompson*). The very administrator who got them going in the first place may be too busy to listen to their proposals. If he listens, he may not understand them. If he understands them, he may reject them. If he accepts them, they still have to cope with other administrators. The opposition to Frederick Taylor by the operating managers of Bethlehem Steel was not the last occasion of vigorous resistance to planning specialists. Many administrators regard it as a personal insult that a planning specialist may come up with ideas as to how *they* should perform their work. The feeling of resentment may be particularly deep if they suspect that the specialist is correct. It may be still deeper if the specialist has obtained his ideas from the line administrator without giving him due credit (*Dalton,* 1959, p. 76).

Third, as planning processes become more sophisticated, the number of specialized planning positions and units increases. Engineers, budgeters, accountants, personnel officers, lawyers, economists, operations researchers, and many others all start developing a variety of plans. When the planners deal with entirely separate activities or when one set of planners achieves monopolistic control over a certain field of activity, competition among the planners may be avioded. In many areas, particularly when the specialized planners merely deal with single aspects of the same operation, such competion becomes unavoidable. Under these circumstances, the administrator may try to cope with the problem by setting up a super planning position, unit, or committee to coordinate the planners. This device will rarely settle matters. The most it can do is help structure a situation which can be handled only by his active personal participation.

"In any democratic structure," write Simon, Smithburg, and Thomp-

son concerning government organizations, "specialized long-range planning units must always remain the most vulnerable units in the
administrative organization" (1950, p. 447). The same statement may be
made about any specialized planning unit set up to initiate major changes
in a private corporation. In both cases vulnerability is increased by a
widespread tendency to ignore the planning functions of others in the
organization and to develop ultraprofessionalized delusions of grandeur.
On the other hand, it must be recognized that many a so-called "planning
office" is merely a relatively harmless fact-gathering or fact-analysis unit
parading under a more honorific title.

B. *THE COMMITMENTS*

Commitment to a future course of action is a very personal matter.
Many people will not commit themselves quickly or very far to plans
that they themselves have not had a part in developing. The imposition
of legitimate sanctions to back up such plans may lead to a significant
amount of commitment under duress. But this may be counterbalanced
to some extent by noncommitment in the form of open or latent opposition.

Under such circumstances it is only natural to find many activities
that often masquerade as full-fledged plans but nonetheless fall far short
of genuine commitments:

1. Precommitment steps. Here we find the collection of information,
its processing and interpretation. One or all of these survey activities
may be the exclusive function of planning advisers or specialized planning
units.

Usually based on a survey, the forecast goes one step further. It
suggests, with varying degrees of confidence, the nature of probable
future situations or sequences. It may even indicate the varying desirability
of different developments, but without reaching the stage of proposing
objectives.

The next step is the actual proposing of objectives. This may be
done in terms of full sequences from the immediate to the distant future,
of longer-range objectives or of more immediate steps toward achieving
already accepted objectives. In any case, this is a long step beyond the
mere making of forecasts, a step which involves considerable risks for
individuals and units that prefer to "stick to the facts." Some may try
to define an in-between area by limiting themselves to an identification of
alternatives and an analysis of the advantages and disadvantages of each.

2. Formal decision. Here a plan of action is formally accepted by
those in the appropriate positions of high authority—a President, a board

of directors, a central committee, a national legislature, or a municipal council. But this does not necessarily mean commitment even by those who have formally made the decision. The ratification of proposals for new programs may be a mere gesture—as is often the case of economic development plans formally adopted by national governments and land use plans embodied in municipal ordinances.

As we look back over precommitment and formal decision activities, we see immediately that each of them may contribute substantially to the process of developing organizational purposefulness. Hence any one of them may be called "preplanning." When all of them are found together the result may even be called "quasiplanning." Yet to the extent that they do not lead to genuine commitment, the more appropriate designation would be "pseudoplanning."

3. Central or broad commitment. Here we come much closer to purposefulness and action orientation. Indeed, if we accept the myths of central omnipotence, we have arrived; the will of the masters is the will of the organization. Yet, as has already been demonstrated in previous chapters, this is an acceptable hypothesis only in small or extremely weak organizations. Commitment by those in the highest positions of formal authority is an extremely favorable condition for the development of organizational purposefulness. Under certain circumstances (there are some who would say all circumstances) it may even be an essential condition. But it is never sufficient. The commitment of the top decision-makers must also be internalized as part of the desired objectives of those individuals and groups with a significant degree of power throughout the organization. This, in turn, usually implies a two-way relation: namely, that the commitments of the top decision makers also reflect the perceived interests or objectives of many others in the organizations.

4. Overcommitment. In turn, overcommitment is both the fruit of past plans and a barrier to the making of current and future plans. When a plan is thoroughly "sold" to all who are involved in its operations, it tends to take on a "life of its own." The sunk costs invested in the development of purposefulness may make its scrapping, or even any major change, seem inordinately expensive—as in the case of a battleship which is half constructed. All the logic at a certain level of rationality and, more important, all the social power that has been mobilized work toward doing what was planned even if the planners themselves have changed their minds. In *The Guns of August* Barbara Tuchman shows how both sides in World War I became the prisoners of defective war plans that had been worked out years ahead of time by their general staffs. "Once settled," VonMoltke told the Kaiser with respect to the Schlieffen Plan, "it cannot be altered" (*Tuchman*, p. 79). Although Kitchener disagreed violently with France's Plan 17, he was forced to accept it because "with the troops already on the water . . . , it had to be accepted because there was no time to make another" (*Tuchman*, p. 204).

C. *THE ACTION SEQUENCES*

We turn now to the sequence of actions to which flexible or rigid commitments may be made. Here the typical difficulties involve the use of planning documents, the extent of detail and the nature of long-range plans. The ever-present problem of the clarity-vagueness balance has already been discussed in Chapter 11.

1. The script and the play. Some form of planning document is essential in all but the simplest of plans. The written word is valuable in recording the actions that are to be taken and the reasons for them. Without it, there is no possibility of supplementing the defective memory of people and of providing effective communication among them, particularly on details. This value may increase when supplements are provided in the form of tables, charts, diagrams, and pictures. Well constructed and sharply presented planning documents provide an ideal way of recording action sequences that could not otherwise be communicated.

The planning documents may also be largely designed to swell professional pride or impress external sources of support. This is often the case with the "master plan"—whether a master plan for a new or expanded factory, urban redevelopment, or economic development. Yet, the master plan can never express the major elements of purposefulness; by the time these points are written down and doublechecked, they are out of date. A master plan can only be up to date when it represents a "planner's" vision upon which little or no action is being taken. If the master plan is beautifully printed, with elaborate charts, tables, and pictures, one may be sure that it does not represent what is going on or that—as is often the case—nothing is going on.[1]

2. Details. The extent of detail in a plan, whether or not recorded in a document, is subject to serious limitations. An organization's general plan can include little more than selected generalities or meaningless detail that will weigh oppresively upon operating units or be ignored by them. The meaningful detail can be developed and kept current only by subordinate units. When we look at plans at these lower levels, the same phenomenon reappears. In absolute terms, of course, a plan such as a train schedulé, a production schedule, or a procedure for placing purchase orders may seem unbelievably detailed. The amount of detail usually fades,

1. See earlier discussion of "script and play" on p. 405.

however, when placed against the tremendous complexity of daily operations. Train schedules are limited to departure and arrival times; they do not include the number of passengers to be carried to each destination. If the plan is that the train move only when filled, this would mean an abandonment of prior scheduling of departures and arrivals. Production schedules often concentrate on quantity and speed at the expense of quality. If quality is to be emphasized, speed may have to be sacrified. At any rate, no preplanning of quality attributes can afford to be anything but extremely selective among all the many possible quality specifications that may have to be included. Purchase procedures, in turn, no matter how detailed, can never hope to prejudge the quantities to be purchased or the prices to be paid. The former is left to specific purchase programs, the latter to negotiation. In all of these cases, it should be noted, the important element is the *strategic* nature of whatever detail is included.

3. Time change. Myopia and utopia provide two simple ways of avoiding the selection of strategic details. The myopic plan concentrates entirely on certain aspects of the immediate future. Strategy is rendered impossible by the inability to appreciate the broad reality of the present or to be concerned at all with the future. The utopian plan concentrates upon remote situations with no attention to the intermediate sequences that are necessary to bring them about. Or else it is based upon commitments to desired situations that are simply impossible to obtain. In this latter case, the elaboration of presumed methods of attaining the unattainable may serve to make the plan more plausible, even though not a bit more feasible. The fact that a plan may be utopian need not prevent its reaching the stage of central decision and commitment. National political leaders often make "pie in the sky" promises as the only way to distract attention from current suffering. While such promises may lead to bitter disillusionment, they may also start the wheels going around on more realistic planning processes.

A more sophisticated avoidance of strategic selection is sometimes found in the use of comprehensive long-range projections. In a business organization these may take the form of projected income statements and balance sheets, with special attention to sales forecasts, expenses and revenues for all products. In national economic planning organizations they usually take the form of projections of major items in the national economic accounts. Yet such projections are usually too general to be operational objectives. Their importance derives from two uses. First, they provide considerations that may be used in developing a strategic decision. Second, they may help in evaluating the consequences of a strategic decision. The strategic acts themselves, however, cannot possibly be comprehensive. They are rather a set of very incomplete segments of the future—those selected segments which are regarded as having significant causative power.

Even in the longest-range planning, however, the most strategic details are those relating to the present and the short-range future. The most critical part of any plan is its link with the present. "The object of planning . . . is to decide what should be done now in light of the best present estimate of how the future will look. Planners think about the future in order to act wisely in the present" (U.S. Senate Subcommittee on National Security Staffing and Operations, 1963, p. 5). Flexible commitments to long-range objectives are significant only because they serve as a guide to the present. This guide is particularly important when the current action may itself be a long, drawnout affair or may have serious future implications. It is also important when the long-range objectives serve to mobilize support for current actions.

Chapter 24

ACTIVATING:
NOT BY COMMANDS ALONE

*H*OW TO GET ACTION under plans? This question is easiest with respect to the nonhuman world. Materials can be moved around by the direct application of energy. Machines can be activated by the provision of fuels and the application of energy directly or in the form of coded commands. Animals can be trained to obey commands through the use of "the carrot and the stick." In each of these cases the characteristics of the materials, the machines or the animals place limits on what you can reasonably expect them to do. One cannot readily get steel to evaporate, a sewing machine to cut timber, or a horse to fly.

To activate people is far more difficult. Lead them to water in an effort to make them drink and some, misunderstanding your message, may swim away. Others may give your message the "file and forget" treatment. Those who are spurred to action may take a sip and then try to hold your head under. Those who comply obediently may respond with inertia or resistance on the next occasion. Some may be more interested in activating *you* than in being activated *by* you. Your chances of success are best if you try to get them to do what they were going to do anyway. When the action you desire means a significant change in customary behavior, resistance is inevitable. The selection of appropriate methods of activation is extremely difficult. Although activation is the use of power, or influence, this is not a mere matter of turning on a switch. The methods of using social power themselves help determine how much power there is to be used.

To help probe the mysteries of activation, it is helpful to distinguish between the use of persuasion and pressure, the promotion of self-activation, and campaign leadership.

A. *PERSUADING*

In using either persuasion or pressure the activator tries to communicate a message with two basic components: (a) a desired course of action and (b) the probability that the recipient of the communication will achieve some form of interest satisfaction (or avoid some form of dissatisfaction) by acting as desired. With persuasion the desired course of action is itself presented as the source of the satisfaction. The intrinsic incentives are embodied in it rather than the threat or promise of contingent action by the activator or his agents.

1. Expectation. The simplest way to activate someone is simply to expect that he behave in a certain manner. This is particularly effective when the expectation is shared and expressed not only by the activator but also by many others. The tremendous power of mere expectation is illustrated by the extent to which people cling to behavior patterns expressed in traditions and in informal roles and codes. This power stems from the dissatisfaction created by disapproval and the gratification resulting from approval. It is greatest when the expectation is shared by the "activatee" himself. It is weakest when there are conflicting expectations and other strong incentives bearing upon him.

2. Example. Another powerful—although often overlooked—form of activation is providing an example to be followed or imitated. An administrator who "loafs" has a hard time getting others to work hard. The example that he sets may be more influential than anything else he does.

The power of example rests in the satisfactions that people obtain from identifying themselves with a person or group whom they admire or envy. This has often been referred to by political scientists as the "bandwagon effect," by economists as the "demonstration effect." Moreover, providing an example has the additional advantage of communicating far more clearly than may be possible in words the exact nature of the action to be taken.

3. Advice. The adviser activates people by suggesting a course of action. This may be done by a direct proposal or by indirectly discussing alternatives. The incentive lies in the frequently implicit assumption—which may or may not ever be clearly stated—that acceptance of the advice is in the interests of the advisee. Advice is most readily accepted when it shows people how to do what they want to do or to organize their conflicting wants. The process of acceptance is usually quicker if the advisee is led to believe that the suggested course of action is really his own idea.

Sometimes, as with command, advice will be listened to only when coming from someone authorized to offer it. The authoritative nature of advice also has a major bearing on the likelihood of its acceptance. When a person is confident that professional advisers are directly concerned with his interests and that there is no conflict among them, the presumption is that the rejection of authoritative advice will lead to some form of dissatisfaction. Under these circumstances, which are fulfilled in many practitioner-client relations, advice approximates command.

Like expectation and example, advice is multidirectional. Many administrators see a major function for themselves in helping their assistants and advising their advisers. While much advice may come from external sources, much may flow the other way.

4. Explanation. One of the most effective methods of persuasion is the presentation of data explaining a desired course of action. Sometimes advisers and others, instead of making specific proposals, will merely present data indicating the desirability of a definite course of action. Often, explanation is carried much further. In legal briefs, position papers, budget justifications, and plan proposals, data are presented to (a) explain the details of a proposed course of action, (b) indicate how and why it will satisfy the interests of the "activatees," and (c) show how and why alternatives are unfeasible or undesirable. Where no counter documents are presented, these documents may be extremely persuasive. When many such presentations are made, no point of view will be taken seriously unless backed up by some sort of brief. Even if a brief is too long to be read or too complicated to be understood, its very size and the presumed competence of its compilers may serve to inspire confidence in the proposal.

5. Propaganda. In a colloquial sense "propaganda" is often used to refer to someone else's efforts at persuasion, while one's own are described as informational or educational activities. Even in a more technical sense the line between propaganda and explanation is hard to draw. Data must always be to some extent structured. They clearly become propaganda only when the facts are strongly "slanted" or a serious effort is made to appeal to emotions and feelings. Any symbols, slogans, or acts identifying the desired course of action with the interests and aspirations of the activatees may be used to do this.

Some administrators become effective leaders within their organizations by themselves becoming the personal symbols of their followers' interests. Those who have learned this secret of modern-day charisma do not merely persuade people; they convince people by establishing an emotional link with their deeper interests. Similarly, many organizations try to become symbols of interests widely shared by outsiders. This is the object of institutional advertising.

It is not always easy to tell whether propaganda is designed more for an external or an internal audience. Much public relations and publicity ostensibly for external consumption has its greatest utility in keeping the members of the organization persuaded. Election propaganda, it has long been observed, is often listened to mainly by a party's supporters. The public relations activity of the U.S. Forest Service "is intended to affect the internal forces acting *on* the Rangers while it strengthens 'inside' them, by heightening their identification with the organization, their tendencies toward conforming with agency decisions" (*Kaufman*, p. 196-197). Some propaganda probably has its greatest effect upon the self-image and self-confidence of the propagandists.

B. *PRESSURING*

In using pressure, the activator makes the course of action he desires more desirable to others by assuring contingent intervention to reward them if they take such action or punish them if they do not. Sometimes more emphasis is placed on the satisfactions to be obtained through rewards, sometimes more on the dissatisfactions resulting from punishments. In either case, the difference between the two forms of incentive is not very sharp. The withdrawn carrot may be a punishment, the unused stick a reward.

The use of pressure depends less on the magnitude of various incentives than on their relevance to the interests of the specific people who are to be activated (*Zaleznik, Christensen and Roethlisberger; Lombard*). People who are more interested in leisure or comradeship than in money cannot be readily spurred to action by bonuses or fines. People who are deeply interested in escaping responsibility and in being guided by others cannot be quickly activated by the possibility of a more responsible position. Above all, a satisfied need may cease to be a motivator. Sometimes, before incentives can be used, it is first necessary to stimulate jaded or latent interests.

The degree of certainty is also important. Severe sanctions mean little when there is no likelihood of applying them. If the reward-punishment system is automatic and no followup is needed, all the activator needs to do is demonstrate the inevitable results of a given course of action. Pressure has thus been reduced to persuasion.

1. Bargaining. In bargaining the process of using pressure works in both directions. Both the activator and the activatee wield incentives.

Each modifies his promises or threats in the light of the actions of the other. Moreover, the desired action itself, as well as the rewards and punishments, is also subject to negotiation.

The power of bargaining as a form of activation lies in this flexibility. Both the *quid* and the *quo* may be adapted to the actual needs and strategies of the people involved, as they are discovered and modified in the light of shifting relationships. The activator escapes many of the resentments and frictions that may easily result from one-way activation. Both inside and outside an organization bargaining on specific points becomes the basis of such cooperative relations as reciprocity, logrolling, or the exchange of favors. It also enters into the formation of longer-term alliances and coalitions.

2. *Manipulation.* In manipulation the activator uses pressure to get action without directly stating what he wants done. He creates situations and influences that impel the activated to move in the desired direction. The successful coquette may use negative signals in order to induce positive action by the ardent male. A central bank may manipulate the money supply and the interest rate in order to obtain certain desired changes in economic activity without direct *fiat.* "Because command is a more ostensible, direct, person-to-person relationship, perhaps it can offend status, self-respect, and dignity of individuals more than does manipulating of operating penalties," Dahl and Lindblom observe. "Manipulation of field seems to be more suitable for creating 'permissive situations,' i.e., situations in which a particular response is attained although the individual can choose among a variety of rewards and penalties" (1953, p. 121).

Manipulation also has its drawbacks. Like command, it also is dependent upon the availability of rewards and penalties. Moreover, indirection is often perceived as a form of trickery or insincerity. People often prefer to stand up against open order-givers rather than unseen manipulators.

3. *Command.* A command (or order, instruction, or direction) is a direct presentation of the desired course of action backed up by at least an implied threat of punishment if the action is not taken. Because other forms of activation are so widely used, command is often a residual method used only when nothing else will do. When used, moreover, it is often closely associated with expectation, example, advice, data presentation, persuasion, bargaining, or manipulation.

Under some circumstances, command is the best method of activation. No other method can be as useful in times of emergency or in any situation when rapid action and coordination are needed. Some people will respond only to command. Orlando in Shakespeare's *As You Like It,* after bursting in on the Duke's forest retreat and trying to commandeer his food at sword's point, explains his action as follows: "I thought that all things had been savage here, and therefore put I on the countenance of stern command" (Act II, Sc. 7).

There are many preconditions for the effectiveness of commands. As all officers learn in military training school, a command must clearly specify the action to be taken. It must be feasible; the impossible can be expected of no one. If there is time, a command may also be explained and justified; one's action in carrying out a command is not hampered by being persuaded of its desirability. It must come from a legitimate source; an army officer will not usually obey an unintelligible, feasible, and well-justified command given him by a newspaper reporter. It must be acceptable. In the language of Barnard and Simon, it must be within the receiver's "zone of indifference" or "area of acceptance." Finally, the command giver must be prepared to check on what is actually done and take corrective action wherever needed.

There are also main limits to the effectiveness of commands. First of all, command is one-directional. You can give orders to a subordinate but not to an associate, superior, or competitor. A government agency may give orders to outsiders only under limited situations defined by law or regulation. Second, the power of an order rests upon the availability of punishments. Few people can draw upon all the punishments needed to back up reliance upon command as the sole means of activation. Available punishments may be evaded. Hence the finding of Dahl and Lindblom that "command is possible only under conditions of social organization that prevent subordinates from fleeing the reach of the superior" (1953, p. 103). When evasion is not possible, as shown by experiences in prison administration, repeated punishments often lose their sting; they may even be converted by the punished into badges of glory (*Sykes*, p. 51). Third, the "countenance of stern command" is ineffective in many situations. The use of commands and directive leadership is usually resented by professional and scientific people (*Baumgartel*, 1956 and 1957; *Brown; Marcson; Weiss*) and by people in higher positions of status and prestige (*Pearlin and Rosenberg*). Others may come to rely so much on commands as to lose their ability to act without instructions from others.

4. Physical force. The use of physical force, or coercion, is one of the oldest means of influencing the actions of others. It is based on two unpleasant but unavoidable facts. The first is that the application of force often creates intense dissatisfactions which, when felt or feared, may serve as a deterrent. The second is that when applied in certain forms—such as confinement, crippling, murder, or destruction—it may reduce or eliminate the recipient's capacity to act at all.

With the advent of the industrial and administrative revolutions and the accompanying decline in slavery and forced labor, physical force has been largely eliminated in the managing of most organizations. Even the most authoritarian administrators of the modern world no longer dream of relying on the whips of the taskmaster. More effective modes of pressure are always available and are generally used. Even when used as a last resort, physical force is accurately seen as something that, at best, has negative value only, and, at worst, may unleash counterforces which may damage if not destroy the one who uses it first.

Although the area in which physical force is used has narrowed considerably, it has by no means disappeared. In family life, where prolonged infancy and childhood guarantees the greater physical strength of adults, physical force is still used as an "honored" instrument for influencing children's behavior. In various games the skillful use of physical force, sometimes by highly organized groups, is the requirement for victory. Criminal organizations use violence in appropriating property from others, resisting law enforcers, and maintaining internal discipline. Revolutionary organizations use it to capture the positions of highest authority in government. Above all, government's traditional monopoly on the legitimate use of organized violence has been maintained. Coercion is still the ultimate sanction in the enforcement of laws. Nation states, indeed, now invest more resources than ever before in building military organizations capable of using physical force in operations ranging from pinpoint conflicts to worldwide devastation. The development, training, guidance, and continuous reequipment of these organizations inevitably creates a vast network of other organizations with vested interests in military postures, problems, and expenditures.

C. *PROMOTING SELF-ACTIVATION*

One of the unique characteristics of people, as distinguished from machines, is that they are self-activating. Although dependent upon their environment for necessary inputs, they can take steps by themselves to obtain them. They do not have to rely as do machines, upon messages from makers and operators. Both the individual cells which form the organism and the organism as a whole are independent systems of energy, systems which will recharge themselves and even grow in power until the inevitable day of disintegration. There is thus a realm of self-activation beyond direct pressure or persuasion, coercion or seduction.

To penetrate this realm, administrators use persuasion and pressure to get people to activate themselves by self-administered rewards and punishments.

1. Participation in decision-making and planning. The most immediate way to promote self-activation is to involve people in the process of themselves determining the desired course of action. To the extent that a decision or plan is regarded as one's own, activation boils down to getting one's self to do what one wants to do. Although this may not be easy, particularly when wants are conflicting and capacities limited, the problem of interpersonal influence is largely bypassed. Also the problem of accurately communicating the nature of the action to be taken is tremendously eased.

It should therefore be no surprise that many studies have demonstrated that various forms of broad participation in decision-making and planning have reduced turnover (*Burling*), eased adjustment to changes in production methods (*Coch and French; French* et al.; *Mann and Williams*), raised output (*Melman*), provided better environment for professional employees (*Goss; Lefton* et al.), and increased member participation in union activities (*Kahn and Tannenbaum*). Other studies and reports have revealed the value of external participation in building support for a controversial program (*Selznick*, 1949), developing national economic planning without formal central controls (Hackett and Hackett), and coordinating international operations (*Salter*).

The framework for participation is provided by the structural distribution of roles and functions. The more decentralized the structure, the greater the participation of each part in planning its own affairs. Participation in the innumerable decisions and plans that cut across the divided units and positions can be provided by the polyarchic relations of dispersed responsibility (particularly consultative procedures) and shared responsibility. Hence most actions to promote increased participation involve some form of adjustment in the formal or informal structure. At the higher levels of organizations they usually involve the operation of a "management committee" or "management team." Participation by external organizations is similarly provided for through consultative procedures, representation and membership in joint committees.

The use of such methods to promote self-activation is fraught with technical difficulties. Wide decentralization requires greater central efforts to keep decentralized operations in line with general policy. The more informal polyarchic relations require amounts of time and energy and still larger expenditures of patience and skill. The more formal ones seem to require long and frequent meetings, carefully prepared agendas and strong supporting services (*Guetzkow*). Both involve constant experimentation.

The greatest difficulty, however, is the danger of either bluff or breakdown. On the one hand, "participative" techniques are often used to provide ritualistic rather than genuine participation. Administrators may merely want to give members or outsiders a "sense" of participation in order to manipulate them into accepting as their own predetermined decisions and plans. Similarly, many representatives on consultative committees, both intraorganizational and interorganizational, are mainly interested in the prestige accruing to themselves or their constituents through symbolic rather than actual participation. On the other hand, too much participation may lead to organizational breakdown. As Selznick points out in his TVA study, leadership needs participation in order to get cooperation but "if participation is allowed to go too far, the continuity of leadership and policy may be threatened" (*Selznick*, 1949, p. 261). This danger is particularly great in the case of participation by external groups eager to penetrate an organization and divert it to other purposes.

The possibility of avoiding these two extremes probably depends to an important extent upon human attitudes and abilities. People who are personally insecure, who have grown up in authoritarian environments, or whose personalities are authoritarian may not respond to opportunities for participating in decisions they feel should be made by others (*Vroom*) or are not legitimate for themselves (*French et al.*). They will certainly not be anxious to have others participate in decisions they feel should be made by them. The administrator who favors wide participation must be able to cope with the fact that the decisions and plans that emerge can never be precisely known in advance. He must be able to take the risk that for better or worse the self-activators may decide to go in directions that he had never contemplated. He must be willing to share power in order to get the opportunity to build a larger system of power.

2. *Training and education.* The most fundamental way to promote self-activation is to influence people's knowledge, abilities and interests. To the extent that this may be done, they will be more capable of rational participation in decision-making and planning. They will acquire more confidence in the handling of their own tasks and in cooperating with others on shared tasks.

For many centuries large organizations—particularly in the field of religion and the military—have operated extensive training programs. Many of the earliest schools and universities were created to supply trained personnel to church and government. With the administrative revolution the interest of administrators in training and education increased immensely. For a considerable period the emphasis was mainly upon technical subjects. More recently administrators have come to be concerned with training and education—both in their own organization and in schools—in administration itself.

Behind the tremendous variety of training and education programs, it is possible to note two significantly different approaches. The first aims at self-development. People may be encouraged to learn how to deal with new and more challenging situations. They may be helped to broaden their perspectives and seek creative solutions through learning on the job and formal education. The result may be creative individuals. The second approach aims at conformity. By drill and indoctrination people can be trained to respond quickly to direct incentives. By more extensive training processes, coupled with careful selection of personnel, managers may try to "control what goes on inside each individual organization member, to get them to do of their own volition what the managers want them to do, and to equip them with the resources of skill and knowledge for these duties" (*Kaufman*, p. 160). In military and conspiratorial organizations special efforts may be made to foster the loss of previous identity (*Bidwell*) and develop unqualified allegiance to the organization (*Selznik*, 1952). When efforts of this type are backed up by sustained use of the instruments of persuasion and pressure, the result may be stereotyped "organization men." In varying proportions and degrees these two divergent approaches are often combined in the training and education activities promoted by administrators.

D. *CAMPAIGN LEADERSHIP*

The strategic problem of the activator is how—in the light of specific plans, people and situations—to combine the various instruments of persuasion, pressure and self-activation into a rational "activation mix." The administrator who does this well enough to get people to follow his lead regularly will usually be called a "leader."

While the personal characteristics of leaders have received much attention, the more important aspects of leadership are independent of personality. No matter what else they do, leaders initiate action. More important, their activation efforts are not confined to single, sporadic acts. They take the leadership in initiating sustained sequences of events. They invariably see such an operation as a campaign—that is, a flexible sequence of interlocking events that may be continually beset by uncertainty, inertia, and conflict.

1. Mobilizing support. The first law of campaign leadership is to mobilize and maintain sources of support. Norton Long has pointed out very effectively that subordinate officials in government cannot depend upon their superiors for the power needed to carry out their tasks. They therefore "fend for themselves and acquire support peculiarly their own. A structure of interests friendly or hostile, vague and general or compact and well defined, encloses each center of administrative discretion. This structure is an important determinant of the scope of possible action" (1949, p. 257-258). This statement may readily be broadened to cover nongovernment organizations as well and to include the search for support both within an organization and in the external environment.

The mobilization of support is always a challenge to leadership's sense of strategy. Support cannot be realistically sought from the entire world. The potentialities are limited, the effort to exploit them costly. The leaders must therefore choose the key points of strength to be developed, locate the "fences" to be built, and design the network of alliances to be woven. In so doing, they apportion their attention among existing supporters (whose support may wither if they are neglected), neutrals (who might be won over), and opponents (who might be divided or neutralized). In making these choices, major attention is usually given to those groups and individuals whose suport is essential for the mobilization of resources. Faithful supporters are often taken for granted, while the squeaking wheels get most of the grease.

The mobilization of support always has a significant influence upon the very substance of decisions and plans. The processes of bargaining and participation both involve decisions on "what" as well as "how." Neither logrolling nor alliances can be achieved without substantive adjustments. As as plan is carried into action, in fact, it will tend to reflect the interests of its most energetic and best organized supporters. The support base provides the very premises for judging the plan's desirability. The possibility of sufficient support enters into any calculation of its feasibility. The exigencies of getting support from divergent sources create its internal inconsistencies.

2. Timing. Time is the medium in which operations are led. "What time is it?" is the ever-present question in the minds of the leaders.

The first question is when to start a campaign. If one waits until plans are perfected and all the needed support is obtained, valuable time may be lost. The best way to improve a plan may be to test it in action. The best way to get support may be to demonstrate that something is really under way. On the other hand, it is sometimes better to wait until a situation "boils over" and people are complaining about the lack of leadership. This may provide the most favorable situation for leaders to initiate action.

Once action is started, it is important to keep the initiative. In simpler operations this means maintaining a tempo of action that provides continuous results. It means setting deadlines and dealing directly with problems that might lead to a breakdown. In situations of conflicting pressures and bitter controversy, a major problem is how to respond to criticism and attack. To keep the initiative, it is often essential to ignore some attacks, refusing to be put on the defensive. Sometimes the best defense is a counterattack on another front, the formation of a new alliance, or capitulation on one front in order to advance on another.

Although persuasion and pressure are invariably mixed, leaders must make continual decisions as to the precise proportions. Sometimes the only way to get timely action is to endure the delays of participative methods. Sometimes, when the ability to command is unquestioned, example, expectation or data presentation may be much more effective. Often, if any activation mix is to be useful, it is essential to make vigorous use of drastic sanctions. It may make sense to keep a loaded gun in reserve for use only as a last resort, but not if the trigger gets rusty and one never practices marksmanship.

3. *Exploiting crisis.* In Chinese the word "crisis" is written with two characters, one signifying "danger," the other "opportunity." In the life of organizations this two-sided nature of crisis is clear. Many studies have shown that the response to crisis may be withdrawal (*Gouldner,* 1954; *Grusky,* 1958), anxiety (*Sofer*), a contraction in the recognition of authority (*Snyder and Paige*), rigidity in adherence to previous plans (*Tuchman,* p. 209-211), or a reduction in communication channels (*Janowitz,* 1959, p. 76). Psychologists have often found that when emotions and drives are heightened by serious stress people tend to solve problems in stereotyped fashions. One survey of the subject suggests that these dangers of breakdown are particularly great in the case of unexpected or unanticipated crises (Hermann, 1963).

On the other hand, crisis may provide the best opportunity to get things done that would otherwise be impossible.

> Communities under stress, with their labile and intense emotions and shifting systems of belief, are ripe for change. While this is a situation fraught with danger because of trends which may make the stress become worse before it gets better, there is also an opportunity for administrative action that is not likely to be found in more secure times. Skillful administration may be able to seize the moment not only to guide spontaneous shifts in constructive directions but even to achieve extensive changes that would otherwise be impossible or extremely difficult (*Leighton,* p. 359-360).

The great changes in the evolving personality of individuals come as a response to a long series of crises throughout the life cycle—from birth, early weaning, and toilet training to puberty, adolescence, marriage, entry into work groups, advancement, and senescence. The great changes in society—including the birth of nations—come at a time of crisis. The opportunity for these changes can be explained in part by the tremendous motivating power of acute dissatisfaction. More significant, the opportunity aspect of crisis is probably rooted directly in its breakdown aspect. "At periods of great emotional stir the individual human being can undergo farreaching and permanent changes in his personality. It is as if the bony structure of his systems of belief and of his habitual patterns of behavior becomes soft, is pushed into new shapes and hardens there when the period of tension is over." (*Ibid.*). The opportunity for initiating extraordinary action is created by this softening. By exploiting this opportunity administrators can, by seizing the initiative, both unify their followers inside and outside the organization and divide and surprise their opponents. As Hirschman has pointed out in his discussion of social reform, "crisis may make it possible to take action against powerful groups which are normally well entrenched and invulnerable, [and] . . . may stimulate action and hence learning on a problem on which insight has been low and which for that very reason has not been tackled as long as it was in a quiescent state (Hirschman, 1963, p. 261). Above all, in time of crisis administrators themselves must act. The crisis calls a halt to the many prior acts of postponement and avoidance. In discussing United States participation in international relations, Cleveland points out that "the President, the Secretaries of State and Defense, the Director of Central Intelligence and several dozen other men do spend a very large part of their time working on the crises of the moment." He adds that "it is often at moments of crisis that the most basic long-range decisions about foreign policy are made" (1963, p. 3). The same observation is probably relevant to the top officials of any organization operating in a turbulent or rapidly changing environment.

To exploit crisis, experienced administrators are usually continuously alert for sources of stress. To be forewarned is to be forearmed; the penalties are great for not recognizing a crisis until too late. Long-range planning—particularly contingency planning—provides one way of getting prepared to deal with crises. Yet long-range plans will never anticipate the profile of the actual crises that emerge. Contingency plans "must normally deal with many contingencies which do not, as things work out, come to pass" (Cleveland, 1963, p. 4). The utility of the plans, rather, is that their preparation may help develop a more "ready" organization or at least an administrative group better geared to facing uncertainties.

When administrators see a crisis, they usually try to get others to share their perception. They may even enlarge crises not of their own making. They may create crises by their own efforts. Whenever administrators initiate an extremely risky operation, the fear of failure may serve to create a sense of crisis throughout the organization. An equally intense crisis may be created whenever the organization's members are induced to set themselves ambitious goals that might be seriously frustrated. Thus stringent deadlines and high quality standards are everyday instruments of crisis creation.

The exploitation of crisis, however, has serious limits. Crises cannot be regularly scheduled every Thursday morning or at the beginning of every fiscal year. If the administrator assumes the role of Cassandra too often, he may end up talking to himself. When he succeeds in creating a widespread perception of crisis, the consequences may go far beyond what he himself may readily perceive. He may himself be caught up in a turbulent field whose nature he cannot comprehend. If the sense of crisis becomes too much internalized within himself, his own actions may become rigid and stereotyped. Instead of being able to exert leadership, he may himself become one whose inertness is open to exploitation by others.

Chapter 25

EVALUATING:
BASIS OF CONTROL

*H*OW WELL (or badly) is the plan or program progressing? How effective (or ineffective) are the actions of this organization, this unit, or this administrator?

To ask these questions and find answers to them is an integral part of governance. Administrators may rarely assume such perfection in planning and activating that the satisfactory nature of ensuing action may be taken for granted.[1] To compensate for past errors and adjust to new conditions, control efforts are invariably needed in the form of additional activation, changes in plans, or both. These, in turn, may require certain changes in personnel or organizational structure. By evaluating past and current action, administrators may complete the circle and undertake these control activities.[2]

Efforts at rational evaluation, however, may easily go astray. The

---

1. A glaring example of what may happen without a check on actual performance is provided by the following story: "An Egyptian platoon commander who had been in charge of a number of Archers [British tank] was asked why, when abandoning his guns, he had not spiked them. He insisted that he had done so; he really believed it. And when he was taken back to his own guns and shown them intact and in perfect fighting order, he could not understand it. Of course they had been spiked; he had told somebody to do it" (Henriques, 1957, p. 58).

2. The evaluation of future action is an integral part of the choice aspect of decision making. Hence many of the considerations in this section are relevant also to section A-2 of this chapter.

criteria used may be invisible or irrelevant. The information to which the criteria are applied may be seriously distorted. Their application—particularly in the form of negative criticism—may be used as an opportunity for the catharsis of pentup feelings, the luxury of personal exaltation over the object of criticism, the expression of hostility, or the projection of personal feelings of guilt. Like planning, evaluating may become a substitute for activating. Like activating, it may lose contact with planning. Evaluation and control systems may indeed impede the kind of action they are supposed to promote and promote the kind they are presumably designed to prevent. When highly effective in certain respects, they may produce undesirable consequences that escape evaluation.

A. *USING EXPLICIT CRITERIA*

The global matrix of purposes include all the basic concepts needed to define the performance of an organization. Throughout Part V, these concepts have been viewed primarily in terms of purposes—that is, commitments to desired future states. It is now time to shift the emphasis and deal with their use in establishing explicit criteria, or standards, for evaluating the performance of organizations and administrators.

1. Advantages. There are many advantages in explicitly stating the criteria of evaluation. First of all, identifiable criteria provide the best basis of looking for relevant information on performance. Indeed, they provide the standard of relevance needed to make the problem of information collection and evaluation manageable.

Second, the effort to state criteria explicitly provides some protection against evaluations stemming from personal bias or unanalyzed likes and dislikes. Even when criteria are used to mask or justify personal bias, debates about explicit criteria may serve to bring the bias into the open.

A third advantage of explicit criteria is that they may help clarify cross-purpose disputes. As shown in the table on p. 597, these occur when one person defends (or criticizes) on the basis of certain criteria and the other retorts with a criticism (or defense) based on other criteria.

The same kind of cross-purpose dispute may also arise with respect to the many dimensions of each of the subcategories listed. The appraisal of satisfactions for outsiders may be linked to many different interests of a large variety of "interesteds" (Chapt. 12). The evaluation of output quality may be related to four levels of product specification and to many different facets within each (Chapt. 14). Output per direct man hour may rise while output in relation to direct labor costs remains stable and output in relation to total labor costs declines (Chapt. 16). Profit data may be expressed in terms of total or unit profits and may be related to net worth, total assets, or sales (Chapt. 16). When we come down to administrative rationality, we find that criteria may be formulated with respect to many detailed techniques relating to any aspect of decision-making, communicating, planning, activating, or evaluating. When such specific criteria are brought into the open, useless disputes may often be converted into fruitful debates on the relevance of alternative criteria. When a set of specific criteria is agreed upon, it then becomes easier to (a) consider the relative weights that should be assigned to each, (b)

CROSS-PURPOSE DISPUTES

Evaluation Categories	DEFENDER: *We do*	CRITIC: *You do not*
1. Satisfaction of interests		
a. Member's interests	provide fine working conditions	
b. External interests		meet the most important needs of the most important clients
2. Output		
a. Kind	produce a balanced line	
b. Quality		maintain high quality
c. Quantity	meet difficult deadlines	
3. Efficiency		
a. Partial relations	reduce labor input per unit	
b. Broad relations		reduce total costs per unit
4. Viability		
a. Survival	manage to survive	
b. Growth		invest enough in the development of the organization
5. Mobilization of resources		
a. Physical	get the best equipment	
b. Human		recruit the best personnel
6. Observance of Codes		
a. Internal	provide "due process" protection for members	
b. External		conform with external regulations
7. Rationality		
a. Technical	keep up with modern technology	
b. Administrative		give enough attention to long-range planning

appraise each in terms of its desirability, its feasibility, and its consistency with other criteria, and (c) focus attention on the adequacy of information relevant to each.

Fourth, if explicit criteria are formulated in the light of the entire matrix of categories, many dangerous oversimplifications can be avoided. Although the most important criteria are those relating to the satisfaction of human interests, the necessity of relying upon surrogates makes them exceedingly hard to apply. The more quantitative information relating to output or input-output relations may attract too much attention unless counterbalanced by information relating to other criteria. Criteria dealing with technological and administrative methods have presumptive implications for other aspects of performance; yet they may easily lead evaluators astray unless a careful eye is kept on the results to which they are presumed to lead.

Fifth, a multidimensional approach to organizational behavior provides the necessary background for evaluating the knowledge, abilities, interests, and other personal characteristics of individual members. The evaluation of particular individuals—for purposes of recruitment, job assignment, training, or advancement—is always an ongoing activity of administrators. It may easily be conducted in terms of criteria based mainly on tradition, habit, prejudices, or the desire of administrators to fashion others in their own image. Better perspective may be obtained by viewing personal traits in terms of the kind, quality, and quantity of services to be performed (Chapt. 15). Output criteria, in turn, can best be viewed in terms of the broader pattern of organizational performance as a whole.

Finally, the explicit use of criteria may itself contribute to the development of constructive purposefulness. In addition to reinforcing organizational purposes, it may break general purposes down into more operational objectives, goals, and norms. It may contribute to the widespread communication of purpose information among the units and members of an organization. It may help considerably in the ongoing process of purpose adjustment and redefinition.

2. *Difficulties.* The explicit use of criteria is inevitably impeded by all the difficulties confronting anyone who attempts an explicit formulation of an organization's purposes. The ordinary language of administration is insufficient to deal with the multiple dimensions of desired performance. Yet sophisticated use of the many concepts expressed in the global matrix will not by itself solve the problem of coping with conflicting and changing purposes. Many purposes and criteria must be deliberatetly shrouded in vagueness. Many defy precise formulation. Hence the question "What are your criteria?" is often apt to prove

as embarrassing as "What are your purposes?" or "What is the problem?"

In addition, even the most clearly formulated purpose will serve only as a partial criterion. If a unit's norm is to complete a given operation in ten days, completion in nine days will indeed indicate a fine record. But not if five days would have been a more justifiable norm! The evaluator must be able to make the jump from actual goals or norms to those goals and norms that, in his best judgment, should have been established in the first place.

Moreover, many criteria can be explicitly stated only at the end of an evaluation process. This is particularly true in those cases in which the purposes sought are never really known before the time of attainment. Even with external evaluators, who are not themselves involved in purpose formulation, it may not be possible before the very last stages of evaluation, after all the facts are collected and interpreted, to determine the relevance of various criteria and the levels at which they might be set.

Finally, overemphasis upon explicit criteria may lead to serious consequences. Precise criteria of lesser significance may "take on a life of their own" entirely apart from the larger purposes of the organization. They may detract attention from vague criteria of greater significance. Precise data that are readily available may deflect attention from criteria requiring information that is hard to get, thereby themselves predetermining the selection of criteria.

B. GETTING INFORMATION

What are the facts on actual performance?

To apply any criteria, some answer must be sought to this question. For sophisticated and refined criteria, the search must be rather strenuous. It requires costly efforts, inevitable tensions, and—particularly in any larger organization—a large amount of records and procedures that will be damned as "red tape." The results at best may be—in the frank words used by a statistician to define statistical analysis—"a delicate dissection of uncertainties, a surgery of suppositions" (Moroney, 1956, p. 3). Sometimes there is even greater relevance in Clausewitz's description of information obtained by commanders in time of battle:

> A great part of the information obtained in war is contradictory, a still greater part is false, and by far the greatest part is doubtful . . .
>
> The timidity of men gives fresh force to lies and untruths. As a general rule, everyone is more inclined to believe the bad than the good. . . .
>
> This difficulty of seeing things correctly, which is one of the greatest sources of friction in war, makes things appear quite different from what

was expected. . . . This is one of the great gulfs that separate *conception* from *execution* (1950, p. 51-52).

1. Collection. The hard core of information collection by administrators consists of formal reporting systems based on written records that provide regular, selective and timely information of a statistical, financial or narrative character. Specialized personnel often concentrate upon collecting, processing and interpreting this information, so that it can be readily handled by administrators. Yet many of these reporting systems —particularly those dealing with accounting data—were originally established as a protection against internal dishonesty or as a means of providing information to external controllers and supporters. Old reporting forms that have outlived their usefulness become "precious islands of tangibility" (Chapt. 15, section B-1), to be built upon but not easily replaced or abolished. The addition of information more pertinent to current evaluation often leads to uncontrolled expansion and a loss of selectivity. As the specialist guardians of various information systems become more dedicated to informational accuracy, they often tend to lose their sense of selectivity and timeliness. To combat this tendency administrators mount recurrent campaigns to cut down and speed up the flow of information.

Under certain conditions, however, regular reporting systems can be ineffective instruments for obtaining information on what goes on inside an organization. These conditions may exist whenever (a) there is serious resistance to the collection of information, (b) the information is of an unusual or nonrecurrent nature, (c) the collectors are not sure what kind of information they want, (d) the expense of regular collection is not warranted, (e) preliminary exploration is needed to provide the basis for regular reporting, or (f) regular reporting systems are themselves being evaluated. Hence administrators usually try to prevent themselves from becoming the spoon-fed prisoners of internal reporting systems. They exploit many other formal and informal channels of communication. They try to seek information from conflicting sources. Like Clausewitz, they may feel that it is "fortunate if these reports in contradicting each other produce a sort of balance and themselves arouse critcism" (1950, p. 51). They make frequent use of field trips and personal inspection trips, often wishing that they could do so in disguise after the fashion of Haroun El-Raschid in the Arabian nights. Above all, they initiate special inquiries or investigations. These may be designed merely to "get the real facts" or may be seen more broadly as a way of developing new plans. They may be conducted openly or *sub rosa*. They may be handled by members of the organization or "impartial" outsiders. Information-hungry administrators have even been known to exploit for their own informational purposes the investigatory efforts of external control agencies.

Regular reporting systems of organizations are still less reliable with respect to information concerning suppliers, clients, competitors and other aspects of the environment. In some countries, important supplements may be obtained from the statistics collected and made available by government agencies and special associations. But these rarely go far enough to enable an administrator to appraise an organization's changing relations with its immediate environment. Useful "intelligence" of this type usually requires, in addition, an imaginative piecing together of reports from special studies, informal contacts, or even—as the case may be—espionage operations.

2. *Effects of collection.* Entirely apart from its use by administrators, information collection itself has important effects on an organization. First of all, by destroying the possibility of complete privacy and secrecy, it creates a certain tension in the atmosphere. This tension may supplement—and even contribute to—the sense of responsibility on the part of members who might otherwise not be sufficiently responsive to the interests of others or of the organization as a whole. It becomes greater whenever attempts are made to extend the scope of regular reporting systems or whenever special inquiries threaten to explore previously private aspects of behavior. It always leads to a certain amount of grumbling against red tape and "snoopers." When collection efforts are seen as "going too far," the atmosphere is sure to become charged with distrust, suspicion, and resentment.

Moreover, information collection affects not only attitudes and atmosphere but also the very behavior which the data are intended to describe. People behave differently when they know they are being watched or that certain aspects of their behavior will be formally recorded. The nature of this difference varies considerably. In many situations the tendency is to conform with those criteria suggested by the type of information collected. Under these circumstances the collection process itself has a control function, thereby rendering unnecessary a large amount of separate or subsequent control actions. If the criteria suggested by the collection system are narrowly conceived, this control influence may itself promote the neglect of other important aspects of performance (*Argyris, 1952; Blau, 1955; Berliner; Learned, p. 132*). If rewards and punishments are directly associated with the information collected, the result may be an "adaptive effort to make a face showing of compliance regardless of the other costs involved to the organization" (Dubin, 1962,

p. 45). In some situations close surveillance may destroy initiative and spontaneity of action. When seen as an illegitimate intrusion, it may result in a complete stoppage of action.

Finally, collection efforts may also influence the nature of the information collected. Administrators at various levels often withhold information that might be useful to their superiors (*Ulrich, Booz and Lawrence; Dalton,* 1950). They often select or "color" information to enhance their own performance, "pass the buck" to others, or tell their superiors what they would like to hear. "Events that may be interpreted as failures, if reported at all, are skilfully underrated and sandwiched between successes. Through experience the subordinate learns how much to report, what interests the boss the most, how far one can safely go in confession his own failures and in pointing out the boss's mistakes, and how co-workers at the same level report" (Redfield, p. 131). Even statistical and financial reports, despite their appearance of cold objectivity, may be based upon a certain amount of fabricated or distorted information at the point where the primary data is first recorded. As these data move through the various channels of processing and interpretation, the distortion may grow. "Distortion is a cumulative process, starting at the bottom and growing as it ascends the hierarchy, because those at the top foster it through a multitude of expressions and actions" (*Ibid.,* p. 131-132).

C. *QUALIFICATIONS OF EVALUATORS*

As already suggested, the rational evaluation of organizational performance requires a skillful, flexible, and ever-skeptical approach to both the formulation of explicit standards and the collection of relevant information. At the crucial stage of applying standards to information and formulating judgments, moreover, there are other characteristics shown by those adept at rational evaluation.

The first is the subordination of evaluation to the objective of improved performance. Overemphasis upon evaluation may undermine future performance. A retributive approach may stand in the way of future contributions to performance.

The second is an interest in basing evaluations upon an awareness of the whole situation. This means looking for the good as well as the bad. It means being able to formulate judgments in which good, bad and in-between aspects of performance are combined, rather than seeking to reduce multidimensional criteria to a single common denominator. It means taking into account special or extenuating circumstances and not being unduly flustered by small deviations from prescribed standards. It means tempering high expectations with an awareness of what might reasonably have been accomplished under the specific conditions.

Third, the rational evaluator regards the judgments made by others as data to be evaluated rather than as evaluations to be accepted at face value. When a large number of people agree upon a certain evaluation, he tries to find out why. The multiplication of a large number of invalid or irrelevant evaluations will not produce either validity or relevance. There may be safety in numbers, but not necessarily wisdom. A broadly shared judgment may do little more than reflect a broadly shared bias. The evaluations of authoritative experts, of course, deserve serious attention rather than automatic acceptance. This attention is genuinely serious only when directed at the criteria and information on which the experts' conclusions are based.

Finally, rational evaluation is tied up in many ways with self-evaluation. The rational evaluator tries to identify—and evaluate—his own premises and biases. His knowledge of how he himself reacts when being evaluated by others helps him appreciate how others feel when he evaluates their performance. He promotes the flow of "knowledge of results" information among his subordinates so that they may more readily judge how they are doing. He encourages them to develop performance objectives that may serve as explicit criteria. Without evading his own responsibilities, he thereby promotes self-evaluation as a companion to self-activation.

D. *EVALUATING ADMINISTRATORS*

Evaluating the performance of administrators, whether undertaken by outsiders, superiors, or themselves, is perhaps the most important form of evaluation. It is unquestionably the most perplexing.

First of all, in evaluating administrators it is essential to look not only at them but also at the performance of the organizations or units they are expected to guide. Thus none of the problems referred to in the previous discussion may be ignored. In fact, a multidimensional evaluation of organizational performance is particularly important. Otherwise, situations like this may arise:

> Let us look . . . at a series of events which often take place in a department or plant engaged in an operation where performance standards or production schedules can be set. A man is put in charge of such a plant or department knowing that he will be favorably judged and rewarded if his department achieves a high level of production. He puts a good deal of pressure on his subordinates and pushes production up. Measurement of the end-result variables indicate that he is a "fine manager." In a year or two his reputation earns him a promotion to another depart-

ment, where he repeats the performance. In the meantime, hostilities have been developing in his subordinates and those below him in the organization. Just about the time that he moves on, the results of his unreasonable pressure begin to show up in decreased loyalty in the organization, lack of motivation to do a job, turnover, slowdowns, and scrap loss. The new manager reaps the fruit of the promoted manager's behavior and gains the reputation of being a "poor manager," for almost as soon as he takes over, things begin to fall apart . . . (Likert, 1961, p. 72-73).

In organizations whose output cannot be easily measured at all (as with many government agencies), undue emphasis is apt to be placed upon any aspect of organizational performance that happens to attract public attention.

Second, explicit standards are needed as to the kinds, quantity and quality of services expected from the administrator. As pointed out in Chapter 15, E-1, these should be based upon output goals rather than general functions. The standards cannot be mechanically prefabricated, since administration is a unique rather than a standardized service. Often, unfortunately, the standards that are actually used—or at least those that administrators think are being used—center upon certain codes of behavior:

- Don't get into any disagreements.
- Always tell the boss what he wants to hear.
- Appear active, start new projects, and tell the boss what you are doing and how well it is working out. (This will show you have initiative.)
- Always be available when the boss wants you.
- Dress well but inconspicuously (Rowland, 1960, p. 34).

Often, major stress may be placed upon personality traits and personal abilities as revealed in occasional or random contacts with the evaluators rather than in the broad spectrum of total performance.

Third, information is needed on the administrator's actual behavior. Just what did he do during the period under review? At this point the collection of performance information is apt to prove weakest. Formal reporting systems can cover only a small part of administrators' actions; what is covered is apt to be highly colored. The "grapevine" is apt to transmit large quantities of rumors, gossip and "facts" manufactured as weapons in intraorganizational disputes. Administrators are more skilled that anyone else in the arts of laying down smokescreens, doctoring data, building a record, and using persuasion and pressure to establish a reputation for effective performance.

Finally, it is essential to establish some link between the performance of the organization and of the administrator. When an organization has done better by certain criteria, it may have been in spite of a certain administrator. When it has done worse, it may be that it would have declined much further if it had not been for the administrator's performance. These possibilities may be examined only if the evaluator can identify and appraise the major influences other than the administrator upon the organization's performance. Similarly, the administrator may use the latest and most impressive methods of decision-making, communicating, planning, activating, and evaluating. Yet the link between these intermediate administrative services and the end products and other aspects of organizational performance cannot be automatically presumed to exist. The fine-looking technique may, indeed, prove an obstacle to improved performance. This possibility may be explored only by tracing the administrator's services through the product flow and appraising their specific contribution to the total performance of the organization.

THE FUTURE

Introduction

WITH THE ONWARD SWEEP of the administrative revolution
and the gradual maturation of administrative thought, the sheer
quantity of educational services in the field of administration
will undoubtedly grow substantially. This growth will be evidenced
in an increasing number of formal schools, departments, and
courses in which some aspect of administration is taught to
undergraduates, graduates and administrators; organizations
conducting administrative education programs for their own
members; students in both types of programs; and countries
in which these programs are undertaken.

A continued increase in the variety of these programs is also
likely. Product differentiation is promoted by the emergence of
new subject matter and methods, the competition between
institutions, the differing needs of organizations and the personal
touch of creative teachers. "Packaged programs" from the
U.S.A. and Western Europe, when installed in industrially
underdeveloped countries, are inevitably refashioned in the light of
local traditions and conditions. New fads and gimmicks
are constantly being invented.

It is also likely that the future of administrative education,
as in the past, will be extremely uneven. Many schools,
organizations, and teachers will never keep up with advances
in administrative thought. Of those who do, many will be more
interested in research than teaching. Many will never give

serious attention to the difficulties in formulating and achieving quality objectives. In universities and colleges decisions on curricula and courses will often reflect the narrow interests of senior faculty members more than the needs of students or wider publics. In other organizations administrative education programs will often reflect the narrowness of their top administrators. In both environments, the influences toward innovation and creativity will be partly counterbalanced by the pressures toward conformity and stultification. In both, the abilities of the teachers will run the gamut from outstanding to mediocre and poor. Despite the high probability of this broad range of quality variations, there are revolutionary potentials for a major upward shift in the entire spectrum. It is possible that the poor administrative education of the future will be superior to that which is now regarded as adequate. The good programs of the future, emerging from agonizing reappraisals and courageous experimentation in the present, may be superior to the outstanding programs of today. The outstanding programs of the future may make a tremendous contribution toward raising the entire level of administrative education and thereby improving the performance of administrators at the major centers of power in society. These potentials are rooted in a small number of powerful principles concerning the educational process in general and administrative education in particular. These principles relate to the primacy of learners' goals and actions, the significance of abilities and interests as well as knowledge, the combination of work with education, and the role of teachers in helping learners. The extent to which these potentials are developed will depend largely upon the leadership of administrators and teachers in educational institutions and other organizations conducting programs of administrative education.

Chapter 26

THE PRIMACY OF LEARNING—
AND UNLEARNING

*T*HE "PLAYBACK" THEORY has been one of the great fallacies underlying educational activities. By this theory, the teacher occupies the center of the stage. The student is a passive recipient. The teacher pumps something into the student's head. The student's task is to listen or look, remember or imitate, and "play back" accurately. By this theory, the quality of education depends mainly upon the teacher's efforts. Curricula and courses are planned in terms of what should be "given" to the students. Learning processes are subordinated. Teaching rules the roost.

In a certain sense, however, nothing can be taught. Certainly no amount of courses in school or teaching on the job can by themselves produce a good administrator. The most that teaching can do is to assist or guide the learning process. Learners must learn; it is up to them. In all fields of education, including administration, teaching may result in very little learning. For all people, a large amount of learning—from earliest infancy to old age—takes place without the benefit of formal instruction. Sometimes, it takes place in spite of it.

In contrast with the "playback" theory, the greatest principle of modern education has been the idea of the primacy of learning processes. "Teaching may be compared to selling commodities. No one can sell unless someone buys. We should ridicule a merchant who said he had sold a great many goods although no one had bought any. Perhaps there are teachers who think they have done a good day's work teaching irrespective of what pupils have learned" (Dewey, p. 614). From this point of view "the mere act of listening to wise statements and sound advice does little for anyone. In the process of learning, the learner's dynamic cooperation is required" (Gragg, "Because Wisdom Can't Be Told"). The teacher's role is to guide or aid the activities of learners. Thus education is rooted not in teaching but in the "teaching-learning process."[1]

A. *LEARNING AS PERSONAL EXPERIENCE*

Learning is an extremely personal form of human experience.

As the more active and purposeful aspect of growth, learning is related to the broader growth processes of personal development and maturation. Many things cannot be learned until a person is ready to learn them. Learning begins with what one has already learned. Its progress is limited by a person's inherent capacities—and when and if potential capacities are fully exploited.

Learning is dependent upon the private purposes of the learners. "Unless they want to learn, teaching cannot readily take place. And if they do want to learn, nothing any instructor talks about will stop them. All genuine learning, in the final analysis, is self-education" (Cantor, 1946, p. 47). Nor does an individual learn merely by doing. "He learns by doing if what he is doing interests him" (Cantor, 1953, p. 287). He may be interested mainly in "getting by," getting a good mark or getting a promotion, in which case such interests will establish boundaries for the learning process. Interests may be aroused by attention-attracting devices and by an elaborate array of incentives in the form of rewards and punishments. Deeper interests and more effective desires, however, are aroused by "freeing learning from immediate stimulus control." When the fundamental interests of the learner are challenged, he may learn "with the autonomy of self-control or, more properly, be rewarded by discovery itself." Retention also is determined by the learner's interests: "material that is organized in terms of a person's own interests and cognitive structures is material that has the best chance of being accessible in memory" (Bruner, 1962, p. 81-96).[2]

---

1. The most comprehensive statement of the "teaching-learning process" is found in three books by Nathaniel Cantor: *The Dynamics of Learning* (1946), *The Teaching-Learning Process* (1953), and *The Learning Process for Managers* (1958).

2. In discussing self-propelled learning, Bruner summarizes psychological research and theory on the inadequacy of mere stimulus-response behavior as a model for human learning processes.

In learning the learner himself always reshapes what is learned. "No teacher can take a concept, however simple, and plant it intact and usable in the mind of another. The art of communication is too imperfect. From what the teacher says or writes or does, the learner must create his own concept. It may approach that of the teacher, but, like all created things, it will be to some extent original" (Gragg, "Teachers Also Must Learn"). What has been learned is inevitably filtered or transformed in the process. "Every person must uniquely translate whatever he undergoes so that it fits in with his present meanings, needs, and purposes" (Cantor, 1953, p. 293).

Above all, the learner reshapes himself. What has been truly learned is not merely added on; it becomes part of the learner. After significant learning, the learner is no longer the same person. He behaves differently. His personal capacities have developed—perhaps even his personality. It is in this sense that Cantor suggests that "the development of a manager is essentially the development of the person" (1958, p. 10).

B. *THE SOCIAL CONTEXT*

The fact that learning is a highly personal activity does not mean that it should be seen out of its social context. As an individual in a group, the learner is subject to the influence not only of teachers but also of his affiliations with others and their expectations concerning his behavior. The effect of such affiliations and expectations on workers' output has been analyzed in many research studies (summarized in Chapts. 14 and 19). More recently, the extension of such research to schools has revealed that the learning process of students is influenced not only by the actions of school and faculty but also by the norms of informal student groups.

The most relevant research study yet available was conducted by Charles D. Orth on two sections of the first year of the two-year Master's degree program at the Harvard Business School (*Orth*).[3] Orth found that in each of these two sections the students tended to organize themselves to "beat the system" (*Ibid.*, p. 56). Each section developed "image norms" to guide the behavior needed for students to be perceived as successful businessmen. In Section A the image norms were based more on the popular stereotype of the successful businessman, in Section E more on the faculty's image of the businessman as a thoughtful, tough-minded de-

---

3. A previous study in another graduate school is available in *Becker et al.* A similar study among Harvard undergraduates is being made by the Harvard Student Study, Dr. S. H. King, Director. A set of essays on the social aspect of student learning in primary and secondary schools has been provided by Nelson (1960).

cision-maker. Moreover, each section developed "coping norms" to help their members meet the hazards of academic life:

Section A	*Section E*
Don't dominate the discussion by talking too often or too long.	It's all right to bring in outside knowledge if it is relevant.
Don't refute another man's point.	It's all right to take up more than your share of time if you are advancing the discussion.
Don't bring in knowledge from outside of classroom—this is unfair competition.	It's all right to refute another man's point if you do it politely.
You should be conservative—avoid "off-beat" conclusions.	It's all right to introduce off-beat ideas as long as they are logically developed.
Don't try to be too much of a "star" and thereby show up the rest of us.	Points made should be relevant to the preceding discussion.
	It's all right to be a "star."

In Section A these norms tended to discourage, and in Section E to encourage, more vigorous learning efforts (*Ibid.*, p. 111-141).

Student learning was also influenced, Orth found, by the pattern of leadership and membership in informal groups. In Section A the student leaders were selected with more reference to their social attainments, in Section E with more reference to their academic attainments. Student leaders exercised greater influence in Section A than in Section E. In both sections the individual students seem to have been greatly influenced by the degree of social support they received from others, mainly other students.[4] In the case of single men particularly, there was a high correlation between superior academic performance and the extent of a student's acceptance by his peers. Isolates tended to perform badly. Married students tended to perform better than single students. In Section A social support patterns became "frozen" early in the year, with many students "locked in" by a stereotyped role that developed quickly and could not be readily changed. In Section E it was easier for students to shift relations and form close friendships with other students (*Ibid.*, p. 142-207).

On the basis of his observations of both sections, Orth came to the following conclusions concerning student behavior:

4. "The social acceptance dimension of the instructional group can either facilitate or impede the development of effective problem-solving requirements for the achievement of a given set of learning objectives" (G. Jensen, 1960).

1. Students feeling the pressures generated by the required system and undecided about how much and what is necessary, search for common agreements limiting individual performance to safe or reasonable levels.

2. Rewards (social support, and/or influence) are offered by students to peers who conform to agreements reached by the group.

3. Many students feel that rewards from their peers are at least as valuable as those offered by the Faculty. They therefore limit their class performance to a point between the minimum acceptable level set by the Faculty and the maximum acceptable level set by their peers (*Ibid.,* p. 215-220).

C. *THE LEARNING STRUGGLE*

The conflict between faculty expectations and the group norms of the students, as Orth points out, may easily give the classroom environment "more of the flavor of the arena than of the laboratory" (*Ibid.,* p. 116). Yet this flavor stems from still deeper conflicts.

Like decision-making, learning begins with problems. The learner is someone who wants to achieve a certain objective and, because of blockage, cannot do so immediately: "Learning depends upon not knowing the answers" (Cantor, 1953, p. 303). It starts with an emotional state of confusion, restlessness or dismay. The best learners are probably those who in their early lives have had to confront "early challenges of problems to be mastered, of stresses to be overcome . . ." (Bruner, 1962, p. 7). The best learning, particularly in a field such as administration, probably takes place when the learners feel the challenge of the unknown and the debatable. "For if education may be defined in a word, that word is controversy. Where concord reigns, learning withers: where conflict rules, it flourishes."[5]

The deepest conflicts in the learning process are probably the internal conflicts of the learner himself. Since learning means change, it is only natural that there be inner resistance to change. This resistance becomes stronger when, as in the use of case study discussions, teachers impose greater responsibility upon students for their own learning processes. "Not all students can bear the strain of thinking actively, of making independent judgments which may be challenged vigorously by their contemporaries" (Gragg, "Because Wisdom Can't Be Told"). The experience of the Harvard Business School indicates that it often takes a long period of gruelling struggle before a student can conquer his own tendencies to rely upon being "spoonfed" by teachers. On the other hand, the more authoritarian types of teaching promote the learner's flight from shouldering his own responsibilities. Instead of struggling to achieve self-discipline,

5. Inscription facing frontispiece of McNair, 1957.

he withdraws from active learning and concentrates only upon those aspects of learning demanded by passive adjustment to the reward-punishment system of teachers and peers. Under these circumstances, he learns "how not to learn" (Cantor, 1946).

D. *THE IMPORTANCE OF UNLEARNING*

In discussing the teaching of logic, a philosopher once wrote:

> . . . logic ought certainly not to infect eager and trustful young minds with fundamental confusions, confusions which determine the setting of consequent philosophizing. If this negative precept seems unimportant, it is well to remember that modern hospital methods were revolutionized by Florence Nightingale, I believe, by this very insistence that, whatever else hospitals may do, they should not spread disease (Cohen, 1956, p. 16).

In administration the germs of fundamental confusion have affected not only the eager and trustful. The battleworn and skeptical are sometimes affected more profoundly. They have already learned too many half truths and untruths, too many abilities to do the wrong thing at the wrong time, too many narrow interests and negative attitudes.

Under these circumstances it is hardly enough to stand on the single negative precept that administrative instruction should not spread additional confusion. Some courses and much coaching have already added appreciably to the folklore and fancy of administration. An additional negative precept should be added: at least part of the training of administrators should be aimed at cauterizing past infections.

Thus "unlearning" is itself a part of learning. It is one of the most important aspects of a learner's struggle with himself, an aspect that may be particularly painful in unlearning how not to learn. In fact, unlearning is a positive rather than a negative process. To cast off old illusions is to open before one's eyes the vistas of new and challenging possibilities. The immediate loss is the security of holding fast to comfortable fiction and friendly habits. The attainable gain is the rare delight—not unmixed with peril—of creative growth.

Chapter 27

WHAT SHOULD ADMINISTRATORS . LEARN?

W HAT SHOULD PEOPLE learn in order to qualify for administrative roles? What should administrators learn to perform more effectively and/or qualify for more responsible positions?

In trying to answer such questions, educational institutions have sometimes overemphasized the acquisition of knowledge. This tendency was lampooned in Gragg's apt limerick ("Because Wisdom Can't Be Told"):

> A student of business with tact
> Absorbed many answers he lacked.
> But acquiring a job,
> He said with a sob,
> "How *does* one fit answer to fact?"

A veteran administrator, in government as well as business, might comment on the limerick by stating that the school of experience, not a university, is the only place one finds answers to fit the "facts of life." Any such comment, however, would confuse the environment of learning with what is learned. The more significant reply to the student's sob is to tell him that knowledge is not enough, since successful administrative performance also requires the acquisition of certain abilities and interests.[1]

As indicated in Chapter 20, there are many levels of knowledge,

---

1. The distinction between these three objects of learning was first stated at length in Charles E. Summer's penetrating analysis (1956) of the objectives of over ninety courses in general administration at twenty American universities. Summer, however, uses the more narrow concept of attitudes rather than the broader concept of interests.

abilities, and interests. Knowledge ranges from simple facts to concepts and theories. Abilities range from simple skill to art, judgment, and wisdom. Interests run the entire gamut of the individual interests discussed in Chapter 8 and the public interests discussed in Chapter 12.

It would be extremely misleading to weave various types of knowledge abilities, and interests together into an ideal of what all administrators and would-be administrators should learn. No one can aim to be—and no school should try to develop—the all-around, perfect administrator. The ideal pattern of learning purposes should always be a selective one. It is always the one best suited for a particular person or group at a particular level of personal development and administrative responsibility in a particular environment. The following discussion merely highlights some of the learning objectives that should be considered in formulating such selective patterns.

A. KNOWLEDGE

As an important basis for the exercise of abilities and the growth of interests, knowledge is not limited to what is clearly known. Genuine understanding can usually be achieved only with a large component of the tacit knowledge that knowers may rarely be able to state explicitly.

1. *General background.* A good background of general knowledge is helpful to any administrator. At the higher levels of responsibility, it is indispensable. Otherwise, an administrator is ill-equipped to deal with either the immediate or social environment in which his organization operates. Herein lies the large kernel of truth in the old tradition in some countries of regarding general education as the best preparation for future administrators.

Any serious knowledge of administrative theory, moreover, is much broader than indicated by the over-simple dichotomies that sprinkle many debates concerning education in business and public administration. Either of these fields can be—and has been—presented in an extremely narrow framework. Yet neither business nor public administration can be adequately presented except against the broad background of the many disciplines from which administrative thought derives its sustenance.

2. *Technical knowledge.* As indicated in Chapter 9, considerable technical knowledge may be needed to handle positions at the lower levels of administrative responsibility. As the specialist-administrator advances, it is less possible—and less important—for him to "keep up" in his previous specialty. As a coordinator of specialists in many fields, however, it is particularly important that he learn something about a large number of technical fields. This "something" should not be the specialized knowledge of the expert. It should rather be the broader "knowledge about" that

will help coordinate experts, encourage their personal growth, and evaluate their performance. It should help him see the potentialities of new techniques as they emerge, while protecting the organization against faddism and the expert's frequent proclivity for the "oversell."

3. Jobs and organizations. An administrator must know the requirements of his job and the structure and operations of the organization. Indeed, the more responsible his role, the more he must learn about many jobs and many organizations, particularly those in his own organization's immediate environment. Moreover, "what" he knows, as the novitiate quickly learns, may not be as important as "whom" he knows.

4. Administrative concepts and theories. It is particularly important that administrators acquire something more than tacit knowledge concerning organizations and their management. They should become familiar with the growing set of explicit concepts in the language of modern administrative thought, with the diverse and rapidly expanding body of currently useful generalizations, and with the major values that govern administrative behavior. A bare minimum may be found in the major elements in the emerging consensus in administrative thought, as set forth in Part I of this book. A more desirable—and more useful—level of knowledge is outlined by the basic ideas in Part II on environment, in Part III on structure, in Part IV on performance and Part V on administrative processes.

5. Self-knowledge. An experienced teacher of administration indicates that a major objective of one of his courses is "a greater understanding of one's self. This includes an awareness of the typical defenses we use to protect ourselves from threats . . . it also means an awareness of what one's impact is on other people" (Tannenbaum, in Summer, p. 29).

Knowledge of this type is not easy to come by. Even with the help of a psychoanalyst, many aspects of self-knowledge may be fully beyond one's reach. What one thinks one knows about one's self may range anywhere from supposition to delusion. Yet for all its difficulties the effort to attain some degree of self-knowledge is essential to attaining knowledge of the behavior of others. The understanding of one's own biases is the first step in attaining objectivity. The understanding of one's own limitations is a prerequisite for acquiring additional knowledge, abilities, and interests.[2]

B. *ABILITIES*

In an extremely general sense, we may say that administrators should acquire the ability to overcome internal and external obstacles and get

---

2. Mental health has been defined, in part, as the recognition and acceptance of one's own limits (*Levinson et al*, p. 193-195).

the members of an organization to work together in formulating and achieving certain purposes. More specifically, they should be able to guide action toward all the purposes in the global matrix. Still more specifically, they should acquire abilities in decision-making, communicating, planning, activating, and evaluating. This list could be elaborated still further by developing the high points in each of these processes (which has been done in Part V).

To avoid endless lists of desirable abilities, we shall concentrate instead on certain minimum abilities underlying effective participation in all the administrative processes.

1. *Working with others.* Because of the obvious nature of this particular ability there is an unfortunate tendency to regard it as something single-faceted .and invariable. This ability is often dependent upon the kinds of "working" and of "others." Some people are better able to work with others on an individual basis—as a superior, subordinate, or colleague. Some are able to subordinate themselves in the way necessary to be useful members of a work team. Some can work well only with certain types of people. In any case, the ability to work with others does not always come naturally. When it does, it can always be developed to higher levels. Wisdom in this area can probably be achieved only by genuine understanding of others and interest in them.

2. *Handling conflict.* To work with others for a sustained period of time, a person must be able to withstand the stresses of inevitable friction. The administrator, however, must be able to do more than merely absorb punishment in a passive fashion. He must be able to *handle* conflict. This means making decisions or standing by them under situations of personal stress. At the very least, it means skill in avoidance and compromise. At best, it means art or wisdom in resolving conflicts through integration.

3. *Intuitive thought.* Many specific abilities enter into the arts of decision-making. Of these considerable attention is often focused on conceptual and analytic ability. Conceptual ability makes it possible for the administrator to make fine distinctions between situations that might superficially appear identical. Analytic ability makes it possible for him to see a problem in its broader aspects and break it into its component parts. Both provide the solid basis required for the exercise of intuition and the checking of its results. Yet overemphasis upon either can detract attention, as Bruner has pointed out, from the development of effectiveness in intuitive thinking. "Intuition implies the act of grasping the meaning, significance or structure of a problem or situation without explicit reliance on the analytic apparatus of one's craft. The rightness or wrongness of an intuition is finally decided not by intuition itself but by the usual methods of proof. It is the intuitive mode, however, that yields hypotheses

quickly, that hits on combinations of ideas before their worth is known" (Bruner, 1962, p. 60). Bruner goes on to call for much more research on intuitive processes in various fields and in ways of encouraging them.

This objective of promoting intuitive thinking is increasingly recognized in the teaching of mathematics and physics. In administration, where greater uncertainties must be dealt with and the tools of analysis are weaker, this objective is still more important. Without intuitive thinking administrative decision-making can never get beyond mere skill and reach the heights of art, judgment and wisdom.

4. Communication. The great value of the study of literary classics, an important aspect of preentry education under the Confucian, English, and Indian civil service systems, has been their contribution to skills of verbal and written expression. Contemplation of this subject has led Drucker to the following observation:

> The only tool whereby managers get people to do things is the use of words and numbers. Managers have to learn to know language, to understand what words are and what they mean. Perhaps most important, they have to require respect for language as man's most precious gift and heritage. The manager must understand the meaning of the old definition of rhetoric as "the art which draws men's heart to the love of true knowledge." Without ability to motivate by means of the written and spoken word or the telling number, a manager cannot be successful (1954, p. 346).

More specifically, administrators and would-be administrators need to learn how to communicate—both orally and in writing—complex, new or unpleasant information to different types of recipients. This ability goes far beyond the arts of self-expression. As outlined in the discussion of aids to communication in Part V, it includes the ability to repress, as well as express, one's views as one learns to listen to others and empathize with them.

5. Learning. As organizations and their problems change, the administrator's own pattern of change must have some relationship to his changing environment. He should learn to see things and react in new and different ways. He should be able to learn from his own experience (particularly his mistakes) and from the observation of others. Above all, he should unlearn whatever skills he has acquired in avoiding learning. He should strive to learn the art and wisdom of learning.

C. *INTERESTS*

The development of interests is probably the most fundamental form of learning. A person's interests are the most dynamic factors in motivation. They guide and structure the acquisition of knowledge and abilities. They are the keys to a person's personality and attitudes.

1. Action-orientation. Some people are more interested in thought or contemplation rather than other forms of action, in preparation for decisions rather than making decisions. This is particularly true of many intellectuals, professionals, and people of academic bent. It is the limitation of many a staff adviser, armchair generalist and remote-control adviser. Such people can become effective administrators only if they develop a direct interest in a more active life. In some situations, this may mean turning one's back on intellect and contemplation. Yet the extent to which this is true will usually be exaggerated by "practical men" glorifying their own limitations. In some situations the best administrators are those who have learned to synthesize their interests in both thought and action.

2. Self-confidence. The ideal administrator is probably one whose interests in survival, commergence, and self-development are so well satisfied that he may concentrate upon self-development. Short of this ideal, it is particularly important that administrators still fighting for security, acceptance, prestige, and power feel reasonably confident in their ability to keep up the fight. In negative terms self-confidence may be defined as freedom from the inner sense of self-contempt, inadequacy, or guilt. In positive terms it implies self-respect. This is quite different from complacency or braggadocio, either of which may be the external expression of an inner lack of confidence. The overwhelming importance of self-confidence is that without it an administrator cannot stand up to the rigors of decision-making in the face of change and opposition. Without it, he cannot have sufficient confidence in others to encourage the self-development of subordinates, stand up to superiors, and cooperate with colleagues.

3. Responsibility. More than most other people, administrators must also learn to accept responsibility *for* certain actions and *to* certain people. Both dimensions of responsibility are rooted in self-confidence. But they go beyond one's attitudes toward self; they are also based upon attitudes toward others. Nothing can be less responsible than the "me first—law of the jungle" approach. To avoid this extreme does not require going to the other extreme of self-effacement or self-abasement. Fundamentally, administrators can learn to be more responsible only by broadening their interests and adjusting them to the interests of others. The most responsible administrators are those who try to guide an organization toward serving the interests of members through actions that satisfy broad public interests as well.

Chapter 28

WORK–EDUCATION COMBINATIONS

ONE OF THE MORE significant trends in modern society is the gradual blurring of the dividing line between work and education. Work is coming to demand continuous education, while education is coming to be seen not as preparation for life, but as a way of living.

In administrative education closer relations between work and education are particularly important. The kinds of learning discussed in the previous section cannot be attained through formal schools or the "school of experience" alone. Both are required. Each has a distinctive contribution to make to the development of administrators.

To make their distinctive contribution, considerable effort is needed to narrow the gap that often exists between the two. Otherwise, the learning in schools will be too remote from the necessities of organizational life and the pressure of daily work will impede the learning that can take place only on the job.

A. IN SCHOOLS

A major role of schools—whether formal educational institutions or special schools set up by other organizations—is to help people acquire administrative concepts and theories. This can often best be done by asking learners to apply them to (or discuss them in) typical situations faced by administrators. This may help them develop the entire range of desired knowledge, abilities and interests.

1. Vicarious experiences. The case study is the traditional method of bringing into the classroom a representation of a "slice of life." In essence, a case study is a written description of an event or series of events in the life of an organization. It deals with specific people, facts and situations. At times, a succession of cases is used to provide the illustrative "flesh and blood" for lectures and discussions that would otherwise be unduly abstract. At times, they are used to confront students with a mass of unstructured problems that they must try to cope with on their own. In many business administration schools cases have been used to help students to develop abilities to analyze problems, recognize their own limitations, cooperate with others, express themselves orally and in writing, and take a responsible attitude toward their own learning processes. Other purposes, as indicated by one of the pioneers in preparing public administration cases, may be "to show the difficulties of applying textbook principles to real-life situations, to develop an understanding of the commingling in real life of factors which are usually studied as separate subjects in universities, to use life materials for better understanding of existing theory, and to convey substantive knowledge" (Bock, p. 95).

While case studies provide for the verbal representation of administrative experience, role playing offers a more active form of vicarious experience. Various members of a group (which may include the teacher as well as students) step into the defined roles of various individuals in a specific case. They then continue the case in their own way. For the observers this technique can bring abstract cases and problems to life in a vivid and unforgettable manner. It demonstrates a delicate variety of human actions and reactions, thereby approaching some of the insights into human nature that are otherwise attainable only through drama and literature. For the participants it can be even more meaningful. It provides a vehicle for trying out one's abilities in an environment in which one can accept critical comment more readily than in real life. It is an excellent device to help people comprehend the views of others—particularly when "role reversal" and "role rotation" are used.

A more highly structured form of role playing is provided by the management game. This technique places a number of people before a given problem (usually involving competition or conflict) and provides a set of rules through which their relative performance may be judged. Historically, it derives from the "war games" extensively developed by nineteenth- and twentieth-century armies. It has been more recently adapted to business administration.

The great advantages of the management game lie in its potential for providing (a) a true-to-life simulation of complex situations, (b) a series of problems in which every decision has an effect upon subsequent problems, (c) emphasize upon the use of strategy and tactics under conditions of pressure, and (d) a high degree of personal involvement and motivation (Cohen and Rhenman, 1961). The use of computers in certain business games has made it possible to handle large masses of quantitative information more rapidly than would otherwise be possible. Their overuse has also led to an overstructuring and overnarrowing of the games.

The further development of management games can lead to the maturation of a teaching instrument which will be as indispensable in administrative education as mock battles are to armies. Business games can be broadened to include problems of internal organization and human relations as well as market competition. Exciting games can be developed to cover almost any aspect of public administration.

2. Field studies. The field study takes the student out of the classroom and places him as a direct observer of organizational behavior and administrative problems. Although what is observed may be less detailed and multisided than what is provided on a silver platter by the carefully-prepared case, it is by virtue of this very fact less synthetic. Moreover, if enough time and resources are allocated, a field study may penetrate a situation far more deeply than a carefully-prepared case.

Field studies also provide excellent links with personal organizational experience. In internship programs an intern's work may consist of a special field study for the organization to which he is assigned. Or else, upon return to formal studies, he might prepare a study linked with his work experience. Also, one of the greatest challenges for experienced administrators is to prepare comparative studies on the operations of their own organizations. Empirical studies of this type may well become the basis of formal theses submitted in fulfillment of requirements for advanced university degrees.

B. *ON THE JOB*

In operating their own schools for administration, many noneducation organizations, uninhibited by frozen academic traditions, have often pioneered in using the above methods to bring practical problems into the classroom. Yet sometimes their interest in formal classroom types of training has diverted them from the important task of enhancing the all-important learning opportunities more closely associated with regular work.

1. Internships. The most intimate combination between work and education is often provided by internship for young people. In its purest form, internship gives work experience before the completion of a formal educational program (as with student teachers and social workers) or, if a degree is actually given, before full acceptance as a qualified professional (as with medical interns and law clerks). In either there is some extent of qualified supervision over the intern's work, together with the possibility of disqualification for those whose performance is substandard.

In its looser forms internships may also be provided without any tie-up with an educational organization or responsible supervisors. In these forms (as often developed for purposes of training in government) they are more to be regarded as supplements to formal education than as something integrally related to it.

A "sandwich" program is a more advanced form of internship. It provides for recurrent periods of work experience interwoven with recurrent periods of formal education. Because of the intricacies of operation, however, this program is rare and has thus far been confined to general or technical, as distinguished from administrative, education.

2. Job rotation. The rotation of younger people from one position to another probably started in dynastic organizations in which heirs and "crown princes" were moved around from one position to another in order to prepare them for future rule. It has been most highly developed by the "elite corps" personnel systems of armies, foreign services, and the general civil service of various countries. Negatively, it has the advantage of not being dependent upon the teaching activities of supervisors; a good man can learn something from bad superiors also. Positively, rotation may provide a great variety of experiences from which one may learn. It may get one out of the rut of established positions and routines. It may develop a self-image of resilience, adaptability, and initiative, and skills and attitudes adapted to dealing with the unknown and the unexpected.

Some people, of course, will learn little more from rotation than would a spinning ball. Hence the success of such a program depends upon considerable care in the selection of personnel and in the planning of their various movements from post to post.[1] It also implies a rather large-scale operation and high degree of central power in the hands of those who handle the routine machinery. In more mobile societies, however, the more mobile individuals may reap the advantages of rotation through their own unsupervised perambulations.

3. Coaching. With or without rotation, people can learn more on the job when their superiors consciously coach them in the arts of administra-

---

1. Unfortunately, there is a serious lack of either theoretical or empirical studies of the operation of "elite corps" personnel systems. The problems of operating rotation systems—and the alternative patterns of variation in job experiences—have therefore not been explored in an across-the-board fashion.

tion. "The supervisor has dual responsibilities; on the one hand he has the administrative responsibility to see that the agency work is carried out; on the other hand, he has a teaching responsibility to help those whom he supervises to carry out their jobs with ever-increasing competence" (Committee on Social Work Organization and Personnel, 1958, p. 1). This quotation comes from an organization striving toward professional standards of administration in the field of social work. With but a minor rephrasing to clarify the point that teaching responsibility is *part* of administrative responsibility (rather than something parallel to it), it is applicable to any type of organization.

In coaching, the supervisor does more than merely help a subordinate perform his job with ever-increasing competence. The coach's aim is to help someone else exploit his potentialities as a self-developing individual. He gives his subordinate increasing opportunities to perform difficult tasks on his own. This usually involves tasks that are far enough beyond the subordinate's capacity to break him down. It also involves enough counselling to help the subordinate keep afloat but not enough to save him the painful effort of self-propulsion and self-instruction (Mace).

4. "Refresher" and "retooling" programs. In professional fields it is now recognized that people whose formal studies ended a long time ago cannot catch up with modern development without concentration possible only in an atmosphere of fulltime study. Hence "refresher" courses for doctors, schoolteachers, engineers, and others. For some people the difference between what they already have learned and what they should be expected to learn is so great that the harsh term "retooling" is probably more appropriate.

In the earlier executive development programs it was thought that the refreshing and retooling process could be initiated in seminars lasting from two to thirteen weeks. The fact that initiation does not guarantee a full-blown continuation of the process is reflected in the eager response of past participants to take part in occasional "reunions" or "follow-up seminars."

The next important phase in the maturation of executive development programs will be the staged series of seminars or courses. These will be based on the principle that every administrator should have the opportunity to accelerate his learning processes through intensive participation at least once every two years in a teaching program outside his own organization. They will be geared to the needs of different levels, from those who have not yet assumed administrative responsibilities to the top executives and members of directorates, and of different types of organizations and administrators. They will provide recurring opportunities for the reflective thought which is needed for someone to consolidate, and learn from, his own experiences.

C. *ADVANCEMENT-LEARNING LINKS*

We have referred above to the *opportunity* to accelerate one's learn-ing processes through the teaching programs of educational organizations. It is now relevant to emphasize the administrator's *responsibility* for the continuous improvement of his knowledge, abilities, and interests through exploitation of all available learning opportunities. An important objective of administrative education should be to develop a set of rather sophisti-cated expectations concerning the learning processes of one's self and others.

The crucial expectation is that *an individual's progress within an organization should be at least partially dependent upon his progress in learning.* The crystalization of this expectation, and its embodiment in practices with respect to job assignment, promotions and recruitment, can have a tremendously invigorating effect upon the intensity and direction of individual motivations to learn.

The principle of advancement-learning linkage, however, cannot be translated into any universally applicable formula. In some circumstances it is wise to prescribe certain academic degrees as the basis for increased responsibility or salary—as in public school systems and universities. With the maturation of executive development programs in universities and the modernization of tradition-bound approaches to academic degrees, this method should also be experimented with in connection with administra-tive posts.

In other circumstances it is more suitable to provide for "barrier tests" that must be passed before promotion. In military organizations these are usually tied in with the formal teaching programs of officer training schools. In the case of flight crews for airlines and air forces this is done through careful checkups on the quality of individual performance under defined conditions. Here the care invested in these tests stems from the physical dangers to life and property that can result from low-quality performance. In the case of administrators generally the dangers are less obvious—but are serious enough to warrant efforts at equally careful testing.

The disadvantage of relying upon completion of formal courses is that degrees, certificates, and grades do not provide an adequate indication of what a person has really learned. The disadvantage of actual or simu-lated tests is that they are usually too limited in scope. The firmest link between individual learning and individual progress can probably be pro-vided when the two methods are combined in an atmosphere which en-courages individual growth and creativity for their own sake.

Chapter 29

THE ASCENT OF
ADMINISTRATIVE TEACHING

*I*N EMPHASIZING THE PRIMACY of objectives for learning and the importance of work-education combinations, our purpose has not been to denigrate the work of teachers.

On the contrary! Within this framework it is easier to appreciate the strategic role of the teacher. The possibility of a revolutionary increase in the quality as well as the quantity of administrative education depends largely upon the future quantity of high quality teachers both in educational organizations and in the "school of experience." This in turn requires an acceleration of present trends toward professional teaching, the development of practitioner-teachers and the recognition of administration itself as a teaching-learning process.

A. *THE PROFESSIONAL TEACHER*

Like administration, teaching is an emerging rather than a fully developed profession. It is not yet based upon a strong enough body of organized knowledge, codes of ethics that clearly recognize obligations to students, or organizations clearly devoted to the promotion of professional standards.

In institutions of higher education the professional approach to teach-

627

ing is usually at its lowest point. "In the faculties of major universities in the United States today, the evaluation of performance is based almost exclusively on publication of scholarly books or articles in professional journals as evidence of research activity." Although hired and paid to teach, the university teacher is rarely encouraged to improve his teaching performance. In fact, there is a tendency "for his superiors to punish successful performance of the tasks for which he is hired" (*Caplow and McGee*, p. 83, 221). In many other countries the teaching aspects of a professor's activities are given even less attention. This neglect is generally rationalized by the fallacious argument that a good or outstanding researcher (whether judged by the volume of publication or by more meaningful tests) is *ipso facto* a good or outstanding teacher. The fact that there is a grain of truth in this over-simplification does not render it any more valid than the fallacy that a good specialist must be *ipso facto* a good administrator.

Like administration, teaching cannot become an all-encompassing profession. It also is tangential. A professional approach to teaching has no meaning except in relation to what the teacher is helping students to learn. A professional teacher must be wedded both to teaching and to his subject matter. Hence the professional teaching of administration requires a "double professionalism." The teacher must have a professional approach to both administration and teaching. He must try to "keep up" in both fields and advance the development of each.

One of the signal achievements of university teachers of administration during recent decades has been the impetus they have given to the advent of this double professionalism.

While dedicated to the promotion of professional administration, many of them have also given an unprecedented amount of time to the improvement of instructional techniques. Still greater progress will be made when the teachers of administration recognize more clearly the primacy of learning and the teacher's role in helping learners orient themselves toward knowledge-ability-interest objectives.

To promote active and responsible learning by others, the professional teacher of administration must himself be actively engaged in learning. The excitement of learning cannot be imparted to others by teachers who have come to "the end of the road." Rather, it is spread by contact with teachers who themselves are trying to acquire more or better knowledge, abilities, and interests. Research may be an important part of this effort. But it would be a very limited viewpoint that saw research as the only opportunity for learning by teachers and neglected the fact that teaching itself may be a way of learning. One of the oldest truths in education is that teaching a subject may be the best way to learn it. The most professional teaching of administration is done by teachers who see their teaching as a positive contribution to their own learning processes.

There are three key aspects to learning about administration by teaching it. First of all, working with people of varied administrative experience provides any teacher with invaluable opportunities to benefit from their experience and insights. One of the great byproducts of executive development programs, in fact, has been their educational impact upon academic teaching staffs.

Second, pre-entry teaching presents the teacher with a formidable challenge. To help inexperienced students learn something about administration, a teacher must do more than keep "one chapter ahead." He must be really good—like the modern mathematics teacher who brings the theory of numbers into the elementary school. He cannot rely upon the fuzzy ideas that will serve in dealing with people who already know something about the subject. If he is to be at all effective, he must push forward on the frontiers of administrative concept formation and theory.

Finally, he can learn about learning and teaching. Every course and classroom in administration is itself an experimental laboratory. Here the creative teacher can set out to perfect old methods and develop new ones.

These opportunities for learning by teaching provide the link between the teacher's personal interests and those of the students. If teaching serves the teacher's interest merely as a form of self-expression before a captive audience or of self-aggrandizement at the expense of a cornered set of scapegoats, it can scarcely serve the student's interests. Nor can these interests be well served by a humbler-than-thou attempt at self-effacement. The best incentive for creative student learning is the opportunity to work with a teacher eager to exploit student learning processes in order to learn more himself about both subject and method.

B. *THE PRACTITIONER-TEACHER*

In well-established professions the teachers are themselves practitioners. Medical students are taught by doctors. Law students are taught by lawyers. There is something shocking about the idea that medicine or law could be taught by teachers without practical experience. The professional immaturity of administrative teaching, in contrast, is indicated by the fact that many teachers of administration are completely lacking in administrative experience and even in organizational experience outside the halls of Academia.

A share of the blame for this sad situation may be placed upon administrators themselves. It is they, above all others, who tolerate its continuation. They often become so embedded in their own rut that they never gain a broader sense of social responsibility. Or else their own standards of competence are so low that they are willing to go along with the outworn idea that good administrators can be developed by experience alone.

Yet no matter how one chooses to explain the present unfortunate situation, the future requirements are clear. The teachers of administration must include many more practitioners. They must be people who have had direct personal experience in organizations other than schools and who have shouldered significant administrative responsibilities. The more varied and intensive this experience, the better.

There are two corollaries to this. First, educational organizations seriously interested in the future of administrative education must look more and more to seasoned administrators as members of their teaching staffs. This does not mean that experience itself is a sufficient qualification. Many practitioners lack the desired breadth of interests and theoretical grasp. It does mean that practitioners with these qualities must be given ample opportunities for full-time, part-time, or recurrent service in teaching and research posts.

Second, the administrator-teachers who enter academic life must never be allowed to become too long or too far removed from involvement in the activity of other organizations. Like Antaeus, they will lose their power if unable to get their feet back to the ground.

C. *ADMINISTRATION AS TEACHING AND LEARNING*

This chapter has thus far given too much attention to the teaching that goes on in educational organizations. We shall now try to redress the balance by returning, in these final words, to the teachers in the school of experience.

One point of view toward the difference between the school of experience and the educational organization is expressed in Bernard Shaw's classic witticism "Those who can, do. Those who can't, teach." It is still true, unfortunately, that many of those who teach administration could not administer anything. But if one refers to high-quality administrative action, the Shavian barb must be tempered. Those who act most effectively as administrators do so in part *by* teaching.

This does not mean that the teacher-administrators consciously see themselves as such. The school of experience is still the school with the largest number of teachers who are not clearly aware of their teaching roles. Intuitively, however, most administrators know that they cannot get organizational action by orders alone. They give more instruction than instructions. They activate people by assisting them in the learning process.

But we can no longer afford to let the learning process in the school of experience take care of itself. We should no longer tolerate the failure of teachers in the school of experience to recognize their role or give it but a partial measure of devotion. We must expect administrators themselves to take the initiative in the teaching of administration, just as doctors and lawyers have taken the initiative in building medical and law schools. In doing this, administrators should demand assistance from educational organizations and volunteer their services as administrator-teachers. Yet they must remember that the formal school is merely an accessory and support to the school of experience. They should operate on the principle that organizational action is a process of continual learning. They should learn continually improved methods of promoting this process. Above all, they must themselves set an example of continual learning. They must recognize that when an administrator thinks he has learned enough or is no longer capable of learning more, he is ready for retirement.

Educational organizations can also contribute to this process. In past decades they have often ignored the subject of administration. Or else, with the rising flood of administrative teaching, they have tilled the narrow gulleys of staff services, techniques, and procedures or danced on the mountaintops of high policy. Without excluding these matters, the central task of schools of administrative education is to help build the image of the administrator as the person who guides an organization's activity. This they cannot do if they presume that their own distinctive role in research and theory confers upon them some mystic monopoly over administrative teaching. One of their central contributions to the creation of the new profession of administration will be to help their students learn that every administrator must also be a teacher.

As noted in *Managing of Organizations*,[1] the onward sweep of the administrative revolution means ever-greater complexity in the operations and interactions of organizations and ever-changing rates of change in various aspects of both. The future of administrative society, therefore, rests to a large degree upon the learning processes of the administrators of large-scale organizations and their ability to learn the multiple roles of Doer and Teacher. If their rate of learning is too slow or the pattern of learning is askew, there will be little prospect of achieving organizational democracy and professional administration. The future will be one of organizational regimentation more than organizational individualism, national drift rather than national purpose, and an international holocaust instead of an international community.

1. "The Challenge of the Administrative Society" (Chap. 3).

Centuries ago in a far simpler world a great philosopher saw a vision of the day when philosophers would be kings. "Until philosophers are kings, or the kings and princes of this world have the spirit and power of philosophy, and political greatness and wisdom meet in one . . . cities will never have rest from their evils—no, nor the human race, as I believe. . . ."

The day envisioned by Plato never came. Nor have his kings survived. Their power has been dispersed among the myriad administrators of organizations.

But the idea of the philosopher-king can be restated today in the more feasible ideal of the administrator-teacher. Already, the men and women who guide thousands of today's organizations are people whose powers stem from understanding, wisdom, and breadth of interests. We have reason to hope that they may become more confident in their "voluntary management of voluntary bipeds," and that their number may increase. To the extent that this should happen, the human race will not have rest from all evils. But it can only benefit from the tremendous power for good—far greater than that emanating from fission or fusion of the atom —that is released by the self-propelled learning of self-developing men and women.

A BIBLIOGRAPHICAL REPORT

RESEARCH STUDIES IN
ORGANIZATIONAL BEHAVIOR

*T*HIS REPORT PROVIDES a bird's-eye view of efforts to learn about organizations and their administration by analyzing organizational behavior. It does this by (1) identifying about 150 research studies in organizational behavior, (2) indicating the major dimensions of each study,[1] and (3) in most cases, summarizing findings or conclusions. It thereby provides a substantive backup for the many places in the text where reference is made to these specific studies.

The citations included in the report have been obtained by searching the published literature of sociology, anthropology, psychology, economics, political science, public administration, and business administration. This includes a canvass of most English-language professional journals in these fields from 1940 through 1962.

In assembling these citations no study has been regarded as dealing with organizational behavior if confined only to (a) the interactions among organizations, without looking at their inner structure, (b) the results of an organization's activities, as revealed in the balance sheets of a business enterprise, the policies of a government, or the decisions of a

---

1. For a brief summary of the major dimensions dealt with, or neglected, by these studies see pages 848-853 in "The Emergence of Administrative Science" (Gross, *The Managing of Organizations*, Chapt. 31).

court, (c) the formal constitutions, charters or rules of organizations, (d) loose aggregations of organizations or broad systems such as a country's "public service" or a society as a whole, or (e) the opinions or attitudes of organization members, without linking such opinions or attitudes to some aspect of actual behavior. Moreover, in the interest of feasibility, it has been necessary to (a) exclude the thousands of case studies prepared primarily for research purposes, (b) exclude the untold numbers of studies (mostly unavailable) prepared primarily to help improve performance in specific organizations or as a means of external control over them, (c) include only those organizational histories written with a clear orientation to problems of organization and administration, (d) include studies

Organizational Type	Articles	Books	Total
I. *Business (excluding research)*			
Goods	114	42	156
Services	28	12	40
Outside U.S.A.	27	9	36
Total	169	63	232
II. *Government (excluding Education, Health, Research)*			
Ch. Exec., Central Coord.	3	7	10
Military	42	9	51
Civilian	42	27	69
Outside U.S.A.	9	3	12
International	3	1	4
Total	99	47	146
III. *Public Service*			
Education	18	6	24
Health	48	10	58
Social Work	3	2	5
Total	69	18	87
IV. *Associations*			
Trade Unions	28	10	38
Political Action	13	9	22
Trade and Prof.	0	2	2
Frat., Cult.	5	1	6
Religious	2	2	4
Coops	3	2	5
Total	51	26	77
V. *Research*	17	5	22
VI. *Cross-type Comparisons*	11	1	12
Total	416	160	576

of experimental groups only when set up as part of an organization's regular operations, and (e) include only a small portion of empirical studies in the behavior of legislatures and political parties. Exclusion is not meant to imply lack of relevance. A careful sifting through of the data and conclusions in these five areas would unquestionably add considerably to generally available knowledge of organizational behavior.

Each citation includes at least the major dimensions of organizational or administrative behavior covered by the researcher. In ţhe case of books and extremely detailed journal articles, minor dimensions have been omitted. In this sense the report is an annotated bibliography.

Most of the citations go still further and indicate the major findings and conclusions. In this sense the report is a set of abstracts. Where findings or conclusions are too extensive for a brief summation (as in many of the books) or where their significance may seem limited, less detail is provided.

It should be noted that there are always alternative ways of classifying or referring to the subject matter or findings of any research study. Information is invariably retrieved in terms of the kinds of information in which one is interested. In this report the "sieve" is provided by the concepts used throughout the text.

In the preparation of this bibliographical report, 576 documents were abstracted—416 journal articles and 160 books. Of these only a little more than a quarter—those directly referred to in the various chapters of this book—are included in this report. Yet the total number is significant, since it shows how large this field of research has grown. Moreover, the distribution of these studies by type of organization—as shown on the previous page—indicates the areas that have received the most attention and those that have been relatively neglected.

Anderson, Theodore R., and Seymour Warkov. "Organizational Size and Functional Complexity: A Study of Administration in Hospitals," *American Sociological Review*. Vol. 26, 1961, p. 23-27.
The relative size of the administrative component of veterans administration hospitals (1) decreased as total size of the organization increased, (2) increased with increasing organizational complexity as measured by number of places and tasks in the organization.

Arensberg, Conrad, and Douglas MacGregor. "Determination of Morale in an Industrial Company," *Applied Anthropology*. Vol. 1, 1942, p. 12-34.
Design engineers of company that designed and manufactured electrical measuring instruments felt that as a result of changes in organizational structure necessitated by company growth, they were too much supervised, too much subjugated to sales policy, and too little consulted.

Argyris, Chris. *Impact of Budgets on People*. Ithaca: School of Business and Public Administration, Cornell University Press, Controllership Foundation, 1952.
Inherent problems of budget-making process and its observed effects on supervisors and workers of departments who were recipients of the budgets and on members of budget departments themselves. Suggestions how some of the difficulties created by budget-making might be avoided by prior consultation and acceptance.

Argyris, Chris. *Executive Leadership*. New York: Harper, 1953.
Description of an industrial leader by himself and by an observer, with reactions of twenty supervisors to the leader's behavior. The plant employed six hundred people and produced custom-made products. Highly successful behavior pattern of leader who interacted frequently with supervisors, kept them separate from each other in their relation to him and dependence on him, controlled transmission of important information, set realistic goals. Effect on supervisors was to increase their dependence on leader for the six organization processes of reward and penalty, authority, communication, identification, perpetuation, and workflow. Although certain amount of such dependence is intrinsic in subordinate-leader relationship, extent of dependence relates to whether leader is more or less "participative." As organization became more successful and tension decreased, leader became more relaxed in his behavior to supervisors, interacted less, and encouraged more independence.

Argyris, Chris. "The Fusion of an Individual with the Organization," *American Sociological Review*. Vol. 19, 1954, p. 267-272.
Comparison of two departments of bank in a middle Atlantic city. Those meeting the public and working self-sufficiently have lower personal expression and organizational fusion than those in department with strong informal relationships, even though management frowned upon the informal relationships.

Argyris, Chris. "The Individual and Organization: An Empirical Test," *Administrative Science Quarterly*. Vol. 4, 1959, p. 145-167.
Pride in quality and interest in work, less spoilage, less emphasis on money, and more on-job friendships found directly related to skill of workers. Creation of informal employee culture modified organization appreciably.

Argyris, Chris. *Understanding Organizational Behavior*. Homewood, Ill.: Dorsey Press, 1960.
Plants X and Y, roughly similar plants of a large corporation, each with low- and high-skill subsystems, studied for informal employee culture, psychological predispositions, and morale of employees and foremen, before and after introduction of tightening-up procedures by management. These studies presented together with detailed methodological discussion to illustrate techniques of analyzing organizational behavior.

Babchuk, Nicholas. "Work Incentives in a Self-Determined Group," *American Sociological Review*. Vol. 16, 1951, p. 679-687.
Well integrated, stable eighteen-member selling unit in a mens' clothing department of a Detroit department store disrupted by new wage system creating differentials. Resultant sales grabbing and interference lowered morale, but group's own system of pooling sales and distributing commission re-established high morale.

Baker, H., and R. R. France. *Centralization and Decentralization in Industrial*

Relations. Princeton: Princeton University Press, Department of Economics and Sociology, 1954.

Majority of chief executives in 135 companies favored decentralized management in local plants to gain efficiency, better adjustment to local conditions, clear personnel responsibility and better personnel relations. Those who opposed it stressed uniformity and economy as benefits of centralization. Industrial relations managers preferred a variable balance between these extremes in light of specific conditions. Union officials preferred centralization (and executives disliked it) in collective bargaining.

Bakke, E. Wight. *Bonds of Organization: An Appraisal of Corporate Human Relations.* New York: Harper, 1950.

A representative sample of 1,022 management and employee respondents in fifteen local exchanges in the Southern New England Telephone Co. and the officers and members of the Connecticut Union of Telegraph Workers, the employees' union, interviewed in depth to determine their attitudes to five areas of the social system of the organizations or Bonds of Organization: (1) Functional Specifications, (2) Status System, (3) Communications System, (4) Reward and Penalty System and (5) the Organizational Charter. Formal and informal aspects with respect to each bond of organization are described and found to be not separable and subject to constant modifications, both formal and informal, by all the participants.

Banfield, Edward C. *Government Project.* New York: Free Press, 1951.

Failure of a government-sponsored attempt to rehabilitate about fifty unemployed families on a 4,000-acre cooperatively-run farm described historically. Root of failure held to be ceaseless struggle for power among settlers and between settlers and management. Other important factors: management's failure to understand psychological needs of settlers and concentration on economic factors; novelty of situation and lack of knowledge on all sides of how to act; and the lack of effective leadership, which was partly inherent in the economic inability of the government to pay for really good leadership.

Banfield, Edward. "Organization for Policy Planning in the U.S. Department of Agriculture," *Journal of Farm Economics.* Vol. 34, 1952, p. 14-34.

The succession of planning agencies established in Agriculture Department from 1939 to 1951 for the formulation of long-term departmental programs had little connection with actual policy-making and were in some instances rationalizations for failure to develop long-term programs.

Barnes, Louis B. *Organizational Systems and Engineering Groups: A Comparative Study of Two Technical Groups in Industry.* Boston: Graduate School of Business Administration, Harvard University Press, 1960.

Two small engineering departments of roughly similar size and purpose analyzed for similarities and differences in their effect on management and group member behavior. Major difference between relatively closed system in Department A—with autonomous activities discouraged, few opportunities for interaction and mutual influence; and relatively open system in Department B, which encouraged above factors. Reference group affiliations in each group determined by interview data and reinforced by Allport-Vernon Study of Values scores. High congruence of status factors studied in Department A reinforced effect of closed system and tended to reduce mutual influence and interaction; lower congruence in Department B reinforced opposite effect. So did formal organizational structure of each and the patterns of in-group competition and goal orientation.

Baumgartel, Howard. "Leadership, Motivation, and Attitudes in Research Laboratories," *Journal of Social Issues.* Vol. 12, 1956, p. 24-31.
Directive leadership of chiefs found less effective leadership pattern in twenty laboratories of large medical organization, resulting in subordinates with less sense of progress than under participatory leadership. Scientific performance and motivation of research chiefs influenced scientific motivation and sense of progress of subordinates but not attitudes toward chiefs. Attitudes influenced by chiefs' conformity to role preferences of subordinates.

Baumgartel, Howard. "Leadership Style as a Variable in Research Administration," *Administrative Science Quarterly.* Vol. 2, 1957, p. 344-360.
Attitudes and performance of scientists in twenty laboratories of research organization directly affected by leadership style, with participatory method resulting in higher research performance and motivation, more favorable attitudes towards laboratory director and freer feelings on part of workers. Laissez-faire leadership had lowest commitment to research, less progress and less favorable attitudes toward laboratory director, while laboratories under directive leadership relied on director for motivation and performance.

Becker, Howard S., Blanche Geer, Everett C. Hughes, and Anselm Strauss. *Boys in White: Student Culture in Medical School.* Chicago: University of Chicago Press, 1961.
Medical students at Kansas Medical School develop their own perspectives (not necessarily those of faculty) on how and what to study, what kind of clinical work is most important for them, what their future professional life will be, and what type of hospital in which to intern. The idealistic aim of students at beginning of medical school to learn "everything" slowly changed, first by fraternity affiliates, then by independents, to aim of "learning what the faculty wants." The aim of medical responsibility for patients is pursued throughout medical school and is deeply felt by both students and faculty.

Belknap, Ivan. *Human Problems of a State Mental Hospital.* New York: McGraw-Hill, 1956.
Primary responsibility of the state mental hospital for the custody of mentally ill and other mentally deficient and welfare patients seen as functioning at expense of psychotherapeutic function because of attendants' informal organization of those patients able to work. Frequent turnover of supervisory and medical staff, partly due to above situation resulting in ineffectual professional rewards, contributed to actual, as contrasted with nominal power of attendants over daily life and therapeutic treatment, if any, of patients.

Bennis, W. G., N. Berkowitz, M. Affinito, and M. Malone. "Authority, Power and the Ability to Influence," *Human Relations.* Vol. 11, 1958, p. 143-155.
Relationship between degree of influence and ability to control perceived and actual rewards and punishments, from a study of ninety nurses in six outpatient departments in a large Eastern city. Supervisors in hospitals with an effective reward system more influential with subordinates and successful in maintaining nurses in their jobs; where supervisors lacked control over reward systems, they were unable to exercise formal control over subordinates.

Berliner, Joseph S. *Factory and Manager in the USSR.* Cambridge: Harvard University Press, 1957.
From reports of refugees and published material on period 1938 to World War II, basic aim of Soviet factory managers to win premium for overfullment of production plan seen to be impossible to attain without continual violation of state laws, industrial regulations, and Party pronouncements. Such violations normally overlooked by inspectors because of vested interest in the achievement of the

factories they patrol. Inefficiencies engendered by violations served to counter the lack of realism in the official output targets.

Bidwell, Charles E. "The Young Professional in the Army: A Study of Occupational Identity," *American Sociological Review.* Vol. 26, 1961, p. 360-372.

The majority of eighty-four professional men drafted into the army were involved in role-set conflicts when they were given jobs with the minimal utilization of their training or that used them as technicians and did not recognize the civilian status of their professional training.

Blau, Peter M. "Patterns of Interaction among a Group of Officials in a Government Agency," *Human Relations.* Vol. 7, 1954, p. 337-348.

Agents rated by superiors as most competent among sixteen in department of government law enforcement agency were more integrated into interpersonal structure of department, were consulted more frequently by other agents, participated more widely in department meetings, and had more contact with people outside department than those rated less competent. The latter needed special effort to become integrated since unofficial status and quality of performance were closely related.

Blau, Peter M. *The Dynamics of Bureaucracy.* Chicago: University of Chicago Press, 1956.

Cohesion, effectiveness, and conflict among fifteen interviewers in a department of an Eastern state employment agency (1949). Performance, evaluation, cohesiveness, and informal procedures in lives of eighteen field agents in a department of a federal enforcement agency (1948). Functional and dysfunctional effects on the employment agency work of the preparation of periodic statistical reports of interviewers' work, such as competition among interviewers or lack of it, equitable treatment of clients, better relations between employees and supervisors, patterns of reciprocity with specialists who were given handicapped and difficult clients to handle. Investigators of the law-enforcing agency developed informal patterns of interaction and consultation among themselves, set up norms for time worked and refusal to take bribes, and in other ways reacted to formal lines of authority, annual civil service ratings by their supervisors, and the operations of the reviewing section.

Blau, Peter M. "Social Integration, Social Rank, and Processes of Interaction," *Human Organization.* Vol. 18, 1959, p. 152-157.

Frequency of received contacts among seventeen officials of federal agency positively related to (a) social rank as expert, (b) participation in discussion at meetings, (c) assuming a dominant role with colleagues, (d) extent of interaction with outsiders, and (e) detachment toward clients. Data on case workers in public welfare agency confirm only last two relations. Difference attributed to association of hierarchal rank with frequency of received contact in federal but not in welfare agency, and to greater identification with work and emphasis on procedural conformity in federal agency.

Brown, Wilfred. *Exploration in Management.* London: Heinemann, 1960.

Organizational structure, procedures and philosophy of Glacier Metal Company, London, as presented by its Chairman and Managing Director. The executive system of company is a social organization based on "an analysis of the work to be done and the techniques and resources available." It is supplemented by (1) a representative system which permits workers to participate in decision-making, (2) a legislative system consisting of shareholders, customers, representatives and executives, and (3) an appeals system.

Burling, Temple, Edith M. Lentz, and Robert N. Wilson. *The Give and Take In Hospitals*. New York: Putnam's, 1956.
Each department of a mixed group of general hospitals minutely analyzed to determine how it functions in itself, in relation to the hospital as a whole, and in relation to the patients and the outside community. As hospitals have grown in recent years, many structural and functional changes have occurred in each department which have mainly tended towards specialization, depersonalization and longer lines of communication. This tendency clashes with the necessity for very active widespread interrelations between the various departments. Those departments that, by the nature of their work (such as in laundries, or operating rooms), encourage teamwork and informal as well as formal cooperation, tend to have less turnover and be more desirable places to work. In other departments, special efforts by administrators accomplish the same thing.

Caplow, Theodore and Reece J. McGee. *The Academic Marketplace*. New York: Basic Books, 1958.
Department chairmen and faculty members of nine major universities indicated that prime criteria in filling 215 vacancies in two consecutive years were prestige and promise of prestige deriving from future publications, although professors were hired ostensibly to perform teaching functions. Patterns of mobility indicated generally high mobility in lower ranks, with mobility at higher levels linked with prestige of the institution. Hiring procedures reveal loosely defined power structures, power residing with those able to harness and wield it.

Carlson, Richard. "Succession and Performance Among School Superintendents," *Administrative Science Quarterly*. Vol. 6, 1961, p. 210-227.
Difference between "career centered" superintendents—who tend to succeed as "outsiders"—and "place centered" superintendents—who will be "insiders"—is seen, in the four districts studied, to affect performance, professional standing, salary level, and general outlook.

Caudhill, William. *The Psychiatric Hospital as a Small Society*. Cambridge: Harvard University Press, 1958.
Results of three studies of the fifty-bed Yale Psychiatric Institute on influence of the hospital on the doctor-patient relationship, problems of communication in administration, perceptions of the hospital among patients and staff, and the handling of administrative conferences. Overt informal and formal structure and covert emotional structure seen as variables affecting the functioning of this social system. Consideration given to the problem of multiple subordination and dual control, both administrative and therapeutic. The effect on patients of conflict between the two groups is clearly detrimental.

Chandler, Alfred D., Jr. *Strategy and Structure*. Cambridge: M.I.T. Press, 1962.
Case studies of long-range adaptation of formal structure to growth patterns in four companies (DuPont, General Motors, Standard Oil, N. J., and Sears Roebuck), with general survey of over seventy other industrial and merchandising corporations. Four historical phases revealed in case studies (1) the mobilization of resources through a loose combination or holding company, (2) consolidation into a centralized, vertically integrated, and functionally departmentalized structure, (3) product diversification and territorial expansion to employ resources partially or inadequately used, and (4) the creation of a decentralized structure with autonomous operating divisions and a central office confined to general planning and control. The fourth phase innovators were younger men with engineering backgrounds and experience outside as well as inside the firm. Their innovations were accepted only after crisis conditions and turnover of top management. The decentralized multidivisional structure has spread widely among large companies selling highly diverse products to differentiated groups of customers. Com-

panies with fewer markets and simpler marketing processes tend to maintain centralized, functionally departmentalized structures.

Cline, Ray S. *Washington Command Post: The Operations Division.* Washington: Department of the Army, 1951. (Part of series on United States Army in World War II.)
Transformation of the War Planning Division, which had been in existence for decades, into the Operations Division "charged with the preparation of strategic plans and coordination of operations throughout the world." Changing structure and functions of the OD, with specific case histories on the Bolero Plan for the defeat of Germany and planning the end of the war against Japan.

Coates, Charles H., and Roland J. Pellegrin. "Executives and Supervisors: Contrasting Self-Conceptions and Conceptions of Each Other," *American Sociological Review.* Vol. 22, 1957, p. 217-220.
Self-conceptions of fifty top-level executives in thirty large business, government, and educational institutions were largely favorable, with emphasis on decisiveness, aggressiveness, and an orientation toward reality. Fifty line supervisors in the same organizations generally saw the executives in the same terms, but supervisors saw themselves as handicapped in terms of training, education, and socioeconomic background, were seen by the executives as having less energy and initiative, being less alert, aggressive, and responsible.

Coch, Lester, and R. P. French, Jr. "Overcoming Resistance to Change," *Human Relations.* Vol. 1, 1947, p. 512-532.
Workers resisted job changes at the Harwood Manufacturing Co., Marion, Virginia, 1600-employee pajama factory, because of consequent large turnover. Experienced workers took longer to learn new jobs than new operators, lost hope of regaining former production rates on piecework pay scale. Experimental group method for instituting changes showed rate of recovery after production change directly proportional to workers' participation in change.

Covner, Bernard. "Management Factors Affecting Absenteeism," *Harvard Business Review.* Vol. 28, 1950, p. 42-48.
Employee absenteeism in thousand-employee manufacturing concern related to quality of supervision and size of department, with larger departments having greater absenteeism. No relationship found with poor work, age, sex of worker, or type of work, whether in office or factory.

Crockett, Walter H. "Emergent Leadership in Small, Decision-Making Groups," *Journal of Abnormal and Social Psychology.* Vol. 51, 1955, p. 378-383.
Leaders other than those officially designated emerged in seventy-two business, government, and industrial decision-making conferences when officially designated leaders did not set goals, seek information, and propose problems. Leaders emerged when cliques were present, and there was little congruence of motivation. Emergent leaders seen to be highly motivated, experienced, of high rank within larger organization, and well thought by other members of their group.

Cumming, Elaine, and John Cumming. "The Locus of Power in a Large Mental Hospital," *Psychiatry.* Vol. 19, 1956, p. 361-369.
The informal power structure of a 2,000-bed, state-supported mental hospital is one in which the formal authority of the medical staff is undermined by the power of the custodial staff, especially of those who control the distribution of scarce goods and services.

Dale, Ernest. *Planning and Developing the Company Organization Structure.* New York: American Management Association, 1952. Research Report Number 20.
Analysis of formal structure in seven companies ranging from very small to very large. A specific organizational problem identified at each size level: a small grocery store (3-7 employees), the division of work; a plastics corporation (25 employees), the accommodation of personalities; a machine tool company (125 employees), the span of control; an owner-manager company (500 employees), the staff assistant; a paper-board company (1,500 employees), the staff specialist; a steel company (5,000 employees), group decision-making; and an automobile company (450,000 employees), decentralization.

Dale, Ernest. *The Great Organizers.* New York: McGraw-Hill, 1960.
Major changes in formal organization of four large industrial corporations. Growth of Du Pont characterized by shift from "Caesar" management to group management, with increasing emphasis on scientific methods. General Motors structure developed by Alfred P. Sloan on basis of decentralized operations and centralized planning and control. National Steel built up by Ernest Weir with "egalitarian oligarchy" at top. Westinghouse Electric reorganized by A. W. Robertson on decentralized basis, with early use of flexible budgeting that allowed cost standards to vary with volume changes.

Dalton, Melville. "Conflict Between Staff and Line Management Officers," *American Sociological Review.* Vol. 15, 1950, p. 342-351.
Conflict between staff officials, responsible for research and used as advisers, and line officials, responsible for production, in three factories employing 4,500 to 20,000. Staff personnel ambitious, had high turnover, moved in different social circles than line officials. Staff expressed need for self-justification by suggesting improvements in production, but line officials jealously guarded their authority in production area.

Dalton, Melville. "Informal Factors in Career Achievement," *American Journal of Sociology.* Vol. 56, 1950-51, p. 407-415.
Selection and advancement through management hierarchy in careers of 225 salaried managers in a factory not dependent on age, years of service, or schooling but alleged by lower and middle level managers to be related to religion, national origin, and social and political affiliations. Most managers fulfilled many qualifications thought necessary for advancement by lower level managers, who were seen to advance themselves by conforming to patterns of behavior of upper levels.

Dalton, Melville. "Managing the Managers," *Human Organization.* Vol. 14, 1955, p. 4-10.
Informal means of implementing formal control recognized as necessary by central office executives and officials of individual unit of large corporations when (a) unit did not gear maintenance work with operations, since executives with equal formal rank but varying authority caused fluctuations in repair work completed, (b) department set up within unit to control maintenance work was unsuccessful, (c) central office took over control, but slowed up successful operation by too frequent interaction, and (d) informal actions of unit executives thwarted formal control of central office.

Dalton, Melville. *Men Who Manage.* New York: John Wiley, 1959.
Covert participant-observer of three industrial and one retailing organization showed how major recurring social problems of operation were threshed out by combinations of official and unofficial action, were involved in relations of advisory experts and line executives, were affected by (and affected) the priority of local interests over wider fealty in union-management affairs, the routes to

careers, and the task of distinguishing requital from theft in compensating exceptional help that cannot be officially recognized or rewarded. Individual managers could not escape some measure of internal conflict, since they were subject to mixture of frequently contradictory rational, emotional, social, and ethical claims. The "strong" or more effective and adaptive types contrasted with "weak" or more routinized and formal types in the extent to which each type helped to shape the role assigned formally and the multiple informal roles possible to him.

Davis, Arthur K. "Bureaucratic Patterns in the Navy Officer Corps," *Social Forces*. Vol. 27, 1948-49, p. 143-153.
Navy bureaucracy seen as having little function in peacetime, falling back on elaborate authority structure, written rules, ritual, and formality. Regulations followed rigorously as only defense of individual. Responsibility avoided and passed up through hierarchy, while work is passed down. Working and living areas close together, leads to families' involvement in social and ritual operations of bureaucracy.

Davis, F. James. "Conceptions of Official Leader Roles in the Air Force," *Social Forces*. Vol. 32, 1953-54, p. 253-258.
Leaders and their followers found to hold widely different conceptions of leader's roles at two nonflying Air Force posts. Followers held conceptions of roles of officially designated leaders based on factors other than follower adjustment.

Davis, Keith, and Edward E. St. Germain. "An Opinion Survey of a Regional Union Group," *Journal of Applied Psychology*. Vol. 36, 1952, p. 285-290.
Communication on day-to-day problems caused greatest worker dissatisfaction among members of A.F. of L. construction equipment operators' local. Members also dissatisfied with business agent's job assignments and local bargaining contract.

Devons, Ely. *Planning in Practice: Essays in Aircraft Planning in War-Time.* Cambridge: Cambridge University Press, 1950.
World War II planning activities in Britain's Ministry of Aircraft Production involved coordination among the production divisions of the ministry, other ministries, and the suppliers of aircraft and components. Plans were always products of conflicting forces and compromises between unrealistic targets and realistic estimates. Same figures often served as estimates of both requirements and production prospects. Huge margins of error in data were neglected as statistics became instruments of negotiation propaganda and sanctification. "Those who were best at planning and coordination in M.A.P. were those who realized that over-all planning and coordination by one directorate was quite impossible."

Dill, William R. "Environment as an Influence on Managerial Autonomy," *Administrative Science Quarterly*. Vol. 2, 1958, p. 409-443.
Managerial autonomy in two Norwegian firms of about 250 employees each varied with ease of formulating independent tasks and control over access to information about production and general company problems. Founding family of clothing firm involved in management, with market relatively unchanged. Sales-engineering firm growing and changing rapidly, with expanding and increasing market for products and services and greater autonomy for managers.

Donald, Gordon. "A Study of a Consumer's Cooperative," *Applied Anthropology*. Vol. 2, 1942, p. 22-28.
Success of group of middle-class families, mostly civil servants and professionals, in establishing a cooperative grocery store in Albany in 1940, attributed to the willingness of members to buy at the store despite its inconveniences, to their

willingness to do much volunteer work, to the help given by the Eastern Co-operative Wholesale, and to their success in organizing committees willing and able to administer effectively.

Dornbusch, Sanford M. "The Military Academy as an Assimilating Institution," *Social Forces.* Vol. 33, 1954, p. 316-321.
Both formal and informal codes at Coast Guard Academy aimed to foster loss of previous identity as quickly as possibly, regulate behavior and promote growth of bureaucratic spirit. Informal codes proved more effective.

Dunham, H. Warren, and S. K. Weinberg. *The Culture of the State Mental Hospital.* Detroit: Wayne State University Press, 1960.
The Columbus, Ohio, State Mental Hospital in 1946 had patient population of 2,500 and employee population of 327, of whom 193 were attendants. The employee culture, particularly of the attendants, found to be mainly oriented toward control of the patients. This culture resisted therapeutic or other innovations which threatened its structure, and tended to assimilate professional workers, who thereby lost their therapeutic value. The patients also developed a kind of cultural organization which functioned to (a) ease their initial adjustment, (b) initiate them into the hospital routine and requirements, (c) protect them from the more undesirable attendants, and (d) make known the techniques and devices which facilitate release. The character of social life, goal orientation, and the degree of tolerance varied from the hopeful to the chronic to the disturbed wards.

Ellsworth, John S., Jr. *Factory Folkways: A Study of Institutional Structure and Change.* New Haven: Yale University Press, 1952.
Early history of over hundred-year-old small industrial factory in New England characterized by strong paternalism, close-knit integration between management and work force and between the factory as a whole and surrounding community. Growth of business led to increase in administrative work and consequent increase in distance between management and work force, breakdown of older traditions, depersonalization, and establishment of a union. With growth of depersonalization, antagonistic cooperation became means of achieving overall aims of organization.

Evan, William M. "Due Process of Law in Military and Industrial Organizations," *Administrative Science Quarterly.* Vol. 7, 1962, p. 187-207.
The Inspector General Complaint system seen as a lateral rather than vertical communication principle, open to all members of the army. The IG system, which served as incentive to officers to conform to rules, was objected to by them as incompatible with the chain of command principle. Use of the system is positively correlated to satisfaction with the army, belief in military justice, and authoritarian principles. Comparison with the grievance procedure in industry showed the norms of due process more institutionalized, but less internalized, in the army.

Fenno, Richard B., Jr. *The President's Cabinet.* Cambridge: Harvard University Press, 1959.
U.S. Cabinet as extra-Constitutional advisory committee to President. Historical material, particularly from Wilson to Eisenhower period, revealed the Cabinet a usually weak instrument for providing President with advice, coordinating departments, unifying the President's party, or developing public prestige and confidence for President. Stronger Presidents tend to have weaker cabinets, and vice versa.

Francis, Roy G., and Robert C. Stone. *Service and Procedure in Bureaucracy: A Case Study.* Minneapolis: University of Minnesota Press, 1956.

Bureaucracy among one hundred people in a major Southern city office of the Louisiana Division of Employment Security characterized by competing or conflicting patterns. Procedures used as a means to serving a client where workers felt this was necessary, or to deny service when that end was sought. Skills, decision-making, and a work ethic found to be functionally related in the agency, resulting in conflict between norm of service and tendency for rules to become ends in themselves. Although the bonds of organization stressed impersonality, there was a well-knit system of personal interactions.

French, Cecil L. "Correlates of Success in Retail Selling," *American Journal of Sociology*. Vol. 66, 1960, p. 128-134.
Of sixty-five retail salesmen in a large retail furniture store observed over a four-year period, those with the highest sales volume and most money earned were those readiest to violate group norms. Tendency highly correlated with possession of higher reference groups than those of other salesmen.

Gardner, Burleigh B., and William F. Whyte. "The Man in the Middle: Position and Problems of the Foreman," *Applied Anthropology*. Vol. 2, 1945, p. 1-28.
From many studies the authors concluded that effective foreman is one who thinks and acts in terms of teamwork; builds up a free and informal system of two-way communication with the workers; builds up a feeling of mutual responsibility; and originates action with confidence and decision. The effectiveness of the foreman is increased if his superiors treat him in like manner.

Gold, Bela. *Wartime Economic Planning in Agriculture: A Study in the Allocation of Resources*. New York: Columbia University Press, 1949.
National economic planning in federal agencies concerned with food and agriculture during World War II. Long- and short-term objectives, administrative organization, and pressure of political expediency in such agencies, with "major emphasis . . . on evaluating the apparent achievements and shortcomings of agricultural mobilization."

Goldstein, Joseph. *The Government of British Trade Unions*. London: George Allen and Unwin, 1952.
Constitutional provisions and working rules of British Transport and General Workers Union (1948) seen as severely limiting members' eligibility to vote and for union office. Aided by membership apathy, this undermines democratic control and strengthens oligarchic rule. Observer-participant in randomly chosen but unusually suitable local Branch shows how almost invariable absence of vast majority of Branch members at local meetings, combined with faithful attendance by self-chosen tiny minority, results in the minority having (a) complete control of local ordinary activities, (b) monopoly of offices and (c) opportunity to limit drastically number voting for area officers. Paid officials of International take advantage of weak popular base of Branch officials to exercise power of "veto" over them, thus further "eating away the union's democratic base."

Goss, Mary E. W. "Influence and Authority Among Physicians in an Out-Patient Clinic," *American Sociological Review*. Vol. 26, 1961, p. 39-50.
Problem of reconciling hierarchical supervision of doctors in a large out-patient clinic with maintenance of their individual authority solved by giving doctors freedom in professional but not administrative matters, and by viewing supervision as a formal consultation relationship.

Gouldner, Alvin W. *Patterns of Industrial Bureaucracy*. New York: Free Press, 1954.
Problems of a new manager seeking to change an ingrained indulgency pattern

in a plant with two basic operating divisions: a subsurface gypsum mine and surface factories processing the gypsum. Problems include: the outside successor and the "Rebecca myth," strategic replacements of "old lieutenants," and lack of internal communication because of exclusion from informal relations in organization. Three types of bureaucratic solutions attempted by the successor—mock, representative, and punishment-centered—are analyzed in terms of purpose and effectiveness.

Gouldner, Alvin W. "Cosmopolitans and Locals: Toward an Analysis of Latent Social Roles–I," *Administrative Science Quarterly*. Vol. 2, 1957, p. 281-306.
Two forms of latent social behavior, local and cosmopolitan, described among 130 faculty and administrative personnel of a thousand-student cooperative college. Cosmopolitans, having high commitments to professional skills, low organizational loyalty, and an outer reference group, had greater influence within the college than locals. The latter, having high organizational loyalty, lower commitment to professional skills, and an inner reference group, participated more in community activities and showed higher rule tropism.

Gouldner, Alvin W. "Cosmopolitans and Locals: Toward an Analysis of Latent Social Roles–II," *Administrative Science Quarterly*. Vol. 2, 1958, p. 443-480.
Further development and factor analysis of local and cosmopolitan types, producing four types of locals and two types of cosmopolitans. The locals were identified as (1) those *dedicated* to organizational ideology, (2) *bureaucrats* desiring additional formal regulations, (3) the *homeguard*, composed of middle administrators and those who returned to their alma mater to teach, and (4) the *elders*, sometimes committed to the organization by virtue of age. The cosmopolitans were identified as (1) the *outsiders*, academically oriented and "in but not of" the organization, and (2) the *empire-builders*, increasing department strength and seeking other employment possibilities.

Gross, Bertram M. *The Legislative Struggle*. New York: McGraw-Hill, 1953.
Formal and informal structure and procedures of U.S. Congress and its interrelations in the legislative process with other government organizations, private organizations, and political parties. Special emphasis upon the mobilization of power and support and the making of strategic and tactical decisions at each stage in enacting or defeating legislative proposals.

Gross, Edward. "Some Functional Consequences of Primary Controls in a Formal Work Organization," *American Sociological Review*. Vol. 18, 1953, p. 368-372.
Symbiotic groups were found to be more cohesive than consensual groups in a Chicago plastics factory and at an Air Defense Command site. Symbiotic groups defined as those whose members were interdependent because each satisfied some needs of the others, consensual groups as those whose members shared some common goal or viewpoint. Symbiotic groups were found to be composed of men of unlike or contrasting characteristics. Consensual groups were composed of men of like characteristics.

Gross, Neal, S. Ward Mason, and W. Alexander McEachern. *Explorations in Role Analysis*. New York: John Wiley, 1958.
One hundred and two school superintendents and 508 school board members in Massachusetts were interviewed in an investigation of role conceptions and role conflicts in these reciprocal groups. Results supported theoretical conclusions about role expectations and conflicts. Denial of the assumption of role consensus allowed for investigation into the question of varying role expectations and the

formulation of a theory of conflict based on the dimensions of perception of legitimacy of expectations of sanctions resulting from nonconformity, the orientation of the individual to these dimensions, and his behavior. Questions of multiple incumbency of many roles and of positional and personal evaluative standards were investigated.

Grusky, Oscar. "Role Conflict in Organization: A Study of Prison Camp Officials," *Administrative Science Quarterly*. Vol. 3, 1958-59, p. 452-472.
Replacement of treatment-oriented with custodial-oriented supervisor in 65-inmate Midwestern prison camp resulted in formalization of camp procedures, increase in hostility, immediate property damage of $400, and highest escape and transfer rate in 2½-year history of camp.

Grusky, Oscar. "Corporate Size, Bureaucratization, and Managerial Succession," *American Journal of Sociology*. Vol. 67, 1962, p. 261-269.
Positions of board chairman, president, treasurer, controller, and secretary in twenty-six largest and twenty-seven smallest business corporations among top five hundred in United States examined over a ten-year span to determine extent of succession in each office. Findings indicated frequency of succession positively related to size of firm.

Guetzkow, Harold. "Interagency Committee Usage," *Public Administration Review*. Vol. 10, 1950, p. 190-196.
Four factors found directly related to effectiveness of thirty-three committees operating between federal department and other federal agencies of mutual concern and overlapping authority: (a) frequency and (b) length of meetings, (c) precision of the agenda, and (d) type of supporting service provided.

Haire, Mason. "Biological Models and Empirical Histories of the Growth of Organizations." In Mason Haire, ed. *Modern Organization Theory*. New York: John Wiley, 1959.
Effort to apply biological and physical growth models to organizations. Rising employment in four companies of different sizes analyzed in terms of equations used in measuring population growth. Employment of people dealing with external relations found to increase by the power of two, employment of those with internal functions growing by the power of three. Rise of staff functions explained in terms of need for bracing material where destructive forces are greatest.

Halpin, Andrew W. "The Leadership Behavior and Combat Performance of Airplane Commanders," *Journal of Abnormal and Social Psychology*. Vol. 49, 1954, p. 19-22.
Evaluation of performance of aircraft commanders among fifty-two B-29 crews by superiors and subordinates based on divergent expectations. Negative correlation between crew chiefs' ratings by their superiors and their personal relationships with their crews, as perceived by them. Positive correlation between ratings by superiors and the crews' perceptions of leader's behavior in organizing activity and in relating to them.

Halpin, Andrew W. "The Observed Leader Behavior and the Ideal Leader Behavior of Aircraft Commanders and School Superintendents." In R. M. Stogdill and A. E. Coons, eds. *Leader Behavior: Its Description and Measurement*. Columbus: Ohio State University, 1957.
The beliefs of 64 educational administrators and 132 aircraft commanders of how they should behave as leaders were not highly associated with their behavior as described by their subordinates.

Hammond, Paul Y. "The National Security Council as a Device of Interdepartmental Coordination," *American Political Science Review.* Vol. 54, 1960, p. 899-910.

The National Security Council, designed to advise the President in formulating defense policy, hampered by political pressures, conflicting loyalties of members to other agencies, and lack of control over execution of policy. Much of the valuable work done by nonpolitical NSC staff members.

Herbst, P. G. *Autonomous Group Functioning.* London: Tavistock, 1962.

Detailed study of composite work organization, rooted in earlier traditions, spontaneously emerged in British coal field. Group takes complete responsibility for total cycle of operations in mining at coal face, in contrast with work techniques based on task segmentation, differential status and payment, and extrinsic hierarchical control. Various interrelations traced among output rate, work rate of team members, level of group integration, stress, task involvement, and performance satisfaction.

Hittle, J. D. *The Military Staff: Its History and Development.* Harrisburg, Pa.: Military Service Publishing Co., 1949.

Growth of military staff organizations as part of armed services of Germany, France, England, U.S.A., and Russia, with attention to similarities and differences in earlier centuries.

Horsfall, Alexander B., and Conrad M. Arensberg. "Teamwork and Productivity in a Shoe Factory," *Human Organization.* Vol. 8, 1949, p. 13-25.

Few formal organizational lines and extensive informal groupings among twenty-eight workers in Bottoming Room of a thousand-employee shoe factory. Informal arrangement by employees of work allocation, equalization of pay and output restrictions. Interaction greater within each group, with most active groups not most productive. Work room leaders took initiative for interaction within and external to their groups, with groups to which they belonged showing excess of both internal and external levels of interaction.

Jackman, Norman R. "Collective Protest in Relocation Centers," *American Journal of Sociology.* Vol. 63, 1957, p. 264-272.

A system of self-government established in Japanese relocation centers during World War II was actually subservient to administration. Exclusion from decision-making in matters pertaining to their welfare led to group protests and irrational behavior. In 115 incidents, differences were successfully negotiated when channels of communication were open and utilized. Strong protests developed when communications were closed.

Janowitz, Morris. *The Professional Soldier: a Social and Political Portrait.* New York: Free Press, 1960.

Analysis of United States military community in terms of career patterns, ideology, political behavior, techniques for communicating with civilian sector, and projected role in light of contemporary technological and political changes. Important changes in military establishment over past half century: shift from authoritarian domination to greater reliance on manipulation, persuasion, and group consensus; skills and orientations common to civilian sector now required; broader social base for officer recruitment and high competence leading to professional elite. These factors contribute to strain on traditional self-images and growth of military as managerial organization.

Jaques, Elliott. *The Changing Culture of a Factory.* London: Tavistock, 1951.

Analytical and historical record of three-year joint project of the Glacier Metal Company management and a research team from the Tavistock Institute on both plant's consultative machinery and general working conditions. Main areas of concentration around the evolution of the Works Council and its integration into the company policy-making system, clarification of the problems of the workers' representatives in the Works Committee and their difficulties in communicating with fellow-workers, the difficulties of the Superintendents' Committee in establishing a valid function and its dissolution with the emergence of a viable Works Managers Meeting, and finally, the problems of the top managers themselves and eventual clarification of roles and procedures which preceded the establishment of two-way communication within the executive chain.

Kahn, R. L., and A. S. Tannenbaum. "Union Leadership and Member Participation," *Personnel Psychology.* Vol. 10, 1957, p. 277-292.
Membership participation in four Michigan industrial union locals positively correlated with stewards' leadership skills in communicating with the men, involving them in decision-making, providing "help" for them, and taking personal interest in how they got along on the job.

Katz, Daniel, Nathan Macoby, and Nancy Morse. *Productivity, Supervision and Morale in an Office Situation.* Ann Arbor: University of Michigan, 1950.
Interviews with 24 section heads and 419 nonsupervisory employees of the Prudential Insurance Co., Newark, N.J., indicated most differences between high and low productivity groups related to supervision. Heads of high-producing sections are likely to: receive general rather than close supervision; like the authority and responsibility they hold; spend more time in supervision; give general rather than close supervision; be employee- rather than production-oriented. Few differences in employee attitudes in high- and low-producing groups. High group employees have more pride in their work.

Kaufman, Herbert. *The Forest Ranger, A Study in Administrative Behavior.* Baltimore: Johns Hopkins, 1960.
Decision-making pattern of the U.S. Forest Service and intensive examination of five ranger districts. Tendencies toward centrifugal fragmentation in the Forest Service are: (1) widely-varied conditions, (2) difficulties of communication and supervision due to scattering of units, (3) recent highly accelerated growth of Service, (4) adaptation to different local conditions, and (5) personal differences among Rangers. Central office has successfully counteracted these tendencies by (1) advance decision-making (authorization, direction, prohibition), (2) detection and discouragement of deviation, and (3) use of psychological integration— i.e. they do by themselves what the organization wants them to. Conscious and deliberate strategy of leaders, aided by fortuitous factors (e.g., technical developments), responsible for success in achieving integration.

Landsberger, H. "The Horizontal Dimension in Bureaucracy," *Administrative Science Quarterly.* Vol. 6, 1961, p. 299-332.
Application of an adaptation of Bale's Interaction Process Analysis to the middle management of comparable companies indicated averages of 39% and 48% of the interactions were horizontal. Evidence that equivalent departments in different organizations take the same positions in controversies explained by postulating presence of underlying basic dilemmas (stability vs. flexibility, long-range vs. short-range considerations, diffuse vs. specific costs and gains, and organizational vs. other goals) common to both organizations.

Lauterbach, Albert. "Perceptions of Management: Case Materials From Western and Northern Europe," *Administrative Science Quarterly.* Vol. 2, 1957, p. 97-109.
In 134 interviews most managers in private, public, and cooperative organizations of varying size in Britain, Norway, Sweden, and West Germany believed there were no significant differences in management functions, no increase in restrictions, and skill was equally effective in public or private enterprises.

Lawrence, Paul R. *The Changing of Organizational Behavior Patterns.* Boston: Graduate School of Business Administration, Harvard University, 1958.
Medium-sized supermarket chain "decentralized" its supervisory hierarchy by changing function of district managers to a less directive and authoritarian role and creating new role of store manager as resident general manager in each supermarket. Accompanying these changes: a reorganization of chain's top management and fundamental changes in top control procedures. Management used a variety of mechanisms to help evolve the desired change, and during two-year period basic behavior patterns of middle-management people changed slowly in desired direction.

Learned, Edmund P., David N. Ulrich, and Donald R. Booz. *Executive Action.* Boston: Graduate School of Business Administration, Harvard University, 1951.
Social situation, problems, and behavior of higher executives, as shown in study of twelve unnamed companies. Executives preoccupied with operating problems that cut across organizational dividing lines, often ignoring the human context of the cooperation necessary for the problems' solution. Older concepts of executive role changing, with some executives becoming more "playwrights" than "actors." Executive behavior showed great variations with respect to delegation, communication, control and measurement, use of specialized staff, and organization building.

Lefton, Mark, Simon Dinitz, and Benjamin Pasananich. "Decision-Making in a Mental Hospital: Real, Perceived, and Ideal," *American Sociological Review.* Vol. 24, 1959, p. 822-829.
Actual influence of professional personnel of the Columbus Psychiatric Institution and Hospital on decisions concerning patient treatment not highly correlated with their perceptions of their influence, except at the highest professional levels. Staff perceived their participation in decision-making in terms of their professional group membership rather than as individuals.

Leighton, Alexander H. *The Governing of Men: General Principles and Recommendations Based on Experience at a Japanese Relocation Camp.* Princeton: Princeton University Press, 1945.
Relocation of 18,000 West Coast Japanese, a mixture of Isseis, Niseis, and Kibeis, shortly after Pearl Harbor, at Poston in the Arizona desert was hampered by many difficulties both inherent in the problem and through fortuitous circumstances. The Japanese suffered total disruption of former life, internal divisions increased, and they were subjected to intense and diverse forms of stress. The Administration itself was divided in its aims and methods and by conflict with other government agencies. A spontaneous strike of one unit occurred and, as a partial result of successful efforts to settle it peacefully, many of the adverse influences were counteracted and self-management by the evacuees was achieved to a greater extent than previously. Individuals and social organizations under stress were analyzed and conclusions drawn concerning the "governing of man."

Leighton, Alexander H. *Human Relations in a Changing World: Observations on the Use of the Social Sciences.* New York: Dutton, 1949.
Foreign Morale Analysis Division functioned as staff aide to the Office of War Information and the War Department on the psychological and social factors pertinent to the Japanese war effort. Staff numbered thirty, for the most part trained social scientists, as well as a number of Japanese experts. Work of Division widely circulated and advocated when in agreement with conclusions of policy makers in OWI, ignored when contrary to general policy. Other difficulties: lack of opportunities for direct study of Japanese and contact with other intelligence organizations in the U.S. and policy officials' lack of interest in opinions and findings of Division.

Levinson, Harry, Charlton R. Price, Kenneth J. Munden, Harold J. Mandl, and Charles M. Solley. *Men, Management and Mental Health.* Cambridge: Harvard University Press, 1962.
Eight hundred seventy-four workers in different parts of a widespread Midwestern utilities company interviewed over two-year period to determine psychological effects of work environment. Workers chiefly concerned with efforts to achieve a satisfactory interdependent relationship with company, comfortable interpersonal relationships with fellow-workers, and ability to deal with change reasonably well. These goals inherent in the mutual expectations of workers and company and form the "psychological contract" worked out through the reciprocation process.

Likert, Rensis. "Voluntary Organizations," Chapter 10 in *New Patterns of Management.* New York: McGraw-Hill, 1961.
One hundred four local Leagues of Women Voters studied, as representative of all 1,100 local leagues, to measure relation between membership activity and type of leadership, relative influence of various parts of League, and relation between size of local League and effectiveness per member. Up to four hundred members, effectiveness of members increased; above this figure, president and board members much more effective, membership relatively less. This found to be true also in size of resource units; i.e., optimum size fifteen to twenty for highest effectiveness per member.

Lipset, Seymour M., Martin A. Trow, and James S. Coleman. *Union Democracy: The Internal Policies of the International Typographers Union.* New York: Free Press, 1956.
The ITU has, over the past seventy years, developed the only institutionalized two-party system in a trade union. Factors favoring this: borderline status of printers between the working and middle classes that provided the political split between "radical" and conservative groups; its genesis through the federation of existing locals which strive to remain autonomous and may be sources of opposition; the large degree of homogeneity in the status, working hours, wages, and interests of the members. Independent nonpolitical clubs facilitate the existence of opposition, and this opposition facilitates the independence of the clubs. Internal conflict revolves around bargaining and control of power; members tend to divide according to experience and wage differences, and into "in" and "out" groups.

Loken, Robert D., and C. J. Thake Winfield. "How Many Managers Are There?" *Current Economic Comment.* Vol. 14, 1952, p. 18-27.
In eighty-two Midwestern business firms 13.3 per cent of all employees found to have managerial responsibilities. Smaller companies (those with five hundred employees or less) averaged 18.4 per cent, as against 9 per cent for the largest (those with five thousand employees or more). Larger percentages also found in financial and transportation firms, with smaller percentages for those in the processing and wholesaling of food and allied products.

Lombard, George F. F. *Behavior in a Selling Group: A Case Study of Interpersonal Relations in a Department Store.* Boston: Graduate School of Business Administration, Harvard University, 1955.
Twenty salesclerks in highly successful children's wear department of large Eastern department store observed to have established informal ways of organizing their work and selling habits which was in many ways directly opposed to the expectations of management. Management's belief that money incentives would assure desired behavior not borne out in practice but the personal needs of salesgirls and ways in which they fulfilled them resulted in effects satisfactory both

to management and the girls themselves. Salesgirls' relations to customers based on the effect of their self-evaluation and tended to reinforce such self-evaluations. The efforts of supervisory staff to improve service to customers not very successful since this aspect of salesgirl-customer relations was not understood.

MacMahon, Arthur W., John D. Millett, and Gladys Ogden. *The Administration of Federal Work Relief*. Chicago: Public Administration Service, 1941.
Growth and operations of Works Progress Administration, the emergency agency set up in 1935 to provide work for able-bodied unemployed throughout U.S.A. Attention given to political controversy on scale of program and conflicts with other government agencies, with examination of role of President Roosevelt as arbiter and participant. Formalization of structure and procedures as agency grew, but with continuing internal frictions. Emphasis upon "rival claims of hierarchy and specialty" and the necessity of dual command "as the solution of the operation of decentralized activities in a large enterprise."

Mann, F. C., and L. R. Hoffman. *Automation and The Worker: A Study of Social Change in Power Plants*. New York: Holt, 1960.
Comparison of two power plants, one recently modernized and destined as a standby system, the other more powerful, more efficient, and considerably more equipped with automatic feedbacks and other self-regulatory machines, with particular emphasis on the workers' attitudes to job changes, shift work, and supervisory attitudes and behavior. In general, the workers in the automated plant were more satisfied with work content and conditions, job opportunities, security, and their supervisors; the foremen, also, felt that they had greater responsibility in the automated plant and better relations with the men under them.

Mann, F., and L. Williams. "Observations on the Dynamics of Change to Electronic Data-Processing Equipment," *Administrative Science Quarterly*. Vol. 5, 1960, p. 217-256.
Light and power company with 1600 employees changed to electronic data-processing equipment during 1953-58. Detailed planning of graduated steps, process of change as test of firm's participative management policy. Problems of retraining and reassigning personnel.

Mansfield, Harvey C. *The Comptroller General*. New Haven: Yale University Press, 1939.
Historical review of the first seventeen years of the General Accounting Office, under the direction of the Comptroller General, from its inception under the U.S. Budget and Accounting Act of 1921. The functions of the agency (with particular attention to the mixture of audit, control, and reporting functions), its internal staffing and organization, and the personal influence of John R. McCarl, the first Comptroller General.

Marcson, Simon. *The Scientist in American Industry*. New York: The Industrial Relations Section, Department of Economics, Princeton University, and Harper, 1960.
Examination of the career development, professional needs, and interaction among scientists, and analysis of the conflict between scientific and corporate goals in a thousand-employee industrial research laboratory. Increasing dependence of industry on internal research resulted in some modifications of customary hiring procedures, organizational forms, authority procedures, emphasis on developmental versus basic research, and new forms of prestige rewards; but not enough to satisfy the inherently unassimilable goal needs of the scientists.

Medalia, Nahum Z. "Unit Size and Leadership Perceptions," *Sociometry*, Vol. 17, 1954, p. 64-67.
Unit members of fifty identically organized squadrons of varying size in the Air

Defense Command perceived the human-relations mindedness of their site leaders as decreasing as size of unit increased.

Melman, Seymour. *Decision-Making and Productivity*. Oxford: Blackwell, 1958.
Employers in the Standard Motor Company, while retaining "dominant role in decision-making on whether and what production shall be carried out," seen as leaving "details of conditions of production" to employees and their union, with consequent favorable effects on productivity without expansion in size of managerial group.

Morse, Nancy C., and Everett Reimer. "The Experimental Change of a Major Organizational Variable," *Journal of Abnormal and Social Psychology*. Vol. 52, 1956, p. 120-129.
Decision-making opportunities on a wide range of activities, including work methods and personnel policies, increased in two divisions of rank-and-file clerical workers of an industrial organization and decreased in control group of two other divisions. Self-actualization, job and work satisfaction increased in decision-making groups and decreased in control groups. All groups gained in productivity, but the significance was greater in control groups, without decision-making power.

Neustadt, Richard E. *Presidential Power*. New York: Wiley, 1960.
President's power seen largely as persuasive. Even sharp commands—such as Truman's recall of MacArthur and seizure of the steel mills and Eisenhower's use of troops in the Little Rock segregation case—are incidents in broader process of persuasion. Chief Executive's persuasive power based on bargaining, vantage point in government, personal reputation among government "professionals," public prestige, and his own efforts to obtain power.

Nourse, Edwin G. *Economics in the Public Service*. New York: Harcourt, Brace, 1953.
The organization, operations, and problems of the Council of Economic Advisers, as seen by its first Chairman. Work of Council in its early years impeded by political pressures, disagreements among Council members, and President's lack of interest.

Orth, Charles D., 3rd. *Social Structure and Learning Climate*. Boston: Graduate School of Business Administration, Harvard University, 1963.
Norms, group membership, and leadership patterns in "student culture" undermine assumption that "the educational institution and its faculty generate and control the rate and kind of learning produced." Students in two sections of first year of two-year Master's program organized themselves to "beat the system." Each section developed different norms concerning learning and social activities. "Image norms" related to behavior needed in order to be perceived as a successful businessman. "Coping norms" designed to cope with hazards of academic program. In one section coping norms discouraged, and in the other encouraged, vigorous learning efforts.

Orzack, Louis H. "Role Implications of Change in a New Organization." Paper presented to Fifth World Congress of Sociology, International Sociological Association. Washington, 1962.
A paradigm for the analysis of role change in organizational settings illustrated by a study of a newly opened hospital and treatment center for severely retarded children. Points emphasized: location of fluid and stable roles, sources of change in role content, timing and phasing of change, prescribed and informal mechanisms of change, and types and modes of role change.

Page, Charles Hunt. "Bureaucracy's Other Face," *Social Forces*. Vol. 25, 1946-47, p. 88-94.

Informal system of control, rules, groupings, and sanctioned systems of procedures existed in Navy alongside the formal, rational, and bureaucratic structure but resisted exposure to outsiders. Informal system provided channels of communication and circumvention of formal procedures, informal solutions to problems, and encouragement of spontaneity. Navy units in isolated areas differed from those in populated centers, the latter required to adhere more closely to strict regulations of the formal organization. Tradition served to stimulate loyalty, pride, and as a means of judging achievement. Personality peculiar to the system developed.

Pearlin, Leonard I. "Sources of Resistance to Change in a Mental Hospital," *American Journal of Sociology*. Vol. 68, 1962, p. 325-334.

Resistance of higher-level nurses of large mental hospital to proposed changes in patient care aroused when change seen interfering with desired relations with patients. Resistance of lower-level nurses when change conflicts with ward maintenance functions. Resistance less likely on ward with advanced patient-care policy and leadership friendly to change.

Pearlin, Leonard I., and Morris Rosenberg. "Nurse-Patient Social Distance and the Structural Context of a Mental Hospital," *American Sociological Review*. Vol. 27, 1962, p. 56-65.

Emphasis on subordination of mental patients to nursing staff in a large mental hospital most frequent among staff of relatively high position who are obeisant toward superiors and whose mobility is blocked. Emotional indifference to patients most frequent among nurses assigned to wards of their own sex where prevailing age of patients differs from their own.

Read, William H. "Upward Communication in Industrial Hierarchies," *Human Relations*. Vol. 15, 1962, p. 3-15.

Significantly negative relationship found between upward mobility among 104 middle-management executives in three large industrial companies and the accuracy with which they communicate problem-related information upward in the organizational hierarchies. It was modified by the degree of the superiors' influence as perceived by their subordinates and by the degree of interpersonal trust held by these executives for their superiors.

Rice, A. K. *Productivity and Social Organization: The Ahmedabad Experiment*. London: Tavistock, 1958.

Experiments in both social and technological changes in an automatic weaving shed and in a group of nonautomatic loom sheds undertaken by the Ahmedabad Mfg. Co., in collaboration with the Tavistock Institute of Human Relations and carried out over a period of three years. As a result of changes in social and economic conditions of the Company, partly a result of above changes introduced in the weaving sheds, disturbances occurred in management, were analyzed, and suggested improvements in management organization agreed upon.

Rice, A. K. *The Enterprise and Its Environment*. London: Tavistock, 1963.

Consultant's report on changes in formal management structure of Ahmedabad textile plant over eight-year period of growth and modernization, and of family-related group of chemical and pharmaceutical companies emerging out of a single enterprise. In both cases, with rapidly changing and environmental conditions and increasing differentiation of functions, reorganization became a "steady state." Conclusions concerning open system theory of organization and necessity of structural changes in the light of an organization's "primary task," the constraints on its performance, and differentiation by unbroken processes.

Richardson, Stephen A. "Organizational Contrasts on British and American Ships," *Administrative Science Quarterly*. Vol. 1, 1956-57, p. 189-207.
Comparison of differences in training, authority structure, and social distance of crews of British and American cargo ships. American training through maritime school or sea experience; crew orientation toward union, with suspicion of authority and less emphasis on authority symbols, which strengthen social distance, than the British. The latter's training through apprenticeship, with conditioning to accept authority, orientation toward company, and greater social distance between officers and men than among the Americans.

Robson, William A. *Nationalized Industry and Public Ownership*. London: Allen and Unwin, 1960.
Analysis and evaluation of structure and operations of major public corporations administering British nationalized industries, with attention to motives for nationalization, legal status, formal organization, size and units, control by government and legislature, governing boards, consultative councils, finance, labor relations, research, and development. Criteria of performance found to include social and political purposes as well as profitability and efficiency. Despite many defects, British public corporations found to have performed well—particularly in mobilizing capital for investment and in improving wages and working conditions.

Roethlisberger, F. J., and William J. Dickson. *Management and the Worker*. Cambridge: Harvard University Press, 1939.
History, analysis, and interpretation of the studies at the Hawthorne plant of the Western Electric Company between 1927 and 1932. These studies dealt with (1) the output of workers, as influenced by physical, economic, and social factors, in three small experimental groups (the Relay Assembly Test Room, the Second Relay Assembly Group, and the Mica Splitting Test Room); (2) the sentiments and feeling underlying workers' complaints, as revealed in over 21,000 non-directed interviews; and (3) the internal organization of a work group (the Bank Wiring Observation Room). For detailed summary of these studies, see Chapter 7.

Ronken, Harriet O., and Paul R. Lawrence. *Administering Changes: A Case Study of Human Relations in a Factory*. Boston: Graduate School of Business Administration, Harvard University, 1952.
Design, development, and production of the Amicon tube, a radically changed electronic device manufactured by the American Magnolite Company, beset by many difficulties, technical, administrative, social, and psychological. Greatest difficulties caused by changes in relationships among people involved and by deficiences of communication between them. Real progress achieved only by increased self-awareness on the part of the administrators and the employees.

Salter, J. A. *Allied Shipping Control*. Oxford: Clarendon, 1921.
Analysis of origins, organization, and operation of Allied Maritime Transport Council, as joint organization to control shipping activities of U.S., Britain, France, Italy, and other Allies during World War I. Special attention to Council's methods of coordinating but not replacing the departments directing the merchant marines of the member countries.

Seeley, John R., Buford H. Junker, R. Wallace Jones, Jr., N. C. Jenkins, M. T. Haugh, and I. Miller. *Community Chest: A Case Study in Philanthropy*. Toronto: University of Toronto Press, 1957.
Failure of Indianapolis Community Chest to meet fund-raising goals partly due to (a) overambitious goals, (b) overdependence on corporate donations and leading donors, (c) inequity in standards for executive giving, (d) nonparticipation of top status people in leadership, (e) overcentralization of Chest staff, (f) unsettled relationship between lay General Chairman of campaign and General Man-

ager of Chest, (g) insecurity of welfare staff, (h) inadequate staff promotion system, and (i) unclarity in Chest values and standards.

Selznick, Philip. *TVA and the Grass Roots.* Berkeley: University of California Press, 1949.
The TVA doctrine of grass roots, decentralization, managerial autonomy, and cooperation with existing area agencies and institutions is analyzed functionally with major emphasis on the cooptation process, or the integration of various elements affecting an organization's existence and growth into its leadership and policy-making functions. The cooptation process is analyzed by examination of TVA activities involving citizen participation in administration through voluntary organizations and through a review of its relationship with its administrative constituency of land grant colleges and farm organizations.

Selznick, Philip. *The Organizational Weapon: A Study of Bolshevik Strategy and Tactics.* New York: McGraw-Hill, 1952.
Operating methods used by small disciplined "combat party" to thwart constitutional limits on exercise of power in different kinds of organizations examined through published materials and self-analyses by bolshevik elites. In identifying the nature of bolshevism as reflected in the organizational objectives and practices of the communist party, the following factors were examined: the ideological operational code of the communists; the function of indoctrination and persuasion as tools used to fulfill power ends; the relationship between the vanguard and the mass; defensive strategies used to ward off threats and conceal subversion; the strategy of access employed by the the bolsheviks to mobilize diffuse population masses and to infiltrate existing organizations; the use of shared power as a basis for a coup d'etat; the vulnerability of institutional targets; and the development of a program of counteroffensives against bolshevist tactics.

Sills, David. *The Volunteers.* New York: Free Press, 1957.
The National Foundation for Infantile Paralysis is a philanthropic corporation operating through permanent local service chapters and an annual March of Dimes fund-raising campaign run by specially appointed officials. Chapters and campaigns run almost exclusively by lay volunteers. Since infantile paralysis is no longer a major threat, the Foundation has succeeded in transforming itself into a permanent institution with many health goals, and in developing in volunteers a sense of participation in and responsibility for an important social movement.

Simon, Herbert A. "Birth of an Organization: The Economic Cooperation Administration," *Public Administration Review.* Vol. 13, 1953, p. 227-236.
The processes of "cell multiplication and power struggles" through which ECA grew in four months from fifteen people to over seven hundred in Washington and fourteen hundred abroad. Tasks, environmental influences, and political alliances more important than organizational structure planned in advance by Bureau of the Budget.

Simpson, Richard L., and William H. Gulley. "Goals, Environmental Pressures, and Organizational Characteristics," *American Sociological Review.* Vol. 27, 1962, p. 344-350.
Data on 211 voluntary associations affirm hypothesis that internal characteristics of organizations will vary with range of external pressures. Organizations facing the widest range of pressures will tend to (a) less centralization of authority, (b) more emphasis on membership involvement in organizational activities, and (c) more attention to internal communication.

Sofer, Cyril. "Reactions to Administrative Change," *Human Relations.* Vol. 8, 1955, p. 291-316.
Examination of staff reactions to new roles and duties and the changes in formal

regulations that accompanied the nationalization of hospitals in three British hospitals—a local hospital, a private hospital and a local mental hospital—five years after nationalization. Changes in formal structure without accompanying changes in internal structure gave rise to anxiety among all the hospital staffs. The superseding of local and private people by regional and national supervision resented by the local and the private hospital staffs, but the local mental hospital noted an improvement in conditions and staff quality and welcomed the focusing of attention on problem of mental health.

Sofer, Cyril. *The Organization from Within*. London: Tavistock, 1961.
Three cases in which author, as consultant, initiated radical examination and reconsideration of organization's tasks and resources and ways of relating the two. Role of crisis in forcing change upon an organization, the effect of organizational change upon environmental relations, the opposition to change, the changing attitudes and defense systems of an innovating group, the constructive potential in conflict, the role of leaders, and the role of outside consultants.

Somers, Herman M. *Presidential Agency—The Office of War Mobilization and Reconversion*. Cambridge: Harvard University Press, 1950.
Antecedents and special characteristics of Office of War Mobilization and Reconversion described. Problems of allocating resources and coordinating manpower programs within these agencies discussed, with emphasis on conflict between civilian and military authorities, and, finally, planning for the change-over to a peacetime economy.

Stanton, Alfred H., and Morris S. Schwartz. *The Mental Hospital: A Study of Institutional Participation in the Treatment of Psychiatric Illness*. London: Tavistock, 1954.
Participant-observer study by psychiatrist in administrative charge of small disturbed ward in private mental hospital and temporarily attached sociologist over two-year period of the ward in particular, in context of hospital as a whole. Exploration of formal and informal structure of hospital and ward, with special emphasis on problems of communication between staff and patients, between staff members and between patients, and the effect of blockage of communication on the patients' progress. Results of both overt and covert disagreement among staff members with regard to individual patients are discussed: hidden and often unconscious disagreements affect patients more strongly and disastrously than overt conflicts. The power structure of the hospital, with emphasis on the making and enforcing of decisions, is analyzed.

Stouffer, Samuel, *et al*. *The American Soldier*. 4 vols. Princeton: Princeton University Press, 1949.
Attitudes of U.S. soldiers during army's expansion from a quarter of a million in 1940 to over eight million in 1945, as revealed in four years of attitude surveys by social scientists in army's research branch. Vol. I, *Adjustment During Army Life:* Adaptation of new recruits to methods, hierarchy, and status system of army, with emphasis on attitudes toward promotion, job assignments, "relative deprivation," officers, and war itself. Better-educated tended to be more committed to war and more critical of promotion opportunities and officers. Vol. II, *Combat and Its Aftermath:* Attitudes of different categories of troops toward combat, noncombat troops, and civilians. Major combat incentives of enlisted men reported as "ending the task" and "solidarity with group." Formal controls strongly supported under stress by informal codes based on mutual dependence and affection. Vols. III and IV, respectively, analyze problems in experimental studies in communication and in the methodology of measurement and prediction.

Strauss, George, and Leonard R. Sayles. "Occupation and the Selection of Local Union Officers," *American Journal of Sociology*. Vol. 58, 1952-53, p. 585-591.
Existence of a prestige hierarchy among informal work groups affected the formal structure of twenty union locals in four northeastern communities with the volunteer union officers being drawn from the higher-status workers. Such leaders came from those who were higher paid, had more skill, more seniority in the plant and union, belonged to dominant ethnic groups, were male, and had jobs enabling them to circulate within their plants. During temporary period of disequilibrium, new locals were formed and lower-status workers obtained leadership in them but were able to maintain control only as long as the disequilibrium continued.

Sykes, A. J. M. "The Effect of a Supervisory Training Course in Changing Supervisors' Perceptions and Expectations of the Role of Management," *Human Relations*. Vol. 15, 1962, p. 227-243.
Supervisory training course, at the suggestion of consultants, given for the supervisors in a medium-sized contracting firm failed to achieve success when the supervisors' changing perceptions and expectations of role of management were not met by corresponding changes in management attitudes. High turnover resulted among supervisors.

Sykes, Gresham M. *The Society of Captives: A Study of a Maximum Security Prison*. Princeton: Princeton University Press, 1958.
The New Jersey State Maximum Security Prison, with three hundred custodial, clerical, and professional state employees and twelve hundred adult male criminals, seen as a single system of total power concentrating primarily on custodial care as opposed to retribution or rehabilitation. Structural defects in the prison's system of power threatened achievement of purposes: lack of sense of duty among prisoners, limited efficacy of rewards and punishments, strong pressures toward corruption of guards by friendship, reciprocity, and transfer of duties into hands of trusted inmates. Inmate solidarity, based on structure of social relationships, helped mitigate pains of imprisonment, while cohesively oriented prisoners did much to maintain prison's equilibrium.

Tannenbaum, Arnold S. "Control and Effectiveness in a Voluntary Organization," *American Journal of Sociology*. Vol. 67, 1961, p. 33-46.
Data on 109 local Leagues within League of Women Voters support the hypotheses that the extent to which an organization fulfills its objectives and preserves its means and resources is directly related to (a) the degree to which control is dispersed through hierarchic levels and (b) the total amount of control exercised at all levels.

Tannenbaum, Arnold S., and Robert L. Kahn. *Participation in Union Locals*. Evanston, Ill.: Row, Peterson, 1958.
Four Michigan industrial union locals compared on membership participation. Active member tends to be older than others, more highly skilled, better paid, married, more satisfied with his job, and more accepting of union norms and values. Active unions characterized by greater emotional attachment of members, consensus of opinion and action, higher degree of control and leadership skill of officers than the inactive unions.

Terrien, Frederic, and Donald L. Mills. "The Effect of Changing Size Upon the Internal Structure of Organizations," *American Sociological Review*. Vol. 20, 1955.
Data collected from nine hundred California school districts suggest that the relative size of an administrative component increases when the size of the containing organization increases.

Thompson, A. Victor. *The Regulatory Process in OPA Rationing*. New York: Kings Crown, 1950.
Activities of wartime Office of Price Administration in formulating and communicating rationing rules. Organizational structure considered in light of the various functions of agency and its external relations, with particular attention given to personality of planners, and external pressures as influences upon planning process.

Thompson, James D. "Authority and Power in 'Identical' Organizations," *American Journal of Sociology*. Vol. 62, 1956-57, p. 290-301.
Real power structure differed from the authority structure in two similar Air Force wings, with operations directors in both wings having unauthorized power over squadron commanders. In one wing the commander let others take leadership initiative, power was concentrated in a few hands, there was little cooperation among the officers, confusion prevailed, and there was limited communication between officials at the top and lower level personnel. The other wing commander exercised leadership initiative, with cooperation among the officers and better communication between top officers and the lower echelons.

Trist, E. L., G. W. Higgin, H. Murray, and A. B. Pollock. *Organizational Choice*. London: Tavistock, 1963.
In traditional single-place working, each miner was self-supervising and multi-skilled. In mechanized conventional longwall systems, management took over coordination and control, established formal division of labor with specialized tasks done by groups of varying sizes. This system marked by low productivity and job satisfaction, poor management-labor relations, high costs, and high rate of absence. Composite longwall system, consistent with higher levels of mechanization, allowed workers to exercise responsible autonomy by allocating men to shifts and tasks and released higher officials for support operations and long-term planning.

Tuchman, Barbara. *The Guns of August*. New York: Macmillan, 1962.
The first month of World War I, with special emphasis upon the plans, internal operations, communications problems, and errors of the German, French, English, and Russian General Staffs. Failure of both the German Schlieffen Plan and the French Plan 17, neither of which could be changed once in operation, "produced deadlock on the Western Front."

Turner, Arthur N. "Interaction and Sentiment in the Foreman-Worker Relationship," *Human Organization*. Vol. 14, 1955, p. 10-16.
High foreman-worker interaction consisting of informal matters in addition to job-centered comments found to be associated with savorable worker attitudes toward foremen in two automobile assembly plants. Workers reporting more frequent contacts with supervisors above foremen level had more favorable attitudes toward upper levels of management, while workers with infrequent interaction expressed a desire for noninterference from their foremen.

Turner, Ralph H. "The Navy Disbursing Officer as a Bureaucrat," *American Sociological Review*. Vol. 12, 1947, p. 342-348.
Situation in which navy disbursing officer operates characterized by (1) frequent conflict between regulations and orders from superiors, (2) superior rank of many of his clients, and (3) such informal structures as genuine friendship patterns, simulated friendships, especially from superior officers, and the exchange system (which is distinguished from bribery and functions under its own code). Disbursing officers react to these pressure by behaving along four general patterns: strict enforces of regulations; the opposite type with little regard for strict enforcement; naively sincere type largely unaware of pressures and con-

flicts; and the realist who uses the regulations with unimportant clients but knows how to do "legally" what influential officers want.

Udy, Stanley H., Jr. "Administrative Rationality, Social Setting, and Organizational Development," *American Journal of Sociology*. Vol. 68, 1962, p. 299-308.
In thirty-four organizations in nonindustrial societies seven characteristics assumed to induce rationality: (a) limited objectives, (b) segmental participation, (c) performance emphasis, (d) specific job assignment, (e) specialization, (f) compensatory rewards and (g) central management. These scaled in cross-sectional comparative analysis to suggest that rationality involves cumulative emphasis on specificity of roles and decision rules. Rationality related positively to independence from social setting, negatively to traditional elements in social setting.

Vroom, Victor H. *Some Personality Determinants of the Effects of Participation.* Englewood Cliffs: Prentice-Hall, 1960.
One hundred eight line supervisors in the New York and Chicago plants of a large delivery company corroborated the hypothesis that participation in decision-making has positive effects on attitudes and motivation. It was further shown that the magnitude of these effects is a function of the authoritarian or equalitarian personality characteristics of the participants—the former being much less affected.

Walker, Charles R., and Robert H. Guest. *The Man on the Assembly Line.* Cambridge: Harvard University Press, 1962.
Study of worker satisfaction with job conditions from interviews with 180 workers on an automobile assembly line. Assembly line jobs found to be disliked to the extent that they embodied repetitiveness, mechanical pacing, and isolation from other workers; pay and job security main reasons for liking assembly jobs. Rotation of jobs, increase in content of job, and reducing depersonalization are suggested steps toward increasing worker satisfaction.

Warner, W. Lloyd, and J. C. Low. *The Social System of the Modern Factory.* New Haven: Yale University Press, 1947.
Shoemaking industry, dominant in small industrial New England community since end of nineteenth century, changed from family-owned, community-centered factories to organizations controlled by absentee owners and managers and oriented toward the outside world. At same time production process in the factories changed from emphasis on craft skills to almost complete mechanization with resultant change in status of workers, both within the factories and in the community. Generally bad economic conditions in early thirties, aggravated by above factors, led to unionization of workers into industrial-type union and a community-wide strike which was entirely successful in uniting workers, mobilizing community support, and achieving better economic conditions.

Weiss, Robert S. *Processes of Organization.* Ann Arbor: Survey Research Center, University of Michigan, 1956.
Essential organizational processes in a government research bureau sponsoring scientific research on national defense, with emphasis on allocation of work and responsibility, adaptation to and acceptance of job assignments, and formal and informal coordination patterns. Scientific personnel, mainly recruited from universities, dependent on informal legitimation based on education level, seniority, scientific experience, and sex, in order to undertake policy-making functions of scientific administrators. Administrative personnel, mainly recruited from military and government bureaus, concerned with job responsibility and organizational channels, tended to look to chief for orders.

Whyte, William F. *Human Relations in the Restaurant Industry.* New York: McGraw-Hill, 1948.
Social and organizational problems peculiar to the restaurant industry as they occur in a group of twenty-five restaurants, including cafeteria, counter, and self-service but mostly fairly large service restaurants. The industry seen as aid to upward mobility of some groups and as refuge for other groups who are going down the social ladder. Attention given to the position of the waitress (or waiter) and the need to reconcile often conflicting needs of kitchen staff and customers, the even more complicated problems of the supervisors, and the more general problems of race relations and trade union organization.

Wohlstetter, Roberta. *Pearl Harbor: Warning and Decision.* Stanford: Stanford University Press, 1962.
Detailed analysis of intelligence operations within various units of U.S. army and navy before Japan's successful surprise attack on Pearl Harbor in December 1941. Information on deteriorating relations with Japan obtained by cracking Japanese secret code and other sources. Proper interpretation before the event was impeded by greater interest in the European theater of operations, by conviction that major threat in Hawaii was local sabotage rather than external attack, by Japanese secrecy and bluff, and by a huge amount of competing and contradictory clues. Last-minute handling of information at Washington slowed down by insufficient cooperation among army and navy intelligence and operations unit, by insufficient knowledge of American foreign policy by intelligence officers, by War Plans Division's reluctance to accept communications from junior signal corps officers, and by army and navy failure to follow up on last minute warnings to Hawaiian forces. Last-minute warnings by army radar, naval submarine, and naval air patrol impeded by technical deficiencies, personnel shortage, and inadequate training.

Worthy, James C. "Organizational Structure and Employee Morale," *American Sociological Review.* April, 1950, p. 169-179.
Large number of Sears-Roebuck employees indicated that trends toward increasing size of administrative units and increasing complexity of organizational structure were detrimental to employee morale and operating efficiency. These trends made effective integration difficult and contributed to deterioration of management-employee relations.

Zaleznik, A. *Foremen Training in a Growing Enterprise.* Boston: Graduate School of Business Administration, Harvard University, 1951.
Tony, newly appointed foreman of a line in a plant reorganization, was not helped in his efforts to be an effective supervisor by the supervisory training conferences in which he participated. Tony's inability to modify his beliefs and actions in accordance with his experience prevented his growth and development on the job, and negative relationships that existed between him and people he worked with precluded the possibility of help from them. The training conferences, concerned mainly with abstract theories and rules of behavior, did not help supervisors learn from their own experiences and from shared discussions.

Zaleznik, A. *Worker Satisfaction and Developments: A Case Study of Work and Social Behavior in a Factory Group.* Boston: Graduate School of Business Administration, Harvard University, 1956.
Interrelations of the working and social patterns of a fourteen-worker machine tool workshop and its foreman. The function of the social organization is to insure survival for the group and fulfill two basic requirements: (1) meeting minimum expectations of management, and (2) satisfying social needs of workers

at level they have come to expect from previous experience (i.e., "status"). Group studied had necessary characteristics: well-defined and interrelated structure, informal and formal leaders, and harmony with group purpose. In absence of challenge from outside, work group will tend to become frozen at this minimum level, with possible ultimate dissatisfaction with the adjusted pattern of work life.

Zaleznik, A., C. R. Christensen, and F. J. Roethlisberger. *The Motivation, Productivity, and Satisfaction of Workers: A Prediction Study.* Boston: Graduate School of Business Administration, Harvard University, 1958.

Interactions of 45-member department of medium-sized manufacturing company observed and analyzed in terms of predictive theories of worker motivation. External and internal determinants of worker motivation, respectively: external rewards satisfy workers' needs for job satisfaction, status, and recognition; internal rewards satisfy needs for support, interaction, approval, and belonging. Congruence between various components of social status seen important for workers' group membership and satisfactions. Productivity and satisfaction more strongly affected by internal rewards, but these rewards tended to keep productivity to the minimum that management expected.

GENERAL BIBLIOGRAPHY

Ackoff, Russell L. "Operations Research and National Planning," *Operations Research*. 1957, p. 457-468.

Adams, Brooks. *The Theory of Social Revolution*. New York: Macmillan, 1913.

Adams, Richard N., and Jack J. Preiss, eds. *Human Organization Research*. Homewood, Ill.: Dorsey, 1960.

Adorno, T. W., Else Frenkel-Brunswik, D. J. Levinson, and R. N. Sanford. *The Authoritarian Personality*. New York: Harper, 1950.

Advisory Committee on International Organization. *Staffing International Organizations*. Washington, D.C.: Department of State, 1963.

Alexander, Sidney S. *Five Monographs on Business Income*. New York: American Institute of Certified Public Accountants, 1950.

Allport, Floyd H. *Social Psychology*. Boston: Houghton Mifflin, 1924

Allport, Floyd H. *Theories of Perception and the Concept of Structure*. New York: Wiley, 1955.

Allport, Floyd H. "A Structuronomic Conception of Behavior," *Journal of Abnormal and Social Psychology*. Vol. 64, 1962, p. 3-30.

Allport, Gordon. *Pattern and Growth in Personality*. New York: Holt, Rinehart and Winston, 1961.

Almond, Gabriel A. "Introduction: A Functional Approach to Comparative Politics." In Gabriel A. Almond and James S. Coleman, eds., *The Politics of Developing Areas*. Princeton: Princeton University Press, 1960.

Almond, Gabriel A., and James S. Coleman, eds. *The Politics of Developing Areas*. Princeton: Princeton University Press, 1960.

AlMulk, Nizam. *The Book of Government*. Hubert Drake, tr. London: Routledge and Kegan Paul, 1960.

American Hospital Association. *Hospital Nursing Service Manual*. New York: National League of Nursing Education, 1950.

American Political Science Association, Committee on Political Parties. *Toward a More Responsible Two-Party System.* New York: Rinehart, 1950.

Andrews, Kenneth R. "University Programs for Practicing Executives." Frank C. Pierson *et al., The Education of American Businessmen.* New York: McGraw-Hill, 1959.

Anthony, Robert N. *Management Accounting,* Revised. Homewood, Ill.: Irwin, 1960.

Appleby, Paul H. *Big Democracy.* New York: Knopf, 1945.

Appleby, Paul H. *Policy and Administration.* University, Ala.: University of Alabama Press, 1949.

Appleby, Paul H. *Morality and Administration in Democratic Government.* Baton Rouge: Louisiana State University Press, 1952.

Appleby, Paul. *Public Administration in India, Report of a Survey.* New Delhi: Government of India Press, 1957.

Apter, David E. *The Gold Coast in Transition.* Princeton, Princeton University Press, 1955.

Aranow, Edward R., and Herbert A. Einhorn. *Proxy Contests for Corporate Control.* New York: Columbia University Press, 1957.

Argyris, Chris. *Executive Leadership.* New York: Harper, 1953.

Argyris, Chris. *Personality and Organization.* New York: Harper, 1957.

Argyris, Chris. *Understanding Organizational Behavior.* Homewood, Ill.: Dorsey, 1960.

Aristotle's Politics. B. Jowett, tr. New York: Modern Library, 1943.

Arnold, Magda B. *Emotion and Personality.* 2 Vols. New York: Columbia University Press, 1960.

Arnold, Thurman. *The Folklore of Capitalism.* New Haven: Yale University Press, 1937.

Arrow, Kenneth. *Social Choice and Individual Values.* New York: Wiley, 1951.

Ashby, William Ross. *An Introduction to Cybernetics.* London: Chapman & Hall, 1958.

Ashby, William Ross. "General Systems Theory as a New Discipline," *General Systems Yearbook.* Vol. 3, 1958. p. 1-17.

Babbage, Charles. *On the Economy of Machinery and Manufactures.* London, 1832.

Bailey, Stephen K. "A Frank Statement of Affairs," *Public Administration Review.* Vol. 9, 1949, p. 51-53.

Bailey, Stephen Kemp. *Congress Makes a Law.* New York: Columbia University Press, 1950.

Bain, Joe S. *Industrial Organization.* New York: Wiley, 1959.

Baker, Helen. *Centralization and Decentralization in Industrial Relations.* Princeton, N.J.: Princeton University Press, 1954.

Bakke, E. Wight. *Organization and the Individual.* New Haven: Yale University Press, 1952.

Bakke, E. Wight. *A Norwegian Contribution to Management Development.* Bergen, Norway: Norwegian School of Economics and Business Administration, Administrative Research Foundation, 1959.

Bales, Robert F. *Interaction Process Analysis.* Reading, Mass.: Addison-Wesley, 1950.

Barber, Bernard. *Social Stratification*. New York: Harcourt, Brace, 1957.

Bar Hillel, Yehoshua. "An Examination of Information Theory," *Philosophy of Science*. 1955, p. 86-105.

Barnard, Chester. *The Functions of the Executive*. Cambridge: Harvard University Press, 1938.

Barnard, Chester. *Organization and Management*. Cambridge: Harvard University Press, 1948.

Barnard, Chester. "Elementary Conditions of Business Morals," *California Management Review*. Vol. I, 1958, p. 1-13.

Barnes, Louis B. *Organizational Systems and Engineering Groups*. Boston: Graduate School of Business Administration, Harvard University, 1960.

Barnett, Homer G. *Anthropology in Administration*. Evanston, Ill.: Row, Peterson, 1956.

Baumol, William J. *Economic Theory and Operations Analysis*. Englewood Cliffs, N.J.: Prentice-Hall, 1961.

Bavelas, Alex. "Communication Patterns in Task-Oriented Groups." In D. Cartwright and A. Zander, eds., *Group Dynamics*. Evanston, Ill.: Row, Peterson, 1953.

Beard, Charles A. *Public Policy and the General Will*. New York: Rinehart, 1941.

Beishline, John R. *Military Management for National Defense*. New York: Prentice-Hall, 1950.

Belknap, Ivan. *Human Problems in a State Mental Hospital*. New York: McGraw-Hill, 1956.

Bendix, Reinhard. *Work and Authority in Industry*. New York: Wiley, 1956.

Bentham, Jeremy. *The Theory of Legislation*. New York: Harcourt, Brace, 1931.

Bentley, Arthur F. *The Process of Government*. Bloomington: Principia Press, 1949.

Bentley, Arthur F. *Life, Language, Law: Essays in Honor by Arthur F. Bentley*. R. W. Taylor, ed. Yellow Springs: Antioch Press, 1957.

Berle, Adolph A., Jr., and Gardiner C. Means. *The Modern Corporation and Private Property*. New York: Macmillan, 1932.

Berle, Adolf A., Jr. *The 20th Century Capitalist Revolution*. New York: Harcourt, Brace, 1954.

Berle, Adolph A. *Power Without Property*. New York: Harcourt, Brace, 1959.

Berliner, Joseph S. *Factory and Manager in the USSR*. Cambridge: Harvard University Press, 1957.

Bertalanffy, Ludwig von. "General Systems Theory," *Main Currents in Modern Thought*. 1955, p. 75-83.

Bethel, Lawrence L. and others. *Essentials of Industrial Management*. New York: McGraw-Hill, 1955.

Bienstock, Gregory, Solomon M. Schwarz, and Aaron Yugow. *Management in Russian Industry and Agriculture*. New York: Oxford University Press, 1944.

Bierman, Harold, Jr. *Managerial Accounting—An Introduction*. New York: Macmillan, 1959.

Blaisdell, Donald C. "Pressure Groups, Foreign Policies, and International Politics," *The Annals*. 1958, p. 149-157.

Blau, Peter M. *The Dynamics of Bureaucracy*. Chicago: University of Chicago Press, 1955.

Blau, Peter M., and W. Richard Scott. *Formal Organizations*. San Francisco: Chandler Publishing Co., 1962.

Blum, Milton L. *Readings in Experimental Industrial Psychology*. New York: Prentice-Hall, 1952.

Bock, Edwin A. "Case Studies about Government: Achieving Realism and Significance." In Edwin A. Bock, ed., *Essays on the Case Method in Public Administration*. Brussels: International Institute of Administrative Sciences, 1952.

Bock, Edwin A., ed. *Essays on the Case Method of Administration*. Brussels: International Institute of Administrative Sciences, 1952.

Bock, Edwin A. and Alan K. Cambell, eds. *Case Studies in American Government*. Englewood Cliffs: Prentice-Hall, 1962.

Bock, Edwin A., ed. *State and Local Government: A Case Book*. University, Ala.: University of Alabama Press, 1963.

Bornstein, Morris. "The Soviet Price System," *American Economic Review*. Vol. 52, 1962, p. 64-103.

Boulding, Kenneth E. *The Organizational Revolution*. New York: Harper, 1953.

Boulding, Kenneth E. *The Skills of the Economist*. Cleveland: Howard Allen, 1958.

Boulding, Kenneth E. "The Present Position of the Theory of the Firm." In Kenneth E. Boulding and W. Allen Spivey, *Linear Programming and the Theory of the Firm*. New York: Macmillan, 1960.

Boulding, Kenneth E., and W. Allen Spivey. *Linear Programming and the Theory of the Firm*. New York: Macmillan, 1960.

Bradshaw, Thornton F., and Charles C. Hull. *Controllership in Modern Management*. Chicago: Irwin, 1950.

Brech, Edward F. L. *Management: Its Nature and Significance*. 3rd ed. London: Pitman, 1953.

Brech, Edward F. L., ed. *The Principles and Practice of Management*. New York: Longmans, Green, 1953.

Brech, Edward F. L. *Organisation*. London: Longmans, Green, 1957.

Brecht, Arnold, and Comstock Glaser. *The Art and Technique of Administration in German Ministries*. Cambridge: Harvard University Press, 1940.

Bridgman, Donald S. "Company Management Development Programs." In Frank C. Pierson and others, eds., *The Education of American Businessmen*. New York: McGraw-Hill, 1959.

Bridgman, Percy Williams. *The Logic of Modern Physics*. New York: Macmillan, 1946.

Bright, James R. *Automation and Management*. Boston: Harvard University Graduate School of Business Administration, 1958.

Brijs, A. *Comment est concu et organisé le mouvement ouvrier chrètien en Belgique*. Brussels: Mouvement Ouvrier Chrètien, 1957.

Brown, Alvin. *Organization: A Formulation of Principle*. New York: Hibbert Printing Co., 1945.

Brown, Alvin. *Organization of Industry*. New York: Prentice-Hall, 1947.

Brown, D. Mackenzie. *The White Umbrella*. Berkeley: University of California Press, 1958.

Brownell, Drucker. *The Human Community.* New York: Harper, 1950.

Brownlow, Louis. *The President and the Presidency.* Chicago: Public Administration Service, 1949.

Brownlow, Louis. *A Passion for Politics.* Chicago: University of Chicago Press, 1955.

Brownrigg, William. *The Human Enterprise Process and Its Administration.* University, Ala.: University of Alabama Press, 1954.

Bruner, Jerome S. *The Process of Education.* Cambridge: Harvard University Press, 1961.

Bruner, Jerome. *On Knowing.* Cambridge: Harvard University Press, 1962.

Bruner, Jerome S., Jacqueline J. Goodnow, and George A. Austin. *A Study of Thinking.* New York: Wiley, 1956.

Bryson, Lyman. "Notes on a theory of Advice," *Political Science Quarterly.* Vol. 66, 1951, p. 321-339.

Buber, Martin. *Moses, the Revelation and the Covenant.* New York: Harper, 1958.

Burkhead, Jesse. *Government Budgeting.* New York: Wiley, 1956.

Burnham, James. *The Managerial Revolution.* New York: John Day, 1941.

Burns, Tom. "Management in Action," *Operational Research Quarterly.* 1957, p. 45-60.

Bursk, Edward C., ed. *The Management Team.* Cambridge: Harvard University Press, 1955.

Bush, George P., and Lowell H. Hattery, eds. *Scientific Research: Its Administration and Organization.* Washington, D.C.: American University Press, 1950.

Bush, Vannevar. "As We May Think," *Atlantic Monthly.* August, 1945.

Canfield, Bertrand R. *Public Relations.* Homewood, Ill.: Irwin, 1956.

Cannon, Walter B. *Wisdom of the Body*, Revised. New York: Norton, 1939.

Cantor, Nathaniel. *Dynamics of Learning.* Buffalo: Henry Stewart, 1946.

Cantor, Nathaniel. *The Teaching-Learning Process*, New York: Holt, 1953.

Cantor, Nathaniel. *The Learning Process for Managers.* New York: Harper, 1958.

Caplow, Theodore. "Organizational Size," *Administrative Science Quarterly.* 1957, p. 484-505.

Carlson, Sune. *Executive Behavior: A Study of the Work Load and the Working Methods of Managing Directors.* Stockholm: Strömberg Aktielbolog, 1951.

Cartwright, Dorwin, ed. *Studies in Social Power.* Ann Arbor: University of Michigan Press, 1959.

Cartwright, Dorwin, and Alvin Zander, eds. *Group Dynamics: Research and Theory.* Evanston, Ill.: Row, Peterson, 1953.

Cassinelli, C. W. "The Totalitarian Party," *Journal of Politics.* 1962, p. 111-141.

Castiglione, Baldesar. *The Book of the Courtier.* French Simpson, tr. New York: Ungar, 1959.

Cattell, R. "Concepts and Methods in the Measurement of Group-Syntality," *Psychological Review.* Vol. 55, 1948.

Catton, Bruce. *The War Lords of Washington.* New York: Harcourt, Brace, 1948.

Caudill, William. *The Psychiatric Hospital as a Small Society*. Cambridge: Harvard University Press, 1958.

Chamberlain, Neil W. *The Firm*. New York: McGraw-Hill, 1962.

Chapman, Brian. *The Profession of Government*. London: Allen & Unwin, 1959.

Chapple, Eliot D., and Carleton S. Coon. *Principles of Anthropology*. London: Jonathan Cape, 1947.

Chapple, Eliot D., and Leonard R. Sayles. *The Measurement of Management*. New York: Macmillan, 1961.

Churchman, C. West, Russell L. Ackoff, and E. Leonard Arnoff. *Introduction to Operations Research*. New York: Wiley, 1961.

Clark, J. Maurice. *Studies in the Economics of Overhead Costs*. Chicago: University of Chicago Press, 1923.

Clawson, Marion. "Reminiscences of the Bureau of Land Management," *1947-48 Agricultural History*. Vol. 33, 1959, p. 22-28.

Cleveland, Harlan. "The Blurred Line Between 'Public' and 'Private.'" In Conference on Science, Philosophy and Religion in Their Relation to the Democratic Way of Life, *Ethics and Bigness*, New York: Harper 1962.

Cleveland, Harlan. "A Philosophy for the Public Executive." In Edmund N. Fulker, ed., *The Influences of Social Scientific, and Economic Trends on Government Administration*. Washington, D.C.: U.S. Department of Agriculture, 1960.

Cleveland, Harlan. "Crisis Diplomacy," *Foreign Affairs*. 1963, p. 3-14.

Cleveland, Harlan, Gerard Mangone, and John C. Adams. *The Overseas Americans*. New York: McGraw-Hill, 1960.

Clinard, Marshall B. *The Black Market*. New York: Rinehart, 1952.

Cohen, Kalman J., and Eric Rhenman. "Management Games in Education and Research," *Management Science*. Vol. 7, 1961, p. 131-166.

Cohen, Morris Raphael. *A Preface to Logic*. New York: Meridian Books, 1956.

Cole, Arthur H. "A Note on Continuity of Enterprise," *Business History Review*. Vol. 1, 1961, p. 75-88.

Committee on Foreign Affairs Personnel. *Personnel for the New Diplomacy*. Washington, D.C.: Carnegie Endowment for International Peace, 1963.

Commission on the Organization of the Executive Branch of the Government. *Budgeting and Accounting*. Washington, D.C.: Government Printing Office, 1949.

Committee on Political Parties, American Political Science Association. *Toward a More Responsible Two-Party System*. New York: Rinehart, 1950.

Committee on Social Work Education and Personnel. *The Supervisor of Caseworkers in the Public Welfare Agency*. Chicago: American Public Welfare Association, 1958.

Commons, John R. *Institutional Economics*. New York: Macmillan, 1934.

Commons, John P. *The Economics of Collective Action*. New York: Macmillan, 1951.

Copley, Frank B. *Frederick W. Taylor: Father of Scientific Management*. 2 Vols. New York: Harper, 1923.

Corwin, Edward S. *The President: Office and Powers, 1787-1948* 3rd ed. New York: New York University Press, 1948.

Coser, Lewis A. *The Functions of Social Conflict*. New York: Free Press, 1956.

Coser, Lewis A. "The Termination of Conflict," *Conflict Resolution.* Vol. 5, 1961, p. 347-353.

Cottrell, Fred. *Energy and Society.* New York: McGraw-Hill, 1955.

Cruttwell, Patrick. *A Matter of Succession.* New York: Macmillan, 1962.

Cyert, Richard M. and James G. March. *A Behavioral Theory of the Firm.* Englewood Cliffs, N.J.: Prentice-Hall, 1963.

Dahl, Robert A. "The Concept of Power," *Behavioral Science.* Vol. 2, 1957, p. 201-215.

Dahl, Robert. "A Critique of the Ruling Elite Model," *American Political Science Review.* 1958, p. 463-469.

Dahl, Robert A. *Who Governs? Democracy and Power in an American City.* New Haven: Yale University Press, 1961.

Dahl, Robert A., and Charles E. Lindblom. *Politics, Economics and Welfare.* New York: Harper, 1953.

Davis, Hiram S. *Productivity Accounting.* Philadelphia: University of Pennsylvania Press, 1955.

Davis, John P. *Corporations.* Reprint, New York: Capricorn, 1961.

Davis, Ralph C. *The Fundamentals of Top Management.* New York: Harper, 1951.

Dean, Joel. *Managerial Economics.* Englewood Cliffs, N.J.: Prentice-Hall, 1951.

Denison, Edward F. *The Sources of Economic Growth in the United States.* New York: Committee for Economic Development, 1962.

Dennison, Henry S. *Organization Engineering.* New York: McGraw-Hill, 1931.

Deutsch, Karl W. *The Nerves of Government.* New York: Free Press, 1963.

Dewey, John. *Intelligence in the Modern World.* New York: Random House, 1939.

Dewey, John, and Arthur F. Bentley. *Knowing and the Known.* Boston: Beacon Press, 1949.

Dimock, Marshall E. *The Executive in Action.* New York: Harper, 1945.

Dimock, Marshall E., Gladys O. Dimock, and Louis W. Koenig. *Public Administration.* New York: Rinehart, 1958.

Dimock, Marshall E., and Howard K. Hyde. *Bureaucracy and Trusteeship in Large Corporations.* Washington, D.C.: U.S. Government Printing Office, 1940. (U.S. Temporary National Economic Committee. Investigation of Concentration of Economic Power. Monograph, No. 11.)

Donaldson, Elvin F. *Corporate Finance.* New York: Ronald Press, 1957.

Donham, Wallace B. "The Theory and Practice of Administration," *Harvard Business Review.* Vol. 14, 1936, p. 405-413.

Dorsey, John T. "An Information-Energy Model." In Ferrell Heady and Sybil Stokes, eds., *Papers in Comparative Public Administration.* Ann Arbor: The University of Michigan, 1962, p. 37-57.

Drucker, Peter F. *The Concept of the Corporation.* New York: John Day, 1946.

Drucker, Peter F. *The New Society.* New York: Harper, 1950.

Drucker, Peter F. *The Practice of Management.* New York: Harper, 1954.

Drury, Horace B. *Scientific Management, A History and Criticism.* New York: Columbia University Press, 1915.

Dubin, Robert. "Industrial Conflict and Social Welfare," *Conflict Resolution*. Vol. 1, 1957, p. 179-199.

Dubin, Robert. *The World of Work*. Englewood Cliffs, N.J.: Prentice-Hall, 1958.

Dubin, Robert, ed. *Human Relations in Administration*. 2d ed. Englewood Cliffs, N.J.: Prentice-Hall, 1961.

Dubin, Robert. "Business Behavior Behaviorally Reviewed," In C. Argyris *et al.*, *Social Science Approaches to Business Behavior*. Homewood, Ill.: Dorsey-Irwin, 1962.

Duverger, Maurice. *Political Parties*. Barbara and Robert North, trs. New York: Wiley, 1954.

Easton, David. *The Political System*. New York: Knopf, 1953.

Easton, David. "Limits of the Equilibrium Model in Social Research," *Behavioral Science*. Vol. 1, 1956, p. 96-104.

Edel, Abraham. *Ethical Judgment*. New York: Free Press, 1955.

Eells, Richard. *The Government of Corporations*. New York: Free Press, 1962.

Egger, Rowland. "Fable for Wise Men," *Public Administration Review*. Vol. 4, 1944, p. 371-376.

Eisenhower, Dwight D. *Crusade in Europe*. Garden City: Doubleday, 1948.

Emery, F. E., and E. L. Trist. "The Causal Texture of Organizational Environments." Mimeographed. London: Tavistock Institute of Human Relations, 1963.

Emmerich, Herbert. *Essays on Federal Reorganization*. University, Ala.: University of Alabama Press, 1950.

Encyclopedia of Associations. 3rd ed. Vol. I. Detroit: Gale Research Company, 1961.

Encyclopedia of the Social Sciences. New York: Macmillan, 1930-1935.

Erikson, Erik H. *Childhood and Society*. New York: Norton, 1950.

Esman, Milton. "The Politics of Development Administration." Prepared for the Comparative Administration Group Seminar. Boston, 1963.

Etzioni, Amitai. *A Comparative Analysis of Complex Organizations*. New York: Free Press, 1961.

Etzioni, Amitai, ed. *Complex Organizations: A Sociological Reader*. New York: Holt, Rinehart and Winston, 1961.

Ewing, David W., ed. *Long-range Planning for Management*. New York: Harper, 1958.

Fainsod, Merle. *How Russia Is Ruled*. Revised. Cambridge: Harvard University Press, 1963.

Fayerweather, John. *The Executive Overseas*. Syracuse: Syracuse University Press, 1959.

Fayol, Henri. "The Administrative Theory of the State." Sarah Green, tr. In Luther Gulick and L. Urwick, eds., *Papers on the Science of Administration*. New York: Institute of Public Administration, 1937.

Fayol, Henri. *General and Industrial Management*. Constance Storrs, tr. London: Pitman, 1949.

Ferber, Robert, and Hugh G. Wales. *Motivation and Market Behavior*. Homewood, Ill.: Irwin, 1958.

Ferrero, Guglielmo. *The Principles of Power*. Theodore Jaeckel, tr. New York: Putnam, 1942.

Fesler, James W. *Area and Administration*. University Ala.: University of Alabama Press, 1949.

Festinger, Leon. Cognitive Dissonance," *Scientific American*. 1962, p. 93-102.

Finer, Samuel E. *Anonymous Empire*. London: Pall Mall Press, 1958.

Finney, Harry A., and Herbert E. Miller. *Principles of Accounting, Advanced*. Englewood Cliffs, N.J.: Prentice-Hall, 1934.

Finney, Harry A., and Herbert E. Miller. *Principles of Accounting, Introductory*. 5th ed. Englewood Cliffs, N.J.: Prentice-Hall, 1957.

Finney, Harry A., and Herbert E. Miller. *Principles of Accounting, Intermediate*. 5th ed. Englewood Cliffs, N.J.: Prentice-Hall, 1958.

Fitzgibbon, Russell H., and Kenneth F. Johnson. "Measurement of Latin American Political Change," *American Political Science Review*. 1961, p. 515-526.

Follett, Mary P. *The Speaker of the House of Representatives*. London: Longmans, Green, 1896.

Follett, Mary P. *The New State*. London: Longmans, Green, 1920.

Follett, Mary P. *Creative Experience*. London: Longmans, Green, 1924.

Follett, Mary P. *Dynamic Administration: The Collected Papers of Mary Follett*. Henry C. Metcalf and Lyndall Urwick, eds. New York: Harper, 1942.

Fortes, Meyer, and E. E. Evans-Pritchard, eds. *African Political Systems*. London: Oxford University Press, 1940.

Foulke, Roy A. *Behind the Scenes of Business*. Revised. New York: Dun and Bradstreet, 1937.

France, Anatole. *Penguin Island*. New York: Modern Library, 1933.

French, John R. P. "A Formal Theory of Social Power," *General Systems Yearbook*. 1957, p. 92-101.

Freud, Sigmund. *Civilization and Its Discontents*. J. Riviere, tr. London: Hogarth Press, 1953.

Friedrich, Carl J. *Constitutional Government and Democracy*. New York: Ginn, 1941.

Friedrich, Carl J., and associates. *American Experiences in Military Government in World War II*. New York: Rinehart, 1948.

Friedrich, Carl J., ed. *The Public Interest*. New York: Atherton Press, 1962.

Fromm, Erich. *The Sane Society*. New York: Rinehart, 1955.

Fromm, Erich. *The Art of Loving*. New York: Harper, 1956.

Galbraith, John Kenneth. *American Capitalism: The Concept of Countervailing Power*. New York: Houghton Mifflin, 1952.

Galbraith, John Kenneth. *The Affluent Society*. Boston: Houghton Mifflin, 1958.

Gange, John. *The Secretariat Function: A Staff Aid for Executive Management*. Chicago: Public Administration Clearing House, 1953.

Gantt, Henry L. *Organizing for Work*. New York: Harcourt, Brace, and Howe, 1919.

Gardner, Burleigh B., and David G. Moore. *Human Relations in Industry*. 3rd ed. Homewood, Ill.: Irwin, 1955.

Garfinkel, Harold. "The Rational Properties of Scientific and Common Sense Activities," *Behavioral Science*. Vol. 5, 1960, p. 72-83.

Gaus, John Merriman. *Reflections on Public Administration*. University, Ala.: University of Alabama Press, 1947.

Gaus, John Merriman, Leonard D. White, and Marshall E. Dimock. *The Frontiers of Public Administration*. Chicago: University of Chicago Press, 1936.

Gettell, Raymond G. *History of Political Thought*. 2d ed. Revised. New York: Appleton-Century-Crofts, 1924.

Ghoshal, U. N. *A History of Indian Political Ideas*. London: Oxford University Press, 1959.

Gierke, Otto. *Political Theories of the Middle Ages*. Frederic W. Maitland, tr. New York: Cambridge University Press, 1958.

Gilbert, Milton, and Irving B. Kravis. *An International Comparison of National Products and Purchasing Power of Currencies*. Paris: Organization for European Economic Cooperation, 1953.

Gilbreth, Frank B. *Primer of Scientific Management*. 2d ed. New York: Van Nostrand, 1914.

Gladden, Edgar N. *The Essentials of Public Administration*. London: Staples Press, 1953.

Glover, J. D. *The Attack on Big Business*. Boston: Graduate School of Business Administration, Harvard University, 1954.

Glover, John D., and Ralph M. Hower, *The Administrator: Cases on Human Relations in Business*. Revised. Homewood, Ill.: Irwin, 1952.

Glover, John G., and Coleman L. Maze. *Managerial Control: Instruments and Methods in Industry*. New York: Ronald Press, 1937.

Goetz, Billy Early. *Management Planning and Control: A Managerial Approach to Industrial Accounting*. New York: McGraw-Hill, 1949.

Goffman, Erving. "Characteristics of Total Institutions." In M. Stein, A. Vidich and D. M. White, eds., *Identity and Anxiety*. New York: Free Press, 1960.

Goldstein, Kurt. *The Organism*. New York: American Book, 1939.

Gollancz, Victor. *Man and God*. Boston: Houghton Mifflin, 1951.

Goode, Cecil E. *Personnel Research Frontiers*. Chicago: Public Personnel Association, 1958.

Goodnow, Frank J. *Politics and Administration: A Study in Government*. New York: Macmillan, 1900.

Gordon, Robert A. *Business Leadership in the Large Corporation*. Washington, D.C.: Brookings Institution, 1945.

Gordon, Robert A., and James E. Howell. *Higher Education for Business*. New York: Columbia University Press, 1959.

Gore, M. S. "The Nature of the Adaptive Demands Confronting the North American Social Worker Serving in Developing Countries," Work Paper Outline for 1961 Annual Program Meeting. New York: Council on Social Work Education, 1961.

Gouldner, Alvin W., ed. *Studies in Leadership: Leadership and Democratic Action*. New York: Harper, 1950.

Gouldner, Alvin. "Red Tape as a Social Problem." In R. K. Merton, *et al.*, *Reader in Bureaucracy*. New York: Free Press, 1952, p. 410-418.

Gouldner, Alvin. "Organizational Analysis." In R. K. Merton, L. Bloom and L. Cottrell, eds., *Sociology Today*. New York: Basic Books, 1959.

Gragg, Charles I. "Teachers Also Must Learn," *Harvard Educational Review*. January, 1940.

Gragg, Charles I. "Because Wisdom Can't Be Told," *Harvard Alumni Bulletin*, October 19, 1940. Reprinted in M. P. McNair, ed., *The Case Method at the Harvard Business School*. New York: McGraw-Hill, 1954, p. 6-14.

Gragg, Charles I. "Whose Fault Was It?" *Harvard Business Review*. Vol. 42, 1964.

Granick, David. *Management of the Industrial Firm in the USSR*. New York: Columbia University Press, 1954.

Granick, David. *The Red Executive*. New York: Doubleday, 1960.

Granick, David. *The European Executive*. New York: Doubleday, 1962.

Graves, W. Brooke. *Public Administration in a Democratic Society*. Boston: D. C. Heath, 1950.

Gross, Bertram M. "The Coming Revolution in Economic Thought?" *Life, Language, Law: Essays in Honor of Arthur F. Bentley*. Yellow Springs: Antioch Press, 1957.

Gross, Bertram M. "Operation Basic: The Retrieval of Wasted Knowledge," *Journal of Communication*. Vol. 12, 1962, p. 67-83.

Guetzkow, Harold, George Kosmetsky, and George Tyndall. *Centralization and Decentralization in Organizing the Controller's Department*. New York: The Controllership Foundation, 1954.

Gulick, Luther. *Administrative Reflection on World War II*. University, Ala.: University of Alabama Press, 1948.

Gulick, Luther, and Lyndall Urwick, eds. *Papers on the Science of Administration*. New York: Institute of Public Administration, 1937.

Hackett, John, and Anne-Marie Hackett. *Economic Planning in France*. Cambridge: Harvard University Press, 1963.

Hagen, Everett. *On the Theory of Social Change*. Homewood, Ill.: Dorsey, 1962.

Haire, Mason. *Modern Organization Theory*. New York: Wiley, 1959.

Hall, Edward T. *The Silent Language*. New York: Premier Books, 1961.

Hammond, Peter B. "The Functions of Indirection in Communication." In James D. Thompson and others, eds., *Comparative Studies in Administration*. Pittsburgh: University of Pittsburgh Press, 1959, p. 183-194.

Hansen, Harry L. *Marketing*. Homewood, Ill.: Irwin, 1956.

Harbison, Frederick, and Charles Myers. *Management in the Industrial World*. New York: McGraw-Hill, 1959, p. 69-73.

Harbrecht, Paul P. *Pension Funds and Economic Power*. New York: Twentieth Century Fund, 1959.

Hare, A. Paul. "Interaction and Consensus in Different Sized Groups." In D. Cartwright and A. Zander, eds., *Group Dynamics*. Evanston, Ill.: Row, Peterson, 1953, p. 501-518.

Harsanyi, John C. "Measurement of Social Power, Opportunity Costs and the Theory of Two-Person Bargaining Games," *Behavioral Science*. Vol. 7, 1962, p. 67-79.

Harsanyi, John C. "Measurement of Social Power in n-Person Reciprocal Power Situations," *Behavioral Science*. Vol. 7, 1962, p. 81-91.

Hart, Liddell. *Strategy*. New York: Praeger, 1954.

Hartley, Eugene, and Ruth Hartley. *Fundamentals of Social Psychology*. New York: Knopf, 1952.

Hartmann, Heinz. *Authority and Organization in German Management*. Princeton: Princeton University Press, 1959.

Hazard, John N. *The Soviet System of Government*. Chicago: University of Chicago Press, 1957.

Henderson, Laurence J. *Pareto's General Sociology*. Cambridge: Harvard University Press, 1935.

Henriques, Robert. *A Hundred Hours to Suez*. New York: Viking, 1957.

Hepner, Harry W. *Modern Marketing*. New York: McGraw-Hill, 1955.

Hermann, Charles F. "Some Consequences of Crisis Which Limit the Viability of Organizations," *Administrative Science Quarterly*. Vol. 8, 1963, p. 61-82.

Herring, E. Pendleton. *Group Representation before Congress*. Baltimore: Johns Hopkins, 1929.

Herring, E. Pendleton. *Federal Commissioners: A Study of their Careers and Qualifications*. Cambridge: Harvard University Press, 1936.

Herring, E. Pendleton. *Public Administration and the Public Interest*. New York: McGraw-Hill, 1936.

Hilgard, E. R. "Creativity and Problem Solving." In H. H. Anderson, ed., *Creativity and its Cultivation*. New York: Harper, 1959.

Hirschman, Albert O. *The Strategy of Economic Development*. New Haven: Yale University Press, 1958.

Hirschman, Albert O. *Journeys Toward Progress*. New York: Twentieth Century Fund, 1963.

Hitch, Charles. "Operations Research and National Planning—A Dissent," *Operations Research*. 1957, p. 718-723.

Hittle, J. D. *The Military Staff*. Harrisburg: Military Service Publishing Corp., 1949.

Hobbs, Edward H. *Behind the President: A Study of Executive Office Agencies*. Washington, D.C.: Public Affairs Press, 1954.

Hogben, Lancelot. *Mathematics for the Millions*. 3d ed. London: Allen and Unwin, 1951.

Holden, Paul E., Lounsbury S. Fish, and Hubert L. Smith. *Top-Management Organization and Control*. Palo Alto, California: Stanford University Press, 1948.

Homans, George. *The Human Group*. New York: Harcourt, Brace, 1950.

Horney, Karen. *Neurosis and Human Growth*. New York: Norton, 1950.

Horney, Karen. *Our Inner Conflicts*. New York: Norton, 1955.

Hoselitz, Bert F. *A Reader's Guide to the Social Sciences*. New York: Free Press, 1959.

Hoxie, Robert. *Scientific Management and Labor*. New York: D. Appleton, 1915.

Huff, Darrell. *How to Lie with Statistics*. New York: Norton, 1954.

Huxley, Aldous. *Brave New World*. New York: Harper, 1932.

Huxley, Aldous. *Brave New World Revisited*. New York: Harper, 1958.

Hyneman, Charles S. *Bureaucracy in a Democracy*. New York: Harper, 1950.

Inkeles, Alex. "Social Stratification and Mobility in the Soviet Union." In Reinhard Bendix and Seymour M. Lipset, eds., *Class, Status and Power*. New York: Free Press, 1953.

Institute of Cost and Works Accountants. *The Accountancy of Changing Price Levels*. London, 1952.

International Labor Office. *Introduction to Work Study*. Geneva, 1957.

International Labor Office. *International Standard Classification of Occupations*. Geneva, 1958.

Ireson, William G., and Eugene L. Grant. *Handbook of Industrial Engineering and Management.* Englewood Cliffs, N.J.: Prentice-Hall, 1955.

James, William. "The Moral Equivalent of War," *Memories and Studies.* New York: Longmans, Green, 1934.
James, William. *Principles of Psychology.* New York: Dover, 1950, Vol. I.
Jaques, Elliott. *The Measurement of Responsibility.* London: Tavistock, 1956.
Jensen, G. "The Sociopsychological Structure of Instructional Groups." In Henry Nelson, ed., *Dynamics of Instructional Groups.* Chicago: University of Chicago Press, 1960.
Johnson, Donald M. *The Psychology of Thought and Judgment.* New York: Harper, 1955.
Johnson, Wendell. "You Can't Write Writing." In S. A. Hayakawa, ed., *Language, Meaning and Maturity.* New York: Harper, 1954.
Johr, W. A., and H. W. Singer. *The Role of the Economist as Official Adviser.* London: Allen and Unwin, 1955.
Jouvenal, Robert de. *La Republique des Camarades.* 1914.
Jucius, Michael J. *Personnel Management.* 3d ed. Homewood, Ill.: Irwin, 1955.
Juran, Joseph M. *Bureaucracy: A Challenge to Better Management.* New York: Harper, 1944.

Kahn, Herman. *On the Thermonuclear War.* Princeton: Princeton University Press, 1960.
Kai Kaus ibn Iskandar. *A Mirror for Princes.* New York: Dutton, 1951.
Kaplan, Abraham. *The Conduct of Inquiry.* San Francisco: Chandler, 1964.
Kapp, William K. *The Social Costs of Private Enterprise.* Cambridge: Harvard University Press, 1950.
Karr, David. *Fight for Control.* New York: Ballantine Books, 1956.
Katz, Elihu, and Paul F. Lazarsfeld. *Personal Influence.* New York: Free Press, 1955.
Kautilya. *Arthasastra,* 6th ed. Shamasastry Mysore, tr. Mysore Printing and Publishing House, 1960.
Kemeny, John G. "Mathematics Without Numbers." In Daniel Lerner, ed., *Quality and Quantity.* New York: Free Press, 1961.
Kendrick, John W. *Productivity Trends in the United States.* National Bureau of Economic Research. Princeton: Princeton University Press, 1961.
Kent, Allen. *Textbook on Mechanized Information Retrieval.* New York: Wiley, 1962.
Kent, Allen, and James W. Perry. *Centralized Information Services.* Cleveland: The Press of Western Reserve University, 1958.
Key, V. O. "The Lack of a Budgetary Theory," *American Political Science Review.* Vol. 34, 1940, p. 1137-1144.
Key, V. O. Jr. *Public Opinion and American Democracy.* New York: Knopf, 1961, p. 536.
Khera, S. S. *Government in Business.* Bombay: Asia Publishing House, 1963.
Kimball, D. S., and D. S. Kimball, Jr. *Principles of Industrial Organization.* 6th ed. New York: McGraw-Hill, 1947.

Kinnard, Willam N., and Zenon S. Malinowski. *The Turnover and Mortality of Manufacturing Firms in the Hartford, Connecticut Economic Area.* Washington, D.C.: Small Business Administration, 1960.

Kitto, H. D. F. *The Greeks.* London: Penguin Books, 1951.

Kluckhohn, Clyde. "Toward a Comparison of Value Emphases in Different Cultures." In Leonard White, ed., *The State of the Social Sciences.* Chicago: University of Chicago Press, 1956, p. 116-132.

Koontz, Harold, and Cyril O'Donnell. *Principles of Management.* New York: McGraw-Hill, 1955.

Kornai, Janos. *Overcentralization in Economic Administration.* John Knapp, tr. Oxford: Oxford University Press, 1959.

Kornhauser, Arthur. "The Problem of Bias in Opinion Research," *The International Journal of Opinion and Attitude Research.* Vol. 1, 1947, p. 1-13.

Krech, David, and Richard S. Crutchfield. *Theory and Problems of Social Psychology.* New York: McGraw-Hill, 1948.

Kuhn, Thomas. *The Structure of Scientific Revolutions.* Chicago: University of Chicago Press, 1962.

LaBarre, Weston. *The Human Animal.* Chicago: University of Chicago Press, 1954.

Landis, James M. *The Administrative Process.* New Haven: Yale University Press, 1938.

Lane, Robert E. *The Regulation of Businessmen.* New Haven: Yale University Press, 1954.

Lansberger, Henry. *Hawthorne Revisited.* Ithaca: Cornell University, 1958.

Lasswell, Harold D. *Politics: Who Gets What, When, How.* New York: McGraw-Hill, 1936.

Lasswell, Harold D., and Abraham Kaplan. *Power and Society.* New Haven: Yale University Press, 1950.

Latham, Earl. "The Body Politic of the Corporation." In Edward S. Mason, ed., *The Corporation in Modern Society.* Cambridge: Harvard University Press, 1960.

Le Breton, Preston P., and Dale A. Henning. *Planning Theory.* Englewood Cliffs, N.J.: Prentice-Hall, 1961.

Leighton, Alexander H. *Human Relations in a Changing World.* New York: Dutton, 1949.

Lenin, Vladimir I. *Selected Works.* Moscow: Foreign Languages Publishing House, 1946.

Leontief, Wassily W. *The Structure of the American Economy, 1919-1939.* New York: Oxford University Press, 1941.

Leontief, Wassily. "The Problem of Quantity and Quality in Economics." In Daniel Lerner, ed., *Quality and Quantity.* New York: Free Press, 1961.

Lepawsky, Albert. *Administration: The Art and Science of Organization and Management.* New York: Knopf, 1949.

Lerner, Daniel, ed. *Quantity and Quality.* New York: Free Press, 1961.

Levy, A. B. *Private Corporations and Their Control.* London: Routledge and Kegan Paul, 1957.

Lewin, Kurt. *A Dynamic Theory of Personality.* Donald K. Adams and Karl E. Zener, trs. New York: McGraw-Hill, 1935.

Lewin, Kurt. *Resolving Social Conflicts.* Gertrude Lewin, ed. New York: Harper, 1948.

Lewis, Clarence Irving. *An Analysis of Knowledge and Valuation.* LaSalle, Ill.: Open Court, 1946.

Lewis, John P. *Quiet Crisis in India.* Washington, D.C.: Brookings Institution, 1962.

Leys, Wayne A. R., and Charner Perry. *Philosophy and the Public Interest.* Chicago: Committee to Advance Original Work in Philosophy, 1959.

Lifton, Robert J. "Methods of Forceful Indoctrination: Psychiatric Aspects of Chinese Communist Thought Reform." In M. Stein, A. Vidich and D. M. White, eds., *Identity and Anxiety.* New York: Free Press, 1960.

Likert, Rensis. *New Patterns of Management.* New York: McGraw-Hill, 1961.

Lindblom, Charles E. "The Science of 'Muddling Through,'" *Public Administration Review.* Vol. 19, 1959, p. 79-88.

Lin Mousheng. *Men and Ideas.* New York: John Day, 1942.

Lin Yutang. *The Wisdom of Confucius.* New York: Modern Library, 1943.

Lin Yutang. *The Wisdom of Laotse.* New York: Random House, 1948.

Lippitt, Ronald, Jeanne Watson, and Bruce Westley. *The Dynamics of Planned Change.* New York: Harcourt, Brace, 1958, p. 142-143.

Litchfield, Edward H. "Notes on a General Theory of Administration." *Administrative Science Quarterly,* Vol. 1, 1956.

Little, I. M. D. *A Critique of Welfare Economics.* London: Oxford University Press, 1950.

Litwak, Eugene, and Lydia F. Hylton. "Interorganizational Analysis," *Administrative Science Quarterly.* 1962, p. 395-420.

Livingston, Joseph A. *The American Stockholder.* Philadelphia: Lippincott, 1958.

Long, Norton. "Power and Administration," *Public Administration Review.* Vol. 9, 1949, p. 257-264.

Luce, R. Duncan, and Howard Raiffa. *Games and Decisions.* New York: Wiley, 1957.

McCamy, James L. *The Administration of American Foreign Affairs.* New York: Knopf, 1950.

McClelland, David. *The Achieving Society.* Princeton: Princeton University Press, 1961.

Mace, Myles L. *The Growth and Development of Executives.* Cambridge: Harvard University Press, 1950.

McGregor, Douglas. "An Uneasy Look at Performance Appraisal," *Harvard Business Review.* 1957, p. 89-94.

McGregor, Douglas. *The Human Side of Enterprise.* New York: McGraw-Hill, 1960.

Machiavelli, Niccolò. *The Prince and the Discourses.* New York: Modern Library, 1950.

MacIver, Robert M. *The Web of Government.* New York: Macmillan, 1947.

Macmahon, Arthur W. *Administration in Foreign Affairs.* University, Ala.: University of Alabama Press, 1953.

Macmahon, Arthur W. and John D. Millett. *Federal Administration.* New York: Columbia University Press, 1939.

Macmahon, Arthur W., John D. Millett, and Gladys Ogden. *The Administration of Federal Work Relief.* Chicago: Public Administration Service, 1941.

McNair, Malcolm P. *The Case Method at the Harvard Business School.* New York: McGraw-Hill, 1954.

McNair, Malcolm P., and Elinor G. May. "Pricing for Profit," *Harvard Business Review.* 1957, p. 105-125.

Maier, Norman R. F. *Principles of Human Relations: Applications to Management.* New York: Wiley, 1952.

Malinowski, Bronislaw. *Crime and Custom in Savage Society.* New York: Harcourt, Brace, 1926, p. 40-41.

Malinowski, Bronislaw. *The Dynamics of Culture Change.* New Haven: Yale University Press, 1945.

Mann, James. "Psychoanalytic Observations Regarding Conformity in Groups," *International Journal of Group Psychotherapy.* Vol. 12, 1962.

Mannheim, Karl. *Man and Society in an Age of Reconstruction.* New York: Harcourt, Brace, 1948.

March, James G. "An Introduction to the Theory and Measurement of Influence," *The American Political Science Review.* Vol. 49, 1955, p. 431-451.

March, James G., and Herbert Simon. *Organizations.* New York: Wiley, 1958.

Marrow, Alfred J. *Making Management Human.* New York: McGraw-Hill, 1957.

Marshall, Alfred. *Economics of Industry.* 4th ed. London: Macmillan, 1909.

Marshall, Alfred. *Principles of Economics.* 8th ed. London: Macmillan, 1949.

Marx, Karl. *Capital.* New York: Modern Library, 1936.

Marx, Karl. "Theories of Surplus Value," *A History of Economic Theories.* New York: Langland Press, 1952.

Marx, Karl, and Friedrich Engels. "The Communist Manifesto," In Max Eastman, ed., *Capital the Communist Manifesto and Other Writings.* New York: Modern Library, 1959.

Maslow, A. H. *Motivation and Personality.* New York: Harper, 1954.

Mason, Edward S. *Economic Concentration and the Monopoly Problem.* Cambridge: Harvard University Press, 1957.

Mason, Edward S. *Economic Planning in Underdeveloped Areas.* New York: Fordham University Press, 1958.

Mason, Edward S., ed. *The Corporation in Modern Society.* Cambridge: Harvard University Press, 1960.

Maynard, Harold B., ed. *Industrial Engineering Handbook.* New York: McGraw-Hill, 1956.

Mayo, Elton. *The Human Problems of an Industrial Civilization.* Boston: Harvard Business School, 1933.

Mayo, Elton. *The Social Problems of an Industrial Civilization.* Boston: Graduate School of Business Administration, Harvard University, 1945.

Mayo, Elton. *The Political Problem of Industrial Civilization.* Boston: Harvard University, Graduate School of Business Administration, 1947.

Mead, George H. *Mind, Self and Society.* Chicago: University of Chicago Press, 1934.

Mee, John F., ed. *Personnel Handbook.* New York: Ronald Press, 1955.

Melman, Seymour. "The Rise of Administrative Overhead in the Manufacturing Industries of the U.S. 1899-1947," *Oxford Economic Papers.* 1951, p. 62-112.

Merriam, Charles E. *Public and Private Government.* New Haven: Yale University Press, 1944.

Merriam, Charles E. *Political Power.* New York: Free Press, 1950.

Merton, Robert K. *Social Theory and Social Structure*. Revised. New York: Free Press, 1957.

Merton, Robert K., Ailsa P. Gray, Barbara Hockey, and Hanan C. Selvin, eds. *Reader in Bureaucracy*. New York: Free Press, 1952.

Michels, Robert. *Political Parties*. New York: Free Press, 1949.

Miller, George A., Eugene Galenter, and Karl H. Pribram. *Plans and the Structure of Behavior*. New York: Holt, Rinehart and Winston, 1960.

Miller, James G. "Toward a General Theory for the Behavioral Sciences," *American Psychologist*. 1955, p. 513-531.

Millett, John D. *The Process and Organization of Government Planning*. New York: Columbia University Press, 1947.

Millett, John D. *Management in the Public Service*. New York: McGraw-Hill, 1954.

Millis, Harry A., and Royal E. Montgomery. *Organized Labor*. New York: McGraw-Hill, 1945.

Mills, C. Wright. *The New Men of Power*. New York: Harcourt, Brace, 1948.

Mills, C. Wright. *The Power Elite*. New York: Oxford University Press, 1956.

Mills, C. Wright. *The Sociological Imagination*. New York: Oxford University Press, 1959.

Mocius,"Works of Mocius," Kuo-Change Wu, *Ancient Chinese Political Theories*. Commerical Press, 1928.

Mooney, James D. *The Principles of Organization*. New York: Harper, 1947.

Mooney, James D., and Alan C. Reiley. *Onward Industry*. New York: Harper, 1931.

Moore, Wilbert E. *The Conduct of the Corporation*. New York: Random House, 1962.

Morgan, Clifford T. *Introduction to Psychology*. New York: McGraw-Hill, 1956.

Morgenstern, Oskar. *On the Accuracy of Economic Observations*. Revised. Princeton: Princeton University Press, 1963.

Moroney, M. J. *Facts from Figures*. London: Penguin, 1956.

Morris, Charles. "Axiology as the Science of Preferential Behavior." In Ray Lepley, ed., *Value: A Cooperative Inquiry*. New York: Columbia University Press, 1949.

Morstein Marx, Fritz. "The Bureau of the Budget: Its Evolution and Present Role," *American Political Science Review*. August 1945, p. 653-684; October, p. 868-898.

Morstein Marx, Fritz, ed. *Elements of Public Administration*. New York: Prentice-Hall, 1946.

Morstein Marx, Fritz. *The President and His Staff Services*. Chicago: Public Administration Service, 1947.

Mosca, Gaetano. *The Ruling Class*. Hannah D. Kahn, tr. New York: McGraw-Hill, 1939.

Mosher, Frederick C. *Program Budgeting*. Chicago: Public Administration Service, 1954.

Mosher, William E., J. Donald Kingsley, and O. Glenn Stahl. *Public Personnel Administration*. 3d ed. New York: Harper, 1950.

Mowrer, O. H. *Learning Theory and Behavior*. New York: Wiley, 1960.

Mumford, Lewis. *The Conduct of Life*. New York: Harcourt, Brace, 1951.

Murdock, George P. *Social Structure*. New York: Macmillan, 1949.

Murphy, Gardner. *Human Potentialities*. New York: Basic Books, 1958.

Murray, Henry A., and associates. *Explorations in Personality*. New York: Oxford University Press, 1938.

Myrdal, Gunnar. *The Political Element in the Developn·ent of Economic Theory*. Cambridge: Harvard University Press, 1954.

Nadworny, Milton J. *Scientific Management and the Trade Unions*. Cambridge: Harvard University Press, 1955.

Nagel, Ernest. *The Structure of Science*. New York: Harcourt, Brace, 1961.

National Organizations of the U.S. Vol. 1, Encyclopedia of Associations, 3d ed. Detroit: Gale Research Co., 1959.

Needler, Martin C. "The Political Development of Mexico," *American Political Science Review*. June, 1961, p. 308-312.

Neiswanger, William A. *Elementary Statistical Methods*. Revised. New York: Macmillan, 1956.

'Nelson, Henry, ed. *Dynamics of Instructional Groups*. Chicago: University of Chicago Press, 1960.

Neumann, Sigmund. *Permanent Revolution*. New York: Harper, 1942.

Newman, William H. *Administration Action*. New York: Prentice-Hall, 1951.

Newman, William H., and Charles E. Summer, Jr. *The Process of Management*. Englewood Cliffs, N.J.: Prentice-Hall, 1961.

Nigro, Felix, ed. *Public Administration Readings and Documents*. New York: Rinehart, 1951.

Nigro, Felix A. *Public Personnel Administration*. New York: Holt, 1959.

Northrop, F. S. C. *The Meeting of East and West*. New York: Macmillan, 1946.

Odegard, Peter H. *Pressure Politics: The Study of the Anti-Saloon League*. New York: Columbia University Press, 1928.

Ogburn, Charlton. "Merrill's Marauders," *Harper's Magazine*. January, 1957, p. 29-44.

Ogden, Charles K., and I. A. Richards. *The Meaning of Meaning*. 8th ed. London: Kegan Paul, Trench, Trubner, 1946.

Oppenheim, Felix E. "Degrees of Power and Freedom," *American Political Science Review*. 1960, p. 437-446.

Orwell, George. *Nineteen Eighty-four*. New York: Harcourt, Brace, 1949.

Packard, Vance. *The Hidden Persuaders*. New York: Pocket Books, 1957.

Pareto, Vilfredo. *Les Systèmes Socialistes*. Paris, 1902.

Pareto, Vilfredo. *Mind and Society*. Arthur Livingston, tr. New York: McGraw-Hill, 1935.

Parkinson, C. Northcote. *The Evolution of Political Thought*. Boston: Houghton Mifflin, 1958.

Parkinson, C. Northcote. *Parkinson's Law or the Pursuit of Progress*. London: John Murray, 1958.

Parsons, Talcott. *The Structure of Social Action*. New York: Free Press, 1949.

Parsons, Talcott. *The Social System*. New York: Free Press, 1951.

Parsons, Talcott. *Essays in Sociological Theory.* Revised. New York: Free Press, 1954.

Parsons, Talcott. *Structure and Process in Modern Societies.* New York: Free Press, 1960.

Parsons, Talcott, and Edward A. Shils, eds. *Toward a General Theory of Social Action.* Cambridge: Harvard University Press, 1951.

Pearce, Charles A. *Trade Association Survey.* Washington, D.C.: U.S. Government Printing Office, 1941. (U.S. Temporary National Economic Committee, Investigation of Concentration of Economic Power, Monograph, No. 18.)

Peck, Merton J., and Frederick M. Scherer. *The Weapons Acquisition Process.* Boston: Graduate School of Business Administration, Harvard University, 1962.

Pepper, Stephen C. *The Sources of Value.* Berkeley and Los Angeles: University of California Press, 1958.

Perry, Ralph Barton. *General Theory of Value.* Cambridge: Harvard University Press, 1926.

Perry, Ralph B. *Realms of Value.* Cambridge: Harvard University Press, 1954.

Person, Harlow S. ed. *Scientific Management in American Industry.* New York: Harper, 1929.

Petersen, Elmore, and E. Grosvenor Plowman. *Business Organization and Management.* 3d ed. Homewood, Ill.: Irwin, 1953.

Pfiffner, John M. *The Supervision of Personnel.* New York: Prentice-Hall, 1951.

Pfiffner, John M. "Administrative Rationality," *Public Administration Review.* Vol. 20, 1960, p. 125-132.

Pfiffner, John M., and R. Vance Presthus. *Public Administration.* 3d ed. New York: Ronald Press, 1953.

Pigors, Paul, and Charles A. Myers. *Personnel Administration.* New York: McGraw-Hill, 1947.

Pigou, A. C. *The Economics of Welfare.* 4th ed. London: Macmillan, 1952.

Plato. *Republic.* B. Jowett, tr. New York: Modern Library, 1941

Plato. *The Statesman.* J. B. Skemp, tr. New York: Liberal Arts Press, 1957.

Polanyi, Karl. *The Great Transformation.* Boston: Beacon Press, 1957.

Polanyi, Michael. *Personal Knowledge.* Chicago: University of Chicago Press, 1958.

Political and Economic Planning, *Economic Planning in France,* Vol, 27, No. 454, August, 1961.

Prasad, Beni. *Theory of Government in Ancient India.* Allahabad: Indian Press, 1928.

President's Committee on Administrative Management. *Administrative Management in the Government of the United States.* Washington, D.C.: Government Printing Office, 1937.

Price, D. G. Bureau of Naval Personnel, Letter to Bertram M. Gross, November 29, 1960.

Price, Don K. *Government and Science.* New York: New York University Press, 1954.

Pringle, J. W. S. "On the Parallel Between Learning and Evaluation," *General Systems.* Vol. 1, 1956.

Pritchett, C. H. "The Paradox of the Government Corporation," *Public Administration Review*. Vol. 1, 1941, p. 381.

Pritchett, C. Herman. *The Tennessee Valley Authority: A Study in Public Administration*. Chapel Hill: University of North Carolina Press, 1943.

Radcliffe-Brown, A. R. *Structure and Function in Primitive Society*. New York: Free Press, 1952.

Radcliffe-Brown, A. R. *A Natural Science of Society*. New York: Free Press, 1957.

Randall, Clarence B. *The Folklore of Management*. Boston: Little, Brown, 1959.

Rapoport, Anatol. *Operational Philosophy*. New York: Harper, 1954.

Rathenau, Walter. *In Days to Come*. E.: and C. Paul, trs. London, 1921.

Rautenstrauch, Walter, and Raymond Villers. *Budgetary Control*. New York: Funk and Wagnalls, 1950.

Redfield, Charles E. *Communication in Management*. Chicago: University of Chicago Press, 1953.

Riesman, David, Nathan Glazer, and Reuel Denny. *The Lonely Crowd*. New Haven: Yale University Press, 1951.

Riggs, Fred W. "Agraria and Industria—Toward a Topology of Comparative Administration." In W. J. Siffin, ed., *Toward a Comparative Study of Public Administration*. Bloomington: Indiana University Press, 1957.

Riggs, F. W. *The Ecology of Public Administration*. Bombay: Asia Publishing House, 1961, p. 75-76.

Robbins, Lionel. *An Essay in the Nature and Significance of Economic Science*. 2d ed. London: Macmillan, 1948.

Robinson. E. A. G. *The Structure of Competitive Industry*. Chicago: University of Chicago Press, 1957.

Roethlisberger, F. J. *Management and Morale*. Cambridge: Harvard University Press, 1941.

Roethlisberger, F. J., and others. *Training for Human Relations*. Boston: Graduate School of Business Administration, Harvard University, 1954.

Rogers, Carl. *Client-Centered Therapy*. Boston: Houghton Mifflin, 1951.

Rokeach, Milton. *The Open and Closed Mind*. New York: Basic Books, 1960.

Rokeach, Milton. "Authority, Authoritarianism and Conformity." In Irwin A. Berg, and Bernard M. Bass, eds., *Conformity and Deviation*. New York: Harper, 1961, p. 230-257.

Rokeach, Milton. "In Pursuit of the Creative Process." Paper delivered in February 1962 at Mackenzie Symposium on the Creative Organization.

Rosenstein-Rodan, P. N. "International Aid for Underdeveloped Countries," *The Review of Economics and Statistics*. 1961, p. 107-137.

Rostow, Walt W. *The Stages of Economic Growth*. New York: Cambridge University Press, 1960.

Rowland, Virgil K. *Managerial Performance Standards*. New York: American Management Association, 1960.

Roy, Robert. *The Administrative Process*. Baltimore: Johns Hopkins, 1958.

Rubinstein, Albert H. and Chadwick H. Haberstroh, eds. *Some Theories of Organization*. Homewood, Illinois: Dorsey and Irwin, 1960.

Ruggles, Richard. "The U.S. National Accounts and Their Development," *American Economic Review*. March 1959, p. 85-95.

Ruml, Beardsley. "Corporate Management as a Locus of Power," *Social Meaning of Legal Concepts*. New York: New York University School of Law, 1950, p. 219-241.

Russell, Bertrand. *Power*. London: Allen and Unwin, 1938.

Russell, Bertrand. *The Principles of Mathematics*. London: Allen and Unwin, 1950.

Ruttenberg, Harold J. *Self-Developing America*. New York: Harper, 1960.

Saint-Simon, Henri Comte de. *Selected Writings*. F. M. H. Markham, ed. New York: Macmillan, 1952.

Sayles, Leonard R. *Behavior of Industrial Work Groups*. New York: Wiley, 1958.

Sayre, Wallace. "The Triumph of Technique Over Purpose," *Public Administration Review*. Spring, 1943.

Sayre, Wallace S. "Trends of a Decade in Administrative Values," *Public Administration Review*. Vol. 2, 1951, p. 1-10.

Sayre, Wallace S. "Premises of Public Administration: Past and Emergent," *Public Administration Review*. Vol. 18, 1958, p. 102-105.

Schachter, Ruth. "Single Party Systems in West Africa," *American Political Science Review*. June, 1961, p. 294-307.

Schell, Erwin Haskell. *New Strength for New Leadership*. New York: Harper, 1942.

Schelling, Thomas C. *The Strategy of Conflict*. Cambridge: Harvard University Press, 1960.

Schlesinger, Arthur M. *The Coming of the New Deal*. Boston: Houghton Mifflin, 1958.

Schoeffler, Sidney. *The Failures of Economics: A Diagnostic Study*. Cambridge: Harvard University Press, 1955.

Schubert, Glendon. *The Public Interest*. New York: Free Press, 1961.

Schultz, Theodore. "Capital Formation by Education," *Journal of Political Economy*. Vol. 68, 1960, p. 571-583.

Schultz, Theodore. "Investment in Human Capital," *American Economic Review*. Vol. 51, 1961, p. 1-17.

Schutz, Alfred. "The Problem of Rationality in the Social World," *Economica*. Vol. 10, 1943, p. 130-149.

Schwartz, Bernard. *An Introduction to American Administrative Law*. London: Pitman, 1958.

Scott, James A. *The Measurement of Industrial Efficiency*. London: Pitman, 1950.

Scott, William G. *Human Relations in Management*. Homewood, Ill.: Irwin 1962.

Seckler-Hudson, Catheryn, ed. *Process of Organization and Management*. Washington, D.C.: Public Affairs Press, 1948.

Selekman, Sylvia K., and Benjamin M. Selekman. *Power and Morality in a Business Society*. New York: McGraw-Hill, 1956.

Selye, Hans. *The Stress of Life*. New York: McGraw-Hill, 1956.

Selznick, Philip. *Leadership in Administration*. Evanston, Ill.: Row, Peterson, 1957.

Selznick, Philip. *Private Government and the Corporate Conscience*. Paper prepared for Symposium on Business Policy Conference, Harvard Graduate School of Business Administration, 1963.

Shakespeare, William. *The Tragedy of Troilus and Cressida*. Revised. J. J. Campbell, ed. New Haven: Yale University Press, 1956.

Shannon, Claude, and Warren Weaver. *The Mathematical Theory of Communication*. Urbana: University of Illinois Press, 1949.

Shao, Liu. *The Study of Human Abilities*. J. K. Shryock, tr. American Oriental Series, Vol. II. New Haven: American Oriental Society, 1937.

Shapely, L. S., and Martin Shubik. "A Method for Evaluating the Distribution of Power in a Committee System," *The American Political Review*. Vol. 48, 1954, p. 787-792.

Shartle, Carroll. "Job Analysis and Job Evaluation," *Personnel Handbook*. John F. Mee, ed. New York: Ronald Press, 1955.

Sheldon, Oliver. *The Philosophy of Management*. New York: Pitman, 1923.

Shera, Jesse H. "Pattern, Structure and Conceptualization for Information Retrieval." In Jesse H. Shera, Allen Kent, and James W. Perry, eds., *Information Systems in Documentation*. Vol. 2. New York: Interscience Publishers, 1957, p. 15-38.

Simmel, Georg. *The Sociology of Georg Simmel*. Kurt H. Wolff, tr. New York: Free Press, 1950.

Simmel, Georg. *Conflict*. Kurt H. Wolff, tr. *The Web of Group-Affiliations*. Reinhard Bendix, tr., New York: Free Press, 1955.

Simon, Herbert. *Administrative Behavior: A Study of Decision-Making Processes in Administrative Organizations*. New York: Macmillan, 1947. Second edition, with new introduction by Simon, 1957.

Simon, Herbert. *Models of Man*. New York: Wiley, 1957.

Simon, Herbert A. *The New Science of Management Decision*. New York: Harper, 1960.

Simon, Herbert, and Clarence Ridley. *Measuring Municipal Activities*. Chicago: International City Managers' Association, 1938.

Simon, Herbert, Donald W. Smithburg, and Victor A. Thompson. *Public Administration*. New York: Knopf, 1950.

Simon, Herbert, Harold Guetzkow, George Kozmetsky, and Gordon Tyndall. *Centralization vs. Decentralization in Organizing the Controller's Department*. New York: Controllership Foundation, 1954.

Small, Albion W. *The Cameralists*. Chicago: University of Chicago Press, 1909.

Smith, Adam. *The Wealth of Nations*. New York: Modern Library, 1937.

Snow, C. P. *The Two Cultures and the Scientific Revolution*. London: Macmillan, 1959.

Sofer, Cyril, and Geoffry Hutton. *New Ways in Management Training*. London: Tavistock, 1958.

Spriegel, William R. *Industrial Management*. 5th ed. New York: Wiley, 1955.

Stagner, Ross. "Personality," *Encyclopaedia Britannica*. 1960 ed. Vol. 17, p. 605-610.

Stahl, O. Glenn. *Public Personnel Administration*. 4th ed. New York: Harper, 1956.

Stein, Harold, ed. *Public Administration and Policy Development: A Case Book*. New York: Harcourt, Brace 1952.

Stein, Harold. *American Civil-Military Decisions*. University, Ala.: University of Alabama Press, 1963.

Stinchcombe, Arthur. "On the Use of Matrix Algebra in the Analysis of Formal Organizations." In Amitai Etzioni, ed., *Complex Organizations*. New York: Holt, Rinehart and Winston, 1961, p. 478-484.

Stouffer, Samuel A. "Some Observations on Study Design," *American Journal of Sociology*, Vol. 55, 1950, p. 356-359.

Studenski, Paul. *The Income of Nations*. New York: New York University Press, 1958.

Sturmthal, Adolf. *Workers Councils*. Cambridge: Harvard University Press, 1964.

Summer, Charles E., Jr. *Factors in Effective Administration*. New York: Graduate School of Business, Columbia University, 1956.

Swerdlow, Irving. *Development Administration, Concepts and Problems*. Syracuse: Syracuse University Press, 1963.

Szasz, Thomas. *The Myth of Mental Illness*. New York: Hoeber-Harper, 1961.

Taft, Philip. "Democracy in Trade Unions," *American Economic Review*, Vol. 36, 1946, p. 359-369.

Tannenbaum, Arnold S. "An Event-Structure Approach to Social Power and to the Problem of Power Comparability," *Behavioral Science Review*. Vol. 17, 1962, p. 315-331.

Tannenbaum, Arnold S. "Control in Organizations," *Administrative Science Quarterly*. Vol. 7, 1962, p. 236-257.

Tawney, Richard H. *The Acquisitive Society*. London: G. Bell, 1927.

Taylor, Frederick. *Scientific Management*. New York: Harper, 1947.

Taylor, Henry. *The Statesman*. New York: Mentor Books, 1958.

Tead, Ordway. *The Art of Leadership*. New York: McGraw-Hill, 1935.

Tead, Ordway. *Human Nature and Management*. 2d ed. Revised. New York: McGraw-Hill, 1940.

Tead, Ordway. *The Art of Administration*. New York: McGraw-Hill, 1951.

Terry, George R. *Principles of Management*, Homewood, Ill.: Irwin, 1953.

Thompson, D'Arcy Wentworth. *On Growth and Form*. Abridged edition. Cambridge at the University Press, 1961.

Thompson, James D., *et al*. Staff of the Administrative Science Center. *Comparative Studies in Administration*. Pittsburgh: University of Pittsburgh Press, 1959.

Thompson, James D. "Common and Uncommon Elements in Administration," *Social Welfare Forum*. 1962, p. 181-201.

Thompson, John W. "Mental Science, Meteorology, and General System Theory," *General Systems*. Vol. 5, 1960.

Thompson, Victor. *Modern Organization*. New York: Knopf, 1961.

Tilles, Seymour. "Understanding the Consultant's Role," *Harvard Business Review*. 1961, p. 87-99.

Timberg, Sigmund. "Corporate Fictions: Logical, Social, and International Implications," *Columbia Law Review*. Vol. 46, 1946, p. 533-580.

Timberg, Sigmund. "The Corporation as a Technique of International Administration," *University of Chicago Law Review*. Vol. 19, 1952, p. 739-758.

de Tocqueville, Alexis. *Democracy in America*. New York: Oxford University Press, 1947.

Tolman, Edward C. *Purposeful Behavior in Animals and Men.* Berkeley: University of California Press, 1951.

Tout, Thomas F. *Chapters in the Administrative History of Medieval England.* Manchester: The University Press, 1920.

Towne, Henry R. *Transactions of the American Society of Mechanical Engineers.* Vol. III, 1886.

Trevor-Roper, Hugh R. *The Last Days of Hitler.* London: Macmillan, 1956.

Truman, David. *The Governmental Process.* New York: Knopf, 1951.

Turner, V. W. *Schism and Continuity in an African Society.* Manchester: Manchester University Press, 1957.

Tyler, Gus. *Organized Crime in America.* Ann Arbor: University of Michigan Press, 1962.

United Nations, Department of Economic and Social Affairs. *A Manual for Economic and Functional Classification of Government Transactions.* New York, 1958.

United Nations Secretariat, Statistical Office. *International Standard Industrial Classification of All Economic Activities.* (Statistical Papers, Series, M, no. 4.) New York, 1949.

United Nations Secretariat, Statistical Office. *A System of National Accounts and Supporting Tables.* (Studies in Methods, Series F. no. 2, rev.) New York, 1960.

United Nations Secretariat, Statistical Office. *Standard International Trade Classification.* (Statistical Papers, Series M, no. 10 Rev.) 2d ed. New York, 1951.

Urwick, Lyndall. *The Elements of Administration.* New York: Harper, 1943.

Urwick, Lyndall. *The Life and Work of Elton Mayo.* London: Urwick, Orr and Partners, 1960.

U.S. Bureau of the Census. *Census of Population: 1950,* Washington, D.C.: U.S. Government Printing Office, 1946.

U.S. Bureau of the Census. *Statistical Abstract of the United States.* Washington, D.C.: U.S. Government Printing Office, published annually.

U.S. Bureau of the Census. *Census of Population: 1950,* Washington, D.C.: U.S. Government Printing Office, 1952-1957.

U.S. Bureau of the Census. *Historical Statistics of the United States: Colonial Times to 1957.* Washington, D.C.: U.S. Government Printing Office, 1960.

U.S. Commission on the Organization of the Executive Branch of the Government, *Report to the Congress, no. 1; Budgeting and Accounting.* Washington, D.C.: U.S. Government Printing Office, 1949.

U.S. Department of the Air Force. *The Management Process.* Washington, D.C.: U.S. Government Printing Office, 1954.

U.S. Employment Service. *Dictionary of Occupational Titles.* 2d ed. Washington, D.C.: U.S. Government Printing Office, 1949

U.S. President's Committee on Administrative Management. *Report.* Washington, D.C.: U.S. Government Printing Office, 1937.

U.S. Senate Subcommittee on National Security Staffing and Operations, *Administration of National Security.* Washington, D.C.: 1963.

Veblen, Thorstein. *The Theory of the Leisure Class.* New York: Macmillan, 1899.

Villers, Raymond. *Dynamic Management in Industry.* Englewood Cliffs, N.J.: Prentice-Hall, 1960.

Viteles, Morris S. *Motivation and Morale in Industry.* New York: Norton, 1953.

Von Clausewitz, Karl. *On War.* O. J. Matthis Jolles, tr. Infantry Journal Press, 1950.

Von Justi, Johann. "Political Economy." In Albion W. Small, *The Cameralists.* Chicago: University of Chicago Press, 1909.

Von Mises, Ludwig. *Bureaucracy.* New Haven: Yale University Press, 1962.

Von Neumann, John, and Oskar Morgenstern. *Theory of Games and Economic Behavior.* Princeton: Princeton University Press, 1953.

Waldo, Dwight. *The Administrative State: A Study of the Political Theory of American Public Administration.* New York: Ronald Press, 1948.

Waldo, Dwight, ed. *Ideas and Issues in Public Administration: A Book of Readings.* New York: McGraw-Hill, 1953.

Waldo, Dwight. *The Study of Public Administration.* Garden City: Doubleday, 1955.

Waldo, Dwight. *Perspectives on Administration.* University Ala.: University of Alabama Press, 1956.

Wallace, Schuyler. *Federal Departmentalization.* New York: Columbia University Press, 1941.

Warner, Richard. *The Principles of Public Administration.* London: Pitman, 1947.

Weber, Max. *Essays in Sociology.* H. Gerth and C. Wright Mills, eds. New York: Oxford University Press, 1946.

Weber, Max. *The Protestant Ethic and the Spirit of Capitalism.* Talcott Parsons, tr. New York: Oxford University Press, 1947.

Weber, Max. *The Theory of Social and Economic Organization.* A. M. Henderson and Talcott Parsons, trs. New York: Oxford University Press, 1947.

Weber, Max. *General Economic History.* Frank H. Knight, tr. New York: Free Press, 1950.

Weber, Max. *The Religion of China.* Hans H. Gerth, tr. New York: Free Press, 1961.

Weidner, Edward W. "Development Administration." In F. Heady and S. Stokes, eds., *Papers in Comparative Public Administration.* Ann Arbor: The University of Michigan, 1962, p. 97-116.

Weiner, Myron. *The Politics of Scarcity.* Chicago: University of Chicago Press, 1962.

Weiss, Robert S., and Eugene Jacobson. "A Method for the Analysis of the Structure of Complex Organizations," *American Sociological Review.* Vol. 20, 1955, p. 661-668.

Westbrook, J. H. "Identifying Significant Research," *Science.* October 28, 1960, p. 1229-1234.

White, Albert Beebe. *Self-Government at the King's Command.* Minneapolis: University of Minnesota Press, 1933.

White, Leonard D. *The Federalists: A Study in Administrative History.* New York: Macmillan, 1948.

White, Leonard D. *The Jeffersonians: A Study in Administrative History, 1801-1829.* New York: Macmillan, 1951.

White, Leonard D. *The Jacksonians: A Study in Administrative History, 1829-1861.* New York: Macmillan, 1954.

White, Leonard D. *Introduction to the Study of Public Administration.* 4th ed. New York: Macmillan, 1955.

White, Leslie A. *The Science of Culture.* New York: Farrar, Straus, 1949.

White, William S., ed. *Industry and Society.* New York: McGraw-Hill, 1946.

Whorf, Benjamin L. *Language, Thought and Reality.* Cambridge: Technology Press of M.I.T., 1956.

Whyte, Lancelot L. *The Next Development in Man.* New York: Mentor Books, 1950.

Whyte, William H., Jr. *The Organization Man.* New York: Simon and Schuster, 1956.

Wiener, Norbert. *Cybernetics.* New York: Wiley, 1948.

Wiener, Norbert. *The Human Use of Human Beings.* Boston: Houghton Mifflin, 1950.

Wildavsky, Aaron. "Political Implications and Budgetary Reform," *Public Administration Review.* Vol. 21, 1961, p. 183-190.

Wiles, P. J. D. *Price, Cost and Output.* Rev. 2d ed., Oxford: Basil Blackwell, 1961.

Wiles, P. J. D. *The Political Economy of Communism.* Cambridge: Harvard University Press, 1962.

Williams, Robin M., Jr., *American Society.* Revised. New York: Knopf, 1960.

Williams, Roger J. *Biochemical Individuality.* New York: Wiley, 1956.

Willoughby, William F. *Principles of Public Administration.* Baltimore: Johns Hopkins, 1927.

Wilson, Woodrow, *Congressional Government.* New York: Houghton Mifflin, 1885.

Wilson, Woodrow. "The Study of Administration," *Political Science Quarterly.* 1887, p. 197-222.

Wilson, Woodrow. *The President of the United States,* New York: Harper, 1916.

Wittfogel, Karl A. *Oriental Despotism.* New Haven: Yale University Press, 1957.

Wolin, Sheldon S. *Politics and Vision.* Boston: Little, Brown, 1960.

Woodham-Smith, Cecil. *Florence Nightingale.* London: Constable, 1954.

Wouk, Herman. *The Caine Mutiny.* New York: Doubleday, 1954.

Woytinsky, W. S., and E. S. Woytinsky. *World Population and Production.* New York: Twentieth Century Fund, 1953.

Xenophon, *Memorabilia and Oeconomicus.* E. C. Marchant, tr. Loeb Classical Library, Harvard University Press, 1923.

Zalkind, Sheldon S., and Timothy W. Costello. "Perception: Some Recent Research and Implications for Administration," *Administrative Science Review.* Vol. 7, 1962, p. 218-235.

Zimmer, Heinrich. *Philosophies of India.* Joseph Campbell, ed. New York: Meridian Books, 1956.

INDEXES

NAME INDEX

SUBJECT INDEX

A

Ability (ies), 546, 618-19
Abstraction, 323-5
Abundance, 140-1
Acceptance, 163-4
Accounting, 391
   cash system of, 351-2; Ostrich-, 346-8; and pricing systems, 344-6; and time units, 351-4; *see also* Cost accounting
Action, activation, 581-4, 620
   and theory, 1-28
Activism, 163-4
Administration:
   and decision-making, 169-605 *passim*; defined, 2*n*, 31*n*, 32*n*, 55-8; education for, 586, 589-90, 608-32; as governance, 32-7; informal role in, 640-5; language of, 14-17, 386, 598; and power, 253-9 *passim*; "process approach" to, 42-6; rationality in, 550-3, 554-605; theories (and science) of, 1-28 *passim*, 615-20
Administrative Procedures Act (1946), 537
Administrative Revolution, 142, 312, 495, 608
   and administrators, 589
Administrators:

and coordination of interests, 515-17; education of, 608-32; evaluation of, 601-3; interlocking functions of, 218-19; planning, 574, 581-636; and red tape, 530; and specialization, 216-18; and survival problems, 455
Adversaries, 114, 130-2, 485, 511
Advertising, 485, 584
Advisers, 114, 122-5, 132, 301, 503
Afghanistan, 150
Africa, 12, 161
   GNP in, 138, 139
Agriculture, 143, 210-11
   and industrialization, 435
Algeria, 150
Altruism, 179
American Telephone and Telegraph Corp., 206, 207
Anomie, 146, 151
Anonymity, 7, 39
   in organization types, 250-1
Anthropology, anthropologists, 519-20
Army, armies, *see* Military
Asia, underdeveloped countries of, 139
Aspiration level, 15, 307
   and constraints, 286-8
Assemblies, *see* Representative assemblies